Deaf Studies *Today!*

Montage

CONFERENCE PROCEEDINGS

UTAH VALLEY UNIVERSITY • OREM, UTAH
APRIL 6–8, 2008

Edited by Bryan K. Eldredge, Doug Stringham,
Flavia Fleischer, and Kati Morton

The biennial Deaf Studies *Today!* conference brings together the best and brightest minds in the interdisciplinary field of Deaf studies. Over three days, scholars from around the country (and beyond) present the latest research and thinking in the field in an environment conducive to the open exchange of ideas. Open to everyone interested in Deaf studies, including scholars, educators, students, Deaf people, and parents of deaf children, Deaf Studies *Today!* also aims to provide networking opportunities and promote Deaf-World interests.

Deaf Studies *Today!* includes presentations and workshops that cover a broad range of topics related to Deaf people, their language, culture, and associated issues. Presentations are based on original work and present current research/thinking relevant to the field of Deaf Studies, including but not limited to perspectives from anthropology, history, linguistics, interpretation and translation, education, psychology, sociology, public administration, political science, social work, philosophy, ethics, art, literature, American Sign Language instruction, and any number of other allied disciplines.

Proceedings of Deaf Studies *Today!* are published by the American Sign Language and Deaf Studies Program at Utah Valley University. Opinions expressed by the authors of these papers are their own and do not necessarily reflect those of the editors or of Utah Valley University. Authors are responsible for the accuracy of the references cited. Use of the words '*Deaf*' or '*deaf*' in each paper also follows the authors' original manuscripts. ASL glosses are represented by small caps (e.g. DEAF, not 'deaf'). Deaf Studies *Today!* takes no responsibility for copyright infringements made by or in behalf of presenters or authors, and presenters agree to indemnify the publishers of Deaf Studies *Today!* against any illegal use of original artwork or creation.

The conference exists only because of the thousands of hours of work put forward by many different people. Most of those hours are volunteered by students and faculty at Utah Valley University. This work is dedicated to them.

2008 Proceedings Editors:

Bryan Eldredge, PH.D.
Co-Chair, Deaf Studies *Today!* 2008
ASL & Deaf Studies at Utah Valley University

Flavia Fleischer, Ph.D.
Co-Chair, Deaf Studies *Today!* 2008
ASL & Deaf Studies at Utah Valley University

Doug Stringham
ASL & Deaf Studies at Utah Valley University

Kati Morton
Student Volunteer at Utah Valley University

ISBN 978-0-9762906-2-9. ©2015 Deaf Studies *Today!* American Sign Language and Deaf Studies Program, Utah Valley University, Orem, Utah. All rights reserved; no part of this publication may be reproduced, stored in a retrieval system, or transmitted in any form or by any means, electronic, mechanical, photocopying, recording, or otherwise, without prior written permission of the publisher. Printed in the USA on acid-free paper.

Table of Contents

1   Deafhood, Deaf Studies, and the 'Deaf Reconstruction' Project: An Evaluation of Future Possibilities
PADDY LADD, PH.D.

27   Expedition for a (Deaf) Theory
MJ BIENVENU, PH.D.

45   Deaf Jews and Deaf Muslims
KATI MORTON & CINDY PLUE, PH.D.

57   "The Play's the Thing": American Deaf Theatre's Contribution to Deaf Studies
AARON KELSTONE

65   The HeART of Deaf Culture: Visual and Literary Arts of Deafhood
KAREN CHRISTIE, PH.D. & PATRICIA DURR

81   The Chaos Theory and Implications for the Creation of a Deaf-friendly University Campus
J. FREEMAN KING, PH.D.

85   The "One-dB Rule": The Deaf Community, Hard-of-Hearing People and Audism
DON GRUSHKIN, PH.D.

109   Doctoral Study Experiences of Deaf and Hard of Hearing Professionals Working in Higher Education Institutions
CHRISTOPHER KURZ, PH.D. & KIM BROWN KURZ, PH.D.

121   Education of the Deaf: Mediated by Interpreters
PATRICIA LESSARD

145   The Law, Deafness, and Personhood: Where Hobson's Choice Meet Social Eugenics
DALE. H. BOAM, J.D.

157   Deaf Studies and the Medical Field of Genetic Research: A Collaboration Model for Linguistic and Cultural Minority Populations
PARTRICK BOUDREAULT, PH.D. & CHRISTINA PALMER, PH.D.

169   Dreams and Dilemmas: Anthropological Notes on International Sign
MARA GREEN

181 Incorporating Deaf Role Models in Teacher-Preparation Curriculum
BRIAN KILPATRICK, PH.D. & KATHY WELDON, LMSW

199 A Silent History: Giving Voice to the African American Deaf Experience in the Northwest
HEATHER CLARK

217 The Unity for Gallaudet Protest and the Emergence of Visual Rhetoric in ASL Vlogs: The Medium and the Message
PAMELA R. CONLEY, PATTI DURR, & STEPHEN JACOBS

229 The Purge of Deaf Intellectuals During the Stalin Era
ARKADY BELOZOVSKY

241 Phonocentrism & Audism: Conceptualizing Notions of d/Deaf Identity and Oppression in Ghana
K. WISDOM MPRAH

253 Struggles and Challenges of the Deaf Studies Program at CSUN: 1983 to Present
PATRICK BOUDREAULT, PH.D., JORDAN EICKMAN, PH.D., GENIE GERTZ, PH.D., & LAWRENCE FLEISCHER, PH.D.

273 ASL Literature: Basic Principles of Stories with Handshape Constraints
BENJAMIN JARASHOW

287 An Exploratory Case Study of a Nongovernmental Organization (NGO) Working with the Deaf in Ghana, West Africa
HILLARY MELANDER

315 Bio-Power, Biosociality, and Community Formation: How Bio-Power is Constitutive of the Deaf Community
MICHELE FRIEDNER

325 GALLAUDET TRUE-BIZ ACADEMIC ASL, HOW-qqq
ARELENE KELLY, PH.D., JANIS COLE, BENJAMIN JARASHOW, BRIAN MALZKUHN, SHERI YOUENS-UN

339 'Deaf Interpreter' as a Career Choice within the Realm of the Deaf Studies Curriculum
PATRICK BOUDREAULT, PH.D., & JIMMY BELDON, CDI

349	Deaf Children's Theatre in the United States BRIAN KILPATRICK, ED.D.
395	To the Point of Exclusion: Balancing Lorenza Mazzetti's *Together* between Deaf and Hearing Communities TRAVIS SUTTON
411	Kendall Green: An Enduring Legacy KEITH GAMACHE, JR.
425	Iconicity, Social Types, and Referent Projections in ASL TERRA EDWARDS
443	The Politics and Practice of Voice: Representing Deaf People in Recent Television Dramas JENNIFER RAYMAN
461	What's Up With Helen Keller? EDNA SAYERS, PH.D.
475	Deaf-World Positional Identity Negotiations BRYAN ELDREDGE, PH.D.
497	Toward True ASL Dictionaries: New Developments in Handshape Similarity KAREN ALKOBY
507	Deaf Wannabes: Technologies of Deafness and The Fetishizing of Hearing KRISTEN HARMON, PH.D.
517	Visual Histories: Recording, Preserving and Disseminating and Analyzing Deaf Stories PATRICIA DURR
543	Is There a Place on Children's Educational Television for ASL? DEBBIE GOLOS, PH.D.
567	Deaf Wiki Project JORDAN EICKMAN, PH.D. & SERGEI SIMEONOV

Workshop Presenters

In addition to the presentation of academic papers, Deaf Studies Today! features workshops intended to inform and assist students and professionals in Deaf studies, as well as those aimed at helping Deaf people. Workshops are generally "hands on" in nature and may take a "how-to approach" to some subject matter. Workshop presenters do not submit papers for publication in the proceedings, but the conference organizers wish to recognize them for their contributions. The workshop topics and presenters at the 2008 conference are listed below.

Implementation of Deaf Leadership Studies — A New Era
ANNE POTTER, PH.D. & KARL P. REDDY

Deaf History in ASL on DVD
BOB PAUL

Teacher, Student, and Interpreter Roles For Success in the Academic Setting
LINDA MARIE ALLINGTON

Intercultural Communications Between Deaf and Hearing Cultures
ANNE POTTER, PH.D. & RYLAND WHITE

Using ASL Literature when Teaching Literature in English
KAREN TURLEY

_____t whq
DEAF STUDIES DEGREE DO++
DAVID MARTIN

About Deaf Studies at Utah Valley University

At the time of the 2008 conference, Utah Valley University (UVU) had a student body of over 24,000 students including sixty Deaf students. *U.S. News and World Report* ranked UVU among the top four comprehensive four-year colleges in the West.

Courses
Deaf Studies *Today!* is the creation of the American Sign Language and Deaf Studies Program at UVU in Orem, Utah. The UVU American Sign Language and Deaf Studies program is part of the Department of Foreign Languages. From its birth as a single beginning-level ASL class offered in the evening during the mid-1990s, the program has expanded to offer over thirty courses serving over 400 students each semester.

The program offerings range from beginning ASL courses to advanced classes in Deaf culture, literature, ASL grammar and linguistics, interpreting, Deaf-World discourse and more. The ASL and Deaf Studies Program also administers specialized classes for the college's Deaf students (taught in ASL), which teach them English literacy and math in preparation for entering college-level courses. The program is also home to the innovative Advanced Interpreter Certification Preparation Program (ACIPP) and the Novice Level Interpreter Preparation Program (NLIPP), which aim to enrich the lives of Deaf people by preparing truly professional interpreters.

Degrees
UVU offers a four degree choices in Deaf Studies:

- Deaf Studies Major (B.A.)
    a. Emphasis 1: General Deaf Studies
    b. Emphasis 2: Interpreting
- ASL & Deaf Studies Education Major (B.A. — secondary education)
- A minor in Deaf Studies
- An ASL emphasis in Integrated Studies (B.A.)

Of course, many students majoring in other fields take ASL courses to fulfill the language requirements for B.A. degrees.

Information
More information about the UVU ASL & Deaf Studies Program is available at www.uvu.edu/asl.

About the 2008 Conference

The second Deaf Studies *Today!* Conference was held at Utah Valley University, Orem, Utah, April 6–8, 2008. Over 800 people participated in the 2008 conference. Highlighting the conference were keynote addresses by distinguished performer Patrick Graybill, Rochester Institute of Technology (retired); Dr. Marlon Kuntze, The University of California at Berkeley; and Dr. Scott K. Liddell, Gallaudet University. The conference also featured the presentation of over thirty papers on topics ranging from ASL sociolinguistics to Deaf history and art and a panel discussion on "The Place of Deaf Studies in the University." (Most of these papers are included in these proceedings.)

Deaf Studies *Today!* was born out of a desire to bring scholars from the many disciplines comprising the field of Deaf Studies to a single academic conference. In addition to paper presentations, Deaf Studies *Today!* 2008 included tradeshow-like expo, a live modern dance performance based on Debbie Rennie's ASL poem "Black Hole: Color ASL," and the debut of Dr. Sam Supalla's one-man show "Deaf to Deaf: The Birth of American Audism."

Participants also viewed the premiere of "Paint It Loud." This documentary film by Emily Sternberg features Deaf artists Betty G. Miller and Susan Dupor. Ms. Sternberg and Ms. Dupor were on hand to answer questions following the screening and a number of Ms. Dupor's original works and prints were on display.

Sponsors
Deaf Studies *Today!* expresses gratitude to the organizations that made this conference and these proceedings possible through their generous support:

Sorenson Communications
Salt Lake Community College
Brigham Young University
The Gallaudet University Regional Center at Ohlone College

Institutional sponsors: Utah Valley University, The Office of the Academic Vice President, The School of Humanities, Arts, and Social Sciences, The Department of Foreign Languages, Conferences and Workshops.

Volunteers
Deaf Studies *Today!* would simply not exist were it not for the hundreds of hours of work volunteered by the students of Utah Valley University. They inspire us, and we give them our heartfelt thanks.

Deafhood, Deaf Studies, and the 'Deaf Reconstruction' Project: An Evaluation of Future Possibilities

PADDY LADD, PH.D.

THE NEW CONCEPT OF DEAFHOOD HAS SPREAD RAPIDLY AROUND THE world, particularly in Deaf communities in the USA and certain parts of Europe, and we may summarise part of this impact as having stimulated a search to identify Deaf epistemologies and ontologies. Such impact is in itself revolutionary. But there are other ways in which the concept has revolutionary implications.

One such is that this search for those epistemologies and ontologies requires those developing the Deafhood concept to begin to build bridges to other academic disciplines, several of which have not worked with Deaf Studies scholars before. Examples include the work of Gulliver (2008) in utilising human geography concepts of space and place in a Deafhood context, Emery's work on citizenship and group human rights (2011), Kusters' (2009) research in anthropology, Meller (2010) in sociology, Emery on genetics and Deafhood, and Goncalves' (2010) research in education.

Another implication is the concept's significance for Deaf Studies itself; indeed by its very existence, Deafhood automatically triggers the need, not only for Deaf Studies to review and evaluate its development over the past 30 years of its existence, but serves as a lens through which we might conduct that review. This is the subject of this paper.

I begin with a historical review of Deaf Studies itself, leading to a brief introduction to the Deafhood concept, with a focus on the centrality of the concept of colonialism as applied to Deaf community lives. I then examine another minority studies discipline — Black Studies as practiced in the USA — to see what can be learned from its own development as a discipline to help us rethink Deaf Studies. It should be stressed that this paper spans a very wide range of time and space. But in order to ensure that we take the very broadest picture of the study of Sign Language Peoples (SLPs), I believe that it is necessary for someone to attempt such a wide gaze, not least to help us identify gaps in what we know about ourselves. This in turn assists us in evaluating which of these might be of especial significance, indeed it assists us in determining which questions should be asked. I would therefore very much welcome feedback and discourse around the material developed in this paper which will help qualify and refine its observations.

AN INITIAL REVIEW OF THE HISTORY OF DEAF STUDIES

First I want to pay tribute to all those who have worked on Deaf Studies these past 30 years. I want to especially thank those who have organised Deaf Studies conferences, firstly at the Gallaudet Continuing Education Department-sponsored conferences, and now these Utah conferences, and those who have given, edited, and published papers from those conferences. Achieving funding for Deaf Studies research is, as will be discussed later, extremely problematic, and this has made it difficult for the discipline to develop. So we are particularly indebted to those who have developed papers for these conferences, in the main without attaining research funding for their work.

For similar reasons, we are also indebted to those Deaf Studies courses which have enabled students to develop dissertations, which in themselves form a valuable body of work, albeit one that is not easily accessible. At the Centre for Deaf Studies in Bristol, for example, there are over 50 Masters' dissertations which have been developed over the past 12 years, some of which have been published, and others which contain valuable information and insights for Deaf Studies.

I begin with a simplified historical analysis of 'Deaf Studies' through a Deafhood lens, and posit the following four phases concerning academic study of SLPs.

PHASE 1: CONSERVATISM AND 'PATHOLOGICAL RESEARCH'

I use these terms to describe 'research' on SLPs from the beginning of academic study in the mid 19th century until the mid-1970s.

However, a case could be made for the existence of a phase consisting of studies existing before this date, in which there is at times a more positive perception of SLPs and their significance for wider society; for example, Bulwer (1644), Kitto (1845), and studies relating to the French Enlightenment era in Lane (1984) and Quartararo (2008). However, a more sophisticated analysis would be needed to develop such a case, given that medical research (albeit focusing its attention on 'deafness') also existed during this era.

We would also need to research and understand the nature of the remarkable *American Annals of the Deaf*, now over 150 years old, especially during the first 50 years of its existence in order to ascertain not only its major preoccupations, but also the social and cultural academic attitudes which could be deconstructed from that examination.

With these caveats stated, I suggest that from the rise of Oralism until the mid-1970s, the first clearly observable phase of studies of SLPs was (a) conducted almost entirely by hearing persons, (b) centred around educational, social welfare, medical and technological disciplines, (c) conducted through the lens of the medical model of deafness. Lane (1993) is especially useful in appreciating some of the dynamics of such research on SLPs.

This state of affairs has much to do with the fact that the rise of Oralist discourses occurred at the same time as the development and expansion of what we now know as academia, leading inevitably to an academic hegemony which took a diminished and reductionist view of SLPs. Later, when the disciplines of psychology and psychiatry and others emerged, their work on SLPs was also similarly grounded, as Lane (ibid) illustrates. It is important to note that the idea that SLPs should play an active role in research concerning them, let alone controlling or approving such research (as is now the case with most Minority Studies), would have challenged the very basis of that hegemony. Perhaps this perspective is best summarised by the reaction of 'a professor at Siena' to being challenged about Oralism by Deaf communities during the early years of its implementation:

> Since when do we consult the patient on the nature of his treatment? *(Cuxac 1980, cited in Lane 1984, p. 409)*

Thus, most research (though not all) prior to the advent of Deaf Studies might be said to be 'pathologically' grounded, adopting a medical model of deafness with Deaf people as the researched 'Other,' atomistic beings whose community and culture either had no meaningful existence for researchers, or threatened their hegemony.

I use the term 'research' loosely here, because many of these studies, especially in the 19th century, were more often assertion rather than scientifically gathered evidence, and even when data appeared to be conducted in a scientific manner, was in fact highly flawed. The most notorious example of this, and an example of just how damaging such research can be when its 'subjects' are not heeded, is A.G. Bell's *Memoir Upon the Formation of a Deaf Variety of the Human Race* presented to the National Academy of Sciences on 13 November 1883. I presume most readers are familiar with either the research itself, or its effects on SLPs in respect of the consequent development of both Oralism and eugenics legislation.

Although a second phase began to emerge during the 1970s, it is important to note that Phase 1 has continued to exist right through to the present day with the advent of new forms of scientism: cochlear implantation, stem cell research and genetic engineering. Lane (1993) has provided a useful analysis of how some of these new forms might be deconstructed in his evaluation of the hegemony of the hearing aid and services industries.

As we know, huge financial resources — which dwarf any money invested in Deaf Studies — have been invested in these fields, and much 'research' conducted, again almost all entirely situated within the medical model of deafness. One can argue that in terms of SLP research, their previous hegemony has now been re-asserted, to the point where one now frequently hears comments like 'What is the point of researching sign languages, cultures, and bilingual educational methods? They will soon be removed by the advent of CIs, oral mainstreaming, stem cell procedures and genetic engineering.'

PHASE 2: LIBERALISM AND THE EMERGENCE OF DEAF STUDIES

It is a complex task, one beyond the scope of this paper, to describe the range and complexity of the patterns of Deaf Studies' own emergence and development, not least because numerous courses, especially in the USA, are situated outside of Deaf Studies departments. Nonetheless, Phase 2 might be characterised as 'active academic interest in Deaf communities themselves,' although, as we shall see, not necessarily on their own terms. I read this as arising from what I term the 'liberal impulse.'

Space does not permit me to explicate liberalism in depth, but a brief introduction to my use of the term is necessary. Political philosopher John Gray (1995) identifies four common strands in liberal thought: individualist, egalitarian, meliorist, and universalist. The first strand emphasises the primacy of the individual human being in respect of social collectivism, whilst the egalitarian strand (in theory) asserts equality of moral worth and status to all individuals. The meliorist strand emphasises that successive generations can improve the quality of their lives through certain (read 'liberal') socio-political activities, whilst the universalist strand emphasises a universalist reading of the human species which marginalizes local cultural differences.

Left-wing critics of liberalism point to the emphasis on individualism as being damaging to oppressed groups within societies because of an unwillingness to perceive their need for collective organisation and action, whilst universalism also hinders the recognition of the needs of oppressed cultural groups. The liberal raison d'etre is seen as one which seeks to *reform* the social order rather than radically change it, and which confirms the status of liberals as one of administering 'benevolence' to the 'less fortunate,' rather than encouraging the latter's own autonomous development. Another criticism of liberalism concerns its reluctance to examine issues relating to power, and in particular its own roles in maintaining power structures.

However, it is important to understand that in conservative-dominated eras, liberalism often represented the only realistic way to move forward - radicalism was often quite impossible. Moreover, given the continuation (and indeed extension) of Phase 1 discussed above, one can see that there are many situations in which liberalism is still useful.

Nonetheless, those of us committed to the wider 'liberation project' for SLPs, and trying to re-evaluate the role of Deaf Studies in that process, are required to identify ways in which liberalism may be hindering that development, and to offer more radical readings of both SLPs and Deaf Studies.

Study of other oppressed groups indicates a common pattern, that liberalism was initially helpful, but later became something of a hindrance to progress (cf. the Civil Rights movement of the 1960s in the USA). However, we should also note that some people who behaved as liberals when there was no other realistic option available, became more radical as situations evolved and opportunities for widescale change emerged.

That said, we can now discuss Phase 2 and the development of Deaf Studies as a university 'discipline.' For convenience I use this term, although of course like all minority studies, it in fact encompasses a range of disciplines, each of which have their own departments within academia. Deaf Studies can be said to have emerged in the late 1970s in Europe and the USA, initially as research centres, followed by teaching programmes based on that research in the 1980s. Again, it is important to remember that not all these programmes were located in departments with the formal title of 'Deaf Studies.'

However, in positing such a phase, we do need to know more about the academic activities at Gallaudet from 1865 until the 1970s. Initial investigation suggests that there was little 'Deaf' content to such activities before the emergence of Stokoe's ASL laboratory. We know that courses with a degree of such content came into being within History, Sociology, Education, Theatre and other departments, but the dates of their emergence and their content are not widely known.

In the UK during this period, the first formal Deaf Studies department was created at the University of Bristol. Other universities followed a similar pattern: initial research activities later forming the basis of degree programmes. Some centres have remained research-oriented such as the Deafness, Cognition and Learning (DCAL) Centre at the University of London. Because sign linguistics was the first discipline to recognise that SLPs manifested something of value to society, and because the teaching of sign language and the development of bilingual education were among the most urgent demands of the 1970s, this led to the domination of Deaf Studies by sign linguistics. We shall discuss this in more depth later.

It is intriguing to note that in the USA, Gallaudet resisted the idea of establishing a Deaf Studies department until 1993, and as one who was present during the debate surrounding this proposed department, it was fascinating (and useful for this review) to observe the reasoning processes of those opposed to it. It seemed that resistance included a fear that if Gallaudet went ahead with the proposal, this would lead to a concentration of Deaf and hearing 'radicals' in one department, and that this would somehow threaten Gallaudet's traditional raison d'etre.

This is a subject that deserves further research, since it is possible to conclude that the creation of such a department (and thus Deaf Studies in general) can be seen by others as a 'political activity.' Similar examination of the situations at NTID and CSUN would also prove to be helpful in a review of Deaf Studies.

Thus this second phase can be summarised as a movement away from the medical model towards a liberal, social model of disability, where hearing academics were engaged in training other hearing people to work in what one might term 'services for the deaf,' such as interpreting, with some involvement of Deaf assistants. Research conducted during this phase reflects a similar pattern, whereby Deaf communities were in effect still treated as the 'researched Other,' for example in the growth of sign linguistics, with Deaf people often seen primarily as 'signing Others' to be examined with the assistance of 'native informants.'

The language which the AAD currently uses to describe itself is a useful reference point in terms of the tone of the language used (and can be contrasted with that found in other minority studies, as will later be seen):

> "For 150 years, the American Annals of the Deaf, has been a professional journal dedicated to quality in education and in related services for children and adults who are deaf and hard of hearing. The Annals publishes articles about deaf education and recent research into trends and issues in the field of deafness."

You will notice the emphasis on 'services' rather than all other aspects of SLP community lives. You may also notice other 'outdated' language and terminology. So although the AAD publishes work that arises from the growth in consciousness seen in later phases, its raison d'etre places it in this phase.

PHASE 3: FORMAL RECOGNITION OF 'DEAF CULTURE' AND THE EMERGENCE OF DEAF ACADEMICS

Broadly speaking, this phase can be said to have emerged during the 1990s, and in particular from 2000 onwards, and is characterised by two main developments. The first has been the increase in opportunities for Deaf people in the UK and Europe to undertake advanced study and to begin to assume academic positions.

The second development, the formal recognition of the Deaf culture concept, as described in Padden and Humphries (1988) and (2005), Wilcox (1989), Mindess (2000) and Ladd (2003) among others, marks a shift of focus towards what we might term the 'internal lives' of SLPs, and has begun the process of *validating SLPs as collective entities with their own worldviews.* The increase in the numbers of Deaf academics also laid the ground for an increasing demand for the development of a Deaf-focused model of Deaf Studies, and thence towards exploration of what this process might entail.

Examples of texts situated in other disciplines which reinforced these developments included Lane (1984) and Mirzoeff (1995) in history, Wrigley (1996) in politics, Rutherford (1993) and Sutton-Spence (2004) in folklore and poetry, and 'multi-disciplinary' texts such as Lane, Hoffmeister and Bahan (1996). However, the primary site of academic initiatives to inform their own discipline that the lives, experiences and practices of SLPs might embody important information for wider academia and indeed the human race, continued to be that of sign linguistics.

This phase, while continuing to manifest liberalism, was, in its emphasis on the importance of Deaf cultural activity and SLPs collectively held worldviews and political philosophies, began also to manifest the development of a radicalism which informs the next phase.

PHASE 4: RADICALISM AND THE 'DEAFHOOD STUDIES' ERA

It is too early in the historical process to know for sure whether this phase is part of Phase 3, or is indeed a new phase. I present it as the latter in order to help us understand its potential implications more easily.

Deafhood itself is a concept that requires many months of study to gain a sense of the breadth of its scope, and the rapidity with which some SLPs have taken it up suggests that Deaf communities' desire, need even, for a renewed collective self-perception and appreciation runs deeper than many of us realised. One might parallel the concept to the emergence of the term 'feminism.' Feminism seems to have two main components. One, recognition of past activities and achievements of women, together with the identification of patriarchal and sexist activities, can be said to embody knowledge already known to many women.

However, by the very act of developing the term, and the flagging up of 'women's issues' and the need for 'women's liberation,' feminism empowered women to start to open up and explore new areas and aspects of their being which had hitherto received little attention. Identification of positive qualities embodied by women (in the process negotiating concerns about 'essentialism') developed together with the wider and deeper deconstruction of patriarchy and sexism. These were researched, formally identified, then taught as part of what is now often known as 'Women's Studies' or 'Gender Studies,' a huge global activity.

This is very much what seems to be happening in the Deafhood process, with the same two components. On the one hand it represents a recognition of what we already know of Deaf culture, SLP lives and the political environments in which they live them. On the other, the framing process which the Deafhood term embodies opens up numerous new areas and aspects of those lives for study. These not only widen and deepen the search for the positive qualities manifested by SLPs, but also enables the beginnings of a formal deconstruction of the ways and means by which oppression of SLPs has been conducted and is manifested.

It is the latter that I wish to focus on first. If we understand that the term 'deafness' and others of its ilk represent concepts imposed on SLPs, we can appreciate the need for internal definition, which is represented by 'Deafhood.' However, given that Deaf experiences and cultures have traditionally been influenced by oppression, the Deafhood concept cannot simply be used as a 'feelgood' device, but must take account of that oppression and its role in shaping the concept itself.

Thus in the first instance, the term Deafhood can be said to encompass the total sum of all positive meanings of 'Deaf,' past, present and future; all the largest meanings of what SLPs have been, are, and can become, including all that Deaf people have created in this world, all that they previously created which has been lost to sight following the rise of Oralism, and all that they might create in future.

The term acknowledges that all Deaf persons are engaged in their own individual internal defining and constructing of their Deaf selves. Some are content to reside within the 'boundaries' of existing Deaf cultures and their social positions in their communities; others attempt to stretch those boundaries. They, along with those who were forced to grow up in stricter Oralist and mainstreaming regimes, are embarked on a journey towards deepening and refining their Deaf selves, which can be termed 'the Deafhood process.' Within all of these experiences exist Deaf epistemologies and ontologies, and the Deafhood process can be said to have impelled a focus on identifying these.

In then bringing to the table the formal deconstruction of oppression, I have posited that it is the concept of colonialism which is of greatest relevance and use to us. The term 'oppression' itself has minimal explanatory value. Post-Colonial Studies on the other hand is a discipline we can learn much from. Lane (1993) and Wrigley (1996) began the process of applying colonialism to SLP contexts (the latter including Deaf-on-Deaf colonialism in his analysis) and the concept was formalised in Ladd (2003) and can be examined in greater depth there.

Colonialism itself can be said to be characterised by a sector of a society acting 'on behalf of' the majority society population, who acquiesce in this as a consequence of accepting the hegemonic discourses of the ruling sector. In the colonialism of SLPs, this can be interpreted as 'specialists' acting on behalf of 'lay people,' who have bought into the concept of 'expertise' and thus remain largely unaware of what is enacted upon those communities.

The colonial process itself takes different forms in different societies, including economic colonisation, linguistic colonisation, cultural colonisation, 'social welfare colonisation,' religious colonisation, and 'colonisation of the body.' The most common site for the colonialist process is the Deaf education system, notably (but not exclusively) Oralism. In the UK and elsewhere, social welfare colonialism is also highly influential in shaping Deaf community lives. A key feature of Post-Colonial Studies is the attempts by colonised peoples to understand the effects of colonialism on their own cultures, psyches and identities, and consequently to engage in the recovery of their histories, epistemologies, and ontologies. In some circumstances, decolonisation is accompanied by a conscious 'Reconstruction' programme which attempts to view their society as a total entity and attempt to establish the full range of what rebuilding of that society might require. This requires a *re-envisioning of that society*: the needs of all the classes and groups within it, what might be involved in the rebuilding process, and the consequent ways in which colonial structures need to change for this to happen.

Similar impulses can be said to be emerging in this fourth phase of Deaf Studies. Examples of historical reclamation can be found in Carty (2004) Gulliver (2009) and Murray (2007), whilst Bauman (2008) contains several papers which raise similar questions in respect of other aspects of SLP lives.

I would locate within this phase three other new concepts which inform and extend these dimensions. One is the re-presentation of Humphries concept of audism by Bauman (2004), the challenge to traditional concepts of ethnicity presented by Lane, Pillard and Hedburg (2010) and the new concept of Deaf-Gain (Bauman and Murray 2009) which can be seen as an extension of aspects of the Deafhood concept, focusing on the qualities that SLPs bring to the world.

In respect of academia itself, one of the next steps in developing the Deafhood concept is to apply its gaze to the disciplines which have hitherto dominated the three earlier phases in the study of SLPs, and examine how they might be reconstructed as part of the decolonisation process. Another is the bridge-building to new disciplines as described in the introduction above.

There are now numbers of Deaf and hearing people who share to some extent these radical, decolonising, community-regeneration and reconstruction perspectives. In this fourth phase, the normality of Deaf academic endeavour is being to gain acceptance and Deaf-led research is beginning to emerge. Such research is still very much in its infancy, given that possession of a PhD is the minimum requirement for attaining one's own research funding, and outside of the USA these are as yet very few in number.

Deaf academics are beginning to organise themselves, both within countries and on an international scale. However, at this moment in time, there has as yet been little consideration by them of the need to review the development of Deaf Studies itself, let alone attempt theories of how it might be reconstructed. Hence the next section of this paper is also intended to initiate that process.

MINORITY STUDIES AND RE-ENVISIONING DEAF STUDIES

Before moving on, I would like you to attempt this exercise. It works equally well in the pub as well as the classroom!

Try to imagine what the Deaf-World (and in this case, Deaf Studies) would look like if Oralist colonialism had never happened. Then try to apply your imagination to academic study of SLPs, and consider what different forms it might have taken, comparing those to what presently exists. Now, having briefly reviewed Deaf Studies, and outlined aspects of the wider 'Deaf Reconstruction' project, I now focus on other aspects of that re-envisioning.

Reconstruction of course requires us to understand the extent to which colonialism and audism have shaped the course syllabi, research priorities and methodologies and the beliefs, values and actions of Deaf Studies practitioners themselves. The other crucial dimension in developing such an understanding is to learn about, and understand the patterns of developments, within other Minority Studies themselves. Important examples include women's/gender Studies, various sectors of Post-colonial Studies, disability studies, various native people's studies and Black Studies. In the case of the latter, the USA examples are perhaps of the most use to us, since Black Studies in the UK leads a precarious existence.

USA BLACK STUDIES AND RECONSTRUCTION

Numerous approaches and models appear to exist, but I have chosen one model as a starting point for comparison, Karenga (1993's *Introduction to Black Studies*. (Later editions exist, but the version in the 1993 edition is the clearest for our purposes.) Utilising Karenga should not be read as endorsing Karenga's full 'agenda,' rather, it is the clarity of his frameworking which is most useful to us.

Karenga's stated objectives for Black Studies are:
- To teach the Black experience across time and place in a systematic way.
- To bring Black contributions out from the margins to their own cultures and to mainstream cultures.
- To assemble and create a body of knowledge which will contribute to intellectual and political emancipation. 'Until the white monopoly on Black minds was broken, liberation was not only impossible but unthinkable, for there would be no categorical referent, no way to conceive it.' (p.13)
- To create a body of Black intellectuals dedicated to community service and development rather than 'vulgar careerism.'
- The cultivation and maintenance and expansion of a mutually beneficial relationship between campus and community.
- To establish Black Studies as a legitimate, respected and permanent discipline. (The contents of the remainder of pages 14 and 15 are especial importance.)

Karenga presents seven categories of 'relevance,' where Black Studies is constructed as:
- A definitive contribution to humanity's understanding of itself.
- A definitive contribution to US' society's understanding of itself. (note also what follows here on p.16).
- A challenge to the academy's claim to embody and teach the 'whole truth' in respect of human knowledge.
- A vital contribution to the critique, resistance and reversal of the Europeanization of human consciousness and culture. (note also what follows on p.20).
- The rescue and reconstruction of Black history and humanity.
- Interdisciplinary and thus a paradigm for a multidimensional approach to social and historical reality, a model for a holistic social science, able to draw attention to the inadequacies, omissions and distortions of traditional white studies.

- A contribution to the development of a Black intelligentsia who then make a vital contribution to the liberation and development of the Black community, and thus to society's own liberation.

THE 'FULCRUM' OF DIFFERENCE: COLONISATION AND ACADEMIA

Perhaps the key epistemological starting point is in the parallel offered by Gordon (2000)'s re-evaluation of aspects of Black Studies. As he puts it:

> 'To break out of epistemic closure, one needs to recognise that blacks have points of view of the world' (p. 90).

In his view, oppression views the oppressed in a 'social role,' one which then defines all that society needs to know about them, seeing them solely as 'exterior being.' Its members are 'literally without insides or hidden spaces for interrogation. One [person] thus counts for all.' (pp. 88–89). Thus study of such peoples is at best a study of 'what they do' rather than 'who they are.' This of course resonates with much of what has been said in Section 2.

INTERNAL BEING IN MINORITY STUDIES

Whilst external activities are of course very important, Minority Studies are often concerned with what drives those actions, and to identify:
- The beliefs, values, norms, traditions, philosophies of the minority.
- The effects of colonisation/oppression on each of the above.
- The different 'schools' of thought which exist, and their relationship with colonialism/oppression.

From this basis they can then identify the most appropriate strategies and visions which might arise from that analysis.

DISCIPLINES HIGHLIGHTED IN KARENGA'S CONCEPT OF BLACK STUDIES

Karenga lists and discusses each of the following: history, religion and Afro-centricity, economics, politics, sociology, 'creative productions,' psychology, Black women's studies, and Black multiculturalism (a different concept to that found in white academica).

COMPARISON OF BLACK STUDIES AND DEAF STUDIES

Our next task is therefore to compare these with what is found in Deaf Studies. Which of these fields are little studied or do not exist within Deaf Studies, and vice versa? What might be the reasons for the differences in both cases? Which of those disciplines might have different meanings to those found in majority academia, why and how?

In order to achieve this task it is also necessary to bring to the comparison other disciplines/areas around Deaf Studies which do not appear in Karenga's list above: language/linguistics, education, mental health, social welfare, medicine, technology.

I begin by constructing this diagram to assist our thinking.

History	Established
Philosophy	Very Minimal
Economics	Very Minimal
Politics	Minimal
Sociology/Culture	Minimal
Arts	Developing, but minimal
Psychology	Not yet explored
Women's Studies	Minimal
Black Multiculturalism	Not yet explored
Established (Ebonics)	Language
Minimal	Linguistics
Developing	Education
Developing	Mental Health
Developing	Social Welfare
Minimal	Medicine
Minimal	Technology

In the bottom left column, I have estimated the extent to which those subjects not mentioned by Karenga can be found in Black Studies in other parts of the USA.

COMPARING BLACK STUDIES AND DEAF STUDIES

As you can see, there is much that could be said about what this diagram reveals, but space does not permit a full exposition. For example, the reader understands that Black Studies was established and run by Black academics, whereas this was simply not possible for Deaf Studies.

The first thing we notice in the top columns is how little attention is given in Deaf Studies to Karenga's nine 'disciplines.' Only Deaf history can be said to have been developed to any significant extent, with Deaf arts offering a (slowly) growing body of academic work. By contrast, the bottom columns indicate that of the seven subjects which play a major role in the study of Deaf persons, three are relatively unimportant for Black Studies, and three are beginning to develop, but *from their own epistemologies*, in contrast with what is found in those subjects in respect of Deaf persons.

What might we conclude from this?
- The vast majority of the work produced still casts Deaf communities as objects of the gaze.
- Karenga's nine 'disciplines' are constructed around Black peoples as subjects who gaze.
- Similarly, work on Deaf culture, arts, community and history can, but does not always centre around the Deaf subject and their internal life.
- Questions are raised about the extent to which some disciplines engaged in studying Deaf persons are traditional sites of colonialism.
- Similar questions are raised as to whether some disciplines, and possibly Deaf Studies itself, manifest forms of neo-colonialism.

Decolonisation cannot of course be achieved until those colonised move from researched object to active subjects. I will now briefly explore some of these themes further. But before doing so, one major difference between Deaf/Disability Studies and other minority studies must be highlighted.

UNIQUE SITUATION OF DEAF/DISABILITY STUDIES

Most minority studies, however much they may be oppressed by institutionalised discrimination in academia, do not find their existence actively 'opposed' by any other disciplines. It is impossible to imagine, for example, there being a White Studies, or Men's Studies, whose raison d'etre actually undermines Black and Women's Studies.

But for Deaf (and to some degree, Disability) Studies, we find that disciplines around medicine and other sciences, whenever their gaze alights on Deaf and disabled people, can be said to often actively oppose the raison d'etre of Deaf/Disability Studies, and what they stand for in respect of human diversity. Further, in the case of Deaf Studies, as we have seen, there exists a significant set of discourses within education which also manifest an oppositional stance.

These disciplines are much more powerful than Deaf Studies, and to return to the example above, one needs to imagine such putative White and Men's Studies attracting funding vastly greatly than Black and Women's Studies in order to grasp a fuller picture of academic hegemony, and the extent of the burden and pressure this creates for both Sign Language Peoples and Deaf Studies.

RE-EVALUATING DEAF STUDIES

Given what we have considered so far, how might we then begin to further re-evaluate Deaf Studies? The following domains, issues and or questions are ones that we might address as part of that re-evaluation.

SIGN LINGUISTICS' TRADITIONAL DOMINATION OF DEAF STUDIES

It is fairly self-evident that sign linguistics is the longest established and most prevalent discipline within what is usually seen as Deaf Studies around the world, and there are positive historical reasons for this (cf. Ladd 2003). To briefly summarise some of these, the engagement of sign linguistics with SLPs in effect not only helped to validate the existence of Deaf communities within academia, but also began the process of validating what we might term their 'humanity.' It enabled Deaf people to begin the process of entering academia, has played a crucial role in the development of bilingual education, in turn laying the groundwork for activists to aspire towards official and governmental recognition of sign languages, has formed the bedrock for the development of interpreting programmes, and has also assisting in the process of recognition and emergence of SLPs in developing countries.

In recognising these crucial historical developments, we should note that the ongoing focus of much of what passes for Deaf Studies is the 'service model' of Phase 2, above, the need to teach sign languages to hearing people in order for them to become professional interpreters, welfare workers, and to some extent, educators. This requirement will not diminish in the coming years.

Moreover, for the foreseeable future, opportunities and incentives to develop Deaf Studies will be minimal, compared with, say Black Studies or Women's Studies. The latter, being numerically greater, will be able to draw on a much larger population of Black and female students (even setting asides the hurdles SLPs face in attaining a university education). These greater numbers in turn increase the size and dimensions of those disciplines by creating larger numbers of employment opportunities and career paths for its practitioners.

These factors indicate that there is an urgent need to re-evaluate the role of sign linguistics within Deaf Studies, and how its hegemony might be affecting the development of Phases 3 and 4. The first thing to note is that because of its longevity, its practitioners often occupy the major positions in the field, and wittingly or unwittingly shape the direction of the field, thus 'soaking up' most of the academic research funding available to Deaf Studies. This happens partly because numbers of its practitioners have attained refereeing status within many grant-awarding bodies, and partly because traditional academic audism means that applications of a sociological or cultural nature, for example, are not reviewed by academics within their own disciplines, but are instead referred out to 'experts in deafness,' often, but not always, sign linguists.

Further, it can be said that the discipline has acquired a 'life of its own,' that is, that it is not subject to Deaf communities' approval or even formal national or international input as to what those communities might consider to be their own research priorities. One example would be the latter's requirement of *language* as opposed to *linguistic* research priorities. It is also important to note that those communities have not begun to engage in the re-envisioning of their peoples, the 'Deaf Reconstruction' process, and thus have not yet developed an alternative vision to present to sign linguists.

Informal Deaf discourses often express concerns about this hegemony, but unfortunately, none have yet dared to commit themselves to print. However, examination of sign linguistics literature raises the question: are Deaf people seen as 'signing machines' with no interiority of any significance? And what would a Deafhood-centred Sign Language Studies look like?

DECOLONISATION AND ACADEMIA

We can gather some clues for the questions above if we examine some of the literature concerning other minorities, for example around post-colonialism and anthropology. As Brown notes in his seminal text 'Who Owns Native Culture?'

> Indigenous peoples now perceive themselves as more threatened by outsiders who claim to love their religion than by missionaries dedicated to its overthrow." Brown (2003), p. 23.

We therefore need to ask a similar question: Do SLPs feel more threatened (in certain ways) by those who claim to love their languages?

Brown also indicates what now passes for a standard approach to anthropology:

> Today native nations properly insist on their right to determine who conducts research among them, and to what end — a principle that is fully acknowledged and embraced by working anthropologists. Brown (2003) p. xi.

We thus need to ask 'To what extent do native SLPs have the power to make such decisions' and indeed 'how far are we presently from recognition of the centrality of such native perspectives'? I will give a further example from Karenga, this time in respect of the discipline of psychology, but it applies to most of the other fields within Black Studies:

The concerns of Black psychology revolve around the development of a discipline which not only studies the behaviour of Black persons, but seeks to transform them into self-conscious *agents* of their own mental, emotional and social liberation.' (Karenga 2002, p. 505, my italics)

It is important to note that this reference to agents should not be read from the usual Western individualist gaze, but from an awareness that these agents are part of a collectivist cultural perspective, where the health of the individual is directly related to the health of the community/nation/people/tribe/race.

Thus the quote exemplifies the classic decolonisation/Reconstruction approach to minority studies, and encapsulates the central principles of those disciplines. The reader can easily ascertain how far 'Deaf psychology' is from such a perspective, but in fact the contrast between the overall aspirations and tone of this type of discourse and what is found across the whole of Deaf Studies is very stark indeed.

THE PLACE OF CULTURE, SOCIOLOGY, AND POLITICS WITHIN DEAF STUDIES

We can see from the above that the discipline of politics is essential to minority studies, and that 'political' perspectives lie at the heart of many other disciplines within them (noting that of course 'everything is political' within and without Deaf Studies, and it is existing hegemonies who maintain the position that only dissenting views are deemed to be 'political').

But we can go further. In moving towards a position where the internal being of SLPs can assume a central position in the reshaping of Deaf Studies, we can note for example that Deaf history is still largely focused on external being – on what Deaf people have done rather than what they have thought (Ladd 2007). We can note that it is becoming more acceptable to explore internal being in the disciplines around Deaf arts. But we cannot draw these together into a coherent whole without a major emphasis on the study of Deaf cultures, sociologies and epistemologies. The 'centre' is missing.

CONTRASTING LEVELS OF ACTIVITIES WITHIN THE DISCIPLINES

Broadly speaking, we can observe a set of differences within Deaf Studies, for example, culture, sociology, arts, politics and philosophy on the one hand, and sign linguistics, education, mental health and social welfare on the other. The latter have international journals, formal bodies, national and international conferences and semi-formal Internet groupings. The former have no journals, formal bodies, or international conferences.

Indeed there have been almost no conferences on 'Deaf Culture,' and even for Deaf Studies itself, there have only been two regular national conferences. The first, organised from 1991–2001 by Gallaudet University has remained virtually unknown, and of low status inasmuch as its conference papers were not published by Gallaudet University Press, but by a 'College for Continuing Education' within the university. The second is of course these valuable Utah initiatives, but which are still published with a lower profile than other comparable disciplines.

In contrast to this, other minority studies appear to go from strength to strength in researching and representing their internal being.

ADDITIONAL SIGNIFICANCE OF THIS CONTRAST IN ACTIVITY

The former group of disciplines above represent sites where the daily life experiences of Deaf persons, past and present, individual and collective, can be brought together to form a systematic reflexive praxis for Deaf Studies, without which decolonisation cannot take place.

This is not to say that minority studies have themselves avoided making research Objects of their own people in such fields, as bell hooks (1989, 2000) notes in respect of both Black Studies and Women's Studies, pointing out the minor role played by female knowledge in the former, the minimal role assigned to Black women in the latter, and the elision of the importance of class in both. We should also note that sociology often shies from confronting some of these issues in its actual academic practice. As Staples has stated for Black Studies,

> If white sociology is the science of oppression, Black sociology must be the science of liberation." (1973, p. 168).

We might therefore note that the absence of the very 'centre' required for decolonisation is not a coincidence, but a fundamental characteristic of the present hegemonic discourse systems.

DECOLONISATION AND THE 'CENTRE'

To briefly summarise the narrative thus far, decolonisation/Reconstruction strategies:
- Conceive of the newly emerging nation as a holistic entity,
- View the entire society from that gaze,
- From that position, conceive policies to remove negative effects of colonialism and attempt to replace these with cultural values and beliefs which they consider central to their new societies.

- In so doing, attempt to clarify the role of academia in the liberation process.

In this process, a reflexive praxis which identifies the place of the intellectual classes in relation to other classes is attempted. This may be conservative — seeking to maintain academic/community class divisions after decolonisation — or radical, as in the field of Subaltern Studies (Chaturvedi 2000) etc. But in both cases, it is social analysis and historical awareness which come together to form a 'centre' to motivate and guide their policies and actions.

The danger for both Deaf Studies and wider academia which studies Deaf persons, is that without such reflexive praxis, it may continue to unconsciously replicate inherited oppressive patterns from colonialism.

THE CENTRE AND THE SEARCH FOR DEAF EPISTEMOLOGIES / ONTOLOGIES

If there is one challenge which underpins the Reconstruction process, one which has been tackled by in many other minority studies, it is the need to research and formally identify Deaf epistemologies and ontologies, based on traditionally understood 'Deaf Ways,' yet, following Deafhood principles, be aware of the degree to which these have themselves been diminished by colonialism.

Achieving such understanding is problematic if it is centred around the absence of such envisioning, a state of affairs which characterises much of the existing literature. Much more research with SLPs is required to even attain the basics of what is needed to identify these epistemologies and ontologies. It is interesting to note that for several years now there has been a growing dissatisfaction within Deaf Studies concerning the lack of epistemological progress within the discipline, as reflected in course syllabi, and this can be correlated with the absence of the kind of research which is needed.

This in turn can be correlated with the 'colonial' relationship which exists in respect of the wider institutionalised discrimination of academia as discussed earlier, the hurdles faced in obtaining research funding, the refereeing systems themselves, and especially a phenomenon which little remarked upon — *that majority societies rarely fund research that benefits minorities in and for themselves* — there is almost always a hidden liberal agenda of assimilation into a mono-cultural model of society rather than the development of real multi-culturalism. All these in turn help to explain the relative absence of career pathways for practitioners of Deaf Studies.

PROBLEMATICISING RECONSTRUCTION

Re-evaluation of Deaf Studies also requires us to examine and problematicise the processes of decolonisation and Reconstruction itself if we are to avoid some of the major problems other minorities and post-colonial societies have encountered. In this section, I flag up and briefly discuss some of these challenges.

WHICH NATIVES?

The classic challenge is that of representation. If we insist that Deaf Studies should shoulder its responsibilities to act as the analytical arm of Reconstruction, in partnership with SLPs, the first question that must be asked is how national (and indeed international) Deaf communities should be represented. Ideally representation should emerge from the elected national Deaf associations, but experience teaches us that this is not as simple as one might wish. If we understand that all SLPs have been damaged by 120 years of colonialism, it is logical to expect there to be concerns about those communities' present ability to develop a vision of Reconstruction, and that these concerns will also apply to the associations which represent them.

35 years experience of working with national and international Deaf associations, including discussions with many Deaf and hearing people, has shown me that most of these associations lag behind other sectors of Deaf societies in terms of awareness and understanding of cutting-edge issues. To put it bluntly, the majority of the more forward-looking 'talented tenth' (to use Dubois' classic phrase) are employed outside of those associations. Thus for Deaf Studies simply to co-opt officials from those associations runs the risk of tokenism.

In seeking those more forward-looking Deaf representatives, it becomes clear that many work in academia. However, it would be inappropriate for Deaf community representation to be sought solely from this domain precisely because as yet they cannot claim the support of national subaltern and professional communities, and also because they themselves have not yet developed Reconstruction visions.

Ideally then, one is engaged in a search for partnership. Given that the national Deaf associations already have the ability to nominate representatives who they do not directly employ, the next question emerges, 'how best to achieve representation from Deaf academics themselves?' Ideally national Deaf Academics associations would come into existence in the near future and these would then be able to discuss and nominate their representatives. (To give an indication of historical differences between minorities, the

National Council for Black Studies was established in 1976.) The same process would then apply to the putative relationship between an International Deaf Academics' Association and the World Federation of the Deaf.

In saying this we should note that there are further problematics to be confronted. One lies with national Deaf associations: to what extent does each truly represent subaltern Deaf interests rather than professional Deaf interests? In some countries the most forward-thinking of Deaf organisations are breakaway bodies, formed because of dissatisfaction with the conservative mindset of the associations, such as occurred in the UK with the formation of the National Union of the Deaf (1976–87) (Lee 1991) and the Federation of Deaf People (1998–2003) (Alker 2000). However, as can be seen from the dates above, these bodies can also be short-lived, usually because of the lack of resources they possess.

In respect of Deaf academics themselves, it is possible to identify two broad groupings: those who have emerged from within Deaf communities, and those who have come to academia via mainstreaming. Generally what one notices is that the former are less comfortable with English, and publish less than those who have been mainstreamed. But the latter's abilities to understand and appreciate Deaf cultures itself varies widely, so that there already exists a risk of polarisation; on the one hand, the former understand their communities and respect their traditions, yet do not publish their knowledge of those communities. On the other, the latter are swiftly becoming the most prominent of future Deaf academics without having such a grounding. Problems associated with this lack of grounding include a lack of reflexivity to appreciate their position within SLPs and the historical background which has enabled them to rise to such positions; a lack of awareness that in-depth knowledge of Deaf cultures and communities is of fundamental importance in rethinking Deaf Studies; and a highly individualised world view (born of the travails experienced during mainstreaming) which contrasts hugely with the collectivist cultural perspectives and demands of SLPs.

There are no simple answers to these challenges, although I will present one suggestion shortly. For the moment, our priority is to become aware of these issues, to spend time thinking about them and discussing them, so that other facets, dimensions and routes to potential solutions, can become visible.

HEARING ACADEMIC ALLIES AND RECONSTRUCTION

There is not space here to discuss issues around hearing allies and coalitions in the wider communities; my focus here is on the role of hearing academic allies and Reconstruction.

We understand that there are historical reasons why, unlike Black and

Women's Studies, hearing academics are generally in control of the study of SLPs, and of Deaf Studies itself. We also understand that many continue to make valuable, even essential contributions to the work, whether that be fund-raising, administering, teaching, researching, mentoring and advocacy, and that in many cases Deaf Studies cannot exist without them.

Nor should we attempt a re-envisioning of Deaf Studies that does not include them; they bring perspectives from other disciplines, an understanding of how majority cultures operate and much else that is necessary for a healthy Deaf Studies, one which is both inward and outward looking.

However, just as Deaf communities, associations and academics must reflect on their own situations and roles in respect of Reconstruction, so of course must hearing academics. What might one expect of them, therefore? I would suggest three principles:

- A commitment to study and understand the colonisation process as it operates on SLPs and their allies.
- A similar commitment to understanding the decolonisation / Reconstruction process, and the issues this raises, particularly for academia.
- A commitment to undertaking the role of ally.

Ideally one would also like to see allies committing themselves to setting down and publishing their thoughts and experiences around these principles so that Deaf communities know where each person stands in the overall scheme of things. But this is the kind of issue that can be explored further by others.

As part of the process above, one would also wish to see more research by both Deaf and hearing people into contemporary Deaf-hearing relationships across a wide range of domains and situations, together with a commitment to studying and understanding the dynamics around other minority studies, and an investigation of the literature surrounding the development of alliances and coalitions where they exist in other societies.

REDEFINING SLP ROLES IN RECONSTRUCTION PROCESSES

We now return to the challenge posed at the end of 7.1. If one expects hearing academics to adopt the principles above, it follows that SLPs must make the same commitment towards understanding those processes (and more besides). The question now arises: is there is a way in which we can formalise the development of such an understanding by all parties involved?

DEAFHOOD AND RECONSTRUCTION

Fortunately for us, it is possible to suggest that such a route has begun to emerge, through the Deafhood concept. Given that the concept already incorporates all the post-colonial features we have been discussing, it is but a short step to propose that all the key players, parties and representatives in the various processes of re-envisioning and reconstructing should therefore be required to undergo training courses in Deafhood Studies as a pre-requisite to becoming representatives of the Deaf Studies-Deaf associations partnership. The material contained within the MSc in Deafhood Studies at the University of Bristol would assist in creating the basis of such courses.

Not only would such courses help each individual to acquire the range of knowledge that each needs, and thus help to place all members 'on the same page,' but the learning process itself would throw up numerous new ideas, perspectives and challenges, all of which would form part of the new liberatory discourses. For Deafhood Studies itself is still in its infancy, and teasing out how Deafhood applies to all the facets of Deaf Reconstruction is central to those discourses. (An initial delineation of these can be found in Ladd 2003, chapter 11.)

THE 'APPEASEMENT DECADE' AND THE 'INVASION OF POLAND'

As if all the above were not challenge enough (albeit an exciting one), the emergence of genetic engineering has now placed SLPs and Deaf Studies in a position where the continuing existence of SLPs themselves is now brought into question. This development 'ups the ante' in respect of what might now be expected from Deaf Studies academics. It can be argued that so serious are these threats, that all Deaf and hearing academics may be required to both understand this process (linked as it is to other manifestations of contemporary scientism such as cochlear and stem cell experimentation, and the consequent resurgence of Oralism), and become active in partnership with SLPs in tackling these.

There are several ways in which these developments can be challenged, but it is clear that one will be a need to 'justify' the continued existence of SLPs, whether that be based around what they offer to humanity, or other forms of argument. This in turn adds impetus to the assertion of this paper that Deaf Studies may well be compelled to embrace and investigate the ontological dimensions of SLP existence in order to locate a basis for that justification.

It can be argued that Deaf Studies has by and large slept through a 'decade of appeasement' inasmuch as it has not prioritised research which deconstructs the myths around cochlear experimentation and mainstreaming, and presented their actualities to the world. The passing of the HFEB Act in the UK in December 2007 can be seen as equivalent to the 3rd September 1939: the first shot in a war. To mix metaphors a little, it is encumbent on each and every one of us in Deaf Studies to ensure that another Hiroshima is not created.

The challenges ahead will be severe. But the work required will be stimulating, fascinating, and break much new ground. It also holds the potential to unite Deaf Studies practitioners, both Deaf and hearing, which was a heartening feature of the international academic response to the HFEB. For in the end, Reconstruction cannot occur without unification. And the need to respond to these negative developments can also be seen as a window of opportunity (and a kick up the rear end!) to formally identify the many positive qualities which validate the existence of Sign Language Peoples on Earth.

Deep thanks are expressed to Jannelle Legg for her invaluable assistance with this paper.

REFERENCES

Alker, D. (2000). *Really Not Interested in the Deaf?* Darwen: Darwen Press.
Bauman, H.-D. L. (2004). Audism: Exploring the Metaphysics of Oppression. *Journal of Deaf Studies and Deaf Education*, 9(2), 239–246. doi:10.1093/deafed/enh025
Bauman, H.-D. L. (2008). *Open Your Eyes: Deaf Studies Talking.* U of Minnesota Press.
Bauman, H.-D. L., & Murray, J. J. (2010). Deaf Studies in the 21st Century: "Deaf-gain" and the Future of Human Diversity. *Oxford Handbook of Deaf Studies, Language and Education* (Vol. 2, pp. 210–225). New York: Oxford University Press.
Bell, A. G. (1884). *Memoir Upon the Formation of a Deaf Variety of the Human Race.* National academy of sciences.
Brown, M. F. (2004). *Who Owns Native Culture?* Cambridge, MA: Harvard University Press.
Bulwer, J. (1644). *Chirologia, or, The naturall language of the hand: composed of the speaking motions, and discoursing gestures thereof; whereunto is added Chironomia, or, The art of manuall rhetoricke : consisting of the naturall expressions, digested by art in the hand, as the chiefest instrument of eloquence, by historicall manifesto's, exemplified out of the authentique registers of common life, and civill conversation.* Printed by Tho. Harper, and are to be sold by Henry Twyford.
Carty, B. (2004). *Managing Their Own Affairs: The Australian Deaf Community in the 1920s and 1930s* (dissertation). Griffith University, South Brisbane, Queensland, Australia.
Chaturvedi, V. (2000). *Mapping Subaltern Studies and the Postcolonial.* London: Verso.
Emery, S. D. (2011). *Citizenship and the Deaf Community.* Nigmegen, The Netherlands: Ishara Press.
Goncalves, J. (2010). *The role of Gaucho culture and Deaf pedagogy in rethinking Deaf Education* (dissertation). University of Bristol, Centre for Deaf Studies, Bristol, England.
Gordon, L. R. (2000). *Existentia Africana: understanding Africana existential thought.* New York: Psychology Press.
Gray, J. (1995). *Liberalism.* U of Minnesota Press.
Gulliver, M. (2009). DEAF Space, a History: The production of DEAF spaces emergent, autonomous, located and disabled in 18th and 19th century France (dissertation,

unpublished). University of Bristol, Centre for Deaf Studies, Bristol, England.
Gulliver, M. (n.d.). Places of Silence. In F. Vanclay, M. Higgins, & A. Blackshaw (Eds.), *Making Sense of Place: Exploring Concepts and Expressions of Place through Different Senses and Lenses* (pp. 87–94). Canberra: National Museum of Australia.
hooks, bell. (1989). *Talking Back: thinking feminist, thinking black*. Cambridge, MA: South End Press.
Karenga, M. (1993). *Introduction to Black studies*. Los Angeles, CA: University of Sankore Press.
Kitto, J. (1845). *The Lost Senses: Series 1 - Deafness*. London: Charles Knight & co.
Kusters, A. (2010). Deaf Utopias? Reviewing the Sociocultural Literature on the World's "Martha's Vineyard Situations." *Journal of Deaf Studies and Deaf Education*, 15(1), 3–16. doi:10.1093/deafed/enp026
Ladd, P. (2003). *Understanding Deaf Culture: in Search of Deafhood*. Clevedon: Multilingual Matters.
Lane, H. (1984). *When the Mind Hears: a history of the deaf*. New York: Random House Digital, Inc.
Lane, H. L. (1993). *The Mask of Benevolence: Disabling the Deaf Community*. New York: Vintage Books.
Lane, H. L., Hoffmeister, R., & Bahan, B. J. (1996). *A Journey into the Deaf-World*. San Diego, CA: DawnSignPress.
Lane, H. L., Pillard, R., & Hedberg, U. (2011). *The People of the Eye: Deaf Ethnicity and Ancestry*. New York: Oxford University Press.
Lee, R. (Ed.). (1991). *Deaf Liberation*. London: National Union of the Deaf.
Meller, G. (2010). Funeral Rites in the British Deaf Church: A Case of Disenfranchised Grief? *Journal of Contemporary Religion*, 25(2), 267–280. doi:10.1080/13537901003750951
Mindess, A. (2000). *Reading Between the Signs: Intercultural Communication for Sign Language Interpreters*. Yarmouth, ME: Intercultural Press.
Mirzoeff, N. (1995). *Silent Poetry: deafness, sign, and visual culture in modern France*. Princeton, NJ: Princeton University Press.
Murray, J. J., & Bauman, H.-D. L. (2009). *Reframing: From Hearing Loss to Deaf Gain*. Deaf Studies Digital Journal, 1(1).
Murray, J. J., & History, T. U. of I. (2007). *"One Touch of Nature Makes the Whole World Kin:" The Transnational Lives of Deaf Americans, 1870--1924* (dissertation, unpublished). University of Iowa, Iowa City, Iowa.
Padden, C., & Humphries, T. (1988). *Deaf in America: voices from a culture*. Cambridge: Harvard University Press.
Padden, C., & Humphries, T. L. (2006). *Inside Deaf Culture*. Cambridge: Harvard University Press.
Quartararo, A. T. (2008). *Deaf Identity and Social Images in Nineteenth-century France*. Washington, D.C.: Gallaudet University Press.
Rutherford, S. (1993). *A Study of American Deaf Folklore*. Silver Spring, Maryland: Linstok Press, Inc.
Staples, R. (1973). What is Black Sociology? Toward a Sociology of Black Liberation. In J. Ladner (Ed.), *The Death of White Sociology* (pp. 161–172). New York: Vintage Books.
Sutton-Spence, R. (2004). *Analysing Sign Language Poetry*. London: Palgrave Macmillian.
Wilcox, S. (1989). *American Deaf Culture: an anthology*. Silver Spring, Maryland: Linstok Press.
Wrigley, O. (1997). *The Politics of Deafness*. Washington, D.C.: Gallaudet University Press.

Expedition for a (Deaf) Theory

MJ BIENVENU, PH.D.

Dedicated to Marie Jean Philip.

WE HAVE BEEN ASKING MANY OF THE SAME QUESTIONS. I WENT THROUGH Marie Philip's papers and even though she passed away ten years ago, people are still asking the same questions. I went through her papers, which are dated from the late 1970s, 1980s and early 1990s. This tells us we are not doing it right. Why do people continue to ask the same questions over and over again about Deaf people? These questions include "Is ASL a language?" and "Do Deaf people really have a culture?" as well as "How can bilingualism help Deaf children?" and "What about English?"

Where is our theory? Before we discuss theory, we need to look at how we are framng the discussion. I appreciate the book by George Lakoff, *Don't Think of an Elephant*. The section on framing — which focuses on what we say and how what we say makes an impact on people — made a great impact on me. One example was former president Nixon's famous quote, "I am not a crook." When Nixon responded with this phrase to accusations related to the Watergate scandal, he reinforced suspicions rather than quelled them. This seems akin to the quote most often used during the Gallaudet Protest of 2006, "Not Deaf enough." The more Deaf people tried to counter Dr. Fernandes' comment, the more we reinforced the idea that it was about her not being Deaf enough.

This brings me to the next question, "What is the meaning of "Deaf"? Most English dictionaries would define deaf as a loss of hearing or the lack of the sense of hearing. This reflects the views of most people not familiar with the Deaf-World who understand deafness as an inability to hear. People were confused by "not Deaf enough" when they saw Dr. Fernandes as obviously deaf. Dr. Fernandes and Dr. Jordan had an excellent team of PR people who planted that quote which put us in a position where we had to defend ourselves, and we consequently missed out on the opportunity to take the offensive.

Being on the defense describes the typical experience of Deaf people. We always have to defend ourselves and try to explain to people who we really are, not who they think we were. Maybe it is time to say, "Yes, Jane Fernandes was not Deaf enough." Dr. Fernandes didn't fit the mold of being a Deaf leader; therefore, in Deaf people's eyes she wasn't Deaf enough. Yet, we were afraid to admit it. The question is what are we afraid of? If we want to change the world's perspective of Deaf people, we need to move on and admit it. Maybe if we had responded in the affirmative to the quote, it wouldn't have been used against us as it was.

This is what I mean about framing. How we frame our arguments, our explanations and our definitions, reinforced that we are who they thought us to be. We need to change this.

From my experience being so very involved in the Protest of 2006, I saw firsthand how the media controlled us. The media served as our barrier, our obstacle to bring our message across to the general public. It seemed like the media had their own filter, maybe it should be called "the filter of ignorance." The media had no idea, nor any understanding of the Deaf-World. It needs to be made clear that the Protest of 2006 was not Deaf President Now II. They are completely different. DPN was a much easier protest, as it was easier to tell the world a Deaf president needs to run a Deaf university, not a non-Deaf woman. That was a concrete concept that the general public could understand. However, during the Protest of 2006 we were denied Gallaudet interpreters so we had to settle for non-Deaf people who weren't trained to serve as interpreters. The biggest casualty was that our choice of words and our way of thinking, were inaccurately portrayed to the world.

Two colleagues and I met with the editorial staff of *The Washington Post*. The first time I was there we didn't have an interpreter as they thought we would bring our own. Bilingual, the three of us communicated with the staff members through the use of a laptop. The communication was not efficient because it was not a natural process and all possible discourse rules for a good dialogue were broken. We ended up having only one person typing all our ideas to them and then signing out loud what they said to us. The second trip to the *Post* was better as we had an interpreter. While it was not the interpreter's fault, we still had difficulty as she was an outsider (being from a different state) and it was difficult to follow the names of people we knew.

Luckily, she was a fluent interpreter and that helped a lot in fighting the obstacles. Still the editorial staff couldn't understand us. We were from two completely different worlds and no language could make them understand us. As I look back, I realize that we reinforced the "not Deaf enough" in our arguments. This experience tells me that how we frame our arguments is essential in arguing our perspectives of the protest and who we are.

These experiences — looking through Marie's papers and fighting in the 2006 protest — led me on a journey in search for a Deaf theory. My sources were books, meetings with colleagues, friends, and students. I will like to discuss especially one student, Robert Sirvage.

In many articles and books that I read there were references to the Marxist theory which I found myself struggling to understand. Robert Sirvage is very knowledgeable about the theory and he had developed a vlog on the theory. I also had a face-to-face meeting with him. This helped me to understand the theory and how many theories fall back on Marxist theory. Many people still look at Marxism and quickly think it is related to Communism. It is much more than that. Actually, in simple terms, it is about "social beings."

To help me with this presentation, I chose three different fields of study that I feel will help me with understanding Deaf Studies. Originally, I believed Queer Studies was closely similar to Deaf Studies, but after taking this journey, I realized all three — Critical Race, Feminist and Queer theories — have some similarities to the Deaf World. My personal and shared experience of oppression contributed to this paper. Paulo Freire's "The Pedagogy of Oppression" is also an important source.

DEFINITIONS

Ideology: a) the body of ideas reflecting the social needs and aspirations of an individual, group, class, or culture; b) a systematic set of doctrines or beliefs (OED)

Theory: a system of ideas or statements held as an explanation or account of a group of facts or phenomena (OED)

Ideology seems to be the study of ideas but it is more systematic than this. It is how the system was set up in a way we all had to follow. The system itself is so embedded in us that it defines world, people, and life, and we are expected to abide by the ideologies we acquired. How we are supposed to think was also shaped by the system. Deaf people are stuck in the hearing ideology to a point we believe it is better to be hearing. As Marie said, it is very difficult to analyze ideology. It is hard to understand ideology because we are lured into acquiring the ideal world "they" decided for us. The system tends to be designed to oppress people.

Theory is also difficult to understand. The definition means nothing but what is in one's mind is what counts the most. How we explain, how we analyze, what we propose, and what fits what we think. It is very difficult, almost as difficult as trying to understand ideology.

Three theories — Gender, Critical Race, and Queer — will be discussed and will be used as guidelines to discuss Deaf Theory.

Feminist Theory

> "Male supremacist ideologist encourages women to believe we are valueless and obtain value only by relating to or bonding with men." (hooks, 2000)

> "Sexist ideology teaches women that to be female is to be a victim." (hooks, 2000)

"This is a man's world." We live in an ideological world where we are led to believe that it is better to be a man. The use of language is often subtle showing superiority of the male gender, inferiority of the female. Women are victimized often to believe that whatever happens to them is their fault because they are the weaker gender. Women aren't taken as seriously as men. People mock women because they are women.

We are at a time where we saw a woman and a Black man vie for presidential candidacy within the Democratic party. The media made Hillary Clinton a victim, just because she is a woman. What happened in the primaries showed we are allowed to oppress women. The media made sexist comments towards Hillary Clinton and nobody did anything to stop them. Is it because Clinton a woman? I believe so. What happened in the primaries makes a good analysis of sexism in our country.

There are numerous sources for feminist theory. I selected a few that, in my opinion, are parallel to the Deaf World:

- a political theory and practice that works to free all women from subjugation (Smith, 1992)
- a theory that acknowledges "women suffer discrimination because of their sex, that they have specific needs which remain negated and unsatisfied, and that the satisfaction of these needs would require a radical change…in the social, economic, and political order" (Delmar, 1994)
- initially feminist theory was the site for the critical interrogation and re-imaging of sexist gender roles (hooks, 2000)

These are the theories I use as the foundation when I look at the Deaf-World. For example, we can paraphrase the second theory above and it will fit the Deaf World.

> "a theory that acknowledges 'Deaf people suffer discrimination because they are Deaf, that they have specific needs which remain negated and unsatisfied, and that the satisfaction of these needs would require a radical change'"

This theory covers how we can radically change the old thinking and fight sexism. We can reimage gender and fight oppression. We need to redefine gender roles. What are they? When the woman is a breadwinner, people will say "she wears the pants." This is because "wearing pants" is more male; therefore, a woman who is bringing in money for the family is like a man.

Critical Race Theory

> "that our blackness is a condition from which we must be liberated" (John O. Calmore, 1995)

> "framers of the US Constitution chose the rewards of property over justice." (Calmore, 1995)

> "Whiteness is the norm." (source unknown)

What drew me to that definition is the word 'condition' because it is often the same way that people look at Deaf people. People are seeing blackness as a condition and if a Black person gets away from her/his blackness, s/he will be normal. It is ideology at work where people see skin color as a condition.

I grew up in a segregated school in Baton Rouge, Louisiana. I was raised to believe Black people were different, that they weren't as clean as white people, and that they had a lot of problems. That was what I was led to believe. Now we know better. Unfortunately, there are people who still believe that it is a 'condition.'

It is important to note that the way the US Constitution was written, people of color had a lower status as human beings. Because Black people were classified as 3/5 of a human being, it was acceptable for them to serve as slaves. The lower status was perpetuated throughout the years, even in the justice system. Black people suffered severe punishments for crimes of lesser violence than what white people committed and yet, white people received lesser punishments. The system's inherent design ensures that people of color will suffer more stringent punishment. Americans often don't see the system's failures and blame the people of color, believing that the punishments match the crimes colored people commit.

People of color are seen as the "other." We have seen this in media where it is written "white people and other people," or sometimes they are called "non-white people." We acquired the belief that whiteness is the norm and all others are different:

- CRT begins with a recognition that 'race' is not a fixed term; instead, it is a fluctuating, decentered complex of social meanings that are formed and transformed under the constant pressures of political struggle." (Calmore, 1995)
- CRT challenges the dominant discourses on race and racism as they relate to law (Calmore, 1995)
- "…seeks to demonstrate that our experiences as people of color are legitimate, appropriate, and effective bases for analyzing the legal system and racial subordination." (Calmore, 1995)

CRT challenges the system. It is imperative to look at how CRT discusses, describes and writes about 'race.' CRT challenges how others describe race and how race is described in the law.

The experience of people of color is legitimate, appropriate and provides an effective analysis of their own races. As Deaf people, we can relate to their experience and how they see themselves. People of color experience what Deaf people experience; this discussion here validates their stories of their own experiences. Many Native Americans stories were disregarded and as legends, rather than being validated as their own experience. Because they weren't written, they are considered fiction or their own legends and therefore not believable.

Queer Theory
Straight Ideologies:

- Heterosexuality is viewed as normal and any deviations as abnormal or "queer."
- One needs to get married and have children.
- One is straight until proven gay.

People are expected to be straight in their sexual orientation, but if not, then they are considered deviants. Although I have been out of the closet for many years, I am still asked by people whether or not I am married. They often look uncomfortable when I say I have a partner.

Our ideology states that one needs to be married and have children. Even straight people who get married and choose not to have children are asked when they will start a family and if there are no plans to, then there is something different about them. They are also considered radical for choosing not to have children. People talk behind their backs and come up with possible reasons for not having children. If you read the advice columns you will realize how often people ask questions regarding how to convince young couples to have children so that they themselves or their friends can become grandparents. This reflects the ideology of straight culture: if a couple only has one child, people wonder why the couple didn't have any more.

Lesbians and Gay men are often denied their own identity. They often had to prove themselves to be Lesbians/Gay men. Frequently in articles, or advice columns, many parents ask about their children coming out and question whether or not it is a phase in their lives. "How does one know she is a Lesbian if she hasn't tried men?" But no one asks how one knows s/he is straight if s/he hasn't tried the same gender? That question is not asked because of the ideology that we acquired. The discussion here shows denial of one's identity. Many Lesbians, Gay men, Bisexuals, and Transgendered (LGBT) develop their identity later in life because they were denied the opportunity (and the right) to identify themselves for who they are:

- all sexual behaviors, all concepts linking sexual behaviors to sexual identities, and all categories or normative and deviant sexualities, are social constructs, set of signifiers which create types of social meaning
- challenges the notions of "straight" ideology
- defines sexuality as part of identity, rather than just an activity which one might engage in

Queer theory challenges straight ideology. Also, it challenges the label given to LGBT for a long time: deviants. It discusses identity and how you are straight until proven gay. If one identifies herself/himself as a Lesbian, a Gay man, a Bisexual or a Transgendered, people are usually reluctant in recognizing their identity. It is not about sexual acts, but about personal identity. These theories above, although very much on the surface, help us understand what is to be discussed next. The ideologies that Deaf people live with eventually lead us into a discussion of Deaf theory.

Ideology of the Deaf World

Sense of hearing (perceptual disability). When I use phrase Deaf-World, I refer to Deaf people in our world. In this section, we will focus on the numerous ideologies Deaf people have to live with. For the purposes of this paper, I limit the discussion to just four select ideologies.

People believe that one needs to have all five senses to be considered a "normal" human. If one loses one or two senses, s/he is considered a disabled individual. Based on this thinking, Deaf people are defined by their "deafness" (where people don't look at the person, but rather at the audiological part of the person). A number of other terms have similarly limiting connotations, including hard of hearing, person with a hearing loss, disabled, hearing impaired. We wonder what is so difficult about using the word Deaf? People zero in on describing the ear, the loss of hearing, and forget to look at Deaf people as people. Sadly, many Deaf people have adopted the ideology that it is important to hear, where they feel the need to wear hearing aids, or even to have a cochlear implant surgery.

When I was a student at Louisiana School for the Deaf, I could count how many students had hearing aids. Now it is the other way around; we now can count how many do not. Deaf children are fitted with hearing aids as soon as parents, schools, and audiologists can get them. I personally shudder to think of how few Deaf children will not be surgically implanted 10 years from now. An alarming number of Deaf people are starting to believe that getting an implant is acceptable. It clearly shows how they were drawn into that ideology that the sense of hearing is important to make a person fully human.

The worst part of the belief is that most hearing parents believe that if they have their Deaf children implanted, they will have "normal" children. They innocently oppress their own children to adopt the ideology.

English as the language to learn (linguicism). It is conservative American thinking to believe that English is "the language." English, as a language, has a lot of power. Many Americans strongly believe that in order to succeed, one needs to master English. English literacy is the road to success. Deaf people are believed to possess third grade level English. Seemingly the way to assess Deaf people's English skills is to compare them to native speakers of English. We all know that it isn't an accurate way to evaluate the language level of Deaf people. There is a double standard here, too: approximately 38–40% of Americans struggle with literacy. Non-deaf people have problems with literacy, but what we are hearing is that specifically Deaf people have problems.

Many Deaf people were brainwashed to feel that English is "the language" and then they impose this ideology on many other Deaf people and children. Unfortunately for some Deaf people, the mere mention of English triggers negative emotions from their childhood.

Linguicism in Deaf community is so strong that most, if not all, ASL teachers are tolerant of ASL errors, contrary to their intolerance of minor English errors. Deaf people will correct English but rarely do they correct ASL errors. They see those with ASL errors as people who try hard and should be tolerated. One common excuse for not correcting ASL is that what was said is understood but then, what was said in English with its errors is understood too. It is the ideology that English is the language that is at work here, causing the double standards.

Individualism (denial of collective identity). American Deaf culture grew when schools for the Deaf were established across the country. Deaf people have their own language, their own culture and most importantly, their own identity. When ASL was first recognized and then American Deaf culture, anti-ASL professionals were threatened. According to Paulo Freire, when one gains power, the oppressor reacts to liberation. Backlash then happens. To fight ASL and American Deaf culture, PL94-142 placed Deaf children into public schools, very often being the only Deaf child in the whole school. This strips Deaf children of their ability and opportunity to develop their own identity as a Deaf person.

Deaf people are hearing until proven Deaf. Professionals will make any effort to make a Deaf child hearing — oral training, invention of sign systems, cued speech systems, putting on hearing aids — and in the end, the children are still Deaf. The question is whether these children have an identity? That is in many ways parallel to LGBT experience where society makes every effort to make a person straight. Many Deaf children are robbed of their identity.

Even many Deaf people are frightened to be identified as Deaf because of this very ideology.

As a Gallaudet professor, I see many mainstreamed students in search of an identity. They don't know their own Deaf heritage. Many still don't know about Laurent Clerc or the impact he had on educating Deaf children. In fact, one mainstreamed student only recently discovered that Gallaudet has not always had a Deaf president.

Speech as a form of success and a human attribute (phonocentrism). This is, in my opinion, the most damaging and most volatile ideology that Deaf people have to live with. People are led to believe that to really succeed, one needs to speak. The ability to speak surpasses other ideologies, e.g., ability to read and write English.

I recall the days when I worked at the Linguistics Research Lab (LRL) at Gallaudet where I was told that English possesses numerous words on the sense of sight. I remembered that throughout the years and until just recently, I realized that ASL has numerous signs related to the mouth. It seems ironic, but then again, it is due to the ideology that we live by. The importance of speech and hearing got embedded in ASL because of this very ideology. We need to look at our lexicon to recognize oppression and our experience as oppressed Deaf people. ASL isn't just a signing machine, as stated by Paddy Ladd in his presentation at the Deaf Studies *Today!* conference in Orem, Utah in 2008. ASL uses more than just signs. It demonstrates the *experience* we all have.

Speech is definitely a byproduct of colonization. We have heard enough stories about oral training, our being slapped on the hands for signing and the fear we had of our oralist teachers. There is one story that made an impact on me that I cannot forget. The credit goes to Dr. Lawrence Fleischer who witnessed the event.

There was once an end-of-school event with young children doing skits and stories. One girl, approximately four years old, retold the entire *Goldilocks and the Three Bears* in ASL. People found her adorable, with her tiny hands and her young use of facial grammar. People applauded. When a five-year-old boy stood and spoke only two sentences, "My name is John. I am five years old," people stood up, and applauded him loudly and some were in tears.

How can one be so impressed with John who spoke only two sentences and not with the girl, who narrated the whole story? It is due to the fact that John spoke.

Also etched in my memory is the NAD 100-year anniversary and conference in Cincinnati, Ohio in 1980. While I was working at the booth, working for LRL, collecting ASL samples from Deaf people, Harry Hoemann, the so-called ASL teacher, proudly showed his new videotape of a young Deaf child, titled "I Want to Talk." That was not the intent of the young boy, but they took advantage of him saying that he wanted to talk. He tried to speak a few words and the videotape impressed people. That shows clearly the thinking of Mr. Hoemann and how he took advantage of the child to perpetuate the ideology of speech.

Many Deaf people are led to feel they need speech training. Those who cannot hear a thing and still can speak impress many. This clearly shows the belief that to succeed, one needs to speak.

Here is another example, a story that demonstrates how we can overcome the dominant ideologies. I was at a conference and during lunch two friends and I went to a fast food restaurant. As the three of us approached the order counter, I signed to the person. The woman mouthed to me, "I can't sign." I signed back, "That's fine, maybe we can write." She had no problem understanding me and brought a piece of paper and pen. It went smoothly. Both of them looked at me strangely and asked why I didn't speak. My reply was that I cannot and what's the point? I have my own language and I have the right to use it. The woman didn't have a negative attitude towards me either. They then tried doing the same thing and found it was not hard to do. I also told them we needed to remove that old thinking that we cannot hear and change it to "they cannot sign."

It is an older way of thinking that if one is able to speak, then the service will be better. Many, if not most, Deaf people are not fluent enough to speak. They probably speak a few words and/or speak to those who know them well.

The general public doesn't respond well to subpar speech.

Simultaneous Method of Communication (SimCom) is phonocentric. People say that they use SimCom because they want to include both Deaf and non-Deaf people. It is more a reflection of their attitude: "I can talk and you cannot." One excellent example is the former president of Gallaudet, I. King Jordan when he chose to waste several minutes to set up the microphone so that he could SimCom to Deaf people at the National Association of the Deaf (NAD) conference in California in 2006. It reflected his thinking that he could talk and that he felt superior to Deaf people. This contradicts the belief of the NAD founders who fought against oralism.

It is interesting to note that speech itself contributes a great deal to prejudice against Deaf people. Some people actually believe that speech is one of the most important human attributes. Here are two quotes that clearly shows prejudice in favor of speech and/or oralism.

> "The breath of life resides in the voice…How little they differ from animals" (John Conrad Amman, quoted in Lane, 107/Bauman, 2008)

> "young creatures human in shape, but only half human in attributes." (Lewis Dudley, founder of Clarke School, quoted in Baynton, 52/Bauman 2008)

These two examples are show how the founders and supporters of oralism perceive Deaf people and believe that they are not fully human just because they sign, instead of speaking. This way of thinking still persists even today, in modern times, unfortunately.

SIGNED LANGUAGES

When I talk about sign language, I mean fully developed languages like American Sign Language, British Sign Language, Japanese Sign Language, Brazilian Sign Languages, and other formed signed languages.

All humans gesture. There is a human need for gestures to communicate. Non-Deaf people do gesture when they speak. They shake their heads in negation, even when they speak on the phone. We need to look at what all humans have in common: gestures. We should look at that and take the opportunity to see how Deaf people contribute to the use of gestures and to humankind. Deaf people have made a very complicated system of gestures into a full language. Deaf people have this ability to do this and again, we should take notice of this. We need to see how this is relevant to society, to the world, and to linguistic studies. Like Paddy said in his lecture, it is unfortunate that people analyze sign languages and show the world they are indeed languages, but failed to look at the lives of Deaf people. They miss the nuance in signed languages that reflect the experiences of oppression. Or, even some will study the languages so interpreters can help Deaf people succeed (as if they couldn't on their own). We need to see and show the value of how the use of eyes, the use of sign languages and how that contributes to the greater society, because humans need gestures to communicate. People overlook the fact that gestures contributed to the survival of communication and then Deaf people created a complicated system from gestures.

Research should be conducted in areas beyond sign languages themselves. We need to learn more about how Deaf people see the world, how they interpret it, and again, how all of this can contribute to the betterment of society. I have issues with people assuming they understand my presentation and how I see the world through the use of interpreters. Non-Deaf people see the world through their ears and it is difficult to change their perceptions and help them to see the way I present my ideas. So many people have their own filters so it is difficult to successfully get ideas across to those with totally different experiences and perceptions of the world.

> "Language is yet another way to categorize people and reinforce their dominant and subordinate status." (Schnedewind and Davidson, 2000)

Understanding how sign languages contribute to the world will definitely upgrade its status. No language is better than the other; it is only how people interpret them that influences why they have different statuses. If we understand people, we will understand languages better. People tend to believe that if we understand languages, we will understand people better. It is my belief that it is actually the other way around.

> "What are those unknown languages that double the world's linguistic resources? You, dear reader, do you know? Of course: Sign languages." (Skutnabb-Kangas, 2000)

Only languages that come with power are listed. There are numerous signed languages that are overlooked and that are unlisted. If we list them all, the amount of languages all over the world will double.

Diverse Culture
It is important to discuss diversity within the community. We need to learn from the mistakes from Feminist and Queer Theories/Studies and to not repeat them. When people began these studies, it was primarily about white Women and white LGBT. Women of color and LGBT of color challenged them and asked why they were excluded. Women said they are women first, and anything else came second, third and so on. Black Women challenged this and said, no, they are both Black and Women. People will see

them as Black first before Women; therefore this thinking needs to be challenged. Even Women Studies fall into the trap of white ideology. Women of color do not share many of their experiences with white women; therefore, Women Studies need to be inclusive and study the experiences of diverse women. Women Studies include studies of privilege, race, ethnicity, class and others to understand the various types of Women and their various experiences in this society.

I have observed that when people talk about Deaf Culture, they tend to think about white Deaf Culture. We need to think of diversity in our Deaf Community to include Deaf people of color, Deaf-Blind people, LGBT Deaf people, Oral Deaf people, and others. We need to do studies on experiences of Black Deaf people, Asian Deaf people and others. We need to share how we see the world.

We all have something in common: our visual orientation toward the world. But, I for one will see the world from a white person's orientation and the biases I have developed over the years.

Deaf-Blind people have different experiences. They were visual beings until they lost their sight. We need to get their stories and include them in Deaf Studies because their stories without any doubt will contribute to the understanding of our society. They adapted their way of living, adapted their understanding of sign languages, and so on. We need to understand their experience.

We should gather stories from oral Deaf people who finally understood when they acquired sign languages. We hear many stories about how lives changed after learning sign languages and developing identities. Their stories are valuable assets to developing theories and to the understanding of Deaf people in general. Again, I use myself as an example. I am a native ASL user with Deaf parents. I have privileges and I was never excluded from my family. I took things for granted and it always struck me when I hear about other people's different experiences, which were so different from mine.

To make Deaf Studies stronger, we must include all of the various types of Deaf people, their experiences, and their backgrounds.

Deafhood

Deafhood by Paddy Ladd is a must read for professionals in Deaf Studies. I have unfortunately heard too many say it is too long or that they feel reluctant to read it because they heard it was controversial. To be real scholars, we need to read books even if we don't agree with them. We cannot argue until we read the materials. This is the case with the Ladd's book.

Taking back the center

As discussed in the book, we need to rediscover our own center. We were thrown off from our center due to oppression, audism, and linguicism. The book discusses how we can get our center back.

One good example is when Deaf people get really engrossed in learning about Deaf culture and trying to understand it. Many of us have been doing scholarly work and lots of discussions have been happening. Then, one — it takes only one — hearing person said, "what about me?" That is enough to throw us off our center. It is not about "you, hearing people" but about us getting our center back first. Luckily, our hearing allies know that and they will wait. It is interesting to note that when I read materials on race, they faced the same problem with white people not being able to wait and allow them have their own center. White people do ask the same questions as hearing people, "what about me?" It is the idea that if a person has her/his own center, s/he gains power. That is frightening to those with power, meaning white hearing straight males.

In October 2007, Gallaudet held its annual Enrichment Day focusing on bilingualism. We had two plenary speakers: one was from the University of Ottawa, a bilingual university speaking both French and English and the other was Ben Bahan. The administrators strongly encouraged all to come. When the first presenter was speaking (in English), the auditorium was full. When it was time for Bahan to present (in ASL) on sensory orientation, most of the hearing chairs and faculty members were no longer present. At the chairs meeting, I asked where they were and the response was that they were busy and needed to do paperwork. The point is that Enrichment Day at Gallaudet means they should put their work on hold and learn from others and from each other. The perspective we got is that they stayed for a non-Deaf presenter but felt a presentation by a Deaf person can be missed.

Ladd asks many questions about our experiences as Deaf people. One important topic in the book is colonialism. We have discussed oppression but colonialism is something we all need to look into, how the ideologies of oralists really colonized our minds and us. This is a valuable asset to my teaching.

It is true that the book is full of theories and like Marie Philip said, theories are hard, but we cannot avoid them. It helps us understand different eras and their ideologies, their theories, and so on and how they apply to the present day. The movie shown at the conference in Orem reflected very well the history of Deaf people, just like the book did.

Also it is important to note one other thing about the book which is the introduction to the concept of sub-alterns. Grass root Deaf people are discussed and how their lives are similar or different from elite Deaf people. How their understanding of and analysis of the world were rejected just because they were Deaf. This reminds me of my studies in linguistics way back in the 1980's. I was told it is difficult to study ASL because I have my biases, and I should be neutral in my studies. In reality, no one is 100% neutral; there is no such thing as this. In that case, no non-Deaf linguists studying ASL are free of own their biases either, and why they thought that they would do research on ASL better than a Deaf person could is beyond our understanding. In other words, what they were saying was that the Deaf stories weren't good enough, but in reality Deaf stories are invaluable because they are based on the core of their experiences.

Ladd also discusses the dimensional stages from deafness to Deafhood. Deafhood itself is really a process of understanding one's own identity as a Deaf person.

Identity

> "The power to define ourselves and our world is radical per se." (Calmore, 1995)

> "The parts of our identity that do capture our attention are those that other people notice, and that reflect back to us." (Tatum, 2000)

When Deaf people identify themselves as Deaf people, many people are taken aback that they could identify themselves as such. How many schools for the Deaf, mainstreaming programs, etc. identify Deaf children as Deaf as opposed to the degree of hearing they have? That in itself tells us that they chose to identify us their way rather than allowing us to identify ourselves.

It is time for us let to go of a superficial definition of Deaf culture. People are still describing it by DST (Deaf Standard Time) which is an ethnocentric way of describing the culture. Deaf culture isn't just about tapping shoulders to get attention. We need to look at the people and their perception of the world. These perspectives should take into account the following themes:

- The whiteness of Deaf culture (discussed in diverse culture earlier in the paper).
- Rehabilitation. It was originated to habilitate a person back to normalness, and our services was originally for our veterans who were injured during the World War II. The idea evolved into rehabilitating Deaf people. Vocational Rehabilitation is used to help Deaf people through their college years financially, including myself. Personally I have difficulty with the concept of VR help. It has too much power over the lives of Deaf people. One example is that I was in a several meetings at my university where discussion on possible

new courses focused on whether or not VR will support it. They shouldn't be deciding for us but rather we should decide what is best for our students.
- The fears surrounding us. Many Deaf people are still frightened by how others think of us. That is common among oppressed people. "Should we say this, or not?" One of characteristics of an oppressed person (Freire) is fear of liberation.
- The perceived importance of speech. It is okay not to speak. There is a strong belief among many of us that it is better not to speak than to speak unintelligibly. People react to strange speech. Ironically, if one speaks only two sentences, people are impressed. This itself instills the belief into Deaf Americans that it is better to speak two sentences than to think for oneself.

PARADIGM SHIFT: DEAF MUTE THEORY OF VISUAL BEINGS

In 1913 George Veditz wrote "people of the eye." Ben Bahan used the term "seeing people." Flavia Fleischer came up with "Deaf Lens" for a conference. We heard stories of the "uniqueness of Deaf eyes" where we could see even the smallest things.

Instead of lamenting on the lack of hearing and speech, we need to look at what we possess that others don't. Our extraordinary use of eyes and how we use eyes for language should be the focus of Deaf Studies. We shall challenge the world, the system, and the ideology that we can contribute to the society with how we use our eyes.

Reclaiming Deaf-Mute as our identity, the no-need-for-speech perspective and challenge phonocentrism

People react negatively to this because for many years we have tried to educate people to not to use 'Deaf-mute' when describing Deaf people, including myself. Are we negative towards mute because of the "speech ideology"?

It was said that hearing people react more negatively to the word mute than to deaf. This is something for us to see. In dictionaries, deaf is defined as a loss, an impairment, but we Deaf people still feel comfortable with that identity. We might be able to do the same for mute or would it be more difficult because it is so embedded in our lives which is believing that speech is ultra-important? We can challenge the system and say that mute is an acceptable term and not necessarily negative. We can look at Queer Theory. The word queer is negative, but the community is challenging the ideology and taking the word back. Maybe we can do the same and fight to get our word back to the community.

REDEFINING DEAF, THIS TIME OUR WAY

We can challenge the definition of Deaf and make it a positive term. It is not in the dictionary but we can add a definition to mean 'a sense of identity' for Deaf people who use sign language. We can challenge the colonialism of the Deaf community. We can analyze the various layers of oppression: individual, institutional and systemic oppression and fight colonialism. With the challenge, we can analyze audism and linguicism. CRT analyzes racism and offer ways to fight it. We can do the same, analyze audism and linguicism and offer ways to fight it.

What I have presented here is not my work alone; it is based on discussions with various Deaf colleagues and peers. It is time for Deaf people, and I mean, Deaf people, to have its own think tank and work on Deaf Theory, our experiences, our theories, our hypotheses and propose them. Non-Deaf people who want to know and learn from us will wait. When we are comfortable with our proposition, we can have a dialogue and they can offer different perspectives. That is scholarly work. Women Studies and Feminist Theory were offered by women and then were open for dialogue. The same was done for CRT and Queer Theory/Studies. Let us do the same. Let us Deaf people do our own work and then open it up for a dialogue. The main goal of Deaf-only work is to find our own center. We shall deconstruct how we are defined and reconstruct who we are.

Deaf Jews and Deaf Muslims

KATI MORTON & CINDY PLUE, PH.D.

THE DEAF WORLD INCLUDES PEOPLE WHO DO NOT ONLY HAVE DEAF Culture affecting their identity. They have various ethnicities, sexual orientation and religion influencing the way they live. These are multicultural Deaf people, those who try to balance other cultures in addition to their Deafhood. Two of the world's prominent religions, Judaism and Islam, have Deaf members, and their experiences with their religion are cause for study and exploration. Both the experiences of Deaf Jews and Deaf Muslims are relatively similar in that they are often shut out from their religion and unable to learn the tenets of what their families and fellow congregants believe because services are not provided to accommodate them. Within these two religions there is much to be done to provide equal access, but they are not at the same stage; more progress has been seen in Judaism compared to Islam.

Access to services for Deaf Americans is greater today because of the passage of the Americans with Disabilities Act (ADA) in 1990, so it seems odd that members of church groups are still struggling to gain access to their heritage and religion. The reason for this lack of access is that religious groups are exempt from complying with most of the ADA. While they still have to make accommodations for employees, church groups do not have to provide accessibility for the public (Obligations, 2007). The ADA says the following about the religious exemption:

> "[T]he ADA's exemption of religious organizations and religious entities controlled by religious organizations is very broad, encompassing a wide variety of situations. Religious organizations and entities controlled by religious organizations have no obligations under the ADA. Even when a

religious organization carries out activities that would otherwise make it a public accommodation, the religious organization is exempt from ADA coverage. Thus, if a church itself operates...a private school, or a diocesan school system, the operations of the...school or schools would not be subject to the ADA or [the title III regulations]. The religious entity would not lose its exemption merely because the services provided were open to the general public. The test is whether the church or other religious organization operates the public accommodation, not which individuals receive the public accommodation's services" (Breen, 1992).

As a result, religious groups have not been held to the same standard as have other organizations. They are not held accountable for lack of access and are under no legal obligation to provide services to their members. This has led to the discrepancies seen in Judaism and Islam regarding Deaf followers of those religions.

DEAF JEWS

To analyze the situation of Deaf Jews today, the history of how they have been perceived in that religion needs to be discussed. According to the Mishnah and the Talmud, holy books in the Jewish faith, Deaf people were legally categorized with "the deaf, the retarded, and minors," meaning that they were not considered to be mentally competent, so they could not be held responsible for their actions (Zwiebel, 1994). This paternalistic attitude meant that they were not seen as fully human, as capable of understanding what was going on around them. They needed to be taken care of. However, Zwiebel (1994) goes on to state that this legal status for the deaf only applied to those who could not speak; deaf people who could talk were thought to be on the same level as hearing people. This shows that the perception of people in the Jewish faith at this time was that speech equaled intelligence, rational thought, and that those who did not possess it were to be classed with the mentally retarded because both groups were believed to be incompetent.

While this attitude is seen in Jewish history, there is evidence that not all deaf people were viewed in this manner. The Mishnah discusses Deaf Jews who served in the Temple in Jerusalem in 100 AD, working in ways that required "great learning and understanding" (Zwiebel, 234, 1994). This shows that deaf people understood the Jewish faith even at a time when they were not considered capable of doing so. There is also evidence that there may have been an ancient Jewish sign language and even an interpreter for this language (Henkin, 1986). If there was a Jewish sign language, it means Deaf Jews were not isolated and associated with each other, and also that they were respected enough that there may have possibly been an interpreter that learned their language and was able to communicate with Deaf Jews in ancient times.

While the perspective that deaf people were not on the same level as those who hear began to be debated and contested in later years (Zwiebel, 1994) it still had an effect on the status of Deaf Jews. Schreiber (2001) describes how he was left out of his religion and as a result, unable to pass it on to his children because he was not taught it himself. He was not given the same opportunity to learn about his religion as hearing people are granted; they acquire such information by default because they simply hear it. This shows the dilemma in the transference of religion, that much attention is placed on what you hear and the fact that some members may not be able to is forgotten.

Many Deaf Jews wonder at the lack of sign language interpreters at their synagogues (Simmons, 2007). Without interpretation of the lessons and teachings, it is difficult for a Deaf Jew to gain an understanding of what their religion is about when they go to synagogue. If they are lucky enough to have good communication at home with their family, then they will gain access there, but they are still left out of the services, causing them to miss the messages that are given outside the home. This may cause them to lose their faith and leave the fold of Judaism because they do not understand it, as the following states:

> Since 90% of deaf children are born into hearing families, they rarely have the opportunity to participate in depth in the living and feeling of what it means to be Jewish, whether in the synagogue or in the home. In the synagogue, they are lost amid a sea of auditory activity to which they had no access, and in the home, their parents, once having realized the scope of the task involved with raising a deaf child, naturally put Judaism on the back burner. Never having obtained an intrinsic connection to Judaism therefore, they are less able to identify as Jews or marry Jews, and less inclined then to pass Judaism on to their children (About Us, 2007).

However, things have shifted for Deaf Jews and they are gaining more services. In 1956, the National Congress of Jewish Deaf was established to "bring together individuals who are deaf and hard of hearing and provide opportunities to study and learn about Judaism in an educational and religious environment" (The JDC Story, 2007). They felt a need to bring together people who were Deaf and Jewish so they could teach each other about their religion. In 1960, the Temple Beth Solomon of the Deaf, a Jewish synagogue, was founded in Los Angeles, California (About Us, 2007). This was a set up by a group of Deaf Jews who "molded a place where they could transmit Jewish traditions, customs, and rituals to their children in such a way that they would grow, loving Judaism, identifying with it and also having a place to serve their own spiritual needs, filling the void of Jewish programming suited to the needs of the Deaf" (About Us, 2007). As a result of these efforts to establish a Jewish Deaf society and synagogue, Deaf Jews have much more access to their faith than ever before. There are rabbis who sign, such as the one at the Congregation Ohev Shalom synagogue in Orlando, Florida, and there is a Deaf Jewish group at Gallaudet University (Fuchs, 2005). There is also a Deaf woman rabbi serving in California, the only female Deaf rabbi in the world (Bertholdo, 2006). These are all efforts that are being made within the Jewish community to include those who are Deaf in their worship.

In addition to these organizations, the Hebrew Association of the Deaf was founded in 1970 to "meet the social and religious needs of Deaf Jews in Chicagoland" (Congregation, 2007). This organization founded the Congregation Bene Shalom synagogue that holds as its goal to be a "spiritual and social resource for Deaf and hearing alike" (Congregation, 2007). This is another place where Deaf Jews can go and learn about their religion and not have to wonder what the beliefs of Judaism are because they have direct access to their faith.

There has been significant progress since the days of Schreiber's anguish over his religion, but there are still many who are isolated and not included in the Jewish faith. However, they have more access to their religion than do Deaf Muslims. According to one imam, Metwali al-Saidi, the Qur'an makes no reference to deaf people (Navarro, 2007) so perceptions of those who are deaf in Islam throughout history cannot be analyzed as was previously with Judaism. While more progress has been seen with access to Judaism for Deaf people, the issues Deaf members of both these religions have faced and are currently dealing with are similar.

DEAF MUSLIMS

Deaf Muslims throughout the world struggle to gain access to their religion, and America is no exception. As one Deaf Muslim from Ghana experienced, he came to America hoping to learn how Deaf Muslims were educated here, only to find that the situation was not vastly different from in Africa. "No interpreters at mosques, no Islamic lessons for deaf Muslims." (Abdulai, 2007). Access to their religion is not commonly provided. There is currently an effort to translate the Qur'an into Sign Language (Al Showaier, 2005), but until that takes place, Deaf Muslims will not be able to learn the words of their holy scripture in their native language. This translation is not into American Sign Language, so Deaf Muslims in America will still not be able to experience the Qur'an in their signed language. They will not be able to utilize this translation unless they learn the sign language it is translated to, so until there is an ASL version, there will be little signed access to the Qur'an for Deaf Muslim Americans.

While the experiences of Deaf Muslims are varied, a common thread is found in many of them, and that is lack of access and understanding of their religion, as an American-born Gallaudet student recounts:

> My parents taught me a little bit about Islam. They would bring me to the mosque, but I didn't understand because it was mostly in Arabic. My family wanted me to focus on English. My sisters and brothers know more about Islam than I do because they understand Arabic better and they have an advantage of hearing everything. My parents taught me basically what is right and wrong, halal and haram. But I don't know like, how to pray, the words, how to recite the Quran, or Islamic history. (Muyesseroglu, 2007)

The experience of this student is found in many of the accounts of Deaf Muslims. Access to Islam is often not given to Deaf members as it is to hearing. One of the reasons for this is a lack of Muslim interpreters in America (Legander-Mourcy, 2000). Even if there were interpreters provided in mosques, if that interpreter was not Muslim, or had no knowledge about Islam, they could interpret incorrectly and stumble if the Deaf Muslim asks them a question pertaining to the religion, as Ashia Ahmad (Legander-Mourcy, 2000) points out: "Even if someone asks about Islam, it is really only a Muslim interpreter who could answer their questions from an Islamic perspective. A Christian or non-believer might give inaccurate information or give it from a slanted perspective." Simply finding sign language interpreters does not necessarily mean that access to religion has been granted for Deaf people; interpreters who are also members of the religion they are interpreting for are greatly needed. They will better be able to interpret the message because they will know what is being discussed, while someone who is not a member of that particular faith may get lost in unfamiliar terminology, which could cause them to render an inaccurate message.

There is still much to be done to provide access for Deaf Muslims. The Deaf Jews have organized, and have pushed for their rights and access to their religion, and there are synagogues specifically for Deaf Jews in America. Deaf Muslims are organizing as well, trying to provide education and access to their fellow Deaf Muslims, but there are no fully accessible mosques yet. However, there has been progress. One Muslim center in Virginia began offering interpreters for the Friday Praying (News, 2007). This will provide greater access to the Deaf Muslims of that community, as they will now know what is being said when they go to these services. This is a great step, (albeit a small one), and needs to be done in mosques throughout America.

One of the organizations that is striving to improve the religious situation of Deaf Muslims is The Global Deaf Muslim organization. It states as its purpose that, "...we aim to provide programs to sisters, brothers, and communities worldwide to understand Deaf in Islam to dismantle the barriers of communication, learning, and participation for Deaf Muslims. We undertake these programs in name of Allah and we ask for his blessing upon our works" (Programs, 2007). This reflects the goals of this group, to provide access to Deaf Muslims throughout the world, so they can participate in their religion like others do. This organization has established many programs in an attempt to accomplish this (Programs, 2007). This shows that the needs of Deaf Muslims are being recognized and efforts are being made to give them access to Islam. One example where this is seen is in Egypt.

In Egypt, the mosque of Sayeda Zeinab has a volunteer who interprets the meeting to hundreds of Deaf people who come to participate in Friday prayers. This interpreter, Alaa al-Din al-Sayed, has a Deaf sister and founded an organization to help Deaf Muslims (Navarro, 2007). The efforts of this man show that there is awareness that the needs of Deaf Muslims are not being met and steps are being taken to combat that. In addition, there is a school in Egypt that teaches around 100 Deaf adolescents classes in language and computers, as well as religion (Navarro, 2007). Deaf Muslims are starting to gain access to their religion in that country, and this is a sign of progress. However, this is very small in comparison to the great need for access. The services at this mosque are interpreted by al-Sayed, which is a step in the right direction, but there are between two to four million deaf people in Egypt (Navarro, 2007). They cannot all attend this one mosque. There needs to be many more mosques like this, so all Deaf Muslims can learn about their religion. There has been progress, and there are many efforts being made to improve the situation for Deaf Muslims internationally. There is a vast amount of work to be done, but there are signs of progress and if it continues, Deaf Muslims will gain more access to their religion and become fully participating members of Islam.

RECOMMENDATIONS

In light of the fact that Deaf Muslims and Jews are currently unable to fully participate in their religion in many cases, what needs to be done to provide equal access to Judaism and Islam for the Deaf members of those religions? At the basic level, interpreters must be provided. This is still not a perfect solution; going to religious services and only being able to participate through an interpreter does not provide equal access, but it is a better situation then what is happening now. In addition, these interpreters should not be any professional interpreter, but whenever possible they should also be members of the religion that they are interpreting. This will make the services much more accessible to Deaf Jews and Muslims, because they will not have an interpreter who does not know the teachings of the religion and could therefore get lost and confused and not accurately interpret what is being taught. Having an interpreter at religious services is better than having no access at all to what is being said, but it is much more beneficial to have an interpreter intimately familiar with the doctrines that are being taught, so they will better be able to transmit an equivalent message in ASL.

Having interpreters at religious services is vital in order to provide access to Deaf Muslims and Jews. However, many Deaf members have gone for so long without knowing the teachings of their religion that it is important that they are taught, not through interpreters, but through someone who can teach them directly in their language. A solution would be to offer classes in the religion, be it Judaism or Islam, in American Sign Language, so that Deaf members would be able to learn the teachings of their religion on an equal level, not through interpreters. Someone who is knowledgeable in both the religion and Deaf culture, preferably a Deaf member of the specific religion, should be granted space, accommodations, and any other help they need by the religious group to teach the Deaf members of that particular area. These students would then be able to teach others, to take what they have learned and pass it on to their families. If such a system had existed in Schreiber's time, he would not have had to be embarrassed that he could not teach his children; he could have taught them himself, just like any other Jewish father. If access is granted to these Deaf members, they will be able to teach others and the Deaf communities within these religions will become stronger.

In addition to classes for Deaf members, it would also be beneficial to have religion classes for families and deaf children, so they can learn at home what their religion teaches, and not have to wait for years before they are taught about their religion. Often, there are communication barriers between hearing parents and deaf children, and parents may not know how to teach their children about their beliefs. This is one of the premier goals of the Global Deaf Muslim organization, to educate Muslim parents about how to teach their deaf children about Islam, and they have set up a program in order to do that.

> The program to educate Muslim parents of deaf children is considered to be the most sacred of all programs to GDM because it is written in Holy Qu'ran and said by our beloved Prophet Muhammad (pbuh) that it is the duty of Muslim parents to give their children an Islamic education. There are many Deaf Muslims who receive insufficient religious education to understand the wonders and beauty of Islam. As part of the mission, GDM aims to develop and provide workshops and information to Muslim parents worldwide in different languages about how to raise Deaf children, how to obtain secular and religious educations, to have their children to be part of the community, and how to communicate with Deaf children. We aim to make videos, audio tapes, informative packets, and workshops where Muslim parents can understand the unique needs of Deaf children and how their

minds can be best educated to be good believers. We strive to reach many Muslim parents of Deaf children as possible. An educated Deaf Muslim will make Allah joyful (Programs, 2007).

This statement shows how important it is for Muslim parents to be able to teach their children about the Islamic religion. The Global Deaf Muslim organization recognizes that this program will be vital in improving the education of Deaf Muslims worldwide. If Deaf Muslims are taught in the home, as children, they will better understand their religion and be able to carry it with them into adulthood, even if they do not have access to their religion at their mosque. They will still know what the beliefs of their family and religion are, so they will be able to be strong members of the Islamic faith, because they will not be completely left out of its teachings.

Classes for Deaf members of Judaism and Islam as well as parents of deaf children will greatly help improve awareness of the teachings of their religion for deaf members, but there are many areas where there are not a large amount of Deaf people who are members of Judaism or Islam, so efforts need to be made to reach out to them. In this time of great video access on the internet, congregations of Deaf Jews and Muslims could record their discussions about religion, interpret the holy books, and teach about the tenets of their faith in ASL, and then post those videos onto the internet so Deaf people throughout America could see them. The same could be done by Jewish and Muslim Deaf people worldwide; they could record themselves signing explanations about their religion in the sign language of their country, and then share them with others via the internet. Videos can be accessed throughout the world, so the international Deaf community could teach each other the doctrines of their religion. This is already happening, as a few videos discussing Islam and Judaism in ASL can be found at online.

One of these, titled "Shabbaton," can be found on youtube.com. Its purpose is to explain "what Shabbaton means and the Jewish traditions involved. Terminology is voiced for pronunciation purposes so that interpreters will know how to voice the word/phrase" (SLAVideoCenter, 2007). This is beneficial to Deaf Jews, because it teaches about Judaism, and is also useful for interpreters, so they will understand the terminology they need to know if they interpret a Jewish religious service.

Another website, deafmuslims.org, has two videos that discuss Islamic teachings in American Sign Language. One of these videos is a translation of the story of the Prophet Yunus called *Yunus and the Whale* for Deaf Muslim children (Deaf Muslims, 2007). Videos like this are a great start in spreading the teachings of Islam to the Deaf community, but many more are needed so that those who have not been able to learn their religion will have the opportunity. This is another effort being undertaken by the Global Deaf Muslim organization, to "provide videos with professional sign language users explaining about Islam on many issues such as zakat, marriage, faith, and learning. The videos will be able to educate Deaf Muslims who lack sufficient reading..." (Programs, 2007). Videos are a great way to spread information, especially with signed languages, and their visual nature. Videos are not a perfect solution, as not everyone has access to the internet and other video technology, but they would greatly increase knowledge about the teachings of Islam and Judaism for members of those faiths, as well as promote awareness in the larger Deaf community, as they will also have access to these videos and will have the opportunity to learn about other religions.

In order to facilitate the use of videos to teach religious concepts to deaf people worldwide, it would be helpful to have similar signs used by all to teach about these religions, so people in different countries would know what was being taught in the videos, even if they did not know the sign language that was being used. This is one of the efforts of the Global Deaf Muslim organization, as the following states:

> We aim to establish a universal hand signs for words and concepts that exist in Islam for all users of sign language to use in pursuit of the goal of uniformity in signs. To do that, we must start collecting pictures and videos of Deaf Muslims in many countries to record their signs for words and concepts in Islam to find the most practical universal hand signs to reduce confusion and time spent on translating different hand signs of a same word or concept (Programs, 2007)

This is a tremendous undertaking, and whether it will prove effective remains to be seen. If successful, it would greatly help to educate Deaf Muslims worldwide, as similar signs would be used to explain religious concepts. This would make it easier for organizations to teach Deaf Muslims, because they would not have to translate between the various sign languages, at least as far as religious terminology is concerned. This would make internet videos more effective, as people internationally would be able to understand the religious teachings shown in videos from throughout the world.

While interpreters, classes, and videos will greatly help to provide access to religion, one of the most vital factors that would help to change the situation for Deaf Jews and Muslims is awareness by the religious leaders of these two groups. If rabbis and imams were aware that they had Deaf congregants and made an effort to reach out to them, it would greatly help provide better access. Religious leaders are generally well-meaning people who seek to assist and help all the members of their faith. They often focus much of their energy on trying to retain the people in their area, so it seems odd that Deaf people are slipping through the cracks. While some overt neglect may be the cause of this, more likely it is caused by a lack of awareness. Rabbis and imams possibly do not know that they have Deaf people among them, or if they do know, they might not have an idea as to what to do to accommodate them. If efforts were made to teach them how to work with these members, then they will be able to provide more access. If they remain unaware, these problems will continue.

CONCLUSION

In the Deaf World, there are multicultural Deaf people who have more influences affecting them than Deaf Culture alone, such as ethnicity and religion. Deaf Jews and Deaf Muslims have both struggled to gain access to the teachings of their religion and to understand the teachings of Judaism and Islam. However, much progress has been made, particularly with Judaism, and if efforts to change the situation continue to take place, some day equal access to religion for all Deaf congregants — Jewish and Muslim — will be a reality.

REFERENCES

Abdulai, N. (2007). *Perspectives of a Deaf Muslim*. Retrieved October 17, 2007 from http://salika.wordpress.com/2007/08/25/perspectives-of-a-deaf-muslim/

About Us. (n.d.). Temple Beth Solomon of the Deaf. Retrieved October 17, 2007 from http://www.tbsdeafjewish.org/about.htm.

Al Showaier, H. (2005). *Arab federation for the deaf*. The World Association of Sign Language Interpreters, (1), 1–4.

Bertholdo, S. (2006) Deafness no obstacle for Adat Elohim rabbi. Thousand Oaks Acorn. Retrieved October 17, 2007 from http://www.toacorn.com/news/2006/0202/Columns/

Breen, P.L. (1992). U.S. Department of Justice letter. Retrieved November 14, 2007 from http://www.usdoj.gov/crt/foia/talo57.txt.

Congregation Bene Shalom (n.d.). A warm joyous congregation where all are welcome. Retrieved December 12, 2007 from http://www.beneshalom.org/main.htm.

Deaf Muslims (n.d.). Welcome to DeafMuslims.org. Retrieved December 12, 2007 from http://www.deafmuslims.org

Fuchs, M. (2005, July 23). At synagogues, services open doors for the deaf. *The New York Times*. Retrieved December 12, 2007 from http:// www.nytimes.com/2005/07/23/national/23religion.html

Henkin, A. (1997). The Deaf Jew in the modern world (book review). *Judaism*, 36(4), pp 489 (10).

Legander-Mourcy, B. (2000) How inclusive of the disabled is the Muslim community? *Azizah Magazine*

Muyesseroglu, J. (n.d.) The Deaf Muslim experience. Retrieved October 17, 2007 from http://edf3.gallaudet.edu/diversity/BGG/!ISLAM/Deafan~1.htm.

Navarro, A. (2007). Signs of the times for Egypt's deaf in search of Islam. Retrieved December 11, 2007 from http://www.middle-east- online.com/English/Egypt/?id=22907=22907&format=0.

News (2007). Global Deaf Muslim. Retrieved October 18, 2007 from http://www.globaldeafmuslim.org/achived_news.htm.

Programs (n.d.). Programs of Global Deaf Muslims. Retrieved December 11, 2007 from http://

www.globaldeafmuslim.org/programs.htm.
Schreiber, F.C. (2001). What a Deaf Jewish leader expects of a rabbi. In Lois Bragg (ed), *Deaf world.* (pp. 33–37). New York: New York University Press.
SLAVideoCenter. (2007, May 11). Shabbaton. Seen on http://www.youtube.com/watch?v=qDM6e3-o_Lg
Simmons, S. (n.d.) Ask Rabbi Simmons: Interpreters for Deaf Jews. Retrieved October 17, 2007 from http://judaism.about.com/library/3_askrabbi_o/bl_simmons_deaf.htm
The JDC Story: A Brief History (2007). Retrieved October 17, 2007 from http://jewishdeafcongress.org/story/
The Obligations of Religious Organizations Under the ADA. (n.d.) Retrieved November 14th, 2007 from http://www.ada-il.org/questions/q_religious_orgs.php.
Zwiebel, A. (1994). Judaism and Deafness: A humanistic heritage. In C.J. Erting, R.C. Johnson, D. L. Smith & B.D. Snider (Eds.), *The deaf way* (pp. 231–238). Washington D.C.: Gallaudet University Press.

"The Play's the Thing": American Deaf Theatre's Contribution to Deaf Studies

AARON KELSTONE

RECENTLY OUR ACADEMIC WORK HAS BECOME EASIER DUE TO THE advent of videotape, CD, and DVD technology. But, how can we make discoveries about the eras prior to the invention of recordable media? How can we discover the trends, concerns, and issues that deaf people were concerned about over the past century or even earlier? To some extent that answer may be found by endeavoring to collect, review, and apply effective analysis of Deaf playwright scripts.

Deaf culture is predominately a "face to face" culture. For scholars in the Deaf Studies field this presents a difficult challenge related to the identification of critical influences within Deaf culture in the eras prior to 1950. Deaf playwright's scripts provide a means to circumvent these difficulties by offering ways to identify historical trends, concerns, and issues within the deaf community.

So why has this approach not been tried in the past? Part of the reason may be associated with the ongoing myth that Deaf people do not write plays. There is a long standing assumption that the English language effectively formed a barrier against any effort by Deaf people to write plays. More importantly, there may have been a barrier that gradually developed within the Deaf community itself; pushing the focus away from Deaf playwrights. This barrier has its roots in the establishment of literary societies, which were initially supported by residential deaf schools and later strengthened from a cross pollination process at Gallaudet College. These literary societies provided a place where Deaf performers could hone their performance skills and develop translation and adaptation skills through transforming English texts into sign language. For many generations of the deaf community this was a:

> cultural staple, presented by literary societies at residential schools or by adult organizations...(t)hese diverse forms and performance styles are assembled into a kind of variety or talent show, but here the accent is (or is supposed to be) on the "literary"...because the term "literary" was interpreted very loosely, the literary framework was capacious and flexible enough to accommodate almost anything from nativist ASL art to signed English readings, although it usually contained works that were originally literary (Peters, 78-79).

As students enrolled at Gallaudet College, they brought with them the best of their local performance materials and shared them with other students. Over time the most popular materials would be return to be shared at the local level. This created a traditional body of performance work and was a positive aspect of the literary societies because it provided the means to nurture development of a skilled base of deaf performers. These deaf individuals would be prepared to adapt traditional theatre into what today we either call Deaf Theatre or Sign Language Theatre. But, how did these same organizational groups create the barrier mentioned earlier? Prior to the development of the literary societies I propose there was always a performance element active in the deaf community. What differentiated these performances from what we see on the stage today was how the process for developing performance materials were created by Deaf performers. I have personally observed performing arts activities on the playground, in Deaf clubs, and in skits developed for conventions and clubs. Much of this material was developed through ideas generated from visual observations of the world. For example, Emmanuelle Laborit, current artistic director of IVT in Paris, France has noted that:

> (i)n the beginning, the idea was to create a theatrical piece not from any existing text but from an idea. Take an idea; get a group to improvise on it, and then add their own ideas, but there was never a text. The productions were always based on the actors' concepts and improvisations (250).

A visual concept of what this looked like can be best observed through the work of Charles McKinney and Alan Barwiolek who toured the United States during the latter part of the 20th century as CHALB. According to a close associate of the two men most of their work was created using an improvisational approach supplemented by written outlines. Some examples of their performance work have been preserved in videotape format by Sign Media Incorporated titled "Live at SMI-CHALB."

On the other hand, literary societies and drama clubs focused on a translation process that was based on scripts written in English by hearing playwrights. Many plays selected were from classic or contemporary theatre. This was most likely the result of a cultural need to address the ongoing colonization experienced by deaf people since 1880. Culturally there was, and continues to be, a need to validate deaf art by imitating the valued artistic canon of the dominant culture. As a consequence a strong tradition developed within Deaf Theatre to perform plays adapted from hearing playwrights and essentially ignored a full century of writing by deaf playwrights. An example of how early playwrights struggled to produce their work can be seen through a series of email conversations that I had with Eric Malzkuhn during January of 2005 where he noted:

> At this stage of my life I was often traveling around the Great Lakes area, giving one man shows and leading a small group doing skits, etc. Since I could get about only on crutches, this was over. I decided that since my career as an actor was ended, I would start writing plays, and I produced my first, "And Gladly Teche" (after Chaucer). This was a one-act play about a newly-graduated Gallaudet woman and the vicissitudes of her new teaching career. I sent this to my mentor, Professor Frederic Hughes. I did not hear anything from him, so I wrote a letter, asking for the play back. No answer.
>
> Finally I asked a friend who was teaching at Gallaudet, Jerry Jordan, to get it back. He was able to procure it after promising to show it to no one. I later found out that Hughes objected to the play because of two reasons: one, in it I suggested that the current curriculum for the normal students did not adequately prepare the graduates for the low reading level of their prospective students and two, I had the heroine fall in love with a man who was born deaf. Thus I committed two grievous faults, I dared question the Gallaudet graduate school offerings and I proposed that deaf marrying deaf was just fine. At this time Gallaudet discouraged this practice. So, Hughes had it copied, and distributed to his drama classes (who wanted to stage it forthwith) and labeled it "pinko," and let it sink into oblivion. It was later lost.

This passage illuminates various difficulties that deaf playwrights encounter as they try to market their plays within the Deaf community. Their work is devalued because it is not generated from an English text thus it would not attract a hearing audience (which is where the money is or so goes the general thinking), and it will not generate enough ticket sales. This is the second reason there is an ongoing myth that deaf people do not write plays. If one was to informally poll groups of deaf people about their knowledge of Deaf plays most would mention "My Third Eye" (1969) by the NTD acting ensemble, "Tales from a Club Room" (1980) by Bernard Bragg and Eugene Bergman, and "Sign Me Alice" (1973) by Gil Eastman. Perhaps a few more would be identified but not many.

Ironically, there is a large body of work that has been generated from at least the beginning of the 20th century. With extensive research more plays may be found dating back to earlier centuries. This cannot happen without greater international support. I have collected a listing of plays through a variety of sources. Some have been identified through direct contact with deaf playwrights and additional information has been collected from an appendix listing contained within Dr. Steve Baldwin's book *Pictures in the Air*. As a result I have compiled a listing (by no means complete) of 37 deaf playwrights and 184 plays. In addition ,one female Irish deaf playwright has been found whose work consists of 19 plays, three works of undetermined format, and 9 radio dramas (see appendix A).

Why is it that there is a lack of awareness for these works? Why is there is a lack of understanding for how these plays offer the potential to expand the range of knowledge and understanding of the Deaf experience within Deaf Studies? For one, not all of these plays are stage worthy. As a result many of the plays have never been performed. Some are outdated, and others have simply never had the chance to be supported by any theatre. Secondly, many of the plays languish in filing cabinets of deaf playwrights or theatres, long forgotten because there has never been a process developed to disseminate these works to the deaf community. In contrast hearing playwrights are able to gain support for their plays through the script publishing houses. This provides them with an effective way to market their work to the national network of American theatres. Currently this kind of support does not exists for deaf playwrights other than a few traditionally well known scripts offered by a small group of online and publishing businesses that are deaf owned.

It is possible that a cooperative effort to collect and categorize these plays will develop research processes enabling us to identify, from within the structure of these plays, specific themes, concerns, and issues that were prevalent for deaf people during specific time periods. What we may learn can provide Information that is not available to us in any other manner because Deaf playwrights are a fertile ground for discovering relevant issues within the deaf community. Shakespeare says it best when Hamlet says to the players: "...the purpose of playing, who end both at the first and now, was and is, to hold t'were the mirror up to nature..."

An early review of some plays collected at NTID show a tendency to adapt popular, well known stories and change the content of these stories to reflect the dramatic experiences of the characters through a deaf lens. However, not many of these adaptations have achieved a wide exposure to Deaf audiences with the exception of Gil Eastman's "Sign Me Alice." The primary reason this adaption of "My Fair Lady" and "Pygmalion" was successful was because the play focused on a communication issue that has been a concern within the deaf community. The modification of sign language into artificial forms such as SEE led Eastman to develop his adaptation to challenge the emerging use of SEE in American deaf culture. By using comedy and particular elements of absurdity he effectively addresses the issue. This is important because many Deaf people assign ASL as being the strongest cultural attribute in their cultural experience. The introduction of SEE creates an ongoing tension within the deaf community because it conflicts with the historical development of sign language. As Carol Padden and Tom Humphries explain:

> (n)atural signed languages, like spoken languages, have histories; they have been passed down through generations of signers or speakers...but no individual — not even the Abbe de l'Epee, for all the credit he is given for "inventing" sign language — can hope to match the productivity or complexity of a language constructed over generations of users. By definition, languages are historically created, not invented by individuals (Clark and Clark 1977) (118–119).

Since SEE has continued to be used in educational mainstream programs the issue remains a consistent concern for the deaf community. As a result Eastman's play remains timely for subsequent generations within the deaf community. Another trend is to create historical plays addressing different aspects of the deaf experience. Some examples of this can be seen in Don Bang's "Institutional Blues" concerning residential deaf schools, Gil Eastman's "Laurence Clerc: A Profile," Bernard Bragg and Eugene Bergman's "Tales from a Club Room" and more recently Willy Conley"s "Goya-en Quinta del Sordo." In this way deaf playwrights are extending the "face-to-face" tradition of storytelling to preserve cultural history through the use of theatre.

Other playwrights have created plays that reflect areas of the deaf experience not readily shared within the deaf community such as Michelle Banks' Black Woman's Stories: One Deaf Experience (1992) or Patti Durr"s "Meta" (1993) which addresses the deaf experience during the Holocaust. Some plays reflect gender or sexual preference issues as in Bruce Hlibok's "Women Talk" (1984), and the work of Raymond Luczak. Other Deaf playwrights address areas of cultural discomfort such as the deaf peddler that are found in the works of Mike Lamitola, Aaron Weir Kelstone, and Douglas Burke.

The exploration of works by deaf playwrights also brings focus on Deaf plays that indirectly addressing the deaf experience. Through careful analysis of these works we could explore the cause and effect of these playwright choices. Are these plays generated by an inability to clearly sense the center or a deliberate desire to avoid a direct reference to the deaf experience? This can lead us to discover other questions that may help deaf individuals or the culture as a whole to begin defining how specific issues shaped the development of the Deaf community. Through the use of academic theories or specific fields of study we can gain insight into the cultural journey that deaf people have historically taken to rediscover their deaf center. Post-Colonialism comes to mind as a strong theoretical choice. Afro-American, Feminist, Gay/Lesbian Studies are some of the fields that offer us ways to define our experiences because by extending our gaze outwards we "could learn to articulate relations between cultural patterns of talking and knowing, and, understanding such relations, to make choices (Heath, 13). Playwrights such as Shanny Mow and Raymond Luczak may simply responding to market forces that are caused by the lack of awareness or a reluctance of the deaf community to support their work. This pushes these deaf artists towards creating works that use canonically acceptable universal themes with the hope it translates into universal appeal and financial success.

Other playwrights demonstrate a more "pre-De'VIA" approach to their work. An example of this can be seen with one of the earliest known deaf playwrights, Teresa Deevy (1894–1963), a female Irish playwright who represents, along with Lady Gregory, one of only two women whose works were ever produced by the Abbey Theatre in Ireland. Deevy's work primarily addressed issues within the Irish community but her themes often related to isolation and separation. Could these themes have been generated from her deaf experience or were there larger forces at play at the time? Research into these kinds of questions can help understand the various processes that deaf playwrights struggle with as they produce artistic works from very isolating experiences.

Most of my observations about the plays have been general comments. This is necessary because the current list developed has encountered difficulties in collecting the actual scripts, because these plays have been difficult to locate and some are lost. There has been a general reluctance by playwrights or their estates to release their work due to issues concerning copyright, intellectual property ownership and potential monetary issues. As a result only 50 of the current 184 plays listed has been successfully collected. This situation is not unique because at RIT/NTID we have experienced similar problems developing public websites for deaf visual artists and deaf people who lived during World War II. These two projects, spearheaded by Patti Durr, had to overcome resistance to online public display of visual artist's work and World War II information.

Ironically, when the websites were launched it proved to be a wonderful vehicle for artist recognition and has often increased their opportunities for additional income from their visual work. It has also expanded scholarly examination of deaf peoples during World War II within a Deaf Studies context. This same process is now ongoing for the Deaf playwright project and should create similar results if fully supported.

As their works are identified and made available to the deaf community it creates opportunities to generate interest in historical trends and issues that were part of the deaf experience before colonialism took its toll of the deaf community. It will provide Deaf Studies scholars with the ability to generate a greater amount of analysis and in-depth study of these works eventually leading to questions and answers that have not been achieved through other research methods. It is certainly an area worth nurturing and will require a concentrated effort to clean out attics, discover lost boxes, and search through filing cabinets. It will release a potentially vast reservoir of material addressing the historical development of the deaf experience. The power of the internet will enable rapid expansion of knowledge about these plays and allow this area of Deaf Studies to make a significant contribution to the field of study by globally exploring the historical and current trends within the Deaf community.

REFERENCES

Baldwin, S. (1993). *Pictures in the Air: The Story of the National Theatre of the Deaf.* Washington, D.C.: Gallaudet University Press.

Clark, H., and E. Clark (1977). *Psychology and Language.* New York: Harcouirt Brace Jovanovich.

Heath, Shirley Brice. Ways with words-language, life, and work in communities and classrooms. 1983. 10th ed. Cambridge: Cambridge UP, 1992.

Laborit, Emmanuelle. "Writing My Life." *Sign Language Studies* 7.2 (Winter 2007): 242-252.

Malzkuhn, Eric. E-mail interview. 6 January 2005.

McKinney, J. Charlie, and Alan Barwiolek, perf. Live At SMI: CHALB. Burtonsville, Maryland. 2 January 1993.

Padden, C, & Humphries, T. (1988) *Deaf in America: Voices From a Culture.* Cambridge: Harvard University Press.

Peters, Cynthia L. (1996) "Literary Night: The Restorative Power of Comedic and Grotesque Literature." *Deaf American Literature: From Carnival to the Canon.* Washington, DC: Gallaudet University Press, 78-95.

The HeART of Deaf Culture: Visual and Literary Arts of Deafhood

KAREN CHRISTIE, PH.D. & PATRICIA DURR

THE COLLECTIVE EXPERIENCES OF ALL CULTURES HAVE BEEN PRESERVED, recorded, and conveyed via visual art, literature, and performance. Throughout history, the arts (storytelling, poetry, theatre, fine arts, and film) have been valuable for preserving the traditions, heritage, language, values and norms of cultural and disenfranchised groups. For those cultural groups that possess a strong oral language tradition, the arts take on an even more vital role. All people have generated artistic expressions that are unique to their culture and which can be interpreted as markers of belonging and/or markers of group boundaries.

All peoples create A-R-T for aesthetic purposes. In addition, artistic works express a group's shared collective experiences, record and preserve their culture and history, communicate their cultural values/world view and advocate for sociological and political changes. In the Plenary Address on Language and Culture at the 2003 World Federation of the Deaf Conference, Dr. Carol Padden and Dr. Yutaka Osugi spoke about the three promises of Deaf culture: history, imagination and justice. That is, "the history to understand, imagination for solutions to our common problems, and justice to guide us as we make changes in our world and our communities" (Padden & Osugi, 2003). They describe how indigenous forms of storytelling in natural signed languages have traditionally incorporated "strategies for Deaf children learning to read and ways of interacting with the world." Thus, the linguistic and artistic products of Deaf people's imagination "give voice to the hidden or the unconscious, and give us ways to reorganize and reshape as we look to our future."

A DEAF-THEMED FRAMEWORK

In order to look specifically at how visual and literary arts carry cultural meaning and communicate collective experiences of a group of people, we have worked from analysis of Deaf artists themselves. The Deaf View/Image Art (De'VIA) manifesto was written in 1989 by nine Deaf artists in order to recognize and promote a particular genre of artworks by Deaf people:

> De'VIA represents Deaf artists and perceptions based on their Deaf experiences. It uses formal art elements with the intention of expressing innate cultural or physical Deaf experience. These experiences may include Deaf metaphors, Deaf perspectives, and Deaf insight in relationship with the environment (both the natural world and Deaf cultural environment), spiritual and everyday life. (De'VIA Manifesto, 1989)

Clearly, literary works by Deaf people can incorporate cultural and physical experiences, Deaf metaphors, Deaf insight, and Deaf perspectives of the world. In this way, De'VIA can be seen as parallel to a post-colonial analysis of literary works. Like many post-colonial peoples, Deaf people express feelings of exile, alienation, and experiences of colonialization of one's language and educational systems.

As with feminist, Harlem Renaissance, Chicano, and other art and literary movements, this representation can further be viewed in terms of the cultural themes of affirmation, resistance and liberation. Both artistic and literary works incorporating De'VIA resistance themes can cover audism, oralism, mainstreaming, cochlear implants, identity confusion and eugenics. Affirmation and liberation themes can further address subthemes related to empowerment, ASL, affiliation, acculturation, acceptance and Deafhood (see Durr, 1999/2000, Durr 2007, and Christie & Wilkins, 2007)

Thus, rather than focusing on artistic and literary works created by but not about Deaf or hard of hearing people, we focus on Deaf-themed works themselves, choosing to highlight those works of art and literature which address and record one's Deafhood journey and/or "Deaf worldview." Coined by British scholar Paddy Ladd, 'Deafhood' is a term which describes the de-colonialism process the individual and collective Deaf group travels through as they shift from a medical/pathological understanding of deafness to a cultural, linguistic, political and spiritual understanding of what it means to be people of the eye (Ladd, 2003).

VISUAL ARTS OF DEAFHOOD

While Deaf people have created literary and cinematic works about the Deaf experience prior to the De'VIA manifesto, the visual arts have led the way because there was a collective and conscious effort to NAME Deaf-themed expressions within the visual arts. The term De'VIA itself is interesting because it initially followed the ASL signing of the concept and the English "gloss" did not come about until later. Deaf (culturally centered) View (meaning perspective)/image (meaning the representation) Art (meaning visual art). After coining the term and creating a gloss, the acronym — De'VIA was created giving it a foreign flavor — showing its uniqueness and its roots in a language other than English.

The conceptualization of De'VIA likely originated in the late 1970s, during the time the Spectrum Deaf artists' colony in Austin, Texas. Yet, it was not named until the gathering of artists before the Deaf Way I conference in 1989. Artists have been striving to represent the Deaf experience via paintings, illustrations, photography, sculpture, mixed media, textile art, printmaking, ceramic, digital arts, and other mediums. No medium appears to be absent from De'VIA representation although painting seems to be the most frequently utilized. Below we discuss a number of De'VIA works and explain how they address the theme of the Deaf experience in terms of resistance, affirmation, and liberation. (see also Durr, 2007, "De'VIA: Investigating Deaf Visual Art" from the Deaf Studies Today! Simply Complex 2006 Conference proceedings which examines many more De'VIA visual artworks).

The visual arts works above by Martin and Ford both depict evolutionary processes and different stages of metamorphism. Martin has a series of busts which overemphasize the neck and mouth and often de-emphasize the eyes. However, a few of the busts that have more normal-sized necks and eyes depict a smaller self emerging from the consciousness of the bust. Ford's S KIN/Left has an emphasis on hands being interconnected to form a womb-like shape while his nude figure is in a gestational phase of becoming a new person. He emerges from the cocoon as a Deaf person after to loosing his hearing gradually due to an unusual illness. He is forming a new "skin" via his kinship with the Deaf community and, just as being left handed was stigmatized in earlier days, he is learning to embrace who he is today rather than succumb to the dominant culture's characterization of him.

Thornley's famous "Milan, Italy, 1880" with its inspired composition following fellow deaf artist, Francisco Goya's "Third of May, 1808," puts ASL in the background and under fire during the uncivil war against sign language in deaf education. In contrast, Lentini's student self-portrait, "Snapshot Silent," puts ASL and Deaf culture in the foreground and the hearing world and sound in the background. Both utilize bright colors to communicate a message of hope and perseverance despite being a misunderstood minority.

Ivey's small "Why Me" sculpture and Clark's graphic design "iPain" both tie into iconic imagery and serve to record resistance to the forced hearingization of Deaf children. Ivey's small child with the oversized headset, absent mouth and tied hands is clearly mute in this process. Clark's silhouette of a child placed on a red background with a blazing white cochlear implant additionally illustrates how both children have become a pathology via the field of deafness to the point where the personhood, spirit, and voice of the child is voided.

"Evolution of ASL" by Dr. Betty G. Miller is a wonderful example of liberation De'VIA. Miller is often referred to the Mother of De'VIA because of the volumes of works she has created in this genre and for her endlessly advocacy for the examination of the Deaf experience via the arts. The painting should be "read" from bottom to top. The dark bottom with simplistic outlines of hand shapes shows the dark ages of oralism, when ASL was banned from the classroom. Dr. Miller has incorporated her famous "Ameslan Prohibited" piece into this artwork as a testament to how oralism has enslaved Deaf people and arrested their potentiality.

Despite enduring oralism and audism, Deaf people have continued to be visual people and to cherish ASL and Deaf culture. The middle section of the painting features a black hand in a Y handshape with glowing reddish yellow outline. Further up are colorful handshapes, some with eyes in the center of the palm, with a bright rainbow-like background. The black handshapes indicate a spiritual entity — perhaps, the center of Deafhood itself and from it spring up more liberated Deaf individuals who form the Deaf collective experience and the promise of our future.

With Joan Popovich-Kutscher's resistance piece "Anti-Prisoner," she records and shares the unfortunate and traumatic experience of having been mis-diagnosised as severely developmentally disabled. This was due to the fact that she did not speak and respond in a time frame judged as age appropriate. As a result of being placed in an institution with developmentally disabled individuals, Joan was deprived of access to language and rendered mute. Several years later after seeing Joan create a sculpture of a dog out of spare clay, it was determined that she was simply Deaf and did not have any biological cognitive difficulties. Transferred to the California School for the Deaf, she was introduced to art as a way of to express feelings and as a communication tool. It was a powerful stepping stone in her journey to language development and her Deafhood. Years later after studying art at the California Institute of the Arts and the Caliornia State University, Popovich-Kutscher would utilized print making to represent her Deaf point of view and experiences. Ropes, zippers, and puzzle pieces would become strong motifs in her work.

Pamela Witcher's painting "Sign Language, our roots. Deaf children, our future," is an affirmation De'VIA piece. It shows a town in the distance, and a natural setting in the middle which serves as a background for five Deaf figures. These Deaf individuals form a line to signify our Deaf heritage and the importance of ancestors in forming a community, preserving and fostering a sign language, and resisting oppression. As in many of her paintings and other De'VIA artists' works, the Deaf individuals are earless and bald — De'VIA artists often choose this representation to show a genderless construct and a foreign / alien composition. From the hearts of these beings is again a glowing yellow light which is transferred onward from one individual / generation to the next with the smallest and nearest child looking back over this linage with a smile. The yellow glow, which may be seen as forming the sign for Deaf over the heart, trails out of the frame toward us, the viewer and on to the next generation — an endless endurance of Deaf love and life.

CINEMA OF DEAFHOOD

Three major types of cinema are narratives, documentaries and art films. For the purposes of this paper, we selected an example of each type of film which depicted the Deaf experience. "Don't Mind?" is a 12-minute, short narrative film directed by Patti Durr and Lizzie Sorkin. Patrick Graybill stars in the lead role as an older Deaf man set in his ways until a Deaf neighbor asks him to babysit her daughter. Initially resistant, Graybill's character softens under the carefree guidance of the 5 year old girl, Samantha. While the film represents a universal theme of the power of love and being youthful at heart, the movie also has some very specific Deaf experiences in it. The Deaf community, rather small and close-knit, often results in people who do not know each other very well asking each other for some kind of assistance.

The film concludes with Bill wanting to stay on as Sam's babysitter and then receiving a new visitor at his door who says, "I heard you babysit Sam and I was wondering if you wouldn't mind watching my son..." Deaf audience members usually laugh as soon as they see this new person at the door with a young child on her hip, immediately recognizing how fast news travels via the Deaf grapevine. This feel-good flick affirms the Deaf experience by normalizing it. (The film is viewable at http://ideatools.rit.edu/sktedr/drff/main/Archive/2005 Award-WinningFilms.htm)

"Exodus: A Deaf Jewish Family Escapes the Holocaust" is a twenty-five minute documentary produced by NTID. The film features interview shots of Lilly Rattner Shirey re-telling her Deaf family's flight from Nazi occupied Europe to their internment on Ellis Island for five months with the prospect of being sent back to Austria. Intercut with Lilly's narrative are photos from their family album, the US Holocaust Memorial Museum, and other sources as well as a narrator. The film is designed to give voice to the Deaf experience within the scope of Nazism, the Holocaust, and U.S. immigration policies. The film covers resistance, affirmation and liberation as the Deaf Rattner/Wiener family members forge a new beginning in their new homeland. (The film is viewable at http://www.rit.edu/deafww2).

A short scene from "Paper Airplane," an autobiographical student art film by Adrean Mangiardi, shows the filmmaker turning the lens on his cochlear implant and giving it a life of its own. This 14 minute film is a mixture of home videos from his childhood, current interviews with different non-signing family members, and a mixture of contemporary footage all exemplifying a deaf person's attempt to get a hold on sound. In the middle of the film Mangiardi films himself placing and removing a safety pin to his skull — it sticks in place due to the magnet affect of the internal cochlear implant unit. He then films various tools and dangles his external cochlear implant unit with its magnet over them — one by one the objects are picked up and hang from this device.

Next Mangiardi uses stop motion animation to show himself asleep being dragged out of his bed by his cochlear implant and down a flight of stairs. The magnetic device finally comes to a rest on a metal stair rung having satisfied its thirst. Given that the filmmaker concludes the film with a text frame explaining that he will be getting a second cochlear implant, it is unclear if the overall work is a form of resistance or affirmation. It is clear that there are several moments of turning the lens onto the dominant culture and their artifacts, moments which shift the Deaf person from being object to being subject, and also examining the unexamined — the hearing gaze and its impact. (Film is viewable at http://ideatools.rit.edu/sktedr/drff/main/archive/2005award-winningfilms.htm)

As filmmaking has fallen into the hands of self-taught filmmakers and can easily be distributed via the internet, we see an explosion of works that are exploring the Deaf experience. (For a more in depth analysis of themes and symbols, discourse and aesthetics of De'VIA Deaf cinema, see Christie, Durr and Wilkins, 2007, "Close-Up: Contemporary Deaf Filmmakers" from the Deaf Studies Today! Simply Complex 2006 Conference Proceedings).

LITERARY ARTS OF DEAFHOOD

Deaf literary artists, creating in both English and ASL, use language in a variety of ways to convey a Deaf world-view. In this paper, we use the term "Deaf literature" to refer to those literary creations about the Deaf experience using English. Deaf literature consists of conventional genres or categories of English literature which include fictional and nonfictional prose works as well as poetic works. The genres of ASL literature include folklore which has been passed down in a face to face manner as well as those works recorded on videotape. Genres are useful for discussing and analyzing literary works by grouping together works that share similar forms. Yet, genres are not static, and literary artists often strive to break forms, blend genres, or create new types of literary forms.

Deaf Literature

English Poetic work of the Deaf Experience

The poem, "Lip Service" by Robert Panara which appears in No Walls of Stone (Jepson, 1992) represents one poem created by a Deaf writer about the Deaf experience. This short poem is formatted with two stanzas, each consisting of eight lines. The final stanza is presented here:

> You want to rap
>
> You said you want to integrate
>
> but you decline
>
> to change your line
>
> of crap
>
> from speech
>
> to sign.
>
> — Robert Panara, "Lip Service"

Panara masterfully manipulates the language so that there is repetition (the first two lines in each stanza are the same), rhythm (short lines), rhyming of words (gap/rap/crap), and skillful use of idioms and slang (line of crap/this thing about the communication gap/lip service).

The poem unfolds as a response to a stated desire for social interaction from a member of the speaking-hearing majority ("you want to rap/you said"). In the course of the poem, the poet cleverly unmasks the insincere desire of the speaking-hearing 'you' to 'integrate and communicate' without any effort or intention to learn our language. Thus, the title of the poem reveals the hypocrisy of empty talk which comes from mouths and is not followed by earnest action. This poem describes a Deaf experience in which there is resistance to the social pressures to assimilate, to use speech, and resistance to the pressure to deny a Deaf cultural center. It is acknowledgement that at the cultural borders of interaction, it is the people from non-dominant cultures who are expected to defer to the dominant culture, its language, and its way of being.

Short Story of the Deaf Experience
The short story, "Yet: Jack Can Hear!" was created by Douglas Bullard and published in the *Deaf Way II Anthology* (Stremlau, 2002). In this story, a young Deaf boy returns to school in the fall after undergoing an experimental operation in which he is given a pair of new ears. The story is written with an ironic tone concerning the reverence toward the doctor-god, the desperation of the parents for a miraculous cure, and the description of the new ears (fake looking and hard to keep aligned perfectly on the sides of this head).

Thanks to the efforts of the doctor and the financial sacrifices of the parents, the experimental new-ear operation has been a success!! Now Jack, the Deaf boy who is told he should be grateful, can hear everything perfectly, but, alas can understand nothing at all. The sounds, which he cannot turn off, are with him all day and all night. Finally, after another of many sleepless nights, Jack decides the only way to stop the noise is by jumping from his dorm window. At the last minute, he is yanked back in, and the houseparent and other kids work to figure out how to remove the batteries carefully from the fragile ears. The following is the ending of the story:

> "...Jack beamed Me deaf!
>
> Nothing wrong deaf, Casey agreed with an elaborate shrug that as much as said, what's the big deal.
>
> Me deaf! Jack exclaimed again.
>
> Jaime made to toss the batteries in the trashcan, but Miss Racher said, "let me have 'em. I'll think of a way to make 'em dead and put 'em back in. Nobody will know."
>
> Secret! Exulted, the boys and Miss Racher swore to each other to keep the secret always...
>
> Jack was very happy to be an object of a dangerous secret and to be deaf, finally. Deaf at long last! (Douglas Bullard, "Yet: Jack Can Hear!")

Bullard's short story includes italic renderings of ASL signs as a way of allowing characters to use their language and as a way of showing the insufficiency of English for rendering signed dialogue. Bullard portrays the Deaf experience of the medicalization of Deaf identity and the glorification of attempts at 'cures,' as well as individual affirmation of Deaf identity as natural and desired. The atmosphere of the story gradually transforms into a statement of personal liberation — a subversive liberation which celebrates a secret and collective act of resistance.

Non-fictional work of Deaf Literature

Deaf people from diverse backgrounds have written autobiographies and memoirs relating their life experiences. These works provide a rich ground for Deaf-themed works. One such work, "A Short Narrative of the Life of Mrs. Adele M. Jewel," appears in the collection of early writings about and by Deaf people, A Mighty Change (Krentz, 2000). This narrative is particularly precious because it is one of the earliest pieces of autobiographical writing by a Deaf American, and more so because it is written by a African American Deaf Woman who lived at the time (1834–?) when many African Americans were denied basic human rights.

Jewel shares a number of experiences including impressions and memories of her childhood before she had language. In the excerpt below, Jewel records the first time she meets another Deaf person.

> "She was the first mute I ever saw and the mysterious ties of sympathy immediately established a friendly feeling between us. I was surprised and delighted at her superior attainments... and in a little while taught me the sign language..
>
> ...After I saw Miss Knight I grew very anxious to become a pupil at Flint. (After arriving), I succeeded in making my self understood, and from being an entire stranger, soon became as a member of one large family." (*Adele Jewel, "A Short Narrative of the Life of Mrs Adele M. Jewel"*)

Jewel shares the common Deaf experience of Deaf children growing up in a hearing family alienated from the majority and isolated from their own culture. In many Deaf literary works, the experience of meeting another Deaf person for the first time is a significant cultural moment. Jewel describes the "immediate ..friendly feeling" and "mysterious ties of sympathy" of "self-sameness" (Rutherford, 1993)) and DEAF-SAME (Padden & Humphries, 1990). In addition, Jewel is likely one of the first Deaf Americans to use the metaphor of the Deaf school as home and the feelings of kinship which evolved among the students there (see also Christie and Wilkins for more on this).

Her work describes her early family history, her perceptions as a Deaf person, and her own struggles to support her family Jewel's writing she provides a glimpse into one Deaf person's beginning steps on her journey to Deafhood. While we don't exactly know how her story ends, we do know that she was able to send her Deaf son to a Deaf school, demonstrating the enduring value of Deaf schools as places for cultural growth.

Performance Art Reflecting the Deaf Experience

Performance art that reflects the Deaf experience is also a place where the intersections of Deaf people's use of two languages often occur. Miss America" was created under the direction of Peter Cook and enacted by a group of female students from the Lexington School for the Deaf during the Second National ASL Literature Conference. Its title, "Miss America" refers to the beauty pageant which was won the previous yearby Heather Whitestone.

This performance takes a feminist view of beauty contests as exercises in superficiality (with Hollywood illusions, makeup, and ruffled dresses) and in which one presents a false-self to be judged. Such references suggest for Deaf people, that false self is created by oralism with its focus on form rather than content, and surface appearances rather than the depth of reality. We are judged by the dominant culture in superficial terms: our ability to use speech rather than by the substance of our thoughts.

The performers unmask Heather Whitestone as a speaking puppet (mouthing "Hello, I'm Heather Whitestone") with the arms of another student draped through hers which sign. Her one line is that she does not sign nor need an interpreter in response to a Deaf questioner. The Deaf questioner the smacks Heather Whitestone in her face — perhaps, an ironic comment on the passivity expected of Deaf women. This performance of resistance clearly mocks the values of the dominant culture and others who get caught up in trying to act as "hearing" as possible.

Drama of the Deaf Experience
The classic play, "Tales from a Clubroom," was created by Bernard Bragg, Eugene Bergman and their original cast of actors. The play gives the audience a glimpse into the lives of Deaf people set in the Deaf club — one of the pillars of Deafhood. The play includes a variety of archetypes representing the diversity of Deaf people. The scene below includes the characters of Mark Lindsay, a Gallaudet graduate (who "signs Englishy") and Mary Brannon (the "club deadbeat"):

> Lindsay: I see you don't want to become a member of this club. Neither do I. But I am curious to know why you keep coming here.
>
> Brannon: (Ponders for awhile). It's a love and hate relationship. The larger world — the hearing world — shuts me out, but I loathe the gossip and banalities that prevail in the small, constricted world of the deaf. At the same time, I'm attracted to the deaf. Why? Because they represent my last human contact. In spite of, or rather because of, their bluntness and candor they somehow seem more human than the hearing....I can't help coming here. They're my last human contact. (Bernard Bragg and Eugene Bergman, "Tales From a Clubroom")

This brief interaction gives us insight into the contradictory feelings the character, Mary Brannon, has about the Deaf club. For her, the experience of being in a small, intimate community, feels restricting. It is a view that likely echoes her feelings about herself as a Deaf person — internalizing the belief that the hearing world is a better place where there isn't any "gossip nor banalities." Yet, her description emphasizes that being able to interact naturally allows "human contact" and allows one to be viewed as "human." This affirms the Deaf cultural value of the Deaf club as a safe place with others like ourselves, the value of our right to a natural sign language and the right to personhood.

ASL Literature

ASL Oratorical expression of the Deaf experience
In even the first filmed recordings of ASL by the National Association of the Deaf (1913), oratory plays a significant role. NAD President George W. Veditz begins by greeting "friends and fellow deaf-mutes," describes the approaching endangerment of sign language by the forces of oralism and mentions by name several masters of sign language. An excerpt, as translated by Dr. Carol Padden, appears below: (see http://videocatalog.gallaudet.edu/player.cfm?video=2520 for the full presentation)

> "The German deaf people and the French deaf people look up at us American deaf people with eyes of jealousy. They look upon us Americans as a jailed man chained at the legs might look upon a man free to wander at will. They freely admit that the American deaf people are superior to them in matters of intelligence and spirituality, in their success in the world, in happiness. And they admit that this superiority can be credited to, what? To one thing, that we permit the use of signs in our schools...
>
> ...we American deaf know, the French deaf know, the German deaf know that in truth, the oral method is the worst......They have tried to banish signs from the schoolroom, from the churches and from the earth.... Enemies of the sign language, they are enemies of the true welfare of the deaf. As long as we have deaf people on earth, we will have signs. And as long as we have our films, we will be able to preserve our signs in their original purity. It is my hope that we all will love and guard our beautiful sign language as the noblest gift God has given to deaf people." (George W. Veditz, "The Preservation of Sign Language," 1913)

In this rhetorical work, Veditz presents the Deaf experience in a historical context. At the time of the presentation, the impact of the Milan conference was reverberating across Europe and making its dominating presence felt on the American continent. Veditz shows the intimate connection between Deaf people and our sign languages. Further, he argues that our sign languages are the key to our success and happiness, our intellectual and spiritual growth. He affirms our collective value of sign language as liberating, and naturally bequeathed to Deaf people. Like many other powerful oratorical works, his ideas communicate across the generations to Deaf people today — concluding with a plea that we will cherish and defend our language.

ASL Folklore of the Deaf Experience

The folklore of Deaf people includes ASL narratives, form-driven stories, folktales, Deafsong/cheers and Deaf jokes. Because of the social functions of folklore, "to serve as a metaphor for the group's experience, to transmit group customs, values, and behavior norms, to serve as an educative tool... and to maintain group identity" (Rutherford, 1993, p. ii), this is an area of literary arts which sould be rich in Deaf-themed works. One well-known joke goes by a variety of titles such as "Which Room Was it?," "The Honeymoon Joke," or "The Deaf Couple at the Motel."

> A Deaf couple arrives at a motel for their honeymoon. After unpacking, the nervous husband goes out to get a drink. When he returns to the motel, he realizes that he has forgotten the room number. It is dark outside and all the rooms look identical. He walks to his car, and leans on the horn. He then waits for the lights to come on in the rooms of the waking, angry hearing guests. All the rooms are lit up except his, where his Deaf wife is waiting for him! (MJ Bienvenu, 1989)

While the origin of the joke seems to be lost, this is characteristic of folkloric works from cultures with face to face language traditions. Yet, the joke clearly continues to live on in various retellings and manifestations. Over the years, the motel key becomes a key swipe card and the reason for leaving the room ranges from the need for a corkscrew to the need for a condom. The recent Pepsi commercial, "Bob's House," is still another manifestation of the joke created for television advertising. Bienvenu's analysis (1989) of Deaf humor, highlights this as "creative problem solving" by Deaf people. Our own students call this a Deaf "zap" joke or a joke which celebrates the convenience of being "hearing free and totally visually in tune." While being Deaf in a world dominated by those who hear is often shown to be a disadvantage, our survival humor communicates the positive value of being Deaf and of claiming a sense of justice.

ASL Poetry of the Deaf experience

A significant number of ASL poems address the Deaf experience (see Christie and Wilkins, 2007). The poem we have chosen here is "Hands Folded" by Clayton Valli. The poem appears in his *Selected Works of Clayton Valli* (1995) and is signed by Mel Carter, Jr. Below is a description of selected parts of the poem in English for discussion purposes (It does not represent a poetic translation).

> Ah, these folded hands...Where did that come from?
>
> Folding my hands......Ah, if I think back
> To my Deaf school in the dining hall, I remember...
> we kids sign-chatting around each table,
>
> To which the houseparents' glared: fold your hands like this and be quiet, fold your hands and be quiet, fold your hands and be quiet.
>
> Looking up at them we exasperatingly surrender, complying our hands to fold. And fold, and fold...
>
> Three times a day, folding hands morning, noon and night...
> from elementary to middle school to high school...
>
> Much later in life, when I went out to eat with groups of friends at restaurants, I'd find myself sitting there with my hands folded.
>
> When I went to family gatherings, amidst our visiting,
>
> I'd be oblivious to my hands sitting folded in my lap....
>
> ...Will I ever break this habit, this habit of folding my hands??
>
> (The persona ends the poem by smiling compliantly and unselfconsciously folds his hands; *a partial English description of the ASL poem, "Hands Folded" by Clayton Valli)*

In this poem, the persona bemoans his inability to break the habit instilled in him from his Deaf school days when the students were forced to fold their hands to prevent signing while waiting for meals. The original ASL poem consists of visual images that are expressed with a clear rhythm in their repetition: the number of tables, the number of meals, the number of situations, and the number of times the gesture of hands folding occurs. This rhythm is further reinforced by the frequency of meals and the passing of years which communicates — via the rhythmical form of the poem — the reinforcement of a behavior which becomes an unconscious habit.

From a Deaf cultural perspective, the shackling or quieting of hands is both a linguistic silencing and a physical silencing. The houseparents' demands for folded hands is institutionalized audism which is internalized, and persists years after graduation. In this resistance poem, we see how folded hands can further symbolize the linguistic, mental, and physical colonialization that Deaf people must become aware of and examine before liberation can occur.

CONCLUSION

The 2008 Deaf Studies *Today!* conference closed with an emerging tradition — a reenactment of the "Blue Ribbon Ceremony" which first touched the hearts of Deaf people world wide at the 1999 World Federation for the Deaf Conference. On stage, in Australia and later Orem, Utah, a group of Deaf people stated, in part:

> "...We celebrate our proud history, our arts, and our cultures... we celebrate our survival...And today, let us remember that many of us and our ancestors have suffered at the hands of those who believe we should not be here. We are here to remember them...to pledge...to fight to end that oppression now for all the world's Deaf children and the others still to come." (Ladd, 2003)

These words emphasize the importance of history, culture, and *the arts* to Deaf people. The ceremony, which taps into our collective imagination, confirms our shared history, celebrates our cultural survival, and reminds us of our responsibilities to work for social justice for future generations. In addition to this ceremony, the visual and literary arts created by Deaf people, as we have shown by representative works, become lasting celebrations and tributes which record, preserve, disseminate, nurture and valorize global Deafhood. All these works serve to fortify the heart of Deaf culture and Deafhood.

Photo by Brandon Scates

Author's note: We would like to honor two Deaf visual and literary artists who have been true keepers of Deaf culture: visual artist and advocate Dr. Betty G. Miller and ASL poet and linguist Dr. Clayton Valli.

REFERENCES

Bienvenu, M.J. (1989). Reflections of Deaf culture in Deaf humor. In C.J. Erting, R.C. Johnson, D. L. Smith, & B.D. Snider (Eds.), *The Deaf Way: Perspectives from the International Conference on Deaf Culture*. Washington DC: Gallaudet University Press.

Bragg, B. and Bergman, E. (1981). *Tales From a Clubroom*. Washington, DC: Gallaudet College Press.

Bullard, D. (2002). Yet: Jack can hear! In. T. Stremlau (Ed.), *The Deaf Way II Anthology*. Washington DC: Gallaudet University Press.

Chrisite, K, Durr, P. and Wilkins, D (2007). Close-Up: Contemporary Deaf Filmmakers. In. B. K. Eldredge and M.M. Wilding-Diaz (Eds). *Deaf Studies Today! 2006: Simply Complex: Conference proceedings*. Orem, UT: Utah Valley State College.

Christie, K. and Wilkins, D. (2007). Themes and symbols in ASL poetry: Resistance, affirmation and liberation. *Deaf Worlds*, 22, 1-49.

Christie, K. and Wilkins, D. (2007). Roots and wings: ASL poems of coming home. In. B. K. Eldredge and M.M. Wilding-Diaz (Eds). *Deaf Studies Today 2006: Simply Complex: Conference proceedings*. Orem, UT: Utah Valley State College.

Durr, P. (1999/2000, Fall). Deconstructing the forced assimilation of Deaf people via De'VIA resistance and affirmation art. *Visual Anthropology Review* 15 (2), 47-68.

Durr, P. (2007). De'VIA: Investigating Deaf visual arts. In. B. K. Eldredge and M.M. Wilding-Diaz (Eds). *Deaf Studies Today! 2006: Simply Complex: Conference proceedings*. Orem, UT: Utah Valley State College.

Jewel, A. M. (2000). A narrative of the life of Adele M. Jewel. In C. Krentz (Ed.), *A mighty change: An anthology of Deaf American writing*. 1816-1864. Washington, DC: Gallaudet University Press.

Ladd, P. (2003). *Understanding Deaf culture: In search of Deafhood*. Clevedon: Multilingual Matters.

Miller, B. G. (accessed 3/12/08). DeVIA manifesto. http://bettigee.purple-swirl.com/DeVIA/DeVIA.html

"Miss America." (1996, March 28-31). Performance by students from the Lexington School for the Deaf. Second National ASL Literature Conference. Rochester, NY. (videotape and film still).

Padden, C. A. (accessed 3/12/08). The preservation of the sign language. http://www.rid.org/UserFiles/File/pdfs/veditz.pdf.

Padden, C.A. and Humphries, T., (1990). *Deaf in America: Voices from a Culture*. Boston: Harvard University Press,.

Padden, C. A. and Y. Osugi (2003). The Future of Sign Language and Deaf Culture. *Plenary Address at the 14th World Federation of the Deaf Conference Proceedings*. Montreal, Quebec: Canada.

Panara, R. (1992). Lip service. In J. Jepson (Ed.), *No walls of stone*. Washington DC: Gallaudet University Press.

Rutherford, S. (1993). *A study of American Deaf folklore*. Burtonsville, MD: Linstok Press.

Valli, C. (1995). "Hands Folded," In *ASL Poetry: Selected Works of Clayton Valli*. San Diego, CA: DawnSign Press. (videotape and film still).

Vedtiz, G. W. (1913; accessed 3/12/08). The preservation of sign language. <http://videocatalog.gallaudet.edu/player.cfm?video=2520> (videotape and film still).

ARTWORK

Baird, Chuck. "Art No.2," 1993.
Baird, Chuck. "Heart on X-ray," 1999.
Clark, Adrean, "iPain," 2005.
Ford, Allen, "'S KIN/Left," 2001.
Ivey, Lee, "Why Me," 1992.
Lentini, Camela, "Snapshot Silent," 2003
Martin, Thad, "Articulatus (Read My Lips)," 1994.
Miller, Betty G., "Evolution of ASL," 2000.
Popovich-Kutscher, "Anti-Prisoner"
Scates, Brandon, Blue Ribbon Ceremony at the Deaf Studies Today Conference, Orem, Utah, 2008.
Thornley, Mary, "Milan, Italy, 1880," 1994.
Witcher, Pamela, "Sign Language, our roots. Deaf children, our future," 2004.

Film Stills and Photos:
Bullard, Douglas (photo). Accessed 3/12/08. < www.cidaa.org/obituaries_2001-06.html>
Durr, Patti, "Exodus: A Deaf Jewish Family Escapes the Holocaust," 2006.
Durr, Patti and Elizabeth Sorkin, "Don't Mind?" 2005.
Graybill, Patrick (director). "Tales of a Clubroom," YEAR. Rochester, NY: Lights On! Deaf Theatre, Spring 1992.
Mangiardi, Adrean, "Paper Airplane," 2005.

The Chaos Theory and Implications for the Creation of a Deaf-friendly University Campus

J. FREEMAN KING, PH.D.

EVEN THOUGH UNIVERSITY/COLLEGE PROGRAMS THAT PREPARE teachers of the deaf are, hopefully, Deaf-friendly, this is often not the case with the university/college at large. Recently, the Deaf students, citing a lack of well-qualified and highly certified interpreters, filed and won a major ADA lawsuit against my university. This incidence, more than the popularity of ASL classes, 16 years of Deaf Awareness Weeks and Silent Weekends and a high profile Deaf Education program, raised Deaf awareness across the campus, in the community, and in the state. However, because of the nature of the federal lawsuit, the university was viewed in a negative light and the recruitment of Deaf students was stymied. If the university had consulted the professionals in education of the Deaf and worked with the Deaf students to establish a Deaf-friendly environment on campus, the lawsuit and the resultant negative publicity could have been avoided.

A campus-wide educational philosophy of accommodation, inclusion, and recruitment of Deaf students is necessary to assure that students are provided the most appropriate and least restrictive learning environment. This philosophy should begin at the upper levels of administration and extend to the university faculty. Not only is accommodation and inclusion federally mandated, but also the basic consideration of human rights must be at the forefront related to diversity and learning in higher education.

Because of the lawsuit, positive improvements have been made on this particular campus related to interpreting services. Also, the university now has a Deaf professor who is teaching in the Deaf Education teacher-training program. However, the provision of a Deaf-friendly campus extends beyond just meeting the minimal requirements of federal law regarding interpreting and having a Deaf professor. To truly create a Deaf-friendly campus, the following considerations must also be entertained: the hiring of qualified Deaf instructors/professors; dissemination of information regarding people who are Deaf; the dispelling of erroneous perceptions regarding Deaf students; information regarding the role of interpreters in the classroom; information for the faculty related to specific classroom accommodations for Deaf students; and, the provision, campus-wide, of videophones and other technology-related devices that enhance accessibility.

The experiences, both negative and positive, that have impacted my particular university have universal application to sister universities/colleges. In order to create a Deaf-friendly campus, it is imperative that dialogue be opened and maintained among Deaf students, the university administration, and the faculty, so as to avoid the pitfalls that my university experienced. With this thought in mind, following are suggestions that will prove beneficial in the creation of a Deaf-friendly university campus:

- Employ more Deaf teachers. The presence of qualified Deaf teachers will enhance faculty diversity, provide more insight of the Deaf experience, and provide for viable role models for Deaf students.
- Provide qualified, certified interpreters. It is the inherent right of the Deaf student to have complete access to academics and the entire university experience. This can be accomplished by the university ensuring that only qualified, highly certified interpreters be available for the Deaf students. Student-interpreters are not acceptable unless they are qualified and highly certified.
- Provide competitive salaries and benefits for the interpreters. The interpreters should be paid commensurate with their training, certification, and skills. The position of interpreter should be recognized as a professional position by the university administration, and an appropriate pay scale should be in place, including all of the professional benefits that are available to faculty and staff.
- Encourage the administration and faculty to view the Deaf students as a positive and not as a negative influence. Because of the necessary financial resources that the university must make available for interpreting services, notetaking, etc., the Deaf student might be construed as a negative; certainly, this is not the view that is desired. Hopefully, the administration and faculty can be influenced to view the Deaf student as a positive, as a student who adds to campus-wide cultural diversity, as does the Black, Hispanic, or Asian student.
- Educate university administration and faculty concerning the Deaf students' culture, background, and language. Workshops, sym-

posiums, and informal meetings can be arranged to introduce the administration and faculty to the uniqueness of the Deaf experience, language, and culture.
- Encourage the university administration to recruit more Deaf students to assist in the mandate for a more diverse campus population.
- Assist the administration in understanding that Deafness needs to be separated from the "disability" label. It goes without saying, that the Deaf student is not disabled. If provided an education that is truly least restrictive, linguistically accessible, and appropriate, the Deaf student can achieve on a par with their hearing counterparts.
- Provide the professors who have Deaf students in their classes with information regarding the language and the culture of the Deaf student. A booklet should be provided for the faculty members who will have a Deaf student enrolled in their classes that discusses the sociocultural aspects of the Deaf experience, Deaf culture, the importance of deep and meaningful language accessibility, and how to best use the interpreter in the classroom environment.
- Offer special symposiums for hearing students on Deaf culture, American Sign Language, and the role of the interpreter in the Deaf experience on the university campus.
- Establish and promote ASL as a legitimate language option on campus. Courses in American Sign Language should be offered for university credit and taught by highly qualified, certified instructors. The legitimacy of the ASL classes should be equal to any foreign language class that is taught.
- All visual media that are used in classes should be captioned.
- Have video-phones available at strategic locations campus-wide. Video-phones should be made available in the dorms, in the student center, in each academic building on campus, in the infirmary, and/or other places where telephones are typically available for students.
- Have a strong Deaf club on campus where students (Deaf and hearing) can socialize and celebrate their culture.
- Establish an ASL-floor or wing in a selected student dorm on campus. This should be coordinated with Student Housing and will provide a physical setting where only ASL is permitted. This setting can be ideal for Deaf students and hearing students who are interested in learning the language used by the Deaf community.

The "One-dB Rule": The Deaf Community, Hard-of-Hearing People and Audism

DON GRUSHKIN, PH.D.

AS A LEGACY OF SLAVERY, DURING THE DAYS OF SEGREGATION AND Jim Crow laws, people of African descent were subjugated to the "one drop" rule (Zack, 1993) which held that a person with even one African forebear (no matter how distant in ancestry) was classified (and held subject to rules specific to this population) as Black, even if that person displayed no physical characteristics of African ancestry. In this paper, it is postulated that our audiocentric, or "audist" (Humphries, 1975; Lane, 1992) society employs a "one dB rule," which in a reverse manner from that of the "one drop rule," makes the assumption that if a Deaf or hard of hearing person has the ability to perceive even one decibel of sound, that person automatically "belongs" to Hearing society. Under this paradigm, Deaf and hard of hearing people are assumed to be naturally "Hearing" inside, and it is this "hidden" Hearing person which needs to be drawn forth.

It is at this point that the processes of "normalization" (Lane, 1992) or "Hearization" (Nover, 1993) take place through Auditory and Speech therapy, and educational and social practices are implemented with the goal of encouraging deaf, and especially hard of hearing people, to identify with and behave as Hearing. Therefore, whereas the "one drop rule" was a policy of exclusion (separating those with African ancestry from those of Caucasian ancestry), the "one dB rule" is a policy of inclusion (amalgamating Deaf and Hard of Hearing people, who have had a long-standing visually-centered worldview, with Hearing people). However, the policies of normalization/Hearization have had profound implications for the academic, social and personal identity development of both Deaf and hard of hearing people. Furthermore, this division of the Deaf community by hearing status (deaf/hard of hearing) has occurred at a cost to the political, educational and collective cohesiveness of this community. In order to more fully understand these costs, it is necessary to take a historical, audiological, linguistic, and educational perspective towards hard of hearing people and the Deaf community.

DEFINITIONS AND COMMONALITIES

Before we begin, a brief overview of what the terms "deaf" and "hard of hearing" are taken to mean must be presented. However, the road toward creating a definition of what "deaf" and "hard of hearing" means has long been fraught with multiple "land mines" barring the way towards a satisfactory resolution of the question. One could take a broad perspective such as the Conference of Executives of American Schools for the Deaf's (CEASD) Ad Hoc Committee to Define Deaf and Hard of Hearing in 1975:

> A deaf person is one whose hearing disability precludes successful processing of linguistic information through audition, with or without a hearing aid.
>
> A hard of hearing person is one who, with the use of a hearing aid, has residual hearing sufficient to enable successful processing of linguistic information through audition (p. 509).

The U.S. federal government takes a similar outlook on defining these two populations (Bienenstock & Vernon, 1994). One can immediately see, however, that this definition is extremely simplistic, and does not include any specific, measurable means by which one can state that an individual is deaf or hard of hearing. The difficulty of definition is further compounded by the now-common use of the generic term "hearing impaired," which was defined by the CEASD's Ad Hoc Committee as "indicating a hearing disability which may range in severity from mild to profound: it includes the subsets of deaf and hard of hearing" (p. 509). To further complicate the issue, "hearing impaired" is frequently used as a synonym for "hard of hearing." Hearing loss is also described in medically-oriented terms around the country such as "fluctuating hearing loss," "unilateral hearing loss," "hearing handicapped," "auditorily handicapped," and "severely hearing handicapped" (Bienenstock & Vernon, 1994: 129). Further, within the general public and the media, one can find the terms "deaf and dumb," "deaf-mute," "deaf and mute," "mute," "audiologically handicapped," "hearing-defective," and "non-hearing" (Levitan, 1993).

However, even when utilizing audiological criteria for classifying deaf and hard of hearing individuals, confusion still reigns. Bienenstock & Vernon (1994) observe that for 24 states, eligibility requirements for program placement for deaf and hard of hearing individuals conforms closely to that of the Federal government's. However, the other 26 states consider the degree of hearing loss in their eligibility requirements. Some states utilize a single decibel cutoff, at which point one qualifies as deaf, hard of hearing, or "hearing impaired", with no further distinctions between these individuals being made. Standards have been found to be as low as 20 dB for all groups, whereas the cutoff separating the hard of hearing from the deaf has been as low as 65 dB to as high as 92 dB (Bienenstock & Vernon, 1994).

In addition, there remain differing ways of conceiving an individual as hard of hearing. While most think of hard of hearing individuals as having a loss in both ears, one could also make the case for an individual with a unilateral loss (Bess, 1986; Oyler, Oyler & Matkin, 1988; Ross, 1990) or chronic and/or fluctuating middle ear problems (Feagans, Blood & Tubman, 1988) as being classified as hard of hearing.

Moreover, within the interpersonal realm, measurable audiological definitions frequently possess little meaning. To illustrate, Witcher (1974) states that her daughter has a severe to moderately severe high frequency loss which enables her to hear only some sounds such as thunder and car motors. To many knowledgeable observers, Witcher's description would be indicative of a deaf, not hard of hearing person, yet Witcher declares her daughter to be "hard of hearing."

Due to the "one dB rule," hard of hearing people are encouraged, both overtly (such as by discouraging hard of hearing people from utilizing lip-reading in favor of direct auditory perception of speech; see Ross, 2003) and indirectly (through mainstreamed placement in public schools and denial for placement in schools for the deaf due to having hearing above the cutoff levels for admittance) to affiliate and identify with Hearing people. As a result of such policies, Woodward and Allen (1993) identified hard of hearing and Deaf people as belonging to two different linguistic communities, which they stated should not be aggregated under a single category, such as "hearing impaired."

Yet, while deaf people have long been recognized as having difficulties in developing (spoken and written) language, academic progress, and communication and socialization with Hearing peers, hard of hearing people are commonly believed not to have any such difficulties for the sole reason that they have the capability to hear and develop speech. However, research shows that this is not necessarily the case; indeed, hard of hearing people may have more in common with Deaf people in their academic and personal areas of life than with Hearing people, due to their abilities and needs. Although deaf people have difficulty hearing a broader range of speech sounds, hard of hearing people also tend to have difficulty hearing certain speech sounds, especially high-pitched fricatives (/f/, /v/, /sh/) and affricatives (/ch/, /j/) (Ross, Brackett & Maxon, 1982). Likewise, certain syntactical (grammatical) structures are an area of difficulty for the hard of hearing, just as they are for deaf students (Scholes, Tanis & Anderson, 1976; Stinson, 1978). These auditory perception problems translate into speech production problems, although fewer and less severe in degree than for deaf people (Elfenbein, Hardin-Jones & Davis, 1994) and syntactical production weaknesses (Brannon & Murry, 1966; Brown, 1984; Elfenbein et al., 1994; Levitt, McGarr & Geffner, 1987). Further, although they may possess speech, some of their discourse and pragmatic (language functions) strategies may be delayed or impaired (Kyllo, 1984; Wray, 1986).

As is the case for deaf people, hard of hearing people experience academic delays, although again not to the degree seen in deaf students. For example, hard of hearing people have been found to perform two to three years behind hearing students on standardized academic achievement tests (Brackett and Maxon, 1986), and are commonly held back from grade promotion by an average of one and a half grades (Kodman, 1963). Even for students with mild hearing losses of 15 to 25 dB, the average delay in vocabulary and other language skills has been found to be over one year (Quigley & Thomure, 1968; Reich, Hambleton & Houldin, 1977). Adler (19--) provides a poignant description of the difficulties faced by hard of hearing students in Hearing-based educational settings:

> "When I was in 3rd grade, I had a 1st-grade math and reading level. I was the only hard of hearing student in a classroom with forty-five kids.... Imagine how much a hearing-impaired kid could miss with all the questions being asked and answered behind her back. Imagine when the teacher is talking and writing on the blackboard at the same time, with her back facing the students. How does a hearing-impaired person read the teacher's lips? By the time I was in 6th grade, I had a 2nd grade math and reading level. Meanwhile, my parents and the school just didn't know what else to do" (p. 207-208)

It has been well documented that deaf students often experience difficulties developing appropriate socialization in the mainstream, due to barriers in communicating with peers who do not sign. However, a number of studies (Elser, 1959; Kennedy & Bruininks, 1974; Kennedy, Northcott, McCauley & Williams, 1976) have produced a paradoxical finding: students with more severe hearing losses are often given higher mean (average) social acceptance scores than those with more hearing ability. Ross (1990) offered a plausible socio-psychological explanation of this phenomenon:

> The effect of language complexity, dialectical or poorly articulated speech, distance from the speech source, and poor room acoustics...will

often have a negative effect upon the ability of hard of hearing children to understand spoken messages. This apparently random and unpredictable behavior causes observers to expect communication behavior that is beyond hard of hearing children's ability. Although they may "hear" in almost all situations, they cannot "understand" in many of them...[as a result] children often consider them less than desirable playmates for reasons that neither group really comprehends... (p. 14; brackets added for clarification).

As a result (or combination) of these factors, hard of hearing children in regular classes are commonly found to be less satisfied with their social situation and to have fewer friends than their hearing peers, and this is particularly true for teenagers (Moschella, 1992; Tvingstedt, 1993). Deficiencies in self-esteem have also been found for hard of hearing children and teens (Loeb & Sarigiani, 1986; Shaffer-Meyer, 1990). For an in-depth discussion of the academic, social, and communicative difficulties and needs of hard of hearing students and adults, the reader is referred to my dissertation (Grushkin, 1996).

From the studies cited above, it is clear that hard of hearing people do share many of the same types of problems in the Hearing world relating to communication, education and socialization as deaf people do. These results do not apply to all hard of hearing people; certainly there are cases of individual hard of hearing (as well as deaf) persons who, through differing means, manage to minimize the difficulties created by their hearing loss in their personal and professional lives within the Hearing society. However, these individuals appear to be the exception rather than the rule; in the majority of cases, a hearing loss, regardless of degree, has a significant impact on most, if not all areas of a person's life within a Hearing-centered setting, as the research has indicated.

HISTORICAL PERSPECTIVE

It is fairly clear that as long as humans have been extant upon Earth, there have been humans with hearing loss, whether from accident, illness, aging, or other causes. What is not so clear, however, is when the term "hard of hearing" first arose. When one examines the historical record, it is readily apparent that deaf and hard of hearing people were typically classified together, although variations could exist in terms of etiology, onset, and degree of loss. In the document of Li Chi from China (inarguably a culture with long historic roots), society is charged with educating, caring for disabled groups, including the Deaf (Cheng, 1993). Li Chi's document makes no distinctions between Deaf and hard of hearing. In comparison, the Jewish tradition, which has a history equally as long as that of the Chinese, identified Deaf and hard of hearing people as a special class in need of certain protections. In the Rabbinical discussions ("pilpul"), Deaf people (along with the mentally retarded, "fools" [emotionally disturbed], and minors) were placed within the category of shote, which limits one's legal rights and responsibilities. Those considered to be shote were perceived as helpless, not possessing full cognitive competence and exempt from needing to fulfill all the Commandments and religious responsibilities (Zweibel, 1993; 1994). Interestingly, under Judaic law, the definition of "deaf" was restricted to those who do not speak at all; those who could speak were considered to have rights and responsibilities comparable to those of normally hearing Jews. Yet, even oral Deaf received special protections: while anyone who hurt them were held to blame, if the Deaf person hurt someone else, they were held blameless (Zweibel, 1993). Also of note is the fact that although the definition of "deaf" was restricted to those who do not speak at all (and therefore placed under the category of shote), hard of hearing people who do not talk were still considered normal human beings and given full legal rights.

The Classical (Greco-Roman) period was not much improved for those with hearing losses. Aristotle is famous for his quote "hearing is the sense of sound, and sound the vehicle of thought; hence the blind are more intelligent than deaf-mutes" (Ladd, 2003), while Plato once said "People without speech show no evidence of intelligence. Therefore, deaf people must not be capable of ideas or language" (Benderly, 1980). Thus, it is evident that during this period as well, Deaf people were commonly viewed as being unintelligent and uneducable. Indeed, Aristotle went so far as to say "Those who can not speak are unteachable" (Benderly, 1980: 107). Thus, it is not surprising that the 6th Century Roman Emperor Justinian implemented a Code restricting the rights of Deaf and hard of hearing people. In his Code, he established 5 classes of deafness: 1) The Deaf and Dumb by nature; 2) The Deaf and Dumb by accident; 3) The Deaf from birth who were not dumb; 4) The Deaf not from birth but by accident; and 5) The Dumb who are not Deaf (Gaw, 1907). Under this code, deaf-mutes were prohibited from making wills, manumitting (freeing slaves), entering into contracts, and being witnesses. Yet, if the acquisition of literacy had already occurred, those who had become deaf-mute were permitted to do these legal activities, provided they did so in writing (Ladd, 2003). Of significance is the third category: those who were Deaf from birth but not dumb. Gaw points out that:

> "The members of this class must at some time in life have possessed sufficient hearing to enable them to hear through the ear, perhaps with much difficulty, the use of verbal language; yet they were so hard of hearing as to pass for totally deaf persons when addressed in the ordinary manner. Such cases are not unknown today. Without the aid of any artificial appliances or mechanical devices whatever it is often possible to develop the dormant hearing power of a person supposedly totally deaf" (1907: 9–10)

It is not until the Enlightenment that efforts to educate Deaf and hard of hearing people at more than the individual level began, with the work of Braidwood in England, l'Epee in France, and Heinicke in Germany. These efforts, especially in France, gave rise to a formal, self-identifying Deaf community. Mottez (1993) describes the inauguration in 1834 of a series of banquets hosted by the French Deaf community at which they celebrated their community and language, lobbied politicians on issues of concern to the Deaf community, as well as gathering together to eat, drink, and have a good time. It was at the Paris Institute, where Dr. Jean-Marc Itard, who was brought on to work with the Wild Boy of Aveyron, became interested in the Deaf condition. He developed 5 categories of hearing ability: (1) when the patient was able to understand the auditory message completely; (2) when he merely heard the voice; (3) when he heard sounds only; (4) when he perceived just a noise; (5) when he heard nothing and was completely deaf (Feldman, 1970).

According to Itard, "Semi-deaf persons" (class 2) "are unable to perceive the majority of articulated speech sounds (i.e., consonants), but are still able to distinguish non-articulated speech sounds (i.e., vowels)" For example, they confuse "ba" and "pa", "da" and "ta", etc. (Feldman, 1970). In an ironic aside, the German translator of Itard's paper was obviously annoyed by Itard's statement, commenting: "Thuringians, more often than not, do not differentiate d from t and b from p, v from f....Must we now consider all Thuringians deaf?" (Feldman, 1970: 77)

Across the Atlantic, the Deaf community in America established the New England Gallaudet Association of Deaf-Mutes (NEGADM) in 1854. One of the earliest associations of the Deaf, the NEGADM's Constitution illustrates the common terminology and perceptions of their time. In a section on membership, the NEGADM Constitution stated that its membership would be drawn from among "mutes," those "only deaf," "semi- mutes," and the "semi-deaf" (Chamberlain, 1857). "Mutes" referred to those who were born deaf and could not utilize speech. In contrast, the "only deaf" were individuals who had been born hearing and retained the ability to speak. While it is unclear in the present day what the difference between "only deaf" and "semi-mute" is, "semi-mute" appears to refer to those who cannot hear, but can talk and were likely late-deafened (possibly with some deterioration of speech skill).

Finally, the "semi deaf" denotes those who would, in the present day, likely be referred to as "hard of hearing.' However, Kirk Van Gilder in a personal communication, warns that the identity constructions of these "semi-mute" persons seem to have been more closely aligned with those of the Deaf community of their time, in contrast to the modern era, in which hard of hearing people typically are said to desire more hearing-affiliated identities, as Woodward and Allen (1993) indicated (DeafAcademics Listserv, Retrieved September 16, 2007). Despite these classifications, all were considered part of the Deaf community and welcome to join the NEGADM.

It is significant to note that in the terminology of all of the above discussions and categorizations, none make explicit reference to the ability to hear or difficulty thereof (in comparison to today's terminology such as "hard of hearing," "aurally challenged," "hearing handicapped," etc.); instead, one was viewed as either being Deaf or able to speak (or some variation thereof). The NEGADM's terms (which were quite likely in popular use during that time period) are especially significant in that the ability to hear or speak are not salient to their classification of the Deaf community; rather it is to being Deaf or "mute" (to whatever degree) that they utilize in their criteria. This is consistent with Padden & Humphries' (1988) assertion that the Deaf, as a cultural group, possess a different "center," or worldview from that of Hearing people. In the Deaf worldview, the ability to hear is not the norm; instead, it is the inability to hear and speak like their Hearing counterparts (along with a visually-based way of life) that is held to be "normal." Or, as Ladd (2003) states: "The inability to speak the majority language (was) viewed in the Deaf tradition, as a far more distinctive marker than not being able to hear" (p. 340).

The NEGADM Constitution shows that as far back as 200 years, and quite likely even prior to this point, as evidenced by the Paris (France) Deaf banquets (Mottez, 1993), the Deaf community perceived themselves to be a group discrete from their Hearing counterparts, and hard of hearing people were a mainstay of this community.

Up until around the turn of the 20th century, Deaf and hard of hearing people were typically educated together at schools for the deaf. Within these schools, hard of hearing, as well as the Deaf students, were educated in the same classes and through sign language. Although some individual variation in the ability to hear or speak was commonly noted, Deaf and hard of hearing people viewed each other as belonging to a shared Deaf community. This viewpoint is exemplified by Gloria Pullen, a British Deaf activist in a videotaped segment of a TV show:

> "This the old sign for what we call HOH now — 'Deaf and dumb, hearing (speaking) skilled.' See, everybody was 'Deaf and dumb.' Just some happen to be able to speak, that's all. (Ladd, 2003: 340).

Translated, what Gloria Pullen was saying is that how Deaf people prior to the 20th century referred to hard of hearing people was through a signed phrase describing them as being like them ('Deaf and dumb'), but with the particular (and incidental) skill of being able to speak as well. Another of Ladd's consultants shared a similar viewpoint: "They were all 'proudly Deaf and Dumb' — speech was just an added bonus; the others were Deaf and part of the community, but they could speak, that's all." (2003: 340).

It is evident from these comments (as well as others to be shown later), that not only were hard of hearing and late deafened people part of the same Deaf community in the past, but speech was seen as simply an individual ability. Moreover, Ladd (2003) stresses that this particular skill, along with possession of well developed English literacy, were seen as skills that could be used to benefit the Deaf community as a whole.

THE ORIGINS OF "HARD OF HEARING"

Although there are no definitive records to be found confirming this, it would appear that the widespread usage of "hard of hearing" is of relatively recent origin. While the term itself has been extant in the English language since at least 1564, when a witness at a trial in England was identified as being "hard of hearinge" (Oxford English Dictionary Online), the earlier discussion indicates that "deaf" and "mute" (and variants thereof) were much more widely used. Hard of hearing instead appears to have been a folk term referring more primarily to aged people with diminished hearing ability or those who had experienced a slight hearing loss but could still communicate through oral means with minimal difficulty.

It is quite likely that the relative paucity in use of "hard of hearing" may be due to the fact that up until the modern era, it was quite difficult to measure degrees of hearing loss beyond rough approximations such as Itard's. In addition, Baynton (1996) suggests that prior to the middle of the 19th century, societal attitudes regarded being deaf as a "natural" or God-given condition which did not require medical intervention. However, toward the middle of the century, societal conditions and cultural perceptions began to change in favor of normalizing the Deaf toward a Hearing ideal. In order to achieve this normalization, it became more imperative to innovate ways of assessing Deaf people's potential for hearing so they might be more successfully taught to speak. Feldman (1970) asserts that some developed "...simple tests...by letting a subject repeat spoken sentences or by letting him listen to a pocket watch" (p. 19). Others turned to the use of tuning forks as an aid in diagnosis of hearing loss. However, the accuracy of these tests was not sufficiently reliable, leading others to seek mechanical means of hearing loss assessment. In 1802 Wolke, and later Itard in 1821 developed mechanical acuity meters, but these too did not prove sufficiently accurate. It was not until 1919 that the first electronic audiometers were developed (Feldman, 1970), and the first commercially produced audiometers were sold by Western Electric in 1923 (Kenneth W. Berger Hearing Aid Museum and Archives).

Fairly concurrent with the development of audiometry came the advent of electronic amplification. While previous eras had seen individuals with mild or moderate hearing losses attempting to make do with ear horns, domes, trumpets and collectors, these instruments did little, if anything to truly benefit their users. The first personal electronic hearing aids (prior to this, only tabletop models were available), using a "carbon microphone" used a large battery pack, had problems with sound distortion, and were generally powerful enough only for those with mild to moderate hearing losses (Kenneth W. Berger Hearing Aid Museum and Archives; Valente, Hosford-Dunn & Roeser, 2000). However, in the 1930s, vacuum tube technology became practical and was powerful enough for those with severe hearing losses, although the hearing aid costs were high due to the need for two batteries.

In the 1950s, the development of the transistor allowed hearing aids to shrink in both size and cost, allowing for more widespread use (Kenneth W. Berger Hearing Aid Museum and Archives). The advancements in hearing aid technology allowed educators and other professionals working with the Deaf to promote the idea that all Deaf people have usable hearing (often called "residual hearing") which can be developed for the purposes of acquiring speech and audition skills, leading to the ability to claim a Hearing-based identity.

HEARING LOSS AND STIGMA

Although the Deaf community of the 1700s and 1800s generally had a positive self-image of being Deaf (cf. Veditz, 1913), this was (and remains) hardly the case for Hearing people's attitudes toward hearing loss. For Hearing people, possession of a hearing loss is a negatively imbued deviation from the norm and therefore viewed as a stigmatizing (Goffman, 1963) condition. A person perceived to have a characteristic marking them as "different," according to Goffman, is:

> "thus reduced in our minds from a whole and usual person to a tainted, discounted one. Such an attribute is a stigma, especially when its discrediting effect is very extensive; sometimes it is also called a failing, a shortcoming, a handicap." (p. 3)

In order to minimize stigma, Goffman claims, individuals will often adopt strategies to prevent their being identified as possessing a negatively marked condition such as through "passing" (attempting to present one's self as "normal"), "covering" (minimizing the visibility of the stigmatizing condition), or paradoxically, by allowing members of the public to be aware of the presence of the stigmatizing condition. Thus, Deaf and hard of hearing people who attempt to "pass" will associate exclusively with Hearing people, and use speech while disallowing signs. Alternatively, they may present their difficulty in hearing as some more innocuous problem, such as being absent-minded or daydreaming. "Covering" is accomplished through such means as wearing behind-the-ear hearing aids or even disguising the hearing aid as some other, more ordinary object such as earrings or glasses. An interesting display of the various means by which hearing devices were concealed as such from the 19th through the 21st centuries can be found on the website "Deafness in Disguise" (http://beckerexhibits.wustl.edu/did/index.htm).

Stigma can also be managed by techniques of reframing, or as Goffman says, "to convince the public to use a softer social label for the category in question" (p. 24). He goes on to describe the actions of the New York League for the Hard of Hearing:

> "...the League...staff agreed to use only such terms as hard of hearing, impaired hearing, and hearing loss; to excise the word *deaf* from their conversation, their correspondence and other writings, their teaching, and their speeches in public. It worked. New York in general gradually began to use the new vocabulary. Straight thinking was on the way" (Warfield, 1957: 78).

APPLICATION OF THE "ONE DB RULE"

With the ability of audiology to identify degrees of hearing ability and hearing aids to mitigate the impact of a hearing loss, along with the perception of Hearing people that to be Deaf is to be stigmatized, the "one dB rule" was born. Under the "one dB rule", possession of any degree of hearing capability automatically grants the possessor with the status of "belonging to the Hearing world." This belief is exacerbated by the fact that over 90 percent of Deaf people are born to Hearing parents. The one dB rule is illustrated with high clarity by Mark Drolsbaugh, who was born hearing to Deaf parents, only to gradually lose his hearing as a youngster:

> "When my hearing loss was initially diagnosed, medical professionals took an entirely pathological approach, emphasizing hearing aids and speech therapy...These specialists preached a skewed version of the old "it's a hearing world" philosophy, somehow convincing my hearing relatives and teachers to discourage my Deaf parents from using sign language with me. It was a vain attempt at holding on to what little residual hearing and speech I had left" (1997, p. i).

Torie Bryant, herself a hard of hearing person, recognizes the existence of the "one dB rule" while offering a challenge to it:

> "Yet at the same time that I can participate in the hearing world, I will never

> be able to participate in it completely. I cannot be a part of the hearing world 100 percent. Experts on "hearing impaired" children think otherwise. After all, the prevailing wisdom has been that hard of hearing kids have more in common with the hearing world then (sic) with the deaf world... But is that really true? Certainly I am not functionally deaf, but at the same time, having a bit of hearing does not make me "more hearing than deaf"' (2007, p. 153)

Despite being audiologically hard of hearing, Bryant feels a kinship with the Deaf experience and perspective and questions the motives of the proponents of audist educational practices:

> "I remember reading Ben Bahan's views on how we, the deaf and hard of hearing, should identify ourselves as "seeing" or "sighted" rather than hearing-impaired. That totally lit a bulb over my head and made me want to know: Why have some experts decided that it's better for kids to grow up under a rehabilitative "healthy normal" mentality? (2007, p. 154)

One of these practices is the development of the concept of "residual hearing," which holds that every person, no matter the degree of hearing loss, possesses some ability to perceive sound. As such, this notion is a primary corollary of the "one dB rule", and at its core, it exemplifies the "one dB rule" through its basic premise that Deaf and hard of hearing people are starting from "Hearing." The John Tracy Clinic's famous correspondence course (Tracy & Theilman, 1972) continually reiterates the central tenet that parents should "Talk, talk, talk. Talk just as you would to a hearing child." Mark Ross, a hard of hearing audiologist, embodies this perspective in the following statement:

> The sense of hearing, the perception of sound and its biological purposes, is not therefore a trivial consideration that can be lightly dismissed. On the contrary, SHHH believes that it is a human birthright that must be respected and utilized to the fullest extent possible....Perhaps even more than those with normal hearing, hard of hearing people value what hearing can offer, precisely because they are better able to recognize what they are missing....We regard the sense of hearing as a gift, from our evolutionary forbearers and/or from the Creator depending how we view the world, and it is not for us who possess some measure of this gift to disregard its presence, to whatever degree it is present (emphasis added). (1995: http://www.hearingresearch.org/Dr.Ross/residual_hearing.htm)

Even if the person does not have functional (for purposes of regular interactions within a Hearing milieu) unaided hearing, the illusion of being able to hear as "normally" as possible is created with the provision of hearing aids that amplify sounds to a level wherein the hard of hearing person can perceive them. Often, the use of hearing aids becomes de rigeur for hard of hearing students regardless of whether the student experienced any actual benefit or desire for their use. Trudy Suggs, a hard of hearing person from a Deaf family recalls this experience:

> "My audiologist got upset when I proclaimed my desire to stop wearing hearing aids... The audiologist called my attitudes as having been spoiled by my [Deaf] mother, pointing out that I only had a 35dB loss with hearing aids (80-85 dB without). (Suggs, 2007, p. 206).

Along with hearing, speaking is also viewed as a natural ability for all human beings. For hard of hearing people, it then becomes all the more essential that they be provided with the opportunity to develop this capability. To this end, intensive speech therapy services are provided, and an inordinate concern for the quality of the hard of hearing person's speech is often expressed.

> "There are some organizations – such as Auditory-Verbal International and AG Bell — that fly their banners under the philosophy that the hearing and talking world is the best thing in the world. Their mentality is that hearing and talking gives deaf and hard of hearing kids freedom.... Apparently, they believe life for deaf and hard of hearing kids should be an eternal speech therapy session" (Bryant, 2007, p. 152).

Since the ability to hear (and speak) is regarded as a birthright by the Hearing world, it then naturally follows that Deaf (and especially hard of hearing) people should not, nor desire to, "segregate" themselves within the Deaf world (which has often been referred to by audist interests as a "Deaf ghetto"). Trudy Suggs, a hard of hearing person from a Deaf family, recalls the reactions of the educators at her public school when she expressed a wish to transfer to the local school for the Deaf:

> "When I was about to enter the 6th grade, there were no remaining deaf peers in my age or grade group, because all of them had transferred over to the Illinois School for the Deaf thirty minutes away. I decided I wanted to transfer to ISD, too. School administrators said I would fail in the hearing world if I continued to defy their wishes of learning speech and being as normal as possible instead of being institutionalized." (2007, p. 202)

Suggs' account illustrates the "Deaf ghetto" viewpoint of audist educators. Moreover, not only would "segregation" be unnatural in their view, but it would, they hypothesize, promote the creation of an identity which is not aligned with the "Hearing world." Ross and Calvert viewed the association of hard of hearing and Deaf students as a step towards a "self-fulfilling prophecy" in which the hard of hearing person would take on the characteristics of a Deaf person due to the effect of labels and subsequent behavioral tendencies by educators and caregivers:

> "...labeling a person with nonfluent speech a 'stutterer' can cause him to assume the characteristics of a stutterer... The application of the label seems to set into motion the dynamics of a self-fulfilling prophecy in which the very nature of the prophecy influences the outcome in the predicted direction. The authors...are concerned that similar dynamics can occur either by labeling a child as 'deaf' or by reacting to children with different degrees and types of hearing loss as if they were 'deaf'" (p. 644-645)

> "...a child with a moderate hearing loss who is labeled 'deaf' and treated accordingly can become 'deaf.' That is, he will not understand speech when it has only rarely been directed to him. He will not develop speech but will resort to a special means of communication. He will need to be educated in a special means of instruction... And he will not succeed or excel in intellectual, social, or vocational endeavors. (p. 645)

In their book "Learning to be Deaf" (1986), A. Donald Evans (a hard of hearing individual) and William Falk also express concerns about the creation of a self-fulfilling prophecy and its detrimental effects on the developing child:

> "...with deafness one may be forcibly set apart for differential treatment. In this way, of course, the beginnings of a possible self-fulfilling prophecy are set up wherein a type of labeling occurs: if deaf are different, and I am deaf, then — ipso facto — I must be different." (p. 2)

> A principle (sic) concern of residential school critics is that a type of experiential deprivation may occur if the deaf child is not around hearing children. This could result in a truncated socialization process and the learning of institutional norms and values versus societal ones...One's personality may be negatively affected by immaturity, egocentricity, distorted perception, lacking empathy, more dependency on others and deficiency in intellectual functioning (p. 13–14).

In essence then, the one-dB rule is aimed toward developing a Hearing, rather than Deaf, identity. A variety of techniques, from the subtle to the overt, are employed to instill a Hearing-centered outlook on the world in the Deaf and hard of hearing child:

> "...it was...ingrained in my head that deafness was bad. In a way, I was being behaviorally conditioned. Anytime I was able to understand hearing people or speak clearly, I was praised; anytime I had difficulty understanding others or mispronounced words, all of the hearing people in my life reacted with grave concern." (Drolsbaugh, 1997, p. 35).

Even with all of these concerted attempts to promulgate a Hearing-centered attitude into hard of hearing and Deaf people, for many this goes contrary to their actual experience and ability. Mark Drolsbaugh poignantly recalls his grandfather's concerns for his education:

> "My grades were better than a lot of hearing students, but to my grandfather it wasn't enough. During report card time, he would grill me on every teacher's written comments about how I needed to sit up closer, wear my hearing aid more, and be more involved in class discussion. Never mind how good my grades were. I needed to be more hearing." (1997, p. 60-61).

Torie Bryant, a self-identified hard of hearing person, compares these efforts to a popular play dealing with similar themes: "When the mentality is that our lives should be spent trying to fit into the hearing world, there is something very "My Fair Ladyishque" about that" (2007, p. 153).

Despite these objections, it should come as no surprise then, that audist educators, in order to avoid the creation of yet more "Deaf" individuals, and to promote the development of a "healthy" Hearing identity in as many of their students as possible, would seek to separate those students viewed as potentially benefiting from Hearing-oriented practices from those who had not or would likely not succeed within this model.

SEPARATION OF THE DEAF AND THE HARD OF HEARING

Separation of Deaf and hard of hearing children took primarily physical form. This was initially accomplished in part by the creation of Day school programs, which ostensibly promoted the social integration of Deaf and hard of hearing children with Hearing people by preventing them from associating with each other after school hours. After the development of personal hearing aids, mainstreaming became possible, which served to separate the two groups even further. In the United Kingdom, "Partial Hearing Units" were established around the 1940s for the purpose of educating hard of hearing students through oral means alone. It is significant to note that in the naming of these units, the one-dB rule came into full play: whereas in the 1800s, hard of hearing people might be referred to as "semi-deaf" or "semi-mute," here the emphasis is now on "hearing," however partial it might be.

However, this separation was not only physical, it was psychological as well. Initially, the separation took on subtle forms, such as by choosing hard of hearing students to represent "Deaf" students during demonstrations of Oralist practices. Harlan Lane (1989) describes this practice:

> "Here is how it happens. A traveler visits an articulatory school. A pupil is called up who became deaf at eight or ten. The pupil speaks distinctly or recites a familiar phrase, seems to understand the everyday requests made

of him vocally. The traveler never thinks of testing the pupil's abilities or determining if he is the exception or the rule... Had he asked a teacher of the deaf...here is what I would have said. There are four great traps; they concern the pupil, his interlocutor, the material, and the visitor. Every large institution has a few outstanding pupils who can be trotted out for the visitor. How representative is the pupil? At what age did he lose his hearing? There is a world of difference between a deaf-mute and a semi-mute, between instilling a knowledge of oral language in one who is deaf, and slowing the deterioration of oral skills in someone who once spoke... Is the pupil selected semi-deaf? Can he hear speech addressed to him directly in a loud voice? (p. 301)

While clearly deceptive, the true impact of this procedure upon the relationships between the Deaf and hard of hearing members of the community is not immediately seen. However, Albert Ballin, a Deaf actor, writer, and teacher reported in 1930:

> "...the semi-mutes...were the pets of the teachers and officers. In fact, they were used as decoys to deceive and delude the indiscriminate and gullible public...The officers never explained the differences between these two classes....they deliberately impressed the visitors that these semi-mutes were the same as all the other pupils, and that they owed all their education wholly to the school... At this point I must make it plain that these decoys were not aware of the use to which they were being put. They did not learn of it until long after they had left school. Then it was that they raged and fumed." (p. 19-20, 27, emphasis in original).

Thus we can see the impacts on two levels. First, hard of hearing students were used as tools to perpetuate and justify the oralist practices which the Deaf community had long argued against. On the second level, hard of hearing students become a favored class within the audist institutions, or as Ballin refers to them, the "pets" of the teachers and officers (administrators). While during Ballin's time, the hard of hearing within the Deaf community clearly shared a solidarity with their Deaf peers, the cumulative impact of this unequal treatment would certainly take a toll on their perceptions of each other. More than fifty years after Ballin, a Deaf person dredges up a painful memory of a similar process of division:

> "Throughout my elementary school years, my classmates and I remained together — except for one boy who was moved to a lower track. The school had several tracks for each grade: A was the highest, B next, and so on. Anyway, this boy was as smart as the rest of us but he couldn't speak at all, so they placed him in a lower track. One day, they passed out buttons to all the kids in the A and B tracks that read: I TALK. We were so proud to wear that button walking down the hall. I remember vividly passing that former classmate of mine, seeing him lined up with the other students in the D class. He was standing there looking at my button. He didn't have one because he didn't talk. (Lane, Hoffmeister & Bahan, p. 221)

Even when the splitting was not overtly blatant as in the above example, it could take insidiously psychological forms as well. In a recent vlog, Carl Schroeder recalled having a private discussion with a teacher during his secondary school years, only to be interrupted (unbeknownst to him) by a hard of hearing peer. Instead of telling the other student to wait his turn, the teacher responded to the student vocally even as Carl was signing to his teacher. When Carl protested this treatment, the teacher sent him to talk with his principal, who straightforwardly told him that the educational system was set up to favor hard of hearing students (http://carl-schroeder.blogspot.com/2008/03/that-was-what-my-high-school-principal.html; retrieved 3/28/2008).

T.L. Anderson, a Deaf teacher and leader, observed a similar course of events in 1938 wherein hard of hearing students were being given an advantage in the educational system over their more profoundly Deaf peers:

> "In our schools, the fashion now is to address assemblies bilingually for the benefit of the hard-of-hearing pupils. Undoubtedly, in this circumstance, the hands are used grudgingly. If any slicking over of thought is done, the speaker does it on his hands" (p. 121)

What Anderson is describing, of course, is now called "Simultaneous Communication, or what Johnson, Liddell & Erting (1989) referred to as "Sign-Supported Speech." Much research, which will not be discussed here, has demonstrated that this practice results in a "broken" signed message, which often renders the concepts the teacher is attempting to convey largely unintelligible for many, if not most Deaf students. Anderson makes note of this issue when he went on to say:

> "...enter the "hard of hearing" in greater and greater numbers, many of them well able to hear the teacher's speaking voice in the ordinary room. It cannot be denied that mixed-class teaching technique has been modified for the benefit of these young people who retain usable hearing. The natural effect is to place the non-oral, non-aural pupils at a grave disadvantage" (p. 125).

The solution to the problem, Anderson suggested, was this:

> "Since the entrance of the hard of hearing in greater and greater numbers has brought about the need for this dual delivery, the logical remedy is to segregate the groups in both schoolrooms and assemblies. (p. 129).

While a logical solution from Anderson's perspective as an advocate for Deaf people, he ironically ended up reinforcing the one-dB rule by encouraging the physical separation of deaf and hard of hearing students. It is almost certain that Anderson, as a contemporary of Ballin, had experienced the cultural and linguistic connection between Deaf and hard of hearing people prior to this point. However, it is clear that due to the changed linguistic and educational environment imposed on the schools for the deaf by Oralist advocates, he felt there was no choice but to make this recommendation.

IMPLICATIONS FOR DEAF CULTURE & COMMUNITY

This paper has attempted to describe the one-dB rule, its application, and some of its effects on Deaf education and community. However, a more specific discussion of the implications of the one-dB rule upon the Deaf culture and community as a whole is warranted here.

A oft-quoted maxim of military technique is that to achieve success, a group must "divide and conquer" the opposing forces. As history has shown, this often takes physical and psychological forms, such as through the processes of colonization. The same was true for the Deaf and hard of hearing community, as has been shown in this paper. Whereas the two groups had been fairly unified prior to the Oralist onslaught of the late 19th century, according to Ballin, by physically and psychologically separating the two groups, they became physically and psychologically separate in actuality, as seen in later years by T. L. Anderson and Lane, Hoffmeister and Bahan. Deaf people, who may have come to resent their hard of hearing peers for their apparent status as a "favored group," may have then translated these resentments into a cultural norm or perspective that hard of hearing people are too different from Deaf people to be a part of the Deaf way of life.

Meanwhile, a cursory reading of the hard of hearing literature, as seen in books, magazines, and blogs, often depicts the hard of hearing as feeling somehow "superior" to the Deaf for their ability to speak and non-reliance on sign language. Alternatively, hard of hearing people often express the view that Deaf people actively reject them for having these characteristics alone. However, Dean Sheridan, a hard of hearing person from a Deaf family, notes that fault lies on neither side, since "The Deaf Fencers [hard of hearing people living within Deaf culture] have their own internalized oppression. Both sides of the fence (Deaf and Hearing) have their own set of cultural expectations" (2007, p. 122). While he is referring specifically to hard of hearing from Deaf families, his statement can apply equally well to Deaf and hard of hearing people in general.

More importantly, it must be seen that the current split between Deaf and hard of hearing people is not a natural phenomenon. Rather, it is artificially created and sustained through active ideologies and practices aimed at generating a culture of hierarchy and individualism rather than commonality and collectivism. These practices were instituted by people who did not necessarily have the best interests of Deaf and hard of hearing people in mind. After several generations of life within this paradigm, it will of course today seem as if this pattern was inevitable. As a look through history (past and present) shows, this is not the case at all.

A potential way out of this trap of cultural division lies in the concept of Deafhood as proposed by Paddy Ladd in 2003. Ladd envisioned Deafhood as a search for "Deaf ways of being in the world, of conceiving that world and their own place within it" (p. 81). As such, it is a means of "encompass[ing] all forms of actualization aspirations, whether maintenance or development" (Ladd, 2003; p. 419). Some critics may charge that the application of Deafhood onto hard of hearing people constitutes a reverse "one-dB rule" by making hard of hearing people adopt a Deaf perspective, just as Hearing people have attempted to do to the Deaf. However, this is not the case since Deafhood as conceptualized by Paddy Ladd allows for differing ways of being Deaf while maintaining a common sense of Deaf identity. For example, there are a number of hard of hearing people who have come to find Deaf ways of life to be more liberating than living according to Hearing norms (see Goffman, 1963, p. 24; Seymour, 2007, p. 79).

Should the Deaf and hard of hearing communities become reunified under a common outlook, a number of positive outcomes could result. First and most obviously, the Deaf community would have more political clout to pursue its objectives. With hard of hearing people to count among their numbers, the Deaf community would be able to point to a larger group of constituents which political leaders would find harder to ignore. In addition, the Deaf community's objectives would be able to be achieved more easily without the divisive claims upon resources and courses of action that is currently seen due to the differing needs and beliefs of each group.

Second, the current trend towards mainstreaming and closure of schools for the Deaf could be mitigated or even reversed once hard of hearing people were seen as sharing many of the communicative, social, educational and psycho-cultural needs of Deaf people. Within this perspective, it would be seen that schools for the Deaf offer an appropriate environment for the provision of these needs, just as they have been for Deaf students. The common exclusion of hard of hearing students from schools for the Deaf is an ironic application of the 1 dB rule in that hard of hearing people are deemed "not Deaf enough" to attend these schools. Some opponents of schools for the Deaf may suggest that ASL/English Bilingual/Bicultural (Bi/Bi) approaches will negatively affect hard of hearing students in the communicative and academic domains. However, just as bilingualism has not been shown to harm Hearing people, research such as that of Grushkin (1996) has shown that Bi/Bi education does not have a negative impact upon hard of hearing students.

Another trend is the practice of implanting Deaf people with Cochlear Implants. Although the rhetoric in the Hearing and medical community suggests that Deaf people become "Hearing" once they have an implant, the reality is that at best, most implantees still function on a "hard of hearing" level. Jerel Barnhart, a hard of hearing doctor, recognizes this truth and argues for the inclusion of sign language in an implantee's communicative store as not only a hedge against, but a preventative to communicative deprivation and delays. Recognizing hard of hearing people as sharing the communicative and sociocultural needs of Deaf people lends further support to Barnhart's position.

On a related point, current educational practices such as Audio-Verbal Therapy often view the use of sign as being detrimental to the development and acquisition of speech skills for Deaf and hard of hearing people. Once it is acknowledged that hard of hearing, along with Deaf people, have been subjected to non-culturally appropriate educational practices and methodology due to a misperception of their abilities and sociocultural affinities, then it stands to reason that access to sign language for this group is not only a right, it is a necessity.

The one-dB rule represents an ethnocentric perspective on the Deaf and hard of hearing community that is an outgrowth of ideologies engendered during the late 19th century. Like the one-drop rule that was applied to African-Americans during the same time period, the one-dB rule is a code that should not be allowed to be sustained. If and when the one-dB rule is no longer held to be natural and correct, then just as has been the case for the one-drop rule, the American society, and indeed the world, will be all the better off for it.

REFERENCES

Adler, R. (2007) I Belong. In M. Drolsbaugh, Ed. *On the Fence: The hidden world of the hard of hearing*. Springhouse, PA: Handwave Publications. Pp. 207–209.

Anderson, T.L. (1938). What of the Sign Language? *American Annals of the Deaf* (83), 120-130.

Ballin, A. (1930). *The Deaf Mute Howls*. Los Angeles: Grafton Publishing. Reprinted by Gallaudet Press, Washington, DC, 1998.

Barnhart, J. (2007). *The Window of Opportunity*. In M. Drolsbaugh, Ed. On the Fence: The hidden world of the hard of hearing. Springhouse, PA: Handwave Publications. Pp. 188–191.

Baynton, D. (1996). *Forbidden Signs: American culture and the campaign against sign language.* Chicago, Ill: University of Chicago Press.

Benderly, B. (1980). *Dancing Without Music*. New York: Anchor Press.

Benson, S. (1981). *Ambiguous Ethnicity*. London: Cambridge University Press.

Bess, F. (1986). The unilaterally hearing-impaired child: A final comment. *Ear and Hearing* (7), 52-54.

Bienenstock, M.A. & Vernon, M. (1994). Classification by the states of deaf and hard of hearing students. American Annals of the Deaf 139 (2), 128–131.

Brackett, D. & Maxon, A. (1986). Service delivery alternatives for the mainstreamed hearing impaired child. *Language, Speech and Hearing Services in Schools* 17, 115-125.

Brannon, J.B. & Murry, T. (1966). The spoken syntax of normal, hard-of-hearing, and deaf children. *Journal of Speech and Hearing Research* 9 (4), 604-610.

Brown, J.B. (1984). Examination of grammatical morphemes in the language of hard-of-hearing children. *Volta Review* 86 (4), 229-244.

Bryant, T. (2007). Equality. In M. Drolsbaugh, Ed. *On the Fence: The hidden world of the hard of hearing.* Springhouse, PA: Handwave Publications. Pp. 149–155.

Canadian Cultural Society of the Deaf. Fact Sheet: The Lower Case "d" or Upper Case "D." HYPERLINK "http://www.ccsdeaf.com/indexe.html" www.ccsdeaf.com/indexe.html. Retrieved March 23, 2008.

Chamberlain, W.M. (1857). Constitution of the New England Gallaudet Association of Deaf Mutes. *American Annals of the Deaf* 9 (April), 78-82.

Cheng, L. L. (1993). Deafness: An Asian/Pacific Island perspective. In K. Christensen & G. Delgado (eds.), *Multicultural Issues in Deafness.* NY: Longman Press.

Conference of Executives of American Schools for the Deaf (1975). Report of the Ad Hoc Committee to Define Deaf and Hard of Hearing. *American Annals of the Deaf*, 120(5), 509-511.

Deafness in Disguise. Washington University School of Medicine, Becker Medical Library. http://beckerexhibits.wustl.edu/did/index.htm. Retrieved January 9, 2008.

Drolsbaugh, M. (1997). *Deaf Again.* Springhouse, PA: Handwave Publications.

_____ (Ed.). (2007). *On the Fence: The hidden world of the hard of hearing.* Springhouse, PA: Handwave Publications.

Elfenbein, J.L., Hardin-Jones, M.A. & Davis, J.M. (1994). Oral communication skills of children who are hard of hearing. *Journal of Speech and Hearing Research* 37 (1), 216-226.

Elser, R.P. (1959). The social position of hearing handicapped children in the regular grades. *Exceptional Children* 25, 305-9.

Erting, C. (1992). Deafness and literacy: Why can't Sam read? *Sign Language Studies* 75 (Summer), 97-112.

Evans, D. & Falk, W. (1986). *Learning to be Deaf.* New York: Mouton de Gruyter.

Feagans, L., Blood, I. & Tubman, J.G. (1988). Otitis media: A model of effects and implications for intervention. In F. Bess (Ed.) *Hearing Impairment in Children* (347–374), Baltimore, MD: York Press.

Feldman, H. (1970). *A history of audiology: A comprehensive report and bibliography from the earliest beginnings to the present.* Chicago, Illinois: Beltone Institute for Hearing Research.

Gaw, Albert C. (1907) The development of the Legal Status of the Deaf, Part III: Justinian Legislation. *American Annals of the Deaf* 52, 1–12 .

Goffman, E. (1963). *Stigma: Notes on the management of spoiled identity.* New York: Simon & Schuster.

Grushkin, D.A. (1996). Academic, linguistic, social and identity development in hard-of-hearing adolescents educated within an ASL/English Bilingual/Bicultural educational setting for deaf and hard-of-hearing students. Unpublished doctoral dissertation, University of Arizona, Tucson, Arizona.

Grushkin, D.A. (2002). The Dilemma of the Hard-of-Hearing Within the United States Deaf Community. In L. Monaghan, K. Nakamura and G. Turner (Eds.). *Many Ways to Be Deaf: International Linguistic and Sociocultural Variation.* 114–140.

Harvey, M. A. (1989). *Psychotherapy with Deaf and Hard-of-Hearing Persons: A Systemic Model.* New Jersey: Lawrence Erlbaum Associates.

Humphries, T. (1975). *The making of a word: Audism.* Unpublished manuscript.

Israelite, N., Ewoldt, C. & Hoffmeister, R. (1992). Bilingual/Bicultural Education for Deaf and Hard-of-Hearing Students: A review of the literature on the effects of native sign language on majority language acquisition. Ontario Ministry of Education: MGS Publications.

Johnson, R.E., Liddell, S.K. & Erting, C.J. (1989). *Unlocking the Curriculum: Principles for achieving access in deaf education.* Gallaudet Research Institute Working Paper #89-3. Washington, DC: Gallaudet University, Department of Linguistics and Interpreting and the Research Institute.

Kennedy, P. & Bruininks, R.H. (1974). Social status of hearing impaired children in regular classrooms. *Exceptional Children* 40 (5), 336-342.

_____, Northcott, W., McCauley, R. & Williams, S.M. (1976). Longitudinal sociometric and cross-sectional data on mainstreaming hearing impaired children: Implications for preschool programming. *Volta Review* 78 (2), 78-81.

Kenneth W. Berger Hearing Aid Museum and Archives. http://dept.kent.edu/hearingaidmuseum/ special collections/audiometers.htm. (Retrieved January 11, 2008).

Kodman, F., Jr. (1963). Educational status of hard-of-hearing children in the classroom. *Journal of Speech and Hearing Disorders* 28, 297-99.

Kyllo, V.K. (1984). Responses to explicit and implicit requests for message clarification in hard-of-hearing and hearing children. Unpublished doctoral dissertation, University of Minnesota.

Ladd, P. (2003). *Understanding Deaf Culture: In search of Deafhood.* Clevedon, UK: Multilingual Matters Ltd.

Lane, H. (1989). *When the Mind Hears: A history of the Deaf.* NY: Random House.

_____. Ethnicity, ethics, and the deaf-world. *Journal of Deaf Studies and Deaf Education* 10 (3), 291-310.

_____, Hoffmeister, R. & Bahan, B. (1996.) *Journey into the Deaf-World.* San Diego: DawnSign Press.

Levitan, L. (1993). What do others call us? And what do we call ourselves? *Deaf Life* (May), 18-29.

Levitt, H., McGarr, N. & Geffner, D. (1987). *Development of children.* ASHA Monograph #26, Washington, DC: American Speech-Language-Hearing Assocation.

Loeb, R. & Sarigiani, P. (1986). The impact of hearing impairment on self-perceptions of children. *Volta Review* 88 (2), 89-100.

Moschella, J. (1992). The experience of growing up deaf or hard of hearing: Implications of sign language versus oral rearing on identity development and emotional well-being. Unpublished doctoral dissertation, Antioch College, New Hampshire.

Motoyoshi, M.M. (1990). The experience of mixed-race people: Some thoughts and theories. *Journal of Ethnic Studies* 18 (2), 77-94.

Mottez, B. (1993). The deaf-mute banquets and the birth of the deaf movement. In J. Van Cleve (ed.) *Deaf History Unveiled: Interpretations from the new scholarship.* Washington, DC: Gallaudet University Press. 27-39.

Nover, S. (1993). *Our Voices, Our Vision: Politics of Deaf Education.* Presented at 1993 CAID/ CEASD Convention, Baltimore, MD.

Padden, C. & Humphries, T. (1988). *Deaf in America: Voices from a culture.* Massachusetts: Harvard University Press.

Oxford English Dictionary Online. http://dictionary.oed.com.libproxy.ucl.ac.uk/cgi/ entry/ 50102525/50102525se21?single=1&query_type=word&queryword=hard-of -hearing&first=1&max_to_show=10&hilite=50102525se21 (Retrieved January 11, 2008).

Oyler, R.F., Oyler, A.L. & Matkin, N.D. (1988). Unilateral hearing loss: Demographics and educational impact. *Language, Speech and Hearing Services in Schools* 19, 201-209.

Quigley, S. & Thomure, R. (1968). *Some effects of a hearing impairment on school performance.* Champaign-Urbana, IL: University of Illinois, Institute of Research on Exceptional Children.

Reich, C., Hambleton, D. & Houldin, B.K. (1977). The integration of hearing impaired children in regular classrooms. *American Annals of the Deaf* 122 (6), 534-543.

Ross, M. (1990). Definitions and descriptions. In J. Davis (Ed.) *Our Forgotten Children: Hard-of-Hearing Pupils in the Schools.* Bethdesda, MD: Self-Help for Hard-of-Hearing People.

_____ (1995). Dr. Ross on Hearing Loss: Residual hearing. Originally in *Hearing Rehabilitation Quarterly*. (Retrieved at http://www.hearingresearch.org/Dr.Ross/residual_hearing.htm, March 2008).

_____ (2003). The role of sound: Don't ignore the hearing of hard of hearing students. *Odyssey: New directions in deaf education* 4 (2), 14–17.

_____, Brackett, D. & Maxon, A. (1982). *Hard-of-Hearing Children in Regular Schools*. NJ: Prentice-Hall.

_____ & Calvert, D. (1967). The Semantics of Deafness. *The Volta Review* (69) 10, 644-649.

Scholes, R.J., Tanis, D.C. & Anderson, M.A. (1976). Comprehension of double-object constructions by hard-of-hearing subjects. *Lektos: Interdisciplinary Working Papers in Language Sciences.* 2(1). ERIC Documents #ED 135 251.

Seymour, C. (2007). Transformations, Part 2. In M. Drolsbaugh, Ed. *On the Fence: The hidden world of the hard of hearing.* Springhouse, PA: Handwave Publications. Pp. 78–90.

Shaffer-Meyer, D. (1990). The self-concept of mainstreamed hearing-impaired students. Unpublished doctoral dissertation, University of Northern Colorado, Greeley, CO.

Sheridan, D. (2007). We cloak a lot. In M. Drolsbaugh, Ed. *On the Fence: The hidden world of the hard of hearing.* Springhouse, PA: Handwave Publications. Pp. 122–125.

Stinson, M. (1978). *Use of contextual cues in language comprehension by hearing-impaired persons.* Presented at the Annual Convention of the Genesee Valley Psychological Association, Rochester, NY. ERIC Documents #ED 168 256.

Suggs, T. (2007). Can I Speak Now? In M. Drolsbaugh, Ed. *On the Fence: The hidden world of the hard of hearing.* Springhouse, PA: Handwave Publications. Pp. 201–206.

Tracy, L. & Theilman, V. (1972). John Tracy Clinic Correspondence Course for parents of preschool deaf childen. Los Angeles, John Tracy Clinic.

Tvingstedt, A. (1993). *Social conditions of hearing-impaired pupils in regular classes.* ERIC Documents #ED 368 150.

Valente, M., Hosford-Dunne, H. & Roeser, R. (2000). *Audiology: Treatment.* Thieme New York: Thieme Publications.

Veditz, G. (1913). Preservation of the Sign Language. Burtonsville, MD: Sign Media Inc.

Warfield, F. (1957). *Keep Listening.* New York: Viking Press.

Witcher, B. (1974). She's not deaf, she's hard of hearing. *Volta Review* 76 (7), 428–435.

Woodward, J. & Allen, T. (1993). Models of deafness compared: A sociolinguistic study of deaf and hard of hearing teachers. *Sign Language Studies* 79, 113–125.

Wray, D.F. (1986). Conversational breakdown strategies manifested by hard of hearing students in grades K-8. Unpublished doctoral dissertation, University of Akron, Ohio.

Zweibel, A. (1993). The status of the Deaf in the light of Jewish sources. In R. Fischer & H. Lane (Eds.) *Looking Back: A reader on the history of Deaf communities and their sign languages.* 403-412.

Zweibel, A. (1994). Judaism and deafness: A humanistic heritage. In C. Erting, R. C. Johnson, D. Smith & B. Snider (Eds.) *The Deaf Way: Perspectives from the international conference on Deaf culture.* 231–238.

ENDNOTES

1. It has been a long-standing convention to capitalize the word 'deaf' to refer to the culture of deaf people, and the individuals within that culture. When uncapitalized, the word 'deaf' refers simply to the biological condition of having a hearing loss. However, Lane (2005) and the Canadian Cultural Society of the Deaf make a compelling argument for viewing Deaf people as an ethnic group. As a consequence of this view, they argue, instances of the word 'deaf' should always be capitalized, as it is for other ethnic groups such as Blacks and Jews.

    This stance will be held throughout this paper. Although not conventionalized, 'hearing' is capitalized here to refer to the culture and individuals of mainstream society, most of whom possess a medical or pathological orientation towards the Deaf. When uncapitalized, 'hearing' refers again to the fact of possessing normal hearing ability. On the other hand, 'hard of hearing' is uncapitalized throughout here, because it is not clear at this time whether hard of hearing people have, or will develop, a cultural identity of their own.
2. This suspicion is reinforced by Ballin's (1930) classification of deaf people as either deaf-mutes (born deaf or deafened before age 6) or semi-mutes (deafened after 6 years of age).
3. It is interesting to observe how Dr. Ross's assertion that "the sense of hearing [is] a gift, from our evolutionary forbearers and/or from the Creator" stands in direct opposition to the Deaf community's viewpoint, as exemplified by George Veditz in 1913 that "sign language is God's noblest gift to Deaf people."

Doctoral Study Experiences of Deaf and Hard of Hearing Professionals Working in Higher Education Institutions

CHRISTOPHER KURZ, PH.D. & KIM BROWN KURZ, PH.D.

SINCE THE EDUCATION FOR ALL HANDICAPPED ACT OF 1975 (EHA), later renamed the Individuals with Disabilities Act (IDEA), was enacted and subsequently reauthorized in 1987, 1990, 1998, and 2004, and supported by other legislation such as Section 504 of the Rehabilitation Act of 1973 and the Americans with Disabilities Act of 1990 (ADA), the lives of Deaf and hard of hearing people were changed forever, both inside and outside of the classrooms (Turnbull, Turnbull, Stowe, & Huerta, 2006). Deaf people are seeing increased opportunities to pursue postsecondary education.

DEAF AND HARD OF HEARING STUDENTS IN HIGHER EDUCATION

Although the number of students with disabilities attending higher education has increased in the last thirty years, such students continue to be underrepresented in postsecondary institutions. In the National Center for Education Statistics' (NCES) latest study on college students with disabilities, 428,280 undergraduate students were identified as having disabilities, thus representing six percent of the student body (1999). In addition, 5.6% of the undergraduate students identified as having disabilities in the study were categorized as having hearing impairments. Less than 24 thousand Deaf and hard of hearing students (23,860) attended higher education during 1997–1998 (NCES, 1999).

In his comprehensive survey of Deaf and hard of hearing people on their workplace and educational background, Crammatte (1987) found that the number of Deaf and hard of hearing people who hold doctoral degrees is significantly small. His claim is further backed up by NCES (U.S. Department of Education, 2000) by which statistics on the percent of graduate and professional students reporting disabilities during 1999-2000 are currently available. The NCES statistics show that the percent of doctoral students who reported a hearing impairment is approximately 0.612%, which is less than the national percentage, 1.2%. Furthermore, the percent of professional students who reported a hearing impairment is 0.378%, which is also less than the national percentage, 1.5%. As Deaf and hard of hearing people climb the educational ladder in order to pursue and earn their doctorates and, in turn, work at institutions of higher education, the population of Deaf and hard of hearing people who hold doctoral degrees remains small (see Crammatte, 1987; U.S. Department of Education, 2000). While the number of deaf students pursuing doctoral and terminal degrees is small, those Deaf students pursue doctoral and terminal degrees for a variety of reasons, including the desire to acquire the knowledge and skills needed to advance their academic careers in higher education institutions.

PURSUIT OF THE PH.D./ED.D.

People pursue doctoral degrees for a variety of reasons. Three main reasons for pursuing doctoral degrees are the need for greater expertise, the desire for career advancement, and the desire to conduct research and/or teach (Wilson, Soto, & Joyner, 2003). To become a scholar and researcher in a chosen field, one is expected to earn a doctoral degree (Jerrard & Jerrard, 1998). To obtain an academic position, one is expected to possess a doctorate degree (Schuele, 2004). Most major colleges and universities require their faculty members to hold doctorate degrees and to engage in research and/or scholarly activities. The justifications for the requirement are to insure that the faculty member has sufficient expertise to teach advanced courses and to force him/her to remain current in his/her field (Ezell, 2002).

Faculty members at colleges and universities have three main activities: teaching, conducting research or scholarly projects, and servicing within and outside the institute (Wilson, Soto, & Joyner, 2003; Schuele, 2004). The yearning to perform one or more of these main activities propels people to move up the academic career ladder. Bodner-Johnson and Martin (1999) conducted a nationwide survey to understand why teacher educators in Deaf education strived to move from school classrooms to universities. The majority of survey respondents (49%) chose university settings for employment so that they could pursue research activities and an academic, scholarly life. To pursue scholarship, to influence Deaf education, to become involved in teacher education, and to teach and work in postsecondary institutions were several primary reasons for the respondents to move up to universities. In sum, it appears that some people pursue doctoral study to move up the academic career ladder.

There is but a lack of research on Deaf and hard of hearing faculty members and administrators who have doctoral degrees regarding their perception of their doctoral study experiences.

RESEARCH QUESTIONS

This current study focuses specifically on the population of Deaf and hard of hearing people who hold doctoral degrees and work in a college or university setting. In this study, the doctoral study experiences of current Deaf college and university faculty and staff are examined. Using an on-line survey questionnaire, the researchers strive to find out more about the doctoral study experiences of Deaf and hard of hearing faculty with doctoral degrees, and to identify common threads that emerged from their statements. Specifically this research study seeks to answer the following research questions:

- What are some common experiences and issues Deaf and hard of hearing doctoral students share while they pursued their doctoral degrees?
- What criteria should colleges and universities use to accept Deaf or hard of hearing doctoral applicants?

METHOD

Respondents. This current study focuses specifically on the population of Deaf and hard of hearing people who hold terminal degrees and work in a college or university setting. Forty Deaf and hard of hearing professionals who hold terminal degrees' names were given to the authors with the aid of the Gallaudet University Regional Center at Johnson County Community College, the Kansas State Department of Education, National Association of the Deaf, Gallaudet University, the National Technical Institute for the Deaf at Rochester Institute of Technology, California State University at Northridge, and the Postsecondary Education Program Network project. Seventeen respondents completed the online survey for a response rate of 43 percent.

Fifteen of the respondents identified themselves as Deaf and two identified themselves as hard of hearing (see Table 1). In regards to their primary communication mode, the respondents were not limited to a single choice. Their response tended to depend on their work and with whom they interacted in order to accomplish their educational or career goals. The majority of the respondents reported that they use American Sign Language (52.9% — nine respondents), four respondents (23.5%) indicated they use Pidgin Signed English and/or Contact Signing, and five respondents (29.4%) said they use Simultaneous Communication or Total Communication. The majority of the respondents ranged in age from 36 years to 45 years (35.3% — six respondents). The second largest age range of the respondents was 46–55 (29.4% — five respondents), and 23.5 percent (four respondents) of the respondents were in the age range of 56–65. Only two respondents indicated that they were in the age range of 25–35 (see Table 1). Ten of the Deaf and hard of hearing individuals who responded have doctor of philosophy degrees and the other seven have doctor of education degrees. Eighty-eight percent (15 respondents) of the respondents said they work in a four-year college or university; 11.8 percent (2 respondents) said they worked in a community college; and another 11.8 percent (2 respondents) said they worked in a technical college. Forty-one percent (7 respondents) indicated that they are employed as faculty, 23.5 percent (4 respondents) said they are administrators, 11.8 percent (2 respondents) said they are researchers, while 29.4 percent (5 respondents) said they do all of the above mentioned work — faculty, administrator, and researcher (see Table 1).

Survey Instrument. All information for this research came from one source: a participant survey. The survey contained questions about the participants' feelings and opinions regarding their graduate study experience, their current workplace experience, and opinions about college admission criteria for Deaf individuals who wish to pursue doctoral degrees. The information the survey respondents provided gave a picture of life in colleges and universities for Deaf and hard of hearing doctoral students.

The Deaf and hard of hearing respondents were then asked to explain whether their graduate-level studies were effective or ineffective, and what they would have liked to see improved. Furthermore, the survey asked participants to examine, from their perspective, some of the current trends and issues in regard to pursuing their doctoral degrees in higher education institutions. However, only the respondents' graduate school experiences and their opinions about college admission criteria will be discussed in this article.

Procedure. Deaf and hard of hearing individuals who hold terminal degrees such as a Ph.D. or Ed.D., received the survey in an electronic format that was created and designed on a website. First, electronic mail was sent to the participants asking them to go to the website that contained the survey. All willing participants then entered the website and answered the survey accordingly. For some questions, they were provided several choices to describe their background information, graduate experiences, and opinions. Other questions required that the respondent complete a "fill-out-in-the-box" window to explain their opinions or feelings. When the survey was completed, their responses were sent electronically to the author's email address.

	n	%
Hearing status		
Deaf	15	88.2
Hard-of-hearing	2	11.8
Primary Communication Mode*		
American Sign Language (ASL)	9	52.9
PSE/Contact Signing	4	23.5
Signed English	1	6.0
Oral	0	0
Simultaneous Communication	5	29.4
Age Range		
25–35	1	11.8
36–45	6	35.3
46–55	5	29.4
56–65	4	23.5
Type of Terminal Degree		
Ph.D.	10	58.8
Ed.D.	7	41.2
Type of Higher Education Institution in which Participants Currently Work*		
Four-year College/University	15	88.2
Community College	2	11.8
Technical College	2	11.8
Types of Work Participants Reported*		
Administration	4	23.5
Faculty	7	41.2
Research	2	11.8
All of the above	5	29.4

Table 1. Background Information (*Respondents have chosen more than one answer for some categories.)

RESULTS

Graduate School Experience. During their graduate education, 88 percent (15) of the respondents said that they had some research experience, 23.5 percent (4) said they had done some grant work, 23.5 percent (4) said they had some grant-writing experience, 47 percent (8) said they had some experience in writing for publication, and 17.6 percent (3) said they had an opportunity to serve on one or more committee (see Table 2).

One individual who graduated from a four-year university and is currently a professor at another four-year university said that his graduate school studies did not really prepare him for the type of work he is doing now (see Table 3). In contrast, another person who has the same background and current position felt she was well prepared for the type of work she does today. She wrote, "I did research papers as part of my regular class work, some of which were eventually published and/or presented at conferences. I also had a class in which we were given practice on how to write grant proposals and encouraged to submit one." She felt strongly that her graduate school provided "appropriate coursework in a broad range of fields and topics which allowed [me] to teach on a broader level rather than a narrowly defined one." One person said, "I needed a Ph.D. to teach." Another person commented about how his graduate school experience led him to his life-long career in research. "I conducted some research on attitudes towards Deaf persons that was published in an APA journal before I completed my Master's [degree]. I used the data in my dissertation, which launched a life-long research career. All of these experiences were derived from my association with a federally funded Research and Training Center, rather than from my academic department."

One college graduate indicated that her research interest in language acquisition of Deaf children as well as preparation of the methodology, evaluation, and assessment of students, prepared her for the type of work she is doing now at a four-year university. An administrator at a technical school said he was a part-time university student while working full-time in his current job. He also said that learning about research, analytical skills, problem solving, leadership and organization during his/her graduate work prepared him for his job. A graduate said that while her graduate school was sensitive to her linguistic and cultural needs, she had to fight for accommodations at the current college where she works. She stated that she now realizes how much she appreciates her graduate school's support services and how it prepared her to request such services at other colleges.

> "[The college] provided the essentials I needed in the area of research by means of the common core, and provided specific coursework related to

grant writing, program evaluation, and program development. Also, the program required an internship or the equivalent of one," said a college graduate. Another graduate said, "It [the college] helped me become more effective as a college faculty member in terms of teaching effectiveness, research, publication, presentations, and making contributions to the field."

Some individuals indicated that the graduate courses were not specific to their intended career. One administrator at a college wrote, "As part of my graduate program, I had to take some core courses as part of my cohort. These core courses focused primarily on K-12 educational administration. These were not very applicable to my work, and most of my classmates were aiming for K-12 supervisory certification. However, as I started my electives and emphasis in higher education, the courses I took were relevant. They were in adult education, administration, statistics, business management, and college personnel."

Another graduate talked about how his dissertation work was a significant part of personnel preparation for the work he does today. "The University (state)'s doctoral program in Special Education is both challenging and demanding. Coursework in Special Education completed with general education learning was intellectually challenging. The dissertation work prepared me well for scholarly efforts in my current role." A graduate from another college echoed this message about how her college prepared her for her current work, "Theory and practices learned in various courses. Experience with research (dissertation). Guidance from excellent professors."

	n	%
Research	15	88.2
Grant work	2	23.5
Writing grants	4	23.5
Writing for publication	8	47
Serving on committees	3	17.6

Table 2. Types of Graduate Experience (Respondents have chosen more than one answer for some categories.)

	n	%
Yes	8	47
No	1	6
In some ways	8	47

Table 3. Graduate Work that Prepared for Current Jobs

Deaf and Hard of Hearing Professionals' Opinions about Graduate Schools' Admission Criteria.
The question on the survey asked, "Do you

think colleges and universities should maintain or eliminate their admission requirements (e.g. GRE scores, previous GPA, writing samples) to the graduate-level programs for individuals who are Deaf or hard of hearing?" About 59 percent (10) of the participants felt strongly that graduate schools should keep all admission requirements regardless of the hearing status of the applicant, and the other 41.2 percent (7) believed that graduate schools should either lower or eliminate some admission requirements based on hearing status. None of the respondents felt that all admission requirements should be eliminated (See Table 4).

A university faculty member said, "I think there definitely needs to be some flexibility as to what admissions criteria will determine one's acceptance. I think most standardized tests do not reflect true abilities or motivation of Deaf applicants." A faculty member at another university said, "I think if you want to enter a program, you should be able to meet the requirements. However, I do not feel that these requirements should be hard and fast. We do need to maintain flexibility and take into consideration other evidence of [the] candidate's ability to achieve and contribute to a graduate-level program in those cases where the candidates do not entirely meet the entrance requirements." One faculty member at a college wrote, "I don't favor lowering standards. I worked hard to get my skills where they are and it wasn't easy and nobody should get an easy ride. I do not believe in lowering standards for Deaf people. It is their problem if they party too much in undergraduate courses. I left the Deaf high school field when the majority of students tell me academics do not matter because of Social Security Incomes (SSI). Why should requirements be lowered to reward them for their lack of high expectations? Research shows high standards will result in high performance."

An administrator at a technical college said, "I recommend keeping all standard tests but each case that involves a Deaf and hard of hearing and at-risk student should be reviewed on case by case basis." Another said, "Get rid of Graduate Records Exams but keep written samples and Grade Point Averages." One person said, "I would hate to see the 'dumbing down' of curricula for Deaf or hard of hearing people. That would only lessen our value and create an uneven playing field. I will work day and night to discourage such practice. Deaf people can do what we set our sights to do — learning English is a minimum if we want to function as professionals in the hearing world." Another person commented about how he thought colleges should use nonverbal tests to determine the Deaf and hard of hearing student's potential during graduate school. "The entry level standards should be kept but assessments need to be modified to ensure they are not eliminating students who are actually qualified" said a graduate. A faculty member at a community college said, "Not necessarily lowered or eliminated but rather modified to better fit the experiences of Deaf and hard of hearing people." An administrator at a community college said, "There are many Deaf individuals who are very bright and very qualified. They may not have 'perfect' English, but know how to accomplish results in the workplace. It would be good for academic programs and the workplace to recognize this and allow for a little flexibility in this area. Of course, good English is absolutely critical, and a very low level of English proficiency is not acceptable. I am just talking about 'minor' blemishes in English that should be tolerated."

	n	%
Keep all admission requirements	10	58.8
Lower or eliminate some admission requirements	7	41.2

Table 4. Deaf and Hard of Hearing Professionals' Opinions about Admissions Criteria

CONCLUSION AND DISCUSSION

This article discusses the doctoral study experiences, as derived from a study, of seventeen Deaf and hard of hearing professionals who hold doctoral degrees and work in college/university settings. Looking at the data, several common patterns were evident.

What are some common experiences and issues Deaf and hard of hearing doctorates share while they pursued their doctoral degrees?
Many of the respondents commented they were satisfied or more than satisfied with their graduate school experience. Even though 88% of the respondents said they had some research experience, some felt they were not given enough opportunities to participate in research projects run by their faculty or university, or to participate in actual grant writing processes during their doctoral study experiences. Many felt their strength were teaching and providing service to the collegial campus and community, and that they were lacking in the research area where they have to submit work for the purpose of publication. Less than half of the respondents had an opportunity to write for publication during their doctoral study experience. Doctoral advisors are encouraged to give their students the experience of publishing their work or become co-authors with their students. Another area where the respondents felt was a weakness during their graduate program was lack of application to their actual, every day work.

The area of leadership preparation needs to be addressed at the doctoral level to ensure that all doctoral students are receiving the training and experience they need to succeed in postsecondary educational settings. For example, several people expressed frustration at not being able to get the support services they requested, or not being able to be promoted or earn recognition commensurate with their degrees and the type of work they do from their administrators. Many felt their doctoral programs need to take initiative to offer personnel preparation courses to their hearing students related to the issues of individuals with disabilities who hold terminal degrees.

What criteria should colleges and universities use to accept Deaf or hard of hearing doctoral applicants?
About half of the respondents strongly felt that the admission criteria of D/Deaf and hard of hearing students who wish to pursue higher education degrees should be revised. Those respondents argued that accessibility to graduate and doctoral education for Deaf and hard of hearing students is a problematic issue, and that these students should not be punished on the basis of their less than perfect English skills. They should be evaluated based on their thinking skills and content knowledge. Some called for flexibility in the admission criteria and consideration of other evidence of the candidate's ability to achieve and contribute to the program. At the same time, the other half of respondents strongly felt that the admissions criteria should not be lowered nor eliminated. These persons felt that Deaf and hard of hearing students who wish to pursue higher education degrees should not be treated any differently from their hearing peers. There is no clear answer to this concern.

FUTURE RESEARCH

This study produces more questions than answers. There is a greater need for research that can provide empirical data on Deaf and hard of hearing doctorates, including their doctoral study experiences. Active participation in doctoral programs is crucial to development and application of knowledge and research skills for postdoctoral employment. Further study regarding potential impact of active participation in Deaf students' doctoral programs by the university personnel; partnerships between educational institutions and Deaf community mentoring system for Deaf and hard of hearing doctoral students and Deaf and hard of hearing professionals who hold doctoral degrees and teach in postsecondary settings; job satisfaction and retention of Deaf and hard of hearing doctorates; research priorities among Deaf and hard of hearing doctorates; and potential impacts of technology on job (e.g., Instant Messaging, Video Relay Service, Video Relay Interpreting).

Suggestions for future research include both gathering input and having discussions on the following questions: 1) how satisfied have Deaf doctoral students been with departmental advising and guidance? 2) Were their Ph.D. candidacy exams and preparation a beneficial educational experience? 3) What professional development opportunities did they attend? 4) How should graduate/doctoral admission for individuals with disabilities be improved? 5) Should mentorship opportunities be provided for Deaf doctoral students and recently-minted doctorates and what should this mentorship involve? and 6) Are Deaf and hard of hearing doctoral students being adequately prepared for their future employment requirements in the areas of research, grant development, service, and training.

While Deaf and hard of hearing faculty expressed the need for a solid networking and support system, there is a loosely support group, the Deaf Academics Organization. Such a mentoring system could strengthen or motivate doctoral students to complete their studies and to solidify career path. There does exist a networking system for deaf and hard of hearing doctoral students and professionals who hold doctoral degrees. The Deaf Academics organization was found few years ago, and is currently serving "approximately 200 deaf and hard of hearing academics and researchers, in a range of disciplines and from all over the world." The international organization promotes dialogue between deaf and hard of hearing individuals who are scientists, researchers, instructors, professors, or lectures within an university of laboratory setting, and who are graduate students and other individuals in training, through their website, listserv and biennial conferences.

The purpose of this document is to promote and begin a healthy dialogue among Deaf and hard-of-hearing professionals who work together and help to identify and create some potential solutions to the issues presented.

REFERENCES

Ambrose, S., Huston, T., & Norman, M. (2005). A qualitative method for assessing faculty satisfaction. *Research in Higher Education*, 46(7), 803-830.

Bodner-Johnson, B.A., & Martin, D.S. (1999). Teacher educators in Deaf education: Why they entered higher education and their current priorities and accomplishments. *American Annals of the Deaf*, 144(3), 236-241.

Crammatte, A. (1987). *Hearing-impaired professionals in the workplace*. Washington, D.C.: Gallaudet University Press.

Ezell, H.K. (2002). *Guide to success in doctoral study and faculty work*. Rockville, MD: American Speech-Language-Hearing Association.

Golde, C.M., & Dore, T.M. (2001). At cross purposes: What the experiences of doctoral students reveal about doctoral education. (www.phd-survey.com). A report prepared for the Pew Charitable Trusts, Philadelphia, PA.

Jerrard, R., & Jerrard, M. (1998). *The grad school handbook: An insider's guide to getting in and succeeding*. New York: Perigee Books.

National Association of Graduate and Professional Students (NAGPS). (2001). *The 2000 National*

Doctoral Program Survey. (survey.nagps.org).

National Center for Education Statistics. (1999). *An institutional perspective on students with disabilities in postsecondary education.* Postsecondary Education Quick Information System. Washington DC: US Department of Education. Available at http://nces.ed.gov/programs/digest/d05/tables/dt05_295.asp

National Center for Education Statistics. (2005). *Doctorate recipients from United States universities, 2003, survey of earned doctorates.* Washington DC: US Department of Education.

National Opinion Research Council. (2001). Doctorate recipients from United States universities: Summary Report 2001. Chicago: IL.

Nerad, M. (2004). *The PhD in the US: Criticisms, facts, and remedies.* Higher Education Policy, 17(2), 183-199.

Nerad, M., & Cerny, J. (2002). Postdoctoral appointments and employment patterns of science and engineering doctoral recipients ten-plus years after Ph.D. completion. *Communicator,* VXXXV(7), 1-6.

Olsen, D., Maple, S.A., & Stage, F.K. (1995). Women and minority faculty job satisfaction. *Journal of Higher Education,* 66(3), 267-293.

Padden, C.A., & Humphries, T.L. (1990). *Deaf in America: Voices from a culture.* Cambridge, MA: Harvard University Press.

Turnbull, H. R., Turnbull, A.P., Stowe, M., & Huerta, N. (2006). *Free appropriate public education: The law and children with disabilities.* Denver: Love Publishing Co.

U.S. Department of Education, National Center for Education Statistics, 1999-2000 National Postsecondary Student Aid Study (NPSAS:2000)

Wilson, T., Soto, N., & Joyner, J. (2003). Deciding if and how to pursue doctoral work. In Anna L. Green & LeKita V. Scott (Eds.). *Journey to the Ph.D.: How to navigate the process as African Americans.* Sterling, VA: Stylus Publishing.

FOOTNOTES

Throughout the paper, the authors has decided to identify all Deaf individuals of all degrees by including the capital "D" which represents those who identify themselves as members of a cultural and linguistic group that share common values, traditions, and language (Padden & Humphries, 1990) and some other individuals are more comfortable as identifying themselves as hard-of-hearing. Since our participants' background and their identifications vary, the authors wish to respect everyone by using appropriate identifications such as "Deaf and hard of hearing" labels.

Education of the Deaf: Mediated by Interpreters

PATRICIA LESSARD

BY DEFINITION, DEAF STUDENTS FALL UNDER THE PROVISIONS OF Special Education. However, they also are required to meet the standards of No Child Left Behind. By and large they are placed in regular education classrooms with support services, in particular, sign language interpreters. The key to an effective mainstream education where an interpreter is provided lies in the qualifications of the interpreter. The inclusion of Deaf students in a regular education classroom means that they are in an environment where they do not share the language (in its spoken modality) with the majority of their peers and/or teacher(s). It is the interpreter who must mediate this environment, and as a consequence, mediate their education.

It is hoped that this brief description of recent observations will generate questions as well as encourage discussion about the challenge of training individuals who will eventually work with deaf students in educational environments. The information presented here is from a review of the literature, from data collected over the last 15 years while observing and evaluating students, anecdotal information gathered when speaking with colleagues in other training programs, discussions with peers when working as an interpreter, and comments that have been made during encounters with former students of interpretation who are now working in the field.

NO CHILD LEFT BEHIND ACT OF 2001

To begin, what is the No Child Left Behind Act of 2001? Essentially, the No Child Left Behind Act of 2001 (NCLB) is a reauthorization of the Elementary and Secondary Education Act (ESEA) of 1965. NCLB expands on major reforms, especially state academic standards, student assessment and progress, accountability, and school improvement. It has set out several key performance goals, which state expectations for schools and students:

- All students will be taught by highly qualified teachers by the end of the 2005-06 school year
- All students will attain proficiency in reading and mathematics by 2014, including students with disabilities and English learners
- All English learners will become proficient in English
- All students will learn in schools that are safe and drug free
- All students will graduate from high school

In compliance with the goals stated above, local school districts are required to test their students – all students – to ensure that they are making progress in school. The NCLB refers to this progress as "adequate yearly progress" or AYP. Students with disabilities (as deaf students are categorized in the US) are also expected to make AYP. A key factor to consider when measuring the academic progress of any student is their placement in a program that supports students in their development of critical thinking skills, language, and appropriate and meaningful social interactions. With access to the benefits of this type of program, i.e., access that is provided by a qualified interpreter, a deaf student is better positioned for success.

In order for deaf students to acquire literacy skills and be performing at grade level as required by No Child Left Behind, they must have meaningful communication. Communication requires access to the expressed thoughts of the other party in the conversation. This means that the deaf child must have comprehensible input (from the interpreter) in order to understand the message that the teacher or classmates are trying to impart. Comprehension requires that the interpreter provide intelligible output to the student. Intelligible output requires language fluency. The interpreter needs to understand what the teacher is saying. The interpreter needs to be able to convey the content in a way that the deaf student can understand. If the interpreter does not understand the talk of the teacher or other children in the class, then there won't be an accurate interpretation.

If the deaf student does not understand the content due to errors or omissions made by the interpreter, then there won't be academic progress. Since the NCLB requires a school to measure a deaf student's academic progress – how can the student be fairly assessed for progress if they aren't getting information in a form that they can access or understand?

BACKGROUND

With the expectations established by the NCLB Act of 2001, Deaf children in the public schools are now faced with the daunting task of performing on par with their hearing peers in all aspects of their academic endeavors. There is a growing concern regarding the education of deaf students that comes to them through interpreters who are not competent to work in an educational setting.

Over the last 30 years, more and more deaf students have been placed in mainstreamed settings. According to the 2002 National Center for Educational Statistics, 80% of deaf children in the United States attend local public schools. Placement in an educational institution does not necessarily mean that deaf students will be in an environment where learning takes place for them. "Deaf students in mainstream settings are suffering because the interpreters that they have working with them are either not qualified to be working as an interpreter at all, or minimally qualified to be working in an educational setting with young deaf students." (Marshark, 2005)

Research on working educational interpreters in the U.S. shows that many do not have language and interpreting skills that are commonly considered as minimum standards in the U.S. Research using the Educational Interpreter Performance Assessment (Schick, Williams, & Bolster, 1999; Schick, Williams, & Kupermintz, 2006) shows that 45% of more than 2,000 interpreters did not have sufficient interpreting skills to be in a classroom.

"An interpreted education seems to place additional demands on [a deaf student's] cognitive processing (Schick, 2004). The student must coordinate visual attention between the interpreter and other visual information in the classroom, which means that the d/hh [deaf and hard-of-hearing] student likely receives less information than the hearing students (Winston, 2004). The d/hh student also must figure out who is speaking in the classroom in order to make sense of the message (Schick, 2004), a requirement that is challenging to represent for many interpreters (Schick et al., 2006).

For their part, educational interpreters are typically second-language learners, so the student must deal with a variety of accents and errors. As we know, the interpretation is likely to be a less rich and complex version of the teacher's communication in addition to being riddled with distortions, errors, and omissions (Langer, 2007), which make learning more challenging. The d/hh student must contend with interpreted communication that is not in synchronization with what the hearing teacher and peers are doing, pointing, and looking (Winston, 2004). This short list of increased demands on cognitive resources is clearly incomplete; we really do not know all the factors that may be involved." (Schick, 2008)

EDUCATIONAL CHALLENGES

When deaf children attend a mainstreamed, public school, their success or failure could be the result of the quality of the interpreter employed by the school where they are placed. According to a report on deaf students who were placed in a setting where educational interpreters were employed, published by LaBue (1998), there were five reasons that deaf students gave as to why they have a difficult time following their interpreter:

1. The interpretation, often ungrammatical, and incomprehensible, forced students to depend on their knowledge of English discourse structure and lip reading if they wanted to understand discussions and participate in them.
2. Turn taking in a mainstreamed classroom is usually controlled by auditory cues, which typically don't get (or can't be) interpreted.
3. Many of the cohesive features of spoken English such as repetition, and other discourse markers were not interpreted.
4. Students had a difficult time tracking the topics. They often did not know if the speaker had changed topics or if someone else was talking.
5. Important cues, such as participant relationships and status – ergo the permission to interrupt or not, were not provided.

Qualifications of classroom interpreters vary widely. Based on information gathered from interviews and discussions conducted during my observations and assessments over the years, if there was a spectrum one could use to help categorize the educational interpreters under discussion, they would have been located at any of a number of places. For example, at one end would be an individual who has graduated from an accredited interpreter-training program and who has had years of experience. At the other end are the individuals who have had nothing more than a few sign language courses or have learned sign language exclusively from a book.

What should be the minimum qualifications of an interpreter? To begin with, one must possess English fluency. Secondly, one must have developed American Sign Language (ASL)fluency. Third, one must have bi-lingual fluency, i.e., have the aptitude to take the meaning, explicitly stated or implied, from one language and give its appropriate interpretation in the other.

ENGLISH FLUENCY

Being fluent in the grammar of English is usually not a problem for interpreters. However, when working in the classroom, they must also recognize different types or genres of discourse in English and what the utterances mean beyond the words in order to effectively convey the intended meaning into ASL. Speakers often use different genres of discourse to achieve particular communicative goals. For example, over the course of a few hours, teacher and students could transition from one genre to another. Their talk could be persuasive, expository, procedural, informational or argumentative in nature. They may be in the middle of a lecture where the teacher describes the process for conducting a lab experiment; perhaps one of the students decides this is the perfect opportunity to argue against genetic testing; the teacher, in turn decides to offer the student advice about seeking or refusing medical interventions, etc. These different ways of speaking will have their own characteristics.

In addition to the genre of the speech, there is the tone that accompanies the words. It can be formal, asserting one's status over the other participant; it can reveal irony or sarcasm, indicate ridicule or judgment, etc. There is also a rising or "checking" intonation in English, which is used by a speaker to see if the listener is able to follow the content of the message. The lack of recognition of these extra-linguistic properties of English has been what caused many of the interpreter errors I observed. As a result, there was confusion and misunderstanding on the part of the student.

Could student struggles be mitigated if the interpreter possessed greater ASL fluency? That is, fluency with the grammar; the ability to recognize the different genres of discourse and provide an equivalent translation that includes the communicative intent of the speaker; and a realization of the meaning that resides beyond the word level.

ASL FLUENCY

ASL is a language that is expressed in a modality that differs from the interpreter's spoken language in many ways. It requires years of exposure or training in order to acquire second language (L2) fluency. Acquisition in terms of language refers to the gradual development of ability by using it naturally in communicative situations—long periods spent in social interactions (Yule 1985). As with the young deaf children, such prolonged interactions would allow adult learners to parse the grammar and prosody of ASL into component parts. Once these features have been isolated and identified, they can be rehearsed and successfully incorporated into the interpreted message. There were very few native speakers of ASL in the interpreters I observed and assessed. Details of their language study and acquisition will follow. All of the non-native speakers learned ASL as adults. Native-like fluency takes a very long time and requires intense training to compensate for late exposure and learning. (Morford and Mayberry 2000)

The question that seems to naturally follow is: How difficult is it to learn ASL? The usual response is "about as difficult as it is to learn any foreign language." According to Jacobs (1996) one must consider its degree of foreignness. The Foreign Service Institute and the Defense Language Institute have grouped languages into four categories. Category 1 includes Spanish, French and German, for example. Each successive category requires more time in which to become proficient. The most difficult is Category 4. It includes languages such as Arabic, Chinese, Japanese and Korean. ASL is considered a Category 4 language. The time and aptitude it would take to learn a language in this category, for example, and be comfortably proficient using it, would be on average between six and fifteen years, based on 10 hours of language instruction per week. It is worth noting that a considerable number of the educational interpreters begin working in the classroom with fewer than three years of experience signing ASL. "While aptitude does not appear to play a significant role in first language acquisition, i.e., most people acquire their native language completely regardless of other cognitive abilities that they may possess, it has been implicated in L2 learning by adults. More importantly, aptitude should be a deciding factor when accepting students into an interpreting program." (Quinto-Pozos 2005)

MY OBSERVATIONS

- Most of the educational interpreters interviewed reported they had never had a deaf teacher for their ASL classes.
- Many of them reported that they never had any formal ASL instruction or formal training for interpreting.
- Most were weak in their ability to accurately convey the actual meaning behind the words – they lacked semantic awareness in both ASL and English resulting in a skewing of the speaker's intent.
- Most of them learned ASL when they were an adult, which doesn't make fluency impossible, but they rarely interacted with deaf adults or children outside of work hours, which impeded their language progress. Many of the educational interpreters interviewed reported having very little contact with the Deaf community.
- Many requisite, co-occurring non-manual grammatical features were not realized or incorporated into their signed production. Non-manual markers of grammatical constructions will be discussed in detail in the following section regarding skewing of a speaker's message.

Many interpreters were weak in their visual-spatial abilities. They had a very difficult time when they were required to go from a verbal text to "seeing" a visual representation of it in their mind's eye. Visual-spatial ability involves accurately perceiving an image, comprehending its properties, and then mentally modifying it, and producing a new image in a different form. (Gardner, 1991) For educational interpreters, the different 'form' would be ASL. The linguistic processing by speakers of English is very linear and sequential. The interpreters I observed struggled visibly in working from this linear format into to the three-dimensional and visual way of talking in ASL. It meant that they had to wait for the entire sentence to be uttered in order to understand and correctly align the objects in space. The classroom dynamics did not always allow the interpreters the luxury of this much processing time.

Most of the interpreters were also very weak in their use of classifiers. Classifiers are an integral part of ASL. It is through the use of classifiers that ASL expresses such things as prepositions, location relationships, and plurality. It is also a means to provide adjectival information. "The use of classifiers consists of making a connection between the visual representation of reality in the mind and its linguistic expression. It is not uncommon that the level of mastery in classifiers is perceived as an indication of the degree of mastery in American Sign Language." (Kuntze in Lessard, 2002) It is not uncommon for second language learners of ASL to plateau in their L2 acquisition because they are not able to make much progress in comprehending and producing structures that incorporate classifiers. The three-dimensional properties of classifiers are unlike anything that speakers of English are accustomed to.

BILINGUAL FLUENCY

It has been said that interpreters need "superior linguistic skills and cultural knowledge to function successfully." (McIntire 1990) One of the most noticeable challenges to the interpreters I observed was the lack of training in the pragmatic use of language. When looking at "talk" or text atomically, one can miss the pragmatic influence; the way people intentionally craft their language and word choice, and fail to understand the overall thought or intention.

The goal should be that the interpreted message be a true reflection of the speaker's intent, and not a literal, verbatim stream of meaningless words. "Experienced [interpreters] (5+ years) seemed to intuitively focus on the function of the discourse while paying attention to the meaning, whereas the less experienced interpreters chose words but didn't recognize the function or lacked strategies to show the function. Impact on students: higher level thinking processes not activated when interpretation lacks these processes."

(Dr. Deb Russell, University of Alberta, Supporting Deaf People Conference, 2008)

What makes for a good interpretation? One measure of a successful interpretation is the amount of prosodic information that is included from the source language into the target language. Prosody is the combination of features in any language that produces the rhythm, accent and feel of the language (Winston 2000). Until recently, the function of prosody and its relation to discourse has been largely ignored in second language learning and teaching. In the literature on first language acquisition, however, the development of intonation and of prosody for discourse functions has been an important issue. The features of prosody in a spoken language include those that have linguistic relevance, as in the words themselves and the co-occurring intonation, accent, rhythm, pitch, stress, volume, tempo and speed. Features of prosody in ASL are carried by Non-Manual Signals (NMS). (See Appendix A for a detailed listing of Non Manual Signals in ASL.) In addition, and often overlooked or left out due to cognitive overload on the part of the interpreter, are the paralinguistic features that add meaning, but may not take on the form of a word, e.g., a sigh or moan.

In discourse, sentences need to be linked to other sentences in order to carry an idea through a series of changes in events and temporal contexts (Morgan 1999). One term used to define this technique is cohesion. Cohesion refers to relations that exist between sentences when the interpretation of some element in discourse is dependent on that of another (Halliday and Hasan 1976). This leads to the overall intelligibility of discourse. It is important that an interpreter knows the cohesion devices of both the source language and the target language and how to employ them correctly. An interpreter who is able to successfully incorporate the features of prosody will allow the deaf student to benefit from more native-like discourse.

Gile (1995) posits a set of three requirements for effective interpreting: linguistic knowledge, knowledge of the interpreting process and extralinguistic knowledge. Working at the discourse level requires the interpreter to discern extralinguistic features in the source language and express the equivalence in the target language.

Roda Roberts from the University of Ottawa, who has taught translation and interpreting in many Canadian, United States, and Indian universities, is considered to be an authority on Translation Theory. She has published numerous articles and books on the training of translators and interpreters, terminology/lexicography, and community interpreting. She believes interpreters should be assessed on their ability to perform in the following three domains of competency [italics mine].

Language Competency
1. The ability to work between two languages.
2. The ability to understand the source message and all its nuances.
3. The ability to express correctly the same message in the target language.

Transfer Competency
1. The ability to understand the meaning contained in the source message.
2. The ability to render the meaning of the source message into the target language without distortions, additions or omissions.
3. The ability to render the message from the source language into the target language without undue influence of the source language, i.e., vocabulary is in ASL, but the grammar is English.
4. The ability to render the message in the same style or register.

Subject Matter Competency
1. Since one cannot interpret what one cannot understand, knowledge of the subject or content is required in order to accurately convey the message.
2. Sufficient knowledge of the specialized discourse to interpret effectively.

Errors and Omissions Specific to Language and Transfer Competencies:
- Omissions in terms of instructional content (unintelligible) [L3]
- Skewing of original message which, often intelligible, but did not have the same intent as the speaker's
- Deletion of pronouns when they were needed for clarity.
- Pronoun copy (redundant use of pronoun at the end of a sentence)
- Omissions of critical cohesive devices: very difficult to follow and parse the text; students said that it felt like one long sentence.
- Well-formed constructions of ASL WH- and RH-Q (rhetorical questions), but pragmatically the wrong intent or discourse function (skewed), e.g. when the speaker was giving an imperative disguised as a question as in "Who left the door open?"
- Good sign production, but semantically the wrong sign choice, e.g. a woman who had suffered with Multiple Sclerosis and after several stays in the hospital "finally died" signed with the ASL PAH!, often glossed as finally, entailing success or accomplishment.
- Interpretation on the word level; unprocessed, literal utterances that usually conform to the grammar of English, not of ASL.
- Skewing on the pragmatic level; missing the more subtle use of language and discourse functions.

DISCOURSE COMPETENCIES

When observing the classroom interpreters, a second type of error was noted, not because the interpreter was unfamiliar with the linguistics of ASL or English as delineated in the ASL fluency section, but because the context-specific use of language in which the discourse took place was not correctly realized.

> "In conversation or classroom discourse, there is usually motivation behind what one says. ... [T]he meaning of the source text is inextricably tied to the context of a single communication event, and the interpreter must look to features of this surrounding circumstance for clues to the particular meaning intended by the words as they are used this one time. (Janzen, 2005)

At the discourse level, interpreters need to listen to a full thought — which could be as long as a paragraph, in order to determine the intended meaning, which may or may not have been said explicitly. However, in the classroom, taking into consideration all the different parties involved and the classroom dynamics, the interpreter is rarely afforded the luxury of waiting that long before having to begin to sign.

In addition to the various types of discourse that took place in the classroom, the dynamics of all the parties involved at any given time were difficult for the interpreter to manage. It was not always the content of a lecture that was the challenge, rather the multiple channels of information that were present and active at the same time, e.g.:

- Classroom chatter before, during, after teacher lectures
- Students interactions with other students
- Announcements that were given over the loudspeaker or intercom
- Classroom chatter before, during after the announcements
- Other distractions such as environmental noises, e.g. lawnmowers, kids on the playground, construction on campus or nearby, etc – visual and auditory "noise" that distracted the other students as well as the interpreter and the deaf student
- When the teacher showed a video which had an off screen narrator
- When there were people on the screen who were also talking, sometimes simultaneously with the narrator, but perhaps at a lower volume
- When the video image included an overlay of maps, diagrams or other graphics

The most challenging seemed to be the action scenes, which the students seemed to prefer watching, rather than witness the struggle of the interpreter attempting to describe or reconstruct what was happening.

- Most of the interpreters were very weak in creating maps and other diagrams in their signing space.
- Many of the interpreted texts were confusing because the interpreter did not include a change in viewpoint when there needed to be one.
- When the interpreters went into a Role Shift (or Constructed Action) they did not align the elements of that part of the text with this new character's point of view.

ERRORS IN SPECIFIC CONSTRUCTIONS

A feature of ASL that is elusive to second language learners, easily overlooked, and yet instrumental for the role that it plays in ASL prosody and pragmatics is the set of non-manual signals that accompany the lexical items. It is important that an educational interpreter... "acquire both linguistic and affective facial expressions and ... distinguish their use in discourse." (Reilly, et al., 1990)

There is a construction in ASL that requires extensive use of non-manual signals and is one that I have found to be problematic for educational interpreters, conditional constructions. Conditionals are used to make inferences when the information is incomplete. It contributes to the development of a child's Theory of Mind (see Further Considerations below). In addition, this construction allows one to think about alternative "hypothetical" situations, perhaps counter to what is currently seen in the world. "Understanding the conceptual and behavioral organization of the ability to construct and interpret conditionals provides basic insight into the cognitive processes, linguistic competence and inferential strategies of human beings" (Traugott, et al., p. 3)

Conditional structures are a challenge to learners of ASL. They are complex in their syntactic structures; the non-manual signals of a conditional are much more elaborate than those showing affect; they can be expressed by a combination of a manual signal and a non-manual marker, or they can be shown by the non-manual markers without the sign.

EXAMPLES

Many of the interpreters observed did not listen to the full sentence before interpreting the sentences described below. As a result, there were notable errors that resulted in confusion on the part of the students.

The first example is a type of conditional that is called a *condition hypothetical* where an event or situation will happen provided that the condition is met. In English, the condition is expressed using the word "if" but is just as often expressed using the words "as long as," or "with the understanding that"; and since many of the interpreters were working at the word level, the latter were where the errors occurred:

English sentence: "I wouldn't mind teaching you how to drive if you'll wash my car."
A correct ASL equivalent: (topic) TO-DRIVE, ME TEACH-TO-YOU, DON'T MIND. UNDERSTAND++, (topic) MY CAR, YOU WASH IN-RETURN.

The ASL lexical item denoting the conditionality was UNDERSTAND++. I rarely observed this sign being used in conjunction with the correct non-manuals in the antecedent clause of the conditional.

    The second example is one that should have been interpreted as a conditional (predictive) but because the sentence contained the word "when," the ASL WH-question sign (temporal) was used instead. A good test of a predictive conditional would be to replace the word 'when' with 'whenever.' If the interpreter is working at the word level, or does not have ample time to process larger chunks of talk, i.e., being able to insert the word whenever to test for a conditional, the prediction will be missed and the message will be skewed:

English sentence: You have to wait; when the light comes on, it's ready.
An ASL equivalent: WAIT, (brow raise to mark condition), LIGHT (become bright), READY

The third example is one that should have been interpreted as a conditional but the condition was implied. The English sentence did not contain the word "if." The interpreters gave it a literal translation:

English sentence: [if you are wearing] No shirt, [and if you are wearing] no shoes, [then there will be] no service
An ASL equivalent: (Brow raise to mark conditional), NO SHIRT, NO SHOES, (lower brow), NO SERVICE

The fourth was correctly interpreted as a conditional (cause and effect). It contained the word "if," but because the first clause absolutely caused the second clause, the degree of conditinality was very strong and there should have been a transition sign, e.g., MEAN, used instead of THEN. The ASL sign MEAN is a transition sign used as an indication of the relationship between the first and clause. If the first clause absolutely causes the second, then MEAN is the transition word used. If the second clause might be caused by the first, then MAYBE is used. Very few educational interpreters used MEAN or MAYBE in their versions of this sentence. Most of them had not heard that there was a relationship factor associated with the words.

English sentence: I realized if the tree had fallen across the tracks, [then] the train will hit it and be derailed.
An ASL equivalent: I REALIZE, SERIOUS DANGER, (brow raise to mark condition), TREE FALL-ACROSS TRACK, TRAIN HIT TREE, FLY OFF TRACKS.

FURTHER CONSIDERATIONS

Unfortunately the variables that need to be considered are greater than the length of this presentation will allow.

Not included, but definitely worth exploring further is the effect of the interpreter on the cognitive development of the deaf child, in developing their intuitive understanding of the world and the ability to make inferences.

It is through a strong Theory of Mind (ToM) that children are able to draw inferences. It is what allows them to make sense of what they encounter in the world, i.e., an understanding of cause and effect, and conditions.

A child develops ToM gradually. Even older children have a difficult time understanding irony — why a person says one thing and means another — or why a question form was used with a non-question meaning, as in rhetorical questions.

- What are the implications for deaf children who come from homes that don't share their language?
- And where they are not able to read either at the level or the speed of the captions at the movies or on TV?
- And where their family does not sit and share books with them?
- Or at school where the plot of a story is mediated through an interpreter who may not be fluent?

Because one cannot interpret what one does not understand, it is important that the educational interpreter have a strong academic background. While working with educational interpreters, I have seen far too frequently their lack of general world knowledge and limited English vocabulary. It is difficult to interpret information at educational levels beyond what one understands or has completed in their own educational pursuits. Even worse is to have to interpret unfamiliar content. An education from a four- year institution affords the educational interpreter an exposure to content in a variety of courses. As a student in a BA program, one would have to write papers and demonstrate the ability to clearly express thoughts and ideas. It would also require a lot of reading and perhaps a course on public speaking.

These qualities make for a well-rounded interpreter. Professional interpreters already working in the field in a variety of settings can attest to the value of a good education and its positive effect on their ability to interpret. To this end, at the 2003 RID Conference in Chicago, the membership passed a motion, which will eventually require a Baccalaureate degree in order to stand for future performance interview tests. (See Appendix D for details)

Hopefully with the current requirements for educational interpreter qualifications being put forth in legislation, the evolution of the interpreter education programs to require both English and ASL language fluency as an entrance requirement, as a result to better prepare graduates to analyze ASL and English on a discourse level, and with more rigorous evaluation processes and a higher level of certification passing rates in place as a (minimum) standard for employment, we will find deaf students in the presence of the best people using the best processes (tools) to provide the best product (interpretation) with which to mediate their education.

REFERENCES

Abe, I. (1980) How vocal pitch works. In C. van Schooneveld and L. Waugh (Eds.), *The melody of language: Intonation and prosody* (pp. 1-24). Baltimore, Maryland: University Park Press.

Anderson, D. & Reilly, J. S. (1998) Pah! The acquisition of adverbials in ASL. *Sign Language and Linguistics* Vol. 1, No. 2, 117-142.

Baker, C. (1977) Regulators and Turn-taking in American Sign Language discourse. In LA. Friedman (Ed.), *On the other hand: New perspectives on American Sign Language.* New York: Academic Press, Inc.

Baker, C. & Padden, C. (1978) Focusing on the nonmanual components of American Sign Language. In P. Siple (Ed.), *Understanding language through sign language research,* (pp 27-57), New York: Academic Press.

Bellugi, U. & Klima, E. (1990) Properties of visual spatial languages. In S. Prillwitz & T. Vollhaber (Eds.), *Sign language research and application: proceedings of the International Congress Hamburg March 23-25, 1990.* Hamburg, Germany: Signum Press.

Bellugi, U., Mcintire, M, & Reilly, J. S. (1990) The acquisition of conditionals in American Sign Language: Grammaticized facial expression. *Applied Psycholinguistics,* 11, 369-392.

Bellugi, U. & Reilly, J. S. (1996) Competition on the face: affect and the language in ASL motherese. *Journal of Child Language* 23, 219-239.

Bonvillian, J.D., Orlansky, M.D., & Folven, R.J. (1994) Early sign language acquisition: implications for theories of language acquisition. In V. Volterra & C. Erting (Eds.), *From gesture to language in hearing and deaf children.* Washington, D.C.: Gallaudet University Press.

Coulter, G. (1978) RAISED EYEBROWS AND WRINKLED NOSES: The grammatical function of facial expression in relative clauses and related constructions. In F. Caccamise & D. Hicks (Eds.), *ASL in a Bilingual, Bicultural Context: Proceedings of the Second National Symposium on Sign Language Research and Teaching* (pp. 65-74). Coronado, CA: NAD.

Davies, J. (2000) Translation Techniques in Interpreter education. In C. Roy (Ed.), *Innovative practices for teaching sign language interpreters.* Washington, D.C.: Gallaudet University Press.

Emmorey, K. (2002) *Language, cognition, and the brain: insights from sign language research.*

New Jersey: Lawrence Erlbaum Associates.

Gardner, H. (1991) *The unschooled mind: how children think and how schools should teach.* (pp. 84-112). New York: Basicbooks.

Hatch, E. (1992) *Discourse and language education.* New York, NY: Cambridge University Press.

Hoiting, N., & Slobin, D. (2002) What a deaf child needs to see: advantages of a natural sign language over a sign system. In Schulmeister, R. and Reinitzer, H. (Eds.), *Progress in sign language research.* Hamburg, Germany: Signum-Verlag.

Jacobs, R. (1996) Just how hard is it to learn ASL? The case for ASL as a truly foreign language. In C. Lucas (Ed.), *Multicultural aspects of sociolinguistics in deaf communities.* Washington, D.C: Gallaudet University Press.

Larson, M. (1984) *Meaning-based translation: A guide to cross-language equivalence.* Lanham, MD: University Press of America, Inc.

LaBue, M.A. (1995). Language and learning in a deaf education classroom: Practice and paradox. In C. Lucas (Ed.), *Sociolinguistics in Deaf Communities,* Washington, D.C.: Gallaudet University.

Lieberman, P. (1980) The innate, central aspect of intonation. In C. van Schooneveld & L. Waugh (Eds.), *The melody of language: Intonation and prosody* (pp. 187-199). Baltimore, Maryland: University Park Press.

Marschark, M. (1997). *Raising and educating a deaf child.* New York: Oxford University Press.

Marschark, M., Sapere, P., Convertino, C., & Seewagen, R. (2005). Access to Postsecondary Education through Sign Language Interpreting. *Journal of Deaf Studies and Deaf Education,* 10 (1).

Marschark, M., Sapere, P., Convertino, C., & Seewagen, R. (2005). Educational interpreting: Access and outcomes. In M. Marschark, R. Peterson & E. Winston (Eds.), *Sign Language Interpreting and Interpreter Education* (pp. 57-83). New York: Oxford University Press.

Mather, S. & Winston E. (1998) Spatial mapping and involvement in ASL storytelling. In C. Lucas (Ed.), *Pinky extension and eye gaze: Language use in deaf communities.* Washington, D.C.: Gallaudet University Press.

McIntire, M, (1990) The work and education of sign language interpreters. In S. Prillwitz & T. Vollhaber (Eds.), *Sign language research and application: proceedings of the International Congress Hamburg March 23-25, 1990.* Hamburg, Germany: Signum Press.

Metzger, M. (1999) *Sign language interpreting: deconstructing the myth of neutrality.* Washington, D.C.: Gallaudet University Press.

Morford, J & Mayberry, R. (2000) A reexamination of "early exposure" and its implications for language acquisition by eye. In C. Chamberlain, J. Morford, & R. Mayberry (Eds.), *Language acquisition by eye.* Mahwah, New Jersey: Lawrence Erlbaum Associates.

Morgan, G. (1999) Event packaging in British Sign Language discourse. In E. Winston (Ed.), *Storytelling conversation discourse in deaf communities.* (pp. 59-82). Washington, D.C.: Gallaudet University Press.

Napier, J. (2003) A sociolinguistic analysis of the occurrence and types of omissions produced by Australian Sign language-English interpreters. In M. Metzger, S. Collins, V. Dively, & R. Shaw, (Eds.), *From topic boundaries to omission: new research on interpretation* (pp.99-145). Washington, D.C.: Gallaudet University Press.

Patschke, C.G. & Wilbur, R. (1998) Body leans and the marking of contrast in American Sign Language. *Journal of Pragmatics* 30, 275-303.

Pollitt, K., (2000) Critical linguistics and cultural awareness: essential tools in the interpreter's kit bag. In C. Roy (Ed.) *Innovative practices for teaching sign language interpreters.* Washington, D.C.: Gallaudet University Press.

Pratt, M.L & Traugott, E.C. (1980) *Linguistics for students in literature.* Orlando, Florida: Harcourt Brace Jovanovich, Inc.

Pyers, J. (2003) The expression of false belief in American sign language. In A Baker, B van den

Bogaerde, & O. Crasborn (Eds.) *Cross-linguistic perspectives in sign language research: selected papers from TISLR 2000*. Hamburg, Germany: Signum Verlag.

Quinto-Pozos, D. (2005) Factors that influence the acquisition of ASL for interpreting students. In M. Marschark, R. Peterson, & E. Winston (Eds.) *Sign language interpreting interpreter education: Directions for research and practice*. New York: Oxford University Press.

Ramsey, C.L. (1997). *Deaf children in public schools: Placement, context, and consequences*. Washington, DC: Gallaudet University Press.

Rayman, J. (1999) Storytelling in the visual mode: A comparison of ASL and English. In E. Winston (Ed.), *Storytelling conversation discourse in deaf communities*. (pp. 27-58). Washington, D.C.: Gallaudet University Press.

Reily, J., McIntire, M., & Bellugi, U. (1994) Faces: The relationship between language and affect. In V. Volterra & C. Erting (Eds.) *From gesture to language in hearing and deaf children*. Washington, D.C.: Gallaudet University Press.

Roy, C.B. (1989) Feature of discourse in an American Sign Language lecture. In C. Lucas (Ed.) *The Sociolinguistics of the Deaf Community*. New York: Academic Press.

Roy, C.B. (2000) Training interpreters-past, present, and future. In C. Roy (Ed) *Innovative practices for teaching sign language interpreters*. Washington, D.C.: Gallaudet University Press.

Schick, B. & Williams, K. (1998). Profile of skills at each rating level if the EIPA. http://www.boystownhospital.org/EIPA/index.asp.

Schick, B., Williams, K. & Bolster, L. 1999. Skill levels of educational interpreters working in public schools. *Journal of Deaf Studies and Deaf Education*, 4 (2), 144-155.

Schick, B., Williams, K., & Kupermintz, H. (2006). Look who's being left behind: Educational interpreters and access to education for deaf and hard-of-hearing students. *Journal of Deaf Studies and Deaf Education* 11, 3-20.

Schick, B. *A model of learning within an interpreted K-12 educational setting*. Supporting Deaf People Conference, 2008.

Schley, S. (1996) What's a clock? "Suppose the alarm lights are flashing...?: Sociolinguistic and educational implications of comparing ASL and English word definitions. In C. Lucas (Ed) *Multicultural aspects of sociolinguistics in deaf communities*. Washington, D.C : Gallaudet University Press.

Selkirk, E.O. (1995) Sentence prosody: Intonation, stress, and phrasing. In J. Goldsmith (Ed.), *The hand book of phonological theory* (pp.550-569). Cambridge, MA: Blackwell.

Snow, C.E. (1999) Social perspectives on the emergence of language. In B. MacWhinney (Ed) *The emergence of language*. (pp 257-273). Mahwah, New Jersey

Stewart, D.A., & Kluwin, T.N. 1999. The gap between guidelines, practices, and knowledge in interpreting services for deaf students. *Journal of Deaf Studies and Deaf Education*, 1, 29-39.

Volterra, V. (1990) Sign language acquisition and bilingualism. In S. Prillwitz & T. Vollhaber (Eds) *Sign language research and application: proceedings of the International Congress Hamburg March 23-25, 1990*. Hamburg, Germany: Signum Press.

Wilbur, R.B. (1997) A prosodic/pragmatic explanation for word order variation in ASL with typological implications. In K. Lee, E. Sweetser, & M. Verspoor (Eds.), *Lexical and syntactic constructions and the construction of meaning* (pp. 89-104). Philadelphia: John Benjamims.

Wilbur, R.B. (2000) *Phonological and prosodic layering of non-manuals in American Sign Language*. Festschrift for Klima & Bellugi.

Winston, B. (2000) It doesn't look like ASL! Defining, recognizing, and teaching prosody in ASL. *Proceedings of the 13th National Convention, Conference of Interpreter Trainers: "CIT at 21: Celebrating excellence, celebrating partnership."* Maryland: Registry of Interpreters for the Deaf, Inc.

Winston, E.A. (1994). An interpreted education: Inclusion or exclusion. In R.C. Johnson, & O.P.Cohen (Eds.), *Implications and complications for deaf students of the full inclusion movement*. Gallaudet Research Institute Occasional Paper 94-2. Washington, DC: Gallaudet University.

Yule, G. (1985) *The study of language* (second edition). New York, NY: Cambridge University Press.

APPENDIX A: NON MANUAL SIGNALS

Brow Raise

An ASL phrase that contains raised eyebrows used grammatically and not for affect, is there to describe the background information. It provides the "scene" from which the second clause can be interpreted. This is true for the antecedent clause in a conditional. The raised eyebrows co-occur with each sign in this clause. If the subsequent clause is a yes-no question, the brows do not get lowered as they normally would.

Body Lean

A forward lean can mark that a certain interaction is taking place with the addressee. Perhaps the speaker is expecting a response of some kind. This is true for a yes-no question that contains a forward lean. A forward lean is also present in a rhetorical yes-no question, even though the speaker is not expecting an answer from the listener. Rhetorical constructions will be discussed in a later section.

Eye Blink

Eye blinks are present in conditionals to mark the boundaries between the two clauses. According to Baker and Cokely (1980) this occurs at the juncture between the conditional and the following clause along with other non-manual activity, namely a pause, the lowering of the eyebrows and a shift in the head or body orientation.

Head Rotation

Head rotation refers to the rotating movement of the signer's head either to the left or to the right. It is similar to the way the head moves in a rhetorical question. Head rotation to a greater or lesser degree was consistently noticed in conditional sentences. (Liddell, 1986) The scope of the head rotation is the antecedent clause. It will not occur when there is the side-to-side movement of the head as in a negative headshake.

Head Thrust

This is a term that Liddell coined in 1986 to mean the single outward and downward movement of the head. This non-manual was consistently present in his corpus of ASL conditionals. Even though the head rotation is maintained throughout the antecedent, the head thrust is only present during the final sign of the clause. He also noted that there were when-clauses in his data that had evidence of a raised brow and head-thrust. "When" has also been recognized as a marker of a conditional for spoken languages. During a class lecture, for example, the teacher might say, "When the solution turns yellow, it indicates the presence of carbon dioxide." I have observed educational interpreters using the citation form of the sign WHEN, which represents a wh-question, e.g., "When will we get there?" instead of the correct non-manual marker for conditionality.

Eye Gaze
A change in the direction of the eye gaze is present in some conditional constructions. It is an indication of a new role or character being created in the discourse. As a result of the change in eye gaze (point-of-view or perspective), there is a newly constructed space in which this new character will reside. The narrator moves in and out of this space when performing a particular type of conditional.

APPENDIX B

State required minimal EIPA standards:
New Jersey, Kansas, Kentucky, Louisiana, North Carolina and Wisconsin: 3.0
Arizona, Colorado, Indiana, Maine, Nebraska, and Utah: 3.5
California and Nevada: 4.0

Interpreters require a great deal of training in order to meet minimum standards. Unfortunately, educational interpreting is an emerging profession and educators are only now beginning to understand the range of skills that are necessary to do the job well.

Minimum qualifications of an educational interpreter should include:
- A formal assessment of interpreting skills
  - An Educational Interpreter Performance Assessment (EIPA) score of at least a 4.0
  - Registry of Interpreters for the Deaf (RID) certification
  - NAD-RID certification (NIC) at a certified level
  - NAD certification of at least a 4.0
- Degree or coursework in an educationally-related field
  - BA degree (preferred)
  - Graduate of an Interpreter Training Program

- 24–30 credit hours of educational coursework
- A formal assessment of content knowledge related to educational interpreting (for example, a passing score on the EIPA Written Test)
- The ability to perform as a professional member of the educational team (For example, as stated in the Educational Interpreter Performance Assessment Code of Professional Conduct).

Research shows that even graduates of two-year Interpreter Training Programs may not meet a common standard held in many states, an EIPA rating of 3.5.

Unqualified interpreters cannot provide access to Free and Appropriate Public Education (FAPE). Research shows that interpreters who fall below minimum standards omit and distort much of teacher and peer communication. When an interpreter is not highly qualified, a deaf or hard of hearing student misses vital classroom communication and does not receive adequate access to the general education curriculum.

EIPA RATING SYSTEM

The evaluation team uses an EIPA rating form to evaluate the interpreter's abilities. The samples are rated in the following domains:
1. Grammatical skills: Use of prosody (or intonation), grammar, and space
2. Sign-to-voice interpreting skills: Ability to understand and convey child/teen sign language
3. Vocabulary: Ability to use a wide range of vocabulary, accurate use of fingerspelling and numbers
4. Overall abilities: Ability to represent a sense of the entire message, use appropriate discourse structures, and represent who is speaking

Evaluators use a Likert Scale to assess specific skills. Scores for each skill range from 0 (no skills demonstrated) to 5 (advanced native-like skills). The scores from all three evaluators are averaged for each skill area, each domain, as well as the overall test score. An individual's EIPA score is the summary total score. For example, an interpreter should report her score as EIPA Secondary PSE 4.2, which shows which grade level, which language, and the total summary EIPA score.

DESCRIPTIONS OF EACH EIPA LEVEL

Level 1: Beginner
Demonstrates very limited sign vocabulary with frequent errors in production. At times, production may be incomprehensible. Grammatical structure tends to be nonexistent. Individual is only able to communicate very simple ideas and demonstrates great difficulty comprehending signed communication. Sign production lacks prosody and use of space for the vast majority of the interpreted message. An individual at this level is not recommended for classroom interpreting.

Level 2: Advanced Beginner
Demonstrates only basic sign vocabulary and these limitations interfere with communication. Lack of fluency and sign production errors are typical and often interfere with communication. The interpreter often hesitates in signing, as if searching for vocabulary. Frequent errors in grammar are apparent, although basic signed sentences appear intact. More complex grammatical structures are typically difficult. Individual is able to read signs at the word level and simple sentence level but complete or complex sentences often require repetitions and repairs. Some use of prosody and space, but use is inconsistent and often incorrect. An individual at this level is not recommended for classroom interpreting.

Level 3: Intermediate
Demonstrates knowledge of basic vocabulary, but will lack vocabulary for more technical, complex, or academic topics. Individual is able to sign in a fairly fluent manner using some consistent prosody, but pacing is still slow with infrequent pauses for vocabulary or complex structures. Sign production may show some errors but generally will not interfere with communication. Grammatical production may still be incorrect, especially for complex structures, but is in general, intact for routine and simple language. Comprehends signed messages but may need repetition and assistance. Voiced translation often lacks depth and subtleties of the original message. An individual at this level would be able to communicate very basic classroom content, but may incorrectly interpret complex information resulting in a message that is not always clear. An interpreter at this level needs continued supervision and should be required to participate in continuing education in interpreting.

Level 4: Advanced Intermediate

Demonstrates broad use of vocabulary with sign production that is generally correct. Demonstrates good strategies for conveying information when a specific sign is not in their vocabulary. Grammatical constructions are generally clear and consistent, but complex information may still pose occasional problems. Prosody is good, with appropriate facial expression most of the time. May still have difficulty with the use of facial expression in complex sentences and adverbial non-manual markers. Fluency may deteriorate when rate or complexity of communication increases. Uses space consistently most of the time, but complex constructions or extended use of discourse cohesion may still pose problems. Comprehension of most signed messages at a normal rate is good but translation may lack some complexity of the original message.

An individual at this level would be able to convey much of the classroom content but may have difficulty with complex topics or rapid turn-taking.

Level 5: Advanced

Demonstrates broad and fluent use of vocabulary, with a broad range of strategies for communicating new words and concepts. Sign production errors are minimal and never interfere with comprehension. Prosody is correct for grammatical, non-manual markers, and affective purposes. Complex grammatical constructions are typically not a problem. Comprehension of sign messages is very good, communicating all details of the original message. An individual at this level is capable of clearly and accurately conveying the majority of interactions within the classroom.

APPENDIX C

CI and CT (Generalist) Rating Scales

RID has recently implemented a new rating system for the Certificates of Interpretation and Transliteration performance tests. This system is based on a set of 13 items, called "behaviorally anchored scales." These items represent key behaviors an interpreter must demonstrate in order to be awarded certification. The 13 behaviors are scored on a 1-5 Likert-type scale, with one being low and five being high. They are weighted according to criticality and importance to the task in order to correspond to the St. Paul standard voted on by the certified membership in 1987. There are seven scales/behaviors for the Voice-to-Sign (V-S) section, and six for the Sign-to-Voice (S-V) section. These 13 scales (items) are duplicated for the One-to-One section of the test as the candidate does both V-S and S-V. Therefore a candidate for certification is rated on 26 scales. There are three categories of raters: Deaf consumers, hearing consumers, and certified interpreters. A candidate's tape of their performance is sent to a rater in each of the three categories.

A general description of the seven scales for the Voice-to-Sign segment are:
1. Sign Parameters: correct and consistent production of sign parameters (handshape, palm orientation, location and movement)
2. Flow: comfort level of sign flow; Example: smooth, comfortable for viewing, not choppy with few false starts and unnecessary pauses, not over smooth without appropriate pauses
3. Message Equivalence: message completion with regard to factual information, register and cultural/linguistic adjustments with few minor miscues (omissions/substitutions, additions, and intrusions)
4. Target Language: uses appropriate target language (e.g. signed English for the transliteration test and ASL for the interpretation test)
5. Affect: consistency of facial grammar and affect to source language
6. Vocabulary Choice: conceptually correct sign choices based on meaning rather than form
7. Sentence Boundaries: clear and consistent identification of sentence types and topic boundaries which match source language

A general description of the six scales for the Sign-to-Voice segment of the test are:
1. Enunciation: clarity and consistency throughout task
2. Flow: comfort level for listening; example: few false starts, pauses, and non-linguistic behaviors (distracting mannerisms - uh, um, etc.), not over smooth without appropriate pauses
3. Message Equivalence: message completion with regard to factual information, register and cultural/linguistic adjustments with few minor miscues (omissions/substitutions, additions, and intrusions)
4. Inflection: consistency of inflection to source language
5. Vocabulary choice: conceptually correct sign choices based on meaning rather than form
6. Sentence Boundaries: clear and consistent identification of sentence types and topic boundaries which match source language

---

APPENDIX D

RID Certification Requirements

Degree Requirements Passed at 2003 Conference. Degrees Necessary Beginning in 2008 for Performance Testing Applicants

At the 2003 RID Conference in Chicago, the membership passed a motion, which requires a degree in order to stand for future performance interview tests. It is important to note that these requirements are not immediate. In 2008, applicants who are hearing will be required to have a minimum of an associate's degree in order to be considered a candidate for certification. This means that they can take written or knowledge tests without a degree, but must have the degree in order to apply for the interview and performance sections of any test.

In 2012, applicants who are hearing will be required to have a minimum of a bachelor's degree in order to be considered a candidate for certification while applicants who are deaf will be required to have a minimum of an associate's degree.

In 2016, applicants who are deaf will be required to have a minimum of a bachelor's degree.

Additionally, there will be exceptions to the requirement. Those exceptions will be formulated and publicized no later than 2006.

The following is the text of the motion as approved at conference:
C 2003.05

- RID adopt and publicize the following schedule for when all test candidates must have a degree from an accredited institution to stand for any RID certificate:
- Effective June 30, 2008, candidates for RID certification must have a minimum of an associate's degree. Effective June 30, 2012, Deaf candidates must have a minimum of an associate's degree.
- Effective June 30, 2012, candidates for RID certification must have a minimum of a bachelor's degree. Effective June 30, 2016, Deaf candidates must have a minimum of a bachelor's degree.
- By June 30, 2006, the Certification Council shall establish equivalent alternative criteria allowable in lieu of the educational requirements such as one or more of the following: life experience, years of professional experience, years of education (credit hours) not totaling a formal degree.

The Law, Deafness, and Personhood: Where Hobson's Choice Meets Social Eugenics

DALE. H. BOAM, J.D.

AS THE STORY GOES, THOMAS HOBSON RAN AN INN AND STABLE IN Cambridge, England. A person hiring a horse could choose any horse in the stable, but Hobson always gave the horse nearest the door. Thus Hobson would give you any horse you wanted… so long as you wanted the next horse in line. Hobson's infamous "choice" developed over time to represent a widely accepted legal concept; the term "Hobson's Choice" defines a situation where a choice can be articulated, defined, and explained, but all the alternatives except one are actually unavailable, unacceptable or so vile as to present no actual choice at all. In other words, have any horse you want… so long as you want the one offered. In short, take the horse offered or walk.

This paper will first explore the "Hobson's Choice" offered to persons who are Deaf by federal laws, particularly Title III of the American's with Disabilities Act (ADA). Second, how this "Hobson's Choice" is a predicable result of a history of social eugenics perpetrated institutionally upon the Deaf community. Third, how this institutionalized social eugenics is evidenced by the language of the Title III creating a hierarchy of protection making the application of the law more feasible for other disability groups than for persons who are Deaf. Finally, possible actions persons who are Deaf and organizations focused promoting the rights of persons who are Deaf can engage in to take control of their own legal destiny.

The "Hobson's Choice" presented to the Deaf community can be articulated thusly, a member of the Deaf community may choose to define herself in any manner she wishes, as long as it's "disabled." If she chooses to define herself as a cultural linguistic minority, and not as a person with a disability, she forfeits legal mandates for the aids and services viewed as essential for daily living; including interpreting services, vocational rehabilitation services and accessibility under the ADA. In other words in order to qualify for the "protections" of the ADA a person who is Deaf must choose to identify himself as a person with a disability. This may seem an obvious prerequisite to a person outside the Deaf community. However, a person who is Deaf sees a stark choice: abandon his opportunity to access legal protections or abandon his cultural identity and personal concept of who he is. (This is a vital aspect of human rights and Deafness; Harlan Lane addressed this concept at length in his masterful work *The Mask of Benevolence* and this paper will not seek to restate the full concept here beyond identifying the overt Hobson's Choice presented.)

Title's I, II and III of the ADA require as a threshold to making claim that a complainant first prove that she is a person with a disability as defined by the Law. (USC 42 §12102, (2)(A)-(C). The term "disability" means, with respect to an individual: (A) a physical or mental impairment that substantially limits one or more of the major life activities of such individual; (B) a record of such an impairment; or (C) being regarded as having such impairment.) Many a member of the Deaf community has filed a complaint of job discrimination, or a complaint against a doctor or lawyer only to be confronted with the question "are you a person with a disability." Answer no and risk having her case dismissed on the grounds that she is not a person in need of protection as defined by the language of the law. Answer yes and the person who is Deaf must accept a label that contradicts a vital component of the Deaf understanding of self. Thus, while federal law recognizes that persons who are Deaf require the protection of civil rights laws, such protection will only be provided if persons who are Deaf accept the label of disabled and abandon their cultural identity. In other words, you may define your self in any manner you wish so long as you wish to define yourself as disabled.

To an objective observer, the simple brutality of a person who is Deaf accepting the label of disabled is not readily apparent. To accept the label of disabled instantly places a societal expectation on the person who is Deaf to mitigate or seek a cure for his deafness. This is, of course the core of social eugenics, controlling the cultural or social development of a group by rewarding behaviors that conform to the majority concept of the group and punishing that which deviates there from. The medical model of deafness or deafness as a disability has been the dominant social concept of deafness for much of this country's history.

Deborah Kaplan, director of the World Institute on Disability explains the impact of this medical model of disability thusly:

> The individual with a disability is in the sick role under the medical model. When people are sick, they are excused from the normal obligations of society: going to school, getting a job, taking on family responsibilities, etc. They are also expected to come under the authority of the medical profession in order to get better. Thus, until recently, most disability policy issues have been regarded as health issues, and physicians have been regarded as the primary authorities in this policy area. (http://www.accessiblesociety.org/topics/demographics-identity/dkaplanpaper.htm)

Sociologist Talcott Parsons delineated and later refined the sociological concept of the "sick role." To state it in an oversimplified manner, a person who accepts the label of "sick" must strive to get better. Failure to actively seek a cure categorizes the sick individual as a deviant (Parsons, 1951) Thus when a person who is Deaf accepts the label of "disabled" she may be expected not only to seek, but also to support, medical intervention including medical experimentation in order to cure her underlying "illness"; deafness. Moreover, expressing pride in Deafness most assuredly invites the societal label of deviant. It is the soul of deviance to have pride in an illness.

For an observer accepting the label of disabled may still appear to be an acceptable trade-off in order to gain the person who is Deaf access to the protections of the law. However, a more subjective analysis proves that, for a person who is Deaf, the act of abandoning her cultural identity may not result in any actual benefit; or at least no benefit until so far after the fact that such protections are illusory. For example, suppose that a person who is Deaf requires an interpreter to communicate with his doctor. The person who is Deaf knows what he needs to communicate effectively and is therefore the party most likely to know which aid or service will be required in order to satisfy the legal requirement that the doctor provide "effective communication." However, the law does not require the doctor to honor the accommodation choice of the person who is Deaf. In fact the preamble to the regulations for Title III states:

> The Department's proposed rule recommended that, in determining what auxiliary aid to use, the public accommodation consult with an individual before providing him or her with a particular auxiliary aid or service. This suggestion sparked a significant volume of public comment. Many persons with disabilities, particularly persons who are [D]eaf or hard of hearing, recommended that the rule should require that public accommodations give "primary consideration" to the "expressed choice" of an individual with a disability. These commenters asserted that the proposed rule was inconsistent with congressional intent of the ADA, with the Department's proposed rule implementing title II of the ADA, and with longstanding interpretations of section 504 of the Rehabilitation Act. See, 28 C.F.R. pt. 36, App. B at 703 (2005), (emphasis added).

The preamble continues:

> Based upon a careful review of the ADA legislative history, the Department believes that Congress did not intend under title III to impose upon a public accommodation the requirement that it give primary consideration to the request of the individual with a disability. To the contrary, the legislative history demonstrates congressional intent to strongly encourage consulting with persons with disabilities. In its analysis of the ADA's auxiliary aids requirement for public accommodations, the House Education and Labor Committee stated that it "expects" that "public accommodation(s) will consult with the individual with a disability before providing a particular auxiliary aid or service" (Education and Labor report at 107)… Thus, the Department finds that strongly encouraging consultation with persons with disabilities, in lieu of mandating primary consideration of their expressed choice, is consistent with congressional intent. Id.

Under Title III, public accommodations such as doctor's offices must provide auxiliary aids and services to ensure effective communication access. The regulations include a list: qualified interpreters, note-takers, computer aided transcription services (CART), written materials, telephone handset amplifiers, assistive listening devices, assistive listening systems, telephones compatible with hearing aids, closed caption decoders, open and closed captioning, telecommunications devices for deaf persons (TDDs), videotext displays, or other effective methods of making aurally delivered materials available to individuals with hearing impairments. 28 C.F.R. § 36.303.

While this list includes a variety of communicative methods neither the law nor any of its regulations actually define the meaning of "effective communication." Furthermore, neither the law nor the regulations do more than imply that all methods are not equally effective in all situations.

The one bit of guidance is found in the preamble to the regulations for Title III which states:

> In the analysis of Sec.36.303(c) in the proposed rule, the Department gave as an example the situation where a note pad and written materials were insufficient to permit effective communication in a doctor's office when the matter to be decided was whether major surgery was necessary. Many commenters objected to this statement, asserting that it gave the impression that only decisions about major surgery would merit the provision of a sign language interpreter. The statement would, as the commenters also claimed, convey the impression to other public accommodations that written communications would meet the regulatory requirements in all but the most extreme situations. The Department, when using the example of major surgery, did not intend to limit the provision of interpreter services to the most extreme situations. Id.

The preamble continues:

> Other situations may also require the use of interpreters to ensure effective communication depending on the facts of the particular case. It is not difficult to imagine a wide range of communications involving areas such as health, legal matters, and finances that would be sufficiently lengthy or complex to require an interpreter for effective communication. Id.

While this may be helpful in understanding when an interpreter may be required, the text is not part of the regulation itself. For legal buffs it is good reading but most uniformed doctors, and for that matter lawyers, miss this guidance. To return to the point, a lack of overt, direct guidance leads an uniformed doctor to make the decision based solely on parameters he can easily understand, cost. What doctor is going to proffer the expense of an interpreter when the list includes "written materials," an aid or service which seems to require no overhead expense?

If, despite consulting the person who is Deaf, the doctor determines that "written materials" are the auxiliary aid he is willing to provide, the person who is Deaf must attempt to communicate with the doctor and fail or she has no actionable case, because without this evidence of failure of effective communication there is no evidence that the auxiliary aid or service offered by the doctor was not effective. Because public accommodations are not required to give deference to the aid or service requested by the person who is Deaf, at the time of service a person who is Deaf is presumed to have been provided effective communication, no matter what auxiliary aid or service the doctor provides. The law places the burden of proving that the auxiliary aid or service was not effective squarely upon the shoulders of the patient who is Deaf. Thus the person who is Deaf must struggle through the communication process and show evidence that it failed, or was otherwise legally ineffective, before the ADA recognizes an actionable violation. Even then there is no set standard as to what is considered ineffective. Such a determination is left to the trier of fact, a judge or jury who may or may not have any experience with the Deaf community. A piece of paper with some questions and answers may satisfy the uniformed judge or jury that the communication was "effective."

Even if a person who is Deaf can prove that communication without an interpreter was ineffective she is still faced with a new and brutal Hobson's Choice. Title III of the ADA provides only injunctive relief for a private lawsuit, no monetary damages. Injunctive relief consists of the Court ordering the offender to stop acting in a manner that caused the injury to the Plaintiff. Therefore, assuming that the person who is Deaf goes to the appointment, fails to receive effective communication, files a complaint, and can prove up a lack of effective communication the sole remedy for a private suit is that the doctor provide effective communication on the next visit. Keep that in mind, the sole remedy afforded the person who is Deaf is another appointment with the same doctor she just sued.

Imagine if you will that next appointment. It is often cold and sometimes even hostile. If a person who is Deaf does not want to face that doctor again under those circumstances then he or she has no remedy at all. With no monetary damages under private suit if the Deaf client does not wish to return then the same doctor an injunction has no effect. The doctor can argue that if the person who is Deaf does not wish to return, then there is no danger that the person who is Deaf will be injured again; thus the case is moot. Here we see the Hobson's Choice, you can enforce your rights against an oppressor, so long as want the right to be placed at the oppressors mercy.

And here we come to the crux of the issue. These Hobson's Choices are born of an understanding within the law that persons who are Deaf do not fit neatly into the general category of persons with disabilities. The framers and authors of the law provided for a different category of protection in recognition that their needs are unique when compared to persons with substantial limitations in other areas. But the confines of social eugenics could not allow the writers to extend that recognition of a difference in protection to a difference in relief. I categorize this as an example of social eugenics because it reflects the historic social attitude that persons who are Deaf are expected to read lips in order to fit in with the real world and person who is Deaf who does not is somehow deviant and trying to take advantage of the hearing world.

The Preamble as quoted above states that congress had the opportunity to require private businesses to give primary consideration to the auxiliary aid or service requested by the person who is Deaf, but the writers of the regulations declined to do so because, as they say, it was not the intent of congress to do so. Instead the choice of which aid or service to provide was left to the private business with the understanding that it would consult with the person who is Deaf in determining the aid or service to provide. Faucets of social eugenics are evident on the face of this decision. First, the assumption that persons who are unaware of their own needs and must be taken care of by hearing persons. Second, that persons who are Deaf are untrustworthy and left to their own devices will request aids or services that are not needed at the expense of the hearing business owner.

I believe there is a deeper layer to this decision. I believe that beneath the surface of the text of the law and regulations there exists a generalized level of discomfort as to the very nature of the accommodation being requested by the person who is Deaf. Within the body of the law accommodations are defined as non-personal items, i.e. a ramp, but not a wheelchair. The law is generally written to afford access to the building but not the person. A ramp gives access to the doctor's office, where an interpreter gives access to the doctor. A person who is Deaf, by nature of their "disability" needs only accommodations that give access to the individual. An interpreter is by definition a highly personal item. This is social eugenics incentive within the text; persons who are Deaf should read lips, persons who are Deaf should be responsible to learn to get along in the hearing world, and hearing people should not be held responsible if they don't. A pad of paper and a pen, or even a computer an understandable accommodation because they exist in the environment anyway. An interpreter is an accommodation that requires "the doctor" to pay money so that a patient who is Deaf can have access to the doctor, not the office, but the doctor personally.

This may seem like a radical accusation, but it becomes more evident when the ability to enforce the law by persons who are Deaf is compared to the ability to enforce the law by persons with mobility impairments. I propose that the text of Title III of the ADA and its regulations afford persons who are Deaf a lesser standard of protection than is afforded to persons with mobility impairments. This lesser standard of protection is a result of the authors of the law and regulations, first, creating a separate category of accommodations for persons who are Deaf (auxiliary aids and services) but failing to adequately define the parameters wherein a specific aid or service is required, and second, failing to recognize that a separate category of accommodations requires a separate standard of relief or failing to act to implement such a separate standard of relief.

The separate category of accommodations is defined above, so we now turn to the question of relief. The foundational point of this discussion is in the nature of relief afforded all persons with disabilities who prevail in a private suit to enforce their rights under Title III of the ADA. A private suit can only get "injunctive" relief, not monetary damages. This means that the judge has the authority to order a defendant to do… or not to do something, but not to make the defendant pay compensation for doing, or not doing. This works well for persons with, for example, mobility impairments. If the doctor's office is not accessible, the judge can order that the office remove any barriers to access; build a ramp for example. This fixes the problem, as now the ramp is there.

Under Title III of the ADA persons who use wheelchairs are promised access to doctor's offices, lawyer's offices, museums, stores and many other places of public accommodation by way of such barrier removal. (See 42 U.S.C. § 12181(7)(A)-(L) for a complete list of Places of Public Accommodation.) The parameters of this barrier removal are set in stone, listed and illustrated in a book called the American's with Disabilities Act Architectural Guide (ADAAG). The ADAAG explains to the ½ inch the type and quality of accommodations that must be provided in order for legal accessibility to be achieved. If the entrance to the building looks like X then the accommodation in place must meet the standards outlined in schematic Y. A person using a wheelchair need request that the barrier be removed, he or she need not attempt to access a place of public accommodation which is not structurally compliant and fail prior to being able to enforce the ADA. (This is known as the "futile gesture" doctrine. A person need not make a futile gesture in order to gain the right to enforce the ADA. 42 U.S.C. § 12188(a).) If the accommodation refuses the person with a physical disability has an actionable violation at the moment of refusal. If enforcement is successful and a ramp is built (or a door is widened, or a lift is installed, etc.) the ramp will be in place from that moment forward, until the proverbial "end of time."

By comparison persons who are Deaf have no document comparable to the ADAAG which defines when an interpreter will be required. As stated above persons who are Deaf have limited access to the "futile gesture" doctrine and so must prove injury prior to seeking enforcement. Furthermore, accommodations provided for persons who are Deaf under Title III are by definition short term fixes. Interpreters are not like structural accommodations; modifications which remain as permanent fixtures, like ramps. The provision of an interpreter at one event does not permanently install an interpreter at that venue.

The Deaf community is therefore required to prove the need for an interpreter each and every time access effective communication with doctors, or lawyers or any other entity covered by Title III of the ADA is required. Even if a doctor has provided an interpreter in the past, without some kind of ongoing legal mandate he is under no obligation to do so in the future. The Deaf community is therefore under a continuing obligation to substantiate the need for an interpreter in order to satisfy the requirement for effective communication.

The disparity is clearly illustrated by the case Long v. Coast Resorts. (See, 267 F.3d 918 (9th Cir. 2001).) In this case a new resort in the Las Vegas area completed construction and opened with (among other issues) doorways measuring 32 inches. The ADAAG requires that doors measure 36 inches in order to be considered accessible in satisfaction of the ADA. A group of wheelchair users sued the resort claiming that this deviation from the measurements specified in the ADAAG amounted to a policy and practice of discrimination by the resort in question.

The resort defended itself by claiming the doorways at their present measurement were in fact accessible enough at 32 inches to satisfy the law. The resort hired an expert witness (himself a wheelchair user) who attempted and succeeded in entering a statistically significant number of rooms and testified that the resort's doorways, while admittedly measuring 32 inches in width, may make entry awkward for some wheelchair users but did not bar access to any of the rooms in question. Based upon this testimony the resort argued that having doors that did not measure the stated 36 inches was at best a "technical violation" of the ADA and not an actionable bar to accessibility. The Federal District Court of Nevada agreed and found that the resort had at most committed a technical violation but had not violated the rights of the wheelchair users and was not required to fix the doors. The Wheelchair users appealed this decision to the Ninth Circuit Court of Appeals. The premise of the appeal was that the judge in Las Vegas had made an error in his interpretation of the law because the ADAAG was very specific in its definition of accessible leaving no room for interpretation and certainly no provision for a "technical violation."

The Ninth Circuit agreed and overturned the finding of the District Court stating that the there was no such thing as a technical violation of the ADA and that the law provided the Court with no discretion to find such. "This violation resulted in the very discrimination the statute seeks to prevent: it denied individuals with disabilities access to public accommodations." (Id. at 923) It is significant to know that some of the prevailing plaintiffs had never actually visited to the hotel in question. Their claimed injury was that the 32 inch doors limited their choices in vacation destinations when compared with non-wheelchair users.

It is not the intent of this paper to somehow set persons with mobility impairments against persons who are Deaf, nor do I begrudge their victory. The point is to illustrate the discrepancy in protections this paper alleges. The person with a mobility impairment, specifically a person who uses a wheelchair, need prove no injury beyond by the non-existence of the specific instrumentalities of accommodation set forth by law and the refusal of the place of public accommodation to remedy it according to the specifications of the ADAAG. Lack of this specific instrumentality constitutes and actionable violation of the ADA. The wheelchair user is not required under the law to attempt to access a public accommodation and fail in order to prove that the building is inaccessible. Moreover, the next time the wheelchair user visits the place of public accommodation (or any other wheelchair user for that matter) the repaired doors will still 36 inches in width.

By contrast, at each encounter between a person who is Deaf and a place of public accommodation the proper Auxiliary Aid or Service needed to provide Effective Communication is up for debate. In the end the decision as to which Aid or Service will be provided not given to the person who is Deaf, but to the Public Accommodation. Unfortunately, as was stated, there is no quantifiable definition under Title III for effective communication. Thus the person who is Deaf is under a repeated and ongoing burden to prove actual injury prior to the courts recognizing an actionable violation.

At the signing of the ADA, then-President George H.W. Bush remarked that "[t]his act (the ADA) is powerful in its simplicity. It will ensure that people with disabilities are given the basic guarantees for which they have worked so long and so hard: independence, freedom of choice, control of their lives, the opportunity to blend fully and equally into the rich mosaic of the American mainstream." (For a more complete record of the remarks of President George Bush at the signing of the Americans with Disabilities Act, see the EEOC website at http://www.eeoc.gov/35th/videos/ada_signing_text.html.)

If the words of then President Bush are applied to the textual realities of the ADA in action, a disparity appears in the protections afforded to persons with physical disabilities and promises given persons who are Deaf under the ADA. Persons who are Deaf are promised "effective communication," but neither the text of the law nor the regulations attached to Title III define what effective communication means. Furthermore, the relief afforded to persons who are Deaf under the law have no practical application by reason of the temporary nature of the enforceable accommodations.

When objectively scrutinized, for the Deaf community the long-term detrimental impact of accepting the label of "disabled" in order to gain some possibly illusory federal protection may substantially outweigh any short term benefit federally supported access may provide.

In other words, Deafhood, is a long journey. The label of "disability" is the horse the Deaf community is offered, but not the horse most would choose. It will not get the Deaf community where it wishes to go. To extend the metaphor to its breaking point, it may be better to walk, no matter how long the journey, than to ride the horse the Deaf Community did not choose.

So if the federal laws are deficient, where should the Deaf community look for protection and equity? How does the community deal with the "Hobson's Choice"? The only way it can: refuse to accept the existence of the choice. Walk away, look elsewhere, be elsewhere.

State laws are the many and varied and best place to construct real, culturally appropriate, protections. Think of laws in general like a suit of clothes. Federal laws are like buying off the rack at a national chain store. The clothes must be constructed in a very generic way in order to fit the most number of people. The same is true of federal laws. They must apply everywhere so they may not fit correctly. Now when you buy a suit off the rack it will not fit right. It will fit almost right, sometimes, but never exactly right. You can get it tailored, but it will never fit like it was made for you. Federal laws can be tailored by local federal court decisions, but they will never really fit the needs of the local community.

State laws are made locally. Your legislators are your friends and neighbors (I can see the front door of one of my representatives from the desk where I currently sit to write this). They are available and can construct laws that have local impact. State laws are like clothes made by a tailor. They are made to fit and move with you.

For example, Massachusetts General Law Chapter 66 of the Acts of 2000 states that, "[e]very acute-care hospital, shall provide competent interpreter services in connection with all emergency room services provided to every non-English speaker who is a patient or who seeks appropriate emergency care or treatment." This Act defines a "non-English speaker" as "a person who cannot speak or understand, or has difficulty with speaking or understanding, the English language because the speaker primarily or only uses a spoken language other than English." It can be argued that this does or should include persons who are Deaf and who use ASL as their primary language. (The use of the word "spoken" when referring to the structure of the language has given some analysts pause. However, the author is aware of at least one unpublished opinion when this Act was successfully argued to include persons who are Deaf.)

Utah law requires that judicial or quasi-judicial function of any subdivision of the state provide a qualified interpreter for participants who are Deaf (cf. Utah Code Section 78-24a-2.12 Utah Code Sections 78-24a-2 (1), 78-24a-8.13 Utah Code Section 78-24a-3). Judicial and quasi-judicial functions include, but not limited to, "civil and criminal court proceedings, grand jury proceedings, proceedings before a magistrate, juvenile proceedings, adoption proceedings, mental health commitment proceedings, and any proceeding in which [Deaf] person may be subjected to confinement or criminal sanction." Interpreters appointed by the Court must be screened and certified by the State of Utah, and may be subjected to further 'voir dire' by the Court and the person who is Deaf before being approved to interpret for any specific function. This right to an interpreter does not require the person who is Deaf to prove disability but only to show that he or she is a "…deaf or hard of hearing person who, because of sensory or environmental conditions, requires the assistance of a qualified interpreter or other special assistance for communicative purposes."

These are just two examples, but they give hope to the Deaf community of a future of equity with dignity. That future is a good many miles off and the horse being offered may not take the Deaf community in the right direction. My suggestion? Let's start walking.

REFERENCES

Parsons, T. (1951). The Social System. New York: The Free Press.

Deaf Studies and the Medical Field of Genetic Research
A Collaboration Model for Linguistic and Cultural Minority Populations

PARTRICK BOUDREAULT, PH.D. & CHRISTINA PALMER, PH.D.

GENETICISTS AND OTHER SCIENTISTS HAVE INCREASINGLY TARGETED various communities for biomedical research to identify genetic explanations for various diseases, traits, or characteristics. There have been some well-known successes using this approach, for example, identifying genetic variations that increase risk for breast cancer in Ashkenazi Jews (Neuhausen et al., 1996; Struewing et al., 1995). However, with the focus on involving communities in genetic research comes concerns for possible discrimination of, or harmful consequences to, whole communities; and thus, since the late 1990s there have been increasing discussions about the need for additional protections for communities in biomedical research (Weijer and Emanuel, 2000).

The question that we raise in our presentation is: How to conduct responsible genetic research in cultural and linguistic minority groups? This is an important question because much of deaf genetics research currently being conducted follows a more traditional Western and hearing-centric research model which does not usually take into account the impact of the research on cultural and linguistic minority groups e.g., Sign Language communities.

In the traditional Western research model in general, subjects are thought of and treated as individuals, not as members of a larger, possibly collective, community. Hence, the protection of human subjects participating in traditional research focuses on individual rights. However the traditional approach often overlooks the rights and concerns of collective groups, such as cultural and linguistic minority populations. The traditional view impacts the interactions between researchers and subjects, and the entire research process is formulated through the researchers' worldviews, which is often hearing-centric from the deaf community's perspective. In traditional deaf genetics research, the core focus of research typically is imbued with a deficit model of deafness because the focus is on the hearing apparatus, not on linguistically and culturally unique human beings (Lane, 1992). Evidence for this comes from a review of literature which reveals focus on collecting DNA samples, audiology, and other clinical information from deaf subjects.

In the traditional Western research model, subjects — or members of the community to which subjects belong — do not contribute to the research process in any way except to provide the essential data. Subjects also do not contribute to interpretation of the findings or consult on the impact of those findings; and findings are often disseminated in peer review journals or inaccessible technical literatures, and produced in a language that is different from the native language of that community (e.g., Signed Language as native language). There are two very important aspects of the traditional Western research model when discussing deaf genetics research. First, the research produces genetic information and this information can have profound implications for deaf people (e.g., the UK Human Fertilisation and Embryology Bill clause 14 (4)(9) which was recently passed) (United Kingdom Parliament, 2008.). Second, the research absolutely requires the participation of deaf people, and because of this requirement, the research also involves members of a cultural and linguistic minority group and so can have implications for these communities.

Research has shown that the extent to which one affiliates with the Deaf culture/community affects attitudes toward genetic testing, at least in hypothetical situations where no testing has been offered (Martinez et al., 2003). Not surprisingly, culturally Deaf people have ambivalent feelings towards genetics. On the one hand culturally Deaf people have attributed negative outcomes to genetic testing, such as concerns that it will devalue Deaf people, do more harm than good, and have a negative impact on the Deaf community (Martinez et al., 2003; Middleton et al., 1998). Culturally Deaf people typically have indicated that they do not have a preference for deaf or a hearing child (while hearing people and non-culturally deaf people uniformly indicate that they prefer a hearing child) (Martinez et al., 2003; Stern et al., 2002), and so it is not too surprising that culturally Deaf people are more likely to oppose prenatal testing for deafness compared to non-culturally deaf and hearing individuals (Martinez et al., 2003; Stern et al., 2002). On the other hand, culturally Deaf people also recognize to varying degrees that genetic information may provide benefit to them, e.g., may provide a reason why they are deaf, an opportunity to learn their chance of having deaf or hearing children, for choosing a mate, or to intentionally select for a deaf child (Arnos et al., 1991; Martinez et al., 2003; Middleton et al., 2001; Mundy, 2002; Stern et al., 2002; Taneja et al., 2004).

Culturally Deaf people are also concerned that the research teams studying genetics and deafness have no or very little understanding of their culture or the ethno-cultural views held by many Deaf people (Harris et al., 2009), and increasingly, members of the Deaf community are questioning their Deaf community member's participation in such research projects in which the research team is made up of hearing people constructing research questions that could be used against their culture (McCullough, 2007). The Deaf community desires greater direct involvement in the research design and implementation, and to support research that could benefit or not harm the Deaf community. This phenomenon of community outcry regarding genetics research is increasingly being observed with other minority groups (Ossorio and Duster, 2005; Tallbear, 2007; Tsosie, 2007).

Our framework for conducting responsible genetic research in cultural and linguistic minority communities, e.g., Sign Language Communities, was developed from two literature bases. Deaf Studies informs our framework through its emphasis on empowering and protecting Sign Language communities (Harris et al., 2009). Biomedical Research Studies informs our framework through its emphasis on defining characteristics of communities and relating those characteristics to mechanisms protecting different communities (Weijer and Emanuel, 2000).

Let's step back a bit and think about what we mean by the word "community". Weijer and Emanuel (2000) state that community:

> "...delineates a wide variety of human associations: ethnic, cultural, political, religious, geographical, municipal, professional, artistic, sexual, and even disease communities";

and (Gbadegesin and Wendler, 2006)) defines community as a:

> "...group of individuals who share some common features – a common culture, language, geographical location, religion, political authority, disease, etc. – in virtue of which they regard themselves as part of the same group, distinct from others who do not share these features."

These two definitions reveal two important components of community: it is based on interactions between people who share some common features. Communities can vary on a number of characteristics. Weijer and Emanuel (2000) described 10 characteristics of communities believed to be important for determining appropriate types of protections to embed into the research process to ensure ethical biomedical research in communities. The characteristics are (1) Common culture and traditions, cannon of knowledge, and shared history; (2) Comprehensiveness of culture; (3) Health-related common culture; (4) Legitimate political authority; (5) Representative group or individuals; (6) Mechanism for priority setting in health care; (7) Geographic localization; (8) Common economy or shared resources; (9) Communication network; and (10) Self-identification as community.

Weijer & Emanuel (2000) did not specifically consider cultural and linguistic minority groups, although their schema can be applied to such groups. Here we present a preliminary analysis in order to specifically consider how to conduct responsible genetic research in cultural and linguistic minority groups. For this analysis we consider two distinct groups within deaf community: deaf people as belonging to a disease-community (considering as hearing impaired group for example) and deaf people as belonging to a cultural and linguistic minority community. Our goal is to identify the characteristics of these two groups and to compare and contrast these characteristics to increase our understanding of how to conduct responsible research.

Our preliminary analysis reveals that the medical and linguistic/cultural perspectives on deafness have a big impact on the number of characteristics that make up a community (Table 1). When deaf people are viewed as making up a disease-related community, this view is consistent with only two characteristics that make up a community: (1) Health-related common culture, i.e., deafness; and (2) Representative groups or individuals. On the other hand, when Deaf people are viewed as making up a cultural and linguistic minority group (a Sign Language community), this is consistent with many more characteristics of a community. Specifically, the latter view reveals that Sign Language communities often or nearly always possess: (1) Common culture and traditions, cannon of knowledge, and shared history; (2) Comprehensive culture; (3) Health-related common culture, i.e., being deaf; (4) Representative groups or individuals; (5) A communication network; and (6) Self-identification as a community. The next step is to relate community characteristics to the research process in order to identify appropriate protections based on the characteristics of the community.

Next we bring together the Deaf Studies approach and the Biomedical Studies approach to identify ways to protect Sign Language communities throughout the research process.

Sign Language Communities Terms of Reference (SLCTR) is a proposed guideline for doing research with, for, and by Sign Language communities (Harris et al., 2009). SLCTR has developed six principles: 1) Authority, 2) Acknowledgement, 3) Negotiations, 4) Diversity, 5) Perceptions, and 6) Processes. For complete description for each principles of SLCTR, refer to Appendix A. SLCTR principles discuss the importance of the culturally appropriate and responsible research toward signed language communities based on indigenous terms of reference (ITR) (Osborne and McPhee, 2000).

Community Characteristics	Deaf: Cultural and Linguistic Minority	Deaf: Disease
Common culture and traditions, canon of knowledge, and shared history	Yes	
Comprehensiveness of culture	Yes	
Health-related common culture	Yes	Yes
Legitimate political authority		
Representative group or individuals	Yes	Yes
Mechanism for priority setting in health care		
Geographic localization		
Common economy or shared resources		
Communication network	Yes	
Self-identification as community	Yes	

Table 1. Comparative chart of Deaf as cultural and linguistic minority and Deaf as disease group based on Weijer & Emanuel (2000).

In the Biomedical Research Framework, there are five major categories of proposed protections for communities (Weijer and Emanuel, 2000): 1) consultation in protocol development; 2) process of providing information and obtaining informed consent; 3) involvement in research conduct; 4) access to data and samples; and 5) dissemination and publication of results. These categories are intimately related with the research process from the beginning to the end. There are many suggested protections within each of these categories, and the important thing to keep in mind is that just as communities vary in their characteristics, so must the relevant protections. That is why it is important to identify the characteristics of the community – so that these characteristics can be used to guide the relevant protections for the community.

In our framework for conducting responsible genetic research in cultural and linguistic minority groups, we propose to incorporate the SLCTR principles, which focus on empowering and protecting Sign Language communities, with biomedical protections, which focus on specific elements of the research process as they relate to protecting communities. The critical overlap between these two sets of principles and protections involves understanding and valuing the culture of the Sign Language community, which can only be accomplished by involving the Deaf community (from participants or patients to members of the researcher team) and its values in the research process, and this forms the core of our research framework for the Deaf Genetics Project.

There are areas where the SLCTR principles and the biomedical protections do not overlap. Specifically, the biomedical protections do not specifically include empowerment and protection of Sign Language communities; and the SLCTR principles do not include specific processes for handling data and samples. The Deaf Genetics Project applies the proposed framework of conducting responsible genetic research in cultural and linguistic minority groups by including the non-overlapping elements of SLCTR guidelines and biomedical protections (Figure 1).

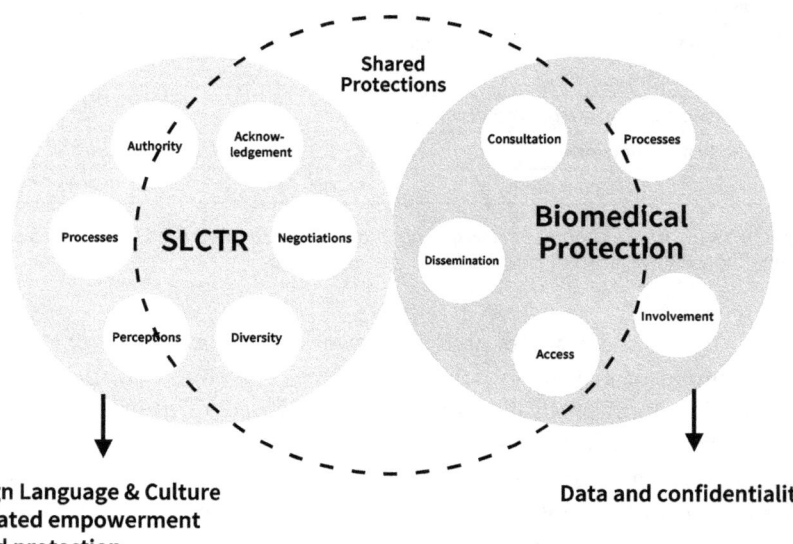

Figure 1. Areas where SLCTR and biomedical protection do not overlap

The Deaf Genetics Project is an example of a collaborative research model. It is a multi-institutional (University of California, Los Angeles and California State University, Northridge) and multi-disciplinary (deaf studies, genetics, linguistics, sign language interpreting, audiology, statistics, and psychology) collaboration of deaf, hard-of-hearing, and hearing researchers. There are two principal investigators: one is Deaf and the other is hearing. Every part of the process is reviewed and analyzed by two principal investigators of the project to ensure the individual and community rights are not breached. An advisory board, made up of deaf individuals from a variety of deaf-related organizations, is also involved. The research team participated in 15 hours of Deaf culture sensitivity training, helping to ensure that the values of the Deaf community would be represented in this research project.

Figure 2 represents the Deaf Genetics Project vision that an all-inclusive responsible deaf genetics research endeavor incorporates three cultural perspectives: 1) academic, 2) hearing, and 3) deaf. As for the individuals and community members of the project, Deaf and hard-of-hearing individuals are in regular communication and information is shared by attending deaf community related events (e.g., Deaf Expo), by giving information session among the deaf and hard-of-hearing community of the project goals and purposes, and by attending deaf and hard-of hearing national or local conferences/workshops, ensuring that the Deaf Genetics Project is working as part of the deaf community instead of working from an Ivory tower as the traditional western hearing-centric model (Figure 2).

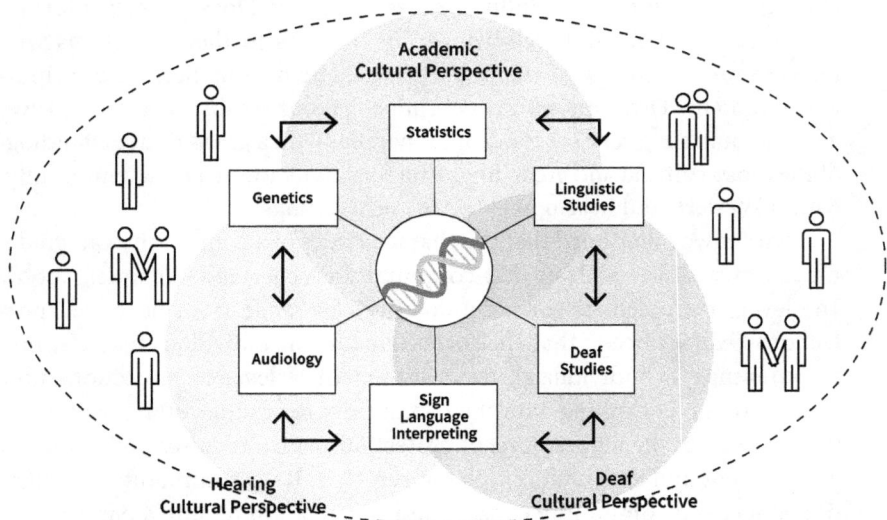

Figure 2. Deaf Genetic Project vision, encompassing academic, hearing, and Deaf cultural perspectives.

The Deaf Genetics Project is unique among deaf genetics research projects. To our knowledge, it is the first genetics research project to directly involve deaf people in the planning and implementation of the project, and to formulate research questions in terms of the meaning of genetic information to deaf people and the Deaf community. The Deaf Genetics Project is culturally Deaf friendly and tri-lingual because it provides on-line study questionnaires in American Sign Language, English, and Spanish. The Deaf Genetics Project has two certified sign language interpreters who are fully familiar with the genetics aspects of this project in order to have effective communication between deaf and hearing researchers, as well as deaf participants and hearing researchers.

The Deaf Genetics Project offers genetic testing for two common genes for deafness: Connexin 26 (Kelsell et al., 1997) and Connexin 30 (del Castillo et al., 2002). The purpose of the project is to understand what this genetic information means to deaf people, and so participants fill out questionnaires before and after they learn their genetic test results. The questionnaires ask about reasons for genetic testing, deaf identity, attitudes toward genetic testing, knowledge and understanding of the genetic information, anxiety, depression, self-esteem, perceived personal control, and what people do with the genetic information.

The data will be able to answer important questions, such as: Is there is a relationship between deaf identity and motivation for genetic testing? Does genetic information influence deaf identity? Does genetic information affect psychological well-being? The answers to these questions will increase understanding of the impact of genetic information on deaf individuals and the Deaf community. We hope that our results will also improve genetic counseling services for deaf individuals with a greater understanding of the cross-cultural and cross-linguistic sensitivity toward Deaf community within Western and hearing-centric medical settings.

Earlier we mentioned that the characteristics of a community can guide the conduct of research in that community (Weijer and Emanuel, 2000). The level of protections for a community can range from no added protections (which means that the focus remains on individual subjects, not a community of individuals), to an intermediate level of protections provided through consulting with the community regarding certain aspects of the research, to the highest level of protections which requires both community consent and consultation for the research. Both community consultation alone, and community consent and consultation require a partnership between communities and researchers.

Our analysis of the characteristics of Sign Language communities through the SLCTR principles and the biomedical protections reveals that a partnership between the community and researchers is required for conducting responsible genetic research in Sign Language communities. Furthermore, analysis of our Deaf Genetics Project reveals that we have approached this research project as a partnership between the community and the researchers and in a manner that provides more protections than simple community consultation. Finally, this examination of the Deaf Genetics Project through a framework of conducting responsible genetic research in cultural and linguistic minority groups allowed us to identify other areas in which to strengthen and benefit this partnership.

ACKNOWLEDGEMENTS

This presentation was supported in part by NHGRI R01 003871 (C.P., P.B. (Deaf)). We thank our Deaf Genetics Team: E.E. Baldwin, M. Fox, A. Martinez, J. Linden (CODA), E. Christensen, R. Trank, L. Dutton, D. Kovacs (Deaf), L. Perez (Deaf), Y. Sininger, J. Sinsheimer, and W.W. Grody. We also thank G. Gertz (Deaf) and L. Fleischer (Deaf) for their valuable comments on the earlier forms of this presentation; and we thank all of the individuals who are participating in the Deaf Genetics Project.

REFERENCES

Arnos, K. S., Israel, J., & Cunningham, M. (1991). A model program for genetic counseling of the deaf. *Annals of the New York Academy of Sciences*, 630, 317-318.

del Castillo, I., Moreno-Pelayo, M. S., del Castillo, F. J., Alvarez, A., Telleria, D., Mendez, I., et al. (2002). A deletion involving the connexin 30 gene in nonsyndromic hearing impairment. *New England Journal of Medicine*, 346, 243-249.

Gbadegesin, S., & Wendler, D. (2006). Protecting communities in health research from exploitation. *Bioethics*, 20, 248-253.

Harris, R., Holmes, H. M., & Mertens, D. M. (2009). Research ethics in sign language communities. *Sign Language Studies*, 9.

Kelsell, D. P., Dunlop, J., Stevens, H. P., Lench, N. J., Liang, J. N., Parry, G., et al. (1997). Connexin 26 mutations in hereditatry non-syndromic sensorineural deafness. *Nature*, 387, 80-83.

Lane, H. (1992). *The mask of benevolence: Disabling the Deaf community*. New York: Alfred A. Knopf.

Martinez, A., Linden, J., Schimmenti, L. A., & Palmer, C. G. S. (2003). Attitudes of the broader hearing, deaf, and hard-of-hearing community toward genetic testing for deafness. *Genetics in Medicine*, 5, 106-112.

McCullough, C. A. (2007). Hearing Researchers: Why do they Study Deaf People? ASC on the Counch. http://www.ascdeaf.com/blog/?p=323. Accessed September 23, 2007.

Middleton, A., Hewison, J., & Mueller, R. F. (1998). Attitudes of Deaf adults toward genetic testing for hereditary deafness. *American Journal of Human Genetics*, 63, 1175-1180.

Middleton, A., Hewison, J., & Mueller, R. F. (2001). Prenatal diagnosis for inherited deafness — what is the potential demand. *Journal of Genetic Counseling*, 101, 121-131.

Mundy, L. (2002). A world of their own. *The Washington Post*, pp. 22-43.

Neuhausen, S., Gilewski, T., Norton, L., Tran, T., McGuire, P., Swensen, J., et al. (1996). Recurrent BRCA2 6174delT mutations in Ashkenazi Jewish women affected by breast cancer. *Nature Genetics*, 13, 126-128.

Osborne, R., & McPhee, R. (2000, December 12-15.). Indigenous terms of reference (ITR). Paper presented at the 6th UNESCO-ACEIF International Conference on Education, Bangkok, Thailand.

Ossorio, P., & Duster, T. (2005). Race and genetics: controversies in biomedical, behavioral, and forensic sciences. *American Psychology*, 60, 115-128.

Stern, S. J., Arnos, K. S., Murrelle, L., Oelrich Welch, K., Nance, W. E., & Pandya, A. (2002). Attitudes of deaf and hard of hearing subjects towards genetic testing and prenatal diagnosis of hearing loss. *Journal of Medical Genetics*, 39, 449-453.

Struewing, J. P., Abeliovich, D., Peretz, T., Avishai, N., Kaback, M. M., Collins, F. S., et al. (1995). The carrier frequency of the BRCA1 185delAG mutation is approximately 1 percent in Ashkenazi Jewish individuals. *Nature Genetics*, 11, 198-200. Erratum in: Nature Genetics 1996 1912:1110.

Tallbear, K. (2007). Narratives of race and indigeneity in the genographic project. *The Journal of Law, Medicine & Ethics*, 35, 412-424.

Taneja, P. R., Pandya, A., Foley, D. L., Nicely, L. V., & Arnos, K. S. (2004). Attitudes of deaf individuals towards genetic testing. *American Journal of Medical Genetics*, 130A, 17-21.

Tsosie, R. (2007). Cultural challenges to biotechnology: Native American genetic resources and the concept of cultural harm. *The Journal of Law, Medicine & Ethics*, 35, 396-411.

Weijer, C., & Emanuel, E. J. (2000). Protecting communities in biomedical research. *Science*, 289, 1142-1144.

APPENDIX A

Six principles of SLCTR by Harris, Holmes, and Mertens (2009)

Principle 1: Authority
The authority for the construction of Sign Language meanings and knowledge rests with Sign Language community members.

Principle 2: Acknowledgement
Investigators should acknowledge that Sign Language community members have the right to have those things that are valued to be fully considered in any interactions.

Principle 3: Negotiations
Investigators should take into account Sign Language community world views are taken into account in all negotiations or dealings which impact on Sign Language community members.

Principle 4: Diversity
Investigators should recognize the diverse experiences, understandings, and way of life (in Sign Language societies) that reflect contemporary Sign Language cultures in the application of Sign Language Communities Terms of Reference.

Principle 5: Perceptions
Investigators should ensure that the views and perceptions of the critical reference group (the Sign Language group you work with) is reflected in any process of validating and evaluating the extent to which Sign Language Communities Terms of Reference have been taken into account.

Principle 6: Processes
Investigators should negotiate within and between Sign Language group(s) with the aim of establishing appropriate processes to consider and determine the criteria for deciding how to meet cultural imperatives, and social needs and priorities.

Dreams and Dilemmas: Anthropological Notes on International Sign[1]

MARA GREEN

THIS PAPER SEEKS TO INVESTIGATE INTERNATIONAL SIGN (IS) FROM A linguistic anthropological perspective that emphasizes interaction and social context. In the first part of this paper I provide a brief introduction to IS, highlighting its characteristic variability. Following a review of the IS literature that focuses on its history, formal properties, and pragmatics, I suggest that how social actors in particular sites and settings communicate in and comment on IS constitutes an important area for further inquiry. In light of this goal, the second part of my paper theorizes what I will call "moral orientation," in order to make sense of ethnographic research from the World Federation of the Deaf (WFD) 2007 General Assembly and World Congress. My hope is that my research, conducted and analyzed within the framework of linguistic anthropology, can contribute to the analysis of IS. In addition, my effort towards an ethnographic account of the relatively unique phenomenon of IS seeks to broaden the scope of linguistic anthropology.

The term "International Sign" broadly designates cross-linguistic communication between signers whose language competencies do not include a shared sign language. The circumstances to which we can apply the moniker IS are therefore diverse. For example, deaf[2] travelers who unexpectedly meet in a foreign city might find that their native sign languages are mutually unintelligible. If, as is often the case, they are nonetheless motivated to engage with each other, and manage to find common ground using visual-gestural resources, their conversations can be considered instantiations of IS. Similarly, a group of researchers, deaf and hearing signers from multiple countries who come together for collaborative purposes, could find it most appropriate or effective not to use a national sign language but rather to conduct their discussions in IS. In a final example, at international meetings, where the audience is made up of deaf people from around the world, a lecture given in either a spoken language or in a national sign language could be interpreted into International Sign to facilitate greater understanding.

Extant scholarship as well as my own ethnographic research clearly shows that what exactly constitutes the phenomenon known as IS — what it looks like — varies considerably, both within and across examples such as those just given.[3] Such variation seems to correlate with a number of factors, including the social background and experiences of the signers as well as communicative situation. For example, where is a signer from? Is this his first time communicating with people from other countries who do not share his native sign language? Or is she an experienced attendee at international events? Where are her interlocutors from? Is an international meeting composed of people from, for example, Europe, Africa, or both? Is the occasion of signing formal, as in a keynote address, or relaxed, as in a chance encounter on a bus or at a bar? The temporal horizon also seems to influence the production of IS.

In the scenarios above, the travelers might chat for several minutes, or spend all day together. In each case, IS would manifest very differently. Similarly, a research group that meets once, and one that convenes regularly, each present different possibilities for the development of a group-specific IS. Madsen (n.d.: 8) points out that geographical location also seems to have an effect on signers' lexical choices. Given the same group of people, the IS used at a meeting in Chicago will probably bear a stronger relation to ASL, while that used at a meeting in London will draw more heavily on BSL.

LITERATURE REVIEW

Here it is helpful to locate IS in its historical development. In the late 1800s in Europe, deaf people from different countries began to come together formally and informally. There is wide agreement that IS has its roots in the forms of communication that started to develop at this time (Madsen n.d.: 1; Webb and Supalla n.d.: 173; Supalla and Webb 1995: 334).

From at least the mid 1900s into the present, deaf organizations, including the WFD, sign linguistics research groups, and sporting leagues, have provided opportunities for large numbers of international deaf people to come together on a regular basis in order to meet and communicate with each other (see Supalla and Webb 1995: 334; McKee and Napier 2002: 28). In 1973 the WFD decided to standardize this kind of communication, and an appointed committee put together a book of international signs, which they called Gestuno. The reaction to Gestuno was largely negative, with complaints that the signs did not reflect people's experiences, and that the Gestuno interpreters were impossible to understand. The WFD accepted this challenge and dropped Gestuno as a project, although researchers have noted that its vocabulary has influenced International Sign as used at WFD events (Madsen n.d.: 3; Supalla and Webb 1995: 335; McKee and Napier, 28–29).

Here it is important to note that the word "international," does not necessarily mean the presence of people from all or even most countries but rather from multiple countries and regions. From the formal establishment of deaf organizations some decades ago, Western Europe, the United States, and, increasingly, Scandinavia, have been the most active participants (Madsen n.d.: 4-5; Supalla and Webb 1995: 348) and as I will explain below, IS bears a strong relation to their national sign languages. Poor and "developing" countries from Eastern Europe, Asia, Africa, and Latin America have played a larger role in international arenas in recent years, a point to which I will return.

In terms of formal analysis, most researchers differentiate between lexicon, on the one hand, and grammar on the other. There is broad consensus that IS has a very small number of repeated, recognized, and stable signs (Madsen n.d.: 6; Moody 1979 cited in Woll 1990: 110; Allsop, Woll, and Brauti 1995 cited in McKee and Napier 2002: 29). Signers' vocabulary is significantly enriched through multiple strategies. They borrow signs from their own and other national sign languages; improvise and invent signs on the spot; and rely heavily on classifiers, role shift, facial expressions, and iconic and mimetic features (ibid; Moody 1994 cited in McKee and Napier 2002: 30; McKee and Napier 40-41). For example, "The food was just disgusting," glossed in ASL as FOOD AWFUL and rendered with appropriate facial expressions, might be conveyed in IS by bringing ones hand, shaped as if holding a spoon, repeatedly to the mouth, chewing, making a disgusted face, and pretending to spit out the food.

Syntactic patterns also appear to reflect national sign languages, especially but not only in the use of space (Webb and Supalla n.d.; Supalla and Webb 1995; Woll 1990; McKee and Napier 2002). In IS, for example, as in ASL, comparisons are made by spatially locating the entities to be compared in distinct regions of the signing space (usually left and right) (see McKee and Napier 2002: 35-36 for transcript analysis). Broadly speaking, researchers concur that in IS the vocabulary is small and flexible, and that IS must exploit the spatial and iconic resources of the signed modality.

Pragmatic analyses have concentrated on how signers use these and other resources to communicate effectively. (For the purposes of this summary, we can consider together utterances produced in interpreted as well as non-interpreted situations.) First, signers are aware of and capitalize on their interlocutors' shared knowledge and experiences, including the social implications of being deaf, national and cultural backgrounds, and the more immediate context of the conference or other event (Madsen n.d.; McKee and Napier 2002). Second, signers pay attention to each others' cues in order to form implicit and explicit consensus on the use of specific signs and to monitor for understanding (ibid). Finally, IS users emphasize the conceptual aspect of their messages by using multiple signs for a single concept; providing examples; and making the abstract concrete through metaphor and metonymy (Woll 1990; McKee and Napier 2002; Rosenstock 2008).

The following frames, taken from video footage of a presentation on women's rights given at the WFD 2007 World Congress in Madrid, help to illustrate some of these properties. In Figures 1 and 2, the woman on the left is lecturing in Spanish Sign Language (LSE); the woman on the right is interpreting into IS. Arguing that deaf women must join together to achieve the goals outlined in the talk, and emphasizing how hard the work had been thus far, the interpreter signs WORK (the IS sign is almost identical to the ASL sign) as well as ROLL-UP-SLEEVES (Figure 1) and SWEAT-DRIPS-DOWN-FACE (Figure 2). This exemplifies the use of iconic signs; the metaphorical and metonymic representation of a concept (hard work) through concrete images (rolled-up sleeves and dripping faces); and repetition.

Figure 1: ROLL-UP-SLEEVES

The works synthesized above represent a variety of analytic frameworks, from linguistic typology (Supalla and Webb 1995) to Gricean implicatures (McKee and Napier 2002); each makes an important contribution to the study of international deaf communities and signed communication. However, while offering sophisticated analyses of syntax, lexicon, and sign production, this literature has tended to neglect interaction and social context. A brief digression on iconicity demonstrates the importance of analyzing these factors. Multiple authors cite iconicity as that which allows communication to occur between people with minimal shared vocabulary; visual reception of an iconic sign enables the addressee to grasp its meaning. Yet for this to be the case, the relationship between that form and meaning must be not only iconic but also known.

As Rosenstock (2008) reminds us, iconic signs are "culturally motivated" and thus "iconic only to those who share the [relevant] cultural knowledge" (144). Iconicity thus asks that we take seriously not only the production of IS but also its reception; this in turn demands attention to how people understand and evaluate IS. Broadly speaking, a full account of International Sign requires further investigation into the processes through which IS produces and is produced by social worlds.

Figure 2: SWEAT-DRIPS-DOWN FACE

ETHNOGRAPHIC RESEARCH

Drawing on ethnographic research and using a linguistic anthropological framework, the rest of this paper seeks to foreground rather than background social actors and the specificity of communicative context. As part of a larger research project, during the summer of 2007 I had the opportunity to attend the WFD's quadrennial meeting, where I engaged in participant observation and conducted formal and informal interviews with other attendees. In addition to participating in the World Congress — a series of panels, speeches, and theater performances attended by literally thousands of deaf as well as hearing people — I also observed the WFD General Assembly, to which I now turn.

The General Assembly, a meeting of the member nations of the WFD, took place in a large auditorium. Following the opening ceremonies, the president and other board members sat on stage, while the assembly itself, comprised of up to two delegates from each voting member nation, sat in alphabetical order by country, facing the stage. The meeting, held over three days, consisted of a one-day workshop followed by two days of formal procedures. These procedures were governed by a language policy of direct communication between deaf people. By this I mean that interpreters — whether deaf or hearing — who might translate from IS to delegates' national sign languages were forbidden.

At the beginning of the meeting, board members explained this policy, and introduced a set of standard signs relevant to GA business (assembly, ratify, etc). As the meeting progressed, many delegates went on stage to ask questions and provide comments, producing greatly varied IS utterances, which board members (and others) monitored for understandability. If, for example, a delegate signed a question in something other than IS, someone would remind him or her to use IS. Occasionally, a board member would wait for a delegate to finish, and then re-sign his or her comments, interpreting from an attempt at IS into a more recognized version of it.

Here it is important to note that not every delegate agreed with the GA policies or with the assumption that IS, at least as produced properly, would be intelligible to all. For example, one delegate, a woman from a Latin American country,[4] requested that the written materials under discussion — projected in English onto a large screen — also be available in Spanish. The board replied that this was, regrettably, impossible. Later that night, the woman reflected on this interaction. She signed: "I don't understand English. I was told, if you can't understand English, then look at the person signing IS. But this doesn't help! I don't understand IS!"

In a separate incident, delegates from an Eastern European country were using an interpreter who was seated next to them. The board interrupted the proceedings to politely ask that the interpreter sit in the back with the rest of the non-delegates; she did so. When the next matter came to a vote, one of the delegates from this country went on stage to announce that if he were forbidden an interpreter, he would abstain from voting. Several other delegates raised green cards (a "yes" vote) to indicate support for his stance.

In seeking to understand these contradictory perspectives, the notion of moral orientation, which I have drawn from several sources, has emerged as a valuable analytic. Hanks (1996) writes:

> In order for two or more people to communicate, at whatever level of effectiveness, it is neither sufficient nor necessary that they 'share' the same grammar. What they must share, to a variable degree, is the ability to orient themselves verbally, perceptually, and physically to each other and to their social world. This implies that they have commensurate but not identical categories, plus commensurate ways of locating themselves in relation to them. (229)

In an article about a man with aphasia, Goodwin (2006) notes that

> [a]ttributing communicative intent to another's sounds and gesture [n.b.: Goodwin refers here to hearing speakers/listeners] and thereby treating that person as a full-fledged human being capable of performing relevant, consequential action, and being willing to do the work to find out what the other is saying, thus has not only a cognitive dimension, but also a moral one. (106)

He adds that other features that contribute to successful communication include shared linguistic code, socially relevant bodies and spaces, shared knowledge, co-occurring activities, and "embodied mutual orientation." These texts suggest that what I am calling "moral orientation" is often or always related to successful communication. By moral orientation (MO) I mean a dimension of communicative practice that is distinct from actual utterances and from abstract linguistic code. While it is related to joint attention and perception, MO as an analytic emphasizes the socially meaningful and productive act of attuning oneself to others. We might think of it as an embodied ethics of communication.

Successful communication, meanwhile, might be said to have occurred when each ratified party considers that s/he has understood and been understood to the degree s/he feels is necessary given the particular situation. When the linguistic code and the ability to produce utterances that accord with it are relatively fully shared, then moral orientation, like many "ordinary" aspects of the social world, gets taken for granted. At moments when, as in Goodwin's case, linguistic performance is compromised, or when the linguistic code is particularly weak, as in IS, then moral orientation in relation to successful communication becomes more noticeable. But in what way or ways are MO and successful communication related?

Let us return to the WFD. In the course of ten days of participant observation, I found that attendees generally agreed that IS is something one must learn, and that the formal variety used at WFD events evidences a strong relationship to Western European sign languages, as well as to ASL (there was some divergence of opinion on the latter among my informants; for similarly diverse opinions see Madsen n.d.: 4; Webb and Supalla n.d.: 183; Woll 1990: 118). This means that those individuals and countries with greater international experience (i.e. the global North) are generally more able to understand and produce WFD-style IS than those with less experience (i.e. the global South).

While the notion of a political geography of IS is generative insofar as it emphasizes the connections between and among spatial and social locations in hearing and deaf worlds, it potentially suggests that people from poor and "developing" nations, on the one hand, and those from countries that have played a larger role in international deaf politics, on the other, hold predetermined and mutually exclusive viewpoints.

An excerpt from an interview with a delegate from a "developing" country in South Asia shows that such a perspective would be inadequate:

> Since flying here to the WFD meeting, I've been attending multiple events and learning so much. Topics have included sign language research, and — let's see, what have the other topics been? Oh yes, deaf women's rights, how it's important to work for inclusion and equality.

When I watch these presentations, there's someone signing IS and someone signing LSE. At first this is a little distracting, but I focus on the IS because I know it, so I am able to really learn from what I'm watching. Here we are in Spain, with people having flown in from countries all over the world. I've met many different people, and we've been able to exchange so much, which is really wonderful.[5]

This translation strongly suggests that social/geopolitical background does not neatly determine how one uses and conceptualizes IS and its place in an international deaf world.[6]

How, then, can we understand the two approaches to IS that I have outlined? I have come to see them as representing two competing theories of communication, both of which place a premium value on successful communication as well as on moral orientation, but which posit different relationships between the two.[7] Theory One claims that successful communication requires moral orientation, which can be achieved by social groups like the General Assembly because of commonalities among deaf people and deaf languages.

Committing to direct communication, monitoring linguistic form, trying to learn IS, and adjusting to its variations are simultaneously made possible by and serve to assert a fundamental likeness among participants. This process of morally orientating is constitutive of and enables communicative success, defined more in terms of how communication happens and less in terms of its referential content.

Theory Two claims that moral orientation requires successful communication, understood primarily as referential content, which can be achieved through national sign language interpreters, written translations, and other means. The acknowledgement of differences in deaf positionalities, knowledges, and languages thus requires communicative strategies — the "how" mentioned above — that in Theory One would be considered antithetical to moral orientation. In Theory Two how communication happens is socially meaningful precisely because in accounting for differences through the implementation of multiple strategies that ensure communicative success, moral orientation is achieved. Theory One, then, emphasizes how deaf experiences are similar, and how deaf and hearing experiences are different; while hearing people need interpreters to understand each other, deaf people do not. This further implies that deaf history, sociality, and personhood cannot be mapped onto hearing models. Theory Two, while in no way contradicting these implications, places emphasis on internal diversity and on the multiplicity of deaf histories and ways of being.[8]

By way of conclusion, let me note that my purpose is not to judge these theories but rather to illuminate them. I hope I have demonstrated that IS cannot be fully accounted for without careful attention to its production and reception in complex and negotiated contexts. In addition, I hope to have shown how theoretical concerns and ethnographic accounts can mutually inform each other. Thinking closely about the dreams and dilemmas of deaf politics and deaf social actors asks that we take seriously what successful communication and moral orientation are, what they do, and how they might be achieved.

FOOTNOTES

1. I would like to extend my sincere thanks to Bryan Eldredge and especially Flavia Fleischer for their hard work in organizing DST! 2008; to Phillipa Sandholm at the World Federation of the Deaf, for her help in bibliographic research; to the NSF GRDF, for its generous financial support of my graduate studies; to Terra Edwards, Michele Friedner, and Orkid Sassouni, for intellectual and moral support; to the audience members at DST for their engagement with my paper and its themes; and last but by no means least to my interlocutors at WFD — especially but not only those who permitted me to videotape them — for their patience, energy, and insights.
2. While it is common practice to distinguish between cultural and audiological D/deafness using capital and lower case letters, most (though not all) articles about IS use only the term "deaf" (sometimes reserving "Deaf" to refer specifically to the U.S. Deaf community). After attempting to use "deaf," "Deaf," and "D/deaf," I have chosen to follow the IS literature's convention for the sake of simplicity. Given the international setting of IS, my decision is

also based on the fact that the non-US deaf community with which I am most familiar (Nepal's) uses the word "deaf" in its official, English-language website (www.nfdh.org.np).

3. The version of this paper presented at DST! included video clips of IS as signed by three people (two from Europe, one from East Asia, each with different international experiences, each signing to different addressees). All videos mentioned in this paper are available on request.
4. For reasons of confidentiality, I have identified delegates by region rather than country.
5. This is my own translation from the video clip presented at DST!
6. It might, however, be productive to enquire more fully into the specific institutional relationships between the countries whose delegates I have quoted and the WFD. This is related to Paddy Ladd's point that it would be worth finding out more about the specific life histories of informants with differing perspectives (personal communication).
7. We can also think of this in terms of metapragmatics. Silverstein (1976) distinguishes between pragmatics — what a language can do — and metapragmatics — what its practitioners say it can do. I understand one aspect of his argument to mean that, while metapragmatic statements do not necessarily accurately reflect on a language's actual pragmatic capacities, metapragmatics can and does influence linguistic structure and performance. We can see this clearly in reference to the narrative by a South Asian signer. In Figure 3 below, the signer begins to articulate the sign that I have translated above as "know" ("I focus on the IS because I know it"). In the first frame, the signer's forefinger is extended, touching the side of his head. In the second and third frames, all four fingers touch the head. The speed with which the former articulation is replaced by the latter, which can be seen on the video, strongly suggests that this is a case of repair. The "mistaken" articulation could be either the ASL, and in some cases IS, sign for THINK, or perhaps a phonological variation of the sign for KNOW in the signer's native language (usually articulated with the first and second finger extended). In either case, what this repair demonstrates is the signer's decision to use IS and to do so properly, given the international setting we were in, despite the fact that I was the sole addressee, and he and I have on past occasions often conversed in his native sign language. Yet the other two delegates mentioned above, their critiques of IS notwithstanding, also communicated their comments in an international setting in what could just as easily be called IS. It is clear that the relationship between performance, pragmatics, and metapragmatics is complex.

Figure 3

8. Thank you to Katie Roberts, who raised the important issue of whether we might understand moral orientation and successful communication in relational, rather than unidirectional, terms. This implicitly asks whether the relationship of opposition between Theories One and Two represents an (ethnographically informed) heuristic device and/or my informants' viewpoint that moral orientation and successful communication are unidirectionally related. I do not yet have an adequate response.

REFERENCES

Allsop, L., B. Woll and J. M. Brauti. 1995. "International Sign: The Creation of an International Deaf Community and Sign Language." In *Sign Language Research 1994: Proceedings of the 4th European Congress on Sign Language Research*, ed. H. F. Bos and G. M. Schermer. Hamburg: Signum Press.

Goodwin, Charles. 2006. "Human Sociality as Mutual Orientation in a Rich Interactive Environment: Multimodal Utterances and Pointing in Aphasia." In *Roots of Human Sociality*, ed. N. J. Enfield and Stephen Levinson. New York: Berg.

Hanks, William F. 1996. *Language and Communicative Practices*. Boulder, CO: Westview Press.

Madsen, W. J. n.d. "International Communication Among Deaf People." Photocopied document received from WFD

Moody, B. 1994. "International Sign: Language, Pidgin, or Charades?" Paper presented at the Issues in Interpreting 2 Conference, University of Durham.

———. 1979. "La Communication Internationale chez les sourds." *Reeducation Orthophonique*, 17, 213-24.

Rosenstock, Rachel. 2008. "The Role of Iconicity in International Sign." *Sign Language Studies*, Vol. 8 No. 2: 132-159.

Silverstein, Michael. 1976. "Shifters, Linguistic Categories, and Cultural Description." In *Meaning in Anthropology*, ed. Keith H. Basso and Henry A. Selby. Albuquerque: University of New Mexico Press.

Supalla, T., and Webb, R. 1995. "The Grammar of International Sign: A New Look at Pidgin Languages." In *Language, Gesture, and Space*, ed. K. Emmorey and J. S. Reilly, J.S. Hillsdale, NJ: Lawrence Erlbaum Associates.

Webb, Rebecca, and Supalla, Ted. n.d. "Negation in International Sign." In *Proceedings of the Fifth International Symposium on Sign Language Research*. Hamburg: Signum Press.

Woll, B. 1990. "International Perspectives on Sign Language Communication." *International Journal of Sign Linguistics*, Vol. 1, No. 2: 107-120.

Further Reading on International Sign

Andersson, Yerker. 1988. "A Special Tribute to Drs. Drago Vukotic and Cesare Magarotto." *WFD News*, No. 1, 5-6.

-----. 1991. "A Turning Point in the Deaf African Heritage." *WFD News*, April, 18-19.

Bar-Tzur, David. 2002. International Gesture: Principles and Gestures. Website: http://www.theinterpretersfriend.com/indj/ig.html

Battison, R., and Jordan, I.K. 1976. "Cross-Cultural Communication with Foreign Signers: Fact and Fancy." *Sign Language Studies*, 10, 53-68.

Bergmann, A. 1996. "Extra Rational Responses: International Sign Language?" *Signpost*, 3(3), 2-3.

British Deaf Association. 1975. *Gestuno: International Sign Language of the Deaf*. Adopted by the Unification of Signs Commission of the World Federation of the Deaf. London: British Deaf Association.

Coppock, P. 1990. "International Sign Language Again." *Signpost*, 3 (1).

Moody, W. 1987. "International Gestures." In *Gallaudet Encyclopedia of Deaf People and Deafness*, Vol. 3, ed. J. V. Van Cleve. New York: McGraw Hill Book Company Inc.

Padden, C. 1993. "Restrictions." *Signpost* 6 (4).

Rosenstock, Rachel. 2004. *An Investigation of International Sign: Analyzing Structure and Comprehension*. PhD dissertation, Gallaudet University.

Incorporating Deaf Role Models in Teacher-Preparation Curriculum

BRIAN KILPATRICK, PH.D. & KATHY WELDON, LMSW

AS SOON AS A CHILD ARRIVES INTO THIS WORLD, HIS OR HER MAIN activity is learning about the surroundings and learning to interact with other similar creatures. Cognitive development happens when children are provided with opportunities to explore their environment. This exploration translates into children's play, which allows children to develop and practice adult-like behaviors and leads to the children's development of thinking. (Vygotosky, 1978) (Piaget, 1929)

Psychosocial development ecompasses several areas and is realized by the child in stages through trial-and-error (Erikson, 1972):

- trust versus mistrust (ages 0–18 months),
- autonomy versus shame and doubt (ages 18 months–3 years): attitudes appropriate to family and culture,
- initiative versus guilt (ages 3–6): experimenting the purpose of life and one's own self, developing self-concept.
- industry versus inferiority (ages 6–12): developing feelings/awareness of competency and positive self-identity,
- identity versus identity diffusion (ages 12–18): ego development, establishing personal goals, developing moral reasoning, self-certainty, self-esteem, performance under stress, and intimacy.

Three other stages follow in adulthood: intimacy versus isolation, generativity versus stagnation, and integrity versus despair.

Deaf and hearing children have the potential for similar development milestones. Healthy identity development is facilitated when deaf children feel comfortable with being deaf and are exposed to role models. (Andrews, Leigh, & Weiner, 2004) Psychologists and educators argue the need for children to emulate and be inspired by good role models. Parents are often mentioned as the child's first role models. Hence if the parents, themselves, are good examples, their children will develop their full potential.

Early communication within the family, particularly conversations about what people are thinking and feeling, are crucial drivers for key areas of a child's development. Children's awareness of other people's thoughts, so called meta-cognition, appears to develop through the experience of talking to other people about other people's thoughts. Many deaf children miss out on these kinds of conversation.

Empowerment processes have to start very early on, and so the empowerment of deaf and hard of hearing adults begins with the empowerment of the families they are born into and in which they grow up. This has numerous implications for the actual realization of any psychosocial collaboration between professionals and the individuals affected (parents and deaf or hard of hearing children): it involves a team effort that analyses the capabilities of the participants, the circumstances in the lives of whoever it is addressing, the way people act and how they search for solutions, in order to provide tailored support models to those concerned. An empowerment-oriented approach has much to do with recognition and acceptance of people: "Acceptance is the background music that sets the mood for the development of autonomy." (Stiemert-Strecker, Teuber, & Seckinger, 2000)

Recent theories have emphasized the importance of environmental factors on the psychosocial development of deaf children. One survey has investigated the impact of the following variables on deaf students' psychosocial adjustment: student-related background and experiential characteristics, parent-related variables, school-related factors, and teacher-related variables. The multiple regression analysis revealed that degree of hearing loss, additional handicap, and age at onset of deafness were negatively related to psychosocial adjustment of deaf students. However, there was a positive relationship between psychosocial variables and some of the independent variables, such as use of hearing aids, speech intelligibility, academic achievement, parental hearing status, and communication methods used at school. The recent findings suggest that it is not deafness per se but that some environmental factors were also influential on the psychosocial adjustment of deaf students. (Polat, 2003)

ROLE MODELS

Joseph Joubert (1752-1824), French essayist said, "Children need models rather than critics." (Joubert, 2005)

How do parents or teachers share stories about successful Deaf people? The changes in technology made this information more accessible than ever before. Anyone is able to search on Google's website and find pictures and stories. Even better, videoclips of actual deaf people sharing their stories can be found on youtube.com.

A personal interview with a mainstreamed deaf adult revealed that only three teachers out of 15 shared stories about successful Deaf adults with deaf children. (Whitworth, 2008) One of them even invited in the classroom Deaf adults who were successful in their careers. All these three teachers are hearing. The person interviewed appreciated the information about how Deaf adults live their lives. He remembered having been introduced to the fact that Deaf adults could lead their lives in the hearing world and not feel deprived of anything. He remembered the stories Deaf adults shared with him about their careers and about the latest technology that enabled them to have access to more jobs in general, and to more white-collar jobs. Another Deaf adult remembered learning nothing about Deaf successful leaders while going through school.

At a workshop for parents of deaf children, a hearing presenter was asked a question by a parent "Can a deaf person become a doctor?" The presenter's facial expression was that of sympathy and the answer was "No." A deaf educator intervened and said "Yes, there are seven doctors we know of right now, there are more preparing to become doctors!" This was just one year ago. Nowadays there are about forty Deaf doctors. Parents were pleased upon hearing this comment at that time, they should be ecstatic now.

Texas Education Code 29.008 explains that schools shall provided role models for deaf children:

> Code 29.008 § 29.307. ROLE MODELS. A student who is deaf or hard of hearing shall be given the opportunity to be exposed to deaf or hard-of-hearing role models. Added by Acts 1995, 74th Leg., ch. 260, § 1, eff. May 30, 1995. (Texas Legislature, 2008)

We are currently unaware of any other state that might have mandated through appropriate legislation the necessity of Deaf Role Models in Deaf Education. However, we hope that other states will follow this initiative.

This article focuses on how teachers can incorporate presenting role models to deaf children in specific studies.

Few would disagree with the idea that adding Deaf Studies to the teacher-preparation adds richness to the curriculum as well as better train teachers to work with K-12 deaf children and youth. But few teacher-training colleges and universities have the resources to provide more than an introductory course in Deaf Studies. Boston University, California State University at Northridge (CSUN) and Gallaudet University were pioneers by being the first degree granting institutions providing the Bachelors degree in Deaf Studies (Katz, 2001). Now Gallaudet University offers a Masters degree in Deaf Studies.

In Beaumont, Texas, Lamar University's Deaf Studies and Deaf Education MA and Ed.D. program implements many projects with the government grant.

This year, the Dishman Art Museum is showing more than 40 works of art by eight Deaf artists from around the country as part of the Deaf Artists in the Community and Schools project, which delves deeply into the culture, the inspiration and the drive behind the artists desire to create. After five years of planning, the dream of the exhibit became reality.

Jean Andrews, professor of Deaf Studies and Deaf Education at Lamar University, said:

> Artists typically work in isolation. This exhibit provides a forum for Deaf artists to discuss their work with each other as well as discuss Deaf art with an audience from the university and local community, including the Deaf community. It will also involve K-16 students-both Deaf and hearing-viewing the work.

Selected artists are Ann Silver of Seattle, Washington; Randy Garber from Boston, Massachusetts; Susan Dupor from Lake Geneva, Wisconsin; Uzi Buzgalo from Superior, Colorado; Paul Johnston from Laurel, Maryland; Chuck Baird and Tony McGregor from Austin, Texas; and Alex Wilhite of Houston, Texas.

The project allows the artists to make presentations about their work, giving the audience a unique opportunity to learn the artists' perspectives about being a Deaf individual using visual art to communicate.

Brenda Schertz, professor of Deaf Studies at the University of Southern Maine, who has curated five national Deaf Artists exhibits and led the panel discussion with the Deaf artists at the Dishman Art Museum, said:

> Deaf Art expresses the values of Deaf Culture: the beauty of sign language and its oppression, the joys of Deaf Bonding, communication breakdowns, the discovery of language, community and the history of Deaf people.

The project — a DVD production — will add long-term educational benefit to the program. The resulting documentary of the exhibits and dialogues produced by graduate students in Art and in Deaf Education will be distributed to the 60 schools for the deaf nationwide free of charge and to an additional 1,000 mainstream programs in Texas for their Art education curriculum. The multimedia product will document the events signed in ASL and captioned in English, with animation, graphics, and digital photographs. A website for teachers and students will be created to allow sharing the artworks, and a teacher's guide will be available to assist teachers in creating similar projects. (Wilhite, 2008)

At these universities, which have a specific Deaf Studies department, the Deaf Education faculty invites Deaf Studies experts to incorporate material from Deaf Literature and ASL Literature into the teacher-preparation curriculum. Deaf Studies courses can be found in other disciplines, such as education, interpreter training, vocational rehabilitation, social work, psychology, nursing, special education, etc. Most sign language classes also incorporate Deaf Studies components. (Katz, 2001)

In contrast, there are more than sixty colleges and universities that primarily enroll hearing students and that offer degrees in Deaf Education for pre-service teachers. Many of these colleges and universities have good libraries with Deaf Culture resources. However, they lack the Deaf Studies specialized faculty to actually teach courses in ASL and Deaf Literature.

The situation is even more critical in public schools and in Deaf Education. Most teachers in K-12 Deaf Education have obtained their degree from one of the hearing universities we previously discussed. As one of the surveys revealed, in schools, Deaf Culture, Deaf Role models, Deaf History, Deaf Art and Literature are rarely incorporated in the Deaf Education curriculum. (Ausbrooks, 2006) This survey is not comprehensive due to the limited sample of schools that accepted to respond to the survey. The same survey would have to test more than half of the size of the deaf community in an area for its results to be conclusive. The survey was answered by 53 current or former graduate students from Lamar University, Deaf Education. 84% of these students are Deaf. Additional bias on the results of this study is also due to the fact that most of the students have similar areas of studies.

In sum, up until now, the responses to this survey lead to the conclusion that more than 50% of the respondents have had no introduction and no exposure to ASL as a language, ASL Literature, including poetry, Deaf Role Models, Deaf Art, Deaf History or, generally, Deaf Culture.

However incomplete and/or biased this survey may be for the time being, as research progresses, children grow up and incorporating more components of Deaf Culture in their school curriculum is only going to better their conscience of the Deaf World, their self-esteem and their confidence. (Ausbrooks, 2006)

Teachers need to be aware that the school library will discard books that are not regularly checked out, due to their limited storage capacity. It is recommended by the authors that teachers keep these special books on reserve or in classrooms to use in teaching deaf children.

School principals require teachers to post homework online, on the school's website. This is an opportunity for teachers to reference websites containing information about Deaf role models and integrate these links in the homework website. Students then will be trained to access the links, search and find this information. This would be an ongoing project for students to find new pictures and links. Parents are free to explore the websites for their own information.

Here are some suggestions concerning the links to websites that contain Deaf culture, studies, history, art and literature information. One word of caution, though, the websites are not permanent. Their content changes and, sometimes, the links become unusable. The best way is to keep the links updated, and to keep searching for new links.

ROLE MODELS AROUND THE GLOBE

On google.com, in the Image search engine, type: "deaf in (country)" to find images related to deaf people in different countries. Clicking on the image will open the website where the image was found, students can then learn more information and find other resources referenced in the website (e.g. books). For example:

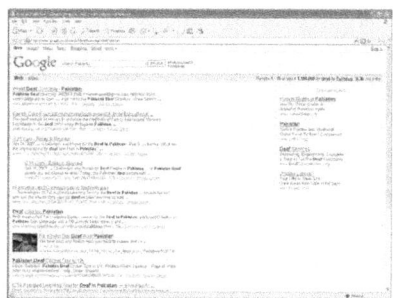
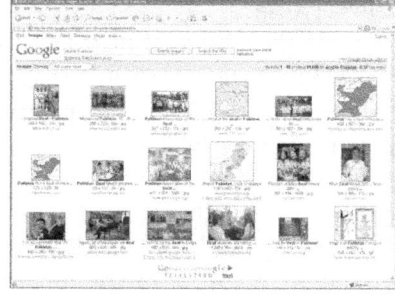

Figure 1. Google search results for "deaf in Pakistan"

Figure 2. Google image search results for "deaf in Pakistan"

ROLE MODELS IN POLITICS

Jean-Ferdinand Berthier, 1803–1886, was an intellectual Deaf Parisian. He unified the French deaf community by setting up a Society of Deaf Parisians.

A google.com image research on keywords "Ferdinand Berthier" shows that Berthier planned and hosted a banquet on November 28, 1886, to celebrate Abbé de l'Epée's 74th birthday and unveil l'Epée's bust.

Figure 3. Ferdinand Berthier

Figure 4. Lithograph of the banquet on November 28, 1886 (Moody, 1987)

When deaf children are first exposed to a picture like the banquet pictured above, and then asked "Are the people in the picture deaf or hearing?," ninety-nine percent responded "hearing." Deaf children are often not exposed to social events where there are numerous deaf adults.

ROLE MODELS IN MATHEMATICS

Oliver Heaviside (1850-1925), British electrical scientist, invented vector and operational calculus a mathematical process to obtain solutions of differential equations. Olof Hanson (1862–1933) was the first deaf architect. A list of building plans attributed to Hanson includes homes, churches, schools, and institutional buildings. He opened his own architectural practice in Faribault. Newspapers note that he also supervised the construction of Faribault's Central and High Schools on 1024 Marshall Avenue in Classical Revival style.

Figure 5. Oliver Heaviside

Figure 6. Olof Hanson

Figure 7. Architectural works by Olof Hanson

ROLE MODELS IN LITERATURE

Laura Redden Searing (1840–1923) used the pen name of Howard Glyndon as a Civil War journalist. She also wrote poems (Moore & Panara, 1996). Doug Bullard wrote the novel *Islay*. He is the first Deaf author to write a novel about deaf experiences. He chose to combine a variety of methods using English and glosses of ASL signs (The New York Times, 1987). Helen Keller, of course, was the famous deaf-blind author who wrote of her introspective views on life.

Figure 8. Laura Redden Searing and her biography *Sweet Bells Jangled*

Figure 9. Doug Bullard

ROLE MODELS IN SCIENCE

There are several Deaf scientists listed in the Lang & Lang biographical dictionary for various scientific fields (Lang & Meath-Lang, 1995). Ruth Fulton Benedict (1887–1948) was a Deaf anthropologist and is the founding member of The Institute for Intercultural Studies in New York. In 1934 she published *Patterns of Culture* which became an American classic. Robert Grant Aitken (1864–1951), Deaf astronomer, described over 3000 binary systems and published in 1932 the comprehensive work *New General Catalogue of Double Stars Within 120° of the North Pole*.

Figure 10. Ruth Fulton Benedict   Figure 11. Robert Grant Aitken

ROLE MODELS IN MEDICINE

Frank P. Hochman is the first known Deaf physician. He wrote Breaking New Ground in Careers for the Hearing Impaired for the Edmund Lyon Memorial Lectureship Presentation at National Technical Institute for the Deaf in 1986.

 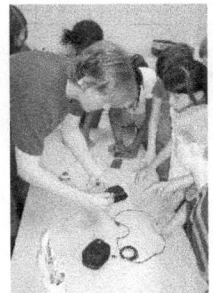

Figure 14. Frank P. Hochman   Figure 15. Michael McKee

ROLE MODELS IN SPORTS

Curtis Pride broke all county records in for soccer, basketball, and baseball by the age of 15. He joined the Detroit Tigers as a baseball player in 1996. These pictures mean a lot to deaf children when they see Curtis wearing a hearing aid. LeRoy Colombo, was a Deaf lifeguard in Galveston, Texas from 1905–1974 who saved 907 lives! He worked for forty years as a lifeguard and continued to swim in competitions throughout his life, for which he received numerous awards. But the most important thing he accomplished by far was to save a whopping 907 lives! He was formerly listed in the Guinness Book of World Records when lifeguarding was a category.

Figure 16. Curtis Pride   Figure 17. LeRoy Colombo

Frances Woods, ballroom dancer (1907–2000), performed several shows with Anthony Caliguire in Broadway shows. They were called "The Wonder Dancers" and won recognition from the Governor of Ohio for their contribution to dance.

Figure 18. Google Image and Search Results for "Frances Woods"

DEAF AFRICAN-AMERICAN ROLE MODELS

Andrew J Foster (1925–1987) was the first African-American enrolled at Gallaudet College in 1951. By studying the year around (regular term at Gallaudet and summer sessions at Hampton Institute) he earned a Bachelor of Arts degree in education in three years. After graduation he went to Africa and established schools for the deaf there.

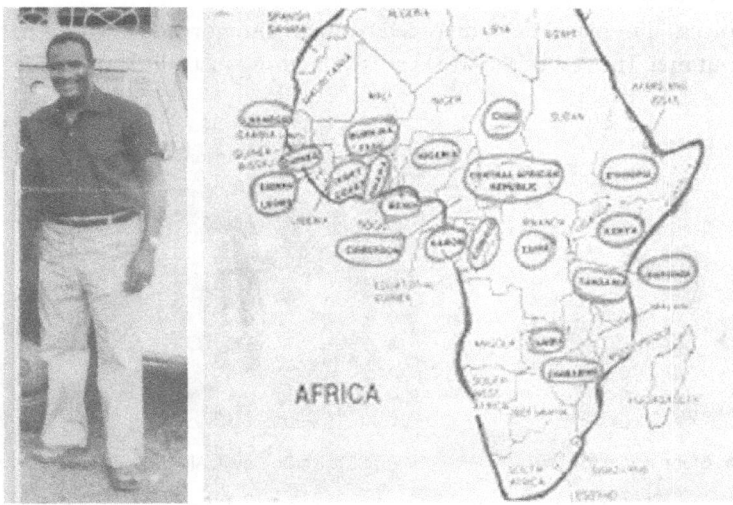

Figures 19-20. Andrew J Foster

During an interview, Foster explained that:

> The deaf in Africa had long been a concern to me. While pursuing the business course, it was my intention to follow that career for a few years, and then work in the same capacity for a foreign business enterprise or mission board in Africa while preaching to the deaf on the side.
>
> But shortly after graduation from the business college, I discovered that there are no schools for the deaf there, except in the politically troubled Northern and Southern portions. So, I deemed it wise to turn toward the Christian education field.
>
> I want to establish schools for the deaf in West, Central and East Africa. I've already organized a foreign mission board (it is the 'Christian Mission for the Deaf Africans,' located at 11704 Griggs).

Dr. Glenn Anderson was the first Deaf African-American male to earn a doctorate degree. Since 1982, he has been Director of Training at the University of Arkansas Rehabilitation Research and Training Center for Persons who are Deaf or Hard of Hearing located in Little Rock. He is also Professor in the University's Department of Rehabilitation, Human Resources, and Communication Disorders. From 1983 to 2006, he served as coordinator of the M.S. degree program in Rehabilitation Counseling with Persons who are Deaf or Hard of Hearing.

Dr. Shirley J. Allen was the first Deaf African-American woman to earn a doctorate in 1992. Her dissertation focused on parental attitudes, education, and other factors that influence their deaf children's aspirations and career choices. "I'm black, deaf, divorced, woman and gorgeous: what's not to like about me? The rest of the world sees something just a little different."

Figure 16. Dr. Glenn Anderson

Figure 17. Dr. Shirley J. Allen

DEAF HISPANIC ROLE MODELS

Dr. Robert Davila, current President of Gallaudet University, is the first Deaf Latino to have received a Ph.D. in 1972. Now, he is the second Deaf President of Gallaudet University since 2007. Dr. Yolanda Rodriguez came from Puerto Rico and is the nations' first Hispanic Deaf woman to earn a doctorate in Deaf Education from Lamar University in Texas in 2001.

DEAF ASIAN ROLE MODELS

Ying Li, Ed.D, is the first Chinese national to receive a doctoral degree in Deaf Studies/Deaf Education at Lamar University, and the first Asian Deaf doctoral graduate.

Figure 23. Dr. Robert Davila

Figure 24. Dr. Yolanda Rodriguez

Figure 26. Dr. Ying Li

ROLE MODELS IN THEATRE

One of the founders in the 1960's of the National Theater of the Deaf (NTD), a deaf actor, director, playwright and lecturer, Bernard Bragg is internationally recognized as a leader in the deaf entertainment industry. In 1956 in Paris, he studied with Marcel Marceau, universally acclaimed as the world's greatest mime. Currently, Bragg is involved in his twelve-city tour with his new one-man show called *Theatre in the Sky* helping raise funds for the NAD and WFD.

Phyllis Frelich is best known as the 1980 Tony Award winner for her portrayal of Sarah in Mark Medoff's *Children of A Lesser God*, and for her Emmy-nominated role as Janice in the 1985 Hallmark Hall of Fame film, *Love is Never Silent*.

Figure 27. Bernard Bragg

Figure 28. Phyllis Frelich

Figure 29. Michelle A. Banks

Figure 30. CJ Jones

Figure 31. Adrian Blue

A native of Washington, DC, Michelle A. Banks is an award-winning actress, writer, director, and producer. Her most recent theatrical appearance includes Big River at the Mark Taper Forum in Los Angeles, CA and at Ford's Theatre in Washington, DC. As a Christopher Reeve Acting Scholarship awardee, Ms. Banks has performed her one-woman show, *Reflections of a Black Deaf Woman* in Los Angeles and Burbank, California as well as throughout the United States.

Having appeared on Broadway stage, in television, video, and on the big screen, CJ Jones, has experienced what he calls the "double whammy" of being an actor who is both deaf and black. CJ vigorously spreads the message to students and adults alike, that being different does not mean being less worthwhile.

Adrian Blue, playwright and director, has performed with the National Theater of the Deaf and has been a consultant throughout the United States on American Sign Language interpretation in the theater, on film, and in television.

ROLE MODELS IN DEAF ART

A new movement of Deaf artists known as De'VIA (Deaf View Image Art) was established at a four day workshop in 1989 at Gallaudet University and presented at Deaf Way 1989.

Figure 32. Betty Miller

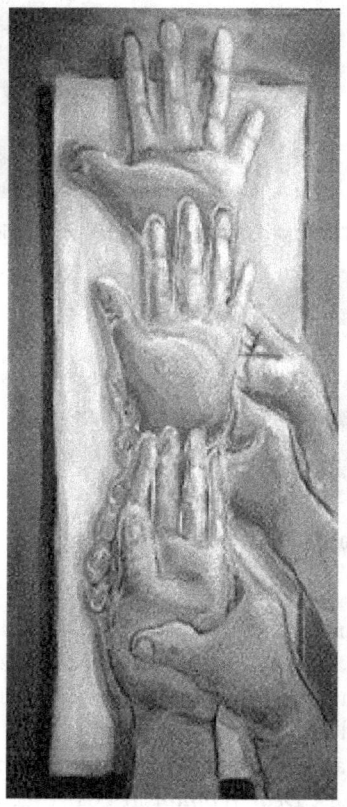

Figure 33. Betty Miller, "Growing with ASL"

Betty Miller is primarily known for her visual representation of her Deaf experience, some of which has been published in *Deaf Heritage* by Jack Gannon (1980). Dr. Miller has become increasingly interested in neon as a medium for her artwork.

Figure 34. Ann Silver   Figure 35. Ann Silver, "Deaf Identity Crayons: Then and Now"

Ann Silver expresses political protest and highlights cultural sensitivity through modifications to such familiar graphic symbols as road signs, license plates and brand name product packaging. She likens the medical and pathological views of Deaf people to the archaic labels of the older style box of crayons in *Deaf Identity Crayons: Then and Now*:

Paul Johnston was the first deaf student to receive a Bachelor of Fine Arts degree (BFA) in Furniture Design and Woodworking from the internationally-known School for the American Craftsmen at the Rochester Institute of Technology (RIT). While at RIT, he studied Deaf Culture and Deaf Literature, courses taught by two terrific professors, Dr. Loy Golloday and Dr. Robert Panara. He also studies Drama, and performed with his close friend, Chuck Baird. Johnston graduated from Penn State University with an Master of Science degree in Art Education, with a minor in Sculpture (1980); and Doctorate in Art Education, with a minor in Philosophy (1988).

After seeing all these pictures, even no more than in this article, imagine a deaf child, who arrives to school everyday, and sees these personalities displayed in the classroom everyday. The feeling of "ability" and "normality" that children experience every time they watch these images will lead them to imprint in their conscience the "can do" attitude.

Also, seeing the pictures, if these pictures are also included in the children's regular homework, their own research of information will lead them to start the process of Deaf identity development. Another influence of these homework assignments and projects will manifest on the children's parents in the sense that they will learn about the Deaf Leaders and how their deaf child is not "impaired" but culturally different, based on the research findings presented in *Deaf People* by Andrews, J., Leigh, I. and Weiner, M. (Andrews, Leigh, & Weiner, 2004)

Figure 36. Paul Johnston

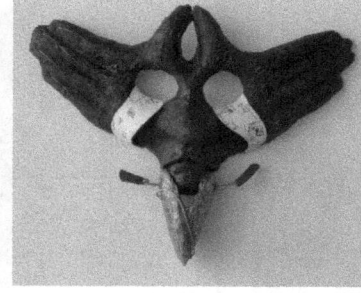

Figure 37. Paul Johnston, "Handscape Mask"

CONCLUSION

Today, more than 80% of deaf children are educated in public school where they might not get an opportunity to learn about their Deaf Culture until they are older and go into their adult Deaf Community.

A more Deaf World conscientious initiative of Deaf Education teachers and of teachers who have deaf children in their mainstreamed classes would be beneficial to deaf children to promote affirming positive self-image, to raise their self-esteem and to help them build a strong Deaf identity.

One cannot imagine not showing the picture of Martin Luther King to a black child. In the same way, one should not imagine that deaf children do not need Deaf Role Models. Deaf children can have better academic achievements and become successful in any career they choose.

REFERENCES

Andrews, J., Leigh, I., & Weiner, M. (2004). *Deaf People: Evolving Perspectives from Psychology, Education, and Sociology*. Boston, Massachusetts: Pearson Education, Inc.

Ausbrooks, M. (2006). *Where's the Deaf in Deaf Education? Building the Case for Curriculum Revitalization*. Beaumont, Texas: Lamar University.

Erikson, E. (1972). Eight Ages of Man. In C. Lavatelli, & F. Stendler (Eds.), *Readings in Child Behavior and Child Development*. San Diego, California: Harcourt Brace, Jovanovich.

Joubert, J. (2005). *The Notebooks of Joseph Joubert*. New York: The New York review of Books.

Katz, C. (2001). A History of the Establishment of Three Bachelor of Arts Degrees Granting Deaf Studies Programs in America. Ph.D. diss. Beaumont, Texas: Lamar University.

Lang, H., & Meath-Lang, B. (1995). *A Biographical Dictionary: Deaf Persons in the Arts and Sciences*. Westport, Connecticut: Greenwood Press.

Moody, W. (1987). Berthier, Jean-Ferdinand (1803–1886). In J. V. Van Cleve (Ed.), Gallaudet *Encyclopedia of Deaf People and Deafness* (Vol. 1, pp. 141–143). New York: McGraw-Hill Professional.

Moore, M. S., & Panara, R. F. (1996). *Great Deaf Americans* (2nd ed.). Rochester, New York: MSM Productions Ltd.

Piaget, J. (1929). *The Child's Conception of the World*. New York: Harcourt, Brace.

Polat, F. (2003). Factors Affecting Psychosocial Adjustment of Deaf Students. *Journal of Deaf Studies and Deaf Education*, 8 (3), 325-339.

Stiemert-Strecker, S., Teuber, K., & Seckinger, M. (2000). Partizipation, Empowerment und Qualität in der Psychosozialen Arbeit. In K. Teuber, S. Stiemert-Strecker, & M. Seckinger (Eds.), *Qualität durch Partizipation und Empowerment. Einmischungen in die Qualitätsdebatte*. (pp. 35–53). Tübingen, Germany: DGVT-Verlag.

Texas Legislature. (2008). § 29.307. Role Models. Retrieved May 4, 2008, from Education Code 1995. Chapter 29. Subchapter A. Special Education Program.: http://tlo2.tlc.state.tx.us/statutes/docs/ED/content/htm/ed.002.00.000029.00.htm#29.008.00

The New York Times. (1987, November 29). Deaf Writer Asks Questions That Echo for Young. Retrieved May 4, 2008, from The New York Times: http://query.nytimes.com/gst/fullpage.html?res=9B0DE0D6103DF93AA15752C1A961948260

Vygotosky, L. (1978). *Mind in Society: The Development of Higher Psychological Processes*. Cambridge, Massachusetts: Harvard University Press.

Whitworth, S. (2008, March 28). Personal Communication at Lamar University. (K. Weldon, Interviewer) Beaumont, Texas.

Wilhite, A. (2008, April 3). Announcement. Email to Brian Kilpatrick.

A Silent History: Giving Voice to the African American Deaf Experience in the Northwest[1]

HEATHER CLARK

MY RESEARCH EXPLORES HOW INDIVIDUALS WHO ARE BOTH DEAF AND African American[2] navigate their many identities. For some of these individuals finding a place to belong is a process of negotiation. I explore the following questions: where do individuals who are African American and Deaf find and make community? To which communities do they perceive they belong? Is their primary identity African American, Deaf or something else? Does belonging to one community conflict with membership in another?

In this paper I use the Community of Practice (CofP) approach since I find that its focus on the role of practices in constituting communities useful when examining identity construction for the people I interviewed (Lave and Wegner, 1991; Bucholtz, 1999; Holmes and Meyerhoff, 1999). The CofP approach emphasizes practice, be it ways of talking, ways of doing things, or beliefs as a way to form community (Holmes and Meyerhoff, 1999). "A CofP is different from the traditional community, primarily because it is defined simultaneously by its membership and by the practice in which that membership engages" (Holmes and Meyerhoff, 1999:174). For the Deaf African Americans I interviewed it was apparent their community of practice — signing — is what seemed to create a sense of cohesion. Regional histories (including demographics, social policies, and educational practices) shape the process through which CofP becomes crucial in these individuals' identity construction. Along with regional histories and CofP, a person's age is important as it relates to the social conditions they have experienced.

There is a prevalent ideology both inside and outside academia that if one is born African American, lives in a predominantly African American community and their immediate family is African American then they would automatically belong to, feel comfortable and identify as such. The work I have done problematizes this ideology because the people I have interviewed do not prioritize their racial/ethnic background. In the most well known literature surrounding African American identity formation (Cross, 1971, 1991; Parham, 1989) disabilities in general and Deafness in particular are overlooked. Alston and Price (1996) take up the challenge of exploring the race/ethnicity and disability intersection. However, not much attention is paid to Deafness in their study. There is one person who is quoted as identifying as a "Black deaf person" (13). Once again this study reinforces the prevailing thought that African Americans who are Deaf prioritize their race/ethnicity in regard to their identity construction.

In the Deaf community there have also been few studies exploring the intersection of race/ethnicity and Deafness (Aramburo, 1989; Valli et al, 1989; Foster and Kinuthia, 2003). Aramburo's (1989) study is the most well known and frequently cited of them. Aramburo interviewed sixty individuals who were both African American and Deaf. The study was conducted in Washington D.C. with a majority of the participants from the East Coast. In this study he found that a large majority (87%) prioritized their racial/ethnic background while the remaining (13%) prioritized their Deafness over that of their racial/ethnic identity.

For those exceptional cases within the study who did prioritize their Deaf identity it was said to be a result of growing up in a Deaf family where they were actively involved in the Deaf community and/or being educated with a predominately white student body. While this may be true in Aramburo's study, I argue that there are other factors that should be examined that may lead some Deaf African Americans to identify by their Deaf identity as opposed to their racial/ethnic one. Some other factors to consider are regional/social history, population of the African American community, experiences with family (including did their family learn to communicate with them in sign language), as well as who introduced them to sign language. In my research, I have found these questions to be crucial in how people constructed their cultural identities.

In contrast to Aramburo's study of Deaf African Americans on the East Coast, I interviewed people who were born and raised in the Northwest. The demographics and history of the Northwest compared to other places in the United States are dramatically different, which can impact how a person chooses to identify. According to the former president of the Washington State Chapter of the National Black Deaf Advocates, there are approximately 2,000 Deaf African Americans in Washington State. This number is problematic because it takes into account those who were born deaf and those who have lost their hearing as a result of old age. It also does not inform us who identifies as culturally Deaf. I believe the older African American Deaf people I interviewed identify as they do in part because the African American population has been so small and at the same time discrimination practices in the Northwest were less institutionalized than in other regions of the United States.

For instance, schools were not racially/ethnically segregated in the Northwest. Due to these and other factors, the people I interviewed identified primarily by their Deaf identity as opposed to their racial/ethnic one even though they were born into and raised in an African American family. As opposed to following the prevailing expectation that their African American race/ethnicity should take precedence, these individuals identified more around their CofP — people with whom they use sign language. In the case of the people I interviewed, sign language was the practice that formed their identity and community membership as opposed to practices related to their racial/ethnic background.

DEFINITIONS

From an outsider's perspective the notion of being Deaf may be understood as simply being able to hear or not hear. However, it is not that cut and dry, and the degree to which a Deaf person has some residual hearing often surprises outsiders. There are Deaf people who are able to use the telephone or use headphones with amplification devices to listen to music. Deaf people identifying as a cultural group is something that is fairly new. It is only within the past twenty years that the debate began regarding how to label the community. The terms to label individuals who cannot hear have been contested; there is "deaf" and "Deaf" — one spelled with a lower-case d, one with a capital D. These different spellings reflect distinctions made regarding individuals who are deaf. The physical condition of not being able to hear is spelled with a lower case "d." This refers to the audiological aspects of deafness and tells us nothing about a person's cultural identity. This contrasts with Deaf spelled with a capital "D" which refers to a cultural Deaf identity, which usually involves knowledge and use of a sign language and participation in a community of other people who sign and identify as Deaf. (Padden and Humphries, 1988; Lane et al., 1996; Senghas and Monaghan, 2002).

Even though this may be the accepted convention, I recognize the two terms are fraught with problems, like most labels. Some believe there is an ideal culturally Deaf person "…It's someone who was born deaf, has deaf parents, learns [sign language] at home, goes to a deaf school…gets married to a deaf person, has deaf children" (Myers, 2006). On the opposite side of this coin is the stereotypical deaf person, seen as someone who does not support the use of American Sign Language (ASL) or ascribe to the norms and beliefs of the Deaf community. They were raised orally: they have not learned ASL, instead they learned how to read lips and voice for themselves.

Since I will be primarily talking about Deafness as a cultural identity and referring to the Deaf community, I am using the capital "D" Deaf. I am also using the self-identified labels of the people I have interviewed. I have not asked them to inform me about, nor am I interested in, their 'hearing' status. Carol Padden insightfully explains why a Deaf person's hearing status is irrelevant when referring to whether a person culturally identifies as Deaf or not: "The type or degree of hearing loss is not a criterion for being Deaf. Rather, the criterion is whether the person identifies with other Deaf people, and behaves as a Deaf person. Deaf people are often unaware of the details of their Deaf friends' hearing loss…" (Padden, 1989:8). Beyond the d/Deaf distinction, there are other ways to differentiate and evaluate people's identities. If a deaf person has more of a "hearing person's perspective" people will sign "thinks like a hearing person" (which is conveyed with the sign for "hearing" placed on the forehead). If a Deaf person has a culturally Deaf perspective and strong ties with the Deaf community they are usually referred to with the "strong deaf" or "fluent ASL" signs (Kannapell, 1989).

In regard to the term "race," anthropology has had a long and torrid relationship with this word and concept. After all, anthropology was one of the first disciplines to support the scientific notion of distinct races (Baker, 1998). Historically the reason for the distinctions was to justify the classification of different groups of people as well as to promote the enslavement of Africans: "Proponents of slavery in particular during the 19th century used "race" to justify the retention of slavery" (American Anthropological Association Statement on Race, 1998). However, since the mid-1900s the concept of different "races" has changed. Scientists have since discovered that genetically there are more differences within a "race" than there are across "races." Researchers acknowledge there are traits which distinguish one group from another that are physical in nature i.e. skin tone, and hair texture, "race does have a biological component, one that can trick us into thinking that races are scientifically valid, biological subdivisions of the human species" (Mukhopadhyay and Henze, 2003:673).

However, even with these defining biological traits the concept of "race" is now understood to be a social construction. But constructs are no less 'real' than biological ones. Thus even though "race" does not exist as a biological category, discrimination and prejudices (racism) associated with these features certainly do exist. "Historical research has shown that the idea of "race" has always carried more meanings than mere physical differences;

indeed, physical variations in the human species have no meaning except the social ones that humans put on them" (American Anthropological Association Statement on Race, 1998). In view of the fact that "race" exists as an ideological category, I use this term to refer to the social meanings that are attached to physical features. Baker (1998) traces how the discipline moved away from the term "race" and used the more inclusive term of ethnicity after the United Nations Educational, Scientific, and Cultural Organization published their statement on race in 1951. Baker says, "This movement in anthropology away from race, even as an analytical and conceptual category, led many anthropologists to use ethnicity as a chief organizing principle for exploring human diversity" (Baker, 1998:211). Ethnicity in and of itself is also a word that can be defined many ways. In my research I have found that people outside of academia most often do not use "ethnicity" when referring to which group they belong to, they use "race."

There are several debated subcategories and ways in which to define ethnicity, including primordial, situational, and instrumental. Scholars who define ethnicity as primordial posit that ethnic groups are natural extensions of biological kinship, that ethnicity has fixed elements which are "defined by the constitutive elements of language, blood and soil" (May, 2001:29). For some this definition is problematic because so many other aspects of identity are believed to be fluid. The primordial point of view does not account for the multiplicity of social groups an individual can belong to, or the historical examination needed to look at ethnic group formation, and how cultural attributes alone make up ethnicity. Situational ethnicity is yet another theoretical approach that defines ethnicity as an individual and group choice, and with fluid boundaries, unlike primordial ethnicity that is perceived as fixed. Also, in this definition the group of individuals have agency to decide its boundaries and who may be considered a member.

One critique of this definition is that it does not take into account how societal structures also play a vital part in structuring an ethnic group. Proponents of this definition also see the forming of ethnic groups as a way to mobilize for political reasons as opposed to finding a place for an individual to fit in. Instrumental ethnicity's definition extends from situational ethnicity in the sense that it is seen as a social and political resource. Proponents of the instrumental ethnicity perspective also see it as malleable. Some skepticism brought up regarding this definition is the notion that ethnicity is fictive and that people only align themselves with an ethnic affiliation depending on its utility and how it benefits the individual (May, 2001).

While to a degree ethnicity can be defined by one's kinship, for the most part it is now seen as fluid by social scientists. The concept of ethnicity does not encompass the prevalence of racist ideologies in society that treat physical appearance and biology as determinants of identity. For this reason in my mind "race" and ethnicity as separate identity markers do not encompass the complexity I am striving for, so when identifying people I have decided to combine the terms throughout this paper. In this convention when using "race" I am referring to the historical and social significance of one's physical appearance. As for ethnicity, I am referring to the fluidity this term invokes as well as recognizing the degree to which it is based on hereditary traits. While the combined term race/ethnicity may be cumbersome, it encompasses both the fluid and the physically defined aspects of identity.

THE RESEARCHER

As a researcher one always prefers to question motives and how fieldwork affects others. One of the questions always asked of an anthropologist is, how can you be objective if you have a vested interest in the community you want to work with? It is one of our struggles with because on the one hand your vested interest is what brought you to study this particular community, and on the other hand you do not want your biases to influence the outcome. My own identity has necessarily shaped how I approach my research. I have worked very hard to become aware of assumptions that might lead me to prejudge, and to hold those assumptions back; I will let people's stories and insights stand on their own while showing connections and implications of these stories.

As for myself, I racially/ethnically and culturally identify as African American; I make the distinction because this is the lens I will be looking through in regard to the issues I raise. I was born and raised in Seattle, WA. I was educated at local public schools, both for my secondary and post-secondary schooling. I am also hearing, and began learning American Sign Language (ASL) in the fall of 1994 and received my Interpreter Training Program (ITP) certificate in the spring of 2003. In some respects I am both an insider and outsider to the African American Deaf community. As a member of the racial/ethnic group I am working with, I am able to gain rapport with members of the community somewhat more easily than someone from a different racial/ethnic background. I am also fluent in ASL so there was not the common language barrier associated with some hearing/Deaf relationships. These attributes expedited my making connections with members of the Deaf community. However, I am hearing, and when I enter some Deaf environments that is the most pronounced identity marker. As a result I have to always be cognizant of my hearing privilege and the oppression hearing people have afflicted on the Deaf community. For some, I am simply another hearing person coming into the community to study and benefit from the stories and experiences of Deaf people. As a member of a marginalized group I can empathize with the members of the Deaf community because historically People of Color (esp. in Africa and Asia) were disproportionately the 'object' of anthropological study; for this reason many People of Color would prefer to reject objectification by researchers. In this way, I am an outsider; I did my very best to be attentive to my positionality and allow this to inform how I interacted with the people I interviewed.

One of the first questions a hearing person is asked when they enter the Deaf community is how you first got interested in learning ASL. Like most stories, mine is long and complicated. The most straightforward answer is that my mother is medically deaf — she cannot hear — she does not identify as culturally Deaf nor does she use ASL. I have found out this is not an uncommon predicament for individuals who are both African American and deaf. Parents want the best for their children, and they also want to give their children opportunities that were denied them. In this respect I have heard from my interviewees that parents of African American deaf children strategically choose not learn ASL nor use ASL as their mode of communication because they are aware of the inherent oppression that comes along with simply being born African American in the United States. For African American girls and women, gender adds another level of disadvantage. In the minds of some parents, the choice was made not to focus on the child's deafness because it can be changed or worked around, whereas you cannot ignore race/ethnicity or gender and the disadvantages that come along with those identities.

In middle school, I was bussed to a predominately white school that housed the Deaf and hard of hearing program; this was my first interaction with ASL. I became friends with a girl who was hard-of-hearing; she taught me some basic signs and the alphabet. After graduating from college I decided to become fluent in a foreign language and remembered how much I enjoyed ASL, so I decided to take classes at a local community college.

I have been active in the Deaf community since I started learning ASL. It was during this time I began recognizing how people in the Deaf community did not recognize race/ethnicity, at least not in the same way hearing people do. When having conversations about racial/ethnic differences in the community many people, regardless of their race/ethnicity would say, "I don't see your race, I don't see people as Black or white, I just see them as people."

This notion of colorblindness was not new for me because it came up in college; however, in college I found it an extremely offensive statement because I felt by denying to see my race/ethnicity then in essence you are denying my history, my culture and my perspective. It also meant that I was just like you, and my reactions to situations would be like yours, so if a disagreement occurred it was somehow my fault because I was looking at it from a different perspective.

When I began to notice colorblindness in the Deaf community I became compelled to look further; it seemed to me that Deaf people in essence were prioritizing their Deafness over their race/ethnicity.

METHODOLOGY

For this paper I interviewed three people, two women and one man. They were ages 50–85 years old. Two of them were born in California, and one was born in Washington State. All currently live in the Seattle area, had little to no linguistic communication with their families growing up and were raised orally. Two of the three were introduced to ASL while they were in their teens. The one man I interviewed has just recently, within the past three years at age 48, been introduced to ASL. For this reason we conducted his interview in English, while all of the other interviews were done in ASL. Each interview (see Appendix A for list of questions) lasted one hour with subsequent follow up via email for clarification. I transcribed the videotaped interviews along with a native Deaf ASL signer who is fluent in both ASL and English, to make sure I was not missing any of the nuances of the language.

After I had written transcriptions I sent them to each interviewee to get their feedback, clarification, and approval. I set up the video camera beside me and so I was not recorded with the participants. Along with videotaping I conducted archival research at the Washington State archival office. I also visited the Washington School for the Deaf in Vancouver, Washington, and at the time of my visit I was able to meet with the Alumni Director who gave me a tour of the grounds and showed me the alumni museum that was recently organized.

I have been a participant, observer, interpreter, student and friend in the Deaf community since I began learning ASL in 1994. Most of my research has been conducted with African American Deaf people ages 22–32 years old. This was the first time I had the opportunity to officially interview older individuals. Given the small sample size it is not my intention to generalize that all African American Deaf people in this age group identify the same, but I do wish to highlight the similarities I noticed with these three individuals. When I originally set out to interview a group of older individuals I created a flyer and emailed it to several people in the Deaf community. I also personally asked for recommendations from people I knew and had worked with in the past. I originally had my age limit set at 60-85 years old, but could only find one person in that age range. After a few weeks of trying to recruit participants I lowered the age range to 50 years old. Even when I lowered the age range I was only able to find two more volunteers. There was another person who was 75 years old whom I wanted to interview, but because of logistic constraints we were not able to meet. Of the supposedly two thousand individuals who fit the criteria of being deaf and African American, how many of them culturally identify as Deaf? This estimate also includes people who were born hearing but lost their hearing because of old age.

It was challenging to find interviewees who were older Deaf African Americans. When I told people what I was working on, invariably someone had a family member who did not hear but did not consider themselves a part of the Deaf community. This scenario follows the reasoning I mentioned earlier about parents deciding to acculturate their children into the hearing world as opposed to raising them with a Deaf cultural or bicultural perspective.

In interviewing Deaf African Americans, I was interested in finding out how their linguistic life history as well as how their self identification had changed over time. In pursuing my research questions I wanted to find out what language they learned first, was this language used by family members, did their race/ethnicity play a paramount role in how they identified, and which community they felt they had more of an affinity with. I wanted the interviews to be open-ended, so I basically asked each person to tell me about their life and how language has had an impact, while I paid attention to these underlying topics. I then followed up with specific questions from my list. There were several themes I noticed with the interviews such as tenuous relationships with family members, feeling isolated at home, and finding comfort in the Deaf community. I see this research as laying the groundwork for understanding issues of cultural identity formation in different segments of the Deaf community.

ETHNOGRAPHIC STORIES

For hearing African Americans, times of family gatherings foster a sense of unity and identity among members of the in-group. However, for individuals who are both Deaf and African American, this same time can be one of isolation, frustration and distance. Individuals I interviewed recalled the frustration they encountered whenever family members would gather. All of them had recollections of trying to be included but feeling as if they were a bother. Phyllis[3] recounts, "…When I was in high school I would go to family gatherings for Thanksgiving and Christmas. Everyone would be talking. I was missing conversations. So I would ask my cousin, 'what are they saying? What is everyone laughing about?' I felt like it was a hassle for them to let me in. They were just "putting up with me" and I thought this isn't fair! I just kind of dealt with the family thing." Darrel has a similar recollection, "Well, actually when I was around family gatherings I will kinda just sit down and watch cartoons all the time you know. I just don't look back cause the more I try to look back you know, I kinda break down cause I wish I was a part of them you know. Actually what I do is watch cartoons or play with my toys, or build my hobby cars just enjoy my own self."

Often out of frustration from not being included in family gatherings some of the interviewees would act out, which is a common story for many Deaf children who are not able to communicate effectively with their families. Sometimes as a last resort the child has a temper tantrum leading not only to lack of communication, but to outright antagonism (Lane, Hoffmeister, and Bahan, 1996). The biggest complaint the interviewees had was that reading lips was out of the question because they were not able to follow the overlapping speech and the many conversations happening at once.

For the Deaf African American people I interviewed living in the Northwest, family gatherings where stories were being told did not create a sense of unity and connection. If anything they felt these times created just the opposite feeling, they felt as if they were an imposition on their families. Like Darrell says, "I wish I was a part of them, you know." For everyone I interviewed, finding a language and community of people who shared that language was the paramount indicator of how they identified themselves, as opposed to the standard race/ethnicity being the crucial identity marker.

For the older group of people, race/ethnicity seemed not to matter as much, language was more salient. As Phyllis says, "I always identified as a Deaf person first. Being Deaf was the biggest part of my childhood. I was more concerned about people accepting me as a Deaf person. It was more important than having a Black identity." For Phyllis, language and acceptance of her deafness was more important than race/ethnicity or kinship in the creation of identity. Mabel recognized that being the only African American student at her predominately white school would be challenging, but being included in a community outweighed her reservations. She says, "being the only Black kid at the Vancouver school was hard but being Deaf like everyone there made it a good experience. They accepted and loved me." Love and acceptance from their families was something the interviewees did not feel.

All of them talked about how not being able to communicate effectively using sign language hindered their relationship with their family members. Phyllis shared with me her first encounter with a hearing family signing to and with their Deaf child. She went to a school friend's home to visit and her entire family signed. It was because of this experience that that she realized her own family was different and that it was possible to communicate with your family despite being Deaf. When she brought this friend to her home and they used ASL during their visit, it was the first time her family saw Phyllis use sign language, and her family simply stared while the two of them signed. However, "after she left, my family was upset I was learning ASL and felt it would ruin my speech. Moving my hands was not pretty for them." Phyllis feels as if she let her family down because she chose to use ASL as her primary mode of communication. She said, "They still show a slight disappointment that I didn't adopt the hearing lifestyle."

Darrell also told of his family's expectation that he would assimilate into the hearing culture and how learning ASL would hinder that possibility. "I feel that if my mom would have put me in the Deaf school I would have learned sign a long time ago but my mother was the type of a woman that wanted me to be involved with the hearing [community]." As a result of his mother's hope to have Darrell assimilate into the hearing community, no one in his family used ASL as a way to communicate with him. A lack of effective communication was something that Darrell spoke a lot about. He still feels very isolated from his family and before learning ASL he felt isolated from others in general. It is his belief that "communication is very important, when you don't communicate you feel lost, you feel like you never exist, you know."

Mabel also had a similar situation to Phyllis and Darrell, as her family did not use ASL at home to communicate. "My family did not learn or try to learn sign language. They never learned to sign by the time they died." It was expected that Mabel would use her voice while with her family at home; however frustrating the situation was for Mabel she did not allow it to overwhelm her because as she says, "I had the Vancouver school as my sanctuary for signing and being Deaf."

A common theme I heard time and time again during my interviews was that more than having race/ethnicity in common it seemed more important to have language as the common denominator, which follows along the lines of how a community of practice is formed and maintained. Darrell talked a lot about feeling isolated in his family because he was not able to hear that well. He said, "...I felt like I was abandoned, feel like my family didn't want to be bothered with me because I was hard-of-hearing." This feeling was in his family but now that he culturally identifies as Deaf, has been involved in the Deaf community, and is learning ASL he exuberantly explains, "Now I feel like I belong because I learned sign language and I can communicate."

Darrell is not the only person who shared how their life changed positively once they were introduced to ASL and the Deaf community. Mabel recalls arriving at the Deaf residential school and being terrified when she first arrived because she was oral and everyone around her knew ASL. But as she puts it, "My oral and Hard of Hearing friends and I slowly learned sign language together. Soon, I was able to communicate so much. My life was better." Mabel went on to tell me that while at home she did not have friends and she was not learning anything but once she became involved in the Deaf community she was able to tell jokes, she began learning and enjoying school and she was so proud when she told me that, "I was able to play basketball." All of these things most hearing children take for granted Mabel and the others cherished. For them language became the vehicle to express themselves and as a result their lives flourished. This joy at finding community through language proved more important than any sense of belonging to any racial/ethnic community.

I want to be careful and not paint a picture that the search for community and identity was over once they learned ASL and became active in the mainstream white Deaf community, because like most things identity is complex and fluid. They all spoke of feeling comfortable in the Deaf community but at times during the interview you could also see that they were ambivalent. Even though race/ethnicity was not an overriding identity marker for them and they felt comfortable in a white Deaf environment, they all mentioned the issue of being different in the Deaf community. Mabel noticed the very first day of arriving at the Deaf residential school that it was not diverse, as she says, "As the only Black kid at the school, I felt lost and lonely. I cried for my mother."

Even though this group of African American Deaf people had positive experiences in the Deaf community one cannot deny that the mainstream white Deaf community mirrors the larger mainstream hearing community with some of its discriminatory practices. Janesick and Moores (1992) declare, "Historically, blacks have not been accepted as full members of the deaf community, or actually of the white deaf community. In many large cities there have been, and continue to be, separate clubs and organizations for the deaf based on race" (53–54). On a national level, some of the major Deaf organizations and institutions did not permit African American Deaf people to join until the 1950s.

The oldest national Deaf organization, the National Association of the Deaf also did not permit African Americans to join until the mid 1900s. African American Deaf people began joining the organization and attending their annual conference; several African American delegates still felt their needs were not being addressed and as a result, they formed a separate organization. In 1982 The National Black Deaf Advocates was established, which is still in existence and very active to this day. It was not only the national organizations that did not allow African American Deaf people to join but Deaf residential schools around the country were also segregated similar to hearing public schools (Gannon, 1981; Hairston and Smith, 1983; Maxwell and Smith-Todd, 1986). On some campuses in the South, there were separate buildings, one for white and one for African American Deaf students. Consequently, even though African American and white Deaf people were raised in the same country, they have different histories (Padden, 2005). The Northwest differs from other regions and Seattle in particular prides itself as being tolerant, liberal, and accepting of all people and lifestyles. After all, there were no blatant Jim Crow laws on the books in the Northwest, there were no racial segregation policies in public schools, and Yesler Terrace (established 1939) was the first integrated public housing community in the country.

It is not that racism does not exist in the Northwest; it just reveals itself differently than in other major cities. Some say Seattle is more "passive aggressive" when it comes to discrimination, that is, discrimination has taken the form of ignoring someone or refusing service, as opposed to overt action or statements of prejudice. During the height of Jim Crow laws in the South, Seattle was not as blatant with its bigotry; one rarely saw "Whites Only" signs in store windows. However, as Quintard Taylor recounts from his research in oral history, in Seattle people recalled certain establishments refusing to serve African Americans if they were not accompanied by a white person (Taylor, 1994).

In Zane's (2001) dissertation, he also elaborates on Seattle's passive aggressive nature when it comes to discrimination. "When he [Calvin] did wander into a restaurant that discriminated, he found himself waiting in vain for service, rather than the rude 'N----r get out!' he could expect in Missouri" (30). Similarly, Mabel, one of my interviewees tells a story of being asked by a white person near campus to be her maid while she was at school in the 1940s. As the story is related to me there is no ill will or discontent on the part of Mabel towards the white person, it was just a job she had during school. I was left wondering, if Mabel did not find it offensive should I? Did this person single her out because she was the only African American girl on campus and they assumed this was the appropriate job for her? Or was it a coincidence? The only African American staff member at the time was portrayed in the school yearbook with the title of 'house boy to the superintendent.'

I highlight these examples because I want to make the point that even though the African American Deaf people I interviewed felt no disrespect from the mainstream white Deaf community, the racial biases that pervaded during this time were also evident in how African American Deaf people were treated in the Northwest. In other areas where the Deaf schools were segregated it was clear that African American Deaf people were set apart because of their race/ethnicity; however, in the Northwest that was not the case. For that reason one could be led to believe that being Deaf created an equal playing field and racial discrimination did not find its way into the community but these examples reveal this was not always true.

What intrigued me while listening to the stories of the older people I interviewed was that they still have more of a rapport with the mainstream white Deaf community than they do with the African American community. As a result of their intense affinity with the language of the Deaf community (ASL), they all prioritize their Deaf identity over that of their racial/ethnic one. This differentiates the Northwest area from many other places in the country, where individuals who are both African American and Deaf tend to identify by their racial/ethnic identity over their cultural Deaf one. The very different histories of social conditions and policies may be what led to this distinction.

For starters, the African American population has always been small in the Northwest, unlike other major cities in the country. Like I mentioned before, the African American Deaf community was not segregated during school so for the people I interviewed, deafness is what set them apart, not their race/ethnicity. Phyllis recalls attending a predominately white mainstream school and not feeling ostracized at all, "I saw other kids wearing hearing aids and I knew I wasn't alone. It felt good being with them. My elementary school was mostly white people…it never bothered me, I felt connected with them, I knew them and they treated me the same." Mabel told me about a few African American Deaf people she knew who moved to the Northwest from Texas, which had segregated schools, who were not accustomed to having a mixed group of friends. "They did not socialize with white people. I'm from Washington State and we always mixed…I was taught to love everyone, it is God's wish."

When Phyllis moved from the Northwest to attend Gallaudet University in Washington D.C. she shared with me her struggle to fit in the African American Deaf community on campus. She was at first excited to find others who shared both her racial/ethnic and cultural identities however, there was still something that kept them apart. When she tried to become involved with the African American Deaf student organization is when the differences came to a head, she told me, "[I] t was always challenging to be friends with Deaf Black people. There was a lot of competition for power because of double identities. I wasn't comfortable with that. They never quite accepted me in their community because I was too 'white.' I finally told the Deaf Blacks they'd have to accept me for who I was." She eventually left the student organization and found other friends of different races/ethnicities, of her new group of friends she said, "People call us the 'international friends' because one is Mexican and Italian and I'm Black. We've been close friends ever since and rely on each other for support." Even though Phyllis could be considered a full member of the mainstream white Deaf community, because she shared their language, she was considered to be on the periphery of the African American Deaf community because she did not practice their language style.

As a result, one can understand why this group of older African American Deaf people would prioritize their identity in such a way. It was the mainstream white Deaf community that gave them a community to belong to, and a language to express themselves. Darrell is the one who most recently was introduced to ASL and the Deaf community, I believe his sentiment is telling of those in his age group and sums up their experience very well: "I began to feel better when I'm around the Deaf community, [they are] always nice, they give me a big hug and it really feels good to be, to be around that community."

CONCLUSION

Thus far in my research, individuals I interviewed in this particular age group who are both African American and Deaf in the Northwest choose to prioritize their Deaf identity over their racial/ethnic one which is different from most findings so far. For many socio-political reasons, the hearing African American families my interviewees were raised in were reluctant to learn ASL, making effective communication with Deaf family members nearly impossible. This, in turn, leaves them with a sense of isolation and being disconnected. Once they were introduced to the mainstream Deaf community they did not simply find a place where they were accepted, they were also taught a language in which to express themselves. Additional interviews I have recently conducted with a younger group of African American Deaf people revealed both commonalities and differences with their older counterparts. This suggests that further study of various groupings within the larger African American Deaf community will help us understand the dynamics of identity construction. I look forward to continuing work with the various groups involved to understand the dynamics of language and identity. Further research into the cultural identity construction among African Americans who are Deaf can tell us a great deal about the role of language and communication and what affects how identity and community are defined. This research can also teach us about how diversity can be better embraced within the mainstream white Deaf and hearing African American community.

ENDNOTES

1. Earlier versions of this paper were presented at the American Anthropological Association's 105th Annual Meeting and the Association for African American Historical Research and Preservation's 4th Annual Conference. I would like to thank Laada Bilaniuk for her assistance with editing and revising the many drafts of this paper to help me get to this point. Funding for this research is from the National Science Foundation Graduate Research Program.
2. I am defining African American/Black as individuals who were born in the United States, have African ancestry, and self identify as African American or Black. I will be using the two terms interchangeably throughout this paper.
3. All names have been changed.

APPENDIX

Range of Interview Questions

- "What was the first language you learned to communicate with?"
- "Was this the language you used in the home with family members? If not, what type of communication did you have in your home?"
- "Do you feel that language was a barrier in communicating with family members and friends?"
- "What language was used in the school you attended?"
- "Has the language you use with your family members has changed?"
- "How do your family members and friends communicate with members of the communities you belong to?"
- "Is language still a barrier with your family members and friends?"
- "Do you feel that the language you were raised with has shaped your identity?"
- "How has the language you use been perceived by the different communities you belong to?"
- "Are there negative or positive reactions? Is language the primary way you identify with other communities?"
- "Does your ethnicity play a paramount role in how you identify?"
- "In the Deaf community do you notice different ways people use sign language?"
- "Do you use different styles of signing when you are in the mainstream Deaf community as opposed to with family and friends?"

REFERENCES

Alston, Reginald J., Sonja Feist-Price and Bell J. Tyronn. "Racial Identity and African Americans with Disabilities: Theoretical and Practical Considerations." In *Journal of Rehabilitation.* 62.2 (1996): 11-15.
American Anthropological Association. "American Anthropological Association Statement on "Race" Page." http://www.aaanet.org/stmts/racepp.html (accessed Feb. 18, 2007).
Aramburo, A.J. "Sociolinguistic Aspects of the Black Deaf Community." In *The Sociolinguistics of the Deaf Community.* Edited by C. Lucas, 103-122. New York, NY: Academic Press, 1989.
Baker, Lee D. *From Savage to Negro: Anthropology and the Construction of Race, 1896-1954.* Berkeley: University of California Press, 1998.
Bucholtz, Mary. "Why be Normal?: Language and Identity Practices in a Community of Nerd Girls." In *Language and Society* 28 (1999): 203-223.
Cross, William E. Jr. "The Negro-to-Black Conversion Experience: Toward a Psychology of Black Liberation." In *Black World* 20.9 (1971): 13-27.
Cross, William E. Jr. *Shades of Black: Diversity in African-American Identity.* Philadelphia: Temple University Press, 1991.
Foster, Susan and Waithera Kinuthia. "Deaf Persons of Asian American, Hispanic American, and African American Backgrounds: A Study of Intraindividual Diversity and Identity." *Journal of Deaf Studies and Deaf Education* 8 no. 3 (2003): 271-290.
Gannon, Jack R. *Deaf Heritage: A Narrative History of Deaf America.* Silver Spring: National Association of the Deaf, 1981.
Hairston, Ernest and Linwood Smith. *Black and Deaf in American: Are We that Different.* Silver Springs: T.J. Publishers, Inc., 1983.
Holmes, Janet and Miriam Meyerhoff. "The Community of Practice: Theories and Methodologies in Language and Gender Studies." In *Language in Society* 28 (1999): 173-183.
Janesick, Valerie J. and Donald F. Moores. "Ethnic and Cultural Considerations." In *Toward Effective Public School Programs for Deaf Students: Context, Process, and Outcomes.* Edited by Thomas Kluwin, Donald F. Moores and Martha Gonter Gaustad, 49-65. New York: Teachers College Press, 1992.
Kannapell, Barbara. "Inside the Deaf Community." In *American Deaf Culture.* Edited Sherman Wilcox, 21-28. Burtonsville: Linstok Press, 1989.
Lane, Harlan, Robert Hoffmeister and Ben Bahan, Eds. *A Journey into the DEAF-WORLD.* San Diego: Dawn Sign Press, 1996.
Lave, Jean and Etienne. *Situated Learning: Legitimate Peripheral Participation.* Cambridge and New York: Cambridge University Press, 1991.
Maxwell, M. and S. Smith-Todd. "Black Sign Language and School Integration in Texas." In *Language in Society* 15 (1986): 81-94.
May, Stephen. *Language and Minority Rights.* Harlow, Essex, England: New York: Longman, 2001.
Mukhopadhyay, Carol and Rosemary C. Henze. "How Real is Race?: Using Anthropology to Make Sense of Human Diversity." In *Phi Delta Kappan* 84 no 9 (2003): 669-678.
Myers, Bill. "Gallaudet President-Select Answers Her Critics." *The Examiner* [Washington D.C.] May 11, 2006, sec. 4.
Nagel, Joane. "Constructing Ethnicity: Creating and Recreating Ethnic Identity and Culture." In *Social Problems* 41 (1994): 152-176.
Padden, Carol and Thomas Humphries. *Deaf America: Voices from a Culture.* Cambridge, M.A.: Harvard University Press, 1988.

Padden, Carol and Thomas Humphries. "The Deaf Community and the Culture of Deaf People." In *American Deaf Culture*. Edited by Sherman Wilcox, 1–16. Burtonsville: Linstok Press, Inc., 1989.

Padden, Carol and Thomas Humphries. *Inside Deaf Culture*. Cambridge, M.A.: Harvard University Press, 2005.

Parham, T.A. "Cycles of Psychological Nigrescence." In *The Counseling Psychologist* 17 (1989): 187-226.

Senghas, Richard J. & Leila Monaghan, "Sign of Their Times: Deaf Communities and the Culture of Language. *Annual Review of Anthropology* 31 (2002): 69-97.

Taylor, Quintard. *The Forging of a Black Community: Seattle's Central District, from 1870 through the Civil Rights Era*. Seattle: University of Washington Press, 1994.

Valli, Clayton, Ruth Reed, Norman Ingram, Jr. and Cecil Lucas. "Sociolinguistic Issues in the Black Deaf Community." In *The Sociolinguistics of the Deaf Community*. Edited by C. Lucas, New York, NY: Academic Press, 1989. 42-66.

Zane, Jeffrey Gregory. "America, Only Less So?: Seattle's Central Area, 1968-1996" PhD diss., University of Notre Dame, 2001

The Unity for Gallaudet Protest and the Emergence of Visual Rhetoric in ASL Vlogs: The Medium and the Message

PAMELA R. CONLEY, PATTI DURR, & STEPHEN JACOBS

IN 1913 GEORGE VEDITZ STATED "IT IS MY HOPE THAT WE ALL WILL cherish and defend our beautiful S-I-G-N-L-A-N-G-U-A-G-E" in one of the films organized by the National Association of the Deaf. Ninety-five years ago, Veditz campaigned for filmed records of Deaf events, performances and day-to-day life to in order to aid in that goal. His dream was limited by the motion picture film technology and the expertise required that were available at that time. Even if there had been widespread access to motion picture cameras, it would have been difficult for the Deaf community to mass produce and distribute those films. Fortunately the films were circulated and later preserved.

With the comparatively recent arrival of high-bandwidth Internet connections to the home, near ubiquitous video editing capabilities on personal computers and inexpensive webcams, the U.S. Deaf Community has achieved a new level of communication and expression. For the first time it is possible to easily distribute messages in ASL for personal expression and/ or public discourse by creating video blogs, or vlogs. In 2006, the phenomenon of ASL vlogging gained momentum as community members on-the-ground and around the world documented and/or reacted to the Unity for Gallaudet Now protests. They initially watched pioneering vloggers contributing their perspectives about the political commotion at Gallaudet and eventually some of them went on to become established vloggers. The numbers of DeafRead viewers skyrocketed on October 13, 2007 when the arrests of protestors were made.

According to blogger Tayler Mayer, DeafRead received over 44,000 pageviews in three hours on Black Friday. Vlogging amongst the Deaf has continued to grow rapidly since; According to one DeafRead statement, 2,243 vlogs were published by July 10, 2007. Currently, over 900 vloggers are members of the DeafVideo.TV forum, a new subsidiary of DeafRead.

DEFINITION OF DIFFERENT FORMS OF RHETORIC:

Spoken/Written Rhetoric

One definition of rhetoric, generally applied to written and spoken argument, is "using language effectively to please or persuade," according to wordnet.princeton.edu. This form of rhetoric originated in ancient Greece, but has been widely practiced in many other languages, including English in the United States. Abraham Lincoln's "Gettysburg Address," a sobering dedication to the Civil War dead with a critical message delivered in 1863 and civil rights leader Martin Luther King's "I Have a Dream" speech delivered on the steps of the Lincoln memorial 100 years later are powerful examples of spoken rhetoric taught to most school children in the United States.

Why isn't anything anyone says spoken rhetoric? Rhetoric is often rich in metaphor and idiom. It often uses spoken rhythm, quotes from classical literature and other sources and/or repeated phrases to help emphasize the speaker's point.

In the Gettysburg address Lincoln says "But, in a larger sense, we can not dedicate — we can not consecrate — we can not hallow — this ground. The brave men, living and dead, who struggled here, have consecrated it, far above our poor power to add or detract. The world will little note, nor long remember what we say here, but it can never forget what they did here" (Abraham Lincoln Online). He uses three words with related meanings and pauses between them for emphasis and points out that deeds are greater than words. (Though in this case, Lincoln was wrong about our memory of his speech.) King's "I Have a Dream" speech uses all the techniques mentioned above. He makes reference to the Gettysburg Address by starting his speech almost identically. He compares the Declaration of Independence to a "bounced check" when it comes to the promise of equality for all men. He repeats the phrases "I have a Dream" and "Let Freedom Ring" to emphasize his points (Carson and Shepard).

These types of uses are what make the work of a rhetorical speaker or writer different than someone who just writes or speaks to express an opinion, talk about their day or have a simple conversation.

Visual Rhetoric

Visual rhetoric is defined as "using visual images (static or moving) to convey cultural meaning for the purpose of persuading an audience." Visual rhetoric can be found in media from Russian political posters to television commercials to motion picture films and everything in-between. Use of familiar corporate styles or logos, combining text and image, using multiple images with subtle alteration, all of these and more can be tools of visual rhetoric. For example, Figure 1 contains a photo found in Adbusters — an image of an American flag with corporate logos on replacing the stars. The message is "Corporations own America. We should be called the United Corporations of America!"

Rhetoric in ASL
In 1972 Marshall McLuhan, the father of media studies, is said to have remarked after seeing Deaf Poet, Robert Panara perform a poem in ASL, "I can see sign language stresses the 'thingness' of things," according to Patti Durr, associate professor of Cultural and Creative Studies at National Technical Institute for the Deaf.

ASL is a visual language that includes static and moving images and grammatical structures encoded within the language itself. ASL also uses body language and facial expressions to add emphasis and finger-spelled words from English to broaden visual vocabulary and add terms not native to ASL. Thus ASL has the potential to combine the properties and the power of both spoken/written rhetoric and visual rhetoric. ASL activists like Ella Lentz and MJ Bienvenu use ASL for the purpose of formally communicating to their audiences. In other media Deaf artists such as Chuck Baird, Susan Dupor, Betty G. Miller and cartoonist Maureen Klusza use both visual rhetoric and ASL rhetoric in their work, See Figures 2-4.

VLOGS AND THE DEAF COMMUNITY:

Steven Holtzman in "Don't Look Back" notes that the advent of the Internet has broken down the barriers imposed by the elite few. Even though the major milestones in the history of mass media (press, radio, and TV) show the benefits of bringing stories to the masses, they still reveal a serious obstruction. For every few stories selected by media producers and paper publishers for public access, numerous stories were rejected. Fast forward to today. It is now possible for ordinary people wishing to share their stories to "self-publish" and make them public to the world.

With the advent of inexpensive, high quality cameras, video capture and editing software as standard applications bundled as part of Windows and Macintosh operating systems editing and web-based video services such as "You Tube" video blogs, or vlogs have become commonplace in the mid-

2000s. Vlogs are short, personal or performance videos, often incorporating supporting text, images, and other metadata, distributed via the Internet. Most vlogs are authored by individuals and some are collaborative efforts.

"IF YOU BUILD IT, THEY WILL COME"

The number of Deaf/ASL vlogs has exploded in the last two years. As stated earlier, over 900 vloggers gather to exchange their thoughts in the DeafRead forum. There are two major factors specific to the Deaf community that have fueled this growth.

First, while it is true for both hearing and Deaf people that availability of high bandwidth connections to the Internet have opened their home to new modes of entertainment and communication; it is specifically true for the Deaf community. Reliable Internet video has allowed members of the Deaf community to use dedicated IP video phones and video communication services such as Sorenson and Purple to make calls. As a result, more and more Deaf people have become accustomed to seeing moving images of themselves and each other in their daily experience. Such communication services have virtually replaced the TTY.

Second, the confluence of Gallaudet University politics and the blogging culture of the Internet created a unique environment that fueled the growth of a blogging/vlogging culture amongst Deaf activists and "average' Deaf citizens alike.

In May 2006, Deaf bloggers like Ricky D. Taylor of Ridorlive* and Elisa Abenchuchan of Elisa Writes* began posting a steady stream of day-to-day messages about what was happening at Gallaudet University, the world's oldest liberal arts college for the Deaf, and the dispute over its process in nominating and electing a new president, Jane K Fernandes. Prior to the announcement of the selection of the next president for Gallaudet University there was a web site created by professor Earl Parks called 9thprez,* which created a great deal of buzz and controversy when analyzing the various prospects for the post (Shapiro). Koko, the signing gorilla was even listed for comedic effect, generating a strong base of support. Previous to the protest, many students, faculty, and staff of color at Gallaudet University had raised important concerns about the lack of diversity in the three candidates in the finalist pool. They were notably concerned about the omission of Dr. Glenn Anderson, a Deaf African-American post-secondary education administrator and educator, from the finalist group. Kristi Merriweather wrote an editorial on this subject in the DeafDC.com blog site. Many others also blogged about the protest in ASL Community Journal*, DeafDC.com and other sites.

Taylor, better known as Ridor, became an overnight sensation with the Deaf community for exposing a myriad of appalling facts about the leaders of Gallaudet, while Elisa, a graduate student from Florida, delivered daily updates. Within the next few weeks, it became clear to the Deaf community outside of Gallaudet that there was serious internal strife about the recent selection of its next president. At around the same time, a coalition called Gallaudet University Faculty, Staff, Students and Alumni (GUFSSA)* maintained a website that has a collection of authoritative and powerful letters and messages from Deaf leaders, groups, and individuals across the United States and other countries in the world showing general contempt towards the Board of Trustees for not fulfilling their obligation in selecting the right president to lead Gallaudet into the 21st century. Through postings and messages exchanged by everyone, it became clear that the input of a certain campus group on candidates was suppressed. Communications from various bloggers evidenced that Irving King Jordan had been too overpowering and was grooming Jane Kelleher Fernandes for the job.

A tent city was set up on campus to visually underscore the students' objection to the presidential selection process and was led by Christopher Corrigan of Maryland. The protest continued until the last day of school. Student bloggers communicated with each other, arguing that the Gallaudet selection process was deliberately postponed until the end of the academic year, according to an article in The Washington Post dated May 14, 2006. The consummate bloggers remained focused on restoring social justice at Gallaudet; they had begun discussing plans for the following fall to continue the protest.

In July 2006, Tayler Mayer and Jared Evans produced a blog aggregator entitled "DeafRead" to continue to share updates on the protests and foster discussions during the summer, remembers Pamela Conley, associate professor of the Department of Liberal Studies at the National Technical Institute for the Deaf. This enabled Deaf people on and off campus to communicate with each other on the situation at Gallaudet. During the evening of the arrests of over 130 protestors at the 6th street entrance at Gallaudet on Friday, October 13, 2006, the DeafRead server crashed due to the high volume of traffic from Deaf people all over the globe wanting to have up-to-the-minute details of the confrontation on Kendall Green. According to an article in Washington Post in October 2006, more than 70 tent cities were set up in response to the unmerited arrests of the Gallaudet protestors.

On May 7, 2007, taylerinfomedia.com introduced a feature making it possible for Deaf people to communicate with each other in American Sign Language (ASL) in the World Wide Wed environment by adding vlog capabilities and eventually allowing for video comments as well ("Happy

Birthday, DeafVideo.TV"). The soaring interest in the "Unity for Gallaudet" (UFG) movement assured Deaf Read an avid following and introduced a large audience of the Deaf to blogging and vlogging in general. It also gave the Deaf community a collective space in which to create, express, share, reflect, analyze, criticize, and process the important events of the Unity for Gallaudet (UFG) protest.

Since then, this aggregator continues to be "the place" to go for the latest news within the Deaf community. A significant portion of culturally Deaf Americans visit Deaf Read daily, mostly to get informed and to comment but not necessarily to author and run their own blog or vlog site. DeafRead has a feature that shows the number of visitors for each of the blogs and vlogs posted in its electronic gathering place. Although the blogs and vlogs vary widely in purposes, audiences, and topics, posts that get the most clicks are on social issues that can either hinder or advance the general welfare of the culturally Deaf people. Commentators are another significant group which contributes regularly to Deaf Read; they either affirm or question about ideas, statements, evidence and actions presented by bloggers and vloggers. The changes made by Deaf Read have effectively attempted to sweep away the general institutional mentality of the 20th century with the UFG protest campaigns. The present-day Deaf community has also immersed themselves in so much virtual activity to delve into their community's past, sharing a common enthusiasm for the roots of Deaf culture.

The potential effects of Deaf/ASL vlogs on Deaf people are unparalleled. For the first time in Deaf history, Deaf people are in or take control of creating a message in ASL for mass distribution to build community, achieve collective consciousness and promote social activism. For the first time since the Little Paper Family (a group of 20th century American periodicals written by Deaf people and printed in shops at schools for the deaf for distribution to parents of Deaf children and alumni of these schools), Deaf people can be in control of the medium and the message. This time they can do it in their preferred/native language.

THE USE OF ASL IN VLOGS

In the early days of the protest most of the information was conveyed via text English in blog sites; however, vloggers quickly taped into ASL rhetoric to make impassioned, impromptu and short ASL messages to share information, raise consciousness, and garner support. Ryan Commerson, a graduate student and one of the protest leaders who was actively involved in media and examining representation, utilized a vlog site called Signcasts and invited other members of the signing community to submit short vlogs or videos to the site. In his "Continuity or Change" vlog, Commerson argued against the selection of Provost Jane Fernandes for numerous reasons: low achievement test scores, no respect for ASL on the campus, while also explaining plans to encourage another vote of no confidence in Dr. Fernandes and the board. In her combined "Gotcha, Jane!" vlog Amy Efron Cohen offered commentaries to different sound bite clips of Jane Fernandes from mainstream media outlets. Political vlogger Joey Baer in his "Afterthoughts" vlog challenged us to better understand the situation at Gallaudet and the current state of our Deaf community by asking us to convene at Deaf clubs for Think Tank meetings.

Most vloggers used a widely popular technique of simply "talking" in front of the webcam. The length of an average ASL vlog lasts five to eight minutes, varying due to a vlogger's style and the content they choose to distribute. Some vloggers produce vlogs that are to the point. On the other hand, some vloggers ramble, which causes some of their viewers to leave before they have a chance to present their ultimate point.

Then there are vloggers who attract viewers despite the duration of their vlogs. These vloggers have an aptitude for using ASL rhetoric no matter what is being talked about. Joey Baer of California is one of these vloggers. He has gained a reputation for making political messages with relevant details and examples, and generally concludes his vlogs with thought-provoking open-ended questions for his viewers to pick up in order to maintain the train of thoughts initiated by this vlogger. Baer's style is to present messages that are thought provoking for all his viewers.

Baer, then a teacher of history and now a media teacher at a school for the Deaf in California, emerged as one of the first vloggers to respond to the Gallaudet crisis. His passionate political messages, conveyed in fluent ASL, prompted other Deaf communities across the country to take appropriate action against the unfairness of the presidential selection process at Gallaudet as uncovered earlier by young bloggers.

Carl Schroeder of Hawaii is another accomplished teacher whose outcry against the Gallaudet upheaval was heard through his attention-to-the-detail and truth-seeking blogs and vlogs. Because his daughter Vivian was a student at Gallaudet, Schroeder was heavily invested in the protest. A stalwart defender of ASL, Schroeder pinned down many illogical fallacies found in speeches and actions of Gallaudet leaders about ASL.

It is now easy to produce a "signing-head" style vlog since the great majority of ASL vloggers use this technique. Viewers' expectations have been raised up a bar though. Viewers are also mindful of the amount of time they spend online. It is time to produce vlogs that are terse and inspiring.

ASL RHETORIC IN VLOGS

Future challenges for vloggers include experimenting with visual rhetoric in effort to present an effective vlog and tapping into the potential influence of sign selection and production on the formation of concepts in ASL and the film techniques on creating engaging vlogs.

Given ASL's natural cinemagraphic nature and the power of video production and dissemination today, ASL vlogs will hopefully and naturally be evolving to more sophisticated vehicles to capture the "thingness" of things that McLuhan spoke of while simultaneously using visual imagery to convey a message to incite a change or reaction.

Presently while most vlogs are still just point-and-shoot "signing-head" shots of people sharing their thoughts, ideas, dirty laundry and more, we have seen an emergence of vloggers using the traditional "signing to the camera approach" while inserting other visual rhetoric to complement and reinforce the overall message and point they are trying to make.

A huge number of visual expressions attempting to document and persuade others about the protest were posted to websites (photographs of tent cities, rallies, marches, etc, video on location almost always with commentary (see signcasts.com and bucknakedbison.com/videos and YouTube.com.) The most effective examples of visual rhetoric in regards to the UFG protest was produced by Mosdeux, a film production company formed by Wayne Betts, Jr and Chad Taylor. They produced several short and extremely creative videos in support of the protesters. "You Must Not Quit," "2,711 Miles Away," and "Let's Meet Gideon" were all artistic works with minimal use of "signing head shots" and relied heavily on visual rhetoric. Each utilized text English to bring the points home and were widely viewed and circulated while they were up online.

Just as with traditional written rhetoric, we look for three strong features to make effective visual rhetoric: V-Logos (visual logic), V-Ethos, (visual character), V-Pathos (visual emotions).

V-Logos

V-logos can be exemplified in Jack Barr's "Three ASL Brothers." Barr's brief vlog blends visual rhetoric and ASL rhetoric to achieve a powerful effect on the viewers. Using ASL, the narrator introduce us to a family, follows this introduction is a brief clip of a mother and three cochlear implanted brothers on local news, we are then referred back to the narrator who advises to pay close attention to one brother's reaction to sound when his implant is activated, we subsequently see the little boy reacting negatively to the activation, and finally, the vlog shifts back to the narrator who takes a final shot at the boys' mother, ending the vlog with a shot of her laughing. A combination of visual rhetoric and ASL rhetoric with special effects amplifies the logical impact on the viewers on the issue of cochlear implants.

Aidan Mack's "Designing A Hearing Baby" vlog is another outstanding example of the v-logos reasoning. This vlogger examines the issue of cochlear implantation from a fresh angle. In this particular vlog, she combines visual rhetoric and ASL rhetoric to argue why cochlear implantation is ineffective. Holding a live infant who is hearing, she poses a rhetorical question to her viewers. She wonders whether her audience would be non-judgmental if she had the baby's head cut open to sever his auditory nerves, causing him to be permanently deaf. The baby is placed in the scene intentionally for the impact of the political statement the vlogger is striving to make.

V-Ethos (Visual Character)
aslpride.blogspot.com provides a depiction of mountains, evoking images of tranquility and authority. In every vlog, the vlogger sits in his office with his legs up on a desk, which creates a sense of intimacy and constancy. The audience feels as though they are also there visiting with the vlogger.

V-Pathos (Visual Emotions)
The "Let's Meet Gideon" vlog produced by Mosdeux is an extended shot showing a little deaf boy named Gideon in a classroom. In this shot, Gideon narrates his future wish in ASL, revealing immediately that, like the futures of many other Deaf children, his future options for college choice may be in jeopardy due to the UFG protest, putting Gallaudet at risk for closing down perhaps for good.

Visual elements of this scene allows the audience to gain a larger perspective of what can really happen to Gallaudet and future generations of Deaf children if nothing is done to take back the social justice that has not been present at Gallaudet, a place that has historically symbolized justice, equality and respect for ASL for a significant portion of Deaf Americans, Deaf people from other parts of the world, and their supporters. The scene with the boy's narrative creates an emotional effect on the viewers.

Clearly visual rhetoric enhances Deaf ASL vlogs and as vloggers become more articulate and sophisticated with the use of the medium and advancing their message, we expect to see a greater use of visual rhetoric in vlogs. It is our hopes that the cinematic nature of ASL storytelling and narratives will also advance the actual cinematography being used to better represent the message and the medium. Given the very short length of vlogs due to size limitations, vloggers will need to learn that "less is more" sometimes and the benefits of taping into visual rhetoric to articulate their message concisely and effectively. It will also allow vloggers to "show instead of tell" more.

It is important to note that even though the events discussed in this paper happened less than three years ago many of the blog sites and videos mentioned have been removed from the World Wide Web and thus are lost to posterity. This indicates the fickle nature of the internet and its posters – "here today, gone tomorrow" seems to be rule of the day and brings with it the mixed blessing of expediency in delivering information quickly and massively while at the same time not inviting reflection and deep thought. It also endangers our ability to look back to analyze and understand what exactly took place.

The Deaf community has been said to be "one generation thick" due to the fact that 95% of Deaf people come from hearing parents. The result is that the Deaf community is often in the position of recreating itself and rediscovering its past in order to inform and shape its present and future. It was said by George Santayana, "Those who do not learn from history are doomed to repeat it" and this has played out to be true in many cases. It is our hope in the future important blogs, vlogs, and videos can be archived and preserved past the very short shelf-life that some creators may desire as these persuasive editorals and visual rhetorics have had a substantial impact on the shape and course of our history and on our collective consciousness. To disappear with the click of a delete button is a shame and leaves us at a disadvantage as a cultural and political group.

```
priceless. The N. A. D. has rendered the deaf an inestimable
service in raising this fund. Not only we American deaf, but the
deaf of England, of France, of Germany, of Italy will benefit from
them. These films are destined to cross the ocean and bring hap-
piness to the deaf of foreign lands.

          As long as there are deaf mutes we shall have signs
As long as these films exist we shall preserve our beautiful
language in its purity. I hope that you all will cherish and
defend this beautiful language as the greatest gift that God has
given us.

                    George William Veditz.
```

Figure 1: Typescript of Veditz' 1913 NAD "Preservation of Sign Language" film

As with any new technology, there is a rough period in which the citizens learn to use and abuse the medium. While vlogs/blogs served a vital importance in advancing the point of view and position of the protestors during the Unity for Gallaudet protest at a time when they often felt powerless and misrepresented in mainstream media, we have seen this very powerful potential also be used against each other. The DeafRead creators added DeafVideo.tv (deafvideo.tv) which has a great deal of potential as an agent for social change. As with any new technology, we must assess if and when it causes more harm than good and we must ensure that we use it for the greater good rather than abuse it. When we achieve this balance then perhaps Veditz's wishes can come true.

Figure 1 is an excerpt from Veditz's typed "Preservation of Sign Language" speech (courtesy of the Gallaudet University Archives); substitute the word "films" for vlog and you will see what a visionary Veditz was and what great prospects the Deaf community has for us and our prosperity. Veditz had envisioned ASL would be documented, preserved, disseminated, cherished and defended via the medium of film. With the proliferation of vlogs amongst the masses, we see Veditz's HOPE materialize geometrically.

REFERENCES

Adbusters. "Corporate Flag." 25 Mar. 2008. http://www.adbusters.org/cultureshop
aslpride.blogspot.com
Baer, Joey. "Afterthoughts." Weblog video entry. 1 Aug. 2006. 12 Mar. 2006. <http://www.joeybaer.com>
Barr, Jack. "Ugly Truth: The Three ASL Brothers." Produced by Darrell Roby. Weblog video entry. Jack's Eyes. 12 Feb. 2007. http://www.jackseyes.com/?p=61
Clouse, Barbara Fine. *The Student Writer: Editor and Critic.* 7th ed. New York: McGraw Hill, 2008.
Commerson, Ryan. "Continuity or Change." Weblog video entry. SignCasts. http://signcasts.com
de Vise, Daniel. "Deaf Advocate Blasts Arrests." The Washington Post, (16 Oct. 2006). Newspaper Source. EBSCO. RIT Libraries, Rochester, NY. 17 Mar. 2008 http://ezproxy.rit.edu/login?url=http://search.ebscohost.com/login.aspx?direct=true&db=nfh&AN=WPT259544363806&site=ehost-live>
Efron, Amy Cohen. "Gotcha Jane!" Weblog video entry. SignCasts. http://signcasts.com
"Happy Birthday DeafVideo TV With Stats and Videos." DeafVideo.TV. http://www.deafvideo.tv/video/2008/05/07/happy-birthday-deafvideotv-with-stats-and-videos
Holtzman, Steven. "Don't Look Back." *Digital Mosaics: The Aesthetics of Cyberspace.* New York: Simon and Schuster, 1997.
Huslin, Anita. "At The Tent City, Time to Pull Up Stakes." *The Washington Post*, (14 May 2006). Newspaper Source. EBSCO. RIT Libraries, Rochester, NY. 17 Mar. 2008. http://ezproxy.rit.edu/login?url=http://search.ebscohost.com/login.aspx?direct=true&db=nfh&AN=WPT001402172206&site=ehost-live.
King, Martin Luther, Jr. "I Have a Dream." Rpt. in A Call to Conscience. Ed. Clayborne Carson and Kris Shepard. New York: Intellectual Properties Management, in association with Warner Books, 2001.
"Let's Meet Gideon." Produced by Mosdeux. http://www.mosdeux.com/blog/?p=26
Lincoln, Abraham. "The Gettysburg Address." Abraham Lincoln Online. 1995-2009. 28 Mar. 2008. http://showcase.netins.net/web/creative/lincoln/speeches/gettysburg.htm

Mack, Aidan. "Designing A Hearing Baby." Weblog video entry. Reason and Enlightenment: In In the Dawn of the Deaf Renaissance. 29 Aug. 2007. http://deaffilmblog.blogspot.com

Merriweather, Kristi. "A Fictitious Protest for Fictitous Reasons." Weblog entry. Deaf DC. 14 Oct. 2006. 17 Mar. 2008 (http://www.deafdc.com/blog/guest-blogger/2006-10-14/ a-fictitious-protest-for-fictitous-reasons).

Mayer, Tayler. "Happy Birthday, DeafRead!" Weblog entry. DeafRead 11 July 2007. 19 Mar. 2008 (http://www.deafread.com/blog/?p=160).

Panara, Robert F. Personal interview. 15 July 2007.

Schroder, Carl. http://carl-schroeder.blogspot.com

Siegel, Robert and Melissa Block, hosts. "Blogs Capture, Amplify Gallaudet Protest." All Things Considered. 26 Oct. 2006. Transcript. LexisNexis Academic. RIT Libraries, Rochester, NY. 14 Mar. 2007. http://www.lexisnexis.com.ezproxy.rit.edu/us/lnacademic

Stein, Wayne, Deborah Israel, and Pam Washington. *Fresh Takes: Explorations in Reading and Writing.* New York: McGraw Hill, 2008.

Veditz, George. The Preservation of American Sign Language. 1997. Videocassette. Sign Media, Inc.

Veditz, George. "The Preservation of American Sign Language," transcription, courtesy of the Gallaudet University Archives.

URL Links No Longer Active:
9thprez.com
ASL Community Journal
Elisa Writes
Error! Hyperlink reference not valid. (gufssa.org)
Ridorlive

The Purge of Deaf Intellectuals During the Stalin Era

ARKADY BELOZOVSKY

CITIZENS OF GERMANY AND FORMER SOVIET-BLOC NATIONS EXPERIENCED great horror at the hands of 20th-century dictators Adolf Hitler and Joseph Stalin, who imposed tragedy and terror upon their countries, senselessly executing millions of people, including Deaf people. Although the Holocaust has been widely reported, there is a long overlooked era in Soviet Deaf history: the untold stories of the 35 Deaf people who were executed during Stalin's reign of terror. Although there have been unsubstantiated rumors and inaccurate details about these men and women, the stories of these 35 people have largely been untold. However, their stories *must* be shared — especially here at Utah Valley University's Deaf Studies *Today!* and at the Deaf History International Conference at Humboldt University in Berlin, Germany in 2006 — so that justice can be served.

The stories of Nazism, eugenics and sterilization during World War II are of course, forever in history books, but little has been told about the 40 million people who suffered in the Soviet Union under Stalin's regime. Intellectual Deaf Russians were also victims of Stalin's efforts to purge the country of German sympathizers or supporters. Among the executed were 35 influential Deaf people such as activists, leaders, intelligentsia, and other pillars of the community.

Before we discuss that, the most important individual involved in this research must be recognized. His name was David Gingzburgsky (Figure 1). I must emphasize that I cannot and will not take credit for the work he did; rather, I want to honor him by continuing and completing the work he started. He was the individual who first alerted me to this hidden, and almost forgotten, story of the Deaf people who suffered during Stalin's years. All this has been his work, not mine.

Gingzburgsky was born in 1914 in Warsaw, Poland, to a hearing Jewish family during the years that Poland was under Russian Empire rule (personal interview, May 29, 1999). During these days, all Jewish families were required to serve in the military, so his father was involved with the Russian Empire army and moved the family to Lugansk, Ukraine, before being sent by the communists to northern Russia, in Petrozavodsk, to operate a steel factory.

Figure 1: David Gingzburgsky (Photo from Volna, May, 1999)

Gingzburgsky became Deaf at the age of four due to meningitis in his new hometown; his family then moved so that Gingzburgsky could attend Deaf School #1 in Petrograd. There, he emerged as a very active leader among his peers. He attended the second VOG (All Russian Deaf-Mute Society) conference in Moscow as a representative of the Pioneer Communist Group, a Deaf youth leadership group from Leningrad.

Gingzburgsky witnessed the tragic turmoil and long-lasting consequences of Stalin's purge, which he shared in a personal interview with me. I first met him by chance, when I taught the first for-credit Russian Sign Language course at National Technical Institute for the Deaf in Rochester, NY. I arranged an immersion-style trip for Deaf students to Russia in May 1999. During the trip, our guide's Deaf grandmother encouraged me to take the students to the local Hillel Club, which had several Deaf people. After some deliberation, I agreed. When our group arrived, Deaf people were in a room, listening to a child of Deaf adults (CODA) lecturing. It is interesting to note that more than half of the people there, mostly senior citizens, were not Jewish; they were there purely for educational and social purposes, and to try and prevent the Jewish history and culture in Russia from disappearing.

The people there had many questions for the American students, and as we interacted with the people there, I noticed this elderly Jewish man sitting and watching me. He was scruffy-looking, resting his chin on a cane, and was wearing a heavy coat even though it was the summer. After the question-and-answer session, he beckoned for me to come closer. As I approached, he said, "I looked into your eyes, and I want to pass on some information to you." Opening up his coat, I saw that there were many papers stuffed into the pockets. He handed me a card showing the Russian fingerspelled alphabet on it, with words of support printed in Russian on the back. Gingzburgsky explained that these cards were given out at hospitals to military people, who had lost their hearing and felt desolate or despondent, in order to provide support and hope that their lives were not destroyed. Many of these servicemen joined the Deaf Society after World War II. After some interaction, I was fascinated and wanted more information, but he said I needed to come to his apartment.

As the students visited the Leningrad Rehabilitation Center (LVTS) in Pavlovsk, I visited his apartment located near the college. When I entered the musty-smelling apartment, I was stunned to see newspapers and other papers piled from floor to ceiling in every part of the dimly lit apartment. As he sat waiting for me, he began to explain about 1937.

Gingzburgsky was director of the Deaf Cultural Society from 1957 until 1963, although he had been involved with the society in different capacities, including theatre, as far back as the 1930s. During World War II, he went to work in a factory in Moscow from 1942-1946. Upon his return to Leningrad, Gingzburgsky immediately went back to the society and continued his long hours of research and work that he often paid with personal funds, including the founding of the Leningrad Deaf Museum in 1980 (located on the third floor of the Deaf Cultural Society building). He initially wanted to name the museum after the people who disappeared in 1937, but was told that it would not be a wise decision, and that the museum should to focus on general Russian Deaf history instead. He obliged, but the Leningrad VOG had looted many of his personal artifacts stored in the museum. Even so, he continued to work to bring honor to the executed and survivors, until his death in 2005. Gingzsburgsky's work is not completed, and this is where I have come in to finish his work, and to share the stories he tried to tell the world.

The Russian Deaf community's history must first be understood in order to understand the full breadth of the executions. St. Petersburg has changed its name four times, although the community has remained the same. The original name, St. Petersburg, was changed to Petrograd, then Leningrad, then back to St. Petersburg; even the name sign for each has changed, but the meaning has always stayed the same.

Figure 2 shows the first Deaf school established in Russia, located north of St. Petersburg in Pavlovsk; this school, Deaf School #1, is considered the birthplace of Russian Deaf education, and was founded in 1806, thanks to the generosity of Empress Maria Fedorovna (1759-1828), the wife of Emperor Pavel (Paul) (Gingzsburgsky, 1998). She donated her family's summer castle for the establishment of this school; however, the building eventually became too small for the school's growing needs, so the school relocated for the second time in 1810, and eventually was located on 18 Gorkhovaya Street, near a canal (Figure 3), in September 1820. St. Petersburg. Deaf School #1 has graduated a high number of Deaf intellectuals who have gone on to become leaders and important citizens.

Figure 2. The school ruins of the original Deaf School #1, donated by Empress Maria Fedorovna in 1806. (Photo taken by Arkady Belozovsky, June 2006).

Figure 3. The second location of Deaf School #1, at 18 Gorokhovaya St., St. Petersburg (Photo from St. Petersburg Deaf Museum Archive, June 2006).

Another important aspect of the Russian Deaf community was establishment of the St.-Petersburg Society of the Deaf-Mutes in St. Petersburg in 1903 by N.L. Deybner (1887–1937), a Deaf leader. In 1904, the organization was officially registered with the Minister of Internal Affairs as the St. Petersburg Union of the Deaf-Mute. When the Revolution took place and the government began to take control of different organizations and services, Deaf people decided they wanted to have their own facilities and programs. They decided to ask the government for a facility that they could use for gatherings, meetings and other purposes; the St. Petersburg Society of the Deaf-Mutes was renamed to the House of Enlightenment of the Deaf-Mutes, after the City of Petrograd donated a palace (Figure 4) in 1922, which was bequeathed to the city by Czar Nikolay II's younger brother, Grand Duke Michael Alexanderovich of Russia.

The facilities — only a portion is shown in Figure 4 — included a library, auditorium, lecture rooms, offices, a basketball court and gym, and much more. Behind the building, in the square, was where Deaf people would gather to socialize and host different events.

Figure 4. The House of Enlightenment, circa 1922. (Photo from the St. Petersburg Deaf Museum Collection, June 2006)

Figure 5. Memorial that hangs in the Deaf Cultural Society. (Photo taken by Arkady Belozovsky, June 2006).

Yet another example of how the Russian Deaf community engaged in intellectual pursuits was the 1916 establishment of *Deaf-Mute World Newspaper*. There were other local newspapers prior to this particular publication, but *Deaf-Mute World Newspaper* was the first local newspaper for Deaf people (personal interview, May 29, 1999). It is important to note that Russia's Deaf community has always had a strong emphasis upon literacy, the arts, and being self-sufficient. During those years Deaf people were repeatedly told they couldn't work at jobs because of being deaf, as a result, they established their own factories for machinery or sewing. All factory foremen, employees and other personnel were Deaf. This remarkably independent community never was an issue with the government until the Revolution took place.

The All Russian Deaf-Mute Union was founded during the first All Russian Union Session in July, 1917, in Moscow before the October Revolution. Due to the civil war taking place, the national second session meeting did not convene again until October of 1922. When the October Revolution occurred, the government required every citizen and company to strictly adhere to government laws and protocols. The Deaf community, accustomed to being self-governing and independent, found this difficult to adjust to. For that reason, the government ordered the All Russian Deaf-Mute Union to restructure the organization to be united with all independently-run organizations of the Deaf. During the organization restructure process, the Deaf activists struggled to unite together to adhere to the government laws and protocols for five years.

The Communist party helped Deaf activists to organize the Second All-Russian Conference in May 1922. But four years later, largely due to the leadership of the first Deaf elected chairperson Pavel Alekseevich Savel'ev, the All Russian Deaf-Mute Society (VOG) was founded in September, 1926 (Palenny, 2003), which was similar to America's National Association of the

Deaf. VOG had a hierarchical structure, and the House of Deaf Cultural Society, formerly the House of Enlightenment of the Deaf-Mutes, became one of its many branches, along with other organizations serving Deaf people.

VOG's sessions became known as VOG Congress, and VOG also coordinated Deaf International Friendship Connections, where Deaf VOG members corresponded with members of Deaf organizations in other countries. In 1929, at the VOG's third Congress, Germany participants were involved. Savel'ev introduced some of the German participants to Eric Tot'myanin, who then helped them forge pen pal-style relationships with Deaf Russians. LenVOG (Leningrad VOG) quickly became a model for other countries, given that Russia's programs were of superior quality and outstanding achievements. As a result, many Deaf foreigners and Deaf people from other regional parts of the Soviet Union came to visit and to study VOG's various programs: athletics, drama, the arts, academics, and so on; countries included Germany, France, Italy, the United States, Central Asia.

Many of the visitors were also ardent communism supporters. There even was a secret society called the Deaf Intellectual Communism Society, which had over 2,500 members from different countries; several members moved to St. Petersburg because of its strong Deaf intellectual community that offered programs and services. Although this society has vanished with very little information and research is ongoing, we know that this community was akin to the community that currently exists near Gallaudet University in Washington, D.C. In fact, many people have continued to stay in the area because of the proximity to a liberal arts college for Deaf and Hard of Hearing people, established as the Leningrad Rehabilitation Center (LVTS) in 1965; it is currently known as the Interregional Center of Rehabilitation for Hearing Problems (MRTS).

The international program created a ripple effect of Deaf-run organizations, and the Soviet government oversaw VOG, closely observing its structure and how Deaf people could have made such strides in their own successes without restriction. But due to the fact that the Deaf-run organizations rapidly expanded every year, the Soviet government started to become more suspicious of Deaf citizens.

In 1937, there was a dark period of time where many Deaf elite leaders disappeared at the hands of Leningrad's secret police, known as People's Commissariat for Internal Affairs, or Narodnoi Komissariat Vnutrennih Del (NKVD Troika ("triplets")). Officially, most of these people were convicted by NKVD Troika through a special court martial. The Library of Congress's Soviet Archives web site reports, "No longer subject to party control or restricted by law, the NKVD became a direct instrument of Stalin for use against the party and the country during the Great Terror of the 1930s."

Gingzburgsky's first exposure to the brutality of the NKVD came when he was at work at the Deaf Cultural Society and the secret police barged into the office of theater director Mikhail Semenovich Tager-Kar'elli (1892–1937), who founded Pantomime Theatre in 1920, to ransack through the director's belongings. The police were angry to find that the theater group had many invaluable artifacts dating back to Russian czars' reigns, such as beautifully intricate swords and outfits; this contradicted and violated the government's position in keeping things as plain and simple as possible. An appalled Gingzburgsky asked the police what they were doing, only to be told, "Shut up! Do you want to be next?" Frightened by this experience, Gingzburgsky, a strong and resilient, never spoke again of these times until 1991 at a conference. Meanwhile, renowned Deaf leaders began to disappear one by one, without much explanation or information (personal interview, May 29, 1999).

Figure 6. Participants at the Second VOG Session in 1929. The two circles show Erich Ritter (left) and William Ross (right). (Photo from personal collection).

Still, Gingzburgsky and others knew that the Deaf people who vanished had disappeared at the hands of NKVD. Figure 6 shows a group of Deaf people after the Second VOG Session in 1929 in Leningrad; on the back of this photo in Gingzburgsky's handwriting are some names of Deaf people who vanished and then were executed. During these years, especially after the Second VOG Session in 1929, some Deaf families moved from Germany to Russia citing political asylum. With the assistance of Deaf organizations, these families lived in communal apartments and were given everything at no cost. German immigrant Albert Blum, who became a pivotal character in this tragic saga later on, was a quiet, humble family man who tended to stay in the background. Some of the Deaf immigrants included Erich Ritter, William Ross, and Italian swimming medalist Roberto DeMarchi. All these families were supportive of the communist ideology because of its collective nature, which was very much similar to the collective nature of the Deaf community, and because of the provisions they received from the Deaf community.

As these families came to Russia, Nikolai Ezhov became the head of the NKVD from 1936 until 1938. During his reign, according to Stalin's Loyal Executioner: People's Commissar Nikolai Ezhov (1895–1940), at least 1.5 million Soviet citizens were arrested, with 700,000 being shot. There was a law passed on July 20, 1937 that required the arrest of all Germans involved in the defense industry. This was done at Stalin's orders, who were paranoid about the Germans' supposed involvement in espionage and sabotage against the Soviet Union. On July 25, Ezhov delivered Order No. 00439, arresting all Germans, focusing primarily on those who worked within the military, at factories or chemical plants associated with the defense industry. On August 1, NKVD's Troika unit launched an operation against kulaks (farmers and other middle-class village people) and criminals. After all, why would Germans want to move to the Soviet Union? Their immigration indicated to the government that the Germans were double agents and/or working against the Soviet government.

While these orders were being carried out, the Deaf people continued their lives on a day-to-day basis, unaware of this new change in law. Eric Michialovich Tot'myanin was the chairperson of the Leningrad Regional Chapter of the All-Russian Union Deaf Society from 1929 until his death, and a very loyal communist. He believed firmly in having new leadership or "new blood" for the new Soviet Union. He supported having Deaf people work for the government and within government standards. Yet, in what was a cruel twist of irony, Tot'myanin was among the first Deaf people executed by NVKD.

Tot'myanin was annoyed by numerous Deaf peddlers who sold paintings and postcards; he felt this made Deaf people look like beggars, especially when there was plentiful employment available. He decided to talk with the police and ask them to try and scare the Deaf peddlers into getting jobs, as part of his support for the new communist ideology. The police agreed, and visited the communal apartment where Albert Blum and many other Deaf people lived. The police, found 14,000 postcards that were used by the peddlers, but also by coincidence, unearthed some of Alexander Stadnikov's German cigarettes that included postcards featuring Hitler. This led the police to mistakenly believe that the Deaf residents were part of the German efforts against Russia, and they quickly made mass arrests, even though most of the people there had primary jobs at the factories and weren't peddlers. Alexander Stadnikov, an innocent bystander who was in the wrong place at the wrong time, was a native of Ukraine, and was one of Blum's apartment mates. He had no involvement with the Germans; he had simply chosen to enjoy some cigarettes brought to him by Blum.

Many of the Deaf people suspected Blum as the one who had falsely tipped the police, since he hadn't been arrested and had quietly disappeared. Unknown to his colleagues, Blum often traveled to Germany to pick up cigarettes for distribution, which were what the police discovered. In fact, when the police stormed the apartments, Blum was in Germany getting more cigarettes – and never returned to Russia.

Starting August 14, 1937 and lasting until November 6, 1937 (Razumov, The Returned Names), the police arrested 54 Deaf people who were interrogated for days, 14–16 hours each day, with three CODAs acting as interpreters; the female interpreters, A.N. Perlova (Dolbilkina), T.D. Simonova (Eroschina), and L.L. Ignatenko (Zaychik), were also imprisoned without parole for two years after the elite Deaf people were shot. Many of the Deaf suspects would not confess anything even though they were physically beaten, because they had nothing to confess. They all referred the police to their local leader, Tot'myanin, especially since he was the chairman of the local Deaf organization and the local advocate and leader who everyone depended on. Tot'myanin — the one who had unintentionally started this whole raid — was then brought in for questioning. Although he denied any and all involvement, the police believed he was lying because all the Deaf people had named him as their leader. In Tot'myanin's tribunal papers, he was labeled as an anti-Soviet fascist member of the Gestapo Terrorist Group run by supposed Gestapo Agent Blum.

If Tot'myanin had never urged the police to try and scare the peddlers, he would probably never have been brought in. As a result, 54 Deaf people were brought in for questioning and jailed. Many of them communicated with each other from their cells, signing through the bars surrounding them whenever possible. A large number finally gave in and made false confessions. They then did not see each other again until December 24, the day of their executions.

According to *Leningrad Martyrology: 1937-1938 Part IV*, Yan Krauze, the head of Leningrad's regional NKVD 'Troika,' didn't target only Deaf people; he also targeted other people, especially foreigners and ethnic groups.

Most of the people brought in for questioning faced a tribunal council and were typically executed within two weeks. Krauze was a psychotic man on a mission; his assistants, whose names are listed on the slide, were the ones who beat the Deaf prisoners, trying to coerce confessions out of them. On December 24, 1937, 34 Deaf people were executed by firing squads. The 35th, David Khorin, was executed on January 11, 1938. It is worthy of note that most of the Deaf people who were executed were intellectuals: artists, photographers, actors/directors/playwrights, highly skilled workers, elite athletes, and teachers. Ten were also women. Their names, as listed in the Moscow Symposium in Deaf History conference proceedings (1991) are:

1. Boleslav Zhelkovsky, 1908-1937
2. Eric Tot'myanin, 1901-1937
3. Vladimir Redz'ko, 1882-1937
4. Andrey Petrov, 1903-1937
5. Yakov Alter, 1907-1937
6. Georgy Zolotnitsky, 1901-1937
7. Nikolay Vasil'ev, 1912-1937
8. Vladislav Dolgotsky, 1902-1937
9. Nikolay Deybner, 1887-1937
10. Elena Pogorjelskaya, 1893-1937
11. Nikolay Bryantsev, 1888-1937
12. Petr Kumme, 1903-1937
13. Maria Mintslova, 1892-1937
14. Alexey Agureev, 1904-1937
15. Alexander Vischkevich, 1909-1937
16. Timophey Kurchavin, 1900-1937
17. Israel Nissenbaum, 1900-1937
18. Alexey Pavlovich, 1910-1937
19. Varvara Lutsenko, 1897-1937
20. Nikolay Dvoynov, 1908-1937
21. Mark Markovich, 1915-1937
22. Ivan Chervinsky, 1891-1937
23. Alexander Stadnikov, 1904-1937
24. Alexander Nekrasov, 1881-1937
25. Mikhail Grigorev, 1909-1937
26. Mikhail Tager-Kar'elli, 1892-1937
27. Nikolay Gurevich, 1885-1937
28. Maria Chausova, 1907-1937
29. Esther Gorfunkel, 1897-1937
30. Antonina Vasileva, 1905-1937
31. Nina Vinter, 1898-1937
32. Valentina Zaks, 1892-1937
33. Antonina Golovina, 1882-1937
34. Elena Kruschevskaya, 1893-1937
35. David Khorin, 1901-1938

There were also 19 others who continued to deny all charges; they were sent to forced labor camps (gulag) for ten years, where they were brainwashed all day long. They were forced into incredibly hard physical labor, in faraway places such as Mordovia and Karaganda, Kazakhstan (Razmouv, 1999). However, in late 1938, after much outcry from people, Ezhov was removed from his position, investigated and then executed among with other Leningrad NKVD 'Troika' militia in 1940. Most of the Deaf prisoners were freed in 1940, except for two, who weren't freed for another three years.

In 1999, Gingzburgsky received a letter from S. Chernov, the assistant head of the Russian Federation Ministry of Security, stating that the cases of the Leningrad Deaf-Mutes were closed in 1940. On December 6, 1955, all 54 victims' and prisoners' names were cleared by the Leningrad Military Tribunal (Gingzburgsky, 1996).

And what of Albert Blum? Blum was still alive at the time of the executions, but was unable to return to the Soviet Union because of the ongoing arrests and imprisonment (personal interview with Harmut Teuber, December 5, 2002). My research shows that Blum remained active in communist circles in East Germany, but continued to lay low. Blum had never been involved in the information given to the police, as many Deaf people mistakenly believed, but had simply taken his family and returned to Germany, where he led a quiet life until his death in the 1960s. Although Blum continues to be a mysterious figure, his name should be cleared of any wrongdoing.

It wasn't until 1991 at the first Moscow Symposium on Deaf History that Gingzburgsky finally worked up the courage to speak of what he had seen and knew about the horrors of Ezhov's actions. He was also frustrated that there had not yet been a memorial created to honor the Deaf victims. He was insistent about sharing these victims' stories, and worked for years studying letters, talking to survivors and their families about the tragedies of 1937-1938. It is interesting to note that many of the survivors and their families continued to insist they didn't know why they were targeted or imprisoned. Finally, Gingzburgsky was able to help create a memorial plaque that now hangs in the entrance area of the Deaf Cultural Society (Figure 5). Unfortunately, Gingzburgsky was unable to attend the memorial unveiling ceremony due to illness, relatives of the victims, friends, and VOG members came to pay their respects at the dedication of the Hall of Victims' Repression of 1937 Memorial on December 23, 1998 (Frolova, 1998).

Even with this memorial, Gingzburgsky felt his work was not complete. He had another goal of creating a memorial at Levaschovskoe Memorial Cemetery, where mass graves of over one million people executed during the Ezhov year are located; the 35 executed Deaf people's graves are there as well, although not identified. There are Catholic, German and Jewish, among others, memorials, but none that mark the graves of the Deaf victims. With the help of interviews, Gingzburgsky's invaluable work, and resources such as the previously mentioned books, it is my hopes that funds raised will go towards a memorial at the cemetery that honors these victims, to finish the work that Gingzburgsky began.

The Deaf intellectuals that Stalin attempted to purge cannot be forgotten or removed from Deaf Russian history, even today, nearly 70 years later.

REFERENCES

Bazoev, V., & Palenny, V. (2002). *Chelovek iz Mira Tischini (A Person from the Silent World)*. Moscow, Russia: Academkniga.
Frolova, E. (1998, December). Den' Pamyati I Skorbi (Memorial and Grief Day). St. Petersburg *Volna*, 4.
Gingzburgsky, D. (1996). Khotelos Bi Vsekh Poimenno Nazvat... (Monograph: I Wish I Could Give All Their Names...). In Pichugin, Y., Zaytseva, G., Kuksin, V., Palenny, V., Skripov, V. (Eds.). *Materiali Pervogo Moskovskogo Simpoziuma po Istorii Glukhix, Moskva. (First Moscow Symposium on History of the Deaf)* (pp. 109-122). Moscow, Russia: Zagrey.
Ginzburgsky, D. (1998, September). Biography of the Soviet Deaf. *Pchela*, 6-10.
Gingzburgsky, D. (1999). Remember Tragedy in 1937. In Razumov, A. (Ed.), *Leningrad Martyrology, 1937-1938*, Volume 4 (pp. 675-678). St. Petersburg, Russia: National Library of Russia.
Ilic, M. (2000). The Great Terror in Leningrad: A Quantitative Analysis. *Europe-Asia Studies*, 52, 1515-1534.
Jensen, M., & Petrov, N. (2002). *Stalin's Loyal Executioner: People's Commissar Nikolai Ezhov, 1895–1940*. Stanford, CA: Hoover Press.
Kozlov, D. (2002, September–December). Leningrad Martyrology: A statistical note on the 1937 executions in Leningrad City and region. Canadian Slavonic Papers. Retrieved April 22, 2005 from: http://www.findarticles.com/p/articles/mi_qa3763/is_200209/ai_n9096856.
Krutsyk, R., Shapoval, Y., & Kravchenko, O. (n.d.). 1934-1938: The Collapse of Ukrainization and the "Great Terror." Retrieved April 21, 2005 from: http://represii.org/eng/1936.html.
"Memorial." (n.d.). Retrieved May 2, 2006 from: http://www.memo.ru/eng/index.htm.
NKVD Memorial Page. (2000). Retrieved May 2, 2006 from: http://www.nkvd.org.
Palenny, V. (2003). *Deaf Russians and Soviet Totalitarianism (1917-1941)*. Presented at Fifth Deaf History International Conference in Paris, France (unpublished).
Razumov, A. (Ed.). (1999). Leningrad Martyrology, 1937-1938 (Vol. 4). St. Petersburg, Russia: National Library of Russia. Ginzburgsky, D. (1999, January). *Remember Tragedy in 1937*, pp. 675-678.
Razumov, A., & Gruzdev, Y. (1999). Letter of the Case of the Leningrad Society of the Deaf. In Razumov, A. (Ed.), *Leningrad Martyrology, 1937-1938*, Volume 4 (pp. 678-681). St. Petersburg, Russia: National Library of Russia.
Razumov, A. (n.d.). The Returned Names. Retrieved June 5, 2006, from: http://visz.nlr.ru/search/lists/t4/index.html.
"Secret Police." (n.d.). Retrieved May 2, 2006 from: http://www.ibiblio.org/expo/soviet.exhibit/secret.html.

Phonocentrism & Audism: Conceptualizing Notions of d/Deaf Identity and Oppression in Ghana

K. WISDOM MPRAH

SINCE I CAME TO THE UNITED STATES IN JULY 2006, I HAVE WONDERED what value systems influence the way Ghanaians and Americans relate their respective Deaf and hard-of-hearing populations. I have observed that there is a vast difference in the general attitude between Ghanaians and Americans towards people who are Deaf and hard-of-hearing.

For Ghanaians in particular, attempts to develop and harness the potentialities of Deaf people started more than 50 years ago. In fact, the first deaf school was established in 1957, the year Ghana gained independence from British colonial rule, but Deaf people are still a colonized population.

Deaf people in Ghana are one of the most marginalized and underrepresented; they are not merely marginalized, but also face stigmatization and oppression. Unlike their hearing counterparts, deaf people lack access to adequate and meaningful information on major issues of national interest. They are cut off from participating in most mainstream activities, placing them at a disadvantageous position compared to their hearing counterparts. This has deprived them access to valued resources such as education, health services, and employment which they need to develop their potentials.

This paper is born out of curiosity and would, by no means, be exhaustive in explicating the lived experiences of individuals who are Deaf and hard-of-hearing in Ghana. In the sections that follow, I will try to locate the sources of stigma, marginalization, and oppression of Deaf people in Ghana in a tradition that has placed word communication or spoken language above all other forms of communications. I will suggest that Ghanaians are phonocentric and espouse audism; as a result, spoken language is favored over sign language, the natural language for Deaf people, and the conduit for social interaction and development of Deaf cultural identity. In other words, the basis of stigmatization and oppression of Deaf people in Ghana is located in Deaf people's inability to hear and use spoken language. I will argue that being able to hear and speak is a prerequisite for being accepted by the dominant hearing culture in Ghana; a lack of it could lead to one being treated less favorable. As a result, Deaf people have no strong cultural heritage and unable to construct a linguistic cultural identity.

GHANAIAN METAPHYSICAL THOUGHT AND WAYS OF BEING DEAF

Understanding Ghanaian metaphysical thought provides a good framework for appreciating the place of individuals on the traditional social ladder in Ghanaian society. Cultural values differ among different ethnic groups in Ghana, but there are general similarities across cultures. Thus although I will focus on the Akan people, which is the largest ethnic group in Ghana, most of the issues I will be discussing on the Ghanaian metaphysical thought, and the way deafness is construed, could be found among other ethnic groups. I will therefore dwell mainly on the Akan metaphysical thought in my explanation of what constitutes a human being in Ghana.

Views on the Akan conception of personhood differ among Ghanaian philosophers, but two main views are discussed in this paper. One viewpoint perceives a person as a dual entity, comprising a biological being and social being. According to Wingo (2006) proponents of this view argue that one is either human or is not. Being human is natural by birth, and therefore, can not be conferred on an individual by society. The social being on the other hand is acquired later in life through ones actions or achievements. Thus social being differentiates one's social and moral qualities from the biological ones.

The second viewpoint perceives an individual as a single entity- just a biological being. Proponents of this view think the dual perspective of personhood violates the principle of equality among humans, and so do not agree with the role society plays on the status of an individual. It should, however, be noted that while the former viewpoint seems to be describing what pertains in the Akan society, the latter viewpoint suggests what ought to be; that is viewing a personhood from human rights perspective.

Perceiving personhood from this dual perspective offers a better understanding of why people are treated differently in the Ghanaian society, because how a person is viewed is influenced by the Ghanaian metaphysical assumptions, which include their normative conceptions of what is human or life. The dual conception, therefore, offers a better framework for conceptualizing the differential treatments people receive in Ghanaian society. Building on this notion, it can be observed how stereotypical labels based on standard norms that one is required to meet affect one's relationships with others. In Ghana, there are numerous norms that control people's behavior, a deviation from which could adversely alter one's social standing in relation to others.

Even opponents of the dual conception of personhood would agree that various Akan labels, expressions, and thoughts about a person's conduct or life seem to confirm the view that personhood has some direct relationship on the extent to which an individual conforms to normative standards of the dominant culture. For instance, the Akan concept "Onnye", (a devalued personhood) instead of the more respectable concept "nipa" is a moral judgment. Nipa indicates that personhood can be acquired or bestowed upon an individual by the degree to which such as an individual is able to meet what is required of him or her (Wingo, 2006).

There are many ways to construct deafness in Ghana, but I will classify them into three broad categories. These are medically deaf, psychosocially deaf and culturally deaf. Medical deafness is depicted as an impairment of the auditory system, a problem located within individuals who are deaf. Psychosocial deafness connotes lack of sensual feelings, stupidity (dumbness), excessive patience, reticence or terse in speech, subservience, indifference or stubbornness. Cultural deafness is the linguistic marker loosely expressed among Deaf elites. All the above categories of deafness denote something negative requiring remedy.

However, the negative and stigmatized attributes associated with deafness is a derivative of the medical category of deafness. That is, the negative value given to deafness is rooted in assumptions underlying the medical model, which sees deafness as having an "inherent essential nature, which can be discovered and which is therefore given the status of 'truth' " (Corker, 1998, p.15). The "truth" is that deafness must "either be 'cured' because it is 'not normal' or it must be hidden because it is a threat to the survival of a strong identity" (Corker, 1998, p. 20).

Thus in spite of the fact that Ghana did not engage in a systematic eugenics practice as was in the U.S. and other countries, traditional values nevertheless shunned those who do not meet normative dominant cultural standards. Particularly, Ghanaian traditional metaphysical thought places personhood within structures that promote ableism, thus conceptualizing ability as a prerequisite of personhood. These assumptions and thoughts have greatly influenced attitudes and perceptions about disability, and the way individuals with perceived impairments are viewed and treated.

PHONOCENTRISM, AUDISM AND OPPRESSION OF DEAF PEOPLE IN GHANA

Phoncentrism is "the belief that spoken word is the ultimate communication [form]" Corker (1998, p.14). Phonocentrism promotes audism, which is a notion that judges one's superiority, ability, and happiness based on one's ability to hear and speak (Bauman, 2004). It is manifested when people, both hearing and deaf, and institutions rationalize and justify injustice or discrimination against individuals on the basis that because such individuals are unable to hear, they are incapable of engaging in a given behavior or occupation. Humphries vividly illustrates this when he states that audism

> ...appears in the form of people who continually judge deaf people's intelligence and success on the basis of their ability in the language of the hearing culture. It appears when the assumption is made that the deaf person's happiness depends on acquiring fluency in the language of the hearing culture. It appears when deaf people actively participate in the oppression of other deaf people by demanding of them the same set of standards, behavior, and values that they demand of hearing people" (qtd. in Bauman, 2004, p. 2).

As outlined in the previous section, in Ghana, one's human status is acquired at birth and social status later in life. Therefore, until deafness in the child is discerned, he or she retains all the human characteristics and has the chances of attaining a high social status. The child is given a name, which is an important social marker or identity. When the child's deafness is identified later, his or her true name either disappears or is used in combination with a label that signifies a new social identity. This new identity stigmatizes the child and put him or her in a situation that will forever limit his or her chances of attaining a status equivalent to his or her hearing counterparts. It should be noted that social status, although different from the physical attributes, does not exist independent of it. The nature of the body, that is, the biological component of a human being, has a strong correlation with the social component; the respect and treatment we receive largely depend on our bodies.

As Davis notes "The point is that the body is not only — or even primarily — a physical object. It is in fact a way of organizing through the realm of the senses the variations and modalities of the physical existence as they are embodied into being through a larger social/political matrix" (p.14). Furthermore, Murphy (1987), notes that disability "is not just a departure from the moral code, but a distortion of conventional classification and knowing" (qtd. in Davis, 1995, p. 14), ensuing from a perceived damaged body.

In the book "Aesthetic Nervousness," Quayson (2007) points out that disability, and for that matter deafness, is framed within a discourse of stereotypes and expectations that serve to erase the identities of the individuals who have been disabled, by obscuring and distorting the true identity of the individual concerned.

And that the treatment of disabled persons reflects relationships between disabled bodies and ethical codes, and how these variables are placed in relation to social, economic, and political power structures. Fundamental to assumptions underlying disability, and for that matter deafness, are the relationships between people. These relationships assume and suggest difference, inferiority, dangerous others, abnormality, and queerness. Such assumptions reflect prejudices, misinformation, and the deliberated quest to maintain, so called, human purity through the rejection of what is considered deviant or abnormal as inconsistent with the natural order of things (Hendriks, 1995). For Ghanaians, any such deviations or abnormalities contradict our metaphysical thought of what constitutes the idea of being human.

It is thus noteworthy that impairment connotes an abnormal condition, a distortion of the expected physical and social rules. Consequently, even what was perceived as normal about a person may acquire a special status after impairment has been discerned. The result is that the person with the perceived impairment is "framed within stereotypes and expectations that serve to efface a person's identity" (Quayson, 2007, p.2). That is, the perceived impairment characterizes the whole being creating limiting, self-fulfilling prophecies about the person's potential.

Thus once deafness in a person is detected, whether in childhood or later in life, the person acquires a new name that signifies the person's devalued social status, which arises from the defect in the body. In Ghana, the term "mumu" is the collective label for Deaf persons. Symbolically, this alludes to the sound made by cattle, indicating the Deaf person's devalued relationship to other humans. The "mumu" is now a person with a spoiled identity (Goffman, 1963): a person less than other humans, not only because he or she cannot hear but because he or she is without spoken language, which is a basic requirement to be human. This perception follows a notable misconception that associates language with speech, and the tendency to erroneously link deafness to lack of speech. The logic then is that speech is language and since Deaf persons lack speech they lack language. Taking this logic further, Brueggermann describes it as follows: "Language is human; speech is language; therefore deaf people are inhuman…" (qtd. in Bauman, 1999, p.11).

Names in Ghana are labels with inherent power or meaning, reflecting the nature or status of the bearer (Agyekum, 2006). In Ghanaian traditional society, names as labels have shaped the conception of many social and biological events, such as pregnancy and childbirth. Labels have also influenced attitudes towards diversity in human beings, and have constrained the need to tolerate disabled persons. Agbenyaga (2002) asserts that labels, such as "mumu" influences the way we perceive disability or deafness, guide our decisions, perceptions, choices, and create impressions that distort reality. Moreover, labels tend to be stigmatizing and may evoke negative connotations about the bearer. Commenting on the disempowering effects of labels Corker (1998) argues that:

> We have enough tension in our lives from the fact that perceptions accompanying the labels 'mentally ill' and 'mental health problems' can collude with a professional's view that a deaf person with 'problems,' or even without them, is powerless to solve problems without 'help', and so these labels can become a very effective and disempowering deterrent for deaf people's choice and participation in service cultures. (p. 101).

And as Davis cited in Braddock and Parish (2001) contends, "disability is not so much the lack of a sense or the presence of a physical or mental impairment as it is the reception and construction of that difference" (p. 12). Disability "overshadow[s] every other trait that the individual possesses, so that the person is no longer a person with an impairment but rather a disabled person; disability thus becomes the paramount characteristic, the inescapable social label of the person" (Sakellariou, 2006. p.102).

For Deaf people, their "mumu" status and the association of speech and eloquence with intelligence has pushed them further to the margins of mainstream society. This perception has led to the belief that Deaf people are slow at learning and cannot handle or manipulate complex problems due to their limited intelligence. Baumann's cautious statement draws illustrates this point:

> Invariably, the most distinctive difference between human and animal is traditionally thought to be language....In itself, saying that language is distinctively human trait does not lead to audism. Yet once language is elevated to the status of a principle defining the human characteristics, how we define language has enormous implications" (emphasis original) (p. 242). Davis (1995) however challenges the reasoning that has given spoken language its superior, for and which reason those who lack it have been treated social 'pariah'. For instance Davis (1998) asserts that "In setting up the commonsense notion that language occurs in two forms and only two forms — speech and writing — we are engaging in a tautology based on an equation of language as such and reason. (p.18)

Relying on Steven Pinker, Davis doubts if there is any association between "the particular language a culture uses and language per se, and that it is erroneous to "link that language to reason or thought" because thought and grammar are human instincts, not particularly dependent on language" (p.19). He further points out that:

> ... the facile equation made between speaking/hearing and writing — all seen as linked to signifying practices — is actually a much more complex set of arrangements. If we look critically, we see that the aural/oral method of communicating, itself seen as totally natural, like all signifying practices, is not natural but based on sets of assumptions about the body, about reality, and of course about power. (pg, 16).

The association between language and intelligence has had serious consequences for Deaf people in Ghana. A major one being that Deaf people should be given special attention and be encouraged to study courses and take up professions which are perceived to be simple, less rigorous and require less analytical skills and procedures. As a result, carpentry, masonry, dressmaking, catering, and metal works among others, have been recommended for them. As to why these courses are perceived as such is another thing beyond this paper, but this perception has deprived Deaf people of the required human resources they need to fight oppression. This has also set in motion a perpetual cycle of poverty, powerlessness, oppression, and domination as prejudices against them persist and their participation in mainstream society curtailed. One of the consequences is reinforcement of negative stereotypes about Deaf people's intelligence level.

From the above, we can see how constructing deafness based on interpretations drawn from assumptions that the Deaf person "is in some sense damaged while the observer is undamaged" (Davis, 1998, p. 14.), portrays the Deaf person as blight to the whole society. To resolve this perceived contradiction, Deaf persons are consequently socialized to internalize their "difference", that is, their abnormal condition (deafness), and struggle with this identity among their phonocentric and audistic families, peers, teachers and other people they interact with in society. Arrangements in all the institutions for socializing children (family, school, church, etc.) reinforce the perception that deafness is bad and must be remedied. The socialization processes either in the home, schools, or churches are structured for hearing people and implicitly or explicitly, express tendencies of audism. So by the time the Deaf child becomes aware of his or her deafness, he or she would have internalized deafness as something bad, something that needed to be corrected and the wish to be a hearing person.

One main reason for Deaf people's oppression in Ghana can therefore be traced to the privileging of hearing norms that compel those who can hear to adjust to it or be ignored. Through this orientation, negative signals of deafness are sent to Deaf persons, portraying deafness as bad and something that must be rejected. For most deaf children their biological families and adults close to them are hearing person "who have not experienced deafness before and who have usually internalized the dominant phonocentric values..." (Corker, 1998, p. 22).

Even institutions specifically meant to socialize Deaf children, such as the residential schools are really not meant to socialize Deaf children into Deafhood. The sign language, for instance, is generally seen as a tool for facilitating communication and the provision of "information in a *hearing environment*" rather than its function as "a native language and transmitter of cultural information in a Deaf environment" (emphasis original) (Corker, 1998, p. 126). It is important to note that laws and policies have legalized the employment for hearing teachers, who can not communicate effectively in the sign language, to teach Deaf children, while prohibiting Deaf people, who are fluent and skillful in sign language from teaching. It is also worthy to note that there are large numbers of hearing people, with the same qualification that has technically disqualified Deaf people from teaching deaf schools, teaching both hearing and Deaf children. Thus by the time deaf children reach adulthood, they would have integrated enough experiences that seeks to uphold the dominant hearing cultural values.

I do not seek to attribute blame to any particular person or group of persons; what I seek to imply is that both deaf people have become part of an institutionalized processed that have oppressed the deaf population. I am inclined towards Corker's cautious statement that:

> [E]xplanations which locate oppression either within the personalities of the oppressed or within those of the oppressors are distractions: prejudice and discrimination are widespread and institutionalized phenomena based on deep-seated oppressive power relations. Reducing everything to individual 'idiosyncrasies' is deeply offensive because if institutionalized oppression is consciously denied, this denial removes the last remaining possibility of its *deconstructions*. (p. 4; emphasis original)

Following Foucault's notion of disciplinary power, however, the above quote also resonates the conditioning of deaf people to conform to a repressive external, "normate" hearing culture that has shaped them into passive and dependent citizens. At the same time we see how the same conditioning has made them active participants, who participate vigorously, advertently or inadvertently, in self-surveillance of their conformity to the normative cultural values of the hearing world. Even though one might not want to apportion blame, one should shy away from naming the oppressor. For, if phonocentric and audistic values are being celebrated at the expense and detriment of the deaf population, then there is a moral justification to name the oppressor. We should also not lose sight of the fact that disciplinary power works on assumptions subscribed by the dominant culture that has institutionalized "the type of relationships which are possible between oppressor and oppressed (Corker, 1998; pg. 69).

The result of these relationships for deaf people in Ghana is the creation of dual sources of oppression: the first being from the hearing world, who view deafness as something to despise, and the other from deaf persons themselves, through a process in which deaf people have been conditioned into "dual being of 'housing' the oppressor" within themselves (Friere, pg. 95).

In other words, "deaf people have been physically and pedagogically coerced into adopting hearing norms, whether they like it or not" (Buaman, 2004, p. 3). They have internalized the oppressor, who is invisibly gazing at them, whenever and wherever, to match the "social character" of the hearing world, albeit grave consequences. They have become their own supervisors exercising power over themselves in their specific duties, attitudes, and behaviors. Specifically Deaf people have been oriented to blame themselves for carrying an inferior gene, a gene which has made them incapable and inferior to their hearing counterparts. This has had vicious and rippling dehumanizing effects on Deaf persons' self-concept and self-esteem. As Friere (1978) suggests,

> "Self-depreciation is another characteristic of the oppression, which derives from their internalization of the opinion the oppressors hold of them. So often do they hear they are good for nothing, know nothing and incapable of learning anything — that they are sick, lazy and unproductive — that in the end they become convinced of their unfitness" (p. 63).

There might not be deliberate policies or programs geared towards such an orientation but the lack of such programs or policies does not make the perception or practice non-existent. All social policies have their underlying assumptions which are expressed in the way they are implemented. Thus a major reason for disqualifying Deaf people from teaching deaf schools, while allowing their hearing counterparts with the same qualification but with little or no proficiency in sign language to teach deaf schools finds its roots in phonocentric and audistic perceptions. Deaf people's condition is 'different', and this warrants remedy to gain equal attention and access to mainstream society.

Their so-called "ignorance and lethargy were the direct product of the whole situation of economic, social, and political domination — and of paternalism — of which they were victims." (Freire, 1978, p. 31). In this paternalism we "find that their identity as persons is submerged by their identity as disabled. All their personal traits and characteristics, their distinctive features and attitudes are of secondary importance; [their] disability is infinitely magnified and overshadows the person" (Sakellariou, 2006, p.103). More Charlton states that:

> Paternalism often must transform its subjects into children or people with childlike qualities. This is the most salient aspect of paternalism as it concerns disability. ... It is most of all, however, the assumption that people with disabilities are intrinsically inferior and unable to take responsibility for their own lives" (p. 53).

Orienting Deaf people in Ghana from paternalistic context has thus contributed to Deaf people's deprivation of equal attention in terms of education health, access to information, and employment. For example, despite the importance government has attached to making information on sexual and reproductive health accessible to the general population Deaf people have not been targeted. All the information channels such as radio, public discussions and television are inaccessible because there are no interpreters and our televisions are non-captioned. The high illiteracy among Deaf people has also made it difficult for this group to obtain information from print materials such as newspapers, magazines, leaflets, posters and billboards.

The mechanisms for constructing deafness and the subsequent oppression and domination parallel thus Friere's (1978) description of the condition of the oppressed:

> They are treated as individual cases, as marginal persons who deviate from the general configuration of a "good, organized, and just" society. The oppressed are regarded as the pathology of a healthy society, which must therefore adjust 'incompetent and lazy' folk to its own patterns by changing their mentality. These marginals need 'integrated,' 'incorporated' into the healthy society that they have "forsaken' (p. 74).

The restrictive conditions under which Deaf people live in Ghana have made it difficult for the Deaf community to develop a coherent social group. A strong deaf identity is therefore lacking in Ghana. The Ghana Sign Language is not well-developed; it is a hybrid of the American Sign Language and signs developed by indigenous Ghanaian Deaf persons. As a result, the sign language is not a strong identity marker and Deaf people generally consider themselves persons with disabilities and not a linguistic minority group, which is the basis of Deaf culture. They have actively taken part in programs organized by the Ghana Federation of the Disabled. The culturally Deaf and clinically (medically) Deaf distinction does not exist in Ghana. Deaf people would also readily welcome any technology that would eliminate or correct deafness, if that would reduce their marginalization, stigma, oppression, and domination. Deafness in Ghana is viewed as a medical condition by both Deaf people and the hearing population, and definition of disability as "functional limitations" in the Ghana Disability Policy Document applies to both Deaf persons and other persons with disabilities. Generally, when Deaf people refer to themselves as cultural group, it is not identification with a linguistic cultural group in the strict sense. The culturally deaf definition is loosely used without any consideration to its implications. We are generally comfortable with terms such hearing impairments.

CONCLUSION

What this paper has argued is that although there are various forms through which language is traditionally expressed in Ghana (spoken, written, dancing, carving, molding, drumming, weaving, and even signing) the social organization in Ghana is arranged around hearing norms, outside the experiences and aspirations of Deaf people. One must hear and speak to be considered "normal" and treated equal as other human beings. This arrangement has marginalized Deaf people whose natural mode of communication is not recognized, exposing them multiple oppression. The often-stated notion that deafness is impairment within the Deaf person, and that the Deaf person is "different" and "abnormal" has imposed on Deaf persons self-devaluing mentality that has weakened their self-concept and self-esteem as a group.

The hope is that with the passage of the Deaf-friendly laws such as the recently passed Persons with Disability Law, the social and economic environment would be less restrictive and more tolerant of Deaf people as persons in their own right. However, such laws must be taken with cautious optimism, as laws do not necessarily change societal beliefs and attitudes. This is especially true when those responsible for enforcing the laws are the same people who hold the negative beliefs and attitudes that need to be changed.

REFERENCES

Agbenyaga S. J. (2002). The power of labeling Discourse in the Construct of Disability in Ghana. http://www.aare.edu.au/03pap/agb03245.pdf

Agyekum, K. (2006). The sociolinguistic of Akan personal names. *Nordic Journal of African Studies*. 15(2), 206-235.

Bauman, L. H. (2004). Audism: Exploring the metaphysics of oppression. *Journal of Deaf Studies and Education*. 9(2).

Braddock, D. L. & Parish, S. (2001). An institutional history of disability. In Albert, G., Seelman, K., Bury, M. (Eds.). *The handbook of disability studies*. CA: Oaks, Sage. pp. 11-67.

Charlton, I. J. (2000). *Nothing about us without us: Disability oppression and empowerment*. CA: University of California Press.

Corker, M. (1998). *Deaf and disabled, or deafness disabled?* Philadelphia: Open University.
Davis, J. L. (1995). *Enforcing normalcy: Disability, deafness and the body.* New York: Verso
Freire, P. (1978). *Pedagogy of the oppressed.* New York: Continuum.
Goffman, E. (1963). *Stigma: Notes on the management of spoiled identity.* New York: Simon & Schuster Inc.
Hendriks. A. (1995). Disabled persons and their right to treatment: Allowing differentiation while ending discrimination. *Health and Human Rights*, 1(2), 152-173.
Quayson, A. (2007). *Disability and the crisis of representation: Aesthetic nervousness.* New York: Columbia University.
Sakellariou, D. (2006). If not the disability, then what? Barriers to reclaiming sexuality following spinal cord injury. *Sexuality and Disability.* 24, 101-111.
Wingo, A. (2006). Akan philosophy of the person. *Stanford Encyclopedia of Philosophy.* http://plato.stanford.edu/entries/akan-person.

Struggles and Challenges of the Deaf Studies Program at CSUN: 1983 to Present

PATRICK BOUDREAULT, PH.D., JORDAN EICKMAN, PH.D.,
GENIE GERTZ, PH.D., & LAWRENCE FLEISCHER, PH.D.

In November 2008, it will be exactly twenty-five years since the Deaf Studies program at California State University, Northridge (CSUN) was formally established. Lawrence Fleischer, CSUN Department of Deaf Studies program chair, presents the following history of the Department. This history includes the eight-year struggle-laden embryonic period between 1975 and 1983, so Deaf Studies at CSUN has actually been in existence for a period of thirty-three years.

The Deaf Studies program initially began under the auspices of the Department of Special Education within Deaf Education. When Fleischer started teaching at CSUN in 1972, he taught within the Deaf Education graduate program. His students did not have sufficient ASL fluency or knowledge about the Deaf-World. Thus, courses were added to address these needs. The amount of added courses made the two-year graduate program turn into a four-year graduate program. This was unfeasible, so two years of the program were moved to the undergraduate level and this led to the creation of the BA degree program. All this was done with the aim to assist future teachers of deaf children.

CSUN: 1975–1976

Between 1975 and 1976, Fleischer visualized and developed the program's initial conceptual framework. This vision had a Bachelor's degree in Sign Language with three tracks of study: 1) sign language interpreting, 2) sign language teaching, and 3) sign language research, and a minor in sign language. However, this vision was more appropriate for a Masters' degree program rather than a Bachelor's degree program. At the time of design, Fleischer was more concerned with fulfilling basic needs rather than with the degree level.

FORMAL ESTABLISHMENT OF THE EDUCATIONAL POLICY COMMITTEE'S SUBCOMMITTEE

This proposal was then presented to the university, which reacted with the attitude of "What is this? We have never heard of this idea at any other school" and rebuffed the proposal. This led to the formation of a subcommittee of the Educational Policy Committee (EPC, the committee at CSUN focusing on university-wide curriculum), after the EPC initially declined to deal with the proposal.

The subcommittee focused on the rationale behind the program's establishment, its structure, organization, and future, the potential courses to be offered, the people to be involved, and what the sign language major entailed. At that time, the program was named Sign Language Studies, rather than Deaf Studies. Another issue was that ASL was viewed as a fad that would soon fade away. At that time at CSUN ASL was known as Ameslan, Lou Fant's term (Fant 1972).

The subcommittee was charged with investigating these topics and in bringing Ursula Bellugi to present before the subcommittee as a response to the subcommittee's skepticism. The first subcommittee meeting took place on March 2, 1978. The pivotal meeting with Bellugi occurred on March 30, 1978. Fant was also present at that meeting (Sakharoff 1978).

Bellugi informed the subcommittee of several significant points regarding ASL, including that ASL has an internal structure and that ASL and spoken languages have parallels in structural similarities. The subcommittee took on board and accepted these points.

FINAL PROPOSAL TO CSU

After the initial idea was developed in 1975, struggling with and running into roadblocks to the program's acceptance at various university positions, finally getting a committee — actually, the subcommittee — set up in order to challenge the university's resistance. Putting forth the formal proposal which was considered meritorious led to the formation of yet another subcommittee. This indicated a lack of trust from the university due to the fear of the program being something "just made up" because of the lack of other existing similar programs. In 1979, the idea of having an ASL/Deaf Studies program was finally accepted.

APPROVAL OF BACHELOR DEGREE PROGRAM IN DEAF STUDIES AT CSUN, NOVEMBER 1983

However, California was experiencing a recession and no new programs were to be established at that time. In 1983, Fleischer was informed that the California State University (CSU where CSUN is one of 23 campuses within the CSU system as of 2008) authority was now ready to accept the final proposal for the program. The proposal was submitted on March 15, 1983. In November 1983, the CSU announced that the Deaf Studies degree program was accepted. It took eight years of struggle to achieve this.

At the time of the Deaf Studies program's establishment, there were students who already were "Deaf Studies" majors, but who were actually not labeled as Deaf Studies majors but rather as "Special Majors." This group moved forward and became the first graduating Deaf Studies class in December 1993 as the old major name was discarded in favor of Deaf Studies.

FOUR GENERATIONS OF THE DEAF STUDIES PROGRAM CURRICULUM

CSUN's Deaf Studies program curriculum is now in its fourth generation. The first generation curriculum, developed during the embryonic stage, was modified to become second generation shortly afterwards just after the approval of the degree program and became effective in Fall 1984, as the curriculum was not exactly to the department's liking after initial experience.

The change from the second to third generation curriculum took place after a longer gap from 1984 to 1992. The main difference between the second and third generation curriculums was the structuring of courses within the program.

The leap to the fourth generation curriculum officially took place in the beginning of the 2007–2008 academic year, and also saw a good number of new courses being added to the program. Two significant changes occurred with the fourth generation curriculum: 1) the ASL requirements were raised to require two courses above ASL IV level and 2) more Deaf Studies content courses were required, due to prior experience with students of the previous two curriculum generations. It was felt that these students were "unfinished products" who had yet to thoroughly absorb and grasp Deaf Studies material.

DEAF STUDIES ACHIEVING DEPARTMENTAL STATUS: 1994

In 1983, the program broadened its scope as Fleischer was named the coordinator and the program was named the Interdiscplinary BA program with a seven-member committee representing different departments in the university and housed within the College of Education. In 1994, the program became autonomous, and not subject to inter-departmental influences on decisions regarding the Deaf Studies curriculum. Between 1983 and 1994, for example, representatives from the Sociology, Psychology, and Communicative Disorders departments came to the program and gave feedback. It was a very difficult struggle at times to reconcile the program's vision with these representatives. If their feedback was not accepted, the program would not change until their approval was obtained.

In 1994, even though autonomy through being a department was achieved, quick change could not take place because the faculty of Deaf Studies needed to ascertain the right direction to go in. This meant patience and slow, gradual change.

DEAF STUDIES CONCENTRATIONS

The previous discussion covered the program's core courses, which are required of all Deaf Studies majors. The program has several concentrations which allow students to specialize in their desired future line of work. The second and third generation program concentrations were:
    I. Communication Sciences & Services
    II. Language & Culture
    III. Human Services
    IV. Special Option

There are more concentrations in the fourth generation program, with each one more clearly and specifically defined, as the second and third generation program concentrations were more broadly defined. An example of this is that Communication Sciences & Services really was the Interpreting concentration but also covering some aspects of the speech/language pathology program. The fourth generation program concentration list reflects that more accurately. The fourth generation program concentrations are:
    I. ASL/English Interpreting
    II. ASL & ASL Literature
    III. Pre-Deaf Education
    IV. Deaf Community Services
    V. Deaf Cultural Studies
    VI. Special Option

Student Statistics
This section discusses the composition of our current students and presents statistics compiled by Patrick Boudreault. The collection of historical data

regarding our students was difficult. Post-data compilation dictated that our report reflects 1994-onwards as no data was collected prior to 1994. The following statistics are intended to give a picture of our student body.

Enrollment Rate

In Spring 2008, the Department had approximately 320 students. About ten percent of those students are deaf (approximately 30). Figure 1 illustrates our program's student enrollment, Full-Time Equivalent Students (FTES), and graduation rates from the 1993-1994 Academic Year (AY) until the present.

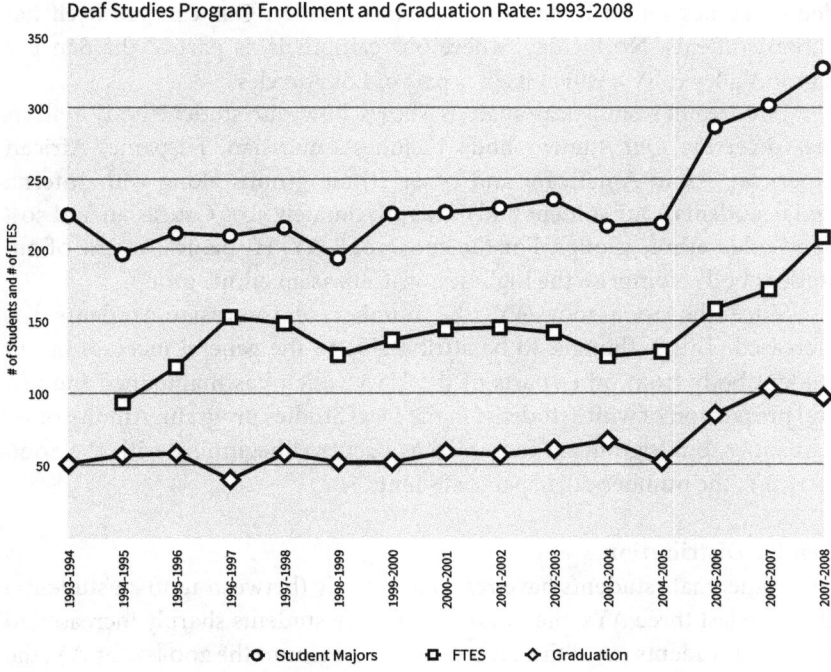

Figure 1. Deaf Studies Program Enrollment and Graduation Rate, 1993–2008

Between the 1993-1994 and 2004-2005 AYs, the number of students in our program fluctuated between 194 and 236 students. During the last three AYs (2005-2006 to the present), the number of students has dramatically increased to the current number of 329 students. This number does not include students who take ASL courses to fulfill elective requirements or their curiosity, or for their enjoyment. Those students who are counted are degree-seeking in Deaf Studies.

A similar jump in the number of our department's FTES occurred over the same range of AYs. From 1993-1994 to 2004-2005, our FTES ranged between 93.73 and 152.87 FTES. During the last AY (2007-2008), our FTES reached a record of 209.1 FTES.

Likewise, between the 1993-1994 and 2004-2005 AYs our graduating classes ranged between 40 and 67 students. Since then, there has been a similar increase, with the class of 2007 establishing a department record of 103 students, breaking the 100 student barrier for the first time.

Ethnicity

CSUN is one of the most diverse campuses statewide in California. Our demographics reflect a very diverse student body. Our campus itself has 35,000 students. Northridge, where our campus is, is part of the San Fernando Valley (SFV), which itself is part of Los Angeles.

Boudreault's statistical analysis shows how our student body reflects that diversity. Our student body includes Caucasian, Hispanic, African-American, Asian-American, and other ethnic groups along with International students. Our student body is approximately 50% Caucasian and 50% of all other ethnic groups. For the 2007-2008 AY, Hispanics, at 22% of our student body, comprise the highest non-Caucasian ethnic group.

Since the 2004-2005 AY, the number of Caucasian students has increased. This is thought to be attributable to the general increase in our student body from other parts of the USA which has maintained the general proportion of white students in the Deaf Studies program. Among other ethnicities, one significant increase has occurred beginning with the 2006-2007 AY: the number of Hispanic students.

Gender Distribution

Over time, male students have remained steady (between 16 to 44 students). Over the last three AYs, the number of female students sharply increased to reach 289 students (as of the 2007-2008 AY). Prior to the 2004-2005 AY, the number of female students ranged from 186 to 209 students. Thus, the great majority, ranging from 85% to 91% over various AYs, of our students continue to be female. The student gender distribution in the 2007-2008 AY is 289 females and 44 males, or 87% female and 13% male.

Age Mean

The majority of our students are between the ages of 21 and 25 years. This is expected as students enter the university and our program from community colleges and generally complete their last two years of their major studies with us, as they are General Education (GE) certified prior to coming to CSUN.

CURRICULUM: PRE-2007

Fleischer previously described the courses offered under our previous four concentration program and the fourth-generation, six concentration program. Figures 2 and 3 look at who has had control over our program courses. Allowing courses offered in other departments outside our program to be used to meet our program requirements is termed as outsourcing.

Figure 2 describes courses offered both within and outside the Department prior to 2007, covering the second and third generation program while excluding the first generation program. The courses are categorized by whether they are core or concentration courses.

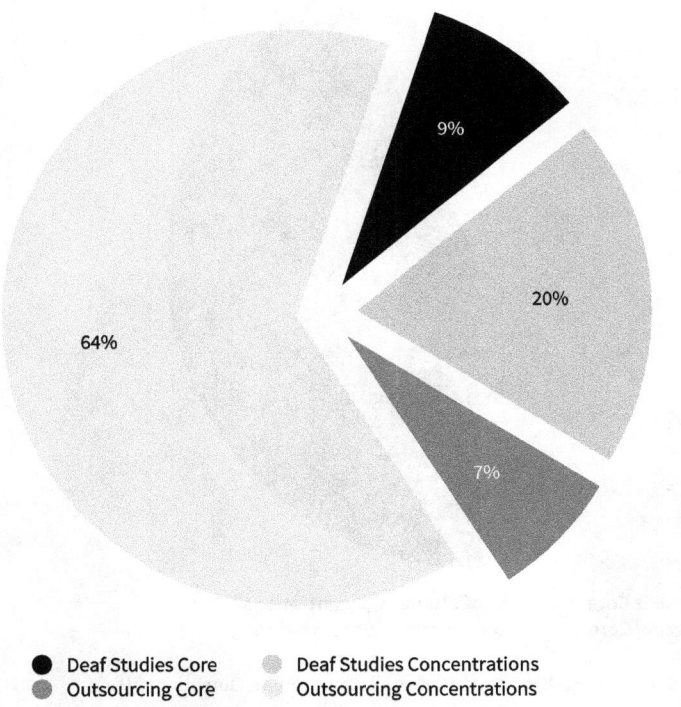

Figure 2. Courses Offered pre-2007: Deaf Studies vs. Department Outsourcing

The core Deaf Studies courses are roughly equally split between those offered within the Department (9%) and other courses offered outside in other departments (7%) such as linguistics or audiology. As for concentration-related courses, 20% were offered within the Department and 64% were offered outside the Department. This means a total of 29% of Deaf Studies program courses were offered within the Department and 71% of Deaf Studies program courses were offered outside the Department.

CURRICULUM: POST-2007

Figure 3 describes courses offered both within and outside the Department after 2007, covering the fourth generation program. As in Figure 2, the courses are categorized by whether they are core or concentration courses.

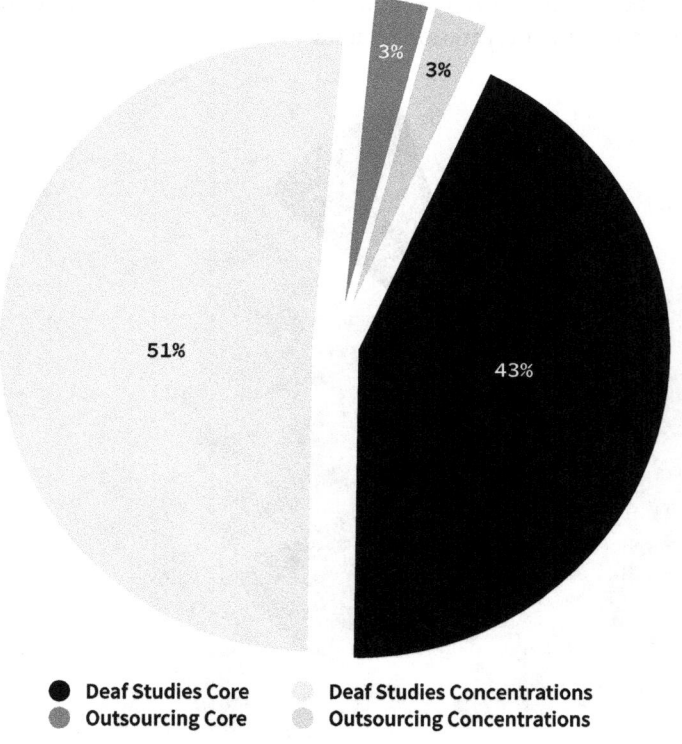

Figure 3. Courses Offered Post-2007: Deaf Studies vs. Department Outsourcing]

Figure 3 indicates that the total amount of outsourced Deaf Studies courses has been reduced to 6%. This represents a change in becoming Deaf-centered. Again, alluding to the discussion taking place regarding Deaf identity centralization, this is a shift to what is really Deaf people's center. Through working within the context of university politics, change was effected over the years with the ultimate goal of establishing a Deaf-centered program.

Figure 3 clearly illustrates and tells us what our Department is doing in establishing our repertoire of courses.

STUDENT LEARNING OUTCOMES

An overview of our Department's eight Student Learning Outcomes (SLOs) is given by Jordan Eickman. The eight SLOs set out the expectations for incoming students in terms of what they will learn and which skills they will acquire before graduating. Also, as part of the accreditation process required by the university, our college and each department within our college have their own SLOs. Appendix 1 lists our SLOs.

The university requires assessment of our SLOs. This basically means measuring the degree of our students' success in achieving each SLO. For example, our most recent assessment measured ASL proficiency. Our advanced ASL course handed out an assignment which required students to go to our ASL Lab to record their own ASL-produced responses to a list of questions. A set of randomly drawn student responses was then assessed by faculty using a rubric. Rubric ratings were then compiled into a statistical report indicating students' success and non-success and then sent to the university.

DEPARTMENT-SPONSORED COMMUNITY EVENTS

Genie Gertz describes in detail the many significant Department-sponsored community events that have taken place over the years.

The principle behind "if the mountain will not go to Mohammed, Mohammed himself must go to the mountain" applies to our department. Our teaching of many courses, in itself, will not fully support and assist students in succeeding in meeting our SLOs. We must provide add-on learning activities. Classroom learning must be supplemented by and connected with the community.

This is because Deaf Studies, itself, is community-oriented and community-based. Understanding the purpose of community, the purpose of Deaf people, and the purpose of activism is a must. Related to our discussion earlier during the 2008 Deaf Studies Today! conference during M. J. Bienvenu's keynote presentation about Deaf identity centralization (Bienvenu 2008), it must be understood that we, the Department of Deaf Studies, centralize and establish our Deaf identity and Deaf principles. From there, our students can learn how to be allies by showing appropriate respect of and understanding of our Deaf principles. Therefore, we must bring together learning and the community. The events we tend to host illustrate how we establish this connection.

DEAFESTIVAL

One example is the annual Deafestival that began in 1990. Each year, Deafestival typically focuses on a different theme. The underlying goal is to celebrate language, art, and poetry. For example, the 1996 Deafestival focused on Deaf folklore. The 1998 edition focused on an original Deaf play. The 2003 Deafestival was centered on two different events with interchanging themes, "Art in ASL" — ASL poetry and "ASL in Art" — ASL produced as artwork. The 2001 celebration was titled "Deaf First." The most important feature of the 2001 poster is the design's focus toward the center — meaning we must focus on the Deaf center. Various topics are distributed around the poster's center. Those closest to the poster's center represent what is the most cherished, the most important to the Deaf center, while those farther away from the poster's center represent those that are furthest away from the Deaf center. The furthest topics are mainstreaming and sign systems, which are not connected with the Deaf center. So, that is expressed through different forms.

DEAF STUDIES-SUPPORTED CONFERENCES AT CSUN

The Department hosted an all-day Deaf Women Conference in Fall 1996. Again, the conference poster has Deaf art within it. The trees represent signs for the different conference themes: communication, understanding, building, and reaching out. For the all-day conference, different speakers were brought in. Throughout the day, discussions were held and attendees interacted with each other. That again emphasizes the connection between classroom learning and the community, through seeing and understanding. The conference also both attracted Deaf community members and was provided for the Deaf community because they are part of that process.

Also, the department hosted a three-day Deaf film event from April 7–9, 2005, which focused on the past, present, and future of Hollywood films and Deaf films. The event also included an analysis of and discussion on how the hearing media has portrayed Deaf characters and the meaning of Deaf films. This event included both people who have worked or acted within the mainstream media and people who are exclusively within the Deaf media, including Deaf filmmakers, those focusing on independent Deaf-centered films.

BIENNIAL JASK PROGRAM

JASK, short for "Just ASK," is our biennial Deaf Awareness Month. Each edition of JASK focuses on a specific theme. Guest presenters are brought to CSUN and faculty, staff, and students collaborate to host various sociocultural events to raise on-campus awareness of and celebrate Deaf culture. JASK originally started out as a week, but later was stretched out to a month, after the realization that only a week was not enough time to carry out a program of satisfactory content.

For example, the 2007 JASK program focused on the Spirit of Deaf Leadership. Presenters were invited to address various topics focusing on Deaf leadership and the meaning of Deaf leadership in different areas such as education, social service, and sports. Sometimes, as for the 2007 JASK program, JASK presenters also overlap as part of our Lecture Series. The 2007 JASK program presenters are included in Appendix 2 which lists the Department's Lecture Series since 2005.

LECTURE SERIES

Since 1980, the Department has hosted various guest presenters within its Lecture Series. Guest presenters visit campus to enrich our students' learning. Oftentimes, a class session from several concurrent Deaf Studies content courses are "plugged into" a lecture. Others within the CSUN and local Deaf community also benefit from attending these lectures. Appendix 2 lists lectures occurring since 2005 as part of the Department's Lecture Series.

A notable recent lecture was Donalda Ammons' presentation, *The Gallaudet Revolution II: An Insider's Perspective*, on the recent Gallaudet protests from "behind the scenes" as a Gallaudet alumnus, faculty member, and a member of the FSSA (Faculty, Staff, Student, and Alumni) group. Her enlightening explanation of the Gallaudet protests is another example of connecting what we see with a real-life person and real experiences, with an emphasis on real life experience.

Another noteworthy lecture was Gil Eastman's *The Importance of Etymology in the Dictionary of ASL*. A moving, poignant fact about Eastman's lecture is that it was his final one before passing away and we feel fortunate he came to CSUN.

INTERNATIONAL LECTURE SERIES

Every year the department brings onto campus an international Deaf guest presenter. Again, Deaf Studies' scope is not limited to the United States, but rather is international in scope and international exchanges do take place. We often discuss that Deaf people themselves are "global citizens", so it is important to show the connection with that. Appendix 3 lists the international Deaf guest presenters that the department has hosted.

STONE DEAF PLAY PRODUCTION

Stone Deaf, our Department-produced play, stage-presented on April 21 and 22, 2006, is about the language oppression Deaf people have experienced. The play's DVD was screened at the 2008 Deaf Studies Today! conference. Again, this is another example of how the Department documents Deaf people's experience through different genres. The project has migrated online at www.stonedeafplay.com for the public's education and benefit.

DEAF STUDIES ASSOCIATION

We also have the Deaf Studies Association where students become involved, and hold their own social activities and organize an annual Silent Weekend, but at the same time support Department-hosted events.

So, in closing, the entire point of describing these Department-sponsored events is illustrating the connection of academic learning with the Deaf community. Including community-based learning within academic learning pulls everything together. In some ways we, as a department, end up doing everything. Other colleges, like Gallaudet or the National Technical Institute for the Deaf (NTID) have departments specializing in various content areas (ie: theatre, art, linguistics, etc.), while we cover these various content areas together within our department because of our belief that we must connect academic learning with the Deaf community. This means our department is deeply committed to our belief in the vision of Deaf Studies.

STRUGGLES & CHALLENGES: PAST

In this section, Fleischer discusses various struggles and challenges the program has faced in the past, is facing in the present, and will face in the future. Commentary regarding each struggle and challenge is given. Three examples for each time — past, present, and future — are addressed.

Our program has faced struggles, mighty struggles. These struggles are not to be considered trivial. Much sweat and hard work has been required to achieve results. The following set of past struggles and challenges occurred prior to the program's establishment:

Struggle: ASL is a fad.
Challenge: Information on ASL is not widely available.
Commentary: As a solution, Ursula Bellugi was brought to CSUN to attest about ASL.

Struggle: Wisdom questioned for an esoteric program in the university.
Challenge: No other Deaf Studies program for comparison.
Commentary: A long gestation period (8 years). If not for the recession at that time, the gestation period would be shortened to 5 years.

Struggle: Different types of deafness into one pot of Deaf Studies.
Challenge: Cultural description of Deaf people nearly nonexistent.
Commentary: One of the representatives from different departments that came to us was a hard-of-hearing sociology professor who did not buy into Deaf Studies at all. This is one of the different views about Deaf Studies that Fleischer had to put up with, as at that time in the 1970s there were no supporting publications to support Deaf-centered Deaf Studies. This led to gradual change throughout the four generations of programs, with the first generation program's peculiar set-up, the second and third generations being a bit closer to the ideal, and finally the fourth generation reaching the Deaf-centered ideal with Deaf Studies having true ownership of the program.

STRUGGLES & CHALLENGES: PRESENT

The present struggles and challenges the Department is experiencing are:

Struggle: Participation in university life generally difficult.
Challenge: Direct communication with non-signing people often limited.
Commentary: Retention, Tenure, and Promotion (RTP) is a fact and a feature of university life. Out of the thirty-five thousand people at CSUN, the four Deaf faculty within our Department and a handful of other deaf individuals on campus are not completely understood by the hearing academic on-campus community. Direct communication with hearing colleagues is not possible as we depend on sign language interpreters. When interpreters are unavailable, proceedings have to be put on hold or CART used, and neither option is desirable. Our hearing colleagues look at us as different from their way of interacting with each other.

Struggle: Accomplishments by Deaf professors not valued.
Challenge: Scholarship assessed for college professors still traditional.
Commentary: Our Department recognizes the importance of involving the Deaf community. For example, Gertz has put in much effort and work in organizing the numerous department-sponsored events benefiting the Deaf community. Our hearing colleagues do not realize the true value of these events. Fleischer has had to defend the importance of these events, particularly as the connection with the Deaf community leads to a better under-

standing of each other. If paper-based publications were produced, they would not be widely understood by or beneficial to the Deaf community. The Department puts the Deaf community first, and helps and supports the Deaf community's growth. As the Deaf community becomes more knowledgeable and comfortable with written English-based literacy, we can shift to a more research-oriented focus.

Struggle: Level of participation in committees/activities strongly tied to interpreters.
Challenge: Finding qualified interpreters to match Deaf professors.
Commentary: CSUN has a large number of deaf people working on-campus: faculty, staff, administrators, and students. Competition is high for interpreter manpower, sometimes interpreters are taken away from CSUN by other job opportunities. At times, this means an interpreter is assigned to us that does not match our level of ASL or cannot understand us, which is frustrating. This illustrates how we feel about our effort to be involved on-campus — it is a struggle.

STRUGGLES & CHALLENGES: FUTURE

The struggles and challenges the Department will face in the future are:

Struggle: Less resources for more students.
Challenge: Additional resources harder to obtain.
Commentary: How can the number of faculty remain the same while the number of students continues to increase? This is a difficult dilemma. It is possible to trigger a university procedure to cap the number of students, but this will create more work for the faculty. A large number of student applications (ranging from 150 to 300 applications) will have to be screened and justification given for each student's selection or rejection. This makes the enrollment cap untenable for our program.

Struggle: Long process to establish a new program-Master's degree in Deaf Studies.
Challenge: Request for new faculty doubly difficult.
Commentary: Our program has the Master's degree program of study visualized and ready. However, in California, it takes time for a degree program to go through the university process to become established and to begin functioning. This process will happen successfully with our program. The more difficult problem is financing the Master's degree program's cost. Overcoming this will mean going through the same experience as when establishing

the Bachelor's degree program. The current number of four full-time faculty members is insufficient as the four are already fully occupied with running the Bachelor's degree program. Hiring more faculty members is necessary.

Struggle: Lower priority for a smaller population.
Challenge: Number not a deciding factor.
Commentary: Yes, our university is very diverse. In Los Angeles, there is a large Hispanic sector of the population, and the funding focus is thus geared toward the Hispanic population. The Deaf population is smaller and more dispersed, resulting in less funding and an attitude of "this will be dealt with later on."

THE DEPARTMENT'S STANCE ON SOCIAL ACTIVISM

The CSUN Deaf Studies faculty has agreed that the Department will partake in social activism. We do not deal with the issue of being "neutral" and just teaching. When we know something is not right, we will do something about it. The CSUN Women's Studies department also has the same social activism philosophy. Other departments will cover both viewpoints of an issue, but Deaf Studies will take a position, and this clearly indicates our activism.

THE DEPARTMENT'S STANCE ON ASL COURSES AND GENERAL EDUCATION

Our Department does teach ASL courses. Our new program requires two ASL courses above ASL IV. Thus, the number of ASL I, II, and III courses offered will diminish and more students will be transferring in from other colleges where they have taken ASL I-III.

However, our ASL courses are not part of CSUN's General Education (GE) courses. We do not want our ASL courses to be part of GE for several reasons. Firstly, if our ASL courses were part of GE, the number of students taking ASL courses would overwhelm our department and redirect our resources toward ASL teaching, effectively making us an "ASL factory." Secondly, many community colleges already offer ASL courses. Thus, we want to focus on Deaf Studies and its meaning as a discipline because Deaf Studies itself is still a new field even though it has existed for some time now. As Paddy Ladd stated in his keynote presentation earlier at the Deaf Studies *Today!* 2008 conference, minority studies should have many established sub-fields (Ladd 2008). Applying this concept to Deaf Studies, the field of Deaf Studies has not yet fully established all these sub-fields. Deaf Studies should not be diverted into solely teaching ASL as a second language. This is the rationale behind our decision not to have ASL courses be part of GE and our focus on Deaf Studies as a major.

PROGRAM REVIEW

Every five years, our college requires a Program Review of our Department, which is a tedious process. Our Department is currently under the Michael D. Eisner College of Education as our Department has its roots within the Special Education department. As part of our most recent Program Review, we discussed proposing a move from the Michael D. Eisner College of Education to the College of Humanities. However and oddly, other minority studies departments within CSUN are not all situated under the College of Humanities. For example, the Pan African Department is within the College of Social and Behavioral Sciences as they have their roots within that College, while Chicano/a Studies are under the College of Humanities. All minority studies departments should be under a "College of People Studies," which was proposed by Fleischer. This proposal met strong resistance from the various departments as they already had positive ties with their College Deans, and felt comfortable and had good political ties within their Colleges. Our Department is curious as to the response from the College of Humanities' Dean about having our Department within that College when we present our proposal. This is a complex issue. We know the College of Humanities is the right place for our Department, but it remains to be seen if this move will be possible even though Deaf Studies has a strong historical attachment to the Michael D. Eisner College of Education.

ASL LAB

The Department has a fully digital ASL Lab with 15 Mac computers with connections to a central server and digital cameras and video viewing capabilities for ASL development work. Technology is part of our program. As the Department and its curriculum's demands change, technology keeps pace in meeting these demands. This facilitates a shift toward more visual-based learning within language teaching.

STUDENT ADVISEMENT

Student advisement has been very time-consuming for the Department's faculty. We believe in providing advisement in ASL. At times, this means new students come in that have very limited knowledge of ASL, and communicating in ASL is very laborious with these students. Advisement consists of many facets. This was despite training advisers within the university advisement center to handle our students, which did not work out too well. These university advisers were still unable to help our students and it ended up that we still had to advise our students. The Spring 2008 semester is the first time we were able to take the yoke of student advisement off, with the hiring of an additional faculty member within our department to focus on student advisement. This new faculty member handled most general student advisement sessions. Fleischer still handled those students who were academically disqualified and other special cases. This took one full-time job off of each faculty's hands. Fleischer, as the chair, is still left with one and a half full-time jobs.

The effect of heavy student advisement meant that the Department's four full-time faculty members found it very difficult to carry out scholarly work, especially with the university asking so much of us. At this point, with the new faculty member handling advisement, the full-time faculty can begin scholarly work.

TEACHING LOAD AND CLASS SIZES

The teaching load is four classes or twelve units per full-time faculty member, which is pretty standard in our field. However, class size is another important factor yet to be mentioned. Class sizes generally begin with twenty students. Some of our content classes have fifty, sixty, or seventy students. Gertz even once taught a class with a hundred students. ASL courses have around thirty students. This is a situation that needs to be improved, and this is another of the Department's struggles.

TOPICS ARISING OUT OF AUDIENCE QUESTIONS/COMMENTS

The audience at our presentation raised questions about many important additional topics and ideas related to running a Deaf Studies program. These topics included covering Certified Deaf Interpreters (CDI) and Deaf-Blind-related content in the curriculum; one-unit courses, ie: Public Signing; Summer Institute/future International Deaf Leaders' two-week conferences; funding for International/Lecture Series Presenters; collaborating with other universities (ie: Gallaudet with the International Deaf Leaders conference); filming/documenting all presenters; improving communication between Deaf Studies departments at different schools to effect quicker Deaf-centered change in the world; teacher exchanges (Visiting Professors) amongst Deaf Studies programs; and future teachers of ASL/California Subject Examinations for Teachers (CSET)-ASL/Masters' program including ASL Teaching.

CONCLUSION

The Department of Deaf Studies' primary objectives are:
1) To convey basic knowledge and understanding about the language and culture of Deaf people including their history and social experiences;
2) To provide students with instruction and training in preparation for advanced degree programs and/or professional careers working with deaf people.

The body of work described above demonstrates the Department has worked toward accomplishing these objectives over the last twenty-five years. This means the Deaf Studies body of knowledge continues to increase and this, in turn, impacts both the Deaf and academic communities by increasing awareness of Deaf people and improving the lives of Deaf people.

REFERENCES

Bienvenu, M. J. (2008, April 11). Expedition for a (Deaf) theory. Presentation made at the 2008 Deaf Studies *Today!* Conference at Utah Valley State College, Orem, Utah.

Fant, L. J., Jr. (1972). *Ameslan: An introduction to American Sign Language.* Northridge, CA: Joyce Media, Inc.

Ladd, N. P. (2008, April 10). Deafhood and Deaf Studies. Presentation made at the 2008 Deaf Studies *Today!* Conference at Utah Valley State College, Orem, Utah.

Sakharoff, M. (1978, March 30). *Minutes of the EPC subcommittee on Deaf Studies/Sign Language.* Minutes of a committee meeting at California State University, Northridge.

APPENDIX 1: CSUN DEPARTMENT OF DEAF STUDIES STUDENT LEARNING OUTCOMES

1) Demonstrate ability to communicate in American Sign Language (ASL) with Deaf people.
2) Identify the major features of and issues in the Deaf Community and Deaf Culture.
3) Demonstrate an understanding of the impact of power, privilege, and oppression on the Deaf community that result in Deaf people's experience of prejudice, discrimination, and inequity.
4) Demonstrate an understanding of how the study of Deaf Studies enables individuals to make informed judgments that strengthen the Deaf Community.

5) Demonstrate an appreciation of the contribution of Deaf arts and humanities for shedding light on what it means to be Deaf.
6) Describe communication between hearing people and Deaf people that is vital to contemporary society.
7) Analyze critically how a Deaf person's social-cultural history influences one's sense of self and relationship to others.
8) Reflect critically on one's abilities in interacting with Deaf individuals, socially and professionally, and evaluate the level of integration achieved.

APPENDIX 2: THE DEPARTMENT OF
DEAF STUDIES' LECTURE SERIES, 2005-PRESENT

Date	Speaker	Topic
November 27, 2007	Seán Herlihy	European Union of the Deaf Youth Programs
May 3, 2007	Jennifer Yost-Ortiz	Deaf Youth
May 1, 2007	Patricia Durr	Deaf Arts & Films
April 25, 2007	Steve Sandy	Deaf Sports
April 23, 2007	Ted Supalla	Deaf Academic Research
April 19, 2007	Ryan Commerson & Alison Aubrecht	Social Justice in the Deaf Community
April 18, 2007	Al Sonnenstrahl	Deaf Visual Technology
November 7, 2006	Donalda Ammons	The Gallaudet Revolution II: An Insider's Perspective
November 6, 2006	Gertrude Scott Galloway	My Thoughts on Language & Communication in Educational Programs for the Deaf
May 3, 2006	Peter Novak	Shakespeare's Bawdy Body: The Bard in American Sign Language
May 1, 2006	Gilbert Eastman	The Importance of Etymology in the Dictionary of ASL
November 29, 2005	Frank Turk	Together, We Build
November 1, 2005	Chris Blum	New Zealand Deaf Community and Culture
October 18, 2005	Jane Norman	Deaf Cinema: Visualizing and Owning the Concept
September 21, 2005	Simon Carmel	Deaf Folklore
April 27, 2005	Claudine Storbeck	The Politics of Language: The South African Deaf Experience
April 26, 2005	Ella Mae Lentz	Laurent, South Dakota: Hopes and Challenges of a Signing Community

April 19, 2005	Paul Johnson	De'VIA: What is it?
April 18, 2005	Todd Czubek	Reading into ASL
April 12, 2005	Chris Wagner	Deaf Leadership & Community Development
April 7, 2005	J. Stan Schuchman	Hollywood Speaks: Deafness & the Film Entertainment Industry

APPENDIX 3: INTERNATIONAL DEAF GUEST PRESENTERS HOSTED BY THE DEPARTMENT OF DEAF STUDIES

2008	Ramon Woolfe	Deaf Media Company Founder & Co-Owner from England
2007	John Bosco Conama	Deaf political theorist from Dublin, Ireland
2006	Riina Kuusk	Deaf leader in Estonia
2005	Paddy Ladd	Internationally renowned Deaf activist from England
2004	Oscar Balmaseda	Deaf leader in Cuba
2003	Roslyn Rosen	Internationally Renowned Deaf Educator
2002	Carol-lee Aquiline	General Secretary, World Federation of the Deaf
2001	Mi Jia-Dong	Deaf Teacher in Beijing, China
2000	David & Rachel McKee	Internationally renowned applied linguists from New Zealand
1999	James Woodward	Internationally renowned sociolinguist
1998	Bruce Gross	President, World Recreation Association of the Deaf
1997	Irene Taylor	Author & photographer, "Buddha in Disguise" (Nepal)
1996	Marilyn Smith	Internationally recognized leader of Deaf women's issues
1995	Ausma Smits	Secretary, Deaf History International
1994	Eric Malzkuhn	Internationally recognized master signer
1990	Peggy Parsons	Deaf Traveler Extraordinaire

ASL Literature: Basic Principles of Stories with Handshape Constraints

BENJAMIN JARASHOW

HOW MANY TIMES HAS AN AUDIENCE SEEN SOMEONE PERFORM ABC stories (also known as A-Z stories) and knew whether or not it was a good story, but couldn't explain why? This is common to the Deaf community. Dr. Tom Humphries pointed this out in his article,

> "We all know Deaf poets that we like and don't like. We all know Deaf artists that we like and don't know. We are less sure why, and we are very unsure what the "why" should be. I think we are still unsure what qualities are that constitute criticism of Deaf art and literature."[1]

ABC stories have been passed on for a long time in the history of ASL literature, but no one is quite sure how to produce or evaluate ABC stories properly.

Dr. Ben Bahan first discussed this issue with colleagues and then made an outline of the basic principles that would be necessary to produce a good ABC story. He was the first to write down the basic principles of ABC stories in his article, "Face-to-Face Tradition in the American Deaf Community: Dynamics of the Teller, the Tale, and the Audience," written in 1999 and published in 2006.[2] I was fortunate enough to have had the opportunity to work with Dr. Bahan as his student and later, his co-worker at Gallaudet University. As storytellers ourselves, we frequently shared with each other our critiques and creative inputs of ABC stories, which led us to producing a DVD, A to Z: ABC Stories in ASL, in 2010. After working with Dr. Bahan, I decided to do this article to expand on his original basic principles of ABC stories, with him as my mentor.

STORIES WITH HANDSHAPE CONSTRAINTS: BASIC PRINCIPLES

Since poetry is considered a composition and is regarded as a branch of literature, ABC stories has been put under the genre of poetry in ASL literature. As have number stories, word stories, and one-handshape stories too. Clayton Valli produced several stories with handshape constraints and published them, on DVD, in his poetry collection.[3] Nathie Marbury[4] and Debbie Rennie[5] did the same thing too. Dr. Bahan took notice of the differences between true poetry and stories with handshape constraints. He brought his findings to several colleagues and after a long discussion followed with some agreements and disagreements, he proposed a new ASL literature genre: Stories with Handshape Constraints. In doing so, he would remove ABC stories, number stories, word stories, and one-handshape stories from the poetry genre. Dr. Bahan considers stories with handshape constraints to be more story than poetry, because poetry is heavily based on distinctive style and rhythm, while stories with handshape constraints is based on limited handshapes.

The goal of each four stories are simple: to create a ABC story based on manual alphabet handshapes; a number story based on manual number handshapes; a word story based on fingerspelling words using manual handshape; and an one-handshape story based on the use of one handshape only. The principles for ABC stories, number stories, and word stories are based on the use of different handshapes while using a system of order. The principles for one-handshape stories are based on the use of the same handshape for each sign.[6]

Stories with handshape constraints are unique to ASL literature because it already has principles set up before the storyteller starts creating his or her story, which has to be told without violating the principles. Basically, the principles were set up to limit the storyteller's choices of handshapes, forcing the storyteller to find a way to successfully tell his or her story.

Dr. Bahan listed the four general principles of stories with handshape constraints, which could also be considered tools of criticism for the stories with handshape constraints genre.[7] The four general principles are:
- Succession Principle
- Minimal Deviation
- Use of Cohesive Devices
- Integrity of the Storyline

SUCCESSION PRINCIPLE

The succession principle is applied to ABC stories, number stories, and word stories only because they all use handshapes already set up in a certain order, as specified by the rules of each type of stories. The succession principle itself is broken down into four parts designated to make sure the order of the different handshapes are effective and appropriate to the particular genre.

Present manual handshapes in successive order
To succeed in telling an ABC story, it must be told in the exact alphabetical order from A to Z. If the storyteller decides to tell a mixed manual alphabet story, this would mean that the storyteller has failed to follow the exact order of the letters of the manual alphabet, and the storyteller's so-called ABC story would no longer be considered a true ABC story. That is the basic principle of the whole sequence of ABC storytelling. However, the storyteller can vary his or her style of telling ABC stories, such as going backward in the sequence of the manual alphabet system. If doing the manual alphabet backward was the storyteller's goal, then it must be done backward in the exact order from Z to A. The same rule applies to number stories and word stories too.

Rhythm/Frequency succession
Storytellers must keep with the rhythm they've chosen throughout the story they are telling. Since our goal is to follow an exact sequence of letters or numbers from the beginning to the end, the storyteller should keep his or her story consistent and use the same rhythm from the beginning to the end.

Most storytellers fail to acknowledge this principle. Here's an example of a common mistake made by storytellers: When a storyteller starts an ABC story about a person going into a haunted house, the story usually goes like this: *the person knocked on the door, but no one answered. So, the person decides to open the door and enter the haunted house. The person walks up the long hallway and upstairs while breathing heavily. Then something darts out right in front of the person.*

Now for the ASL version, if the storyteller disregarded the rhythm/frequency succession principle and told the story this way: (A: hand — knocking on the door), (A: hand — open the door), (B: hallway — description of long hallway), (B: stair — description of stairs going up), (B: feet — walking up stairs), (B: chest — breathing heavily), (C: eyes — shocked, wide-open eyes), and (D: mysterious figure — someone passes by in front of the person).[8] This storyteller signed the letter A twice with two different meanings, then letter B four times with four different meanings. The way the story was done implies that the alphabet has two As and four Bs in it, so it seems as if the alphabet went on like A, A, B, B, B, B, C, D. As we all know, the alphabet has only one A and one B. Therefore, the storyteller has failed to sustain an appropriate rhythm for his ABC story, using a single-letter sequence.

The only handshape that has the right to be signed twice is the handshape for the manual alphabet letters I and J. As seeing both letters have the same handshape, the storyteller can use the handshape twice with different meanings applied to them. One grievous error often made by storytellers is that they often skip one letter by signing the I and the J handshape together as if they were one sign instead of two.

If the storyteller decides to change the rhythm of the ABC story by changing from one letter to two letters from the beginning to end (AA, BB, CC, DD…), it is acceptable as long as the storyteller maintains the same rhythm throughout the story. As long as this principle is followed, the storyteller has the freedom to experiment with different rhythms, i.e., (AA, B, CC, D, EE, F…).

Careful transition between letters and/or numbers
This is the most commonly overlooked problem. Storytellers often do not realize that they are adding extra signs in between the actual manual alphabet and/or number sequence.

Another haunted house story will be used as an example for this: The person opens the front door of a haunted house, goes inside and immediately sees something that really scares the person. This person then tells the other person standing next to him to check out whatever has frightened the first person so badly . Now, in the ASL version, the storyteller signs, (A: hand — open the door), (B: feet — walking), (C: eyes — shocked, wide-open eyes), (B: hand — tapping next person) and (D: hand — pointing at something). The storyteller has added the one small, subtle gesture of tapping the other person's shoulder – as if it's not a part of the ABC sequence. This storyteller has inadvertently added an extra sign between the letters C and D.

When storytellers are on stage telling ABC stories, they must realize that the audience watches their stories very carefully, often checking to make sure that each letter appears in the story. If the storytellers add signs in between letters, the audience may either overlook or notice the inconsistency. They may choose to ignore it, but just because the audience does not often complain about it, doesn't mean the storytellers should be allowed to add signs in between letters.

Order of presenting two lettered or numbered handshapes
Many storytellers like to get creative by using a combination of two handshapes. There's nothing wrong with doing this, since it is a form of creative language play. There are many nifty combinations of two handshapes that can be used in ABC stories, such as the use of 'AB' to describe a heart beating (A: heart — beating) and (B: chest — covering the heart) or 'KL' as a rider on

a bike (K: person — riding on the bike) and (L: bike — moving bike).

However, storytellers need to be careful not to return to the previous letter. This is one of the most common mistakes storytellers make, because it is very easy to do without even noticing. For example: *A person is riding on his bike, and then all of sudden, the rider falls off his bike.* An ASL storyteller may start with the letters K and L to show a rider on a bike (K: person — riding on the bike) and (L: bike — moving bike), then (K: rider — falls off). Then L letter handshape disappears while the storyteller is still signing the K letter handshape. That becomes a failure in the succession of the manual alphabet. It goes the same with signing the next letter early, then going back to the letter that was supposed to come before. That is, starting with L (L: bike — park on the land), then K appears (K: person — walking to bike), then the combinations begin (K: person — riding on the bike) and (L: bike — moving bike). The combination of two handshapes should not be a problem long as the storyteller avoids mixing up the first and second letter in the order.

MINIMAL DEVIATION

How often have audiences noticed that there are certain signs that often appear in ABC, number, word, and one-handshape stories, but are never seen or signed in a normal conversation? Developing and signing stories are not easy; it is challenging to make a whole story come alive with each handshape. There are some handshapes that storytellers often struggle with because there are limited numbers of signs for those handshapes. As a result, storytellers will often come up with a deviated version of that handshape to fit into their stories so they can move on. There are two different methods of deviation, such as changing the handshape a little bit to meet the needs of the story, or using the correct handshape for a sign that we would usually sign with a different handshape. However, the question is: How much deviation is permitted? There are some storytellers who deviate too far from the original handshapes or signs. What we need to do is set a goal to keep deviation as minimal as possible.

Deviations #1: Changing the handshape of the original manual handshape? We know that to follow the manual handshapes is a basic requirement for a successful story with handshape constraints, but sometimes we want to change the handshape a little bit so it can go into the signs that we want to use it for. Take the letter A, we can use the handshape of the letter A to show the act of KNOCKING, WASHING, or PUTTING-A-SHIRT-ON. Those are the perfect signs for the letter A, because in signing those signs, you can clearly use the proper handshape of the letter A. Now, what about using the A handshape with an open thumb? It can be used when signing the following words- CHASING, WHICH, GIRL, and GAME. When we spell out the letter A, do we spell it out with an open thumb? Not typically, although there are a few people who spell out the letter A with an open thumb, but the point is that the appropriate way to sign the letter A is with a closed thumb. Yet storytellers will change the A handshape slightly by opening their thumbs to make more signs accessible. Since using the A handshape with an open thumb is in fact, a minimal deviation, it is still acceptable by many people; so it is not wrong to do this.

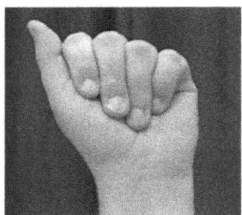
Correct "A" manual alphabet

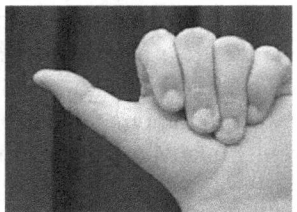
Acceptable "A" minimal deviation

There are storytellers who have deviated handshapes to the extent where it is not acceptable at all. Here's a famous example — changing the T handshape to the "time-out" sign. In doing this, storytellers are attempting to substitute the image of the T as seen in written English for the manual T of ASL. The "time-out" sign does not come close to the T of the manual alphabet and we don't spell out the manual alphabet like this: R, S, "time-out", U, V... Storytellers should always follow the appropriate sign of each letter of the manual alphabet, within the control of acceptable minimal deviation.

Most storytellers argue that the reason why they use the "time-out" sign rather than the T handshape is because they cannot find better ways to sign the T letter handshape. What they don't realize is that they can find better ways to sign the T handshape using minimal deviation.

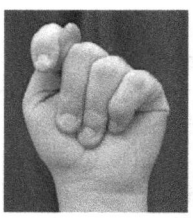
Correct "T" manual alphabet

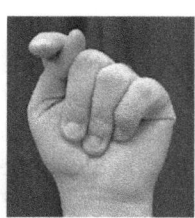
Acceptable "T" minimal deviation

Unacceptable "T" minimal deviation

Movement?
We get the concept of following the handshapes of the manual alphabet to make a story out of it, now what about the movements used to individualize each letter or number? Should we follow the movements of the letters J and Z in an ABC or word story? Should we follow the movements of the numbers ten and higher in a number story? There are some people who consider it a requirement to follow the movement of letters and numbers, while others don't think that it's necessary to follow the movement of letters and numbers, just the handshape.

My point of view on the movement issue is that it is not necessary to follow the letters and number's movements for stories with handshape constraints. Let's look at this from a linguistic view; it follows the four principles of phonology for the ASL signs: handshape, location, movement, and palm orientation.[9] Since the handshape is frozen, we depend on different locations, movement, palm orientation, and as well as non-manual signs to make a story out of the manual handshapes. If we decided to be absolutists for natural ASL fingerspelling components, such as the handshape and movement for the J and Z letters, our options with signing will be much more limited for ABC and word stories. To sum it up, we are not allowed to change the handshape of each letters, but we are allowed to change the movements to enhance a story. Hence, the issue of movement does not matter to me at all, however, it is acceptable if a storyteller wants to follow the exact movements of the J and Z letters and numbers.

Bending the handshapes
It is very common for storytellers to bend the handshapes they're using in order to improve the quality and structure of their stories. There are some handshapes that can be bent, such as B, C, and D while other handshapes cannot be bent, such as A, M, and S. Again, deviation has to be as minimal as possible. For example, the B handshape: if the fingers bend slightly, about one-quarter of the way, deviation will be considered minimal, thus acceptable. If the fingers bend half of the way down, and deviation will be a little more than minimal, and may be not be considered acceptable. However, if the storyteller repeatedly moves his fingers quickly, i.e., the D handshape used for COME-TO-ME, it will be acceptable. If the fingers bends more than halfway down, at least three-quarters of the way, the deviation will be considered too far out and it may be rejected by the majority of the audience.

Deviations #2: Changing the original sign to fit the handshape?
Sometimes when we want to sign something, but are stuck with a handshape that does not go with the signs we want to use. Then we try our best to

change the sign slightly to fit the handshape. Of course, there are some signs that have undergone acceptable minimal deviation and there are also signs where the deviation was overdone to the point where it is unacceptable.

Here are some examples where I have seen some storytellers use minimal deviation for the letter M — they have used it to indicate SWEATING (M: water — trickling on forehead). The number 5 handshape would have been the appropriate handshape to use instead, but most audiences have found the use of the letter M acceptable. Another example is the THINKING sign using the E handshape, (E: think — using both hands, moving all fingers on forehead). The flat-O handshape is what people usually use for the THINKING sign, but in this instance, the storyteller used the E handshape because it's similar to the flat-O handshape, therefore reasonable to most audiences.

There are some signs being used by other storytellers that deviate too far and are unacceptable. Someone once used the A handshape to indicate an airplane (A: plane — flying). People wouldn't be able to see how the A handshape can be used for an airplane, because to sign "airplane," we use the ILY handshape. In using the A handshape for AIRPLANE, the storyteller went too far outside the limits of deviation.

Who decides the limits of deviations?

Storytellers may try to defend their work (i.e., the use of the A handshape for AIRPLANE) by arguing that the sign is similar to a SEE sign or that the airplane is too far from us to be able to see the shape clearly. This leads to the next question, who decides how much deviation is acceptable? There are some who believe the storytellers have the final say because they are the artists and their stories are their works of art. There are also others who believe that the audience has the right to decide how much deviation is acceptable. Personally, I believe it goes both ways. Storytellers should follow the basic principles and please the majority of the audience. If the audience wants to critique the storytellers' work, they have to do it within reason. Both the storytellers and the audience need to agree on a common range of acceptable minimal deviation for stories with handshape constraints.

USE OF COHESIVE DEVICES

The general storytelling principles are a part of the stories with handshape constraints principles, too. It's very important to be aware of how storytellers present their stories to the audience. Their stories will reflect the storyteller's delivery skill; if the storyteller is successful, someone who makes good use of cohesive devices, the story will turn out to be excellent, whilst storytellers who are weak with cohesive devices will turn out second-rate stories. The

cohesive device principles are designed to help the storyteller be able to tell stories smoothly, going from manual handshape to manual handshape or use one-handshape continuously. Whenever a storyteller tells a story with handshape constraints, with a stiff hand as if they were signing each manual handshape individually, that is when the storyteller loses control over his audience. The audience will get bored and start focusing on the storyteller's mistakes, thus notice them more. The cohesive device principles often holds a lot of power because if the storyteller fails to follow this rule, the audience can get distracted easily and lose interest, even if the story itself is a good one. Cohesive devices involve the use of the following:
- Use of space and role shifts
- Use of paralinguistic cues: eye gazes, facial expression, and body movement
- Deployment of 3 Ps: pacing, pausing, and phrasing

Use of Space and Role Shifts

The use of space and role shifts helps the audience follow the story clearly and easily. The use of space helps the storyteller set up a map of the story, such as the location of a tree, house, and lake in the story's setting. Also, the storyteller can set up two things or characters in the story, with one on the left side, and the other on the right side, and from there on, the storyteller can point to the right side and audience will know what or who the storyteller is talking about. To be able to tell a story about two or more people, you have to tell it using clear shifting between two or more roles. Proper role shifting requires you to act as if you are one character, then immediately change to an entirely different person by turning your body around a little bit with a change in where your eyes are fixated, so that the audience can understand the difference between the two characters and can see what is going on between both characters.

Use of Paralinguistic Cues: Eye Gazes and Facial Expression

The direction of eye gaze plays a role in the use of space and role shifting, too. Eye gaze acts as a support for the setting and the people in the story. Where the storyteller's eyes gaze is the key to the audience in many ways. It helps the audience's awareness of what the person in the story is looking at. The storyteller can reveal more information from the story by just using eye contact. Eye contact plays a very important role in showing the mood of the character in the story such as showing fear or curiosity through the different eye expressions. Of course, the storyteller needs to keep the audience involved with the story by making regular eye contact with them during the telling of the story.

Everybody agrees that facial expression is very important for storytelling. However, what some storytellers do not realize is that facial expressions gives them an extra advantage in telling stories with handshape constraints. Since the storyteller's handshapes are limited, they have to use their facial expressions to relay extra information. Going back to the haunted house story as an example of the mistake commonly made by storytellers with the use of their facial expression, (A: hand — open door), (B: feet — walking), (C: eyes — shocked, wide eyes), (B: hand — tapping other person on shoulder) and (D: hand — pointing at something). The mistake is adding another B handshape in between the C and D handshape. How can the storyteller avoid this mistake and let the audience know that the main character in the story is getting the other person's attention? That's when facial expressions comes in and saves the story. After the C handshape, the storyteller can "freeze" the manual alphabet sequence, turn his or her head to the side, make a "Hey, look at that!" facial expression, and then turn back to where the character is pointing at, using the D handshape.

Use of Paralinguistic Cues: Body Movement
There are some storytellers who tell stories using their entire body by moving their legs, bending up and down, using bigger signs, and wiggling their body around, but when it comes to telling stories with handshape constraints (especially ABC stories), they lose the use of their body movement? The use of paralinguistic cues, such as body movements, is the key to giving out extra information in the story, which is what your hands are not allowed to do due to limited handshapes. We are aware of the importance of facial expressions, but we often forget to make good use of the rest of our bodies, such as our legs, while telling stories. To get the audience's full attention, it is always best for the storyteller to put himself in the story, which can be achieved by using his whole body to its fullest potential.

Deployment of 3 Ps: Pacing, Pausing, and Phrasing
Each storyteller must put the following to good use: pacing, pausing, and phrasing, or the stories would be dull. Good stories are told using a range of speed, going from fast to slow, depending on what is happening in the story at certain moments. So storytellers should tell stories using the pacing, pausing, and phrasing methods successfully. This is the area where the most problems appear for many ABC stories, number stories, and word stories because storytellers often tell their stories using the same pace from the beginning to the end. This is where the famous example of the haunted house story comes in again. The storyteller would sign, (A: hand — knocking), (B: door — opening the door), (C: search — searching), (D: hear — hear something), and (E:

scream — screaming in "E" note). A true storyteller would tell the story from A to C in a slow pace, then jump from D to E using a faster pace. Using this method would get the audience interested in the story, but many storytellers tell their stories with the same pace from A to Z, they will use the same pace from A to E, which isn't acceptable.

All in all, storytellers telling one-handshape stories usually have no problem with cohesive devices but most of them will have problems with ABC stories, number stories, and word stories. This may be because the storytellers are very focused on each letter or number during the telling of these stories, as if trying to remember the order of the letters or numbers. When storytellers are this focused on remembering the order of the letters or numbers, cohesive devices are easily forgotten.

INTEGRITY OF THE STORYLINE

It is very important to see how storytellers present the story and to see how the plot of the story is presented to the audience. A very good story plot paired up with a skilled storyteller makes a masterpiece. Since creating new stories with handshape constraints is challenging, it's even more challenging to create a good plot. It requires quite some time to mull over the new story and work out the kinks.

Logically, stories with handshape constraints have to make sense. A story that doesn't make any sense to the audience can't be a good story. How can the audience enjoy stories with handshape constraints if they don't understand the story at all? Unfortunately, this happens, especially with stories with handshape constraints. Storytellers need to study their stories closely to see if it would make any sense to the audience. A basic guideline to follow when going through a storyline would be: Would the audience follow the story easily? Would the audience understand the story without any problems? Would the audiences enjoy the story?

We have to make sure the story with handshape constraints is clear and that the plot is good and easy to follow. To create a story that makes sense involves these three elements:
- Clear introduction and conclusion
- Flow in the stories
- Phrasings that are not forced

Clear of introduction and conclusion
Generally, stories must have good introductions and conclusions, but storytellers seem to struggle with this when it comes to stories with handshape constraints. Most storytellers don't have any problems with the introduc-

tion; they are able to start off well, but many storytellers have a lot of trouble with their conclusions. There are many stories that have been cut short without a proper conclusion. For example, there have been ABC stories that were brilliant until the final letter, Z, when all of sudden, the character simply zooms away in the middle of the story's plot. Granted, there are some stories that end well with the "zooming away" technique. It may be a good way to get away from having to come up with a conclusion, but it doesn't apply to every story. All stories need to be wrapped up with a good conclusion, for a good story is nothing without a good conclusion.

Flow in the stories

The ABC, number, and word stories should have a smooth flow of each letters or numbers in the plot. Since storytellers often have a hard time coming up with ideas of possible signs without breaking the succession principle and the minimal deviation principles, they often can't help but come up with some deviated information in the storyline to get rid of some difficult letters or numbers. Here's a classic example, the use of the T handshape to sign RESTROOM. There are many good ABC stories, but when it comes to the T letter, the story tends to deviate to RESTROOM all of the sudden, then back to the story.

Another example; some storytellers have a hard time with the I and J letter, so they will use the old "I JEALOUS KING" trick with the help of the K letter, which often sticks out of the story plot like an eyesore. Again, storytellers have to make sure each letter or number fits into the plot to ensure the smooth flow of the story. Another one of the most common mistake is using the I letter to show a person walking in high heels. There are some stories that are being told in the masculine form and the storyteller will often end up showing men running, using the I handshape, as if the man is running in high heels. Those men in the stories wouldn't be wearing high heels at all unless the story involves a male character wearing high heels.

Phrasings that are not forced

When storytellers come up with a new ABC, number, or word story, they usually develop the plot letter-by-letter or number-by-number, which is fine, but when they are telling the story, they seem to be emphasizing the order of the letters or numbers over the story itself. Sometimes the process of telling an ABC story shows the storyteller focusing more on getting the letters right rather than on the storyline, which is a mistake. Because of this, the quality of the story is weakened.

The reason that many storytellers emphasize the letters or numbers more than the story itself is because they are trying to remember the right order for each letter or number. Storytellers need to practice, familiarize themselves with the story, and know the story by heart. From there, they can tell the story in a way that focuses on the story itself rather than the letters or numbers, which will make the story a successful one.

TOOLS OF STORIES WITH HANDSHAPE CONSTRAINTS CRITICISM

In conclusion, stories with handshape constraints that are evaluated as a successful story, adheres to the following principles: succession principle, minimal deviations, use of cohesive devices, and integrity of the storyline.

Those basic principles are impossible!
I remember when I first learned the basic principles of stories with handshape constraints from Dr. Bahan in one of his classes; I was overwhelmed.[10] My first response to the basic principles was that it is impossible to make stories with handshape constraints without violating them. In fact, I used to believe that I would not be able to come up with any good ABC stories at all. I am confident that those thoughts apply to most others too. That's how most people respond to the basic principles and it's a perfectly normal reaction.

In reality, we can break some of the basic principles. Making up stories with handshape constraints should be a fun activity for us. We can just ignore the basic principles and make up many good stories. It's all about having fun and the challenge that comes with making up stories with handshape constraints. After people play with creating stories with handshape constraints, they can start picking up some new ideas and techniques without violating the basic principles. It's all about creativity and practice.

When it come to the stage, contests, filming, or any other professional events, storytellers should seriously consider strictly following the basic principles of stories with handshape constraints. Professional storytellers should be able to tell stories with handshape constraints without violating the basic principles. Also, their stories should be models for all those that follow. If the storytellers violate some of the basic principles, others will take that as an example and follow those storytellers, who are supposed to set standards for others. If they are able to follow the basic principles and present good stories with handshape constraints, it will encourage others to practice their stories with handshape constraints correctly.

Creating new standards for critique
These tools of criticism were designed with several reasons in mind, one being to encourage storytellers to create a standard that will in turn bring up the status of stories with handshape constraints in ASL literature. They

were also designed with stability and precision in mind, because with these basic principles, all storytellers alike will be able to produce quality work that can be compared to and evaluated fairly. It also provides proper guidelines for the audience, giving them the opportunity to do sophisticated evaluations instead of second-guessing contestants and storytellers' quality of stories like they have been doing in the past. Also, we would be able to be more effective in teaching others about/how to do stories with handshape constraints. With these basic principles, we will be able to pass our knowledge on to the next generation of storytellers and influence ASL literature as we know it, as well as improve the quality of stories with handshape constraints.

ENDNOTES

1. Humphries, T. "Talking Culture and Culture Talking" in Bauman, H-D. ed. 2008. *Open Your Eyes: Deaf Studies Talking*. Minneapolis, MN: University of Minnesota Press.
2. Bauman, H-D., Nelson, J., and Rose, H. 2006. *Signing the Body Poetic: Essays on American Sign Literature*. Berkeley, CA: University of California Press.
3. Clayton Valli created the following number stories, "Rabbit" and "The Bridge," and word stories, "Flash" and "Something Not Right" in *ASL Poetry: Selected Works of Clayton Valli*. DawnSignPress. 1995.
4. Nathie Marbury created the following number story, "Children's ASL Poems #3" and "Funeral," and one-handshape story, "Children's ASL Poems #1-2" "Ones" in *Nathie: No Hand-Me-Downs*. The Tactile Mind Press. 2005.
5. Debbie Rennie created the following word story, "Veal Boycott" and one-handshape story, "Swan" in *Poetry in Motion — Debbie Rennie*. Sign Media Inc. 1989.
6. Principles for the handshapes in order don't have to apply to just three types of stories. Theoretically, these principles may apply to a composite of ASL Handshapes stories, such as the "ASL Handshape Chart" by Frank Allen Paul at DawnSignPress or others. The same goes for principles for one-handshape stories too, it can also apply to two-handshapes stories, such as Nathie Marbury's "Love Lesson."
7. Bauman, H-D., Nelson, J., and Rose, H. 2006. *Signing the Body Poetic: Essays on American Sign Literature*. Berkeley, CA: University of California Press.
8. This article provides several examples of specific letters in ABC stories. In order to help the reader understand how to sign the examples visually, this article uses a system in written English. It goes like this: (Letter: What the hand will represent — What the hand is doing.) Here is an example of the classic ABC story and a visual example of how it will be signed:
    - The person opens the front door and enters the haunted house. Then this person saw something that really scared this person.
    - (A: hand — open door), (B: feet — walking), (C: eyes — shocked, wide eyes).
9. Lucas, C., Murlrooney, K., and Valli, C. 2005. *Linguistics of American Sign Language: An Introduction, 4th Ed.* Washington, DC: Gallaudet University Press.
10. DST 314: Oral Traditions in the Deaf Community at Gallaudet University, Fall 2002.

An Exploratory Case Study of a Nongovernmental Organization (NGO) Working with the Deaf in Ghana, West Africa

HILLARY MELANDER

SIGNS OF HOPE INTERNATIONAL, A NONGOVERNMENTAL ORGANIZATION (NGO), sends a group of interns to the Demonstration School for the Deaf (DemoDeaf) in Mampong-Akuapim, Ghana every summer. Three interns are assigned to the Junior Secondary School department (JSS). From May to August 2005 an assessment of student, teacher, and volunteers needs took place to find the best way Signs of Hope International interns can best support the school without contributing to the oppression already faced by the minority population.

The assessment led to the development of a mathematics program designed to reinforce basic mathematic skills including counting, addition, subtraction, multiplication and division. The program was evaluated by a researcher/intern and modified and launched again as an after-school program in June of 2007. The purpose of this study is to explore the effects of the supplementary math program on the JSS at students at the Demonstration School for the Deaf.

A predominantly qualitative approach was used to gather data on the perspectives of the students, teachers, and Signs of Hope International volunteers at DemoDeaf to more fully understand the math program and math achievement data context. A discussion of the histories of Ghana, education and Deaf Education in Ghana will be included to contextualize the state of Deaf Education in Ghana. Institutional Review Board (IRB) approval for this study was received in May 2007. Signs of Hope International co-founders and the Headmaster at DemoDeaf approved the study after receiving a copy of the IRB proposal. The department head was also briefed and given a copy of the proposal for review. Suggestions from the local teachers were adapted into the program.

This study has practical significance for Signs of Hope International and other NGOs that work with the deaf in countries with similar educational systems for the deaf. In addition, this study has academic and sociological significance because it includes an ethnography piece on a linguistic minority group that has been set apart from the rest of the larger society and into residential or day Deaf schools in order to protect the "vulnerable population" (Charrow 1975; Lane et al. 1996; Higgins 1996; National 1996). It also demonstrates that protecting deaf children by placing them into an educational system originally designed for hearing students actually perpetuates some harmful effects caused by stratification and status ascription. However, some of the benefits the government may not have anticipated are those that provide students with access to a community with whom they can be a part of and share a common culture with (Bienvenu 1985-1988; Charrow 1975; Lane et al. 1996; Humphrey 2001). The significance of this benefit cannot be stressed enough.

Since 2005 the organization has sponsored three summer missions and is preparing to launch the fourth. Interns work with students in the classroom during and after school providing classroom instruction, one-on-one tutoring, informal conversations and recreational activities. The similarities between ASL and GSL allow interns to quickly adapt to local signs to meet the needs of the students. Signs of Hope International leaders recognize that the presence of the organization on the school campus does not guarantee the positive effects on students (Balliff-Spanvill et. al.2005; Fuhriman et. al. 2006; Ward et al. 2008). The objective of this study is to examine the possible positive or negative consequences that the mathematics program (designed and carried out by Signs of Hope International interns) may have on the Junior Secondary Students at DemoDeaf.

HISTORY OF DEAF EDUCATION

Reading, writing, and the arts of science and mathematics were limited to the elite for centuries. For many years income status, gender, and an individual's physical characteristics determined who would be educated (Ballantine 1997; Brint 1998; Matthaei 1984). Deaf individuals were excluded from the educational system because verbal language was thought to reflect cognitive ability by experts or doctors, and philosophers (Miller and Branson 2002; Higgins 1996, 1980, Harris 1995; Lane 1984).

Instead the deaf were labeled in many parts of the world as misfits and hidden by family members, sent to the country, or taken and locked into asylums (Branson and Miller 2002; Lane 1984, 1992). In the 1770s, Charles-Michel de L'Épée paved the way for deaf education by raising funds to establish Saint Jacques, the first public residential school for the deaf in Paris. However, like medical experts and philosophers of the time he did not appreciate or comprehend the sophistication of the signed language and culture of the linguistic minority (Branson and Miller 2002; Lane 1984, 1992; Lane et al. 1996). Consequently, hearing experts deemed themselves stewards of the deaf and assumed the responsibility of designing their integration into hearing society.

Epée believed that the sign language of the deaf should mirror the grammar of spoken French if the deaf were to learn complex and intense subjects such as science and philosophy (Branson and Miller 2002; Lane 1984, 1996). He developed methodical signs and required all students and teachers to use these signs in the classroom (Branson and Miller 2002; Lane 1984, 1992; Lane et al. 1996). However, when deaf students were among peers or with other deaf adults, students resumed the use of their natural signed language (Lane 1984, 1992).

Eventually sign language was prohibited at St. Jacques and was replaced with the oralist method where the students are taught to rely on speech and lip reading. Harlan Lane (1984) explains that while under the control of Baron Joseph Marie De Gerando, Saint-Jacques was transformed into a hearing school for the Deaf. Enthusiasm for the oralist method heightened in 1880 at the Congress of Milan. The congress consisting of nearly all hearing educators and specialists with no sign language background or experience declared, "...the superiority of speech over signs" (Branson and Miller 2002; Harris 1995; Humphrey 2001; Lane 1984, 1996; Lane et. al 1992). The congress decided that all deaf education would be conveyed through the oralist method, thus forcing all deaf teachers out of the deaf educational system for decades. Senior students with signing experience were separated from younger students for fear of contamination (Branson and Miller 2002; Lane 1984, 1996; Lane et. al 1992). The effects of the decisions made at the Milan of Congress can be seen in Deaf education today.

The violent history of stigma, attempted linguistic genocide, and oppression has had detrimental effects on the quality and type of education the Deaf have received. The main focus and structure of Deaf Education has been based less on content and subject matter and more about on socializing the Deaf to become more "hearing" (Akamatsu 1998; Branson and Miller 2002; Fischer 1998).

Total Communication (TC), mainstreaming, and full integration programs are all means by which hearing experts attempt to integrate the Deaf into the hearing community (Branson and Miller 2002; Corker 1996; Harris 1995; Humphrey 2001). In some way each of these methods assumes the superiority of speech over sign and ignores the social and individual needs of the deaf students' personal development.

Deaf individuals and leaders in the community support Deaf schools as alternatives to mainstreaming and integration programs. Deaf schools include both day schools and residential programs. Deaf schools empower children by providing the opportunity to congregate together, learn sign language, communicate, build relationships, and often receive education in the form of a manual language (Harris 1995; Bienvenu 1988; Corker 1996; Lane 1984, 1992; Lane et al 1996). Residential schools throughout the world have become so salient to the deaf culture that generation Deaf families continue to send their children to the schools (Bienvenu 1988). Residential schools provide the opportunity for the deaf to finally feel at "home" (Bienvenu 1988; Lane; Harris 1995).

The deaf are a linguistic minority born into this world as visual learners and communicators (Charrow 1975; Lane 1992; Lane et al. 1996). The deaf community has a rich deaf culture of at its core. It is unfortunate that even today deaf leaders and community members must actively fight for basic rights such as access to quality education in the primary language of the deaf.

BRIEF HISTORY OF GHANA

The land now known as the Republic of Ghana was under colonial rule since the arrival of the Portuguese in the 15th Century until late in the 20th Century. Control of Ghana switched hands from the Portuguese, Dutch, Danes and then the British Empire. Ghana became the first African nation to receive independence from colonial rule on March 6, 1957 (Britannica 2008).

Since 1957 Ghana's government has undergone several coups. The first elected head of state declared himself dictator in 1964 and in 1966 the Ghanaian army took control of the capitol. In 1983 Jerry Rawlings, a flight lieutenant, lead his regime in another successful coup (Hayne 1991; Babatope 1982). All governmental powers, including the judicial system, were given to the regime. Rawlings established the Provisional National Defense Council (PNDC) which created law 42 which turned the power to the people and abrogated the 1979 Ghanaian constitution (Haynes 1991). The first peaceful transfer of power took place between head of state flight lieutenant Jerry John Rawlings and John Kofi Agyekum Kufuor in 2001.

EDUCATION IN GHANA

A series of legislative acts and reports have contributed to the development of Ghana's Basic Education system. The Education Act of 1961 was designed to make education compulsory for all primary school aged students in Ghana, including those with special needs. The government found compulsory education difficult to enforce due to the high rural population and government instability (Babatope 1982; National 1996). Later, the Compulsory Universal Basic Education Program (CUBEP) was established to reinforce the 1961 Act (National 1996). The World Bank credits the CUBEP with increasing national primary school enrollment by 5.2 percent between 1996 and 2001 (World Bank 2007).

In 2001 there were 12,225 public Primary Schools and 6,418 Junior Secondary Schools. Total enrollment for Primary and JSS was approximately 767,303. The World Bank reports total percent of gross enrollment for students in primary school was at 94% in 2006, vastly different from the 79% enrollment less than a decade ago (World Development Index 2008). The education system in Ghana has made significant improvements during the last two decades it is still struggling with issues such as "poor quality teaching and learning, weak management capacity at all levels to the educational system, and inadequate access to education" (Ghana 2001).

DEAF EDUCATION IN GHANA AND OTHER COUNTRIES

In Ghana, those viewed as disabled include the blind, deaf, deaf and blind, mentally handicapped, and the otherwise severely handicapped. Of the estimated 679,000 to 804,000 disabled in Ghana only .6% receives any form of education (National 1996). These students are often grouped together in Special Schools or Special Education schools because they are viewed as the most vulnerable to social exclusion (National 1996). There are two contributing factors to the development of Special Schools including legislative acts and deaf advocates.

One of the first principles stated under Law 42 mandates adequate schooling facilities for all "to the greatest extent possible" (Haynes 1991 pp. 412). The Basic Education Sector Improvement Program (BESIP) was introduced to "improve access to basic education, especially of girls, the poor and other disadvantaged segments of the population (pg1)." These legislative acts provided funds for the establishment of deaf schools.

In 1957 Dr. Andrew Foster, the first black graduate from Gallaudet University, minister, and founder of the Christian Mission for the Deaf (CMD) came to Ghana to lobby for the establishment of deaf schools. With the efforts of Dr. Foster and other advocates for the Deaf, a Deaf school was established in 1957. Dr. Foster helped to establish thirteen schools for the Deaf in Ghana including one Senior Secondary School (SSS) for the Deaf, and other Deaf schools throughout West Africa. Today, the schools for the deaf are either day schools or residential schools.

Dr. Foster and his colleagues introduced ASL to the Deaf in West Africa, a very controversial action among the Deaf community (Lane et al. 1996). ASL originally taught at the deaf schools has since evolved into Ghanaian Sign Language (GSL), the national sign language today. Ghanaian Sign Language differs from ASL only in lexicon (Gordon 2005) and has come to be considered a legitimate language among linguists. GSL has been listed in several language databases and several GSL dictionaries have been published.

Currently most Special Education teachers in Ghana are college graduates from the University College of Education at Winneba. The College of Education offers a Special Education program where GSL classes are offered. According to graduates from Winneba University students are required to complete one semester of GSL and an internship at a Special Education School before graduating (Melander 2005, 2007).

Deaf schools in other countries such as Nigeria, Greece, and Saudi Arabia have similar standards for teachers of Deaf Education. In Greece, teachers undergo a two-year training program in special education. However, the program does not offer any kind of specialization (Lampropoulou 1989). Emmanuel Ojile claims that the biggest threat to Deaf Education in Nigeria is the lack of qualified teachers (1989). In this report Ojile recalls an article he previously published (1987) where he asserted that at least 37 percent of deaf school teachers in Nigeria lack specialized training and knowledge in their field. This has occurred in a country where Deaf advocates have successfully lead the way for the establishment of 43 Deaf schools. The number of specialized teachers versus the number of schools demonstrates how important educating the Deaf in the primary language of the Deaf is to hearing administrators and policy makers.

SIGN LANGUAGE IN THE CLASSROOM

Low sign language requirements set by government institutions and universities have a series of unintended consequences that effect the population as a whole, teachers of the deaf, and most importantly deaf students.

A false message is conveyed by government and education leaders to the larger society when teachers are not required to become fluent in sign language while in school. The false message down plays the legitimacy of sign languages, its role as a primary language, and the level of importance in deaf schools. As a result family members of the Deaf and community members are mislead to conclude sign languages are inferior to spoken languages. The rich culture of the linguistic minority thus remains oppressed and hidden by the Hearing majority. Moreover the negative stereotype and stigma against the deaf are perpetuated among the oppressors.

Teachers experience unforeseen stresses and experience high levels of inadequacy that threaten their emotional wellbeing upon entering a classroom where they are the minority and are the only persons in the classroom that cannot communicate with the students (DeMarris & LeCompte 1995). Teachers who cannot communicate with students in the classroom struggle to maintain classroom order, build a positive rapport with students, and maintain flexibility in teaching strategy.

The most detrimental consequences of not requiring fluent sign language teachers at deaf schools harm the actual students. Teachers of the deaf who do not sign are attempting to force students to learn a new language and curricula simultaneously. The time the student should have spent learning the material is actually spent decoding what the teacher is saying. High levels of illiteracy, low comprehension, and low test scores can naturally be expected under such circumstances. The shallow gestural conversations with teachers and the absence of communicative adult role models in the classroom make it difficult for students to understand the original purposes for schooling. The forced oppression and isolation robs the students of an education, hampers language and mental development, and contributes to surmounting levels of frustration on behalf of the student (Corker 1996; Senghas & Monaghan 2002; Branson & Miller 2002; Erting 1994; Higgins 1996; Lane 1984, 1992; Lane et al. 1996).

ROLE OF NGOS IN DEAF EDUCATION

The role of non-governmental organizations, or NGOs, has increased significantly and gained legitimacy in the international world. Instead of looking toward government agencies to improve local conditions, communities look to NGOs to represent them and to meet their needs (McMichael 2000). For example, many developing countries with large rural areas depend on NGOs to support community schools or government schools by providing supplemental funding, manpower, or trainings (Ballif-Spanvill et al. 2005; 2006; Ward et al. 2008).

In doing so the risk of imposing western ideals and systems onto the community receiving assistance is very high (Mehmet 1995; Moore-Gilbert 1997; Ward 2008). These ideals can even have harmful effects in educational settings when the assumption is made that any kind of education is better than no education (Balliff-Spanvill et al. 2005; Fuhriman et. al. 2006). NGOs must be responsible for ensuring programs do not have harmful effects on members of the target population or other local society members.

There are additional risks NGOs working with deaf populations must consider. Just as hearing "knowledge leaders" or experts governed decisions, educational policies, and daily life practices of the Deaf minority, NGO leaders and volunteers run the risk of falsely assuming expertise over local deaf knowledge and experience. As a result programs or policies may be established that do not reach the target population or do more harm than good (Branson & Miller 2002; Crouch 1997; McMichael 2000; Solomon et al. 2002; Ward 2008).

To minimize harmful effects on Deaf minorities, NGOs, consisting of mainly hearing members, are obligated to consider both the western and hearing ideals and approaches they bring to the development process. The traditional perspective of Hearing individuals has viewed the Deaf as pathological, people who need to be fixed (Branson & Miller 2002; Charrow 1975; Crouch 1997; Lane 1984, 1992; Lane et al. 1996; Senghas 2002; Quartararo 1995). The Deaf perspective however, holds strong to viewing themselves as a linguistic minority (Crouch 1997; Lane et al. 1996). These two ideologies ultimately determine the kinds of services an organization offers and whether the services result in oppressive consequences in the educational setting.

Organizations following the traditional pathological approach offer more audiological or speech support in the forms of hearing aids, oralist and manual forms of the spoken language, reaffirm the ideal that the deaf are disabled or handicapped, and etc.

NGOs that view the Deaf community as a linguistic minority focus on obtaining access to equal education opportunities, rights to healthcare, and other opportunities for the Deaf. This is done by lobbying for the Deaf at international levels, facilitating networking between Deaf organizations in developed and developing countries, providing experts or facilitating experts on Deaf education and sign language, providing information on fundraising possibilities, etc. (World Federation of the Deaf 2008).

Many hearing NGO leaders and volunteers attempt to follow the guidelines as established by the World Federation of the Deaf however, it is difficult for a hearing person to recognize they live in a hearing world. Brown et al. (2003) describes a similar situation between white middle class America and other American racial minority groups by using this metaphor to emphasize their point, just as it is difficult for a fish to recognize that they swim in water. Thus it is difficult for hearing persons to address the needs of Deaf as perceived by the Deaf because they take for granted the things of the hearing world.

Signs that an NGO is facing this struggle are manifested on websites and organization strategy via word choice ("hearing impaired" versus "Deaf"), have limited Deaf membership or involvement, and sign language choice (natural sign languages versus manual modes of the dominant spoken language in society).

There are many NGOs working with the Deaf Ghana such as World Vision, Growing Connection, Volunteer Abroad, and Ikando that bring training directly to the deaf or provide prospective volunteers with access to Deaf Schools. The literature, however, on the methods and the effects of NGOs on the Deaf community is very limited. The lack of research suggests that the expected benefits of the programs are based on the premise that NGOs produce only positive outcomes by virtue of their altruistic ambitions. Therefore, little evaluation or research on the actual effects is needed by the NGO.

METHODS AND DATA COLLECTION

Research Questions

In this study we will seek to understand the perspectives and experiences of the JSS students and teachers at DemoDeaf. This makes it possible for the researcher to contextualize the mathematics program and its potential effects on students through the eyes of the participants. Researchers are interested in learning if the program increases student participation in their regular math class and the program's potential impact on student confidence. Potential program impact on teachers' perceptions of student ability and teaching strategy will also be addressed. This section will be discussed through qualitative data collected through field notes from the May-August 2005 and May–June 2007 programs.

Researchers are interested in learning if the afterschool mathematics program, which includes one-on-one tutoring and group work, affects participants' mathematic skill level. To answer this question the number of achievement tests successfully completed by students with 100% accuracy at the beginning of the program will be compared to the number of achievement tests completed by the end of the program.

Data Collection

Participants include the 49 student who were present at the JSS at the time. Three students were on a leave of absence due to medical problems and the JSS3 class had completed the school year. Student ages ranged from 13 to 22 years old. Admittance to the JSS indicates the student has demonstrated basic cognitive abilities during his or her primary school experience (Melander 2007). Experience has shown that the students' cognitive abilities range from kindergarten to about third grade (Melander 2005, 2007).

The JSS at DemoDeaf is an ideal setting to conduct this research because of the strong cooperative relationship between DemoDeaf and Signs of

Hope International as well as the familiarity of the classroom settings for researchers and participants. The headmaster, assistant headmaster, and faculty members are always open to teaching researchers the customs and ways of the school by welcoming observers in classrooms, answering researchers' questions, and providing feedback to when asked.

The classroom setting is ideal because it is familiar to both the participants and researchers. They are accustomed to teaching strategies such as lectures, tests, classroom exercises, tutoring, and some group work. Baseline data can be gathered through methods already familiar to students. This minimizes error by avoiding methods unfamiliar to participants (e.g. surveys) (Creswell 2007; Lofland 2006).

As a hearing white American, there are potential stumbling blocks for me as a researcher. I do feel that these barriers were minimized and the students accepted me into their social circles. Initially my background and experiences made students more inclined to trust me. I was born and raised in a family with a Deaf father and I started learning ASL as a baby. Students also made statements such as, "You love Deaf!" in response to my automatic reaction of shock and bewilderment after the students commented, "Oh I am sorry your dad is Deaf." This suggests students appreciated my sincerity. My visits to the school were also my second and third visits to Ghana, to which students replied, "You love Ghana!" My diverse family background and past experience in Ghana only gained the attention of the students. The true tests came at the beginning when students were testing my signing and receptive skills. Each time, however, the students congratulated me on understanding their language.

Trust was maintained as I continued to adapt to GSL, learned more about Ghanaian and Deaf cultures, ate local food such as Kankey and Fufu, and took to learning Twi, the local tribal language. As I learn to enjoy the food and speak the local language, more invitations to both formal and informal social gatherings invitations where I my appreciation for Ghanaian culture , the Culture at DemoDeaf, and Deaf culture increased. Appreciating the many cultures at the school helped to build a rapport with students and faculty that reciprocated respect and trust in and out of the classroom.

During the assessment phase information such as sex, age, estimated onset of deafness, family size, use of sign language in the home, and deaths in the family was documented. To avoid students signing answers to each other as observed in 2005 students testing was done in an isolated room with only the two researchers and two students in it. While testing, the students had limited vision of only one researcher. A third researcher stayed with the class playing getting-to-know-you games. When one student was done with the testing, they returned to class and told another student to come in. The assessment period took longer than expected so the third intern was brought in to help with the pre-testing period.

Student assessment consisted of achievement tests that revealed student ability in the following areas: counting, and single digit, double digit, and triple digit addition, subtraction, multiplication and division. To measure counting ability each individual student was asked to count to one hundred manually using GSL and by writing it down. The researcher recorded how far the student counted and any other interesting patterns observed.

Next, the student was given a worksheet, or achievement test, with ten single digit addition problems. If the student answered all ten questions correctly then other worksheets followed with double digit addition problems. If the double digit worksheet was completed with 100% accuracy the student progressed to triple digit addition exercises. This same pattern of testing was conducted for subtraction, multiplication, and division. Every student was tested for single digit addition, subtraction, multiplication and division, even those who could not count to 100. Again, researchers looked for patterns throughout the assessment phase. If a student could not perform the single digit exercise, they were not tested for the double or triple digit exercises.

Once pre-testing was completed the students were divided into groups based on achievement level. As the 2005 findings suggested, these first groups included counting, addition, and subtraction. The math program then continued as planned. Post tests included the number of achievements test passed throughout the duration of the math program before Signs of Hope International Interns left on July 12, 2007.

DESCRIPTION OF DEMONSTRATION SCHOOL FOR THE DEAF

This portion of the paper is based on participant observation field notes from the May-August 2005 and May-June 2007. Within this portion of the paper are some quotes and ideas that do not necessarily reflect the ideas of the school as a whole nor the consensus of the teacher body.

The Junior Secondary School in Mampong-Akuapim, Ghana, is just one of four departments under the Demonstration School for the Deaf. The other three departments are the Primary School, Deaf and Blind Unit, and Vocational departments. The JSS is housed in the lower level of a two story building. When walking from one end of the building to the other a visitor will first pass the Headmasters office, four main classrooms, and then a teachers' lounge. The girls dorm is located above the JSS classrooms and the boys dorm is located above the vocational department just left of the JSS.

Each classroom is equipped with about seventeen desks, a chalkboard, and sometimes a clock. Each grade level is assigned to one room in which teachers rotate in to teach. A class schedule is posted at the front of the classroom to remind the students which subjects they should be studying. Inside the teachers' lounge written on the chalk board is a detailed schedule listing all the class times for every day of the week.

The JSS is divided into four classes beginning with Pre-JSS, JSS1, JSS2, and ending with JSS3. Students age ranges from the Pre-JSS class to the JSS2 classes are 13 to 22 years. The ages of the JSS3 students were not collected since the students had gone home after completing the school year in early May. Students use any combination of verbal English, Signing Exact English (another mode of English), Ghanaian Sign Language (GSL), pidgin (a mixture of both English and GSL), and Twi (local tribal language) to communicate with teachers and school administrators. Admittance to the JSS indicates the student has demonstrated basic cognitive abilities during his or her primary school experience (Melander 2007). Experience has shown that the students' cognitive abilities range from kindergarten to about third grade (Melander 2005, 2007).

All students at DemoDeaf line up Monday thru Friday at 7:45 am for roll call, morning prayers, student disciplinary action, and school announcements. Class is in session from 8:05 am until 1:45 pm. Class times range from 35 minutes to one hour and forty-five minutes depending on the subject and day of the week. Courses include Religion and Morality Education, Agricultural Science, Sign Language, Leatherwork, Mathematics, Social Studies, English Language, General Science, and Pre-technical Skills. At 9:50 every morning students have a 25 minute break. A few days of the week students receive a snack of biscuits (cookies) or tea. Lunch is generally served at 1:45pm, but it may be earlier or later depending on the day and the cooks.

Teachers at DemoDeaf range from interns just out of the university or teacher training colleges to experienced teachers of over twenty years. Upon graduation from the University College of Special Education at Winneba new teachers are randomly assigned to a special school (Melander 2005). A graduate from Winneba explained a teacher who has studied how to work with the blind has just as much chance of being sent to work at a deaf school as a teacher who has studied to work with the deaf has to be sent to a blind school (Melander 2005).

A commonality between all schools no matter location in the world is that some teachers are less effective than others. At DemoDeaf the attitude teachers have toward their Deaf students seems to be the most influential determinant of whether a teacher successfully conveys knowledge to students or not. Teacher attitudes affect teacher attendance, GSL abilities, expectations for students, teaching methods, and student teacher relationships. The attitudes teachers have toward the Deaf students seem to range from very negative accompanied with very low studen expectations for students to very positive accompanied with high student expectations.

In 2005 it was not unusual to have days where only two teachers would attend a classroom in an entire day. Teacher attendance was much more predictable and reliable in 2007 after the Headmaster addressed the issue a few days after our arrival in a morning faculty meeting. In 2005 and 2007 I learned teacher absence can be contributed to two causes. First the challenges of daily living such as washing laundry by hand, fetching buckets of water, cooking from scratch over fire, having to travel into town for business, and so on may legitimately cause teacher tardiness and occasionally teacher absence. However, some teachers with negative attitudes toward students often abused this privilege of having an accommodating school schedule.

Teachers who view the Deaf as incapable of learning or lazy appear to be more likely to be found in the Teachers' Lounge, talking together even though there are classes to teach. Other times teachers have been observed to have gone to class for a few minutes, written the lecture on the board, and then count that as teaching for the day. One day a teacher came to class after an absence of nearly two weeks. The students asked where he had been, but then the teacher became angry and was offended that the students asked for an explanation of some sort (Melander 2007).

Another similarity among these teachers with pessimistic attitudes towards students is that they were most resistant to learning GSL. This resistance is magnified by feelings of burn-out or feeling as if neither they nor anyone else can offer a solution to improve their situation. A solution to them would include immediate clear communication with students and students who perform better on tests. For them, the prospect of learning GSL at this time is overwhelming. Instead some teachers make excuses for not taking the initiative themselves to learn sign language from the students and other teachers they make excuses. Some believe they are justified because they did not ask to be sent to the Deaf school.

Another excuse is that the teacher does not think they will be at the school long enough to make it worth their while to invest the time and energy into learning. The reasoning that the government does not give enough "monetary incentive" for teachers to learn, however, seemed to be the most popular reason for not learning sign language among these teachers (Melander 2005). Given that most teachers do have to find another source of supplemental income this may be a true concern. However, because the teachers are not necessarily taking advantage of the opportunities to learn while on campus shows that it is more of an excuse than a legitimate reason.

These same teachers who appear to be absent more often and have lower GSL skills have similar teaching approaches. These teachers often rely on the traditional or teacher centered approach of lecturing like most teachers in third world countries (Brint, 1998). The lecture is often delivered through broken English and some signs, SEE, or written on the board. Delivering a lecture outside of the students language posses a real problem for conveying knowledge. After a lecture on one occasion the teacher asked if the class understood. A couple admitted they did not. The teacher asked another student to stand up to explain the concept to his classmate. The second student first explained he did not understand it either, but then shrugged his shoulders, smirked at his classmates, and proceeded to repeat what was written on the board in Signing Exact English and finger spelling. The teacher congratulated him for a job well done, the student sat down and class was concluded. After the teacher left I asked if the students really understood. They were honest and said they did not. They chose to rely on a survival mechanism to appease the teacher by signing UNDERSTAND.

To prepare for the tests given by teachers who rely so strongly on the lecturing method students concentrate on memorizing written words and ideas they have copied from the chalkboard and into their notebooks. Often, the students are not literate enough however, to even grasp the meanings of the words they are memorizing. When teachers rely on anything less than smooth and fluent GSL to teach the anxiety among the students is high and tests reflect more on memorization skills then comprehension.

From these less effective teachers it is not unusual to see them tell the students or hear them tell the students they are "lazy" or in conversations stating they are incapable of learning. One teacher explained that they have lower expectations for the Deaf students than they had to the hearing students they used to teach (Madsen 2007). Another teacher said, "[Deaf students] think slower then hearing students and use shortcuts when speaking instead of using proper English." When students did not perform well on a test some teachers would triumphantly show me their papers and say, "See!" as in I told you so. From observing teacher behavior and conversations it became apparent to the researcher that some of the teachers at DemoDeaf agree with the following perception as stated by one of the teachers, "The deaf actually make better vocational workers but the hearing students make better educated people." The low expectations less effective teachers have for student performance effects the level of engagement teachers will have with the students (Brint 1998).

Because of the low levels of GSL understanding and low expectations some of these teachers create social distance between them. Even the names of students are often unknown to these teachers. This lack of interest or engagement with the class makes teachers oblivious to much of what is happening in the classroom. For example, one day a teacher was upset because she caught one student doing the work for another student who had been absent and was handing it in. Apparently it had been going on for two weeks. Another teacher I was talking to was shocked when I told them I had found something similar had happened in their class. Unfortunately, the realization only fortified his decision that the students were lazy and did not want to learn.

Teachers that appear to be more effective at DemoDeaf are those who have more positive attitudes and perceptions of the Deaf. The words "more positive" is used in the last sentence because some of these teachers that I would categorize as more effective may have thought the Deaf are not capable of learning or are lazy at one time but, as they learn more about the experiences of the students in their family life and at the school, the richness of GSL, and are open to have positive teacher student relationships this perception changes. Their minds are more open to recognizing the needs of the students and acknowledging the role of teachers and their impact on the student's education.

This more positive and open attitude for the Deaf can be found in interns and the most experienced teachers. One day an intern was complaining that the sign language was faulty because there is more than one sign for an object. A senior teacher reminded her that both Twi and English have synonyms so GSL likewise had had synonyms. At first the intern was resistant to that idea, but seemed to sink in. Later conversations with her revealed that she had begun to recognize that GSL was more complex and rich then she had thought. Instead of being overwhelmed by this concept more effective teachers begin to embrace it and start learning the language from the students and by attending GSL teacher courses held once or twice a week at the school.

These teachers also appear to use a more progressive or student centered approach in their teaching style. Most teachers at DemoDeaf do use some kind of drawing or prop when possible to help students visualize what the lesson is about. One of the most effective examples was when a teacher drew very detailed diagrams of the various levels and kinds of soil on the chalkboard. She then lead the class to a construction site on campus where construction workers were digging to build a foundation for a building. The teacher pointed to the different layers in the soil and tried to explain the different layers of soil to the best of her sign language abilities. The students nodded to each other with understanding. These demonstrations generally appear to be very helpful.

Ghanaian Sign Language use is often found in the classes of teachers who are more accepting of their Deaf students. Students can be observed participating in these classes where laughter and enjoyment from being in each other's company is not unusual. It is important to note that the laughter is not at the expense of a student who did not know an answer, but because the teacher is fluent enough in GSL to make a joke or a funny connection in the lecture.

The level of anxiety exhibited among students as they prepare for tests given by teachers who converse with students more freely, teach them in their own language, and come to class more frequently is much lower. The night before a test most students can be found at their desk busily preparing. When students prepare for a test given by a more Deaf friendly teacher students are able to give in depth explanations. However, when the same students are asked to explain a simple word supposedly taught by a less Deaf friendly teacher the students simply respond by signing HARD. The tests and class exercises given by teachers who converse with the students seem to reflect more of learning then rote memorization of words on paper.

The expectations of teachers who engage with students more often and use GSL seem to have higher expectations. In one situation a student did not perform well on his exam. I came into the classroom when the teacher was talking to this student asking him why his score was so low. The teacher knew he was capable of much performing better than he had. This teacher repeated this process of talking to students who performed lower then normally after returning other tests and class exercises.

Teachers do not necessarily have to be fluent in GSL in order to gain the respect of students. When students were asked which teachers they liked they usually named those who made an effort to learn. Their favorite teachers, however, tended to be those who were fluent. Regarding the teachers who did not sign, students usually responded HATE DEAF, meaning, the students thought the teacher hated deaf students.

Student comprehension in the classroom is not guaranteed in classes where teachers are fluent in GSL. Because reading and comprehension was neglected so much in the past and that the Deaf student had most likely been isolated as a child from language and common knowledge shared through conversation, Deaf students may still not understand all the concepts shared in a lecture. For example, one teacher created a make-shift shop right in the classroom to teach students meaning of "profit." His signs were clear and direct. He explained concepts multiple times in multiple ways. Despite the clarity of his signs and sincerity of his teaching the students were still answering the questions incorrectly. Because teachers in the past had not conveyed the ideas of simple addition and subtraction they struggled to understand this concept. It was actually this observation finalized the decision to develop the basic mathematics program.

BASIC MATHEMATICS PROGRAM

Signs of Hope International interns taught day classes in 2005 and evening classes in 2007. Initial findings early on during the 2005 mission revealed students' basic mathematics skills were very low and Signs of Hope International volunteers felt overwhelmed because the differences in subject matter and the educational system from what they were used to. The basic mathematics program was a solution that provided students meaningful skills and a set curriculum for volunteers to teach.

In 2005 interns found it was difficult to meet all the needs of the students through classroom demonstrations because student ability ranged from limited counting to limited subtraction, with only a few students able to multiply or divide. As a solution math achievement tests were used in 2007 to divide the classes divide into three groups or into the first three levels of the program, counting, addition, and subtraction. Three interns, one for each group, were brought into the classroom. Except for those in the counting group, each student is divided into single double, and triple digit sub-levels. Students advance from sub-level and groups by completing with 100% accuracy achievement tests consisting of ten problems in less than three minutes. The counting test consisted of counting one through 100 manually and on paper in three minutes or less.

Interns rely on a student centered approach in the groups and rely on group demonstrations, one on one tutoring and peer tutoring to teach students. Students use small rocks or pebbles, bottle caps, chalk markings on desks, or numerical picture books to practice.

Level 1: Counting	Count to 100		
Level 2: Addition	Single-digit addition (9 + 5 = 14)	→ Double-digit addition (37 + 23 = 60)	→ Triple-digit addition (210 + 100 = 310)
Level 3: Subtraction	Single-digit subtraction (9 - 5 = 4)	→ Double-digit subtraction (37 - 23 = 14)	→ Triple-digit subtraction (210 - 100 = 110)

Table 1: Sequential progression of mathematics learning

FINDINGS

Included in this section is a discussion of reactions of students within the three groups, observed learning and testing patterns exhibited by students, and an analysis of how the mathematics program affects participants' mathematic skill level. Also included in this section are discussions of program impact on student participation in the day-time math classes as observed a mathematics teacher, student confidence, and teacher perceptions of student ability and teaching strategy.

Counting

The students assigned to the counting group seemed eager and excited to start the program. When the child was told they were to review counting, they smiled and excitedly went back to their classroom to get the next student. The students also helped monitor who belonged in which group and notified us if a student had returned to school after being sick so that we could test their skill level and assign them a group too. The students did not seem disappointed when told to go to one group over another.

Within the counting group, the first observation noted the differences in GSL and ASL signs for some numbers. For instance, the ASL signs for 'sixteen,' 'seventeen,' 'eighteen,' and 'nineteen' are of a compound production: they begin with a 'ten' and end in a 'six,' 'seven,' 'eight,' or 'nine,' respectively. In GSL, however, to produce the sign 'sixteen,' one makes the GSL/ASL sign for 'six' but the pinky quickly slides down the surface of the thumb twice. The number 'seventeen' is signed by making the GSL/ASL sign for 'seven' and then tap the ring finger a couple times on the thumb. The pattern continues through 'nineteen.'

Another pattern observed when students were counting 20–30, 30–40, etc. Students tended to count 20, 1, 2, 3, 4, 5, 6, 7, 8, 9, 30, 1, 2, 3, 4, 5..., which continues until they counters reached 100. At first the researchers thought the students were mumbling since it can be tiring to count 1–100 manually. However, because so many students counted in this same pattern even when in separate rooms, researchers began to wonder if it is related to some linguistic rules the volunteers were not aware of. This pattern of counting did cause students to make similar errors when they lost track of where they were in the counting process. By signing 1–9 between 'twenty,' 'thirty,' 'forty,' etc. the signer often forgot if they were counting in their sixties or seventies. Other students would even count something like "70, 71, 72, 73, 74, 75, 76, 77, 78, 79, 6, 7, 8, 9, 80..."

One of the most fascinating observations was that of the fifteen students in 2007 who could not count six could not count past 29, 30, or 31. When questioned about this phenomenon, a student at the nearby Senior Secondary School looked at me like the answer was obvious. He explained that the cause is related to the number of days in a month. Everyday students at the Deaf school update the day of the month in the upper right corner on the chalk board and so the students learn to count at least to 29.

These students who struggled to count past 31 counted 3–10, 3–11, 3–12, 3–13, 3–13.... This may be because the students observed how other students counted in a similar previous pattern 20, 1, 2, 3, 4... 30.... Or, more likely the students recognize the pattern of 11, 12, 13, 14...19 before reaching 20 and are simply attempting to do the same to reach 40 and so on.

To teach counting the intern developed a very specific technique that proved effective in 2005 and in 2007. For those who could not count a chart was prepared for them to study. It consisted of 10 rows with zero through nine written on the first row. On the second line 10-19 third line 20-29 and so on until we reached one hundred. To help the students learn the patterns of numbers the students color-coded the columns where numbers were the same such as 7, 17, 27, 37, and so on. On the margin of the one's column was written "ones." Next to the tens row was written "tens," then "twenties," and so forth. Upon completion of the number chart, the students and the volunteer together read off the numbers in GSL after which the students wrote the number chart again. This helped the students to recognize the basic patterns in counting. Next, the student wrote the chart out by themselves. Upon repeating this cycle an average of five times the students seemed to understand the concept of counting well enough for them to do it alone. At the bottom of the chart counting by 100s and 1000s were included. A week into the counting group students began to be tested on counting by threes, fives, tens, 100s, and 1,000s before moving on to the addition group.

In 2007 only 34 of the 49 students tested could count to 100. Of the fifteen who struggled to count, 13 were post-tested with two missing due to school absence. Of the 13 post-tested, ten were found to be proficient in counting. By the end of the program 43 students could count to 100. Those who did not test as proficient either avoided the class themselves, were absent for an extended period of time, or simply did not improve their math skills after hours of individual tutoring from interns or students.

Other interesting observations were made involving this group. Five of the fifteen students who could not count could actually add single digit numbers together and one could subtract as well. This is logical after considering the highest number possible when adding single digits together is 18 and most students can count past 18. Also, five students in the 2007 counting group had also been in the 2005 counting group two years prior. Each of these five students was able to count by the time of volunteers left Demo-Deaf in 2005. Again, four of these five students tested proficient by volunteer departure in 2007. The one who did not was observed avoiding counting class but still decreased his counting time from 22 minutes to eight. This discovery presents problems of limited short term improvement and sustainability. After speaking to the math teachers about this discovery he suggested that they begin class daily with counting and basic arithmetic reviews to keep the students practicing their new skill.

Ones	0	1	2	3	4	5	6	7	8	9
Tens	10	11	12	13	14	15	16	17	18	19
Twenties	20	21	22	23	24	25	26	27	28	29
Thirties	30	31	32	33	34	35	36	37	38	39
Forties	40	41	42	43	44	45	46	47	48	49
Fifties	50	51	52	53	54	55	56	57	58	59
Sixties	60	61	62	63	64	65	66	67	68	69
Seventies	70	71	72	73	74	75	76	77	78	79
Eighties	80	81	82	83	84	85	86	87	88	89
Nineties	90	91	92	93	94	95	96	97	98	99
	100	101…								
Hundreds	100	200	300	400	500	600	700	800	900	
Thousands	1000	2000	3000	4000	5000	6000	7000	8000	9000	

Table 2: Student progressive counting chart

Addition

Students with limited addition abilities shared common areas of confusion as well. Many students did not have simple addition problems memorized to allow them to answer exercises quickly. To help facilitate memorization researchers used flash cards. With flashcards students were able to test each other and race each other individually or in teams.

The students appeared to be able to count only one digit at a time. To do this some would make small marks on their desks with chalk or on their papers with their pencils and then tabulated all the marks together to get the answer. An intern suggested counting by twos, threes, or fives to speed the process up. However, to count by more than one at a time was a foreign idea that did not make sense to some students. This is when the intern responsible for teaching counting began to teach students to count not only one number at a time but by threes, fives, tens, hundreds and thousands before advancing them to the addition group.

Carrying over in adding double digits was also something the students struggled with when adding large numbers. For example, when adding '27 + 38,' students would answer 515 instead of 65. The volunteer did group demonstrations and had the students show more work. When the program began, 34 of 47 tested could add single digits. Of the 15 who could not add single digits ten could not count to 100. An additional five students learned to count single digit numbers while 11 more students became proficient in double digit addition. The greatest difference can be seen with triple addition. The number of students proficient in triple addition doubled from 14 to 28 students.

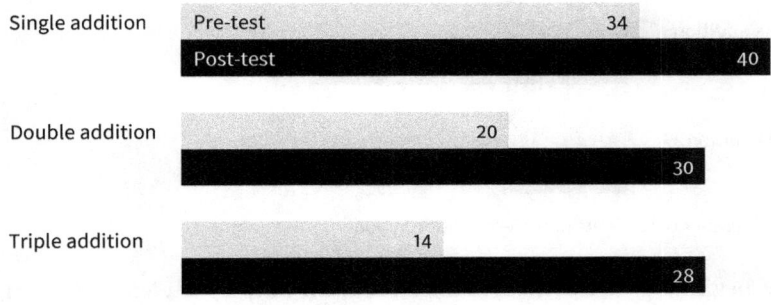

Table 2: Number of students proficient in addition

Subtraction
One common mistake among students involved the concepts of borrowing numbers when subtracting larger numbers. For example, when subtracting 474 from 540 students would be stuck with the 'four minus zero' calculation and write '4' as the answer. To help students understand how to borrow when subtracting, the researcher had the students show their work in the workbooks. However, students were used to working on scratch paper and turning in assignments separately. As students started showing their work they began to answer more of the exercises correctly. Writing the work out also helped the interns see other areas with which students were confused.

Many students did not recognize the meaning of plus, minus, or multiplication symbols. Some students would try to do all three functions on one worksheet of subtraction problems. The symbols were reviewed and then exercises were created in which where they had to insert the correct symbol into the equation such as in 10 [insert symbol] = 3. Doing problems with the students on the chalk board and showing the work on the chalk board was also helpful. One-on-one tutoring not only by the intern but other students who understood subtraction proved to be very important as well.

Student attention was best maintained through the use of group work and games such as "Around the World" and racing against each other to finish their exercises first. Timed tests were successful at keeping students engaged in the learning process also. At first students just cared about completing the tests the fastest and did not focus on correct answers. But after being sent to their desks a few times to correct their work, the students became preoccupied with both speed and accuracy.

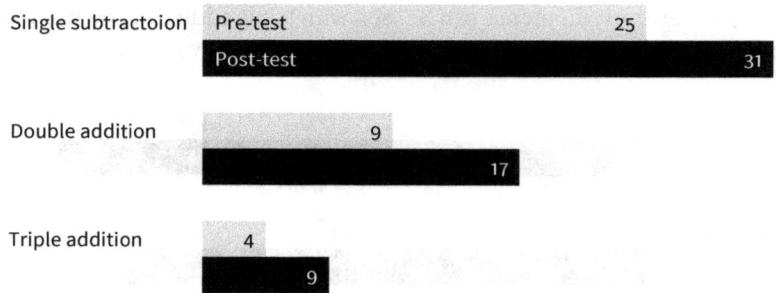

Table 3: Number of students proficient in subtraction

At the beginning of the mathematics program only 25 students of the 47 could subtract single digits. By the end of the program 31 students successfully performed single digit subtraction. Of the 47 students only nine could perform double digit subtraction. Post-testing showed an additional eight students could successfully perform double digit subtraction. An additional five students of the original four became proficient in subtracting triple digits from triple digits.

Multiplication and Division

Eight students performed single digit multiplication. Of the eight, however, only one student could perform triple digit multiplication. Four students were found to successfully divide single digit numbers into another single digit number, however, no students were found to be able to perform triple digit division.

Group work and peer tutoring

During the program in 2005 and 2007 interns facilitated group work. There are several benefits to group work. First, it is helpful for teachers and class management. But perhaps more importantly the students found enjoyment in practicing together or trying to stump each other. The challenge made learning fun. I found that the students seemed to enjoy working together. Students often found way of explaining concepts in much simpler ways than I had. Group work, when compared to strict lecturing in the classroom, seemed to be very effective not only in helping teaching students but in encouraging students to gain confidence as they taught and challenged each other.

Student tutors were also very helpful to reach students because of the varying levels of cognitive ability among students and the different signing vocabulary and life experiences of the by volunteers. Students proven to be proficient in counting, addition or subtraction were given the role as a teacher's aide for a class period and they helped lead one-on-one tutoring sessions with students who were really struggling. The different life experiences often made it difficult for teachers to think of examples applicable to student life in Ghana. Student faces glowed when first asked to help explain a concept to another. These aides seemed to take their duty seriously for the class period to really help.

Participation in daily mathematics course

Both math teachers explained that since the implementation of the math program more students are actually attempting to perform the calculations on their own. They are not shying away as often as they had been instead students are performing their own work. One teacher mentioned exclaimed, "Even Aduwa (pseudonym) is trying!" Still, the answers computed by students are not always correct, however, the fact that the students are trying to do the work is very good news.

Student confidence

Student confidence in their own ability to perform well on math assignments without the help of others does appears to be low. This observation is supported by the high level of answer sharing among students and the quick almost instinctive response of agreeing with classmates when someone explains they are IGNORANT. Another signal that students have low levels of confidence in their scholastic ability is when they say they cannot answer a question or do well on a test because it is too HARD.

The assessment phase and one-on-one testing was deliberately designed to not only minimize student answer sharing but to minimize negative effects on self-confidence caused by repeatedly receiving low scores on tests. Instead the number of tests given and level of difficulty of the tests varied by student. If the student could not add single digit numbers together it was not necessary to check if they could add double or triple digits. So the negative feedback students may have otherwise felt by being forced to take these tests and not be able to answer them is avoided. In addition, students were tested separately from other students so they could not compare who finished first or who looked stumped.

Dividing students into groups by ability also did not seem to have negative effects on students because there were nearly equal numbers in each of the groups and they all had friends in the group and most progressed at similar paces as their friends because they helped each other throughout the learning process. For those who did not progress enough to move from one topic to the next or from one group to the next the interns focused on the progress they did make in other areas such as cutting the amount of time it took them to count.

Another intern started the practice of having the group spend the first and last few minutes of group work repeating over and over again statements like I CAN and I BEAUTIFUL (meaning "I am beautiful" in English). At first the students appeared to not be convinced and were just appeasing the intern. However, towards as intern departure date came closer and closer the students began to gain a look of pride in their eyes and smiles as they said I CAN, a testament to their increased confidence in their abilities.

Teacher perceptions

The math program does not seem to change the perceptions regarding student ability. However, teacher perceptions regarding student ability and appropriate teaching methods for the Deaf do appear to be changing as they converse with the interns about the sophistication of GSL. For many teachers the importance of facial expressions and body movements has never been noticeable to them until conversations with interns. Classifiers and use of space are also new concepts to these teachers.

After first learning about these concepts through conversations and then seeing an intern do it and the students understand what is being conveyed, that is when teachers begin to see that the students can learn. One day a teacher had been trying to teach the students about AIDS and HIV. We had several conversations prior regarding GSL and its depth. The teacher wrote the information on the board and read it back to them verbally with some signs. Students were not responding to the lecture. Another intern stood up and reviewed the lecture with the students. Teachers started gathering around the window and door of the classroom exclaiming, "They understand! They understand!"

Another example occurred when students were taking the national exam. Students did not understand some of the questions, to which the teachers became irate even though they themselves did not understand some of the questions. One teacher approached me and expressed her frustrations that the students could not answer the questions. First she accused the students of being lazy. But as we spoke and discussed the language differences between teachers and the students her facial expressions softened. She began to see how the students need to be first taught the material in their own language before they can understand it.

CONCLUSIONS

This research study has practical significance for Signs of Hope International and other NGOs who work with Deaf schools in countries with similar Deaf education systems as Ghana. Regardless of location, if the stigma and the educational system are not addressing the language needs of students the effects on the students will be the same, low literacy and arithmetic skill level not to mention the plethora of other negative consequences effecting personal and group identity and so forth.

The math program created by Signs of Hope International interns is not necessarily a solution to these problems, only structural changes in the educational system will most likely be able to provide a solution, but the program does provide students with some sort of relief. The program has helped at least 25 students to improve math skills to some degree. Because of the program more students may be able to more easily contribute to the family income by participating in the local economy by selling bananas, oranges, or other goods without having to rely on other people to tell them how much change to give or how much money to charge.

Sustainability is an issue that needs to be addressed. If teachers do not require students to continue to practice throughout the year the things they learned will most likely be forgotten like the students had in 2005. The teachers should have been included more in the program development so that they would have more vested interest in reviewing the material with the students. The math teachers could also have tutored the interns on teaching methods they found to be useful also.

In addition, this research study has academic and sociological significance. As mentioned in the introduction this research provides an ethnographical piece on a linguistic minority group that has not previously been studied. This group has been separated from the rest of the larger society and placed into residential or day schools for the Deaf to protect them against the negative consequences of stigmas, social stratification, and status ascription (National 1996). However, the same oppressive dangers the schools are attempting to prevent are actually perpetuated within the school because many hearing education policy makers, administrators, and teachers continue to rely on educational models more fitting for hearing students rather than Deaf students.

REFERENCES

Akamatsu, C. T. 1998. *Thinking With and Without Language: What is Necessary and Sufficient for School-Based Learning?* Washington DC: Gallaudet University Press.

Babatope, E. 1982. *The Ghana Revolution:From Nkrumurah to Jerry Rawlings.* Enugu, Nigeria: Fourth Dimension Publishers.

Ballantine, J. H. 1997. *The Sociology of Education: Asystematic Analysis (4th ed.).* Upper Saddle River, New Jersey, USA: Prentice-Hall, Inc.

Ballif-Spanvill, B. Carol Ward, Addie Fuhriman, Yodit Solomon, & Kacey Widdison, Jones. 2005. "Human Capital and Community Development: A Case Study of an NGO-sponsored Schooling Program in Mali." *World Studies in Education.* James Nicholas Publishers: v6, No. 2 pp. 29-52.

Bennett, K. A. 1995. *The Way schools Work: A Sociological Analysis of Education.* White Plains, NY: Longman Publishers.

Bienvenu, M.J. & Colonmous, B. 1985-1988. *An introduction to American Deaf Culture.* Burtonsville: Sign Media.

Branson, J., & Miller, D. 2002. *Damned for their Difference: The Cultural Construction of Deaf People as Disabled.* Washington DC: Gallaudet University Press.

Brint, S. 1998. *Schools and Society.* Thousand Oaks: Pine Forge Press.

Brown, M., Carnoy, M., Currie, E., Duster, T., Oppenheimer, d., Shultz, M., et al. 2003. *Whitewashing Race: The Myth of a Color-Blind Society.* Berkeley: Univeristy of California Press.

Charrow, V. R., and Ronnie B. W. 1975. "The Deaf Child as a Linguistic Minority." *Language use and Acquisition* 14 (5):

Crouch, R.A. 1997. "Letting the Deaf be Deaf Reconsidering the use of Cochlear Implants in Prelingually Deaf Children." *The Hastings Center Report* 27 (24):14-21.

deMarrais, K. B., M. D. (1995). *The Way Schools Work: A Sociological Analysis of Education.* White Plains, NY: Longman Publishers.

Fischer, S. D. 1998. Critical Periods for Language Acquisition. *Issues Unresolved: New Perspectives on Language and Deaf Education,* 9-26.

Furhiman, A., Ballif-Spanvill, B., Ward, C., Solomon Y. Kacey, W-J. 2006. "Meaningful Literacy? Gendered Experiences with an NGO-Sponsored Literacy Program in Rural Mali." *Ethnography and Education* 1 (1):103-124.

Ghana. 2008. "Compton's by Britannica."

Gordon, R. G. Jr. 2005. *Ethnologue Languages of the World.* Dallas, Texas: SIL International.

Haynes, J. 1991. "Human Rights and Democracy in Ghana: The Record of the Rawlings' Regime." *African Affairs,* 90 (360), 407-425.

Higgins, P. 1980. *Outsiders in a Hearing World.* Beverly Hills: Sage Publications, Inc.

Humphrey, J., & Alcorn, B. 2001. *So You Want To Be An Interpreter (3rd ed.).* Washington D.C.: Gallaudet Universitiy Press.

Lampropoulou, V. 1988. The History of Deaf Education in Greece. In *The Deaf Way.* Washington D.C.: Gallaudet University Press. pp 97-101

Lane, H. 1992. *The Mask of Benevolence.* New York: Alfred A. Knopf, Inc.

Lane, H. 1984. *When the Mind Hears: A History of the Deaf.* New York: Random House, Inc.

Lane, H., Bahan, B., Hoffmeister, R. 1996. *A Journey into the Deaf-World.* San Diego: DawnSignPress.

Madsen, A. 2007. Field Notes DemoDeaf.

Matthaei, J. A. 1984. *An Economic History of Women in America: Women's Work, the Sexual Division of Labor, and the Development of Capitalism.* New York: Harvest Press.

McMichael, P. 2000. *Development and Social Change: A Global Perspective*. Thousand Oaks, California: Pine Forge Press.
Mehmet, O. 1995. *Westernizing the Third World: The Eurocentricity of Economic Development Theories*. London: Routledge.
Melander, H. 2005. Field Notes Ghana 2005.
Melander, H. 2007. Field Notes Ghana 2007.
Moore-Gilbert, B. 1997. *Postcolonial Theory: Contexts, Practices and Policies*. London
National Report. 1996. "Republic of Ghana International Conference on Education.
Ojile, O.E. 1988. Education of the Deaf in Nigeria: An Historical Perspective. In *The Deaf Way* (pp. 268-274). Washington D.C.: Gallaudet University Press. Pp. 268-274.
Ojile, O.E., & E. Carver. 1987. "Education of the Deaf in Nigeria and Canada: A Comparison." *The ACEH Journal/LA Revue ACEDA* 13:96-103
Okyere, A., & Addo, M. 1988. Deaf Culture in Ghana. In *The Deaf Way* (pp. 97-101). Washington D.C.: Gallaudet University Press.
Philibert, N. 1992. *In The Land of the Deaf*. France: International Film Circuit Release.
Senghas, R. and Monaghan, L. 2002. "Signs of their Times: Deaf Communities and the Culture of Language." *Annual Review of Anthropology* 31 69-97.
Solomon, Y., Ballif-Spanvill, B., Ward, C., Addie, F. 2002. "Outreach, Impact, and Sustainability of Informal Banking: A Case Study of the Ouelessebougou-Utah Alliance Microenterprise Program in Mali." *Journal of Developing Societies* 18 (4):290-314.
Ward, C., Solomon, Y., Ballif-Spanvill, B., Fuhriman, A. . 2008. "Framing Development: Community and NGO Perspectives in Mali."
The World Bank. 1996. "Ghana Basic Education Sector Improvement Project."
———. 2007. ""Ghana on Fast Track to Meet Education Goals"."
———. 1996. "Ghana Education Sector Improvement Sector."
Wiesel, A. (Ed.). 1998. *Issues Unresolved: New Perspective on Language and Deaf Education*. Washington D.C.: Gallaudet University Press.

Bio-Power, Biosociality, and Community Formation: How Bio-Power is Constitutive of the Deaf Community[1]

MICHELE FRIEDNER

MICHEL FOUCAULT'S WORK ON POWER AND SUBJECT FORMATION HAS been extremely useful for key theorists within Deaf Studies. In this paper I analyze the ways that certain theorists, specifically Harlan Lane and Paddy Ladd, utilize Foucault's work. I am interested in how, and to what ends, Foucault is used by these two theorists. I then set out to conduct a close reading of Foucault's work on bio-power and subject formation in which I outline the emergence of bio-power as a distinct rationality of rule and I examine the relationship between bio-power and subject formation. I argue, based upon my reading of Foucault, that these works do not go far enough in looking at the ways that power is not just oppressive, that it is actually productive, and that similarly, subject formation and subject positionings involve a constant and fluid process of give and take, back and forth, struggle and resistance. Finally, I examine current works within anthropology that explore the ways that bio-power produces, and creates conditions of possibility for, the emergence of community (and communities) around *bios*, or life.

Inspired by Rabinow's (1996) work, I suggest that the Deaf[2] community can be seen as biosociality, as something produced by, and not in spite of, power. In addition, I also suggest that the Deaf community has developed as a result of a specific form of governance that Nikolas Rose (1999) working through Foucault, calls "governing through community." In this sense, echoing anthropologist Jean Comaroff's work on HIV/AIDS, I suggest that deafness has been *productive*. As Comaroff writes: "I use [productive] in the manner of Marx and Foucault to imply that it has given birth to significant forms of sociality and signification, of enterprise and activism, both negative and positive" (Comaroff 2007, 203). Underlying this paper is a commitment to excavating and salvaging the relationship between 'little d' and 'capital D deafness.' How can we begin to understand the slippage and (productive) tension between 'little d' and 'capital D' d/Deafness?

In his powerful work *The Mask of Benevolence*, Harlan Lane (1999) examines the ways that d/Deaf people are medicalized and made to feel that they are abnormal and inferior by hearing people and institutions. Lane sets up a binary between the hearing audist world and the world of the Deaf and he illustrates how the hearing world oppresses the Deaf world. Indeed, Lane's story is very much one of oppression, colonialism, and paternalism, of d/Deaf children forced to wear hearing aids, sit through individualized education program meetings, and attend specialized schools for the deaf. For him, artifacts such as a hearing test, headphones, and hearing aids are symbols of oppression (Lane 1999, 81).

Lane's story is also one of loss: he writes about how deaf childrens' cultural heritage as Deaf people and their innate and natural language, sign language, are denied. He also writes that as a result of audiological and psychological exams, deaf children are individualized (individually diagnosed and labeled) and as such, the communal nature of the Deaf community as a linguistic and cultural minority is masked (Lane 1999, 81). And so the question is, how does Lane utilize Foucault's work to further his argument about the ways that hearing people oppress the Deaf community? I now include four treatments of Foucault's work.

In examining the ways that the National Association for the Deaf and other Deaf political organizations constantly invoke the 1880 Milan Deaf Congress and fight against cochlear implants, Lane writes:

> Michel Foucault has analyzed the historical evolution in which the control of peoples' bodies came to be seen as a legitimate concern of government. What he calls "bio-power" extends to reach into our civilization in such diverse fields as criminality, psychiatry, education, and family planning. In bio-power, knowledge and power form a regulatory technology whose purpose is to forge a docile body that can be subjected, used, transformed, and improved. (Lane 1999, 84).

In discussing both the process and effects of the testing process that Deaf children must undergo, Lane writes:

> Foucault points out that the psychological examination not only imposes its mark on its subjects, 'holds them in a mechanism of objectification,' but also is itself the ceremony of this objectification (Lane 1999, 81).

And in the same vein, Lane writes:

> ...as Foucault has argued, power not only excludes and oppresses, it pro-

duces reality. Identification, testing, classification, institutionalization, and surgical intervention are successive steps in increasing expropriation of the Deaf child's body, the 'colonization of the body.' (Lane 1999, 82).

Lane writes perhaps most powerfully and succinctly about biopower in his discussion of cochlear implants:

> This is bio-power: massive intervention in the life of the child in an attempt to impose the majority's language, culture, and values. (Lane 1999, 206)

In his landmark text *Understanding Deaf Culture: In Search of Deafhood*, Paddy Ladd (2003)'s treatment of Foucault is similar, if not identical to Lane's although it seems to me that Ladd is perhaps more attentive to shifts in forms of power and he looks at the emergence of bio-power as a rationality of rule. Similarly, Ladd is writing a story not just about "the hearing world" or "audism," but rather, he is looking at the role of the state in creating and perpetuating classification systems that establish binaries of normality and abnormality (Ladd 2003, 123). Spatially and temporally locating bio-power in Western democracies in the 19th century, Ladd calls bio-power an "imperialist-medicalist-scientist triumvirate" which, aided by the accumulation of wealth and the growth of mercantilism, led to the creation of oral schools to educate deaf children. This education was designed to increase state power through creating an educated deaf elite as well as an (un)educated Deaf underclass that could work productively in industrial settings; Ladd directly links bio-power with the making of state power (Ladd 2003, 117). Ladd, like Lane, devotes much space and labor to exploring how the state employs medicine, technology, and education to categorize and control deaf children and deaf adults.

Here I want to devote some space and labor to thinking about how Lane and Ladd utilize Foucault's work on bio-power, power, subject formation, and the state. It seems to me that both theorists are working with "impact models" of power through which power moves in one direction: it emanates from either the Audist hearing world, the hearing majority, or the state and it oppresses Deaf people. As a result of bio-power, deaf individuals are alienated from themselves and others like them and they are forced to embody the manners, culture, and values of the majority (hearing world). What is important to take away from this is that for Lane and Ladd, power is oppressive and it creates subjects that, while alienated, are docile and unresisting. These subjects are 'lowercase d' deaf subjects and their ability to become 'capital D' Deaf subjects is squashed through the exercise of power. There is no room within power to resist and as such, it follows that Deaf people then struggle to create alternate forms of community, self, and socialities that are *outside* of power.

It therefore follows that for Lane and Ladd, the Deaf community and Deaf culture are not created or produced by power, they are created or produced in spite of power. These theorists do not see power as being productive in creating the Deaf community and 'capital D' deafness; power can only be seen in terms of submission within and resistance outside of power. I argue that while this reading of Foucault is certainly productive for understanding how deaf children and adults have been individualized, medicalized, and classified, it does not go far enough in exploring how power is productive of forms of community and subject- formation.

Specifically, I argue that such individualization, medicalization, and classification have created the conditions of possibility for the emergence of the Deaf community, 'capital D' Deaf identity, and community politics. The medical diagnosis of deafness ultimately serves as a ticket of entry into the Deaf community. 'Lowercase d' and 'capital D' d/Deafness are closely related; 'lowercase d' deafness can be constitutive of 'capital D' Deafness.

According to Foucault, there is a direct connection between the way that the body is (discursively) produced and practices of government. Writing specifically about the emergence of the modern state in Europe, Foucault explores the formation of a new type of intervention into the field of economy and population (Foucault 1994, 217). This new form of governance is called governmentality, or governmental rationality. This shift towards governmentality was accompanied by a shift in the focus of power. In earlier forms of government, the sovereign exercised his power through killing or the taking of life. This was the power to *take* life and *let* live (Foucault 1978, 138). However, a shift has occurred in which the focus is on the administration and optimization of life: the power to *cultivate* life or to *let* die. Thus a politics of death has been replaced by a politics of life in which the regulation of conduct (the "conduct of conduct"), and of bodies, is the dominant technique of governmentality.

According to Foucault, power over life has two basic forms, developed in the seventeenth century. One form is *anatomo-politics* and the other, which was formed later, was *bio-politics*. Anatomo-politics exists on the realm of the individual while bio-politics targets the entire human species. Both types of politics are concerned with the management and cultivation of life although on different scales. Additionally, both come with distinct techniques and processes designed to subjugate bodies and control populations. For the first time in history, life and politics go hand in hand and biological existence is synonymous with politics.

Subject formation is predicated upon the body, the locus of power. I want to note here that I think that Lane and Ladd engage with this aspect of Foucault's work productively although I think that Lane's understanding of bio-power misses its inherently communal (and not individual) basis. However, I argue that what is also important to take away from Foucault's work on subject formation is the way that this is a contested and fraught *process* that the individual herself participates within. This process takes place within power which according to Foucault can be thought of as a force field within which various nodes of resistances transmit and produce power; power is rendered mutable and it is able to transform itself through encounters with resistance (Foucault 1978, 96). So, to put it somewhat simply, resistance exists and operates within power and it should not be seen as the opposite of power. Similarly, relations to and within power transcend the crude binary of submission and resistance. According to Foucault:

> "Power is not something that is acquired, seized, or shared, something that one holds on to or allows to slip away; power is exercised from innumerable points...
>
> Relations of power are not in positions of exteriority with respect to other types of relationships (economic processes, knowledge relationships, sexual relations), but are immanent in the latter...
>
> Power comes from below; that is, there is no binary and all-encompassing opposition between rulers and ruled at the root of power relations, and serving as a general matrix
>
> no such duality extending from the top down and reacting on more and more limited groups to the very depths of the social body. One must suppose rather that the manifold relationships of force that take shape and come into play in the machinery of production, in families, limited groups, and institutions, are the basis for wide-ranging effects of cleavage that run through the social body as a whole" (Foucault 1978, 94).

What is important to take away from the above extended quote is that power is not uni-directional and that it can and does operate from below, and more importantly, that it produces subject positions. It is within, and not outside of, this force field of power that subjects form. As Foucault writes: "There are two meanings of the word subject: subject to someone else by control and dependence and tied to his own identity by a conscious or self-knowledge" (Foucault 1983, 212). These concepts of "identity" and "self-knowledge" seem to me to be key for this analysis. As the individual develops her own identity, she begins to act on herself through techniques of the self. This is how governmentality is deployed — through conduct of conduct, through taking care of oneself. In thinking about Foucault's writing on the ways that sexuality is produced and subsequently deployed through rationalities of rule, I argue that deafness functions similarly. Similar to the ways that the category of homosexuality, initially defined as deviance, was productive in creating both identities and communities (the queer community as a cultural and political community is an excellent and obvious example), I argue that deafness as a category creates identities and communities—specifically the Deaf community. It is important to take away from Foucault an understanding of the relationship between power, self (formation), and community (formation); as the body becomes a key site for exerting power, it also becomes an important site for examining how subjects, identities, and communities are created through power.

Here I want to move on to Paul Rabinow's concept of biosociality as I believe that Rabinow's (1996) work on biosociality offers us some insights into this relationship between subjects, communities, and power. Rabinow, working through Foucault, and writing about the intersection of biopower and governmentality, argues that people are developing new modes of relating to each other and fostering relationships based on shared biological characteristics. As he writes, in an inversion of sociobiology, "...in biosociality nature will be modeled on culture understood as practice" (Rabinow 1996, 99). Rabinow's work on biosociality examines how communities form through shared biological characteristics; culture is modeled upon nature (and 'little d' becomes 'capital D'). The Deaf community can be seen as an example of Rabinow's biosociality and again, we see the ways that power can be considered to be productive of community. Bio-power sets up the conditions of possibility for biosociality.

In a similar vein, Nikolas Rose's (1999) work on government through community has stakes for how we think about Deaf communities. Rose (1999) sets up an "ideal type" of a late liberal, or neo-liberal, government and examines the ways that government in its modern form governs through practices of community formation through which individuals "become what they already are" and align themselves with others like them through processes of self-awareness (Rose 1999, 172). An example of this would again be medically deaf people who as a result of becoming aware of their Deaf identity transform themselves into cultural Deaf communities.

Rose creates a temporal argument and states that government through community has replaced social or welfare governments in which the state took care of people through social welfare programs. Instead of a social worker, institution, or other government apparatus looking after them, under late liberal forms of governance, individuals and communities take care of themselves. So in this sense, we can say that perhaps Lane and Ladd do not look at the shift from social or welfare forms of rule to looking at late modern, or neo-liberal, forms of governance which are based upon governing through community. Their work seems more focused on analyzing earlier forms of rule in which the medical and rehabilitation apparatus played a more significant role. Thus, the Deaf community rather than being seen as outside of power, can be seen as a tool for creating or perpetuating certain late liberal, or neo-liberal, rationalities of rule.

Let us keep in mind that neo-liberalism, according to David Harvey (2005) is an economic and political project in which the state decreases its role and allows the private sector and the market to play a larger role in the provision of services. As the state's role decreases, the private sector, and individuals and communities, come to play a crucial role in governing themselves. The discourse associated with neo-liberalism is very much about inclusion, participation, and empowerment; people learn how to conduct themselves as rights bearing citizens with specific cultural identities (eg Mohan and Stokke 2002).

People, and communities, are required to be sufficiently empowered to participate in providing their own services and securing entitlements and rights. And so here I want to ask if we can see organizations such as the National Association of the Deaf and the World Federation of the Deaf as neo-liberal organizations3? What role do these organizations, and other Deaf created and designed institutions play in perpetuating neo-liberal forms of rule? Through biosociality, technologies of self, and government through community, Deaf individuals ostensibly develop new relationships to themselves, the state, and to others.

Here I am arguing that it is important to look at the ways that the Deaf community and concepts such as Deaf identity and culture, can be seen as productive of certain rationalities of rule. Recent work in anthropology has looked at the formation of associational communities as a result of shared biological characteristics. I am thinking of Rose and Novas' (2005) work on biological citizenship in which they explore the emergence of communities based upon principles of advocacy, kinship, and care of people with various medical conditions.

Rose and Novas argue that we are seeing distinct citizenship projects, through which people make demands upon the state, based upon biological characteristics, and more specifically, identity derived from biological characteristics. Similarly, Rayna Rapp's (1999) work explores the formation of communities around families with children with disabilities. Downs Syndrome advocacy and support organizations encourage families to embrace and support children with Downs Syndrome and new forms of affinity and kinship develop for these families. More recently, Vinh-Kim Nguyen (2005) has looked at the emergence of communities of people living with HIV and AIDS in Burkina-Faso and he argues that as a result of (neo-liberal) non governmental organization practices, these people are engaging in the formation of new communities; as individuals identity as having HIV/AIDS, they form alliances with others like them. These works, and others, examine how the current bio-political moment has established conditions of possibility for the formation of communities and how bio-politics very much operates through, and not in spite of, communities.

And so when I look at current works within Deaf Studies which argue that the Deaf community, or Deaf culture, exists outside of or in spite of power, I want to argue that it is extremely important to look at the role that power plays in creating this community. I ask how do concepts such as the Deaf community, Deaf culture, and Deaf identity perpetuate certain forms of rule and practices of government? What is the relationship between the Deaf community and neo-liberal forms of government? How can we look at the relationship between internationalist organizations such as the World Federation of the Deaf (WFD) and other rights based organizations which stress the importance of participation, inclusion, and rights, and neo-liberal forms and practices of rule? Is the culturally Deaf subject a neo-liberal subject and if so, what does this mean for how we think about questions of Deafness, identity, and community?

In no way do I want to discount or minimize the work that Deaf Studies, the Deaf community, and Deaf activists are doing in arguing for the uniqueness of the Deaf community as a cultural and linguistic community but at the same time, I also want to think critically about the conditions which have led to this and what this means in this current political moment. I am not trying to argue that the Deaf community is identical to Nguyen's HIV/AIDS sufferers, Rapp's families, and Rose and Novas' biological citizenship in general, but I do think that we can see certain interesting similarities between these community projects and the ways that Deaf people speak about community and I wonder if we can look at these ethical and political projects as emerging from similar political conjunctures.

Ultimately, I am arguing for a closer and more rigorous reading of Foucault's work on power and subject formation and that we explore the ways that 'little d' deaf and 'capital D' deaf are intertwined; 'little d' deafness can be seen as setting up conditions of possibility for 'capital D' deafness, and power can be seen as setting the stage for the emergence (and not the suppression) of the Deaf community and 'capital D' Deafness.

ENDNOTES

1. Many thanks to Mara Green, Terra Edwards, and Theresa Smith for engagement with this paper, and the ideas accompanying it, both before the paper presentation, during, and afterwards. I also want to thank the fabulous conference organizers, especially Flavia Fleischer, and the lead interpreter during my presentation, Clint Behunin.
2. In this paper I try to distinguish between 'lowercase d' and 'capital D' deafness. That is, I try

to use a lowercase 'd' when writing about deafness as a medical condition and I try to use a capital 'D' when writing about the Deaf community as a cultural and linguistic minority. However, at times it is unclear whether to use a lowercase 'd' or capital 'D' and as an analyst I view this as a productive and interesting tension; I sometimes attempt to resolve this tension by writing d/D. As a caveat, I recognize that readers might quibble with, or find incorrect, certain applications of d/D.

3. I note that these organizations were temporally established before neo-liberal practices and policies were developed and operationalized. However, these organizations currently perform roles which include community development, advocacy and leadership training, and service provision which are neo-liberal in nature.

REFERENCES

Burchell, Gordon. (1996). "Liberal government and techniques of the self (Chapter 1)". In Barry A, Osborne T and Rose N, eds. *Foucault and Political Reason: Liberalism, Neo-liberalism, and Rationalities of Government*. Chicago: University of Chicago Press.

Burchell, Gordon et al. (1991). *The Foucault Effect: Studies in Governmentality*. Chicago: University of Chicago Press.

Comaroff, Jean. (2007). *Beyond the Politics of Bare Life: AIDS and the Global Order*. Public Culture 19(1): 197-219.

Foucault, Michel. (1997). *Society Must Be Defended*. New York: Picador.

Foucault, Michel. (1995). *Discpline and Punish*. New York: Vintage Books.

Foucault, Michel. (1994). *Power: The Essential Works of Michel Foucault: 1954-1984*. New York: New Press.

Foucault, Michel. (1990). *Madness and Civilization*. New York: Vintage Books.

Foucault, Michel. (1983). *Beyond Structuralism and Hermeneutics*. Chicago: University of Chicago Press.

Foucault, Michel. (1978). *The History of Sexuality: An Introduction (Volume 1)*. New York: Vintage Books.

Harvey, David. (2005). *A Brief History of Neoliberalism*. New York: Oxford University Press.

Ladd, Paddy. (2003). *Understanding Deaf Culture: In Search of Deafhood*. Clevedon: Multinlingual Matters Ltd.

Lane, Harlan. (1992). *The mask of benevolence: Disabling the Deaf community*. New York: Knopf.

Mohan, G. and Stokke. K. (2000). "Participatory development and empowerment: The dangers of Localism." *Third World Quarterly* 21:247-68.

Nguyen, Vinh-Kim. (2005). "Antiretroviral Globalism, Biopolitics and Therapeutic Citizenship". In Ong, Aihwa and Collier, Stephen J., eds. *Global Assemblages*. Oxford: Blackwell.

Petryna, Adriana. (2002). *Life Exposed: Biological Citizens after Chernobyl*. Princeton: Princeton University Press.

Rabinow, Paul. (1996). *Essays on the Anthropoloy of Reason*. New York: Princeton University Press.

Rapp, Rayna. (1999). *Testing Women, Testing the Fetus: The Social Impact of Amniocentesis in America*. London: Routledge.

Rapp, Rayna and Ginsburg, Faye. (2001). "Enabling Disability: Rewriting Kinship, Reimagining Citizenship." *Public Culture* 13(3): 533-556.

Rose, Nikolas. (1999). *The Powers of Freedom*. Cambridge: Cambridge University Press.

Rose, Nikolas. (1996). "The death of the social? Re-figuring the territory of government". *Economy and Society* 25(3):327-356.

Rose, Nikolas and Novas, Carlos. (2005). "Biological Citizenship." In Ong, Aihwa and Collier, Stephen J., eds. *Global Assemblages*. Oxford: Blackwell.

GALLAUDET TRUE-BIZ ACADEMIC ASL, HOW-qqq[1]

ARELENE KELLY, PH.D., JANIS COLE, BENJAMIN JARASHOW, BRIAN MALZKUHN, SHERI YOUENS-UN

THE TITLE IS TRANSCRIBED IN ASL GLOSSES FOR A REASON. THE TITLE ends with a question for a reason. The team behind this title, consisting of Dr. Arlene B. Kelly, Ms. Janis Cole, Mr. Benjamin Jarashow, Mr. Brian Malzkuhn and Ms. Sheri Youens-Un, hope that it is catchy. The title describes one of the many paths, or montages, that Gallaudet University is taking to place American Sign Language (ASL) and Written English on an equal footing. This essay describes one specific journey toward equality. This essay also reflects the theme of the 2008 Deaf Studies *Today*! Conference: "Montage." The journey described herewith is like a montage, a collage of learning, researching and experiencing.

A BILINGUAL UNIVERSITY?

Chartered on April 8, 1864, the National Deaf-Mute College[2] used two languages: sign language and English, thus it was bilingual by default. But was it truly bilingual in the sense of the concept itself? Gallaudet was created as a unique bilingual university. But what sort of bilingual university was it? Was it more like the University of Ottawa[3] where two high status languages intersected on a more or less equal totality, or like the University of Nairobi,[4] a colonial bilingual university where one language was superior over another? Until 2007, Gallaudet may have been more like the University of Nairobi. However in 2007, Gallaudet seemed to have shifted to be more like the University of Ottawa, or even better.

Over the years at Gallaudet, English was viewed as a superior language and was taught as an academic discipline, yet the information was conveyed through sign language which was also used for everyday communication. However, sign language was rarely discussed and dissected in the classroom in the same way that English was. In 1965, ASL was proclaimed as a bona fide language.[5] That proclamation, however, did not produce much academic discourse. Instead, this proclamation caused chaos;.both Deaf and hearing people resisted the new view of sign language.[6] Additionally, the first credit course on ASL structure for Gallaudet undergraduates did not emerge until 1978.[7] Nor did the 1988 Deaf President Now protest capitulate ASL into the academic arena except for the 1994 formation of the Department of Deaf Studies.[8]

THE MISSION AND VISION STATEMENT

Fast forward to May 2006. The Gallaudet community protested the Board of Trustees' selection of Dr. Jane Kelleher Fernandes as the next president. This protest continued until October when the selection was rescinded. As soon as the protest ended, the Middle States Commission on Higher Education (MSCHE) raised concerns that the university was deficient in the areas of shared governance, campus climate and academic rigor.[9] Additionally, MSCHE also recommended a re-vamp of the undergraduate curriculum. These concerns were actually raised in 2001 during the Irving Jordan administration but unfortunately were never addressed. In addition, as a result of the Vision Implement Program (new footnote here) in 1995[10], the then-existing communication policy was revisited and rewritten which in part read:

> "…Communication among faculty, staff, and students is through the use of both *sign language and written and spoken English*…" (emphasis added)

This statement suggested that using any form of sign language and spoken English in the classroom was acceptable. Furthermore, it trivialized the worthiness of the role of ASL in Deaf lives.

The communal introspection, resulting from both the 2006 Protest and the MSCHE's concerns, prompted the revisiting of the 1995 mission and vision statement during the summer of 2007, reflecting a paradigm shift.[11] The Mission Statement was then rewritten and now reads:

> Gallaudet University, federally chartered in 1864, is a *bilingual*, diverse, multicultural institution of higher education that ensures the intellectual and professional advancement of deaf and hard of hearing individuals through *American Sign Language and English*. Gallaudet maintains a proud tradition of research and scholarly activity and prepares its graduates for career

opportunities in a highly competitive, technological, and rapidly changing world. (emphasis added)

In addition, the Vision Statement also commits the university to

"...offer a welcoming, *supportive, and accessible bilingual* educational environment for teaching and learning..." (emphasis added)

ASL was no longer on the back burner. The new Mission and Vision Statement signified that courses are to be conducted bilingually on an equal footing: ASL and English. For the first time in the university's 143 years, ASL moved from colloquial to academic. Dissection of ASL in the classroom was encouraged. The idea of ASL essays emerged. Exploiting video technology was touted. This paradigm shift also promoted General Studies Requirements (GSR) curriculum changes for Fall 2007, particularly for the incoming freshmen. The upperclass students were/are grandfathered to the older curriculum.

CHALLENGES

The University's Department of ASL and Deaf Studies[12] eagerly faced the challenge of teaching ASL to the incoming freshmen who were already ASL users. The uppermost challenge was creating a brand-new curriculum. Thus, during the summer of 2007, Dr. Ben Bahan developed a new curriculum for GSR 103, a course devoted to issues and themes related to ASL and Deaf Studies. He collaborated with the teaching faculty of GSR 101 and GSR 102, which are First Year Seminar and Critical Reading and Writing (English), respectively. Themes, such as identity and language, to be taught in the 101 and 102 courses were then interwoven into the 103 course.

Simultaneously, it was acknowledged that an ASL Screening Test was needed to place students in appropriate courses. Dr. MJ Bienvenu then undertook the task of creating such a test. Collaborating with the Assessment and Evaluation Unit,[13] the team developed this test with three week's notice, prior to the start of the fall 2007 semester.

Another pressing challenge was staffing. Five individuals were recruited as full-time temporary instructors along with one tenured professor to teach this pioneering course known as GSR 103: ASL & Deaf Studies: Kelly, Cole, Jarashow, Malzkuhn and Youens-Un. Both Bahan and Bienvenu continued to be part of this new endeavor, however, in the somewhat different roles already mentioned earlier (to be described further later in this essay). The fifth instructor, Lawrence Gray, was responsible for other courses needing professors as well as ASL 102.[14]

Another challenge was defining Academic ASL. For years we all have known Academic English; it has been taught from the pre-school level to the college level. We know College Freshman English, College Sophomore English and so forth. English has always been taught in various forms: summary, review, persuasive, critical, poetic and so forth. But what about ASL? Is there such a thing as an ASL essay? An ASL summary? An ASL review? A critical ASL piece? How are these questions going to impact the academic climate at Gallaudet? Needless to say, this paradigm shift led to a necessary transformation in the general curriculum.

GENERAL STUDIES REQUIREMENTS

Under the Old General Studies Requirements (GSR) as listed in the 2006-2007 Gallaudet University Undergraduate Catalog, students were to complete 60–66 GS hours. The range given here was due to Honor students who could take two classes of English as opposed to four courses for most students to satisfy the GSR total. With electives and major of study requiring 58–64 more hours, students needed at least 124 credits in order to graduate with a Bachelor's degree. Below is a quick reference outlining different GS Requirements from the previous year to next:

Old General Studies Requirements (2006–2007):

English Reading & Composition	6-12
Foreign Language	8
Communication Processes	3
Quantitative Reasoning	3
Physical Education	2
Heritage and Self-Awareness	6
Historical and Social Analysis	9
Humanities Inquiry	9
Scientific Inquiry	8
Diversity	6
Total:	60-66 credit hours

The post-2006 Protest and the ensuing accreditation crisis as raised by MSCHE prompted the revamping of the general university curriculum. The substantial reduction of previous requirements allows for more depth in majors of study:

New General Studies Requirements (2007–2008):

Freshman Foundation courses (four courses)	12
GSR 101: First Year Seminar	
GSR 102: Critical Reading and Writing (English)	
GSR 103: *American Sign Language and Deaf Studies*	
GSR 104: Quantitative Reasoning (Math)	
Integrated courses (five/six courses)	24
including one service learning course	
Capstone Experience (one course)	4
Total:	40 credit hours

In the sophomore year, integrated courses are offered through dual department collaboration. For example, two professors from Psychology and Biology departments join forces to teach one course known as "GSR 150: What do we know about sex and gender?: From Biological and Psychological Perspectives."[15] In addition, ASL and English consultants are utilized to evaluate ASL and English for each student. That totals to 24 credits. After successful completion of 24 credits of GSR 150 and GSR 200-level courses, the student then takes a Capstone Experience course in his/her junior year. That completes the general requirements and the student should then be ready to declare a major preferably before or at the same time as the Capstone Experience course.

ASL SCREENING TEST

Historically, during the New Student Orientation period, incoming students took English and Mathematics examinations to determine class placement. For the first time in August 2007, an ASL Screening Test was added during the Orientation week. Because this test was developed on a moment's notice (in three weeks) it was not without flaws. Using computer technology, it tested student's receptive skills only. In addition, there were some "video bugs" and unclear instructions. Nevertheless, a cut-off score was established. Students scoring above the cut-off were enrolled in GSR 103. Students scoring below the cut-off went on to ASL 102 with Malzkuhn and Gray to receive intensive training that developed the signing skills that would prepare them to enroll in GSR 103 the following semester. Most of these GSR 103 students, as realized throughout the pioneering course, knew how to use ASL but were not aware of the intricacies of the linguistic structure itself.

THE COURSE: ITS EMERGENCE AND STRUCTURE

Monday, August 27, 2007 marked the historical birth of the course with Bahan's opening lecture at the Andrew J. Foster Auditorium. The course description and the course structure were both innovative, a first for the University. The course description for GSR 103 reads:

> "The purpose of the course is to prepare students to engage in critical, academic thinking through American Sign Language. Students will be introduced to historical linguistic, literary and academic dimensions of American Sign Language. Students will learn the differences between formal and informal uses of language and gain experiences in critical analysis of American Sign Language texts. This course will also explore the theme of "Deaf Lives" and engage students in thinking about the complexities involved in identity construction and what it means to live Deaf lives today."

The course was structured as a lecture with all the 150 students from ten sections meeting at the Foster Auditorium on Mondays. These lectures were conducted by Bahan and Bienvenu. In addition, Dr. Carolyn McCaskill and Provost Stephen Weiner were guest lecturers. The Wednesday/Friday sessions were conducted as seminars by Cole, Jarashow, Kelly, Malzkuhn and Youens-Un, totaling two classes per teacher. The chart below illustrates the course structure:

- Monday: Lecture, 150 students
- Wednesday: Seminars 1–5, 75 students
- Friday: Seminars 6–10, 75 students

Each lecture and seminar was connected thematically. Deaf Studies themes began with the lecture and subsequently carried over into the seminars for in-depth discussions. Each theme was treated with much thought and they overlapped with each other. Interwoven with Deaf Studies were ASL components. The themes and components are listed below, however not in chronological order as presented in lectures and seminars:

Deaf Studies themes:	**ASL Components**
Audism	Classifers
Ideology	Fingerspelling and numbers
Identity	Grammar
Language	Non-manual signs
Linguistics	Prosody
Linguicism	Register
Places	Sign production
Selves	Structure
Technology	Use of space

ACADEMIC ASL DISCOURSE AND RUBRICS

As stated earlier, the new mission and vision statement brings a new paradigm shift in that the current curriculum addresses an academic ASL discourse in the classroom. This new powerful and exciting curriculum allows ASL to be one of the primary student learning outcomes with the intention that students graduate as competent bilinguals.

Since ASL and English are placed on equal footing, ASL pushes past outdated paradigms to create a genuine bilingual classroom experience. In doing transformational work, it requires inference, syntheses, analysis and evaluation of ASL in an academic setting. Yet, the team remains in the midst of discovering through exploration. Now, to have a formal meta-analysis of ASL brings us to a place in history where we all not only discuss what is not, but analyze and describe what is.

Teaching the incoming freshmen from a L_1[16] position is challenging because of a dearth of literature regarding teaching ASL as a L1 as opposed to the plethora of literature on teaching ASL as a L_2[17]. What was lacking was research validating best pedagogical models to teach ASL as a first language to some Deaf students who have not naturally acquired the language but nonetheless it is their L1, or most natural language. In addition, most of them come from educational settings where sign language was bastardized into coding systems. To unlearn these coding systems and to appreciate ASL as a natural language is the first obstacle to consciously valuing ASL as equal to English.[18] This challenge propelled the team to utilize a L1 perspective.

The team undertook new pedagogical principles to become standard for GSR 103 courses. Because students came from a vast variety of cultures and experienced linguicism,[19] the team was aware and sensitive in providing a clear understanding of ASL structure before discussing on a meta-language level. This skill is seen in American public schools on the elementary level, but here, this is introduced in a post-secondary setting. To validate the idea of discussing ASL on a meta-language level, an assessment tool became critical.

Rubrics are a scoring tool where criteria is listed and scored, providing fair and sound judgment. ASL essays are judged on content, conventions and on a lesser scale, the mise en scéne. The challenging part was setting a scoring range because of a lack of standards in measuring academic ASL. To develop ASL rubrics, both the Department of ASL and Deaf Studies and the team looked at English rubrics as a starting point, which lead to discussions on measuring ASL competency.[20] Adopted by the entire university, this became a benchmark to identify the level of understanding and mastering Academic ASL in the formal academic arena, including listening, speaking, reading and discussing about subject area content material. Written English mechanisms such as format, tabs, font size, length or word count and margins, prompted techniques in ASL videotexts such as appropriate color contrast clothing, background, framing of the signer in the camera lens and so forth. The ASL rubrics also include critical thinking skills, analysis, organization of thought and vocabulary.

VIDEOTEXTS

All the assignments were conducted as videotexts. The teachers developed homework assignments and took turns video-signing the assignments that were posted on Blackboard.[21] By a specific deadline, students video-responded to and submitted the assignments to respective professors. Using the rubrics, the students' content, including an introduction, body and conclusion, and conventions were graded. The rubrics allowed room for teachers' feedback. Some feedback, just like written assignments, was conducted face to face. Written texts can be analyzed and edited, and so can ASL texts; however not many students initially agreed.

All feedback should have been submitted in ASL. It however didn't happen in a formal way due to new technology and time constraints. Another challenge was the technical support often didn't have the capacity or platform support to cross PC and Mac needs. It is predicted that in the near future, all of the interactions with videotext assignments will be implemented more consistently to allow responsive pedagogy and will be completely online to best meet students' need for progress.

Through this process of evaluating submitted ASL work, the team often readjusted the rubrics to reflect what was noted in the students' submissions. These adjustments also affected the pedagogy to fill in gaps in student learning. All of this dynamic work is informed by a loop of constant evaluation and careful analysis. This is the goal and is in the plan to implement in the near future.

REACTIONS AND REFLECTIONS

As mentioned earlier, incoming freshmen and new transfer students underwent ASL Screening Tests for appropriate course placements: GSR 103 or ASL 102. Once these students were told that they were to take an ASL course, they were quick to opine. Their early reactions were fraught with resistance:
- "I am from a Deaf family…."
- "I came from a Deaf school…."
- "I am in honors program, so why should I be required to take ASL…"

- "ASL equal English? Yeah, right...."
- "Why must I learn ASL? It has nothing do with university...."
- "I don't want see myself on video...."
- "Self-correct? My first videotext looks fine...."
- "I don't like video-technology...."

These attitudes clearly signified a lack of appreciation of language and identity. Some students also were uncomfortable in either using or seeing themselves on videos. Language, specifically ASL, was not intrinsically understood as their cultural identity. This challenged the team to engage students in understanding not only their language but identity and culture on all levels of humanity. The team also encouraged the students to become technically savvy.

As part of the final examination, the team solicited from the students their reflections on the course. A shift in their views and thoughts on ASL was definitely detected. They finished their first semester with an appreciation of ASL as a complex and rich language on par with any other spoken language. In addition, they realized that they were deprived of an educational opportunity, expressing a desire for a K-12 ASL curriculum to be implemented in all academic settings:

- "ASL has verbs!"
- "I want to learn more about ASL."
- "I did not realize I have been oppressed."
- "Now I cherish ASL."

THE FINAL EXAMINATION

For the final exam, the team decided to do five questions, with a time limit of three to five minutes per question. It seemed reasonable at the time, seeing it as one of the most common formats for a written final exam is to assign between 15 to 20 questions. What was not thought of was the time factor. For a written test, depending on the required length of the answers to each question, it may take the teacher about thirty minutes to read and grade the tests. In this situation, one student meant five videos, ranging from three to five minutes in length, which in turn totaled 15 to 25 minutes for that one student.

With this, the team reached an even more devastating conclusion - approximately 15 students meant 75 videos and about 3.75 to 6.75 hours of footage per class. What was even more hair-wrenching is that each team member taught two GSR sections, totaling 30 students. That totaled 150 videos and 7.5 to 12.5 hours of footage with only one week to grade them all before submitting final grades to the Registrar. Not just that, two full days of mandatory workshops and presentations were scheduled during that same week, thus subtracting two full days of grading. In addition, there were other classes to grade. All of this made the task of grading the students' works seem impossible, but the team did it!

THE FOLLOWING SEMESTER

As the spring 2008 semester approached, the team had the opportunity to stop momentarily and reflect on the previous semester and consider improvements and adjustments. One major improvement was the use of video recordings of the previous semester's Monday sessions, which were videotaped and became videotexts, akin to print text, i.e., textbooks, articles, etc. Another major improvement was the changes made by Gallaudet's E-Learning Department that improved technology, enabling professors to send video feedback to assignments directly to each student. That meant students would finally get ASL feedback for their assignments.

In addition to the two major adjustments, tweaks were made in the curriculum for the GSR courses, as well as the ASL rubrics. For example, instruction on basic ASL linguistics began earlier in the semester rather than later as it did in the pioneering semester. The fall semester did not allow much time to do a thorough job of setting up the rubric nor for in-depth retrospection, so the spring semester allowed for making revisions where necessary. After reevaluating homework assignments and questions, improvements to those were engendered. Most importantly, the final exam was readjusted to two questions instead of the original five, one reason being that a more thorough evaluation of the students' ASL skills can be performed.

The changes made from the fall 2007 semester to the spring 2008 semester look good and have certainly improved the program, but there is always room for improvement, and that will continue. Another major improvement was the fine-tuning of the ASL Screening Test once more time was available. For example, this test has gone from testing just the students' receptive skills to testing both comprehension and production skills. Within one year, significant changes have been made.

THE BEACON

All in all, it was and is the team's goal to place ASL on an equal footing with English and other academic discourses. Throughout this journey, the team faced surmountable challenges: defining Academic ASL, choosing L1 or L2 pedagogy, developing ASL Rubrics, assigning video activities and dealing with technological limitations in giving feedback on video homework. These challenges prompted the awareness of the link between language and culture, of the complexity of ASL, and of the fact that Deaf people are victims of linguicism. This pioneering GSR 103 course reflects Bauman's 2008 sentiment: "…only the beginning of a cultural and academic exchange that must put Gallaudet firmly on the map of intellectual life in America" (p. 334). It is the aim of this GSR 103 course to achieve bilingualism as stated in the mission and vision statement, as well as academic rigor as recommended by the MSCHE.

There are reasons for the catchy glossed title of this essay. Basically it describes the path, or montage, that the team undertook to formally bring Academic ASL into the classroom. This essay serves as a beacon for all schools, programs, colleges and universities with a deaf and hard-of-hearing population. Teachers and professors are encouraged to refer to this essay as an inspiration, as a guide, and as validation for bringing ASL into the academic arena. The essay ends with a glossed declaration, but without a question mark: GALLAUDET TRUE-BIZ ACADEMIC ASL–q, THAT!

ENDNOTES

1. The Fall 2007 GSR 103 team wishes to acknowledge Gallaudet's Department of ASL and Deaf Studies for the opportunity to teach this pioneering course; Gallaudet's E-Learning Department for technical support; Dean Isaac Agboola and Provost Stephen Weiner for their unwavering support; the 150 freshmen who themselves were pioneers in this experiment. Last but not the least, the team also thanks Dr. Dirksen Bauman and Dr. Ben Bahan for feedback on this essay.
2. The National Deaf-Mute College was renamed Gallaudet College in 1894 and then renamed Gallaudet University in 1986. www.gallaudet.edu/x234.xml
3. http://web5.uottawa.ca/admingov/bilingualism.html
4. See Thiong'O (1995).
5. See Stokoe, Casterline & Croneberg (1965).
6. Maher, J. (1996); Wilcox (2000).
7. See Baker & Battison (1980), xix.
8. For the history of the Deaf Studies field, see Katz (1996), 133-148; Kelly (1998), 188-124; Bauman (2008), 1-32.
9. For a synopsis on the MSCHE crisis, refer to Bauman (2008), 327-336.
10. The Vision Implement Program was an administrative attempt to streamline on-campus programs which had an effect on the Communication Policy.
11. The paradigm shift theory was introduced and popularized by Kuhn (1962). He proposed that revolution, or chaos, engenders a shift to new thinking, new views, new methodologies.
12. In January 2002, the Department of Deaf Studies merged with the Department of ASL to become the Department of ASL and Deaf Studies, also known as ASL/DST.
13. The staff of the Assessment and Evaluation Unit (AEU), formerly known as the Center for ASL Literacy (CASLL), consists of Leticia Arellano, Jean M. Gordon, Toni Parliman, Loretta S. Roult and Marti Edelman Kellner.
14. ASL 101 & 102 focus on signing skills, grammatical structures and comprehension and production skills. For more information see: http://admissions.gallaudet.edu/catalog/07-08/

UG_06_Departments.pdf
15. Dr. Tammy Weiner and Dr. Jane Dillehay16 L1 refers to one's natural language, often acquired from the environment as posited by Cummins, 1991b.
16. L1 refers to one's natural language, often acquired from the environment as posited by Cummins, 1991b.
17. L2 refers to learning a second language as proposed by Krashen, 1981.
18. For further discussion, see Cummins (2006)
19. Skutnabb-Kangas (1988) coined this term to define language oppression.
20. Keep in mind that there is a wide plethora of English rubrics available online while there is not a single ASL rubric.
21. BlackBoard is an e-Learning tool used in colleges and universities to facilitate the exchange of information between teachers and students as well as among the students themselves. Articles and professors' power point presentations, for example, can be posted for the students to read at their convenience. See www.blackboard.com.

REFERENCES

Mission Statement: http://www.gallaudet.edu/mission.xml
GSR Curricula: http://admissions.gallaudet.edu/generalstudies/FAQ/faq.html
http://admissions.gallaudet.edu/generalstudies/spring08/spring2008.html
http://admissions.gallaudet.edu/catalog/07-08/UG_06_Departments.pdf
www.blackboard,com
http://web5.uottawa.ca/admingov/bilingualism.html

Baker, C., R. Battison, eds. 1980. *Sign Language and The Deaf Community: Essays in Honor of William C. Stokoe.* Silver Spring, MD: National Association of the Deaf.
Bauman, D., ed. 2008. "Introduction" and "PostScript." *Open Your Eyes: Deaf Studies Talking.* Minneapolis: University of Minnesota Press. 1-32 and 327-336.
Cummins, J. 1991a. "Conversational and Academic Language Proficiency in Bilingual Contexts." *Association Internationale de Linguistique Appliquee*, v. 8. (75-89).
Cummins, J. 1991b. "Interdependence of first and second language proficiency in bilingual children." In *Language Processing in Bilingual Children*, edited by Bialystok. Cambridge University Press. 70-89.
Cummins, J. 2006. *The Relationship between American Sign Language Proficiency and English Academic Development: A Review of the Research.* The University of Toronto.
Katz, C. N. 1996. "A Comparative Analysis of Deaf, Women, and Black Studies," *Deaf Studies IV Conference Proceedings: Visions of the Past — Visions of the Future.* Washington, D.C.; Gallaudet University College of Continuing Education. 133-148.
Kelly, A. B. 1998. "A Brief History on the Field of Deaf Studies," *Disability Quarterly Studies* 18, 2. 118-124.
Kuhn, T. 1962. *The Structure of Scientific Revolutions.* Chicago: University of Chicago Press.
Maher, J. 1996. *Seeing Signs: The William C. Stokoe Story.* Washington, D.C.: Gallaudet University Press.
Stokoe, W., D. Casterline, C. Croneberg. 1965. *A Dictionary of American Sign Language on Linguistic Principles.* Washington, D.C.: Gallaudet College Press.
Skutnabb-Kangas , T. 1988. "Multilingualism and the Education of Minority Children. In *Minority Education: From Shame to Struggle*, edited by Skutnabb-Kangas and Cummins. Clevedon, Avon: Multilingual Matters. 9-44.

Thiong'O, N. 1995. "On the Abolition of the English Department." In *PostColonial Studies Reader*, edited by Ashcroft, Griffiths and Tiffin. London: Routledge. 438-442.

Wilcox, S. 2000. "Appreciation: William C. Stokoe: July 21, 1919- April 4, 2000" *Sign Language Studies*, 1.1, 7-9.

Deaf Interpreter as a Career Choice within the Realm of the Deaf Studies Curriculum

PATRICK BOUDREAULT, PH.D., & JIMMY BELDON, CDI

THE NATIONAL CONSORTIUM OF INTERPRETER EDUCATION CENTERS is a collaboration of six Interpreter Education Centers funded by the U.S. Department of Education, Rehabilitation Services Administration for the purpose of increasing the number of qualified interpreters and advancing the field of interpreting and interpreting education. The Consortium has established a national partner network of interpreters, educators, and researchers to investigate effective practices in teaching Deaf Interpreting. Together since summer 2006, the team is working to describe the specialized domains and competencies required of the Deaf Interpreter (DI) particularly in the critical areas of language foundations, consumer assessment, decision-making, and interpreting process.

Consortium-sponsored surveys and focus groups of Deaf Interpreters and DI educators have begun to shed light on current and best practices in this emerging field. Planned outcomes of this work are a clear definition of the roles and functions of the DI, domains and competencies required for effective interpreting practice, and the future implementation of a clearinghouse of resources, study, and networking opportunities for DIs. These professional discussions and qualitative data gathering are critical as the field works toward understanding and embracing Deaf interpreting as a vital and valued enterprise: an emerging industry of the interpreting field.

The purpose of this conference presentation was to highlight Consortium findings to date; provide an overview of the tasks performed by the DI; and consider how the Deaf studies curriculum can contribute to the emergence of Deaf Interpreting as a professional career choice and provide core knowledge and foundation for interpreting education.

WHAT IS THE DEAF INTERPRETER'S WORK?

The DI's work may be viewed as involving interpretation or translation between two distinct languages (e.g. LSQ and ASL; or written English and ASL) or within one language employing a variety of communication systems or techniques based on consumer and situational needs. Boudreault (2007) refers to the latter function as "facilitation." In either case, the DI might produce the target language or variety either visually or tactually, as in Deaf-blind interpreting.

In terms of interpreting roles and functions, the DI provides interpreting services in a variety of situations: conferences and lectures; international conferences and events; legal proceedings; employment and vocational rehabilitation; social services; healthcare; entertainment; educational; and interpreting via video, to name several. Additionally, he or she serves as translator (sight or videotext), clarifier or monitor, linguistic and cultural mediator, and may team with or mentor novice interpreters. All of these areas have potential for growth as consumers, ASL-English interpreters, hiring entities, and policy makers learn about the value of Deaf Interpreting. Interpreting via video is one sector where growth is anticipated. The Federal Communications Commission (FCC) recently acknowledged roles for the DI within Video Relay Services (VRS), (FCC 2007) and the Registry of Interpreters for the Deaf (RID), Inc. encourages the use of Certified Deaf Interpreters (CDI) as team interpreters in the VRS (RID 2006).

NATIONAL SURVEY CONDUCTED

With the resources provided by the National Consortium, we have been able to begin to move from anecdotal information about the work of the DI to more tangible data-driven descriptions of who Deaf Interpreters are, where they work, in what languages and communication forms, who their consumers are, and what their educational experiences and needs are. The following reflects some of the findings of an on-line national survey conducted from February-March 2008. Of 199 respondents captured by the survey, forty-seven (or approximately 24%) indicated that they were RID certified (CDI and/or RSC). Forty-seven represents approximately 87% of the total number of current RID certified Deaf interpreters.

While anecdote would have us believe that the DI works primarily with Deaf-blind and semi-lingual Deaf persons, the data indicates that 73% of National Survey respondents reported that the majority of their work was with consumers who are sighted; 51% reported regular or frequent work with monolingual ASL users; and 26% reported that they are regularly or frequently called upon to work with consumers who have little or no language.

Some believe that DI work is limited primarily to the legal setting. In fact, only 18% of National Survey respondents indicated that the majority of their work was in the legal setting; 30% reported working most of the time in healthcare (medical and mental health) settings; and 52% worked in a variety of community settings including social services, professional or business settings, vocational rehabilitation/job placement settings, educational settings, performing arts, and religious settings.

The survey supported earlier assertions about the need for DI education (Boudreault, 2005; Forestal, 2005). Only 14% of the respondents reported having taken a formal interpreting education program. Yet, most of the Deaf Interpreters responding to this survey had college degrees. 67% reported having at least a baccalaureate degree.

More in-depth analysis of the National DI Survey results is forthcoming.

DOMAINS AND COMPETENCIES

While there are many domains in which DI work is akin to ASL-English interpreting provided by hearing interpreters, the National Consortium Work team has begun to identify some critical areas where DI work diverges from ASL-English interpreting provided by hearing interpreters. Like ASL-English interpreters, the DI works one-on-one, in small groups, and in larger groups such as meetings and conferences. Similarly, the DI performs sight translation, translation of frozen texts, simultaneous and consecutive interpretation, shadowing or mirroring, and as feed to another interpreter. Like the ASL-English interpreter, the DI is expected to exhibit such minimum competencies inherent in general interpreting as:

- Knowledge and application of interpreting theory to understand and describe the work itself;
- Effective communication in the languages of the participants including nuances of discourse, culture, race, gender, region, ethnicity, age, and socio-economic status;
- Ability to explain, discuss, and negotiate the role and function of the interpreter and the interpreting team;
- Ability to adjust interpreting approach to the needs of consumers;
- Proficiency with technology used in interpreting;
- Ability to appropriately choose, use, and monitor the effectiveness of different types of interpreting (e.g. simultaneous, consecutive, sight translation);

- Ability to apply academic and world knowledge during interpreting;
- Commitment to ethical conduct and professional development;
- Strategies for managing professional conflicts, boundary issues, personal safety; and
- Knowledge and adherence to interpreting-related laws and professional requirements including credentialing and licensure.

Moreover, the DI is expected to bring additional, further developed and specialized competencies beyond those of day-to-day ASL-English interpreting to meet the challenges offered up by the consumer population the DI is most often called upon to serve. These additional competencies seem to fall into four domains: communication/language foundations, consumer assessment, interpreting process, and ethical decision-making.

Consumer Language Assessment
The Deaf Interpreter commonly encounters a range of language abilities and preferences among Deaf consumers. Currently, the Deaf Interpreter is most often called upon to interpret for Deaf and Deaf-blind consumers over age 16 who have had limited or inconsistent exposure to English or ASL. 82% of survey respondents reported working at least occasionally with monolingual ASL speakers (i.e. consumers who are limited English proficient), and 51% report working regularly or frequently with this population. 73% of survey respondents reported that they use gesture-based communication in their interpreting work; for 42%, the majority of the work requires use of a mixture of ASL and gesture-based communication. 62% report that they work occasionally, regularly, or frequently with individuals who have no language. The Deaf Interpreter must be able to assess the consumer's command of language, culture, information, and situational protocols, as well as factors – physical, cognitive, psychological, environmental, educational – that play into the consumer's communicative needs and behaviors.

Communication/Language Foundations
The range of settings and consumer populations encountered by the Deaf Interpreter requires facility with signed and written English and mastery of a continuum of visual communication strategies from formal ASL discourse to basic gestures, pantomime, role- playing and props. Semi- and a-lingual consumers may require the DI to employ extra-linguistic knowledge and such strategies as cycling back to previous points, distillation of the key concepts, or parsing and restructuring complex questions or statements into several shorter, more easily understood forms. The DI must be able move with ease from one language to another and one sign code to another on a

case-by-case basis. Additionally, the DI must be articulate about the choices he or she makes and the rationale.

Ethical Decision-making
Interpreting requires moment-by-moment decisions. The ethical interpreter has thought critically through his or her own personal tendencies, values, and ethics, and the meaning of professional conduct. S/he is able to recognize ethical dilemmas and to distinguish not only between right and wrong, but also between right and right.

The ethical interpreter will employ decision-making processes to evaluate dilemmas, weigh several options and possible outcomes, and determine the optimal course of action. The DI navigates complex relationships: with him/herself, whose skills and tendencies s/he must know well and manage expertly; with the consumer, whose struggles may generate boundary or role conflicts within the DI which must be analyzed and managed appropriately; with the ASL-English partner interpreter, with whom the DI negotiates in constructing meaning, managing logistics, and sharing power; and with the non-signing party, who is unlikely to understand why the DI is present or what the process is all about. The education of the DI must present sufficient opportunities to explore and think critically about personal and professional ethics as well as decision-making processes to develop ethical fitness.

Deaf Interpreting Processes
In the United States, most of the DI's work (57%) is carried out collaboratively with an ASL-English interpreter. The DI works from signed source language material provided by the ASL-English interpreter on one side and from ASL or gesture-based communication provided by a Deaf or Deafblind consumer on the other side. The DI can also interpret directly from a signing source-language presenter or translate from a written or filmed text.

The complexity of the content, situational protocol, and participant needs factor into decisions on how to conduct the process, that is, whether the interpretation will be simultaneous, consecutive, or quasi. In simultaneous interpretation, the DI renders an interpretation while the source message continues without pause; in consecutive interpretation, the source language message is divided into segments allowing for more in-depth analysis and resulting in a more linguistically accurate and culturally nuanced interpretation. A setting may determine a combination of simultaneous and consecutive in which the interpreting team moves between the two modes.

In the 2006 Deaf Interpreting Critical Issues Forum, our team explored the application of interpreting service models, theories of interpretation including Gile's Effort Model (Gile, 1995) and Vermeer's Skopostheorie

(1989/2004), and pedagogical approaches such as Colonomos' CRP model (discussed in Boines, et. al. 1996), Gish's goal-to-detail, detail-to-goal approach to information processing (Gish, 1984), and Monikowski & Winston's discourse mapping approach (Monikowski & Winston, 2000) as means of illuminating the practice and teaching of Deaf Interpreting and the interpreting team process. Forum presentations are available in summary and PowerPoint form through the Consortium website at: www.asl.neu.edu/nciec/projects.html#di. Here the reader may find more information about the Deaf Interpreting strategies described above, as well as discussion of interpreting process and pedagogical models as applied to Deaf Interpreting.

TRAINING NEEDS AND PREFERENCES

Deaf Interpreters express a serious interest in and a critical need for continuing professional development. As many as 40% of the National Survey respondents would be willing to travel away from home to participate in educational opportunities. 82% indicated that they were willing to participate in online education. While there was some expression of interest in general interpreting education programs (27%) and interpreting teacher training (15%), the majority (59%) were most interested in specialty training in such areas as legal, medical, and mental healthcare interpreting.

CURRENT CRITICAL ISSUES FOR DI

We intend that the work of the Consortium on Deaf Interpreting will affect several issues in the field today:
- While ASL-English interpreters are generally expected to complete two-to-four years of interpreting education before sitting for certification, the RID currently requires only 16 hours of training before a DI is eligible for certification. This may contribute to a high rate of failure on the DI certification test. Additionally, it creates an uneven playing field for the DI and ASL-English interpreter who practice together as a team.
- A number of workshops on Deaf Interpreting are offered each year around the U.S. There is a need to identify and promote content and approaches based in effective practices.
- Interpreting Education for the Deaf Interpreter needs to support the development of the requisite skills and knowledge for effective Deaf Interpreting described above through coursework, internships, and mentoring opportunities.
- The value of the DI in the interpreting process is not well known among members of Deaf Community, ASL-English interpreters, and the gen-

eral public. Deaf Interpreters themselves need information on how to market themselves and how to build careers in this emerging field.

By defining the knowledge and competencies required for effective Deaf Interpreting, the Consortium will help to promote higher standards for DI education. The Consortium's plans to create an Internet based clearinghouse of information and resources for and about Deaf interpreting practice and education will help to advance the field through sharing of information and networking opportunities.

FUTURE PLANS

The Consortium Deaf Interpreting Work-team is currently developing a web-based clearinghouse of resources, study, and networking opportunities for and about Deaf Interpreters, which will be known as Deaf Interpreting Institute. DIInstitute.org will be a focal point for the Deaf Interpreting field, offering information about Deaf Interpreting including definitions and DI domains and competencies; an interactive, annotated bibliography of literature and DVDs on Deaf Interpreting; resources for Deaf Interpreters, the Deaf Community, interpreting education programs, ASL-English interpreters, and the general public; a calendar of events; DI learning opportunities and case studies focused on common issues and challenges in Deaf Interpreting; data collection surveys; and a VLOG to promote networking and discussion among Deaf Interpreter practitioners, mentors, and educators.

THE ROLE OF DEAF STUDIES IN THE
ADVANCEMENT OF DEAF INTERPRETERS

The field of Deaf Interpreting might be well supported by a partnership among Deaf Studies programs, interpreting education programs, and the forthcoming DIInstitute.org.

A solid Deaf Studies curriculum, including such content areas as Deaf and Culture, Deaf history, linguistics of ASL, Deaf-blind community, communication, and culture, dynamics of oppression, ASL literature, sign language acquisition (psycholinguistics), issues and trends in the Deaf Community, law and the Deaf, and foreign Sign Languages would lay a solid foundation for Deaf Interpreting Education. The interpreting education curriculum would then focus on the knowledge and competencies of effective interpreting, however built upon core knowledge and experiences that will expand the DI's schema, foster critical thinking and decision-making skills, help them better understand and assess consumers, and become more conversant in the underlying issues and challenges of Deaf Interpreting. DIInstitute.org will support continuing professional development through the services and networking it will provide. Partnering together, Deaf Studies, Interpreting Education, and the DI Institute would allow for continual professional growth for Deaf Interpreters. These opportunities would also help Deaf Interpreters reach the goal of achieving credentials.

It is important for us all to be involved in driving this initiative forward. Deaf Studies Programs can participate by strengthening the curriculum to incorporate a wide range of courses beyond Deaf Culture. A strong core curriculum will facilitate the emergence of Deaf interpreting as a professional career. When we become unified in doing this at the basic curriculum level, we will see our students develop quickly into successful and professional Deaf Interpreters.

ACKNOWLEDGEMENTS

The current members of the Deaf Interpreting Work Team are Jimmy Beldon, Patrick Boudreault, Cathy Cogen, Lillian Garcia, Eileen Forestal, Carole Lazorisak, Priscilla Moyers, Cynthia Napier, and Debbie Peterson.

We are also appreciative of the contributions of Janis Cole, Jan DeLap, Sharon Neumann-Solow, Terry Malcolm, Mark Morales, and Stacey Storme whose participation and contributions at the 2006 Critical Issues in Deaf Interpreting Forum have supported this work.

Original translation of this conference presentation was rendered by Nanette Wendt.

REFERENCES AND RESOURCES

Boudreault, P. (2005). Deaf interpreters. In T. Janzen (Ed.) *Topics in Signed Language Interpreting: Theory and Practice* (pp. 323-355). Philadelphia: John Benjamins.

Boinis, S. et.al. (1996). *Self-Paced Modules for Educational Interpreter Skill Development*. St. Paul: Minnesota Registry of Interpreters for the Deaf.

Federal Communications Commission (2007). *In the Matter of Telecommunications Relay Services and Speech-to-Speech Services for Individuals with Hearing and Speech Disabilities, Report and Order, FCC 07-186, CG Docket No. 03-123* (p. 81), released November 19, 2007.

Forestal, E. (2005). The emerging professionals: Deaf interpreters and their views and experiences on training. In Mark Marschark, Rico Peterson, & Elizabeth A. Winston (Eds.), *Sign Language Interpreting and Interpreter Education: Directions for Research and Practice* (pp. 235-258). New York: Oxford University Press.

Gile, D. (1995). *Basic Concepts and Models for Translator and Interpreter Training*. Amsterdam/Philadelphia: John Benjamins Publishing Company.

Gish, S. (1984). Goal-to-detail and detail-to-goal. In M.L. McIntire (Ed.), New dimensions in interpreter education: Task analysis – theory and application. *Proceedings of the 5th National Convention, Conference of Interpreter Trainers*, Silver Spring: RID Publications.

Registry of Interpreters for the Deaf (2006) *Video Relay Service Interpreting Standard Practice Paper*, Retrieved April 1, 2008, from http://rid.org.

Vermeer, Hans J. (1989/2004). "Skopos and Commission in Translational Action." Trans. Andrew Chesterman. In Lawrence Venuti. Ed. *The Translation Studies Reader*. 2nd ed (pp. 227-238). New York: Routledge, 2004. 227-38.

Winston, E. & Monikowski, C. (2000). Discourse mapping: Developing textual coherence skills in interpreters. In C.R. Roy (Ed.) *Innovative Practices for Teaching Sign Language Interpreters*. Washington D.C.: Gallaudet University Press.

Information on the National Consortium's work on Deaf Interpreting, as well as its other projects, may be found at these websites:

www.asl.neu.edu/nciec
www.asl.neu.edu/nciec/projects.html#di
www.asl.neu.edu/nciec/resource/docs.html

The National Consortium of Interpreter Education Centers is funded from 2005 – 2010 by the U.S. Department of Education RSA CFDA #84.160A and B, Training of Interpreters for Individuals Who Are Deaf and Individuals Who Are Deaf-Blind.

Deaf Children's Theatre in the United States

BRIAN KILPATRICK, ED.D.

"I think that Deaf children's theatre represents an opportunity to analyze language, to understand the power of ASL, to know that depending on how one uses ASL in politics, in comedy, in any context, this language can become a powerful tool for discourse. Theatre, either for adults, or for children, is a medium. It makes the impossible possible. It brings life to abstract ideas. It is a way children can understand, acquire ASL, and then use it to express their creativity. Theatre makes the impossible happen. Theatre can teach, can make people cry or laugh, or have all kinds of emotions. Theatre is magic. Deaf Children's Theatre is magic." (Czubek, 2003)

Figure 1. The Magical Literacy Camp rehearsal, August 2004.

The history of Deaf children's theatre has deep roots. It has emerged from many previous influences. These influences are ASL storytelling, early performances in churches, and schools, clubs, communities, and universities. Deaf actors, playwrights and poets have also played an important role in the history of Deaf children's theatre.

The use of ASL in performance and storytelling has always been an important part of Deaf culture. American Sign Language stories and Art-Sign, part of Deaf American literature, have been transmitted through the years by way of socializing in Deaf clubs and in schools for the deaf. The first school for the deaf was established in Hartford, Connecticut, on April 15, 1817. We might assume that ASL storytelling began there and was transmitted through faculty and students. As more states established schools for the deaf, ASL storytelling spread throughout the United States.

As early as 1874, a men's literary society was founded at Gallaudet College with the help of Melville Ballard. The society organized performances of skits, farces, and sketches. In 1891 the male students formed an organization, The Saturday Night Dramatics Club, for the purpose of presenting "dramatic entertainment."

By 1893 the female students at Gallaudet had formed their own dramatic organization, The Jollity Club. Interestingly, some male Saturday Night Dramatics cast members dressed up as female characters, while some female Jollity cast members dressed up as male characters. These two clubs operated for many years, until the Jollity Club disbanded in 1928. Under the influence of women's liberation movements, the nature of the Saturday Night Dramatics Club changed its policies to include female participants in 1935. (Tadie, 1978)

During Thomas Gallaudet's period, there were drama groups and organizations such as the Kendall Green Dramatics Club (1893), the O.W.L.S., of whose acronym only members knew the meaning, which later became the Phi Zeta Sorority, functioning between 1930 and 1957, the Kappa Gamma Fraternity, and other groups.

Deaf Clubs were not established simply from a desire to socialize and preserve life experiences, life lessons, and Deaf history. They were also places where deaf people could network to find jobs. Deaf Clubs were an institution of Deaf Culture, providing socialization, literature, networking, and entertainment, responding to almost all the aspects of a deaf person's life. They represented a world that could not be seen and judged from the outside, a safe haven where deaf people could feel "at home."

From 1817 until the 1950s, ASL storytelling was a form of instruction and entertainment at schools for the deaf. We do not have written records of these ASL stories, because they were not captured on film or videotape. (Peters, 2000)

Deaf children became storytellers at residential schools, and later on became storytelling role models for deaf children who were deprived of communication at home.

An important prelude to Deaf theatre was the era of silent films. In fact, Deaf people have participated in the entertainment industry, particularly the silent films, since the early years of the twentieth century. Granville Redmond demonstrated his performance skills next to the most famous stars of the silent film era, Charlie Chaplin, Douglas Fairbanks, and Raymond Griffith. However, by 1935, talking motion-picture films had replaced silent films (Schuchman, 1988). Films became inaccessible to the deaf audience. Therefore, Deaf people started to develop their own entertainment: Deaf Theatre with signing actors. Without access to movies or to plays, deaf people were drawn to the plays and storytelling that were taking place either in someone's home or at the Deaf Clubs.

In 1960, the American Sign Language has been proven a stand-alone language by Dr. William Stokoe. It was not until the publication of Dr. Stokoe's linguistic study of American Sign Language in 1964 that scholars began giving academic acceptance and credence to creative expression that used American Sign Language.

During the 1970s, the professional summer school of the National Theatre of the Deaf worked on developing Art-Sign and poetry. In the 1980s Clayton Valli formalized more extensively the linguistics of ASL, including its artistic aspect, which is used almost exclusively for storytelling. (Baldwin, 1993) In 1976, based on Dr. Stokoe's work, linguist Dr. Edward Klima and psycho-linguist Dr. Ursula Bellugi began exploring the artistic use of sign language, which they termed "Art-Sign." (Bellugi & Klima, 1983)

Legal provisions for accessibility to the theatre for the deaf and hard-of-hearing did not occur until 1973. Accessibility to theater is not just a luxury for deaf people. It is a right. The Americans with Disabilities Act (ADA) states in Title III that all theaters are required to provide "effective communication," to patrons who are deaf or hard of hearing. Therefore, theatres must provide qualified interpreters, assistive listening devices, and other appropriate services to facilitate access:

- Theatrical open captioning — English text
- Amplification systems — English audio
- Performances in sign language with voice interpreters (for hearing and deaf audiences)
- Theatre interpreters who use sign language
- Theatre interpreters for deaf-blind persons
- Shadow interpreting ("twin" actors — one Deaf actor who signs and one hearing actor who talks — representing the same character)

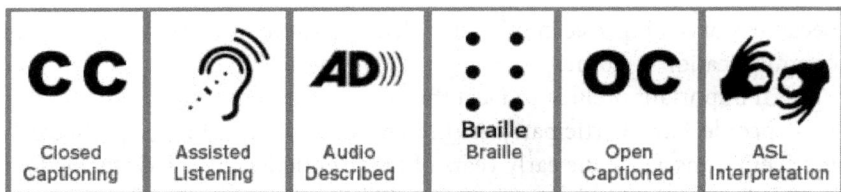

Figure 2. Access Symbols and Terminology. (Cultural Access Consortium, 2006)

Theatrical open captioning is one way to communicate using English text display. However, captioning is not an option for all deaf people. The success of this form depends upon the reading level of the audience.

There is little information about how individuals using assistive devices perceive the theatrical experience. These individuals may have the ability to hear more effectively when provided with sound-amplification devices, such as hearing aids, or other assistive listening devices, such as FM systems and infrared systems. They often refer to themselves as "hard-of-hearing" or "hearing impaired"; many do not use American Sign Language.

Sign language performances are those in which all the characters, whether played by Deaf or hearing actors, use sign exclusively, without voice. Any voicing is performed offstage by a performance-art interpreter who voices for the signing occurring on stage.

Theatrical-arts interpreting is a relatively new art form. It does not merely involve translating words; it is creating a work of art. It is striving to re-interpret the director's vision. In the process it creates a different, more pictorial, staging of that vision. Theatrical-arts interpreting is not merely interpreting, it is performing.

Interpreters for deaf-blind audience members are often Deaf themselves and rely on ASL. They craft their tactile or close-vision translation of the performance. The interpreters also assist the production department in determining the need for and arrangement of auxiliary lighting. These interpreters also prepare for the pre-show tour where the deaf-blind persons can walk around the stage and "feel" the props and costumes.

Interpreting theatre performances for children is fundamentally different that interpreting for adults. For one, the language level of the interpretation has to correspond with the language levels of the children in the audience. In addition, theatrical performances should have a more dramatic action to keep the children focused and interested. Thirdly, the story plots have to be explicit for children to be able to comprehend. Young children may not be able to pick up on ironies or subtleties.

The shadowing style of interpreting places the interpreter directly on stage. In this style, the interpreters are placed within the set, near the actors.

The "shadowed" style of interpreting is inclusive, in that it allows the interpreter a direct link to the action. The interpreters actually echo or "shadow" the actors' every line and move and even their emotions.

Deaf audiences typically prefer to have Deaf actors. Either in an ASL play as independent performers, or in a shadowed performance as shadows of hearing actors, they bring to the audience a more artistic and live theatrical experience. They are also representatives of Deaf Culture and are able to naturally and artistically portray the theme of the production in an appropriate linguistic manner, while adapting the underlying cultural concepts to the Deaf perspective. In an ASL play this adaptation is only necessary if the script of the production belongs to the hearing culture. In the case of shadowed performances, this adaptation is critical to achieving the dynamic equivalence of the theatrical experience for the deaf audience. In addition, Deaf actors are proof of professional excellence, thus being considered role models by the Deaf Community.

The deaf audience feels more immersed in the theatrical experience of a shadowed play than that of an interpreted play. The facial expressions and body language of the shadowing Deaf actors are the bond to the world of ideas conveyed in the play. But this artistic expression and visual imaginary world is brought from behind the hearing actors. Hence, the deaf audience has the feeling that the stage is "crowded" and that the hearing actors are a sort of "visual noise" that interferes in the process of connecting with the acting on stage.

Full ASL productions are the natural way for the deaf audience to dive into the theatrical experience. In these performances, the Deaf actors choose the linguistic level of the play that is best suited for their audience. If the play is addressed to adult audience, then the linguistic level will be adapted function of the characters and ideas contained in the play.

In contrast, if the play is a children's play, then the linguistic level of the play would be brought to match the linguistic level of the young deaf audience. This is the main reason why deaf children prefer full ASL plays for children. Shadowed plays based on children's stories usually employ a higher linguistic level than the one of the young deaf audience because, often times, for the translation of the script, being precise is more important than achieving dynamic equivalence. Therefore, the young deaf audience may miss the actual world of concepts conveyed by the play, and only enjoy the movement and facial expressions on stage.

The Civil Rights movement in the United States brought a new era — the Age of Access, or the Golden Age. Deaf people have equal rights to communication, and equal rights to their own community and social structure. However, the imprint of the oppression of the Deaf minority is left in the most vulnerable institution of the Deaf culture, Deaf education, and more precisely Deaf arts education.

Deaf theatres, besides fighting a yet slow-to-react hearing theatre community, also have to fight the age of technology, where communication in a plethora of forms becomes less and less dependent on human approach and contact. Despite this reality, Deaf theatre is adapting to the new society, which is more and more ruled by economics, and has also instilled itself into institutions of higher education. Most recently, Deaf theatre has extended its reach to both schools for the deaf and public schools, through outreach programs meant to educate artistically, personally, socially, and humanly, deaf and hearing children to accept and work with each other. The hope is to build a future society in which the means of attaining an art form would no longer be judged with prejudice.

For the first time in the Deaf Studies discipline, the history of the birth, evolution, development of six Deaf children's theatre groups and, unfortunately, the recent death of one of these theatre groups, has been revealed. (Kilpatrick, 2007)

LITTLE THEATRE OF THE DEAF

The Little Theatre of the Deaf is a Deaf children's theatre group that emerged from The National Theatre of the Deaf (NTD). Located in Hartford, Connecticut it started with only ten to twelve actors who decided to break into smaller groups to increase the company's revenues.

David Hays thought that the National Theatre of the Deaf needed to diversify its activity in order to provide more work for the company during routine downtimes. To this end he created the outreach program directed toward schools. This program assured that the company would be busy during the fall and spring semesters. The Little Theatre of the Deaf and the National Theatre of the Deaf would perform simultaneously in two different places, thus spreading Deaf Theatre to diverse audiences young and old.

In 1970 a second Little Theatre of the Deaf group was formed on the East Coast. A third Little Theatre of the Deaf was founded in 1978 on the West Coast, based in Los Angeles, California, the Los Angeles Little Theatre of the Deaf, its main objective being to perform for the inner-city schools. Unfortunately, due to lack of funding, the Los Angeles Little Theatre of the Deaf was discontinued later in 1978.

Currently there is only one Little Theatre of the Deaf. The usual LTD performance is one hour long. The performance is given by a group of three Deaf and hearing actors. However, the artistic purposes of entertaining and educating children and adults through the performances of the Little Theatre of the Deaf in schools and in public theatres are still ongoing but with reduced numbers of performances depending on funding availability (Beekman, 2003).

List of Plays and Workshops

By combining sign language with the spoken word, the Little Theatre of the Deaf creates a unique visual language that one critic described as "poetry for the eye and heart." The Little Theatre of the Deaf sculpts words and meanings in the air through sign language and blends them with spoken words in every performance — original works, classic stories, fables, or poems — "You see and hear every word."

Among the most recent collections of stories performed by LTD, *Fingers Around the World*, offers a potpourri of folktales and stories. For three seasons, since 2004, LTD has brought different flavors from distant corners of the world to deaf children. These captivating stories are an educational tool to teach deaf children about the art of storytelling. Another recent performance, *Poetry in Motion*, educates deaf children on the art of ASL poetry. The LTD performances, unlike theatre performance for adults, are less formal. Before the show, the performers engage the audience in a signing warm-up supposed to build cohesiveness of the audience and a more comfortable atmosphere. Also, after the performance, the actors make sure to regain contact with the audience and conclude the show in an open and communicative atmosphere (National Theatre of the Deaf, 2004).

Figure 3. LTD — *Giving Tree and Other Stories*, 2002–2003 season.

Figure 4. ICODA — *Annie Get Your Gun*, 2001–2002 season.

Participants and Audiences

In 1965, based on the need for a touring company to visit schools and encourage drama programs for deaf students, a federal grant from the United States Department of Health, Education and Welfare provided planning funds to LTD. While more than 90 percent of the company's audience is hearing, the theatre fills an important need for deaf viewers as well. The Little Theatre of the Deaf has performed for over 50,000 children and adults all over the United States and in foreign countries such as Mexico, Germany, Russia, India, Japan, the People's Republic of China, and New Zealand. (Daniels, 1992)

Kinds of Skills Taught
A standard performance of the Little Theatre of the Deaf lasts fifty minutes. However, its length is usually adjusted to fit into each school's schedule. Because of its educational orientation, prior to the performances the actors give the schools a study guide book. The exercise and activities contained in the study/resource guide are targeted for school groups from pre-kindergarten through the eighth grade. These activities include engaging deaf children in discussions and games. The techniques are adapted to match and complement the school curriculum. Curricular goals include enhancing organization and sequencing in communicating ideas, developing logic, using imagination, providing an opportunity for group interaction, learning cooperation and problem solving, using varied communication skills, practicing memorization, developing deduction, and learning respect for and sensitivity to other students and their ideas (Little Theatre of the Deaf, 2003).

Conversations with Actors and Participants
LTD organizes yearly, in August, a Summer School Academy to recruit and to train their actors and performers who will be touring with the theatre.

All former cast and Summer School Academy's participants of the Little Theatre of the Deaf had been involved in community Deaf Theatre acting and in the previous summer schools (yearly during June or July) organized by the National Theatre of the Deaf. Some also joined the touring company of the National Theatre of the Deaf before joining the Little Theatre of the Deaf. To an interview question asking "Should deaf children be involved on stage to perform rather than watching Deaf adults performing for them?" Robert DeMayo answered:

> "I also think that exposure to literature is important. Hearing parents are not comfortable signing the stories to their deaf children. Sign language is a visual language and the books are printed in English. Deaf kids have comprehension difficulties. At LTD, we take stories from books, put them into action and make them visual. The children are enthralled by this visual presentation. We become their book. In turn, the children gain motivation to go back to the book and read. This is why I think exposure is important. ... I think deaf children should be involved in theatre during the school year. It would be nice to incorporate that in the regular curriculum. Then every-

thing would intertwine, becoming a holistic approach to education. Deaf children understand everything easier, if it becomes visual."

Shanny Mow, former cast member with the National Theatre of the Deaf and Deaf playwright and director, commented about the influence of theatre education on developing creativity:

> "Theatre can be performed in Sign Language, which is the natural language of deaf children. It is also a wonderful opportunity for deaf children to become creative. Children have natural skills and abilities. Schools don't offer many opportunities for deaf children to use their creativity in a natural way. ... Many deaf children don't have the opportunity to develop social skills, poise and confidence in order to communicate through acting. We can teach them to develop their communication skills in a nice and creative way by involving them in theater, on stage."

Of the directors, actors, and actresses interviewed, many spoke passionately about the value of children's theatre for deaf children — particularly those who are Deaf, as they benefited from it while they were growing up.

Vickee Waltrip, an Academy staff member in her third year with LTD, commented about the necessity of imparting knowledge about theatre:

> "I think it is important for deaf children have that exposure. I had the opportunity to be immersed in the arts within the residential school. I received such a wealth of knowledge; the right thing to do is to share it with others. I've often worked with children and I see where it (theatre) promotes better self-worth, knowledge, creativity, comfort in relating to others, and teamwork. This is why art programs are so important. ... Art itself reflects life. Most hearing children are taught that concept. Deaf children seldom have this opportunity. Deaf children don't understand this concept. So it is important for us to provide initiation in all arts, not just theater, but in all arts. My conviction is that we need community artists to come to schools, expose deaf children to the arts and become their role models. Their influence will remain with the children for a long time."

Ian Sanborn, an Academy staff member in his fifth year, continued Mow's idea, pointing out that exposure broadens the range of career choices later in life:

> "I have noticed that schools focus on more academic topics. But children have creative thoughts. Schools need to provide more programs that would focus on using creative arts. They need to embrace the creative side of children. Children need exposure to arts to become even more creative. Later in life, they may choose not to pursue arts professionally, but we need to provide them the exposure, so that they can make an informed choice. ... Whether children get on stage, in front of an audience, or involved in any way with theatre, it is a valuable experience. The students who are not acting on stage work behind the stage on the technical aspects of theater, and their work is equally important."

Vic Crosta, an Academy staff member in her fourth year and a former cast member with the South Florida Theatre of the Deaf, commented:

> "Not all deaf schools have drama programs. Depends on the staff, whether the kids have access to theatre. At some schools, we have the opportunity to encourage deaf children to join us on stage. They need to feel comfortable on the stage."

INTERNATIONAL CENTER ON DEAFNESS AND THE ARTS

ICODA's founder, Dr. Patricia Scherer, made an important observation about the comparison between the Little Theatre of the Deaf and ICODA. While LTD uses adult actors to play children's theatre, ICODA uses children to play children's theatre. Dr. Scherer said:

> "NTD is adults doing children's theatre ... That is not us. Ours is children doing children's theatre. ... We have a deaf theatre and we add some hearing children to it, so that the focus is always on the deaf child. ... In most of our plays, the deaf and hard-of-hearing play the roles of the actors — the signing actors. The hearing children are the voices. But we put them on the stage with the deaf kids. ... Our goal is that most of the lead roles are played by deaf children."

Dr. Scherer was formerly the head of the Northwestern University Clinic for the Deaf. In 1973, when the university announced its decision to phase out the clinic, Dr. Scherer gave up her position as a tenured professor to create an alternative, the Center on Deafness. She had started with a $1,000 donation and a working relationship with the parents of many deaf children from the center of Chicago to the Wisconsin border. "Scherer's first priority was to start a theatre company, the first in the nation for deaf children." (Liberty, 1991) This company was the Center on Deafness. In 1992 the name was changed to International Center on Deafness and the Arts, or ICODA.

ICODA is a place where deaf, hard-of-hearing, and hearing children are encouraged to imagine, create, and dream through shared artistic expression. The acronym ICODA also stands for (ICODA, 2007):

- *Inspire* creative thinking through Distance Learning
- *Cultivate* character through Museum workshops
- *Optimize* self-continence through Arts Festival competitions
- *Develop* self-discipline through CenterLight Theatre and Dance training
- *Accentuate* talent and quality as an individual through Children's Programs.

Currently housed in a forty-thousand square-foot building in Northbrook, Illinois, the International Center on Deafness and the Arts nurtures the talents of deaf and hard-of-hearing children through drama workshops and theatrical performances. ICODA has currently five departments: CenterLight Theatre, ICODA-Fest (the International Creative Arts Festival, ICODance) the Dance company, Children's Museum on Deafness, and Distance Learning. In 2003 the five ICODA staff employees were Dr. Scherer, Jonnalee Folerzynski (Deaf), the director of the children's theatre program; Carolyn Strejc (hearing), the choreography dance teacher of the dance program; Christine Strejc (hearing), a teacher with the traveling team and the dance team; and Patti Lahey (hearing), the artistic and managing director of the CenterLight Theatre.

List of Plays and Workshops
The CenterLight Theatre's plays have consisted of dramas (e.g. *Crimes of the Heart*), comedies (e.g. *The Odd Couple*), musicals (e.g. *Oliver!* and *Joseph and the Amazing Technicolor Dreamcoat"*), and children's shows (e.g. *Cinderella* and *Peter Pan*).

Figure 5. ICODA — *Alice in Wonderland*, 2004–2005 season.

Figure 6. ICODA — *Everybody Dance*, August 2007.

The Story-&-Sign, part of CenterLight Theatre, is the outreach theatre touring troupe. It is a group of professional actors and performers who perform, through voice and movement, and song/sign interpretation, thirty to forty-five minutes skits, stories, mime, improvisation, and poetry at schools and in community groups throughout the Midwest. The children who attend are helped to develop a sense of awareness about and acceptance of the Deaf World through these performances (Folerzynski, 2003).

Participants and Audiences
The CenterLight Theatre's performances are open to the general public. The

orientation of the plays varies from children's stories to more complex dramatic subjects. The drama and dance classes of the children's program are available to children ages five through twelve. The Story-&-Sign theatre group presentations are suitable for all ages. The ICODance outreach program involves children ages seven through nineteen. The professional company performs one concert each year in a variety of dance styles.

CenterLight's outreach program, Story-&-Sign, brings a unique sign-and-voice style to local and community groups. It interweaves Deaf Culture and the beauty of American Sign Language in this educational and entertaining experience. The program's group presentations are suitable for all ages. A professional troupe of performers who are Deaf, hard-of hearing, and hearing perform stories or poems with voice and sign. In addition, there is an educational component: the actors teach the audience how to sign common words and phrases.

The Children's Museum of Deafness was designed for children grades one through eight, but all ages are welcome.

Still another component of ICODA is the Creative Arts Festival. It is a yearly competition among students with hearing loss. The festival sends applications to hundred of Deaf Education programs around the world. In addition to those from the United States, competitors from Canada, Japan, Finland, Sweden, and Australia strive to be part of the festival. They compete in the areas of visual, literary, and performing arts. The winners of the competition are invited to attend the festival. The Arts Festival is funded through foundations, corporations, service organizations, and private individual contributions from the local community.

Kinds of Skills Taught

The children and adults of ICODA are "encouraged to imagine, create, and dream through shared artistic expression," which results in building self-confidence and awareness.

The annual plays of the CenterLight Theatre Children's program show teachers, parents, and the general public the children's skill improvement in the dramatic arts. This provides children with the opportunity to appreciate the results of their learning process, thus building their confidence and feelings of self-worth.

Education on deafness and Deaf Culture are the main topics of the Story-&-Sign theatre plays. Performances include an introduction to American Sign Language, a question-and-answer portion, and audience participation related to topics on Deaf Culture themes.

The ICODance studio is open to children and adults and is taught in both American Sign Language and spoken English. The members are chosen by audition. The dance studio has year-round classes of ballet, jazz, modern dance, tap, and hip-hop (street dance styles that are part of the hip-hop culture). ICODance produces one dance concert each year.

The two-hour tour of the Children's Museum on Deafness is presented in American Sign Language and spoken English. The tour consists of the museum, a project studio, where children learn scientific considerations about deafness, and a theatrical performance.

A narrator guides the audience through several displays and invites the audience to interact. The audience learns about the scientific perspective on deafness through explanations about sound, about the mechanics of the hearing process, and about the causes of deafness, and engages in hands-on activities like assembling parts of the auditory system into a model and role-playing. The tour continues with a history of American Sign Language, a technology timeline with a "Then and Now" display, and the experience of a Safe House — a model home equipped with visitor-activated assistive devices — which gives the audience the feeling of what it means to be deaf.

Next, the audience learns about Deaf Culture. For instance, they are told about contributions of remarkable Deaf people like I. King Jordan and Marlee Matlin. The audience learns about Deaf View Image Art (De'VIA). De'VIA uses formal art elements with the intention of expressing innate cultural or physical Deaf experiences. These experiences may include Deaf metaphors, Deaf perspectives, and Deaf insights in relation to the environment (both the natural world and the Deaf cultural environment) and to spiritual and everyday life. There are opportunities for the visitors to write questions on the museum's permanent structure, called The Communication Wall. The purpose of this wall is to allow "an ongoing dialogue between the hearing and Deaf communities." In the project studio of the museum, the audience has the chance to create a take-home memento of the museum to show parents or to share in the classroom.

CenterLight Theatre's outreach troupe, Story-&-Sign, performs the original play *Anything is Possible,* written by Patti Lahey. The play is followed by thirty minutes of a question-and-answer session about the play. It is the story of a child having difficulties with the challenges of being deaf. An audiologist, Dr. Earl Lobe and his faithful assistant, Spotakiss, a deaf Dalmatian, shows the boy what can be accomplished if he believes in himself.

The ICODA Fest encompasses a weekend of art display, talent competitions, social events, and workshops led by professional artists and performers who are Deaf and hard-of-hearing. The participants are chosen by preliminary contest. The winners this contest have a chance to spend a weekend participating in the unique experiences provided by these professional artists at the Festival.

The festival also includes display, a talent competition, and workshops by professional Deaf artists and performers. Many professionals attend annually and mingle with the children, thus providing them with the unique opportunity to meet Deaf positive role models. Some of these professionals are Chuck Baird, an artist and former NTD actor; Bernard Bragg, a former NTD actor; Paul Johnson, Jr., a former NTD actor and artist; renowned actress Marlee Matlin; and Liz Tannebaum-Greco, a former member of the Children's Traveling Hands Troupe. The children can ask questions and learn from these Deaf role models. The festival is believed to be an influential way in which ICODA impacts deaf children by exposing them to Deaf Culture and ASL. In addition, the festival has provided the incentive for many talented children to pursue professional careers in the arts.

In 1990 the President's Council was created to advise ICODA so that the festival would maintain the Deaf perspective. In particular, the Council was to ensure that the festival would provide role models for the children. Members of the Council are successful artists and professionals who are Deaf and hard-of-hearing. These individuals serve in an advisory capacity for future performances.

Conversations with Actors and Participants
Here are excerpts from the interviews with some of the ICODA's staff. Dr. Scherer commented:

> "In the deaf community, unemployment is very, very high. I have kept track of our graduates throughout the years. There was almost no unemployment. Most of them are working and have very good jobs, some of the top jobs for deaf people. So we are very proud of them. And I think it's because of some of the skills that they have learned though theatre."

Sandra Harvey, director of the Creative Arts Festival and parent of a deaf child, commented:

> "One of the best things about being involved in the creative arts festival is watching the students grow and mature through the years. The educators have told us that the students grow in self-confidence and become leaders in their schools. Some of the contestants started entering the festival at six or seven years of age and continued through high school! Our past Traveling Hands Troupe contacts me each year asking if they could perform at the festival to show the younger students what they can achieve! What a wonderful tribute!"

Folerzynski commented:

> "In my childhood, hearing theatre was inaccessible to me, because I am deaf. My professional goal has been to become a drama teacher. I wanted to

teach deaf children that they are not alone and that they don't need to hide because they are deaf. Each one of them is special. So I bring them here for them to shine like stars. Their parents are astonished and proud when they see them perform. And this is not for deaf children only. Hearing children also join. Deaf and hearing children act together, form friendships, and shine together. Every child matters. Either deaf or hearing, each child has a unique heart and special skills. When we bring them together, they shine like stars. When children are motivated and perseverant, they can succeed."

IMAGINATION STAGE

Imagination Stage, located in Bethesda, Maryland, is one of the nation's most exciting and innovative Deaf children's theatre centers. Its mission is to make the theatre arts a vital part of every child's life, "to nurture the creative spirit in all children and to cultivate skills that serve them throughout their lives." Imagination Stage is the largest and most respected multi-disciplinary theatre-arts organization for young people in Maryland. It has grown from a handful of children in a single classroom to a full-spectrum arts organization. Its classes, student ensembles, summer programs, and programs of outreach to schools complement a year-round season of professional children's theatre. Bonnie Fogel, its founder and executive director, commented, "The group's mission is to encourage self-expression in a non-competitive, multicultural environment." (Toscano, 2003)

Imagination Stage grew out of Bethesda Academy of Performing Arts, founded as a non-profit organization in September 1979. It was established in response to the need to provide arts education for young people ages five and up. Fogel felt that her children were not exposed to the arts as much as she had been, growing up. "In England," she said, "the arts are a very important part of the school days ... There was clearly an interest, especially in programs like Deaf Access and workshops for youngsters with developmental and cognitive differences." (Imagination Stage, 2003) Fogel believes that the program has a wide appeal because children need arts in their lives.

The company was renamed Imagination Stage in 2001 in anticipation of its move to the Imagination Stage outside Washington, DC, in the downtown area of Bethesda, Maryland, in the spring of 2003. The theatre opened in April 2003. It provides children and youth who are deaf and hard-of-hearing and those who have deaf parents with an ongoing opportunity to use performing as one of the senses.

In September 1990, the Deaf Access Program was established. Its purpose was to improve deaf students' academic, artistic, and social skills, to raise their self-esteem and self-knowledge, and to open the culture of the Deaf to people in the hearing world through theatre performances. The program offers both education and entertainment to the public. During the first five years of this program there was a Deaf Access Advisory committee comprised of deaf and hearing parents, artists, and educators. They provided community connections, resources for marketing and publicizing programming, access to deaf educators in the region, input about the kinds of program offerings desired by the Deaf Community, and technical advice on how to implement the program sensitively, inclusively, and appropriately. (Bailey & Agogliati, 2002)

The Deaf Access Program is run jointly by Lisa Agogliati, its founder, a hearing theatre professional who has an extensive background in dance performance and choreography, and Donna Salamoff, its co-founder, assistant director, and a Gallaudet University graduate. She also works as a Deaf visual dramaturg and sign master. The visual dramaturg looks at the script from the point of view of the deaf audience members to anticipate potentially confusing moments (that hearing people would not even perceive as confusing) and to identify places where audience participation or some aspect of Deaf Culture might be inserted. Salamoff also teaches the young people how to blend sign, mime, facial expression, and gesture to create theatrical sign language.

The initial name Special Needs Program was later changed to Arts Access to take the focus away from "disability," a concept with a generally negative connotation. The founder wanted to emphasize the real goal: making arts accessible to everyone. Arts Access answered to the philosophy of inclusion. Ever since, it has served all young people, regardless of physical or cognitive ability.

But the Deaf Theatre program wanted its own identity apart from the Arts program for disabled children. In due time, Arts Access split into two programs: the Deaf Access Program, serving young people who are deaf, hard of hearing, and KODA, and the AccessAbility Program, serving young people who have physical or cognitive disabilities. (Bailey & Agogliati, 2002)

The Deaf Access program hires contract employees for individual play productions. Fred Beam, who is Black-Deaf, works as a contract choreographer for the Deaf Access program. He is the founder and executive director of Invisible Hands, Inc., an organization promoting Deaf Culture awareness, which contains the international all-deaf dance troupe The Wild Zappers. Susan Robbins works as a sign master for the Deaf Access program. She is also a teacher of the deaf with the Montgomery County Public Schools.

The Deaf Access program provides specific activities for different age groups. These components are the Senior Deaf Access Company, the Junior Deaf Access Company, the Fantastic Folktales, the Drama & Movement, and Just Imagine: Sign and Play Together. The Senior Deaf Access Company is geared towards grades nine through twelve, offering high-school students the chance to be involved in major season productions at Imagination Stage. The intended scope is for students to develop a professional level of expressiveness in theatre skills. The Junior Deaf Access Company offers deaf and hearing students ages eleven through fifteen the opportunity to work together in theatre. Its intended scope is for students to practice the theatrical techniques needed for combining sign language and English on stage. (Agogliati, 2003)

There are also programs for ages six and younger. Fantastic Folktales gathers children ages five and six in a class designed for deaf and KODA students to explore folktales from around the world in sign language and English. This class is supposed to build students' interpersonal skills and self-esteem. Drama & Movement leads children ages three and four to explore stories and characters from a wide of variety of children's literature and to experience dramatic play and movement. Just Imagine: Sign and Play Together is offering toddlers from twenty-four to thirty-six months old storytelling, finger-play, art, and movement to expose them to the beauty of sign language. (Imagination Stage, 2007)

List of Plays and Workshops

The Deaf Access staff consists of both Deaf and hearing artists. These individuals grew cohesive first by learning from and about each other — language, culture, mode of communication — then by learning to value and respect each other's abilities and talents. Agogliati realized that cultural competency was achieved through theatre. Thinking beyond the scope of bridging the Deaf and hearing communities in the United States, she realized that, through theatre, these communities could also learn to appreciate Deaf and hearing cultures from around the world. (Bailey & Agogliati, 2002)

The Deaf Access program seeks advice from cultural experts in order to offer many productions oriented toward multiculturalism, thus providing both cross-cultural and multicultural education. After Agogliati initiated the first multicultural production *Coyote and the Circle of Tales*, which explored the diversity of Native American folklore, other productions explored cultural traditions from four different geographical regions in the United States: *Stories from Tlinget* (from the Pacific Northwest), *Apache* (from the Southwest), *Iroquois* (from the Northwestern Woodlands), and *Cherokee* (from the Eastern and Southern regions). These productions also represented the Four Directions of the Medicine Wheel.

Figure 7. Imagination Stage — *Pinocchio Comedia*, 2002°2003 season.

Figure 8. *Dreams to Sign* by Sally D. Bailey and Lisa Agogliati

Participants and Audiences

The Deaf Access company chooses a new play each year. High-school teenagers from across the country audition in September and make a nine-month commitment to researching, rehearsing, and performing in Bethesda during the winter and at other venues in the spring. Half the performers are Deaf or hard-of-hearing, and the others are hearing teens, often children of Deaf parents (CODA). They attend advanced classes and workshops related to the production. The plays are also toured to local arts festival and national conferences and symposia during the spring and early summer. They have, for example, been presented at the National and Worldwide Deaf Festival under the auspices of the National Theatre of the Deaf in Connecticut, bringing the group's artistry and message of cross-cultural collaboration to a wide range of children and adults.

The Junior Deaf Access Company focuses on children ages eleven through fifteen, both deaf and hearing. Its purpose is to give children the opportunity to work together in theatre. Students also develop visual skills: signs, facial expressions, and mime. The cast performs for an invited audience of family and friends at the end of the rehearsal period. The students are enrolled through audition.

Creative Arts Residencies, yet another Deaf Access component, spans eight to ten weeks. These yearly residencies are conducted for deaf and hard-of-hearing students, ages three through eighteen, who attend Montgomery County Public Schools. The emphasis is on developing students' expressive communication skills by using a combination of sign language, mime, and acting techniques, and on working with classroom teachers to incorporate drama into the curriculum as a learning tool.

Weekend drama classes are also offered to deaf, hard-of-hearing, and CODA students, ages three through twelve, at the Bethesda Academy. These sessions focus on teaching expressive communication, teamwork, and learning how to tell stories through words, body movement, facial expression, and action. A Deaf drama teacher instructs the expressive-arts classes, assisted by members of the Deaf Access Company.

The Deaf Access program also has an adult educational touring company that uses an interactive performance style. The productions explore the beauty and richness of sign language and of Deaf culture while breaking down barriers between the Deaf and hearing worlds. Participation in the Deaf Access program is determined by audition.

Kinds of Skills Taught

Imagination Stage provides theatre-arts classes at elementary schools in the Washington, DC area. These classes are aligned to the philosophy and curriculum of the programs offered on site at Imagination Stage. Sally Bailey, the Arts Access director, and Agogliati used the grant from the United States Department of Education to develop *Dreams to Sign* as a unique educational theatre program for deaf and hearing teens through the Deaf Access program. Its performances blend voice and sign language, bridging the cross-cultural divide between Deaf and hearing communities. The performances cover multi-cultural tales from around the world. The accompanying book and videotape Dreams to Sign describes the Deaf Access process and production guidelines in a well-structured manner. It is illustrated with production photos, scripts, scenario excerpts, and video clips. The book is a valuable resource for hearing and Deaf educators and practitioners working with deaf children, as well as for children's theatre professionals. (Imagination Stage, 2007)

For the company's performances, Agogliati and Salamoff work together to select the script. Then literary and visual dramaturgs help review and analyze the script. Salamoff created these positions in 1999. The literary dramaturgs understand the structure of the script and its function, and then adapt the script by strengthening certain parts while eliminating others. They build clear characters and actions and bring the artistic touch of an appropriate pacing and dramatic progression.

The visual dramaturgs analyze the script from the perspective of the deaf audience. They foresee potentially confusing moments and initiate changes to make the deaf audience feel involved in the performance by inserting aspects of Deaf Culture. For example, a key component might be the use of foreign sign language from the featured foreign culture. *The Magic Babushka and Other Russian Tales* used gigantic Russian dolls as a key visual element to introduce each character at the beginning of the play. The featured artist was a Russian-born guest Deaf actor, Iosif Schneiderman.

The goal of Imagination Stage is to bring together the Deaf and hearing worlds in a nurturing environment where they can learn about each other and work with each other. The six-month long rehearsal and performance period allows students to conduct research for the production, to attend special workshops taught by Deaf and hearing guest artists, and to enjoy socializing together. Each year the company studies a different culture. In previous years they have focused on China, Japan, Russia, Mexico, Spain, India, and other countries. The company works with both Deaf and hearing guest artists from the selected country, learning about their culture, storytelling traditions, visual arts (which are incorporated into the productions), and about the foreign sign language from that country.

Conversations with Actors and Participants

During an interview, Salamoff, the visual dramaturg and sign master, commented:

> "We make all of our services accessible, whether deaf, hard of hearing, KODA, or hearing, anyone who wants to participate with the group. We want to provide 100% accessibility to everyone, whether parents of deaf children or people who work here. I think our goal is to provide the deaf students the opportunity to enjoy theatre and to think for themselves, to be expressive, and to be more confident as deaf people. Our program is accessible to many deaf children who are so frustrated by having to communicate through an interpreter. But our staffs are teachers and all of us sign. It is very valuable and very important to be able to interact in a direct way."

ILLUMINATIONS ARTS

Illuminations Arts started as a small company with big goals, to provide theatre accessibility to deaf and hard-of-hearing people in the Houston area. Beginning in 1990, it has progressively become known in the greater Houston area and has continued to develop its program for deaf children in school districts in and around Houston. It has brought a unifying force to Houston's diverse Deaf, hard-of-hearing, and hearing communities.

In the 1980s, Clarence Russell, a Deaf actor and director, originally from Washington, DC, moved to Austin, Texas, where he helped found the Spectrum Deaf Theatre with Deaf artists. It folded after a few years. He then moved to Houston, where he founded the Houston Theatre of the Deaf (Chimæras). He had gathered a group of talented amateur actors and interpreters involved in the Deaf Community, and they worked in cooperation with local theatres. (Morris, 1983)

Suzie Phillips, administrator of the Alley Theatre in Houston, went to a theatre stage company called StageHands in Atlanta, Georgia. She witnessed the recent innovation in signing and theatre arts — the shadow interpreting — at its source.

The art of shadowing was introduced in Houston in the summer of 1982. The Alley Theatre, with the underwriting of the Pennzoil Corporation, produced Houston's first shadowed performance, *The Unexpected Guest*. Most of the original pioneering professionals are still today involved with Illuminations. Illuminations was established formally in 1984. The original ten board members are Carol Anderson-Bradley, Deaf Education teacher; Debbie Gunter, interpreter; Eric Kantor, tour director of Texas Opera Theatre; Brian and Jackie Kilpatrick, Deaf professional actors from Fairmount Theatre of the Deaf; Alice Morewitz, deaf consumer; Suzie Philips and Mike Serkess, grant writers; Gary Scullin, Stages Repertory Theatre actor; and Charles Trevino, interpreter. Together they formed Illuminations ... Theatre with the Deaf. As related by its director, Illuminations' mission is "to bridge the gap between the Deaf, hard-of-hearing and hearing communities through artistic activities." (Illuminations Arts, 2006)

The Illuminations Theatre has provided the Deaf Community with productions in ASL through theatrical interpreting and shadowed performances, in cooperation and collaboration with Houston area theatres as such as the Alley Theatre, the Express Theatre, the University of Houston Children's Theatre Festival, and A.D. Players. Illuminations Theatre's goal is to make arts accessible to all hearing, deaf, and hard-of-hearing people.

Illuminations has worked diligently on behalf of the Deaf Community, advocating accessibility to a variety of Cultural activities and opportunities for deaf and hard-of-hearing children and adults. The group has brought a unifying force to Houston's diverse Deaf Community. As Jill Beebout remembers, "before Illuminations, there was not an organization in town that appealed to their [Deaf people's] difference. It brought them together." (Beebout, 2003) All Illuminations workers were volunteers who wanted to make something happen for the Deaf Community and gave their time and energy, although they had their own full-time jobs. Illuminations worked with hearing theatres in the Houston area, theatres that need small grants to provide shadow-interpreted productions, including the Texas Opera Theatre, Shakespeare's Globe Outreach at the University of Houston, Children Theatre's Festival at the University of Houston, and A.D. Players.

Jackie and Brian Kilpatrick are the only Deaf professional actors, owing to many years of theatrical training with the summer school of the National Theatre of the Deaf and the Gallaudet University Theatre, Gallaudet Dance Company under the auspices of Dr. Wisher, and to the experience gained with the theatre they have founded, the Fairmount Theatre of the Deaf in Cleveland, Ohio.

Susan Jackson, who is Deaf, is the artistic director. Prior to joining the Illuminations team, Jackson worked for the National Theatre of the Deaf and the Fairmount Theatre of the Deaf (now the Cleveland Sign Stage Theatre). She was a National and Worldwide Deaf Theatre conference administrator at the National Theatre of the Deaf in Chester, Connecticut for two and a half years. She has spent thirty-five years in the performing arts: on stage, in television and film, touring internationally with the National Theatre of the Deaf, and as a freelance artist.

Jill Beebout, who is hearing, was the production coordinator between 1999 and 2003. Beebout had fifteen years of professional experience in theatre and opera, working in production and management positions with regional theatres around the country, including the Dallas Shakespeare Festival, the Dallas Theatre Center and the Alley Theatre. She holds an Associate of Arts and Sciences degree in Interpreting and Transliterating Technology. Beebout is also a Texas state-certified interpreter for the deaf and a member of the Houston Storyteller Guild, a corporation committed to the educational aspects of storytelling. Illuminations' most sought-after program to date is ASL Children's Story Hour, brought in front of deaf and hearing children a Deaf performer and a hearing performer simultaneously storytelling in ASL and telling the story in English.

Throughout this and other programs, the Deaf, hard-of-hearing, and hearing communities are provided with the opportunity to see and associate with successful Deaf and hearing role models in the arts. Beginning with the *Mother/Daughter Storytelling Celebration*, Illuminations encouraged teams of deaf and hearing mothers and daughter to share stories during the performance. When confronted by fathers who wanted to participate, Illuminations created the *Family Fun* event, which showcases stories by any family group that includes at least one deaf and one hearing member. Illuminations Arts is not specifically a children's theatre, although much of its programming is addressed to all ages.

In 2002, Illuminations registered and started to operate under the name Illuminations Arts to reflect the greater scope of the theatre's growing interests in the Deaf-arts community. (Illuminations Arts, 2004)

List of Plays and Workshops
The first performance of Illuminations Theatre with the Deaf was *The Unexpected Guest*, shadow-interpreted and presented at the Alley Theatre.

Other shadowed productions followed: *The Fantasticks* and *Madame Butterfly* with the Texas Opera Theatre; *La Traviata*, produced by the Texas

Opera Theatre; *The Taming of the Shrew* and *A Midsummer Night's Dream* with the University of Houston's Shakespeare Globe Theatre/Outreach.

Quilters, produced in 1987 by the Heinen Theatre in collaboration with Houston International Quilt Festival, was an all sign language performance with off-stage voicing actors. Brian Kilpatrick was the first director. Carole McCann, executive director of Humphreys School of Musical Theatre, choreographed the dance with the help of Jackie Kilpatrick and Kathy Weldon.

Figure 9. Illuminations Arts — shadow interpretation of *The Myrtle* with A.D. Players, 1987-1988 season.

Figure 10. Illuminations Arts — shadow interpretation of *A Midsummer Night's Dream* with the University of Houston's Shakespeare Globe Theatre, 1984-1985 season.

In 1996 the Express Theatre's education department had a dynamic season of events, workshops, and residencies. Weldon is a Deaf counselor for gifted children and for deaf and hard-of-hearing children and former president of Illuminations coordinated with the Express Theatre. She worked to facilitate a theatre-arts residency at T.H. Rogers Elementary School for deaf and hard-of-hearing students in the seventh and eighth grades. Guest artist in residence, Brian Kilpatrick, taught the children drama. This ground-breaking project presented deaf children with the opportunity to be involved in the creative process, as well as to work with an artist who shared their unique physical abilities.

In 1997 Illuminations performed *The Yellow Boat* on two nights, a second sign language production in conjunction with Express Theatre and DiverseWorks, courtesy of the Seattle Children's Theatre. About one hundred deaf, hard-of-hearing, and hearing patrons attended the two-nights run. The plot was touching and dealt with the experiences of an eight-year-old boy diagnosed with Human Immunodeficiency Virus (HIV)/Acquired Immunodeficiency Syndrome (AIDS) and his parents' support during his final days. (Phan, 1997)

In 1999 the Houston Endowment for the Arts awarded Illuminations Arts a three-year grant for OPTICA's Little Hands Theatre Activity. (Houston Endowment, Inc., 2006) This was a theatre camp where children were taught theatrical expression through sign, mime, dance, and song. The first summer activity was the 1999 ASL Kid's Camp, followed by the 2000 Kid's ASL Theatre Day Camp, and the 2001 Hands Can, Too. The thirty students were divided in the three sections according to their grade level: first through third grade, fourth through sixth grade, and seventh through eighth grade.

Figure 11. Illuminations Arts — *Little Hands Theatre Activity*, 2000-2001 season.

Figure 12. Illuminations Arts — *Mothers + Daughters*, 2000-2001 season.

The two-week activities consisted of four different classes: an exercise class to help the body and mind coordinate together; a storytelling class to help children express themselves using ASL, body movements and facial expressions; an acting class to help the kids express their creativity using general mime, finger mime, and rhythm; and a class teaching play development, scenery construction, and makeup. For example, guest artist Brian Kilpatrick, taught the students how to apply and arrange makeup to make an actor in his fifties to look like an eighty-year-old man. The guest Deaf artists were Jackie Kilpatrick, Mindy Moore (the founder and performer of Just Mindy Company), and Kathy Weldon. Deaf and hearing volunteers with good American Sign Language skills teamed with the guest artists. The children attending the camp developed their own play to be performed for their families and friends at the Metropolitan Multi-Service Center festival night.

After the three-year funding ended, Illuminations Arts has not been awarded any other funding due to a decrease in the Deaf Community's support and the existence of the Deaf education program in Harris County. Also, the deaf children's parents found the required transportation to be inconvenient. Illuminations was not equipped with its own transportation means. The parents erroneously thought that the use of sign without voice would hamper the children's speech and language acquisition. Research does not support this myth. In fact, research shows that sign language supports speech rather than hindering it. (Wilbur, 2000)

The Illuminations Arts group has provided interpreters for a variety of cultural events and has coordinated social events for deaf and hearing. They have worked with area schools to bring literacy and literature to deaf children and hosted *Ear News*, a monthly television show that provides a forum for Deaf and hard-of-hearing issues through Houston MediaSource (HMS). Illuminations Arts has an educational mission to serve the public's communication needs by programming educational, political and community shows on cable TV.

During the 2000–2001 season Illuminations Arts collaborated with the Interpreter Training Program and Show of Hands, the sign language club at North Harris College, to present the world-renowned Invisible Hands Wild Zappers, and the African American and Hispanic Deaf dancing troupe from Washington, DC. Along with the Aurora Picture Show, Illuminations presented the first Deaf Film Festival in the country with Spotlight: Deaf Films, and premiered *Interpretations: A Language of Loss* by Deaf playwright Raymond Luczak in honor of World AIDS Day. The group has achieved statewide appeal performing at Southwest Texas State University and at the Texas Storytelling Festival in March 2004 (Illuminations Arts, 2003).

Participants and Audiences

Illuminations Arts provides accessible theatre to the deaf and hard-of-hearing community in Houston. Illuminations Arts has worked with the University of Houston in the Children's Theatre Festival to provide accessibility to public performances.

In October 1999, Illuminations' OPTICA began presenting "Classic $1 Movie Night" once every month on a Friday evening. This series ran until May 2000. These events were open to the general public, deaf people, interpreters, and children, both hearing and deaf. Featured classic movies included *Deaf President Now!* (the history of self-led Deaf protest directed toward instituting the first Deaf President of Gallaudet University), *Mime Time II* (a short film about the art of pantomime, hosted by Robert Panara and Bernard Bragg), and *Sign Mime: The Art of Visual Imagery*.

Illuminations Arts's most lauded effort to date has been the addition of Hand Held Tales, the storytelling troupe that has traveled across the state of Texas and performed stories in American Sign Language and spoken English for audiences young and old. Beebout brought together several teams of one Deaf and one hearing storyteller to work together to reach hearing and deaf audiences through performances that present stories on a variety of children's classic themes.

Figure 13. Illuminations Arts — *ASL Children's Story Hour*, 1998–1999 season

Figure 14. DYDP — 15th Deaf Kids Drama Festival, 2002–2003 season.

In April 2005, Illuminations Arts collaborated with A.D. Players for the shadow-interpreted and captioned production of *The Wind in the Willows* at the Miller Outdoor Theatre. The morning performance was free and open to the public. Over 750 deaf and hard-of-hearing children from the Greater Houston Area school districts and more than 600 other spectators gathered at the outdoor theatre to witness this event. (Illuminations Arts, 2005)

Kinds of Skills Taught

Operating since 1993, Hand Held Tales is a pilot project that offers storytelling in the Fort Bend Independent School District to supplement the existing classroom curriculum. Nearly any subject that is taught in school can be enhanced through story, both signed and spoken. In addition to the storytelling performance, the teacher is provided with printed copies of the stories as supplemental documentation for activities that will reinforce the information and vocabulary introduced through the storytelling performance. A sampling of these programs include *Stories to Be Thankful For*, stories about Native Americans and colonists at the time of first Thanksgiving; *Festival of Light*, stories about the winter festivals of various cultures); African-American Tales, biographical stories about famous African Americans and African folklore; and *Texas Wildflower Legends*, legends based on wildflowers found in Texas.

In 2005 the Humphreys School Musical Theatre, a wing of Theatre Under The Stars (TUTS) in Houston, in collaboration with Illuminations Arts, provided for the first time a one-day theatre workshop. This workshop interweaved American Sign Language and spoken word with choreography and staging to present *The King and I*, a thirty-minutes song and sign performance, to friends and families. The Humphreys School of Musical Theatre worked to find young performing-arts talents in the Greater Houston Area and offered them training opportunities to develop their skills. The one-day acting workshop was open to deaf, hard-of-hearing, and hearing children separately for two age groups: ages seven through twelve and ages thirteen through eighteen. The workshop participation was limited to 15 students per age group. This workshop did not require previous training in signing, dancing, acting, or American Sign Language. Instructors from the Humphreys School along with Susan Jackson and Jackie Kilpatrick, interpreters Debbie Teague and David Haynes, and other volunteers from Illuminations worked with the thirty-six hearing and four deaf students to teach songs and signs and to teach students to choreograph numbers and translate and memorize dialogues in only five and a half hours.

Conversations with Actors and Participants
In an interview, Weldon, after attending *The Yellow Boat* show, said:

> "We were pleased to introduce a number of first-time actors and actresses. My hat is off all the people involved. Countless hours of rehearsal time paid off in this history-making event. For the first time, a theatre allowed Illuminations ... to "take over." The voice cast did a remarkable job as they gave vocal expressions to the beautiful signs on stage. Hopefully, more sign language performances will be undertaken, and the Deaf actors and actresses can help their hearing cohorts to give American Sign Language its proper place in the world of drama. If you never have experienced the ambiance and spirit of a sign language performance, be sure not to miss the next one! Theatre will take on a new meaning. "

Jackson, the artistic director, emphasized the need for arts and drama in education:

> "My opinion of the importance of theatre for Deaf Students is "4 (four) R" meaning Reading, Writing, Arithmetic and Arts. I strongly believe that deaf children should be exposed more to the creativity specific to different arts, in the same way that hearing children are exposed to visual arts, music, and performing arts. ... I notice that some residential schools for the deaf have drama classes as part of the Deaf Studies curriculum, while the mainstream schools do not. I remember when I was growing up, in my residential school, the Deaf teacher, after the school program was over for the day, would spend some more time with us after school, signing stories to us, arranging drama skits, and even setting up performances open to deaf children and adults. We even practiced on weekends. But today, the teachers are not willing to give of their own free time; when the school day is over, their work is done."

Moore, Deaf actress, commented along the same lines:

> "I feel that Deaf children will build their own self-esteem and self-identity into a strong positive model. I would like to see more theatrical classes offered from preschool years to high-school years, but unfortunately, the school curriculum is very strictly structured as far as the planning of the school year is concerned."

In June 2003, at the Children's Museum of Houston, after attending the *Mother/Daughter Storytelling Celebration*, a deaf girl's parent (who desired to remain anonymous) commented:

> "I would like to thank you for inviting us to participate with the performance. I think it is such a good idea to boost the kids' self-esteem and confidence."

A Deaf Education teacher said:

> "The entire morning my students would come to me about yet another deaf student they had met from another school. They had so much fun! Thank you for the experience you provided for our students. It was amazing!"

After *The Princess and The Pea* performance in April 2004, Ms. E. Whitley, a teacher in the Pasadena Independent School District, noted:

> "It was absolutely wonderful for my kids to see a whole audience of people using sign. Too often the younger kids think they will become hearing because they never have the opportunity to see deaf and hard-of-hearing people."

SEATTLE CHILDREN'S THEATRE

The Seattle Children's Theatre, through its Deaf Youth Drama Program has opened new worlds of theatrical expression for deaf and hard-of-hearing youth in the Puget Sound region in Washington State.

Founded in 1975, the Seattle Children's Theatre is the second largest resident theatre for children and their families in Seattle, Washington. It is based on culturally and thematically diverse themes and crafted to capture the attention of children and adults alike. The Seattle Children's Theatre is infused with the belief that theatre is a necessary component in the education of young people, promoting literacy, creativity, self-esteem, and humanitarian values.

In addition to educational programming through a drama school, the Seattle Children's Theatre offers theatre classes. Young people expand their imagination, build self-confidence, and develop their creative abilities. The Seattle Children's Theatre also maintains a touring Education Outreach program that brings theatre directly to students and young people in cities and towns throughout Washington State: Seattle, Spokane, Vancouver, Tacoma, and Everett (Seattle Children's Theatre, 2003).

Linda Hartzell, a hearing actress, has been the artistic director of the Seattle Children's Theatre and head of its education program since 1984.

The Seattle Children's Theatre was surviving on minimal budget when Hartzell took over. Under her leadership the audiences grew, and memberships and profits increased. Hartzell used the increasing budget to raise actors' pay and to add popular and educational programming such as Deaf Youth Drama classes. In addition, two theatre buildings were added to the Seattle's Children Theatre complex: the Charlotte Martin Theatre, completed in 1993, and the new technical facility, Allen Pavilion, in 2000.

The Seattle Children's Theatre had provided ASL-interpreted performances before the establishment of the Deaf Youth Drama Program. In 1992 Billy and Howie Seago, two Deaf brothers who are actors and ASL storytellers, approached Hartzell about establishing a Deaf Youth program. The Seago brothers are the founders and the first program managers of the Deaf Youth Drama Program (DYDP) of the Seattle Children's Theatre, which began in 1993. Before DYDP, the Seagos had also founded the Deaf Moose Theatre in Seattle. The Deaf Moose Theatre was put on hold because the DYDP children group was growing and more time and energy needed to be invested in DYDP.

Billy Seago, the current DYDP director, has acted in professional productions with the National Theatre of the Deaf. He was the featured artist in *Stories in the Attic*, the series produced by Visual Tales Sign-A-Vision Institute. *Stories in the Attic* is a series of signed productions of stories for children and adults.

As the program director, Seago has been artist-in-residence in dozens of deaf and hard-of-hearing classrooms and has directed several Deaf Youth Summer Theatre productions. The artist-in-residence program is organized twice every year. Between eight and ten schools within the Puget Sound region and two schools in the rural area are selected for the Deaf Youth artist-in-residence program. The Deaf Youth Summer Theatre program offers classes and mounts a production. It takes place every summer, from June to August, at the Seattle Children's Theatre.

The Deaf Youth Drama Program has many benefits. It not only empowers young Deaf actors, but it reveals their talents to the hearing world through American Sign Language. DYDP also provides personal and artistic opportunities for deaf and hard-of-hearing youth through theatre-education and theatre-arts training with Deaf theatre professionals. Deaf and hard-of-hearing children in the Puget Sound region and throughout western Washington, who may have little or no experience beyond their hearing family and schools, attend DYDP to build their self-esteem and interpersonal skills with Deaf artists, volunteers, and peers from other schools.

The Deaf Youth Drama Program includes four different programs: the local artist-in-residence program for the Deaf Kids Drama Festival, the outreach artist-in-residence program, the Deaf Youth Summer Theatre, and workshops. Most participants in the Deaf Youth Drama Program are in grades kindergarten through twelve. DYDP also serves their hearing peers, their families, and the deaf and hard-of-hearing communities (Seattle Children's Theatre, 2007).

DYDP has two full-time staff employees. Jacob Fisher is a Deaf theatre major from Gallaudet University and works as artistic and literary assistant. In addition, he has assisted Billy Seago in his school outreach teaching. Lisa McIntosh (hearing) is the program coordinator. A graduate of the interpreter training program at Seattle Central Community College, she has worked as volunteer for DYDP and as a voice interpreter for the children's festival.

Each summer Nat Wilson, a Deaf theatre major from Gallaudet University, who performed with the National Theatre of the Deaf for a long time, was sign coach for the Deaf Youth Summer Theatre production. In addition, he has taught American Sign Language classes in Seattle Central Community College's Interpreter Training Program. (Wilson, 2003)

List of Plays and Workshops
The Deaf Youth Drama Program has produced many American Sign Language performances, among which are *Our Town*, *West Side Story*, *The Three Musketeers*, and *The Crucible*.

Figure 15. DYDP — *West Side Story*, 2003–2004 season.

Figure 16. PAH — *Bird of a Different Feather*, 1996–1997 season.

Participants and Audiences
Seattle has a large proportion of deaf and hard-of-hearing individuals in its population. Therefore it is a ripe area for Deaf theatre. Under the Seattle

Children's Theatre, the Deaf Youth Drama Program teaches drama to deaf and hard-of-hearing students from kindergarten through grade twelve.

The Deaf Kids Drama Festival, which began in 1993, is part of the Seattle Children's Theatre educational outreach department. Some of DYDP's Deaf artists, such as Howie Seago, Dawn Stoyanoff (Deaf dancer), and Nat Wilson went to several different schools (mostly to mainstreamed schools in the Puget Sound region, but also to residential schools for the deaf) to select the children for the festival. Each residency lasts twelve weeks with one-hour classes two or three times a week. At the end of each residency, deaf students perform short pieces at the Seattle Children's Theatre, where their families, peers, and people from the Deaf Community come to attend the show.

The Deaf Youth Summer Theatre offers a four-week training program each summer, customized for four different age groups. Participants come mostly from Washington, and especially the Seattle area. However, some out-of-state participants are willing to pay the travel and lodging expenses to benefit from training with DYDP. Participants learn the basic skills of performing on the stage: acting, improvisation, stage combat, movement, and dance. When the author attended their training in 2003, the older participants' group remained on campus for three more weeks to rehearse the American Sign Language production *West Side Story*. At that time, all the instructors were Deaf. The author had the opportunity to attend the rehearsals for three days before the show opened. The group rehearsed the stage blocking and the dialogue exchange, and hearing and Deaf actors worked together as a team. The rehearsal unfolded the same way as a regular hearing play rehearsal. The performance lasted three days, and every day the auditorium was packed with family members (mostly hearing), peers, Deaf families, and with people from the Deaf Community.

Actors, directors, and stagehands of the Deaf Youth Drama Program staff have traveled to national conferences and theatres. For example, Howie Seago presented the keynote address "Literacy in Life" at the Illinois Teachers for Hard-of-Hearing/Deaf Individuals (ITHI) Conference on March 2, 2007, in Bloomingdale, Illinois. DYDP has became a national model for arts-education programs, sharing information about DYDP strategies with various Deaf Communities. Each Deaf community learned how to implement a Deaf Arts curriculum into their local theatre-education programs. The transmission of Deaf Culture through theatre is the goal of this group.

Kinds of Skills Taught
Acting skills — basic acting, clowning, improvisation, and stage combat — are some of the skills taught at the Seattle Children's Theatre in the Deaf Youth Drama Program. The program offers literature-based workshops, i.e.

Winnie The Pooh, Sideways Stories from Wayside School, a children's adaptation of *Animal Farm*, and other children stories. They also have educator-training workshops and educational professional-development sessions, where classroom teachers are taught drama activities and explore styles of plays, themes, and subjects. The workshops cover a variety of themes such as acting, creative drama, and other specialty workshops. Teachers and educators learn techniques for increasing self-esteem and confidence in students.

The Deaf Youth Drama Program also offers training for teacher assistants for drama schools (Seattle Children's Theatre, 2003). Internships are available. University students act as teacher assistants in drama classes, to teach workshops, and to participate in the plays. Dance and signing songs that are translated to ASL are also skills taught to the actors.

Conversations with Actors and Participants
In an interview, Wilson, sign coach for the Deaf Youth Summer Theatre, commented:

> "I have been involved with the Deaf Youth Drama Program for nine years. I have seen many of the children grow up through the program, and I believe it is a definite plus for those involved. It assists them in becoming much more expressive individuals."

Billy Seago commented:

> "I feel that it is very important to have deaf people in charge of the Theatre for the Deaf. It is okay to have hearing people involved, and perhaps in some positions of authority in operating certain aspects, but I believe that it is ultimately important to have deaf people running the show, as it were. I feel this prevents people from looking and saying:

> 'Oh, it's Theatre for the Deaf, but hearing people are running it. I guess they have deaf people involved who are the Token Deaf. No! It must be theatre *for* the deaf, *of* the Deaf, run *by* the Deaf.'

Seago also clarifies the perspective of The Deaf Youth Program on the meaning of Deaf theatre:

> "Theatre for the Deaf must be delivered in a way that fits Deaf Culture. ... I also feel that Deaf Theatre does not always have to focus on Deaf themes. ... Many Deaf people do not know Shakespeare or other famous playwrights. There are so many beautiful plays that can be performed not just by hearing performers. ... These plays can be modified for Deaf audiences to understand the play and the performance on stage. That is my idea about Deaf Theatre. We do not always have to perform plays with Deaf themes."

About the kinds of participants in the Deaf Youth Drama Program, Billy Seago expressed his openness:

> "We don't want them [hearing children] to just simply view us pathologically as not being able to hear but to help mold positive social views about the Deaf. Often the deaf children will have hearing friends from school who want to become involved. They may not know how to sign very well at first, but they learn rather slowly as we go along. Even if at first they are unable to sign well, that is fine. This is an educational process for us all. We are not professional actors. It is an education both in acting and in Deaf Culture. ... We allow hearing children to be involved. However, the majority of children have to be deaf. ... The main thing is their attitude and desire to be involved with deaf people and not simply just sit back and pity them. We hope that these hearing children will be our ambassadors to the hearing world to help change their perspective on the Deaf."

Howie Seago commented on his attempt to reach out to educators of deaf children for the play *The Skin of Our Teeth*:

> "I would like drama teachers in mainstreamed schools and others in the community to realize, through this play, the various ways the Deaf can be accommodated for performing onstage. ... I hope this play will inspire Deaf students to perform, as well."

Several staff members have commented on the accessibility of the Seattle theatre group as it involves shadowing, captioning, and interpreting. McIntosh made these comments:

> "Brian: Earlier it was said that the SCT provides interpreters for performances. What about shadowing for any of the performances?
>
> Lisa: No, that hasn't been done, at least not in the short time I've been here. Previously Billy himself was on stage and provided some signing and shadowing. He did several different characters all by himself. How he did it I don't know. It was pretty amazing, I'm sure.
>
> Brian: What about captioning for the plays?
>
> Lisa: No, we have the captioning equipment and have used it from time to time during rehearsals to help the students learn their lines and learn words to the songs. To my knowledge it's never been used during any performances."

She also commented on deaf audiences' views of sign interpretation:

> "Brian: In, general, do you believe Deaf people would prefer a sign language performance to an interpreted performance?
>
> Lisa: Yes. I believe so. For one thing, it cuts down on looking back and forth from the stage to the interpreters. However, some deaf people that I have met seem not to care one way or the other. They seem to be able to enjoy the

play with the interpreter off to the side equally as well. However, I think it's obvious that most deaf people would prefer to watch theatre signed in their language and not have to depend on it being interpreted."

About shadowing and sign language interpretation of plays, Wilson said,

"About four years ago at a performance of *The Cider House Rules*. I was asked to be an advisor for the shadowed interpreting for this play. There were some difficult times in matching the interpreting with the acting, but I still feel that shadowing is better than having the interpretation off to the side. If the signing is being done on stage, it's much easier for the deaf person to keep up with what's going on in the performance.

I know of another time, at Central Park in New York, at a Shakespeare festival. They had special bleachers set up for the deaf audience members. An interpreter stood in front of the bleachers, and it was easier to see the stage behind the interpreter. I thought that was a very good design for interpretation of those plays."

PAH! DEAF YOUTH THEATRE

PAH! Deaf Youth Theatre is based at the Wheelock Family Theatre, established in 1981 by Andrea Genser, Anthony Hancock, Susan Kosoff, the artistic director, and Jane Staab. Wheelock Family Theatre was the recipient of the StageSource's 2002 Theatre Hero Award for its impact on Boston's cultural life. It is a non-profit professional organization performing in a 650-seat auditorium located on the campus of Wheelock College in Boston, Massachusetts. (StageSource, 2002)

The Wheelock Family Theatre produces at least three main stage productions each season. Productions include family-oriented modern drama, children's classics, musicals, and original works. The Wheelock Family Theatre offers selected performances interpreted in American Sign Language or open-captioned for the deaf, broadcasted through infrared assisted listening devices for the hard-of-hearing, and audio-described for the blind. Special projects have also provided interpreting for the deaf-blind (VSA Arts of Massachusetts, 2007).

PAH! fosters artistic expression and a sense of personal achievement in young deaf teenagers. Its goals are to:
1. produce proud Deaf adolescents with healthy self-esteem
2. teach theatre arts
3. enhance healthy peer relationships and social skills
4. foster relationships between deaf students and the Deaf Community

The name of the theatre — PAH! — is an American Sign Language expression that means "success!" or "we did it!" The theatre has been using theatre arts to develop communications skills and build personal strengths among the area's deaf adolescents (Coming Up Taller Awards, 1998).

The theatre's co-founders, Jody Steiner (hearing) and Janis Cole (Deaf), have extensive backgrounds in the theatre and care deeply for children. Steiner, the executive director, is a professional American Sign Language interpreter with a strong background in theatre, who worked a few years as an actress at the National Theatre of the Deaf. Cole, a graduate of Rochester Institute of Technology, is a former actress with the National Theatre of the Deaf and a teacher of the deaf. She had found time to organize and run the Deaf Youth Theatre while teaching American Sign Language, Deaf culture and history, Deaf literature, and American Sign Language literature at Boston University in the Deaf Studies Department. She serves as a practicum supervisor for graduate students. Cole also interprets for deaf-blind clients in the Boston community and works as an American Sign Language consultant for the Boston Center for Deaf and Hard-of-Hearing Children.

Although only half of PAH! staffers are Deaf, all are theatre professionals fluent in American Sign Language. Among them are Patrick McCarthy, Deaf professor at Wheelock College in the Interpreter Training Program, actor and ASL consultant for theatre interpreters across Boston; Katy Burns, an experienced teacher of deaf children and children with special needs at Horace Mann School for the Deaf; and Adrian Blue, Deaf playwright, the guest artist who directed and designed the set for the play *A Nice Place to Live*. PAH! also hosted guest artists like Clayton Valli, an ASL poet; John Kovacs, Deaf actor and the director of the Rathskellar Tour Company; Rosa Lee Gallimore, a Black-Deaf actress who runs her own company (The Rosa Lee Show); and Mike Lamitola, Deaf former actor and artistic director of the National Theatre of the Deaf (Steiner, 2007).

In 1998 PAH! received national recognition for its exemplary programs in the areas of art and social service. It won the Coming Up Taller Award from the President's Commission on the Arts and Humanities and the National Endowment for the Arts (Coming Up Taller Awards, 1998).

Although PAH! Deaf Youth Theatre is based at the Wheelock Family Theatre, each year PAH! creates an original production and conducts a public performance which is performed by the PAH! actors in American Sign Language, at the Wheelock Family Theatre.

List of Plays and Workshops
A few of the original productions performed by PAH! include *Bird of a Different Feather*, *Little Red Riding Hood*, *Legacy*, and *A Nice Place to Live*.

Ben Bahan, Deaf professor of Deaf Studies at Gallaudet University, after learning different skills such as dancing, blocking, painting, acting, storytelling, and ASL poetry, adapted and directed *Bird of a Different Feather* to make it into a Deaf story. PAH! students studied the story for one year. They incorporated their own improvisations and ideas, thus gaining experience with Deaf story productions.

Legacy is considered one of the group's most ambitious projects because it was a unique attempt to document the history of Deaf life in the area. In an effort to elicit stories that would be used for the production of the play, nineteen members of PAH! were bussed to the New England Home for the Deaf over the course of three months to interview the senior citizens about their past life experiences (Marx, 1999).

The Wheelock Family Theatre's *The Island Project — Martha's Vineyard*, by Jodie Steiner, producer, was staged between the beginning of September 2003 and June 2004. Martha's Vineyard is an island situated in southeastern Massachusetts, off the southwest coast of Cape Cod. Settled in 1642, it was a whaling and fishing center in the eighteenth and early nineteenth centuries and is now a popular resort area. In the early days, hereditary deafness was common on the island. The sign language used by the Deaf islanders was Martha's Vineyard Sign Language (MVSL), which has roots in the sign language used in the Kent region of southern England. The inhabitants of Martha's Vineyard called their sign Chilmark Sign Language after the village of Chilmark, where there was a good-sized Deaf Community. Chilmark Sign Language was then used in the Hartford School for the Deaf in Connecticut. Later, in Hartford, it was combined with French Sign Language and with the signs used by the Deaf Community in New York to form the basis of ASL. (About.com, 2007)

A Nice Place to Live was a new play by Adrian Blue, Deaf playwright and director, and his wife Catherine Rush, a hearing playwright. It is the resulting showpiece that has toured the Cape and Islands. It is based on the book *Everyone Here Spoke Sign Language: Hereditary Deafness on the Island of Martha's Vineyard* by Dr. Nora Ellen Groce and Joan Poole Nash, the last family generation of Martha's Islanders who uncovered this rich heritage on Martha's Vineyard (The Vineyard Playhouse, 2004).

A Nice Place to Live tells the story of a hearing boy who moves to the island with his family in 1890. He falls in love with a young Deaf woman and must learn to understand a world where deafness is seen in an entirely different light than on the mainland. The production was performed simultaneously by signing actors and voice interpreting actors.

Figure 17. PAH — performance set for *A Nice Place to Live*, 2003–2004 season. (Blue & Rush, *A Nice Place to Live*, 2004)

Figure 18. PAH — *A Nice Place to Live*, 2003–2004 season.

A Visual Language is a two-videotape package that resulted from the collaboration between PAH! Deaf Youth Theatre and VSA Arts of Massachusetts. The first videotape is the *Legacy* project in which different generations of Deaf men and women tell their stories, and the second videotape is *Little Red Riding Hood*. These videos are signed in ASL and open-captioned (Troise, 1999).

Participants and Audiences
In addition to creating and performing original productions, PAH! has presented workshops and drama camps for area schools and interested deaf youth. PAH! also has a touring company, PAH! Troopers, which is composed of recent graduates. This group performs original pieces celebrating Deaf Culture throughout the Boston region. The extent of students' participation ranges from one to four years.

The majority of PAH! students come from hearing families in which there are no deaf siblings. Most of their families do not know sign language. This program is available to deaf people who would not otherwise have an easy access to training in the arts, due to geographical location, disability, economics, and so on.

For the production of *A Nice Place to Live*, the Wheelock Family Theatre selected a team of highly qualified artists and teachers to develop a ten-week curriculum based on a unique period of time in the history of Martha's Vineyard. Damon Timm, a sign language interpreter, actor, and teacher; Norma Tourangeau, a Deaf actress and a kindergarten teacher at the Learning Center for Deaf Children; and Melanie Von Bitten, a teacher and historian, were the staff. For ten weeks, seventy students from the Horace Mann School for the Deaf and hard-of-hearing in Brighton, Massachusetts, and the Learning Center for Deaf Children in Framingham, Massachusetts, combined social studies and history with American Sign Language storytelling and poetry.

During the April 2005 school vacation, nine of those students, cast in the play, traveled to Cape Cod and Martha's Vineyard for staged readings at the Harwich Junior Theatre and the Vineyard Playhouse (Steiner, 2007).

On Monday, June 7, at the matinee performance, there were approximately 480 deaf and hard-of-hearing children from five state residential schools for the deaf (oral and sign language), but also children from mainstreamed schools and some hearing students from public schools. After the play, the cast panelists connected with the audience in an open forum that allowed school children to approach the actors who shared the same school background and exchange questions and ideas.

Kinds of Skills Taught
PAH! classes include the following: acting, African dance and drumming, theatre crafts, poetry, and storytelling. Students meet after school, twice a week, for ten months — the school year — at the Wheelock Family Theatre. This program has included up to forty participants that are generally eleven to seventeen years old. Their participation ranges from one to four years.

Although many of the students begin PAH! without much proficiency in signing, the lessons in acting, storytelling, and stage design are conducted entirely in American Sign Language. Instructors, half of whom are Deaf (theatre professionals fluent in American Sign Language), teach communication techniques and build students' self-confidence. Thus the students will develop skills and raised expectations of what they can accomplish in life. PAH! has created an environment where students can be challenged, express themselves, and grow. In addition to teaching the fundamentals of theatre including lighting, set building, costuming, and performing, instructors also train the youths in conflict resolution and behavior control. Understanding the importance of their Deaf identity and self-respect is what drives PAH! students to expand their horizons in the wider community. PAH! participants interpret other productions, usher at performing-arts centers, and audition for professional productions. Ultimately this program has encouraged deaf youth to embrace American Sign Language and pride in their Deaf Culture. (Marx, 1999)

Although PAH! receives a lot of support for this program from parents, their largest financial and logistical challenge is finding transportation for participants. The program directors must also handle problems dealing with the Boston public school system and a chronic lack of Deaf artists and staff members who are willing to work with children for low pay.

PAH! Deaf Youth Theatre is not just a children's theatre, but a place where students can learn about Deaf Culture and American Sign Language. Students are provided with social interaction that is more useful and less dangerous than the no-control street socialization that our society tends to lean toward nowadays. In this safe environment, they learn better communication skills as well as many different aspects of the art of theatrics, which will help them in their future. Students learn to take pride in their identity as Deaf people and are given an opportunity to take risks and express themselves (Blue, 2004).

The *Legacy* project had a tremendous impact on the language skills of the deaf children who participated. It also provided them with a unique social experience in that they had contact with people two or three generations apart from them, who had a different style of signing or limited signing skills, as most of them were raised with the oral method.

During the first five weeks of the project, students learned techniques for interviewing and video recording. About forty residents of the Home for the Deaf, some well into their eighties and nineties, answered students' questions and contributed to building a collection of oral histories. During the next five weeks, students trained both at the New England Home for the Deaf and at the Wheelock Family Theatre. They built storytelling skills by watching Deaf elders sign their stories and then signing these stories themselves. The last five weeks were dedicated to mounting a production from the stories gathered at the New England Home for the Deaf. Five stories were chosen for inclusion in *Legacy*: a talk between a black child and an elderly deaf resident who had never met another black-deaf person; a tale of injustice at a Connecticut sewing factory; the reunion of an immigrant daughter with her father at Ellis Island; social interaction at a Deaf Club; and an episode in which a deaf boy's hearing parents take their son to a deaf school without telling him where he is going.

Participants underwent tedious rehearsals in the development of the final production, a process of building up communication skills and breaking down fears. More than three hundred members of the community attended the performance, including proud PAH! parents and a significant number of enthusiastic residents from the New England Home for the Deaf. The *Legacy* program also benefited the senior Deaf citizens, who had the opportunity to socialize and to pass their knowledge to young generations by having their stories recorded (VSA Arts of Massachusetts, 2003).

Conversations with Actors and Participants

Steiner, the executive director, said:

> "We, PAH!, wanted to see the children creating their own stories, using their own expressions, feelings, ideas and working with deaf or hearing adults who can sign. Together we create from the children's experiences and go through the important process of developing the final product that will be

performed for the parents and the community. The parents and the community generally respond in awe at what the children can do, and it is very empowering for the children."

Cole, Deaf actress, commented:

"The Wheelock Family Theatre supported us in forming our own troupe with children from the school, to take on tour. We have a dual program and a dual philosophy with regard to Deaf and hard-of-hearing working together. Some of that stems from the Bilingual-Bicultural philosophy. I teach Deaf Studies and Deaf Education in the graduate program at Boston University. Jody's philosophy is Bilingual-Bicultural, meaning that children can read and write English and also know ASL. It is important for them to be adept in both cultures and to truly become Bilingual and Bicultural. They should not be immersed only in the Deaf World, because we are mainstreamed with the hearing society, and it would benefit them to learn from other cultures. Although we do primarily focus on the Deaf World."

Todd Czubek, a hearing teacher and CODA, the creative language director from The Magical Literacy Camp (TMLC) and teacher of language arts at Scranton School for the Deaf in Pennsylvania, said:

"Deaf children's theatre gives them an opportunity to really analyze the language and to understand how powerful ASL is. It germinates the idea of using ASL to make a statement. ASL can be powerful, whether used for political statements, for fun, or for play. Theatre for both adults and children means to me that the impossible becomes possible. Theatre elicits ideas from one's mind, thus releasing creativity. Once the kids understand that they can use ASL to express their creativity and their imagination, there is just something about the theatre that makes the impossible possible. It makes teaching possible. It also frees their emotions, causing them to cry, to laugh, and to feel many other emotions. It's magic. Deaf children's theatre is magic."

Elbert Joseph, a PAH! Deaf actor, proudly exclaimed:

"PAH! has taught me so much about acting, techniques, directing, and teamwork. You have to leave your ego at the door and work together at Wheelock! I am determined to go to New York University and join their directors program. That's it! I'm going to do it!"

Gallimore, the Black-Deaf guest artist in the summer drama at The Learning Center for Deaf Children in Framingham, near Boston, had this to say about Deaf children's theatre:

"I support the idea of Deaf children's theatre. Not only does it help build their self-esteem, but it also helps them develop their language and creativity. Theatre improves their reading skills, because they have to memorize lines. They get to work in groups and learn how to work together. They learn directing skills, writing skills, and reading scripts. This really helps educate the deaf children. I support that.

What does Deaf children's theatre mean? I think it is a theatre run by deaf children, their own theatre. They act, they bring their own creative ideas, they create an artistic image themselves. It means that deaf children are exposed to theatre and expose their theatre for the world to see."

CONCLUSION

When ASL was formally declared a language, deaf people realized that being Deaf meant only belonging to a minority who had been muted by political interests. In the following decade, Deaf people gained pride in their language and in their culture. Deaf theatre, which until then had been just a cultural survival tool, was regarded now as an institution on a par with hearing Theatre. Deaf people wanted the world to see and acknowledge this reality.

Before that time, 1960, the Deaf Community was solely responsible to educate the deaf children, either born in hearing families or in Deaf families with the social support structure and the necessary education in which regards their identity and their belonging to Deaf culture.

As the Civil Rights movement prompted new legislation, deaf children's families were given the option to raise them in the hearing world with access to education, arts, and other components of hearing culture. The necessity for deaf children to gain a Deaf cultural identity became a lesser priority.

In theatre, deaf children are provided with the same kind of accessibility options as deaf adults. In the case of plays for children, even with captioning or interpreting or shadowing at a more child-appropriate linguistic level, the linguistic background of deaf children is so varied that it is hard to predict whether the deaf children will benefit from the theatrical experience. The only way that deaf children could arrive at an appreciation of theatre is for them to become involved in the theatrical experience at an early age, to be provided in advance with a simple script that would ease their entrance into the theatrical experience, and to become involved in the theatrical experience itself, so that their questions would be answered and clarified before they leave the theatre. This would be a suitable educational way to expose deaf children to theatre and to language in a way that would strengthen and build their knowledge through continuous exposure and feedback.

Although Deaf theatres started to flourish throughout the United States and wanted to expand their performances to include children's plays, they had no control over the decisions of the hearing families who had deaf children or of the public schools that could have brought deaf children to the Deaf theatre. In these conditions, Deaf theatres found it financially impossible to provide educational support for deaf children.

Hearing people, who initially worked in different professions in contact with deaf people, realized the need for educational activities suitable for deaf children. Based on the deaf children's need for a strong visual communication process and a deaf-friendly environment, the best way to teach deaf children proved to be through theatre and creative drama activities with Art-Sign and ASL. Hearing people had the financial resources and the structural support to establish Deaf children's theatre companies.

However, hearing people needed the innate knowledge and creativity of Deaf people to be able to provide the proper education for deaf children. So it came about that Deaf actors and teachers became role models for the young deaf generations.

In some cases, hearing people took on the responsibility of teaching deaf children themselves. Although they had a noble mission, they could only teach deaf children the way hearing culture perceives deaf people and deafness. This was not a passage for the children to enter the Deaf World but rather to become fit for the hearing world.

In the meantime, Deaf theatres started to lose the support of the Deaf Community because of the technological advances that allowed people to communicate from the comfort of their homes, and provided easy entertainment by the way of television stations. The new technology offering movies with closed captioning on DVD also had a negative influence on deaf people's willingness to attend theatre performances.

Hearing theatres and Deaf theatres find it hard to make a profit by providing deaf people with accessible performances. Deaf theatres had no other choice than to function under the patronage of hearing theatres, hoping to attract more hearing audiences, so as to be able to continue their operations. Deaf children's theatre had even fewer opportunities and less attention. If Deaf theatres were struggling to stay in business because of the scarcity of a deaf audience, what about trying to attract deaf children who depended on their hearing parents, or on their schools to be able to attend theatre performances? This was nearly impossible. In spite of the financial difficulties, however, the availability of state and federal grants made it possible for Deaf children's theatre to come into existence.

As can be seen from the exploration of the six Deaf children's theatres, across the United States many different approaches have been successful in complementing and completing the education of deaf children through theatre and drama.

In competition with all the media entertainment choices, theatres manage to attract less and less audience. In general, there are not many children's plays compared to the number of theatrical productions addressed to the adult public. And even less common is for theatres to produce plays with children actors. Children's theatre may be hence considered a "minority enterprise." This means that the next generation is not trained to appreciate, first, children's theatre, and naturally, later on, theatre in the larger sense of the concept.

Already we have experiences the Deaf theatre dwindling due to lack of financial support and to diminishing support from the Deaf Community itself. Will Deaf children's theatre companies suffer the same fate? Will there be any Deaf children's theatre or program in the school system? Is there any way to sustain the idea of training with theatre and drama, a very visual medium, to support deaf children's appreciation for theatre as well as language acquisition process for both ASL and English?

These and other questions are critical for the future of Deaf theatre and of deaf children's education. Future research in the fields of Deaf Studies and Deaf education could start from trying to answer these questions and to open avenues for implementing solutions. Deaf children deserve access to theatrical experiences, to arts in general, through their own Deaf cultural perspective and their own language, American Sign Language. They also deserve equal opportunities to access knowledge and to become successful individuals by observing Deaf role models in the theatre.

REFERENCES

About.com. (2007). Deaf History — History of Sign Language. Retrieved July 6, 2007, from About.com: http://deafness.about.com/cs/featurearticles/a/signhistory.htm

Agogliati, L. (2003, July 22). Founder and director of the Deaf Access Program, Baltimore, Maryland. (B. Kilpatrick, Interviewer)

Bailey, S. D., & Agogliati, L. (2002). *Dreams to Sign*. Bethesda, Maryland: Imagination stage, Inc.

Baldwin, S. C. (1993). *Pictures in the Air: The Story of the National Theatre of the Deaf*. Washington, DC: Gallaudet University Press.

Beebout, J. (2003, July 23). Co-director of Illuminations Arts, Houston, Texas. (B. Kilpatrick, Interviewer)

Beekman, B. (2003, August 11). Director of the Little Theatre of the Deaf, Hartford, Connecticut. (B. Kilpatrick, Interviewer)

Bellugi, E. S., & Klima, U. (1983). *Poetry without Sound. Jerome & Diane Rothenberg's Symposium of the Whole: A Range of Discourse Toward an Ethnopoetics* (pp. 291-302). Berkeley, California: University of California Press.

Blue, A. (2004, July 27). Director and scriptwriter from Boston, Massachusetts. (B. Kilpatrick, Interviewer)

Blue, A., & Rush, C. (2004, June). A Nice Place to Live. Wheelock Family Theatre, Boston, Massachusetts.

Coming Up Taller Awards. (1998). PAH! Deaf Youth Theatre. Retrieved May 11, 2006, from Coming Up Taller: Arts and Humanities Programs for Children and Youth at Risk: http://www.cominguptaller.org/awards/program7.html

Cultural Access Consortium. (2006). Image: Showing a List of All the Access Symbols. Retrieved June 29, 2006, from Calendar of Events: http://www.culturalaccess.org/L2/months/jun.htm

Czubek, T. (2003, August 5). Director and founder of The Magical Literacy Camp, Pittsburgh School for the Deaf, Boston, Massachusetts. (B. Kilpatrick, Interviewer)

Daniels, B. (1992, Fall). What is Deaf Theater? *Gallaudet Today — The Magazine*, p. 6.

Folerzynski, J. (2003, July 14). Director of the children's theatre program, International Center on Deafness and the Arts, Chicago, Illinois. (B. Kilpatrick, Interviewer)

Houston Endowment, Inc. (2006). Grantee and Purpose — Illuminations Theatre with the Deaf. Retrieved June 28, 2006, from Houston Endowment, Inc.: http://www.houstonendowment.org/grants/orgsearch.asp?ScriptAction=orgdetail&keyword=Illuminations+&Organization_ID=571998780

ICODA. (2007). ICODA. Retrieved June 8, 2007, from International Center On Deafness and the Arts: http://www.icodaarts.org

Illuminations Arts. (2005, September). A Record 750 Deaf/HH Students Attend Shadowed Performance. *Illuminations Arts Newsletter* 7 , p. 2.

Illuminations Arts. (2006). About Us: Our Mission. Retrieved June 28, 2006, from Illuminations Arts: http://www.illuminationsarts.org

Illuminations Arts. (2004). Fact Sheet. Illuminations Arts: 20th Anniversary: 1984-2004. Illuminations Arts.

Illuminations Arts. (2003, June). Hand Held Tales: Stories in ASL and English. *Illuminations Arts Newsletter* 1 , p. 2.

Imagination Stage. (2007). Deaf Access. Retrieved June 13, 2007, from Imagination Stage: http://www.imaginationstage.org/deaf_access.htm

Imagination Stage. (2007). Dreams to Sign. Retrieved June 13, 2007, from Imagination Stage: http://www.imaginationstage.org/Our%20Classes/dreamstosign.htm

Imagination Stage. (2003, February 13). Production Staff and Faculty. Retrieved May 15, 2006, from Imagination Stage: http://www.imaginationstage.org/Our%20Classes/deaf_access_staff.htm

Kilpatrick, B. R. (2007). The History of the Formation of Deaf Children's Theatre in the United States. Ph.D. dissertation, Lamar University.

Liberty, D. (1991, February 13). Patricia Scherer Frees Children from Silence. TempoNorthwest, *Chicago Tribune*, pp. 7-8.

Little Theatre of the Deaf. (2003). *Study Guide: The Giving Tree and Other Stories*.

Marx, B. (1999, September 12). Many Hands Make Good Theater. *The Boston Globe Magazine*, pp. 18-19, 29-35.

Morris, A. (1983, First quarter). Theater Without Words. *Houston Arts, The Quarterly Publication of the Cultural Council of Houston* 6, no. 1 , pp. 2-17.

National Theatre of the Deaf. (2004). 2004-2005 Touring Season: Little Theatre of the Deaf. Collection of touring packages. National Theatre of the Deaf.

Peters, C. L. (2000). *Deaf American Literature: From Carnival to the Canon*. Washington, DC: Gallaudet University Press.

Phan, S. (1997, Winter). Bravo! Bravo! *Illuminations Arts Newsletter*, p. 5.

Schuchman, J. S. (1988). *Hollywood Speaks: Deafness and the Film Entertainment Industry*. Urbana and Chicago, Illinois: University of Illinois Press.

Seattle Children's Theatre. (2003, February 6). Deaf Youth Drama. Retrieved February 6, 2003, from Seattle Children's Theatre: http://www.sct.org/classes/dramashops.html

Seattle Children's Theatre. (2007). Deaf Youth Drama Program. Seattle Children's Theatre Brochure. Seattle Children's Theatre.

Seattle Children's Theatre. (2003, February 13). Organization Overview. Seattle Children's Theatre Documentation. Seattle Children's Theatre.

StageSource. (2002). Wheelock Family Theatre to Receive the 2002 Theatre Hero Award. Retrieved 2002, from StageSource.org: http://www.stagesource.org

Steiner, J. (2007, June 28). PAH! Deaf Youth Theatre. e-mail to Brian Kilpatrick .

Tadie, N. B. (1978). A History of Drama at Gallaudet College: 1864 to 1969. Volume I. Ph.D. dissertation. New York University.

The Vineyard Playhouse. (2004, April 19). The Vineyard Playhouse Welcomes the Wheelock Family Theatre and PAH! Deaf Youth Theatre on April 23. Retrieved May 12, 2006, from The Vineyard Playhouse: http://www.vineyardplayhouse.org/press/2004/press0402.html

Toscano, M. (2003, May). Theatre Group Finally Gets Its New Home. *The Washington Post*, p. 21.

Troise, A. (1999, September-December). Museum of Science's Message Speaks to All Vistors. Retrieved July 28, 2007, from VSA Massachusetts News 9, no. 24: http://www.accessexpressed.net/articles.php?table=articles&id=179&pageNumber=1

VSA Arts of Massachusetts. (2007). Cultural Access: National Cultural Access Initiative: Pathways to Participation. Retrieved July 25, 2007, from VSA Arts of Massachusetts: http://www.vsamass.org/programs.html

VSA Arts of Massachusetts. (2003). Deaf Legacy Project. Retrieved February 19, 2003, from VSA Arts of Massachusetts: http://www.massbaycfc.org/specarts.htm

Wilbur, R. (2000, Winter). The Use of ASL to Support the Development of English and Literacy. *Journal of Deaf Studies and Deaf Education* 5, no. 1, pp. 81-104.

Wilson, N. (2003, August 7). American Sign Language assistant, American Sign Language sign coach with the Deaf Youth Drama Program, former actor with the Little Theatre of the Deaf. (B. Kilpatrick, Interviewer)

To the Point of Exclusion: Balancing Lorenza Mazzetti's *Together* between Deaf and Hearing Communities

TRAVIS SUTTON

> These films were not made together; nor with the idea of showing them together. But when they came together, we felt they had an attitude in common. Implicit in this attitude is a belief in freedom, in the importance of people and in the significance of the every day (Lichtenstein and Schregenberger 241).

THESE WORDS WERE PART OF A MANIFESTO THAT ACCOMPANIED THE first Free Cinema program at London's National Film Theatre in 1956. This was a program of three short films that had been made with minimal resources outside of the British studio system. Lorenza Mazzetti's film *Together* was released as part of this program, and many audience members celebrated or condemned the film's presentation of deaf people. That same year, British film critic Gavin Lambert observed, "Incensed viewers...wrote that the film was an insult to deaf-mutes and the makers should have their ears cut off" ("Free Cinema" 260). This concern from viewers may have challenged the manifesto's affirmation of "the importance of people" since the content of *Together* appeared to be audist in the way it stereotyped the deaf population.

Lambert justified the presentation of deafness in *Together* because he argued that the film was not meant to document deaf existence. For Lambert, deafness was merely a symbol in the film for a world of "anxiety, helplessness, and solitude" beneath the familiar world of daily life ("Free Cinema" 260). While Lambert may be accurate in his symbolic interpretation, presenting deaf life as a symbol for such negative human conditions reinforces the viewers' concern that the film is socially offensive to members of the Deaf community. However, the movie *Together* has artistic depth and a skillful composition that includes structural elements from the silent film era. Despite Mazzetti's use of these elements from the silent film era that appear to invite a viewing position for both deaf and hearing spectators with a story of deaf characters who communicate through sign language, the content and form of *Together* ultimately maintain an audist perspective that limits deaf representation and excludes deaf spectators.

Together is a fictional narrative about two deaf men who are friends and live in the East End of London. The story in the film is presented in an episodic structure as it observes the two deaf characters in various circumstances. The two friends labor together on the river port, walk in the street, shop at the market, visit a saloon, share a meal with the their landlord, and converse in their tiny apartment. During the various episodes, groups of children from the street repeatedly follow, ridicule, and taunt the two deaf characters. At the conclusion of the film when one of the deaf characters is sitting on a bridge, a taunting child pushes him off the structure, and the deaf man falls into the water beneath the bridge. The other deaf character does not see (or hear) his friend struggling in the water, and as the film fades to a close the spectator is left to assume that the deaf character drowns.

Lorenza Mazzetti, who was not deaf, was a new filmmaker at the time of making *Together*. She collaborated with Denis Horne who had written the script, which was originally titled *The Glass Marble* (*Small is Beautiful*). Mazzetti had to get her project approved through the British Film Institute (BFI) for financial assistance. The BFI Experimental Film Fund was initially designed to aid new filmmakers with a first-time project and had been set up by Michael Balcon, who had been a key figure as a young producer in providing Alfred Hitchcock with directorial opportunities as an early filmmaker (Lambert "Notes" 2). This funding allowed for the introduction of new voices and creative minds in the British film industry. Following the financial approval, Mazzetti began the production of *Together*. She cast two hearing acquaintances, Michael Andrews and Eduardo Paolozzi, as the two deaf characters in the film.

The Institute granted Mazzetti some funds to provide a version of the film without sound before she could obtain additional funding for a soundtrack. Essentially, Mazzetti was asked to create her film about two deaf characters in a manner that could potentially include both deaf and hearing audiences. When Mazzetti completed a silent version of her film, the Institute granted funds for Mazzetti to add a soundtrack. Most of the appended soundtrack for the film is a musical score that serves as background audio for the images on the screen. The score emulates the movies of the silent film era that would typically involve an extrafilmic sound source, such as a piano or orchestra, during the film. Other moments in the film attach atmospheric noise, such as indiscernible crowd noises at the market. There are very few instances of synchronized sound in the film.

Filmmaker and critic Lindsay Anderson began collaborating with Mazzetti on *Together* during the editing process. Anderson was familiar with deafness and audist perspectives on deaf identities. Prior to his collaboration with Mazzetti, Anderson had co-directed with Guy Breton the Oscar-winning documentary *Thursday's Children* (1954). Through narration by Richard Burton, *Thursday's Children* documents the instruction of children at a school for the deaf. The school and techniques that were captured for the film were rooted in audist approaches to education. No one in the film uses sign language, and the various techniques reveal the time and attention given to oralism. Each child's deafness is presented as a tragedy that needs to be overcome. The film's narration promotes the idea about the necessity of the deaf children to learn and vocalize English words in order for them to process thoughts. The film also concludes that each child's ability to talk is his or her only hope to become a fully functioning human being by preventing a life of silence and loneliness. Despite the movie's skillfully crafted production, *Thursday's Children* is a presentation about a colonialist process of changing deaf children to be like hearing children.

The audist perspectives Anderson promulgated through his work on *Thursday's Children* would not be challenged in *Together*. The narration in *Thursday's Children* attributes the oralist environment to be saving the children from "the worst enemy of the deaf: to be alone in silence." The two deaf characters in *Together* have a relationship through their common signed language, but according to the story, their separation and independence from hearing people who do not use sign language leads these characters to sorrow and tragedy. The story presented in *Together* reinforces this idea of loneliness in silence for deaf people who have not been trained in the methods of oralism.

The premiere of *Together* as part of the Free Cinema program in London was very successful. Filmmaker Karel Reisz believed the successful response to the three films in the program was due to the audience's thirst for a different kind of British cinema, a cinema that was aware of the change in British culture after the war (*Small is Beautiful*). For many years prior to World War II, the British film industry had a difficult time establishing its artistic influence on the international movie scene. In the year of the first Free Cinema program, Gavin Lambert wrote some observations about the British Cinema. He recalled a French critic's statement regarding the history of British cinema as saying, "There is no such thing." With this in mind, Lambert conceded, "The British cinema grew up late" (Lambert "Notes" 1). British film historian Alan Lovell describes how England's "negative reactions" against Hollywood's apparent sex and violence resulted in a "low pressure" or bland cinema with little influence on the international film circuit. Thus, documentary films had taken the claim of "art cinema" in Britain, and the documentary movement had established a strong resistance against the entertainment industry. Lovell concludes, "Stranded between two kinds of cinema, the British entertainment cinema has never established a character of its own" ("The Unknown Cinema" 6-7).

It was the frustration of young film critics such as Lindsay Anderson and Karel Reisz that aimed to change the character of British cinema in the 1950s. These critics recognized the stranded state of the British cinema that Lovell describes. Regarding the journal that these critics were involved with, Lovell writes, "Sequence attacked on the one hand the British documentary movement for its drabness and orthodoxy and on the other the British feature cinema for its lack of aesthetic adventure and its conventional ideas about cultural quality" (7). These young critics decided to create their own films that exemplified their principles of filmmaking with movies that captured what they felt the British cinema had chosen to neglect. These critics began with making documentary films and later started the Free Cinema movement to exhibit their work. After the Free Cinema programs they directed fictional narratives with features such as *Saturday Night and Sunday Morning* (1960) and *This Sporting Life* (1963). Many of these feature narratives would be classified as "kitchen sink" dramas because they took an interest in working-class issues and representation (Nichols 32). Lorenza Mazzetti did not become associated with this group of movie critics and filmmakers until Lindsay Anderson agreed to help with *Together* during the editing process.

Because *Together* premiered in the first Free Cinema program with Lindsay Anderson's *O Dreamland* (1953) and Karel Reisz and Tony Richardson's *Momma Don't Allow* (1955), which are documentary films, *Together* is frequently generalized to be a documentary film as well. The first Free Cinema program inaugurated a series of programs with short films that were noted for their observational documentary styles. In his history of the documentary film, Eric Barnouw comments, "The film makers were observers, rejecting the role of promoter. New, light equipment made possible an intimacy of observation new to documentary, and this involved sound as well as image" (231). In *Studies in Documentary*, Alan Lovell and Jim Hillier describe this type of filmmaking as "reportage" (143). *Momma Don't Allow* (1955) observes the activity of youths dancing at a jazz club; however, several instances in the film are clearly staged, such as the various opening scenes with characters leaving their place of work to attend the club or the scene of a young couple quarreling at the club later that evening. *Refuge England* (1959) is also unusual as a documentary because it follows a fictional Hungarian refugee in England who is in search of a vague address. The audio in Refuge England is the main character's first-person narration of his thoughts and confusions regarding the British society as an outsider. Robert Vas, the director of the film and himself a Hungarian refugee to England in 1956, perhaps inserted autobiographical elements into the piece. Many generalize the Free Cinema programs as a collection of documentary films and part of Britain's documentary film movement, but some of these films blur the boundaries of fiction and reality so as to challenge a documentary label.

Several of the episodes in *Together* incorporate observational shots of a non-staged reality in East End of London, such as the marketplace or the docks on the river. Many of these shots were influenced by Anderson and his collaboration with Mazzetti in the editing process. Anderson suggested an inclusion of additional footage that would make the film less plot-driven and more a "poetic and atmospheric evocation" of the East End of London (*Small is Beautiful*). The observational shots in *Together* serve to capture the tone of the story, a story that poetically shifts to fantasy spaces outside of reality. In fact, the movie's opening dedication describes the film as a "tale." Nevertheless, the film *Together* received recognition at the Cannes Film Festival as an investigative documentary film, research film, or "Mention au film de recherche — court métrage, 1956" (Cannes Festival). However, unlike the programmers at Cannes and other film critics of British cinema, I cannot describe *Together* as a whole to be a documentary film.

The movie *Together* has a construction that is more easily described as a fictional narrative with an influence from Italian neorealism. Italian neorealism is a film movement after World War II in which certain Italian filmmakers would use limited film resources and non-professional actors to capture a fictional story in the war-torn urban areas of Italy. These films, such as *Rome, Open City* (1945) and *Bicycle Thieves* (1948), focused on the experience of the working class and aimed for an influence in politics during the post-Fascist rebuilding of Italy. Cesare Zavattini, a key proponent for Italian neorealism at the time, wrote, "The cinema's overwhelming desire to see, to analyse, its hunger for reality, is an act of concrete homage towards other people, towards what is happening and existing in the world. And, incidentally, it is what distinguishes 'neorealism' from the American cinema" (218). Even with a fictional framework, a way to emphasize people and represent reality for Italian neorealists is through capturing the world, which is also done in documentary filmmaking. However, the films that are connected with Italian neorealism are not documentary films.

Mazzetti lived in Italy during the height of Italian neorealism after World War II. After this period, Mazzetti moved to London to study art and painting. When she returned to Italy after her work in Free Cinema, she collaborated with Zavattini on other film projects (Lovell and Hillier 169). The film *Together* captures much of the atmosphere and character of the East End of London through imagery of the crammed buildings, bombed-out corners, and dirty streets. The neglect of this area by the rest of London is poignant in the imagery of children playing in the concrete rubble of a war scene from the past. The images of the damaged city, the focus on the working class, the inclusion of non-professional actors, and the use of minimal film resources to present a fictional story by an Italian director contribute to the association of *Together* with Italian neorealism. This connection is important for the film's distinction from a simple identification with the British documentary movement. Although film styles and movements can blur in their boundaries, to label *Together* as a documentary could be misleading and potentially more damaging to the hearing community's perception of the Deaf community because of the film's presentation of deafness.

REPRESENTATION AND THE DEAF CHARACTER

Together was released in a period of limited deaf representation with other films that include *Thursday's Children* and Ealing Studios' fictional narrative *Crash of Silence* (1952). Both of these films present deafness as a tragedy in need of support and remedy from the hearing world, and *Together* contributes to this cultural assumption. This prevalent cultural perception can be recognized a decade later in the United States with Hollywood films such as *The Heart is a Lonely Hunter* (1968). Richard Dyer writes:

> How a group is represented, presented over again in cultural forms,...[has] to do with how members of groups see themselves and others like themselves...How we are seen determines in part how we are treated; how we treat others is based on how we see them; such seeing comes from representation. (Dyer 1)

Much of the hearing community learns about the deaf community through cultural presentations, so it is important to acknowledge how deaf people are being presented. How hearing people see and treat deaf people influences education, medicine, work, and other levels of social interaction.

Because the writer, director, and performers in *Together* are all hearing, they rely on stereotypes of deaf people to present the story. Dyer reminds his readers that stereotyping is a function of human existence. It is part of the human mind that seeks to categorize and make sense of the information it encounters. He writes that it is not stereotypes that are "wrong, but who controls and defines them, what interests they serve...partial knowledge is not false knowledge, it is simply not absolute knowledge" (Dyer 12). It is the British hearing community of the 1950s that accepts and reinforces the images presented in films such as *Together*.

Many of these types of representations can be found today as they serve those who benefit from audist perspectives of deafness. Harlan Lane writes, "In the hearing stereotype, deafness is the lack of something, not the presence of anything. Silence is emptiness" (7). In contrast to this stereotype, Lane rehearses a 1988 United States survey in which "two-thirds of deaf adults interviewed…thought their social life was better than hearing people's" (9). Although this is a study from a different period of time in a different country, during the era of Free Cinema in Britain, deaf people satisfied with their social experience rarely made it to the movie screen. The hearing community, which dominates the viewing audience in the film industry, pleasurably responds to films where deaf people pursue identities to be like the hearing community. In these stories it is typically the responsibility of the deaf person to change his or her identity and sociality. From an audist perspective, this change can only be done through the good graces of hearing people. It can be pleasurable for a hearing spectator to be situated in a position of privilege through watching a story of enabling others who are different by eliminating that difference.

In *Together*, Michael Andrews' character is the central character of the story, and a central theme of the film is this character's loneliness and isolation despite his friendship with Eduardo Paolozzi's character. Andrews' character remains uncomfortable with his deafness and desires a hearing identity. His signing dominates screen time over Paolozzi's character; however, his embarrassment about communicating through sign language is apparent at the meals with his landlord and the hearing environment of the saloon.

Paolozzi's character does not seem to be bothered with his identity as a deaf person, but this apparent satisfaction with a deaf identity comes at a cost for deaf representation. Paolozzi's character is diminished cognitively so that he is equated with the level of the children in the film. He cannot control his temper during the taunts of the other children, which is manifested when he lifts one of the children in anger. This action places Paolozzi's character at their level. Though he is a grown man, he behaves as though he were a child who wishes to defend himself against the other children around him. Paolozzi's character is also equated with the other children when he collects the marbles that he finds in the street. When he returns to the apartment, he empties his pockets to find the marbles and in the process finds a variety of other items a child would find fascinating.

The relationship between the two men also manifests a hearing perspective of deafness. Andrews' character is a paternal figure for Paolozzi's character. His maturity in contrast to Paolozzi's character is revealed in the instances when he assists Paolozzi's character with his shoes or instructs Paolozzi's character to shave, which is something adult males are expected to do. Paolozzi's contentment with his deafness is thus associated with the naivety of a child, while Andrews' paternal-type character is aware of the reality of the hearing world and thus interprets their deaf existence to be a tragedy. Andrews' character embodies the hearing perspective that even though most deaf people are content with their identity, as hearing people "we can give them a thousand reasons why they can't be" (Lane 9).

The two deaf characters maintain a friendship, but for Andrews' character the relationship is not satisfying. Throughout the film he is intrigued and distracted by the hearing women around him. There are no deaf women in the story, and Paolozzi's character is never presented as having sexual desire for women or men. This is another way Paolozzi's character is associated with the disposition of a child. When the two deaf characters are at the saloon, Paolozzi's character plays with the marbles and takes no notice of the dancing men and women around him. At the same time, Andrews' character is intrigued with the woman who speaks at him, which words he cannot understand. Following this instance when Andrews' character is in bed, he allows himself to fantasize a romantic encounter between himself and the hearing woman he had seen at the saloon. He moves his mouth as if he were talking, which manifests his desire for a hearing identity. This fantasy is prior to his final moment of loneliness on the bridge where the children push him into the water. For the presentation of this film, deafness not only means a loss of hearing but can also mean a loss of desirability, maturity, and connectivity. A hearing interpretation on the limits of deafness also comes in that final moment of the film when Paolozzi's character cannot hear Andrews' character struggling in the water.

With such an audist perspective of deafness, one must question the purpose deafness serves in the film. As mentioned earlier, Lambert interpreted the film to be about two parallel worlds in which a world of sorrow may go unnoticed in the world of the everday. Mazzetti emphasized in an interview that she "had to do this story." As a native Italian in London, she felt like an outsider, and she was intrigued with the "world of silence" within a world of sound. Mazzetti claimed to have projected her own feelings as an outsider upon these two characters, but it appears that she projected her fear of deafness as well (*Small is Beautiful*). This fear fuels the repeated cycle of deafness being presented as lack, loneliness, and loss. This cycle of representation is destructive to the way hearing people see and treat deaf people and may influence how many deaf people perceive themselves.

"VISUAL ACOUSTICS" AND THE DEAF SPECTATOR

Because the initial construction of *Together* was silent, it includes elements of visual cues that had been typical during the silent film era, a period in which deaf and hearing audiences mutually enjoyed the phenomenon of the motion picture. In her essay "Sounding Images in Silent Film: Visual Acoustics in Murnau's *Sunrise*," Melinda Szaloky identifies the ability of skilled filmmakers in the silent era, specifically F. W. Murnau, who could convey the experience of sound entirely through the moving image, such as a flock of birds rising after an image of a gun to visualize a gunshot (Szaloky 113). She quotes Victor Oscar Freeburg in the opening of her essay. "'High-brow' critics and apologists for the spoken drama have been known to sneer at the silent drama. Let the cinema composer [i.e., director] attune their ears to the sounding beauties of that silence" (Szaloky 109, Freeburg 99-103).

Szaloky reminds her reader that the term "silent film" did not develop until movies had reached a point of including sound with the image (109). Prior to this technological addition, movies were recognized as moving pictures and did not necessitate a distinction based on auditory difference. Movies were regarded as inherently visual, although extrafilmic sound typically accompanied exhibition of a film with music or sound effects. Extrafilmic sound sources were typically expendable, and when they were omitted they did not impose a great loss to the spectating experience. The moving image was accepted as a visual medium and deaf and hearing spectators mutually responded to the images. When language was able to distinguish the difference manifested in the films after the swift evolution to the "talkies" or movies with sound at the end of the 1920s, the exclusion of the deaf community from hearing audiences had already taken place.

Through an exploration of theories related to phenomenology, Szaloky skillfully crafts a framework for perception that can be valuable for understanding the experience of the deaf spectator. Phenomenology can be described as "the study of things as they are perceived, acknowledging the existence of phenomena in the world but arguing they don't 'exist' for us until we perceive them" (Swenson 252). For the spectator of a film, phenomenology highlights the meaning-making process within the consciousness of the spectator. In essence, a film is not created for the spectator until this process occurs during the reception of a film.

Szaloky adopts this exploration of cinematic reception to examine what she calls "visual acoustics" or "visualized sound." Szaloky writes, "What I will call visualized sound is the pictorial rendering of narratively significant acoustic phenomena, a kind of acoustic close-up that, like the close-up in general, serves to guide and organize spectatorial attention and to help the viewer comprehend the story" (Szaloky 113). The moments a spectator experiences visualized sound are moments typically crafted by the filmmaker because those moments are significant to the story. Visualized sound is one of the many tools a filmmaker can use to cultivate a specific response in the spectator at certain points in a film.

Szaloky does not recognize the process of deaf spectators experiencing the phenomenon of visual acoustics. In fact, in the thesis of her essay she specifically excludes deaf spectators from this process. She writes, "I will argue that silent cinema was never silent because it was never meant to represent a mute world addressed to deaf spectators; nor did spectators understand it as such" (110). Szaloky is perhaps accurate in the assumption that filmmakers during the silent era did not aim to target the minority of deaf spectators in the viewing audience. However, deaf spectators were included by the very nature of the film form. It is just as likely to assume that studios did not distinguish between deaf and hearing audiences because both audiences, prior to the introduction of sound in movies, could be targeted as a single body of people for ticket sales. "Hollywood had not planned to accommodate deaf viewers — it had just happened" (Schuchman 22). Deaf actors could also participate alongside hearing actors in this medium of entertainment (Schuchman 21).

The way Szaloky phrases her argument, in an essay that focuses on such concepts as imaginary hearing, alternative sense perception, and phenomenology is puzzling. Szaloky praises the visual language of silent cinema and its capacity to address audiences of various cultures and languages; however, the inclusion of the deaf community during silent cinema and their spectatorial pleasures during such films, which would include visualized sound, explicitly evades her main argument (110). Aside from her thesis and a rhetorical question about "deaf and mute characters…in a soundless space," Szaloky does not elaborate on how the theoretical principles that are discussed in her essay do not include deaf spectators (111).

I suggest that the principles of visual acoustics do involve deaf spectators. Through their language and experience, members of the deaf community are accustomed to communicating and experiencing phenomena visually. Returning to the description of phenomenology, the meaning-making that occurs in the consciousness of a deaf spectator as he or she encounters visualized sound may be different than with a hearing spectator. However, visualized sound is not entirely about matching an auditory memory with the soundless image on the screen, although many hearing people may use their remembrance of sounds as they construct a meaning in their consciousness. The deaf spectator may experience acoustic or other sensory phenomena as he or she constructs the meaning in his or her consciousness. To provide an example, a similar exercise of visualizing sound can be done in American Sign Language. Non-manual cues such as "intense," "puff. cheeks," and "pow" can be used to intensify the energy of a sign (Baker-Shenk and Cokely 20-24). This energy can be understood by the receiver of the message, as he or she perceives the message and creates its meaning, as an experience of visual acoustics.

Visual acoustics relies on the inner processes of the mind and body during cinematic reception. Szaloky relates an important concept for this type of reception: synaesthesia. Synaesthesia has been medically associated with "spontaneous physical sensations" of one sense that have been triggered by another sense, but synaethesia has "metaphoric (and artistic) associations" as well. Szaloky explains, "This metaphorical aspect of synaesthesia implies an inner hearing that, independent of immediate physical stimuli, relies on memory, imagination, and inference making on the basis of lived experiences" (113). The inner hearing of visual acoustics does not require an experience of physically responding to sound but can be created in the mind of the spectator as he or she creates meaning and mental associations of the concept of sound. Synaesthesia recognizes the body's ability to experience the idea or energy of sound through an alternative means, such as a visual modality.

In this way, visual acoustics is not entirely about visually showing something that typically makes noise. As Szaloky states, it's "a kind of acoustic close-up," even for phenomena that may not necessarily generate sound, such as human emotions. Szaloky describes how the framing of a barking dog in Murnau's *Sunrise* represents the volume and noise of the main character's guilt (123). The human emotion of guilt does not generate auditory sound waves for the inner ear to capture; however, Murnau presents a visualized sound through the acoustic and visual close-up of the barking dog for the spectator of his silent film to recognize the presence of an invisible emotion. Both the deaf and hearing spectator can recognize the intensity of the visualized sound during this moment and this visual moment can produce inner responses in the spectator beyond visual recognition.

Mazzetti's film has a number of moments where visualized sound is presented. These include instances of the tormenting children, shots of empty London streets, and a jarring sequence captured from the back of a truck. One of the most obvious segments is the concluding sequence of the film. While Andrews' character sits on the wall of the bridge, he stares at the water. This image is followed by a close-up of the water and its fluid, rhythmic waves. The children quickly arrive to torment the deaf character, and the editing and mise-en-scene alternate between the serenity of the water and the chaos of the children on the bridge. The children are shown running up to the camera and making faces, waving their fingers, or running in circles.

Their energy rises as the film approaches a climax and introduces another visualized sound: the industrial machines. This second visualized sound presses against the lone character on the bridge who is associated with the peaceful rhythm of the water. The low visual angles of the chain and shovel extracting dirt from the river maintains in conjunction with the images of the children a contrast of "silent" sounds to the visualized sound associated with Andrews' character.

After Andrews' character is pushed into the water, the children scatter. Their disappearance into the city alters the visual acoustic but not the tension of the moment. Paolozzi's character returns to the bridge and his calm confusion is contrasted with an image of Andrews' character splashing in the water below the bridge. The visualized sound of Andrews' character falls silent beneath the river, and Paolozzi's character's acoustic fades as he waits. The visualized sound of the industrial machine conqueres and concludes this final sequence of the film as a barge pulls away into the river. "So an image in itself very ordinary, the barge passing along the Thames at the end, carries tragedy with it: a symbol of time, indifference and oblivion that seems unforced and deeply sad" (Lambert "Free Cinema" 260).

An instance earlier in the film can be interpreted to convey the imaginary sound that Szaloky attributes to the Man's guilt as the barking dog in *Sunrise*. In *Together* Andrews' character leaves the apartment by himself because Paolozzi's character prefers to stay in bed. Andrews' character arrives to the carnival. The film provides a close-up of Andrews' face as he looks at the attractions. This image is followed by a shot of the rotating carousel. These two images are emphasized, and the visually acoustic close-up of the carousel communicates an association with Andrews' character's state of being. The visually loud rotation conveys his disorientation with the hearing world, and this disorientation is followed by the images of the dancer at the carnival. Andrews' character is enticed by the hearing world, and this moment of disorienting visualized sound, which is not the sound of the carousel but an imaginary sound of its own, prepares the spectator to be introduced to the sexual drives and yearnings of this particular character as he observes the female dancer.

When Mazzetti does reach the point of adding auditory sound to the film, she again models the silent cinema by providing a simple musical score for the background of the narrative, in the same manner as a piano or orchestra would provide an extrafilmic sound source during a motion picture of the silent film era. This activity would perhaps enhance the viewing experience for the hearing and deaf spectator; however, the extrafilmic sound during silent films and the musical score attached to Mazzetti's film does not directly exclude the deaf spectator from the story.

In other instances during *Together*, Mazzetti's use of sound qualifies for what Rudolph Arnheim calls "a double soundtrack" (Szaloky 112, Arnheim 215-216). Arnheim explores the role of auditory sound with the moving image because of the apparent "uneasiness" hearing audiences initially had with the combination. He believes the "two media are fighting each other instead of capturing [the audience] by united effort" because "the spectator's attention [is] being torn in two directions" (Arnheim 199). For Arnheim, sound must be in a complete fusion or "parallelism" with the image in order to avoid the uneasiness of the spectator (209). He writes, "...an interruption of the dialogue can only take the form of an interval; it cannot be justified as a temporary shift from audible to visible action" (208). Parallelism occurs when the auditory sound or dialogue is complete on its own and compounded with a complete image. Arnheim would most likely be critical of Mazzetti's shift of auditory elements to silent visual elements throughout the film, which can be interpreted as Mazzetti's exploration of "the world of silence" she associates with the deaf identity.

However, Arnheim affirms that there must be a reason for compounding the independently complete "visual and auditory elements...[the combination] must serve to express something that could not be said by one of the media alone" (215). In this way, merely adding an auditory element of what a visual element already presents results in a "double soundtrack." If the combination of the auditory element with the visual element does not change what the visual element already communicates, then there is no need to communicate the same thing twice. The moments where sound simply parallels the image on the screen as a "double soundtrack" in *Together* would be the instances of atmospheric noise. These are the scenes of the children playing in the street, the saloon, the market, and the final crane in the river. Very little sound is synchronized in the film. One instance would be a man who is singing at the saloon where the music matches his vocalization.

In a couple of other moments in the film, Mazzetti avoids the pitfalls of a double soundtrack by adding sound that is not communicated in a visual manner. She uses audio signals for their own effect and independent from what is conveyed on the screen. Despite this exploration of auditory possibilities in a motion picture, this decision excludes deaf spectators from moments of the story in *Together*. One scene is when the two deaf characters are walking down the street and a vehicle honks its horn for the two deaf men to move out of its way. The street is wide enough to pass because another car passes in the opposite direction. The driver gets out of his vehicle to express his anger at the two deaf characters, who concede to stepping aside. Without the auditory cue of the honking horn, this interplay between the deaf and hearing characters could be confusing to the spectator.

Another moment of exclusion through auditory signals is when the children are chanting a racially violent rhyme. Without a visual manifestation of this chant, the children appear to be playing in the same manner as any other moment in the film. This racially violent rhyme reveals the cultural impression of violence against people who are different. There is also an instance at the saloon where Andrews' character as a deaf white man is associated with the one black character in the film. In that moment, a hearing white woman at the saloon flirts with the black man before she flirts with Andrews' character. The repeated racist chant of the children, which is juxtaposed with the two deaf characters laboring at the docks, provides an understanding of the violent action performed by the children at the conclusion of the film. Without this auditory cue, the spectator may be bewildered by the random act of violence performed by the group of children at the conclusion of the film.

Certainly, Mazzetti, as a free artist in this film movement, could address whatever to whomever she wanted. But to single out members of a community for the topic of a story would certainly interest members of that community, and that is a consideration that should have been taken. Perhaps it was because the film comes so close to being an inclusive text for both deaf and hearing audiences that the appended auditory signals that privilege the hearing spectators in a story about deafness appears to be discriminatory and exclusive.

Previous studies on Free Cinema typically evaluate the body of short films as a whole without fully acknowledging the uniqueness of *Together* with its fictional narrative, presentation of deafness, and its exercise in manipulating sound and image to predominantly include two types of spectating positions. Though the film is constructed in many ways to include both deaf and hearing audiences, the content and form of *Together* favors one spectating position to the point of excluding the other. The film reveals more about the hearing community's audist assumptions and fears regarding deafness than it does about deaf identities.

REFERENCES

Arnheim, Rudolph. *Film as Art*. Berkley: University of California, 1957.

Baker-Shenk, Charlotte, and Dennis Cokely. *American Sign Language: A Teacher's Resource Text on Grammar and Culture*. 1980. Washington DC: Gallaudet University, 1996.

Barnouw, Erik. Documentary: *A History of the Non-fiction Film*. 2nd Revised ed. 1974. Oxford: Oxford University, 1993.

Bicycle Thieves. Dir. Vittorio De Sica. Ente Nazionale Industrie Cinematografiche (ENIC), 1948.

Cannes Festival. Online Archive. *Together* (1956). 20 Mar 2008.
    <http://www.festival-cannes.com/index.php/en/archives/film/3654>

Crash of Silence or Mandy. Dir. Alexander Mackendrick. General Film Distributors (GFD), 1952.
Dyer, Richard. *The Matter of Images: Essays on Representation*. 2nd Ed. 1993. London: Routledge, 2002.
Freeburg, Victor Oscar. *The Art of Photoplay Making*. New York: Macmillan, 1918.
Heart is a Lonely Hunter, The. Dir. Robert Ellis Miller. Perf. Alan Arkin. Warner Brothers/Seven Arts, 1968.
Lambert, Gavin. "Free Cinema." *As Found: The Discovery of the Ordinary*. Claude Lichtenstein and Thomas Schregenberger. Eds. English ed. Baden, Switzerland: Lars Muller, 2001.
Lambert, Gavin. "Notes on the British Cinema." *The Quarterly of Film Radio and Television*, Berkeley: University of California.Vol. 11, No. 1. (Autumn, 1956), pp. 1-13.
Lane, Harlan. *The Mask of Benevolence: Disabling the Deaf Community*. New York: Vintage, 1993.
Lichtenstein, Claude and Thomas Schregenberger. Eds. *As Found: The Discovery of the Ordinary*. English ed. Baden, Switzerland: Lars Muller, 2001.
Lovell, Alan. "The Unknown Cinema of Britain." *Cinema Journal*. Austin: University of Texas. Vol. 11, No. 2. (Spring, 1972), pp. 1-8.
Lovell, Alan, and Jim Hillier. *Studies in Documentary*. New York: Viking, 1972.
Momma Don't Allow. Dir. Karel Reisz and Tony Richardson. British Film Institute, 1955.
O Dreamland. Dir. Lindsay Anderson. British Film Institute, 1953.
Rome, Open City. Dir. Roberto Rossellini. Minerva Film SpA, 1945.
Schuchman, John S. *Hollywood Speaks: Deafness and the Film Entertainment Industry*. Urbana: University of Illinois, 1988.
Small is Beautiful: The Story of the Free Cinema Films Told by Their Makers. Dir. Cristophe Dupin. British Film Institute, 2006.
Szaloky, Melinda. "Sounding Images in Silent Film: Visual Acoustics in Murnau's Sunrise." *Cinema Journal*. Austin: University of Texas. Vol. 41, No. 2. (Winter, 2002), pp. 109-131.
Thursday's Children. Dir. Lindsay Anderson and Guy Breton. British Information Service, 1954.
Together. Dir. Lorenza Mazzetti. British Film Institute, 1956.
Zavattini, Cesare. "Some Ideas on the Cinema." *Film: A Montage of Theories*. Richard Dyer MacCann, ed. New York: Dutton, 1966.

Kendall Green:
An Enduring Legacy

KEITH GAMACHE, JR.

KENDALL GREEN IS THE NAME OF THE PROPERTY THAT GALLAUDET University is situated on. It also houses the Laurent Clerc National Deaf Education Center that includes the Kendall Demonstration Elementary School and the Model Secondary School for the Deaf. The campus is considered a Deaf Mecca because of what it represents to the people of the Deaf World. The title was previously reserved for American School for the Deaf (ASD) in Hartford, Connecticut, the birthplace of American Sign Language and early Deaf education. When the Columbia Institution and Gallaudet College grew in popularity, its role expanded, and ASD slowly stepped back. Kendall Green is also not the Deaf Mecca owing to the differing perspectives of deaf communities who maintained that there are many other "centers" across the country and in the world.

I became interested in this project when the Unity for Gallaudet (UFG) protest began in May 2006. I was a witness to the protests from its inception to its conclusion. I observed many dialogues between students, faculty, staff, and administrators in their attempts to define the university. I became disturbed when I came across students discussing that Edward Miner Gallaudet didn't serve the needs of the Deaf and thereby discrediting his many accomplishments. I also noticed that many people were not familiar with Gallaudet's history. I searched the university bookstore and the archives to see if they have a comprehensive and contemporary history of Gallaudet University in print. I was surprised to learn that none existed, leaving only books that were either outdated or those that reflected only a small part of the whole picture. It became my challenge to tackle this monumental task of collecting information and to publish a work in an attempt to define this Mecca, the one we call Gallaudet.

Five hundred hours of research time was spent in the Gallaudet University Archives poring through newspapers, documents, and other related memorabilia (also known as Gallaudetiana). Sources were cited from the following: American Annals of the Deaf, The Deaf American, On the Green, The Buff and Blue, The Silent Worker, and The Silent World. It was no easy task. The college newspaper, The Buff and Blue, for instance, was kept in circulation since 1892. I also gathered information from the following books: Gallaudet College: 100 Years by Albert Atwood, Gallaudet College: 1857-1907 by Edward M. Gallaudet, Deaf Heritage by Jack Gannon, The Gallaudet Almanac by W. Edington, D. Peikoff, H-D. Baumert, and J. Gannon, The Gallaudet College Centennial Commemorative Edition (produced by the Gallaudet College Alumni Association), and Gallaudet yearbooks.

KENDALL GREEN GEOGRAPHY

When a person thinks of Gallaudet, an image of the Tower Clock immediately comes to mind. A probable explanation comes from the old entrance near the gatehouse on Florida Avenue. It was the only entrance in the old days and you see Tower Clock the first thing when you enter the campus. As the college grew, the campus closed that particular gate and opened four others. They are called the Florida Avenue entrance, the Seventh Avenue entrance, the MSSD entrance, and the KDES entrance. When you enter Gallaudet from the current Florida Avenue entrance, you see Fowler Hall instead of the Tower Clock. The front portion of the campus is called the "historical district" of Gallaudet University. Fowler Hall is one of the three connecting buildings along with Chapel Hall and College Hall on the left. As you walk on the terrace or the corridors of Chapel Hall, you can only wonder about its eyes looking upon thousands upon thousands of students who obtained academic knowledge here. There was a story back in the Sixties that the Tower Clock was relied as an alarm clock for the surrounding communities. One day it ceased to function in its proper order and the neighborhood was thrown into chaos. It appears that those people decided to get their own alarm clocks instead.

The first bird's eye view drawing of Kendall Green was made in 1857 detailing frame houses on the property built by the owner, Amos Kendall. It included the Kendall Mansion that was situated on Knob Hill, now home to Ballard North and West dormitory buildings. There was another drawing in 1885 detailing the institution with the outcropping of new buildings and changing landscape. The first known aerial photo of the campus grounds was taken in 1922. A third of the estate was still woodland. In the most recent aerial photos, the whole campus was engulfed with buildings and the surrounding communities were already established. It is so different from the old days when there was nothing between Kendall Green and the Government Accountability Office (located two blocks west of Union Station). Gallaudet went through certain building stages starting with the said Historical District. The Greater Gallaudet Era during the Fifties and the Sixties brought a massive building program on campus. Dormitories, KDES, and MSSD began to appear more intensely in the Seventies and the Eighties. There are a lot of new buildings that replaced old ones, with continuous improvements being made today.

The 1885 aerial drawing of Kendall Green was missing Thomas Gallaudet/Alice Cogswell statue in front of Chapel Hall. That is because the statue didn't exist, only to appear four years later. There were orchards, farms, and livestock all over campus. They were eventually abolished to make way for a more academic setting, marking a change from a trade-oriented program to a liberal arts program. The 1885 map included Houses 5 and 6 (part of the Faculty Row) that doesn't exist today. They were demolished to make way for a parking lot. Commodius (a laboratory building north of Chapel Hall), Farm House (northeast of Kendall Mansion), and several other farm-related buildings appear on the map. When farming was removed from the curriculum in 1945, the structures that supported it slowly faded into oblivion. The Commodius was removed to mark the landscape design similar to the Capitol Mall. There weren't any established fields for athletic sports like football, track, baseball, or tennis back then. However, the college of years past allowed students to roam the landscape with untold adventures.

NAMES OF BUILDINGS

The names of Kendall Green changed over time. When Amos Kendall took over the reins over the defunct school for the deaf and blind in the District of Columbia area in 1856, he endeavored to create his own school that was later known as the "Columbia Institution." The National Deaf Mute College was created in 1864 out of necessity for higher education; its creation was approved by Congress and signed by U.S. President Abraham Lincoln. The Columbia Institution was informally changed to The Kendall School in 1885 when the Kendall School building was built on campus north of Fowler Hall. In this sense, the institution functioned two separate departments, the primary department and the collegiate department. After a heated debate between the students and the faculty, the college changed its name to Gallaudet College in 1894. There were discussions to name the college Clerc

College at some point. However, the school name was still recorded as an institution until 1957 when it was changed into Gallaudet College. In the same year, Gallaudet College obtained its first accreditation, vaulting itself, making the Kendall School a part of its program instead of a dual existence. The mission of the Kendall School was expanded nationally with the creation of Kendall Demonstration Elementary School in 1969 and Model Secondary School for the Deaf in 1970. Graduate Studies were implemented in 1964, thus paving the way for the college to receive its university status later in 1986.

AMOS KENDALL

Kendall Green's first benefactor was Amos Kendall. Raised in Massachusetts, he graduated from a law school to practice law. He was inclined in politics and was an advocate of Jacksonian democracy. He became a member of Andrew Jackson's cabinet as a postmaster general. He operated a newspaper called the "Kendall Expositor" which circulated in the District of Columbia area. Making his stay in the political circle of Washington, Amos Kendall bought the Brentwood Farm in 1841 that was hereafter known as Kendall Green (it is also sometimes called Garlic Grounds). Because of a strong garlic presence, it took years to root out the taste in crops, even cow's milk, whose diet was tied to grass in the land. Kendall invested in the telegraph business with Samuel Morse and garnered a fortune that launched his philanthropist efforts in the last years of his life. Kendall became a trustee for a district house for the deaf and the blind that only failed after a year. Kendall took charge of the five deaf orphans by adopting them and sought to provide education for them by creating the institution. He was actively involved in the school and the community upon his death in 1869. He entrusted the future of the school to Edward Miner Gallaudet and his able assistants.

Kendall originally allowed two of the boarding houses to be used for the school. The operating costs of the school were funded through the government. The two dwelling buildings were called The Stickney House (known as the Rose Cottage) and The Kendall House. William Stickney (for which the house was named after) was a son-in-law of Kendall and helped operate the school as a board of director. Funded by Kendall, The new school building was the first erected building for the school in 1859 that annexed itself with the old Kendall House. The Rose Cottage was then used for the college before being demolished to make way for Chapel Hall and its terrace. The old Fowler Hall was built piecemeal around the new school building thus demolishing the old Kendall House. Stickney House is called Rose Cottage because a bed of roses was in between the two dwelling houses in the early days. There used to be a first playground between the present Fowler Hall and Dawes House. Kendall School didn't expand further until 1952 when segregated buildings were built for black students only to have it scrapped two years later. The school functioned in different buildings until KDES and MSSD were constructed.

The first five orphaned students that were taken in care by Amos Kendall were William H. Blood, John Quinn, James Henry, Isaac Winn, and Annie Szymanoskie. Blood left Washington after he finish school to work in the cabinet business. Quinn went through college, dropped out, and lived in Baltimore. He was known as the first person that established the flag tradition at Kendall Green. Henry died in the 1870s in a streetcar accident. Winn was mentioned to have graduated from the college in 1870, though there was no more information given. Annie's background was more extensive because Edward M. Gallaudet made mention of her in one of his addresses that was preserved. She was one of the few female students who entered college though she lasted only a year. She eventually worked for the government, married to a deaf man, and died soon afterward.

EDWARD MINER GALLAUDET

The dream of having a college for the deaf was envisioned by Edward Miner Gallaudet. The faculty members at the American School may have influenced him for the Deaf (ASD). ASD is known to have a "high class" program, something in between high school and college. When Edward became a superintendent of the institution, he campaigned for a college education on campus. At first, Amos Kendall disputed that Edward was a dreamer in this regard. Raised and schooled by his parents, Thomas Hopkins Gallaudet and Sophia Fowler, he gained ambition and understanding towards deaf education. He pursued college studies at Trinity College in Hartford, Connecticut. He was hired to work at ASD for two years before being snatched up by Kendall for the Columbia Institution. By this time, Edward was only twenty years old and single. It would not be until 1911 when he retired and returned to his hometown at Hartford.

Edward proved to be a tireless leader advocating for the rights of the deaf in education. He gave his time, talents, and his life to cement the foundations of the schools on Kendall Green. He wrestled with many prominent politicians of Washington to get enough support to secure the necessary appropriations for the future of the institution. He toured Europe a few times gathering information about and support for deaf education. He wove a strong web of connection between Columbia and many other deaf institutions across the country, thus drawing qualified students for the college.

He married twice and had six children, however, he was able to ingrain his family with the school. He was considered a master storyteller and a skilled "sign-maker" by many of his former students and deaf colleagues. He was one of the most revered figures in the deaf community during the latter end of his life. Edward explained to several people that in order for him to become an articulate speaker in a procession at the school, he has to practice his signs in front of a mirror. He saw deaf people as equals, not only by opinion, but he acted on it by his interaction at many social functions. He brought Kendall Green to national prominence through his 53 years of service.

With some opposition from Congress, the college was chartered in 1864 to begin conferring college degrees to deaf candidates. The college started with five students and three faculty members. John Carlin, a noted deaf artist, received the first honorary degree from the college in 1864. It was not until two years later when Melville Ballard was the first college graduate. A graduate of ASD, he worked as a teacher at Columbia while pursuing his degree and eventually a masters' degree in 1870. He was one of the oldest teachers who taught for a span of 52 years at Kendall School, still teaching until his death. He noted that when he started college, he was the only student for several months. Students began to stream in to the number of thirteen at the end of the first year. He recalled two female students, Annie Szymanoskie and Annie Sparks in his first year. The faculty of the college was inconsistent in its first ten years.

The first two instructors were Richard Storrs and Roswell Parish who left only after a year. Succeeding instructors include the following: John Chickering (natural science), Amos Draper (math), Edward Fay (history and ancient languages), Edward Gallaudet (moral and political science), Joseph Gordon (mathematics and chemistry), A.B. Greener, John Hotchkiss (English language and literature), John Patterson (astronomy), Samuel Porter (mental science and philosophy), Lewellyn Pratt (math and natural science), and James Spencer (math and physiology). Hotchkiss became the first alumni that became a faculty of the college. Gallaudet, Fay, and Hotchkiss made up the famously known "We Never Die" group. The group accumulated 151 years of service at the college (43 for Gallaudet, 52 for Hotchkiss, and 56 for Fay). Draper, Gordon, Gallaudet, Hotchkiss, and Fay were also recognized and recorded in a 1913 National Association of the Deaf's "Preservation of Sign" video collection.

FEATURES OF KENDALL GREEN

Kendall Green included buildings that were erected in different periods of Gallaudet history. The Historical District (buildings prior to 1895) included

Chapel Hall, College Hall, Fowler Hall, Dawes House, Kendall Hall, Ole Jim, President's Residence and the Faculty Row. Chapel Hall was designed to be a public hall and a refectory. It evolved to become a social center among other functions. The building attained national historical landmark status in 1966. Inside the halls included the popular Gallaudet Hall of Fame until 1972 when it was removed due to renovation. Only portraits and busts of Gallaudet presidents and prominent leaders that had supported the school now existed. The room has a doorway to the Tower Clock annex. The staircase is covered with graffiti of the names of the college students spanning many decades. It is currently restricted because of concerns to its stability. The Tower Clock is one of the 27 sites in the Washington, D.C. area to be allowed to fly the flag night and day. The first College Hall (or the East Wing) on the left was originally built in 1868. The second College Hall was made in 1877 in response to rapid growth of the college. The college adapted its school colors from having the buff and blue tiles in College Hall that was placed in honor of the Civil War Union soldiers. The building also has an intriguing "coffin door" on the south that spurred many legends.

The Bison Statue

College Hall's' "coffin door"

Fowler Hall

The Old Fowler Hall (honoring the institution's first matron, Sophia Fowler) was demolished in 1919 because of unsafe safety conditions following the College Hall fire of 1910. The present Fowler Hall architecture reflected the old one with its somewhat odd dimensions. Presidents of the college and their families dwelt at the President's Residence (or House One) over the years. On the right is a line of faculty residences called "The Faculty Row." The original row included seven houses; now only three remain. They include the Ballard House, the Fay House, and the Dennison House that were built between 1867 and 1875. Ole Jim, of Queen Anne design, was so named because of how deaf students pronounced "Old Gym." Erected in 1880, it housed the second oldest indoor swimming pool in the United States, next to Harvard University. It functioned as a social and cultural center for the students at the college after College Hall and before the present Student Academic Center. It was eventually remodeled and converted into the Peikoff Alumni House.

College Hall

There were some items of interest in the president's office in College Hall that merit storytelling. The office displayed one of the first doorbells used in the dormitory rooms of college hall. That was before the invention of the doorbell lights that didn't occur until 1976. There also stood a display of a mace made of wood and decorative silver with Tower Clock on the top demonstrating the authority of the college. The mace was symbolically designed in 1969 to include three types of wood — one from American School for the Deaf, one from the Tower Clock staircase, and one from a 16th century church in Feuges, France where L'Epee had served. Next, a display of an iron dog was meant to illustrate Diamond, a tan and gray terrier (or the English Toy Terrier) who was considered the first mascot of the college. Owned by Mr. Wright in 1888, Diamond became a comfort and a guardian to the students of Kendall Green. Being a favorite of Dr. Gallaudet himself, the dog was present to many football games and social gatherings. Countless class and organizational pictures include the statue on the steps of Chapel Hall.

Statue of Alice Cogswell

The Thomas Hopkins Gallaudet/Alice Cogswell statue was created by Daniel Chester French. He was the same sculptor that created the Lincoln statue for the Lincoln Memorial and the Garfield Memorial in Chapel Hall. Commissioned for the job, he negotiated with Gallaudet to have the statue right on where an apple tree once stood. Gallaudet refused to remove the tree for the sake of his children who played there. Incidentally, a lightning strike destroyed the tree. French won the argument stating that it is the will of the heavens. However, he had to extend his work because he made mistakes on the legs of the statue due to distractions of a wedding engagement for another year. The Edward Miner Gallaudet statue north of Chapel Hall was established in 1969 through the college alumni. Here is the only known college to have two statues of father and son in the same college.

The Edward Miner Gallaudet statue north of Chapel Hall (established in 1969)

The Gallaudet/Cogswell statue at Chapel Hall

As the college grew, traditions began to emerge with chiseled class memories in 1869. Ivy was planted next on the ground below the engravings. Only seven such inscriptions survived the ravages of time on the walls of College Hall and Chapel Hall in diverse places. The last surviving one was in 1879. The buildings were later covered with ivy coming from those class ivies. It was later removed because its spread posed a threat to the building. Instead of ivies and inscriptions, students decided to place class slabs and trees on campus. Spring break trips by the students and the faculty began in 1869 attending the nearby Great Falls between Virginia and Maryland on the Potomac. Juniors began a tradition called "Cremation of Mechanics" which eventually ceased in 1897. They detested a course called mechanics and reveled in its demise with a very detailed ceremony. It was replaced with Junior Promenade (Prom, for short). It is a very possibility that the ceremony spurred future rat funeral activities. Since 1890 succeeding graduating classes evolved their differing ways to celebrate their college experience. Past traditions led to the present rat funerals, slab day, banner day, tree day, and a senior trip.

Gallaudet College went through a lot of changes during Edward Gallaudet's tenure. Co-education allowing female students in the college started in 1887. The Normal School or training of teachers for the deaf was created in 1892 to meet the demands for teachers on the national level. The college shifted from a manual school to a combined method instruction including sign and articulation. It may have saved the school from being swallowed whole by the oralist establishment. The college at one time exhibited feelings that they were the last bastions using sign language in education in a sea of opposing ideologies. The college was also threatened with railroad tracks in the middle of campus in 1895 only to have it averted with the founding of Union Station nearby. Of the many student experiences at Gallaudet one in particular deserves mention here. Amos Draper, one of the faculty members at the college, went berserk one morning when he found a cow in his classroom. Mischievous students crept through the night and snatched the animal from the college farm. The classroom was off limits for a few days until a thorough cleansing could be made.

ATHLETICS

Gallaudet athletics began with Kendall Baseball Club in 1867. The players (also known as the Nines) played against many other prominent teams and on such grounds like the one at the White House. Kendall Athletic Association was eventually created to manage a growing number of sports that were starting to encroach with each other. The name was changed to Gallaudet Athletic Association in 1894 when the college name was changed. GWAA (Women's association) was established in 1911 to address concerns to women's sports only to be disbanded in 1933 when both men's and women's organizations were merged into one. Sports events were first placed in the Rose Cottage, Ole Jim, Hughes Gym, and then the current Field House. Mascots began with Diamond with a succession of a number of dogs in the next few decades. Mascots changed hands with the Blues, Blue Bisons, and currently Bisons since being officially recognized by the college in 1957. The current Gallaudet Bison Song could be derived from its original roots in 1886. There were different adaptations until 1960 when Dorothy Miles, a student at the time, coined the now famous song.

Gallaudet football began as a Gallafukindet rugby club in 1874. It evolved into the Kendall Eleven in 1883. Faculty members John Chickering and John Hotchkiss both were credited for bringing football to the college. Uniforms were red flannel shirts and with knitted caps along with knickerbockers. The traditional molly-coddle clash (football games among freshmen and sophomores) continued the sport's popularity. Track emerged with the Hare and Hounds Club of 1880. It is a combination of cross-country running and a game. From its roots sprouted track, field, and cross-country for both men and women. Women students brought basketball to the college because they couldn't play outdoors initially. The story about the Five Iron Men was one of the legendary basketball stories at the college. The last seeded team in a tournament, Gallaudet's five players played three straight games without replacements to win the conference championship in 1944. Wrestling was brought to Gallaudet due to some players who could not compete in football. Thomas Clayton, a coach for 31 years, brought his wrestlers to many championships. Gallaudet also included volleyball, cycling, tennis, golf, intramural activities, soccer, swimming, and hockey.

CAMPUS LEADERSHIP ORGANIZATIONS

Gallaudet provided avenues for students to exhibit their creativity and leadership potential through various organizations. One of the first was The Buff and Blue. It functioned as a literary magazine and a newspaper for more than 100 years. Student Body Government began as a financial department and then a joint administration connecting students with the college administration. Initial concerns included dating hours, revival of a football team, and reducing types of punishments. The Tower Clock, which began as a Senior Annual in 1912, continued a series of unforgettable memories recorded in a book since 1941. In those pages lies thousands upon thousands of pictures defining the Gallaudet experience of students past and present. Fraternities and Sororities played a big part of campus culture, fostering a sense of identity, unity, and empowerment. Societies began with Kappa Gamma (also known as HOSS and Xi Phi Sigma) and Phi Kappa Zeta (also known as OWLS) and eventually led to new societies to the present day. Special interest organizations captivated Gallaudet at one time or another through its history with the example of Saturday Night Dramatics Club and Jollity Club. They are both men's and women's drama clubs since they do not mix in the old days.

PRESIDENTS OF GALLAUDET UNIVERSITY

Percival Hall
Percival Hall carried the mantle of Edward Miner Gallaudet as the second president at Gallaudet, leading the college for the next 35 rough years. A graduate of the normal department, a player on the Kendall football team, he was also a friend to the deaf community. He focused on developing a liberal arts education and adding various branches of learning. He helped create the financial aid department in 1925. However, the college struggled with stagnant growth through two world wars. Alumni members remarked that during this administration there was a declining presence of signing faculty. Sign language became almost nonexistent in residential schools and many students were not prepared for the rigorous study at the college. Dur-

ing Hall's tenure, there was a high rate of dropouts, and many students didn't possess a minimum level of English mastery. Prospective candidates also view their limited career choices being veered from education to trade jobs. We cannot leave this era without mentioning Douglas Craig, black deaf orphan raised at the institution. Craig worked all his life at Gallaudet and was beloved by students and faculty. He was a man of all trades who was also known as a master of mechanics and a trickster.

Leonard Elstad

Leonard Elstad followed Hall's steps in 1945 as the third president of the college. He ushered the "Greater Gallaudet" era. It included a massive building program with nineteen new structures on campus. He led program developments and services to make the students' college experience more feasible. Enrollment skyrocketed fivefold from two hundred at end of Hall's tenure to 1,000. Elstad was the last in a series of presidents who had a background with the deaf people prior to coming to Gallaudet until Irving King Jordan. A graduate of the normal department, he became a teacher and then a principal of the Kendall School. He led the Minnesota School for the Deaf at the time he became president of the college. His first test was to battle the National Capital Park organization to have the college remain on Kendall Green, instead of moving south. He fought for greatness of the school not by building, but modernizing the curriculum. Agriculture was abolished in favor for more research-based programs. The college's accreditation status in 1957 was a mixed success because it promoted two contradictory sides: recognition of a legitimate educational institution for the deaf but bringing in faculty and administrators who knew little or none about deaf people.

Gallaudet became research-oriented with its first research department in 1937. Future research and support led to national research foundations in deaf education with KDES and MSSD. Sign language began to be viewed as a research subject with the establishment of Linguistics Research Lab in 1971. Gallaudet Research Institute, created in 1978, led the college with research priorities connecting to deaf people that continue to the present day. National Deaf Education Network and Clearinghouse (now known as Laurent Clerc national Deaf Education Center since 1999) was created in 1980 to create an accurate centralized source of information regarding to deaf education. Center on Deafness was set up in 1980. The Laurent Clerc National Deaf Educational Center was founded in 1999. Because of its research interests and mountains of data, the university became internationally recognized as a center of knowledge pertaining to deaf people.

When Merrill retired in 1969, the college revolved through the following presidents: Edward Merrill (1969–1983), Lloyd Johns (1983), Jerry Lee

(1983–1987), Elizabeth Zinser (1988), Irving King Jordan (1988–2006), and Robert Davila (2007–present). Merrill came from the University of Tennessee where he was a professor and a dean. Jerry Lee was a professor of Gallaudet for 13 years when he was asked to be interim president after Johns. Zinser was a professor at North Carolina when she started at Gallaudet briefly in 1988. Robert Davila created a new milestone being the first alumni to become a president of the college. During those leadership changes, Gallaudet went through social changes as well. Social centers Rathskellar and Abbey popped up in 1971 serving food, games, and entertainment. Co-ed dorms were allowed in 1973. A new post-office substation was placed in Student Union Building since 1974. Academic Bowl became popular among college students, leading to university academic bowls and high school academic bowls. In a sense, they celebrate the ingenuity and intelligence of deaf people in an academic setting from so many different places. Though an exchange program existed since 1971, Hearing Undergraduate Program (HUG) first admitted students at Gallaudet since 2001.

SIGN LANGUAGE ON KENDALL GREEN

The use of sign language has always brought headlines at Gallaudet. During the early days, they are called the language of signs, the picture language, the sign-maker, or the slang-signer. The first mention of sign language classes was given by Elizabeth Peet in 1921 out of concern on the deterioration of signs from students who entered the college. There was a flurry of correspondence from newspaper articles starting in 1937 regarding the use of substandard signs on campus. Written papers first appeared in 1957 citing that sign language by the faculty ceased to be a guiding force for the students. However, sign language went through a linguistic study by William Stokoe that produced a publication in 1960 discussing its findings. The first known sign dictionary called "Sign Text" was published by Gallaudet in 1966. However, students and faculty continued to express their struggles with ASL recognition for many years to come.

The Sign Communication Proficiency Inventory (SCPI) was first introduced in 1971 in response of concerns about faculty members who cannot sign. Gallaudet hosted its first sign language conference in 1974 addressing various related topics. The ASL Proficiency Inventory (ASLPI) was created in 2005 in design to look at ASL language features. Gallaudet now has various branches of study in American Sign Language, Deaf Studies, Interpreting, and Linguistics.

Gallaudet also produced many breakthroughs that we take for granted today. Edwin Nies of the Class of 1911 became the first Gallaudet graduate to obtain a doctorate (in dentistry) in 1914. Boyce Williams was the first deaf board of trustee for Gallaudet in 1950. The first counseling center (now known as Academic Advising) began in 1960. Eleven deaf students were first admitted into the graduate school of education in 1962 when prospects for deaf teachers began to improve. The college received its computers during the same year. Computers evolved to the VAX systems to the more modern computers with Internet access and networking. New Student Orientation began in 1968 in promotion to smooth the transition experience for new students. Classes began to produce class jerseys in 1972. Email systems were created on campus starting in 1979. TDD pay phones were installed on campus beginning in 1990. Skytel pagers were the rage on campus in 1997 producing many diverse technological gadgets that are present. Videophones made a permanent indentation on campus recently and transformed the preferred dialogue between the printed word and the visual screen. Campus features grew more prominent with various services including Gallaudet University Press, Consortium of the DC Area, Mental Health Center, Library/Archives, to name a few.

The list is endless. What has been discussed is just a fraction of what is in store. Two revolutions within twenty years of each other on campus had transformed Gallaudet to define its mission more clearly and to serve the needs of the deaf community better today and in the future. This work will be a memorial to reflect the symbols the university had been, now is, and will be to the people who get its influence. Such is the legacy of Kendall Green, the Mecca of the Deaf World.

Iconicity, Social Types, and Referent Projections in ASL

TERRA EDWARDS

WHILE QUESTIONS ABOUT ICONICITY ARE FOUND THROUGHOUT THE sign language literature, what it means for a form to be iconic is often taken as relatively self-evident. Sandler and Lillo-Martin use the term to mean "a direct or transparent relation between form and meaning" (2006:496). They assume that as far as spoken languages are concerned, linguistic signs have an arbitrary relationship to their referents. They state however, that "Sign languages are indeed different. They have gestural origins and are perceived visually, both of which contribute to pervasive motivatedness in form at the level of the sign" (p. 496).

Direct relations between form and meaning are not only taken to be self-evident, but also natural in the sense that iconic forms are assumed to reproduce natural aspects of a given world external to language in relatively uncomplicated ways. Senghas, et. al. in their study of the origin of Nicaraguan Sign Language clearly articulate this assumption in stating that,

> "...[N]on-linguistic representations such as maps and paintings derive their structure iconically, from their referent... Unlike language, such nonlinguistic representations are typically analog and holistic" (2004:1780).

In examining iconic representations of motion events, they state that, "such gestures (unlike speech) are fully available to deaf observers, likely providing raw materials to shape into a sign language" (ibid). In these treatments of iconicity, there are two domains considered: the world, which is taken to be natural, concrete, and self-evident; and language, which is taken to be abstract and arbitrary. Although this approach takes formal structure into account, it neglects the social and historical activity out of which iconic forms have arisen, as well as the ideological motivatedness of iconic signs (Hanks 1996:230-8)[1]. Resemblances are often deeply cultural, and bodies are not homogeneous within any given culture. Rather, they are disciplined by institutions through which individuals are socially ordered and stratified, such as military or educational institutions that, "[obtain] holds upon it at the level of the mechanism itself- movements, gestures, attitudes..." (Foucault, 1975:137). Institutions leave their mark on the way bodies move, and to some degree or another, we are able, as social beings to recognize those movements in our readings and others' retellings of social scenes.

Counter to the idea that iconically motivated forms are 'natural input' on a unidirectional path toward arbitrary linguistic structure, is the idea that iconic forms rely on a kind of resemblance that involves cultural and arbitrary relations to begin with. Resemblance, in terms of both expression and perception, involves an analytic process whereby parts of something are juxtaposed to another disassembled object. This is different than assuming that iconic forms involve a direct replication of a "holistic" object. Furthermore, which parts are chosen and whether they resemble each other can often only be understood in culturally relevant terms. As Sandler and Lillo-Martin point out, "The ability to select the salient aspect, to make iconically motivated representations of it with parts of our own bodies (the hands), and to understand and conventionalize these representations, is abstract in the sense that it is symbolic. Our ability to symbolize at will in this way appears to be uniquely human" (2006:499).

Although they make this observation, they continue to dichotomize the more formally fluid dimensions of language such as mimetic facial expressions and gestures and "abstract," "linear" linguistic structure. With respect to the face, they note, "As referent projections use the body to represent animate beings, they are more mimetic and less abstract..." (p. 506). They assume that "as a sign language 'ages' it begins to develop the kind of morphology more typically found in spoken languages: morphology that is both arbitrary and sequential" (ibid). I would like to call into question the assumption that mimetic facial expressions should necessarily be considered less abstract than other dimensions of signed languages, as well as the expectation that iconic forms including mimetic facial expressions should disappear as signed languages age.

Pietrandrea (2003), although she does not include movement or any non-manual aspects, examines iconicity and arbitrariness in Italian Sign Language. She notes that even at the basic level of formational parameters, ISL makes wide use of iconic relations. An example she uses is the sign NAPKIN, which is articulated with a flat hand (the shape of a napkin) on the mouth (the location where napkins are prototypically thought to be useful). So both parameters of handshape and location for this sign show a high degree of iconicity. However, she notes that, "In spite of the high degree of iconicity, the LIS lexicon is characterized by a deep arbitrariness. First, the iconicity present in the lexical organization is phonemized, that is the depicting of referents can be conveyed only by the few phonological patterns the language allows" (2002:312).

In addition, "given a formational parameter, it is not possible to predict the formational parameter's meaning because it is not possible to predict which aspect of its form will be used for the expressive purpose. In the same way, it is not possible to predict which sign will be used to express any given referent (Klima and Belugi 1979) because it is not possible to predict which aspects of the referent will be selected for linguistic purposes" (Pietrandrea, 2002:314-15). In addition, cultural meaning attributed to physical forms can be represented iconically. An example given is the sign BIRTHDAY, which is articulated at the ear. In Italy there is a tradition of pulling someone's ear for every year they have lived (p. 308). These points illustrate nicely some of the interplay between iconicity and arbitrariness, as well as the role of culture in producing resemblances.

I am interested in extending this kind of analysis to features of ASL articulated with the face, in the production of referent projections. It has been assumed that grammaticalization in ASL entails a transition from iconic to arbitrary forms (Frischberg, 1979). Referent projections, being mimetic uses of the face, can be located on the more iconic and more "emergent"[2] edge of language near things like gesture as opposed to the more fixed, more "schematic" end of the spectrum like many manual lexemes, or grammaticalized non-manual features, such as marking basic grammatical relations with eye gaze. In everyday interaction, these more iconic, emergent forms are used with great frequency and therefore might be expected to tend over time toward arbitrariness.

However, it is possible that they continue to exist precisely for the attributes that those ambiguous realms tending toward categories like gesture lend to discourse functions. Further, to conceive of this realm as closer to nature is misleading. As Hanks argues, "This proximal zone of an activity has the appearance of concreteness, but it is a false appearance. The relation between an agent, the agent's body, the location of action, and the conventional categories of language and gesture is a social construction par excellence" (1990:7). Despite claims that in nascent sign languages, gesture provides raw input to the linguistic system which will become more arbitrary as it becomes more 'linguistic' (Senghas, et.al, 2004), iconicity remains pervasive in conventional sign languages such as ASL.

The data I will present in this paper suggests that iconic forms do not represent natural origins in a unidirectional flow toward phonologically shortened, semantically bleached, and morphologically bound forms (Hopper and Traugott, 2003). Iconic forms, those that have generally been located on the margins of 'language proper' such as ideophones, gestures, and mimetic (if stylized) facial expressions, I will argue, can be seen not as beginnings which will disappear as they evolve, but as a well maintained linguistic category kept for the usefulness of its fluidity, which can wrap around details of fleeting moments, reproduce and negotiate stereotypes without overt mention of them, and more generally achieve the kinds of subtlety in discourse that more schematic aspects of communicative practice cannot.

In contrast to a notion of arbitrariness that guarantees to society, "the availability of a flexible tool of meaning generation instead of a rigid one tied to extralinguistic depictions" (Pietrandrea, 2002), we could attend to the ways that iconic forms offer a different kind of flexibility that allows language users to do things. This approach moves both activity and ideology from their assumed positions as logical extensions of form, and gives them a constitutive role in our understanding of referent projections, and further, of iconicity in signed languages.

ICONICITY, MODALITY, AND SOCIALITY

Iconicity and modality are linked in crucial ways. Visual modalities lend resources that auditory channels do not. This may be important also in analysis of spoken languages, where attending only to sound can limit our understanding of language and communication at a fundamental level. Haviland points out some of the differences at a very general level applicable to both modalities:

Contrasted with the linear flow of speech units, gesture unfolds in four dimensions, and easily combines multiple simultaneous signing vehicles (gaze, facial expression, posture, as well as hands and other extremities) in a miniature and multifunctional orchestra of expression. Gesture has a dimensionality, a potential persistence, and a spatial immediacy in the context of utterance not similarly available to sound. (2006:1)

So if we take into account the social functions of visually iconic, relatively emergent forms, we would have to move away from arbitrariness as "emancipating" (Haiman, 1980), and see instead different discourse functions for which iconically motivated forms may be more or less useful. Although this gets us no closer to a positive explanation of the origins of language, it may explain why not everything has become arbitrary, shortened, bleached, and bound by now.

Here, I will look at referent projections as an area of American Sign Language where forms that seem to resist incorporation into schematic domains are employed to accomplish things in particular fields of social practice. I will argue that their iconic form is not only motivated, but also motivating in a pragmatic sense, which may be why they remain available as a semiotic resource. If this is the case, taking iconic forms as natural origins in a unidirectional process of grammaticalization is disrupted by considering alternate (social, interactional, and historical) forces at work in the maintenance of structures that 'should be' disappearing if arbitrariness is where all of these resemblances are going.

REFERENT PROJECTIONS

In order for a referent to be projected, the referent must be able to be identified by the addressee. This is accomplished through a mechanism that has been called many things including perspective shift and role shift defined as, "a pervasive aspect of Sign Language communication marked by subtle shifts of gaze and posture that allow the signer to convey the utterances, thoughts or actions of other people." (Hoiting and Slobin, 2002:10). According to Janzen, "Overt perspective-coding options available to ASL signers are numerous. First, the signer's options include potential perspectives equal to the number of participants involved in the action depicted by the particular verb in a given clause." (2004:152). The shifts are marked and decoded through phonological and morphological cues embedded in the verb complex (Janzen, 2004:152). These shifts in perspective require cognitive work on the part of both the signer and the addressee to mentally rotate space throughout a stream of discourse, which can be triggered more overtly though using clusters of phonological and morphological features in concert (such as eye-gaze, head-tilts, and torso shifts) or more subtly using less of those features (Janzen, 2004).

Although the grammatical signals that mark shifts in perspective, and the mimetic use of the face and body are temporally proximate, they are formally and functionally dissimilar. The conflation of the two phenomena has led to limited analyses of the latter, and therefore, the latter is the focus of this paper. While the cues that signal shifts in perspective are grammatical, and are not mimetic, once the referent has been identified, the face can be used mimetically to attribute particular characteristics, attitudes, beliefs, or emotions to that referent. These mimetic uses of the face, or referent projections[3] (RPs) might be considered extralinguistic. However, they seem to be in some ways comparable to categories of spoken language that may be formally liminal, but are linguistic nonetheless, such as ideophones. Some of the formal and semantic evidence for ideophones as a class are their strange phonological behavior, as is the case in Yoruba and Bantu languages (Samarin 1971:136), and in Japanese where palatal consonants occur only in 'mimetic' vocabulary (Hamano 1994:154). They can also exhibit morphological idiosyncrasies. For example, repetition of roots can convey repetition over time and extension in space (Basso 1985:66) or expected affixation patterns might be disrupted (Kita 1997:383-85). In terms of syntax, they tend to be less integrated structurally and 'supplement' the predicate rather than predicating on their own (Nuckolls, 1999:241). They can also be restricted to certain sentence types (Childs 1994:188). In terms of pragmatics, they are often set apart by pauses and prosodic peaks, and their meaning can be 'difficult' because of its specificity and nuanced character (Nuckolls, 1999).

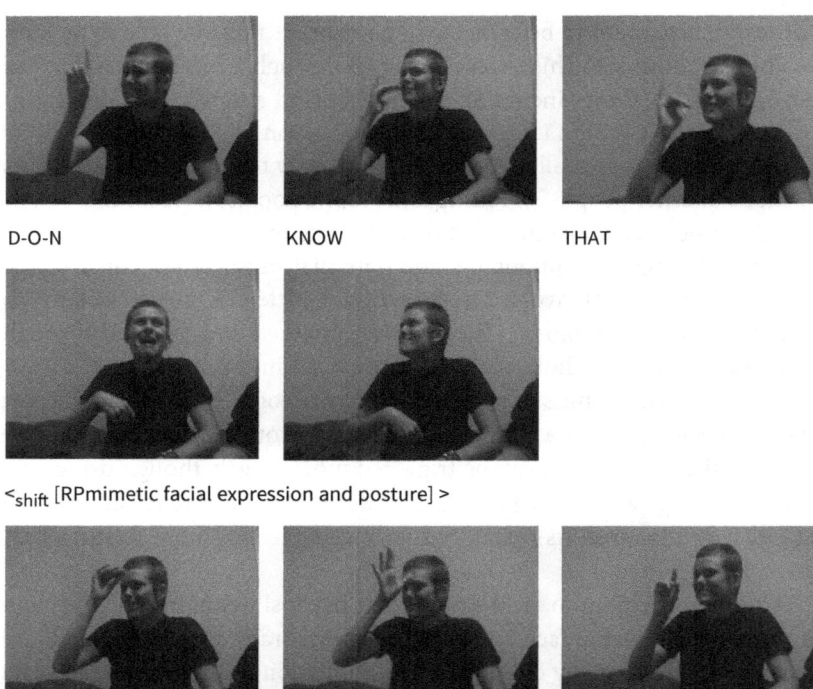

D-O-N   KNOW   THAT

<shift [RPmimetic facial expression and posture] >

BOY   MAN   D-O-N

Rough Translation[4]: You know Don? He's that "looks-like-this" boy man.

Referent projections show some of these same idiosyncrasies. The face in particular, may or may not fit into well-defined formational parameters such as location, orientation, or non-manual features. Rather, the face can be used in highly specific, less-repeatable, and less-stable ways in order to capture details of a remembered or imagined event or person. In the following example, a specific person is indicated by imitating a typical facial expression known to people who have spent time around that person:

In this case, in the second set of frames, the formational parameters of ASL do not seem to be adhered to. The handshape, torso, and mouth, for example, exhibit idiosyncratic, mimetic characteristics that are emergent, as opposed to schematic. In other words, we are not likely to find the non-manual signals in the second row of frames above in multiple contexts, exactly as they appear here. Functionally, however, the facial expression is linguistic in that it has a modifying function, restricting the class "boy/man" to a specific person who "looks like this." One way that RPs are not entirely phonemized, is that they tend to violate restrictions on signing space as can be seen in the following example where Don, once identified, is reported to have taken part in an activity (pounding on a table in frame one, and then waving for the crowd's attention in frame two):

Notice that the signing space (the area of the body that signing is usually restricted to) is greatly extended. In addition, the face, hands, mouth, eyes, and torso, as articulators, are not formed in ways that are fixed (schematic), but rather are wrapping around a remembered, imagined, and stylized retelling of an event (emergent). In the next example, I would like to look at how referent projections can be useful to social actors as forms for conveying very abstract meanings. As I have stated, the fact that they use formally fluid, less-fixed features of the language might be precisely why the category to which they belong is not only maintained, but pervasively so. This troubles an assumption that because they are iconic, they represent a "raw" origin of abstract linguistic structures.

REFERENT PROJECTIONS AND SOCIAL TYPES

In the next narrative, the signer is explaining her experience of coming into the residential school for the Deaf. After years of schooling where the mode of communication was spoken English, she was left without any real command of language (including both spoken and signed codes). When she finally transferred to the school for the Deaf, where the mode of communication was American Sign Language, she had to start over as if she was a child, learning basic language skills. In order to interpret the narrative represented in the clips below, the addressee must be familiar with tensions within the American Deaf community between people like the signer, who do not have early access to language, and are therefore set back in their education, and those who are exposed to language early on, and are therefore more likely to advance quickly in their education. In the frames below, this tension is referred to, using referent projections. The glosses should be read with close attention to the facial expressions and postures in the pictures they are aligned with.

Also important is the use of physical space to represent social space. Following the glosses are translations. Signs that are represented with more than one English word are written as hyphenated strings. The signer, in these frames, is signaling shifts to various perspectives through grammatical cues on the face and body such as eye gaze and posture, as was discussed previously. Each shift in perspective is marked by <SHIFT>. Each RP is marked with [RP]. Lastly, classifier predicates are marked with the following: CL. It should be noted that the perspective taken by the signer is often not identical with the referent indicated by the mimetic use of the face. For example, in the first two frames below, the signer signs SMART-SMART-SMART. She is looking from this outsider's perspective toward a place in space she has established in the previous frame as representing the "smart" category. As is particularly clear in the third frame, the face mimetically indicates a particular manner or attitude that, for our purposes here, we could gloss as "snobby." This attitude is attributed not to the perspective taken by the signer, but the one referred to. Therefore, the referent projection is understood as being projected from a particular social perspective (those who were not exposed to language until later in life).

In (3), the sign ME indicates an actual person (the signer at the time of the reported event), but the RP LOOKING-SNOBBY places this referent within a larger social matrix, visually actualizing social categories. However, these categories are actualized only to have their stability immediately undermined. The face is "mimetic" because in order for the utterance to be interpretable, the addressee must recognize a resemblance between the facial expression and a social type. However, embedded in this resemblance is a visual form of social commentary (or what Hanks calls the "ideological" or "evaluative" aspect of practice). The commentary is understood as coming from a perspective named and established in space earlier in the stream of discourse. This perspective is signaled grammatically through phonological

Iconicity, Social Types, and Referent Projections in ASL

UP-THERE   _{shift} SMART-SMART-SMART

CL-GROUP [RP: shows   _{shift} [RP looking down]
attitude of "smart" group   STUPID DOWN-THERE>
from an outsider perspective>

ME _{shift} HEY!   STUPID? [RP: shows critical   SMART-SMART-SMART?
                            appraisal of being thought of   [RP: shows indignant
                            as "stupid"]   attitude of group made to
                                                             seem "stupid"] >

Translation: "Just because I didn't have language, I was taken to be one of those "stupid kids." But the kids who already knew sign language, and were good at school didn't understand where we were coming from."

Description: The only manual lexemes produced in this utterance are SMART, STUPID, and ME. However, these signs are produced as part of three verb complexes, each one marked by a grammatically signaled shift in perspective. The referent projection is nested in the verbal predicate as a simultaneous, morphologically idiosyncratic form. The entire utterance is difficult to represent in two dimensions, however, I have attempted to capture a useful level of translation for each of the three predicates below. (1) is from the perspective of the "stupid" category, (2) is from the perspective of the "smart" category, and (3) is from the perspective of the "stupid" category again.

(1) (THEY) _{shift}"GO-AROUND-IN-A-GROUP [RPLOOKING-SNOBBY]">
(2) _{shift} "STUPID DOWN-THERE">,
(3) ME _{shift} 'HEY! WE-STUPID? YOU-SMART? >"

and morphological cues embedded in the verb complex (in this case, a simultaneous shift in eye-gaze, head-tilt, and posture, orienting alternately toward the space established as "smart" space, which is physically higher, and that established as "stupid" space, which is physically lower). The manual signs are naming these perspectives as "smart" and "stupid," as well as expressing an "event" or "verb" (the act of looking at, and naming another social category) without which a shift cannot be signaled, and an RP cannot be embedded.

It is important to note that the force of the utterance, in this example, is derived from the mimetic use of the face and body, as well as the metaphorical use of physical space (smart is "up," stupid is "down"). Significance does not accrue to the manual lexemes with the same force as it does to the face and body. In fact, it seems that the force of the utterance is riding on the words more than it is contained in them. Manheim argues that iconicity serves to naturalize "one set of semiotic distinctions by referring it to another that is believed by the speakers to be more basic, essential, outside volitional control, or outside culture " (1999:107). In the example above, however, iconic properties of RPs are used to contest the nature of the "smart"/ "stupid" social distinction that have arisen out of socio-historical processes in residential schools for the Deaf. Therefore, it does not serve to naturalize, but it is effective in contesting naturalized categories because the RP allows the signer to operate in the same formal domain as that which seems natural. Referent projections like the one examined here, offer a semiotic resource that lends itself to projects like this because facial expressions are often taken to be more "basic, essential, outside volitional control, or outside culture" (ibid).

FACES OF THE NEW ECONOMY

The next narrative is taken from an ethnographic interview conducted in the summer of 2006 with Douglas.[5] The man in the narrative is Deaf-Blind, and is a member of the Seattle Deaf-Blind community. In his community people use "Support Service Providers" or "SSPs," who translate visual information in the immediate environment into tactile or visually modified ASL. SSPs are used for activities like grocery shopping, clothes shopping, managing finances at the bank, people-watching, voting, and other practical activities. Over the years, in my involvement in the Seattle Deaf-Blind community, I began to notice that the shortage of SSPs was a growing concern for Deaf-Blind people there.

Prior to the frames you will see below, I asked Douglas for his thoughts on possible causes of this shortage. His feeling was, essentially, that the economy had made it very difficult for people to devote extra time to work that was either not lucrative, or not paid. He compares the effects of the 1984 economy on the numbers of available SSPs to the effects of the 2006 economy on SSP availability through the use of RPs. The first shift is to the perspective of the signer (in 1985), the second shift is to that of SSPs in general (in 1985), and the third shift is to the perspective of the signer at the time of the reported event. The fourth shift is to the perspective of SSPs in general (in 2006), and the fifth shift is to the perspective of the signer at the time of the reported event.

A verb complex is obligatory for a shift in perspective to be accomplished. The referent must be doing something, in order to be doing in a particular way, with a particular manner. However, in the first, second, third, and fourth shifts, there is no manually encoded verb. Instead, the RP mimetically performs an act of speaking, which in English would be marked first with "s/he said," "s/he thought," etc. The reported event in the fifth shift is the signer, at the time of the reported event, "looking" at SSPs in general in the 1980's. The status of this event as actual or not actual is not important at the level of interpretation (also true for the four shifts previous to this one). What is important is the evaluative manner expressed on the face of the signer (along with the manual sign wow), both of which are understood as evaluations or feelings directed at SSPs at that time, because the space associated with them is where the "looking" is directed. In this sense, the verb LOOK-AT has a structural function because it establishes the subject and object of evaluation. The larger event being reported, discursively, is an effect of changes in the economy, which we are meant to understand through this abstract act of looking.

Because the signer uses RPs, as opposed to other semiotic resources available to him, we see a "resemblance" operating, but it is not between the face of the signer, and a specific SSP that the signer remembers. The RP illustrates the effects of economic changes on the Deaf-Blind community in Seattle, via a mimetic representation of the prototypical facial features of an SSP at that time, as well as the manner of expression in the Deaf-Blind person's response to the SSP. There is substantial arbitrariness that obtains between the RP produced by the signer, the structure and content of the argument being put forth, Deaf-Blind people and SSPs, generally as categories to which feelings and manner are attributed.

At this point, it is useful to revisit Jansen's take on "perspective shift," which is analytically bound up with referent projection. He states, "Overt perspective-coding options...include potential perspectives equal to the number of participants involved in the action depicted by the particular verb in a given clause." (2004:152). In light of the examples above, it becomes suspect to refer to SSPs or Deaf-Blind people as "participants" in a reported event. In addition, the shifts in perspective, in combination with lexical forms that occur with the RP, (VOLUNTEER, 12 DOLLARS AN-HOUR, ME-VOLUNTEER, WOW, WORK-WORK, RENT EXPENSIVE, and I-LOOK-AT-THEM WOW) are reported utterances, thoughts, and actions that imply verbs of saying, thinking, and acting. However, the verb in each clause does not constrain the number or possible perspectives. Instead, the verb serves a more or less structural purpose in establishing an intersubjective relation between abstract categories that refer to social types, as opposed to actual people.

1985	_{shift1} [RP12 DOLLARS AN-HOUR]>	_{shift2} [RPOH, NO!]
ME-VOLUNTEER!]>	<shift3 [RPWOW]>	2006
_{shift4} [RPWORK-WORK	RENT EXPENSIVE]>	_{shift5} [RPI-LOOK-AT-THEM WOW]>

Translation: In 1985, if you offered people money to work as an SSP, they'd turn it down. They were happy to volunteer. Now, in 2006, people have to work to pay their rent. They get second jobs to pay their mortgages. They don't have time.

Therefore, perspective-coding options are not constrained by the depicted action, so much as the verb is constrained by its capacity for embedding the chosen RP in a recognizable social field. In addition, the "action" is not remembered, but asserted, at a level of abstraction not recognized in prior accounts of perspective shift. This is at least partially due to the conflation of perspective shift as a phenomenon, with referent projection. In addition, this is a result of reducing a complex communicative practice, which at once includes structure, activity, and ideology, giving form, and sometimes "function" primacy.

A STIGMATIZED DEAF-BLIND FIGURE

The following narrative is another example where an RP resembles an abstract social category, as opposed to an individual, and the signer is comparing, over the course of a narrative, the experience of being Deaf-Blind with what others seem to assume being Deaf-Blind means. First there is an explanation of an experience that is presented as emblematic of her current experience of being a Deaf-Blind person. Then, in the frames below, there is a grammatical shift to a different hypothetical perspective through the use of an RP. The RP does not indicate an actual participant in an actual reported event, but rather a non-actual referent that stands for what the signer is putting forth as a socially dominant perspective. Below are frame grabs (a transcript of the narrative out of which they were taken is available as an endnote).

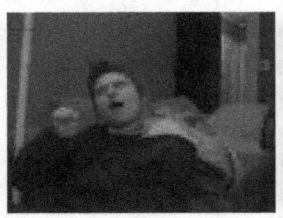 

_{shift} [RP(walking with a cane; movement is back and forth)]>   (signer laughs)

Description: The signer has been taking the perspective of herself at the time of the reported event. She indicates the referent seen in the first frame above as a "stigmatized Deaf Blind person" who is mimetically represented as walking with a cane. She then laughs at the absurdity of the figure in the second frame. The overall translation of this, with more distance from the actual form, is something like:

Translation: "… It's not like we fit the stereotyped, stigmatized image of a person with some horrendous disability, like what people must imagine Deaf-Blindness to be."

The figure of a stigmatized Deaf-Blind person as a social category is predicated through a non-actual event from the perspective of non-actual Deaf-Blind person. The event being this imagined referent walking with a cane in a particular manner (a prototypical activity for a stereotypical figure). It is understood that this event is less actual than the description of an actual Deaf-Blind experience, which has constituted the first portion of the story.

One could imagine that "real" and "non-real" worlds might very well be a matter of perspective (in a social sense). This signer is shifting perspective grammatically, but is also asking her audience to shift perspectives pragmatically.[6] In these frames, the "stigmatized Deaf Blind person" is a figure we are expected to 1) recognize, and 2) correlate with stigma. The correlation is arbitrary, in the sense that it relies on the assignation of social meaning to arbitrary physiological characteristics. However, it is recognizable because it is the product of historical, collective activity. The RP is presented at the end of a detailed description of the signer's own experience as an actual Deaf-Blind person in order to juxtapose the two, bringing the stigmatized status of "Deaf-Blind" as a category questioned, negotiated, and at least partially uprooted from its visual correlate.

CONCLUSION

There is a complex interplay of iconicity and arbitrariness represented in the examples I have presented, which becomes apparent at the level of discourse function. However, discourse function, in turn has explanatory power in terms of the persistence of iconicity in ASL at other levels of linguistic analysis. If iconicity is based on a sort of formal mirroring of something, or at least parts of something, what is it that is being mirrored in these cases? These facial expressions are indeed iconic, if iconic signs are, "signs that try to reproduce some aspect of their referent" (Duranti, 1997:17). However, they are also as arbitrary (or symbolic) as we take the social order to be. In this way, the "referent" in the cases cited above might better translate as a "figure" than a person.

According to Donna Haraway, " 'to figure' means to count or calculate and also to be in a story, to have a role" (1997:11) Figures "pertain to graphic representations and visual forms in general." They "do not have to be representational and mimetic, but they do have to be tropic; that is, they cannot be literal and self-identical. Figures must involve at least some kind of displacement that can trouble identifications and certainties... Figures are performative images that can be inhabited." (ibid). Figures, then, are social as opposed to situational, and as such are not "an epiphenomenal product of the situation," (Manning, 2001:64) but rather move beyond their immediate contexts, can be inhabited, traced, and importantly, used.

While these 'figures' and categories of people can and are represented formally by manual NPs such as 'stigmatized Deaf-Blind person' and 'SSPs in the '80s', the projects pursued in these examples are hard to imagine being as convincing without exploiting the shifty, fluid, formal domain where referent projections masquerade as, or critique that which seems "natural." So if particular domains have pragmatic uses that can be linked to formal properties characteristic of those domains, why would we expect them to become more arbitrary with time? In addition, assumptions made that gesture, and other less fixed, less formulated ways of using the body to communicate constitute raw input for linguistic systems seem suspect in light of the evidence presented in this essay. Therefore, in conclusion, I would like to propose the following definition for Referent Projections:

An iconic feature of ASL, signaled with perspective shifts that are marked and decoded through phonological and morphological cues embedded in the verb complex. Once a perspective has been grammatically signaled, the mimetic capacity of the face and body is drawn on, through the use of referent projections, in the evocation, description, construction, and contestation of people and social figures. Circulation of these figures is constrained by the relational dynamics of the body of the signer, the properties of the language, and the fields of social practice in which the language is used, including the socio-historical matrix through which particular resemblances have come to seem natural.

ENDNOTES

1. Hanks (1996) proposes the following three elements of practice as objects of analysis (p.230):
    1. Formal structure: language as a formal system
    2. Activity: what actors actually do.
    3. Ideology: actor's evaluations of 1 and 2.

    It is important to note that ideology, in this case, is informed by Bourieu's habitus, and as such, is not merely a contemplative matter. Ideology is "embodied both in corporeal practices and in mental representations....distributed over what the Cartesian perspective takes to be the different domains of mind and body" (234). Although each of the three dimensions of communicative practice should be considered integral to the production of social facts— no element being reduced to the byproduct or the cause of any other (231), they each require a different mode of analysis. Activities can't be treated as formal systems, language can't be treated as a temporary product of activity, and ideology can't be treated as "the projection of verbal categories or the misconstrual of action." (p.231). In this paper, I argue that engaging Hanks' analytic improves our understanding of RPs as a sociolinguistic phenomenon, including, but not limited to formal structure.

2. Hanks (1996) distinguishes between schematic and emergent aspects of practice. Schematic aspects are relatively stable, perduring, and underspecified. Social actors have access to these

aspects of practice prior to particular engagements, and beyond those engagements as well (233). They pre-exist, and yet are unfinished prior to activity. Emergent aspects, on the other hand, are coeval with actions or engagements. They are unstable, relatively specific, and not given prior to activity (ibid).
3. See Enberg-Pedersen (1993) and Aronoff et al (2003).
4. All translations are the author's unless otherwise stated.
5. All names are pseudonyms.
6. I would like to thank Dr. Pattie Epps for the phrasing of this observation, which she suggested after I presented this example in her Linguistic Typology class at the University of Texas at Austin.

REFERENCES

Aronoff, M. I. Meir, C. Padden and W. Sandler. 2003. Classifier Constructions and Morphology in Two Sign Languages, in K. Emmorey (ed.), *Perspectives on Classifiers in Signed Languages. Proceedings of the NSF Conference on Classifier Constructions in Sign Languages*, April 14-16, 2000, Lawrence Erlbaum Associates, Mahwah NJ, pp.53-84.

Basso Ellen, B. 1985. *A Musical View of the Universe*. Philadelphia: Univ. Penn. Press.

Childs, Tucker, G. 1994. *African ideophones*. See Hinton et al 1994, pp.178-204.

Duranti, Allesandro, 1997. *Linguistic Anthropology*. Cambridge University Press. Cambridge, UK.

Engberg-Pedersen, Elisabeth (1993). *Space in Danish Sign Language: the semantics and morphosyntax of the use of space in a visual language*. Hamburg: Signum Press.

Fernandez, James, W. 1986. The Dark at the Bottom of the Stairs: The inchoate in symbolic inquiry and some strategies for coping with it. In *Persuasions and Performances: The Play of Tropes in Culture*. Indiana University Press. Bloomington.

Foucault, Michel. 1975. *Discipline and Punish: The birth of the prison*. Random House. New York.

Haiman, John. 1980. The Iconicity of Grammar: Isomorphism and Motivation. *Language*. 56(3), p. 515-540.

Hanks, William, F. 1996. *Language and Communicative Practices*. University of Chicago Press. Chicago.

Hanks, William, F. 1990. *Referential Practice: Language and Lived Space among the Maya*. Chicago: The University of Chicago Press.

Haviland, John, B. 2006. Gesture, Sociocultural Analysis. In *Encyclopedia of Language and Linguistics*.

Haraway, Donna, J. 1997. Modest_Witness@Second_Millennium. FemaleMan©_Meets_ OncoMouseTM. Routledge, New York.

Hamano Shoko. 1994. *Palataliziation in Japanese sound symbolism*. See Hinton et al 1994, pp. 148-57.

Hopper, Paul J. and Elizabeth Closs Traugott. 2003. *Grammaticalization*. Cambridge.

Janzen, Terry. 2004. Space Rotation, Perspective Shift, and Verb Morphology in ASL. *Cognitive Linguistics*, 15:2, 149-174.

Klima, Edward and Ursula Bellugi. 1979. *The Signs of Language*. Harvard University Press. Cambridge, Mass.

Kita Sotaro. 1997. Two dimensional semantic analysis of Japanese mimetics. *Linguistics* 35:379-15.

Liddell, Scott. K. 1980. *American Sign Language Syntax*. The Hague: Mouton.

Mannheim, Bruce. 2000. Iconicity. *Journal of Linguistic Anthropology* 9(1-2):107-110.

Manning, Paul, H. 2001. On Social Deixis. *Anthropological Linguistics*, (43)1.

Pietrandrea, Paola. 2002. Iconicity and Arbitrariness in Italian Sign Language. *Sign Language Studies*, Vol. 2. No. 3.

Samarin W. 1971. Survey of Bantu ideophones. *African Language Studies*, 12:130-68.

Sandler, Wendy and Diane Lillo-Martin. 2006. *Sign Language and Linguistic Universals.* Cambridge University Press. New York.

Senghas, Ann, Sotaro Kita, Asli Ozyurek. 2004. Children Creating Core Properties of Language: Evidence from an Emerging Sign Language in Nicaragua. *Science.* Vol. 305, p. 1779-1782.

Voloßinov, V.N. 1973. *Marxism and the Philosophy of Language.* Cambridge, Mass: Harvard University Press.

The Politics and Practice of Voice: Representing Deaf People in Recent Television Dramas

JENNIFER RAYMAN

IN THIS PAPER, I EXAMINE THE PRACTICES OF REPRESENTING DEAF 'voices' to hearing audiences in two recent US television crime dramas. More literally I look at how American Sign Language is framed and made visible on the screen through various production decisions. Drawing examples from an episode of *CSI: New York* that aired in 2006 and an episode of *Law and Order: Criminal Intent (CI)* that aired in 2007, I examine how the practices of filming Deaf people and the use of American Sign Language intersect with the production of a political Deaf 'voice.'

The problem of representing a Deaf 'voice' on the screen is akin to the problem of representing other minority languages. Producers have to make choices about whether the majority audience of English speakers will have access to the minority language or not. In the face of this dilemma media producers have approached this in several ways: subtitling foreign speech, translating foreign speech through other characters, or leaving the language inaccessible except to those who use it. The additional difficulty with representing national sign languages is that both the language and the recording medium are visual. Sometimes, filmmakers make the choice of leaving some portions of the signed dialogue inaccessible to a naïve hearing audience. On the one hand this choice could indicate a devaluing of the signed communication, as its specific content is considered irrelevant to the plot. On the other hand it could indicate that Deaf people have a right to be visible on television using their own language without accommodating hearing people. A number of choices made in the filming and editing can subtly undermine positive representations of Deaf 'voices' particularly to a Deaf audience. These choices often construct an image of sign languages as objectified, exoticized, disjointed, incomplete, or even a code for spoken language. Simple choices of such as using simultaneous speaking and signing by deaf characters, cropping the scene, translating or not translating the dialogue have powerful implications for the ways that Deaf 'voices' are becoming more visible in the 21st century. Typical filming and editing conventions effectively silence the Deaf 'voice.'

The silencing of voice is more than just a production element. It also has political implications. When I use the word 'voice' in relation to deaf characters on the screen, I intend it to reflect many possible senses of the word — in the practical sense of voices speaking and being heard, or from a signing perspective of hands and bodies expressing and being seen, as well as in the political sense of having the right to be seen and heard. A voice is both literal — sounds emitted from the throat shaped by the mouth to form words as well as figurative — representing power, participation.

Having a voice is also about empowerment and visibility. Voice is more than sounds emitted from the vocal folds in the throat shaped by configurations of the mouth to form spoken words. It is more than visual movements of the hands and face combining to articulate signs. In a personal and political sense, it is about having the right to be seen and heard. It is about taking a stance and fighting for recognition. In some sense, in the act of watching television audience members are seeking recognition. This recognition is twofold: first it is about self-recognition and identification, and second it is about the hope of being recognized by the others and understood more fully.

SPOKEN MINORITY LANGUAGE REPRESENTATIONS ON THE SCREEN

First, I want to briefly examine recent portrayals of spoken minority languages in dramatic fictional television programs. Many of the same production techniques used in representing sign languages are also used when representing spoken foreign languages. This is especially true with regards to questions of audience access to the languages. Yet there are distinct differences due to modality — auditory versus visual. Because sign languages are visual languages, it is more critical that their full expression be visible on the screen, whereas with spoken languages the speech can still be audible and accessible even if the source is not visible on the screen. In the case of the representation of foreign spoken languages, the auditory modality is always available to the audience, so even if focal point of a scene is not on the character speaking the foreign language, it is still audible and accessible to the foreign speaking audience. Of course, there are issues as to whether the actors are actually fluent enough in the spoken minority language to have appropriate pronunciation and inflection. The English-speaking audience that doesn't know the language is excluded from recognizing whether the minority language representation is accurate or fluent and usually assumes that it is both. This would also be the case for representations of American Sign Language (ASL) to naïve hearing audiences. However, with spoken minority languages it is obvious that the language is a full language separate from English whereas with sign language so many misconceptions still abound about the nature of ASL as a complete and separate language. Hollywood representations generally do not contradict these misconceptions but only reinforce already held views on what ASL constitutes in the minds of audience members as a universal gestural system or a manual code for English.

In a rather unusual move for Hollywood industries, two recent popular serial dramas in primetime television have key characters that use languages other than English in extended scenes. It is likely no coincidence that these programs fall into the genre of sci-fi/fantasy. As it might be expected that audiences for these types of programs may be more tolerant of innovative practices and alternative ways of representing diversity.

The dramatic serial *Lost* is a complicated program about a group of plane crash victims surviving on a mysterious island. Often the format of the show focuses on a few characters and then, through a series of flashbacks, provides background information on the characters that pertain to the 'present day' storyline. One such episode is "In Translation" from the first season, where a native Korean couple is showcased.

From the first episodes of the program, the couple only speaks Korean. The producers/writers made a conscious decision that if the other characters didn't understand what the Korean couple was saying to each other, then the audience would be left in the dark as well. Later in the storyline, it is revealed that the wife, while in Korea, actually secretly learned English from her lover without her husband's knowledge. After she reveals her knowledge of English, she periodically functions as a translator for her husband.

In a particular episode showcasing the background of the couple as it took place in Korea, the producers and writers made the decision for all of the action to happen in the Korean language, as it naturally would have, and to add subtitles for audience accessibility. As the actors are Korean-born, we can assume that their language production is fluent and accurate. In a particular scene, as the couple converse on their wedding day, the camera cuts between the two characters. Sometimes the camera is on the woman's reaction while the audience hears the man's voice and sees the subtitles revealing the content of his speech. But whether the camera is on the speaker or not, a hearing audience can still tell who is talking by the nature of his/her voice and a deaf audience can deduce who is speaking by attending to whether the person on camera is moving his/her lips.

In another television program, *Heroes*, inspired by the comic book genre, several characters are foreign born and, at times, speak in their character's native language. This show portrays a time when genetic mutations begin to appear in the human population, yielding various superhero powers such as time travel, flying, self-healing, and invisibility. One such character is an unobtrusive Japanese office worker named Hiro. He discovers he has the ability to transport himself through time and change the course of history. He interacts in Japanese with other office workers in Japan, including his best friend Ando and his businessman father.

Actor Masi Oka (Hiro) was born and raised in Japan until he the age of six; actor James Kyson Lee (Ando) moved to the United States from Korea at the age of ten and memorizes Japanese dialog phonetically; actor George Takei, best known for his portrayal of Lieutenant Sulu in the original *Star Trek* sci-fi genre series which originally aired in the United States from 1966 to 1969, is of Japanese heritage but has lived in the US since childhood. All of the actors have varying fluency in spoken Japanese.

On several blogs and vlogs, fans that are also familiar with the Japanese language and Japanese culture complain about sloppy accents, unintelligible speech, and inaccurate cultural information found in the show. This type of commentary is similar to complaints found in the Deaf community when non-deaf actors are used to play deaf characters or when inaccurate cultural information is portrayed in Deaf themed episodes.

What is particularly interesting about the show *Heroes* is the way it provides access to the scenes spoken in foreign languages. This may derive from its inspiration from the comic book genre. When spoken Spanish is used, the subtitles are yellow; when spoken Japanese is used, the subtitles are white. Additionally, in the spoken Japanese scenes, a stylized font is used and though the producers do not go as far as inserting comic book style speech balloons, the words almost look like they are emanating in space from invisible speech balloons on the screen near the characters that are speaking. This style of subtitling actually 1) gives a deaf audience clearer access to the fact that different languages are being spoken and 2) clarifies who is doing the speaking. In this manner, the techniques of subtitling use visual representations to try to capture both the idea that different languages are being spoken by using different colors and font styles as well as that different characters are doing the speaking by spatially locating the subtitles near the characters doing the speaking.

In both these portrayals of spoken minority languages on the screen, it is evident that the minority voices are made visible whether or not the speaker is visible on the screen. The fact that their speech is foreign is marked for the audience both by unfamiliar sounds and by the use of subtitles, which already provide a familiar practice for representing foreign speech.

Foreign speech directors, producers, and editors typically do not have to adjust their visual style of presenting images of the characters because no matter how they edit the images together, both the audio and subtitle track will maintain the presence of the language throughout scenes. Through force of habit, media producers may maintain their phonocentric patterns even when approaching the portrayal of sign language on the screen.

SCHUCHMAN'S HISTORY OF DEAFNESS IN THE FILM INDUSTRY

In the twenty years since John Schuchman's *Hollywood Speaks: Deafness and the Film Entertainment Industry* was first published in 1988, many of the same stereotypes of the dummy, the perfect speaker, the expert lip-reader, the fake, and the unhappy hearing impaired still prevail. Schuchman's critiques of editing techniques still apply to more recent portrayals of deaf people on television. As editing techniques have evolved over the years from more reliance on wide and medium shots to frequent intercutting of closeups, the tendency to cut sign language off the screen and out of the comprehensible view of the audience may have increased.

There have been some positive trends in the depiction of deaf characters on the screen. Schuchman (1988) discusses an early shift in the use of the dummy stereotype, where initially the stereotype simply indicated that deaf people were dumb in a portrayal like the one in *Johnny Belinda* (1948) where she is transformed from an isolated dummy into a capable communicating young woman. Today, it is rare to find the dummy stereotype used and, when it is invoked, it is often challenged in some way within the framework of the portrayal itself (for example, in the episode of *CSI: New York* discussed here, a hearing ex-boyfriend scoffs that he would never marry a deaf girl implying that she was defective and he is rebuked by the detective as a "jerk").

Another significant shift in the portrayal of Deaf people discussed by Schuchman is the precedent set in the 1970s, when deaf actress Audrey Norton complained to the Screen Actors Guild about the hiring of hearing actors to play deaf characters. Today, it is an unspoken policy that deaf actors are hired to play deaf characters and it is rare to find a counter example, except perhaps in cases where the character is a non-signing deaf character as in the film *In The Company Of Men*. This is a significant triumph for the deaf acting community. It means that when there was an increase in the number of deaf characters on television between more deaf people were hired. In Schuchman's (1988) conclusion, he pointed to the fact that deaf people were almost always depicted as isolated rather than members of a wider deaf community. Since that time, in recent episodes of several crime dramas such as *Conviction*, *CSI: New York*, *Law & Order: Criminal Intent*, and *Cold Case* have all depicted deaf people as part of a vibrant deaf community and culture.

RECENT PORTRAYALS OF DEAF PEOPLE ON TELEVISION

During the two seasons of US broadcast and cable television between August 2006 and April 2008, 50 episodes of ten different serial dramas portrayed signing deaf characters. Three of these dramas had on-going deaf characters that appeared in a number of episodes throughout the seasons, while seven dramas portrayed deaf people in a one-off episode with a deaf theme. See the charts below.

Initial season air date	Program and Season	# of episodes
August 14, 2006	Weeds, Season 2	5
Sepember 20, 2006	Jericho, Seasons 1 & 2	17
January 28, 2007	The L Word, Seasons 4 & 5	21

Table 1. Dramas with ongoing Deaf characters during the 2006–2008 US television seasons

Initial air date	Program; Season (Episode)	Episode Title
April 7, 2006	Conviction; 1(6)	"Madness"
December 13, 2006	CSI: New York; 3(12)	"Silent Night"
April 3, 2007	Law and Order: Criminal Intent; 6(18)	"Silencer"
April 12, 2007	Scrubs; 6(16)	"My Words of Wisdom"
October 8, 2007	CSI: Miami; 6(3)	"Inside Out"
February 18, 2008	Medium; 4(64)	"Do You Hear What I Hear"
March 30, 2008	Cold Case; 5(14)	"Andy in C Minor"

Table 2. One-off episodes with signing Deaf characters during the 2006–2008 US television seasons

The majority of the one-off programs were crime dramas focusing in some way on the cochlear implant controversy in the deaf community. All of the six crime dramas all but one, *Medium*, included the topic of cochlear implants. Even in the case of *CSI: Miami*, a minor deaf character, only on the screen for less than a minute, had a cochlear implant. She relied on lipreading and signing to use some information to her advantage and could just as easily not have had an implant as had one. Surprisingly, even the medical comedy *Scrubs* focused on the cochlear implant controversy where the doctors suggest to the deaf father that his deaf son, in for treatment of a minor ailment, should get an implant. In three of the crime dramas, cochlear implants were at the heart of the reason for the crimes.

Ironically, though the shows with ongoing characters often allow the deafness of the character to be incidental to their role, it is the one-off crime dramas with a deaf theme that accomplish the feat of showing deaf people relating with one another as members of a vibrant community and culture. Often, in ongoing series, deaf characters remain isolated from the deaf community and their interactions with other deaf people are sparse. Though communication issues and realities about deaf people's lives are touched on the reality of their social lives in the deaf community is left absent.

ANALYZING TWO CRIME DRAMAS

In this article, I examine how filmmakers use both sound and video editing in two crime dramas to create an image of American Sign Language. Filmmakers use both of these editing techniques to mark the experiential difference between hearing and deaf characters. In an obvious approach, they often rely on distorting or muting the sound in certain scenes in order to project the auditory perspective of either deaf or hearing characters vicariously onto the audience. In addition, they use extreme close-ups on the hands or lips to emphasize the visual nature of communication through signing or lipreading. This technique marks the difference between two different modalities of language manual and vocal (ASL and spoken English)

OPENING SCENES SETTING THE STAGE FOR DEAF THEMES

CSI: New York and *Law and Order: Criminal Intent* take different approaches to leading the audience into the deaf-themed storylines. By examining the opening scenes of each program, we can see how the production choices guide the audience into a certain perceptual understanding of what it means to be deaf and to communicate visually. Both programs use editing techniques to alert the audience to the difference of deafness.

In an episode of *CSI: New York* entitled "Silent Night," a conflict between a young deaf man and woman who were formerly romantically involved is portrayed. The murdered young woman does not want her deaf baby to have a cochlear implant while the killer ex-boyfriend who has a cochlear implant believes that it is the best option for his child. In a plot twist, the young woman's deaf parents initially pass their grandchild off as their own in order to save the social embarrassment of their young daughter's unwed pregnancy.

In the opening scene, it is slowly revealed that the victims of the intruder are deaf. In the first three minutes, no sign language is used; however, each shot reveals another clue that the characters do not hear. The scene opens on a snowy New York cityscape and floats to a closeup of a storybookhouse that morphs into a toy. As the camera zooms out, we see the toy house is enclosed in a snowglobe. Gina (portrayed by actress Marlee Matlin), in pajamas, walks barefoot down the wooden floored hallway to check on a baby and a woman asleep in her bedroom. As she turns back down the hallway to her own bedroom, we see an intruder walk across the hallway bumping a table where the snowglobe rests, jarring it to crash and shatter on the floor.

Undisturbed, Gina continues to walk into her bedroom and sit barefoot on the edge of her bed. The baby crier light flashes, she wiggles her toes and senses something through the floorboards as the audience hears muffled shotgun explosions. Walking back down the hallway, she notices the shattered globe, sniffs the air smelling the shotgun. She turns to see the woman's bed empty and then the baby standing calmly at the edge of her crib. Gina glances down and we see her scream but the audio is muted and we only hear the dramatic sound track. The baby doesn't react to the scream.

At each point along the way, there are 'sound' cues to the deafness: the lack of response to the shattered globe, the floorboard vibrations, the flashing baby crier lights, the muted scream, and the lack of reaction from the deaf baby (though one might think that witnessing your own mother be shot would cause some reaction!) It is not until the next part of the scene that it is overtly revealed that Matlin's character is deaf.

Though no sign language is used to clue the audience or the recently arrived detectives that the victims of the crime are deaf, the interactions that follow demonstrate various visual clues and visual communication strategies that can be used between deaf signers and non-signers. The CSI unit's leader, Detective Taylor, notices Matlin's character trying to track what is going on by lipreading another policeman as he speaks into the walkie-talkie. The camera first reveals Gina holding the baby and making every effort to maintain eye contact with the officer in the car communicating on the radio. This is intercut with shots of the detective noticing her and a closeup image of the officer's mouth moving with no sound. Detective Taylor then identifies Gina as deaf and states that an interpreter is needed.

Once he approaches her, he makes sure that he has her eye contact and maintains eye contact with her as he is talking. As he speaks, sometimes his voice is muted through sound editing to offer the audience a vicarious experience of her deaf perspective while she lipreads him. He also hands her a notepad so that she can communicate with him, where she writes "Find my daughter's killer." At no point does he expect her to speak or ask her if she can read lips. At the close of the scene, she lightly touches his chin to get him to look at her and then she speaks, "Please help me."

The episode of *Law and Order: Criminal Intent (CI)*, entitled "Silencer," is also ultimately about a conflict between a deaf man and a deaf woman over cochlear implants. In the end, it is revealed that the deaf woman is exploring the possibility of a cochlear implant. Her boyfriend, projecting the past hurt of his hearing sister leaving him behind to go off and live her own life, doesn't want his girlfriend to leave him once she gains hearing. The boyfriend shoots the doctor in the hand to prevent him from being able to perform the surgery, and then accidentally kills him by crushing his voice box without realizing that, even though his mouth was open in an apparent scream, the surgeon wasn't making a noise.

In this episode, there is no slow reveal to the deaf theme; the audience is clued in immediately by the extreme closeup on the interpreter's signing hands and the expert cochlear implant surgeon testifying in a malpractice suit. Some signs are visible and understandable, but the movement of the camera makes tracking them more challenging. As the interpreter continues signing, the camera pans from a right profile shot of the interpreter around her back blocking the view of the signs and then goes in for a closeup on the surgeon in the witness box. Some parts of the interpreter's hands are visible, but the only intelligible signs are 'prosecutor-ASKS-witness' and 'witness-says-NO' (given in response to the question of whether the surgery should have been performed on the baby). This is visible in the right corner of the frame, which is a medium shot of the witness sitting on the stand.

This panning style of camerawork and editing sets the visual style for the show. At this point, there are several shot cuts to reactions of the defendant and the audience. The courtroom is then disrupted with the defendants' attorney objecting and the defendant standing in an outburst. The courtroom then erupts with signing and verbal discussion. There are various shots of deaf people signing in the courtroom audience, some intelligible such as when Melia, one of the main deaf characters, says, "what's he SAYING?" During this sequence the sound is edited so that a shot of the hearing judge speaking is silent, intercut with a noisy reaction shot of the crowd and then we see a few shots of muted hearing people reacting. This gives a sense of the deaf characters not having access to what is going on in the confusion.

As with the *CSI: New York* interaction between the hearing detective and the deaf victim, the sound in the courtroom scene is alternately muted as the camera flashes between different characters including several signing deaf people providing the audience with a deaf auditory perspective. During this sequence and the next, no access to the ASL conversations between deaf people is given to the naïve hearing audience. Unlike the *CSI: New York* opening scene, in the opening scene of *Law & Order: CI*, ASL is visible as the preferred language of deaf people amongst themselves.

In the next part of the opening sequence, we see the conclusion to Larry, the deaf playwright's deaf-themed play spoofing the dean of the school. Melia, the star of the play in a closing monologue signs as the interpreter voices for her, "In our deaf world we find our peace and our power. If you cannot understand this, then go!" And the chorus chants: DEAF POWER! DEAF POWER! As the scene is filmed, only a few elements of the signed performance are visible between shots of the audience and the interpreter. This leads to a montage of post-performance interactions between deaf signers edited together to a musical soundtrack with no other environmental or speech noises, emphasizing the reliance on visual means of communication.

SETTING THE STAGE FOR USING INTERPRETERS

Now that the stage is set in each episode for the deaf theme and the deaf characters are revealed, each drama next sets the stage for the use of interpreters in witness interviews and suspect interrogation scenes. It is a positive step that both crime dramas indicate the need for the use of qualified interpreters. In *CSI: New York,* immediately after recognizing that one of the victims is deaf, the detective states, "We need an interpreter," and does not attempt to interview her until the situation is arranged with an interpreter present. The same is true in *Law & Order: CI*. One of the supervisors on the scene asks the female detective, Eames, "Your partner signs?" And she replies, "Not enough for a witness interview. We called for an interpreter."

Both of these vignettes indicate that interpreting from ASL into English and vice versa requires a certain level of skill (in contrast to the episode of *Cold Case* where an officer learns ASL overnight by studying the book *ASL for Dummies*). Unrealistically, however, the interpreters in both shows are officers of the police department. In the case of *CSI: New York,* the interpreter is a uniformed officer, while in the case of *Law & Order: CI*, the interpreter introduces himself as "Detective Peter Lyons, Community Affairs. You need an interpreter?"

Aside from the fact that the majority of ASL interpreters are actually women, interpreters also are usually called in on a contract basis and are not simultaneously trained officers of the law *and* certified ASL interpreters. When looking at the actual sign production and translations of these two interpreters/officers, it is easy to spot that the "interpreter" in *CSI: New York* is an actor who has picked up a few signs and does not have the fluency of a certified interpreter. What little we see of his sign interpretation doesn't demonstrate much more than translating the signs from English in a word for word format.

In contrast, the interpreter in *Law & Order: CI* is a natural signer and his translations demonstrate finesse and skill in conceptual accuracy. For example, in one instance when interviewing a suspect, the detective says, "There's a lot of people pointing their finger at you." The interpreter's literal representation is ALOT THINK YOU GUILTY. While there has been some progress on the front of hiring deaf actors, we still may have further to go in terms of hiring skilled hearing signers to act as interpreters or represent other skilled hearing signers as part of the community.

SCENE ANALYSIS METHODOLOGY

In taking a closer look at a scene from each episode, we can see exactly how the filming and editing techniques work to create an image of sign language. I have chosen comparable scenes where a deaf individual is interviewed or interrogated by the police using a sign language interpreter. In each scene, it can be assumed that all the communication is happening in both English and ASL through an interpreter so, at all times, some signing should be occurring. In transcribing the scenes, I noted each point when the editor spliced different camera angles adjacent to each other (where there is a shift in camera perspective from one angle to another). Because of the different visual aesthetics in each program, I also noted where the screen time of each character shifts. This allowed for a better comparison between the two programs as the number of splice edits was markedly different in the two programs. I included both glosses of the ASL signs visible on the screen as well as transcribing the flow of the spoken English. This enabled me to count how many separate shifts in screen time segments contained signing and how much of these were completely visible in medium shots.

CSI: NEW YORK WITNESS INTERVIEW SCENE

In the first signing scene, Gina (Matlin) is brought in for an interview with Detective Taylor and a signing interpreter/signing uniformed officer. The scene opens with a medium shot on Detective Taylor as he asks her, "What do you think woke you up?" The shot cuts to an extreme close up of her face and hands and pans to only the hands as she signs FOOTSTEPS. Then the scene shifts to an over-the-shoulder medium shot of the interpreter where we can still see her signing VIBRATIONS and then it cuts to a closeup of her face as she signs ALLISON NOISE. Though these signs are cropped, they are still decipherable as they happen near the face. Throughout this sequence, the interpreter speaks, "Footsteps, I felt vibrations. I thought maybe it was Alison."

Next there is a closeup on Detective Taylor's face as he asks Gina why her family moved and whether she had family in the area. During his question, the camera shifts to a closeup reaction of Gina listening, back to a closeup on Taylor's face, and then to a medium shot of the interpreter translating the last part of the question. Next, while Gina responds, the camera quickly cuts from a medium shot to a closeup side view of the hands to a closeup bird's eye view of the hands to a close up of Gina's face with most of the signs outside of the frame. See the transcript below:

[medium shot] NOT PLAN HAVE MORE CHILDREN
[closeup side view of hands] PREGNANT
[closeup from bird's eye view] DECIDE RAISE ELIZABETH
[closeup Gina's face signs out of frame] SAFE

While this sequence plays out the interpreter voices, "My husband and I weren't planning on having any more children. When I got pregnant my husband and I decided to raise Elizabeth outside of the city where it's safe."

The kind of quick cuts between closeups, medium shots and reaction shots of other characters sets the visual aesthetic for this episode of *CSI: New York*. In this particular clip, the camera shifts shot angles no less than 50 times in the space of one minute and 34 seconds. Yet there are only 12 conversational turns back and forth between the two characters. This makes for a number of intercut reaction shots, interpreter shots as well as within turn close-ups and other angles on the same character. If only counting shifts in screen time on a particular character (despite any close-ups or perspective changes on the same character) then there are still 37 shifts in focus between different characters during the scene. There are 22 shots that contain some element of signing yet out of all of these, we only see Gina in a medium shot with all of the signing space visible four times for approximately two seconds each. Though signing is occurring during every communication via the interpreter or Gina, less than half of the shots contain signs and 18 of these are closeups from various angles. This scene is highly emotional; Gina is clearly upset with the recent murder of her daughter. The filming techniques add to this sense of chaos, disjointedness, with a rollercoaster of feelings. In the sequence described above which lasts for a 15-second stretch there are nine different shots spliced together All of this occuring while she is communicating in sign language gives the signing viewer a disjointed feeling, jumping to different perspectives every couple of seconds.

The closeups in this clip varied from closeups on the face, which cut out part of the signs, to closeups on the hands caught in different perspectives from a front, side, top or even table top reflected upside-down view. Some of the other shots were over the back shoulder of Gina catching a rear view of the signs as the camera is aimed in a medium shot of the detective and interpreter. The overall result from a signing perspective is a disjointed jumble of signs leaving the impression of chaos and heightened emotion. One deaf viewer during the conference presentation showing this clip indicated that the closeups on the hands and the quick cuts to different perspectives made sign language seem animalistic.

In some ways this can be seen as an exoticization of the signs making them look surreal, drawing attention to the body parts displaying the signs and objectifying them. While such objectification may seem harmless to a naïve hearing audience or media producer — a mere materializing of the felt amazement at signed communication moving at such a pace. But if we were to propose a hypothetical parallel situation where a Korean character is speaking in her native tongue and we are shown extreme closeups and quick cuts jumping from an image of the lips moving to the tongue tapping the teeth to a side close up of the mouth to an overhead image from the top of the head — this type of portrayal would immediately be felt to be a dehumanization of Korean people and likely labeled racist. In the case of sign language, is it merely thought of as visual artistry?

LAW & ORDER: SUSPECT INTERROGATION SCENE

Law & Order: Criminal Intent has a different film aesthetic. The scene selected is an interview with a potential suspect in the murder of a cochlear implant surgeon. The deaf man, Larry, is an activist and playwright. Sitting at a table with his lawyer across from the male detective Goren and the interpreter with the female detective Eames standing to the side. Unlike the *CSI: New York* scene there are no quick cuts between shots. Instead the camera takes longer shots panning around the table. Even when there are cuts to slightly different angles, the camera continues to pan in the same direction as the previous shot, giving the illusion that almost the entire scene is one shot. In this 45-second scene, there are only five cuts to different camera angles. Even though this is a shorter scene than the *CSI: New York* scene, it still contains significantly less editing cuts. However, the act of panning the camera around the room — even in a continuous shot — serves to break up the scene further as the camera pulls focus zooming in on different characters while it pans.

For the purposes of this analysis, in addition to dividing the scene at shifts in camera angles performed through editing, I also divide the scenes at shifts in camera angles focusing on different characters. As the camera moves to focus on a different interlocutor (serving the same purpose as a shift done through editing), this brings the total shifts in camera angles to ten.

At several points throughout this *Law & Order: CI* episode, the cinematographer uses the same technique of zooming into an extreme closeup on the hands and then pulling out to see the signer. But in this particular scene, all of the visible signed sequences are filmed in medium shots. While this is positive (because we can actually see the whole message including hand and face), the act of panning behind the backs of seated characters while Larry is signing blocks some of his message just as much as shifting the edit to a reaction shot would do. Of the ten shots, only one shot does not contain any signing: when Detective Eames reacts to Larry's demands and incredulously says, "A deaf cop?"

While all of the other shots contain some signing, only two signed interchanges are not interrupted by some sort of body block. Ironically both of these shots occur when the hearing detective is speaking. The first is the opening shot. The camera, in a wide shot on five characters, opens on their reflections in the mirrored window located in the interview room. As the camera pulls back into the room, it spins around and pans across the Detective Eames' face to settle on Detective Goran. While Goran begins talking, the shot widens out to include the interpreter sitting next to him and catch the signed translation. Goran says, "Larry? There's a lot of people pointing their finger at you." After a bit of lag time, the interpreter signs, A-LOT PEOPLE THINK YOU GUILTY.

OVERALL COMPARISON OF THE TWO SCENES

For both scenes, there were only four segments with unobstructed medium shots of signers in the act of signing. In the case of *Law & Order: CI*, this might be considered a good showing as there were only nine segments in the entire scene, eight of which contained signing, thus yielding a 50% visibility of the signs (whether or not the signs were fully visible) during the entire stream of the conversation. In the case of *CSI: New York*, with its higher ratio of segments split by different camera shots, 22 segments contained signing, yielding a ratio of only 18% visibility of signs. Though this analysis is limited to only one scene for comparison, it does reveal that both episodes prioritize the spoken language stream of information over the sign language stream of information.

	CSI: New York	Law & Order: Criminal Intent
Time duration of the clip	1:34	0:45
# shifts in character conversational turns	12	10
# edited camera shots to different angle	50	5
# shifts in screen time of the characters (edited or panned)	37	9
Total # screen time segments with signing	22	8
# medium segments with signing fully visible	4	4
# segments containing close ups of signs, cropped off signs or blocked	18	4

Table 3. Count comparison between the two scenes

Filmmakers come from a hearing framework of film production where language equals sound on an audio track. Within that framework, sound editing is separate from video editing and can provide continuity between disjointed visual shots. But this kind of reliance on sound to provide the linguistic continuity fails when confronted with representing American Sign Language on the screen. The soundstream of translated English words may provide continuity for the hearing audience, but if left to rely on what is available in the visual modality, deaf viewers may have to rely on closed captioning to understand the dialog even when it is portrayed in their own language. Disjointed scenes showing quick cuts between different angles on a signed dialog and flashing between reacting interlocutors leaves the signing audience with a view on a silenced protagonist.

RECOMMENDATIONS

How can media producers give voice to sign language on the screen? First there needs to be an awareness and concern amongst these same media producers that there is actually value in taking the care required to make sign language visible and accessible to the signing deaf audience and perhaps raise more awareness among the naïve hearing audience. It may be entirely possible to maintain a similar visual aesthetic to the programs and still make sign language visible.

In both examples used above, careful planning and choreography of the filming and editing of the scenes would make this possible. In the quick cutting style of frequent closeup shots found in *CSI: New York*, it would be necessary to either reduce the number of closeups and/or make sure that the cloeups were wide enough to include enough of the signs to maintain intelligibility as with signs that are made near the face. In addition, medium shots of the interpreter or the interpreter and the hearing speaker would have to become the rule of the day in order to make the interpreted spoken language accessible as well. Over-the-shoulder shots of signers are possible as well as long as the back of the signer does not obscure understanding of the signs. In order to avoid objectification of sign language, extreme closeups of the hands should be avoided unless similar objectifying shots are also made of hand gestures and body parts of hearing people during conversation. In addition using a different visual aesthetic of panning continuous shots such as those found in *Law and Order: CI*, care would need to be taken not to obstruct the signs while circling behind other participants. Other possibilities include adapting the visual aesthetic of *24* (another United States crime drama) where multiple shots taking place simultaneously are projected onto the screen. In this manner, reaction shots and full shots of the signing can both be visible.

Aside from careful shot choreography, hearing media producers need to rely on excellent ASL/Deaf culture informants during all stages of the production; typically, cinematographers, directors, and editors likely do not know how to make sure that signs are not obscured. Simultaneous signing and talking by deaf and hearing characters should be avoided as this method of communication only confirms in the minds of hearing signers that sign language is merely a code for spoken language. Instead, hearing media producers can more creatively rely on interpreters in mixed settings or subtitling when conversations occur between deaf characters occurs. Subtitling is already a marker for foreign language and may alert naïve hearing audiences to the fact that sign language is a full language, not merely a code for English. Using these kinds of techniques as a matter of policy when filming signing deaf people will enable the signing voice some of the visibility that the deaf community desires.

REFERENCES

Ashcraft, B. (2008). Night Note: "Heroes" is all kinds of dumb. Retrieved March 30, 2008 from Infinite Undiscovery, Kotaku: http://kotaku.com/360264/heroes-is-all-kinds-of-dumb.

Caron, G.G. (Creator). Arquette, D. (Director). (18 February 2008). "Do You Hear What I Hear." [Television series episode]. In *Medium*, Season 4, Episode 64.

Chaiken, Ilene. (Writer), [Television series] *The L Word*, Season 4.

Chbosky, S., Schaer, J. & Steinbert, J.E. (Creators) 2006-7) [Television series] *Jericho*, Season 1 & 2.

Green, Walon (Writer), & Deschanel, Caleb (Director). (April 7, 2006). "Madness." [Television series episode]. In Carter Harris (Producer). *Conviction*, Season 1, Episode 6. New York: NBC Studios.

Harris, Gavin. (Writer), & Szwarc, Jeannot. (Director). (March 30, 2008). "Andy in C Minor." [Television series episode]. In *Cold Case*, 107 Season 5, Episode 14.

Haynes, John & Nayar, Sunil. (Writers), & Lamar, Gina. (Director). (8 October 2007). "Inside Out." [Television series episode]. In John Haynes & Melissa Black. (Producers), *CSI: Miami*, 124 Season 6, Episode 3. Raleigh Manhattan Beach Studios. CBS Broadcasting Inc & Alliance Atlantis Productions Inc.

Japanese in Heroes — Part 1. (October 8, 2007). Retrieved March 30, 2008 from Rocking in Hakata: http://www.rockinginhakata.com/2007/10/08/212/.

Kohan, J. (Creator) [Television series] In Burley, M. (Producer), *Weeds*.

Lawrence, B. (Creator) & Nelli Jr, V. (Director). (12 April 2007). "My Words of Wisdom." [Television series episode]. In *Scrubs*, Season 6, Episode 16.

Lenkov, Peter, M., & Humphrey, Samantha (Writers), Zulker, Anthony E. (Story), & Bailey, Rob. (Director). (December 13, 2006). "Silent Night." [Television series episode]. *CSI: New York*, 59 Season 3, episode 12. CBS Broadcasting Inc & Alliance Atlantis Productions Inc.

Mockett, M. (August 25, 2007). My Hero My Hiro. Retrieved March 30, 2008 from Japundit: Japan — A whole lot more than: http://japundit.com/archives/2007/08/25/6806/.

O'Shea, Marygrace. (Writer), & White, Dean. (Director). (April 3, 2007). "Silencer." [Television series episode]. In Mary Rae Thewlis (Producer). *Law and Order: Criminal Intent*, 129 Season 6, Episode 18. New York: Universal Network Television.

Schuchman, J. S. (1988). *Hollywood Speaks: Deafness and the Entertainment Industry*. Urbana & Chicago, Illinois: University of Illinois Press.

Schuchman, J. S. (2004). The Silent Film Era: Silent Films, NAD Films, and the Deaf Community's Response. [Electronic version]. *Sign Language Studies*, 4(3), 231–238.

Shakespeare, T. (1994). Cultural representations of disabled people: Dustbins for disavowal. [Electronic version]. *Disability & Society*, 9(3), 283–299.

What's Up With Helen Keller?

EDNA SAYERS, PH.D.

HELEN KELLER IS UNDOUBTEDLY THE BEST KNOWN DEAF PERSON IN history and one of the most accomplished ever to have lived: an internationally known author, lecturer, fundraiser, and goodwill ambassador. When the museum exhibit "Through Deaf Eyes" traveled around America, it was rumored that the most common comment made in the visitor's log was surprise that the exhibit did not include Helen Keller. We didn't include Keller's life and accomplishments in that exhibit, and we don't normally teach Keller or her works in courses on Deaf literature, Deaf history, or Deaf studies: not only was Keller simply not Deaf, but she was an active oralist. So we ignore her. But that's not what the Deaf community did in the years Keller was in the news, from 1888 to the 1920s. Far from ignoring Keller, Deaf Americans one hundred years ago invited her to visit their clubs and schools, and they wrote about her education, her tours, her health, and her speech. Articles about Keller that appeared in various Deaf papers during these years are a window onto the Deaf World in the dark years when the fallout from Milan had taken hold all over America.

When Keller became deaf and blind in 1882, it was certainly not inevitable that she would fall into the hands of oralists. The American Asylum in Hartford, Connecticut, had had a signing deaf-blind woman, Julia Brace, in residence from 1825 to 1860. Brace attracted some regional attention, but the school under Lewis Weld and subsequent principals did not publicize its "success stories" or use its students as "poster children" to raise funds. Brace therefore remained relatively unknown outside of New England (Nielsen "Was Helen Keller Deaf?" 24-25).

In contrast, the deaf-blind woman in residence at the Perkins Institution for the Blind in Boston, Laura Bridgman, had been taught English by Samuel Gridley Howe through fingerspelling and with raised-letter labels attached to objects, and she was exploited extensively for fund raising. Her consequent fame attracted Charles Dickens to visit her when he was in Boston and to include an account of her in his American Notes of 1842. Kate Keller knew that Laura Bridgman read and communicated in English because she had read about it in this book by the world-famous Charles Dickens, but she knew nothing of Julia Brace, who communicated in what must have been Early ASL. When an eye doctor sent the Kellers to consult A. G. Bell and Bell in turn referred them to the Perkins Institution, which sent them Anne Sullivan, who had been trained by Howe and had worked with Laura Bridgman, the Kellers would have assumed that fingerspelling English was the only available educational method.

Before Sullivan's arrival in the Keller household, however, Helen was inventing home sign and teaching it to her mother and playmates.

> Was it bread that I wanted? Then I would imitate the acts of cutting the slices and buttering them. If I wanted my mother to make ice-cream for dinner I made the sign for working the freezer and shivered, indicating cold. My mother, moreover, succeeded in making me understand a good deal. I always knew when she wished me to bring her something, and I would run upstairs or anywhere else she indicated. (Keller, Story of My Life 23-24)

As a sophomore at Radcliffe, Keller could not remember the name of her playmate, "a little colored girl ... the child of our cook," though she certainly remembered signing with her (Nielsen, ed. Helen Keller: Selected, 78-80). Calling the little girl "Martha Washington," Keller recalls the two of them hunting in the grass for guinea-fowl eggs:

> I would double my hands and put them on the ground, which meant something round in the grass, and Martha always understood. When we were fortunate enough to find a nest I never allowed her to carry the eggs home, making her understand by emphatic signs that she might fall and break them. (Story 25)

The examples of home signs BREAD and ICE CREAM are classic; the ability to sign a conditional sentence — "If you carry the eggs, you might fall and break them" — demonstrates advanced syntax. If Keller had been placed in a signing environment, she would have been signing excellent ASL in a matter of months. She was certainly not "helpless and dependent" (Perry 11) — on the contrary, she was inventing language to understand and manipulate her environment.

How Sullivan taught Keller English — commonly referred to, in that day, as "language" — has been extensively documented, but Sullivan's own account, written for the *American Annals of the Deaf and Dumb* in 1892, is perhaps the best source. During Keller's lifetime, the public believed that she had been taught English through speech (Holcomb & Woods) but Sullivan, and Keller herself, were always clear that the language was taught through fingerspelling. According to Sullivan, she started fingerspelling to Keller immediately upon arrival at the Kellers' home, beginning with nouns, proceeding to verbs, then to sentences. At the level of simple sentences, Sullivan had an inspired idea: instead of teaching simple sentences with words Keller already knew, as had been done with Bridgman, Sullivan began to spell fluent English sentences into Keller's hand, flooding the child with idiomatic English. Sullivan tells us, "I talked to her almost incessantly," and "I talked … with my fingers as I should have talked to her with my mouth" (Sullivan 136). She also gave Keller books with raised letters (since Braille was not yet in wide use) — as a pastime, not a lesson (Sullivan 137). Sullivan offered two reasons for Keller's success with English: one was that the child had a great deal of aptitude, and the other was immersion in conversational and written English. Laura Bridgman, who was taught English words but not exposed to conversational English, never attained the fluency in English that Keller did.

Sullivan never intended to teach Keller to speak or lipread. Keller herself recalled that "friends" tried to discourage her attempts to speak until she finally convinced Sullivan to take her to a speech teacher, Sarah Fuller, at the Horace Mann school in 1890, when she was ten years old and a pupil at Perkins (Keller Story 60). Sullivan wrote that she "repress[ed] this instinctive tendency" of Keller's to vocalize (Sullivan 132) until realizing that the child had better have speech lessons if she was to persist in using her voice (133). Sarah Fuller corroborates these accounts of Keller's initiative. Considering the experience with speech lessons of even the most motivated "oral successes," this account is difficult to believe. But Keller's near-total isolation as a deaf child in the oral world of the blind at the Perkins Institution and her complete ignorance of what speech lessons would actually entail make it easier to understand a small girl's desire to fit in.

Keller's real experience with speech training is hidden in her letters to close friends, while her public statements on speech are rosy, to say the least. In her autobiography, for example, published in 1903, she describes "the thrill of surprise, the joy of discovery" when she spoke her first word (Keller Story 61). But in an 1896 letter to a hearing, sighted friend, Keller admitted difficulties with speech training and efforts to fight natural discouragement (Keller Story 198), and in a 1915 letter to her speech trainer, admitted that "my voice has not brought me the happiness that I anticipated" (Lash 421). These private letters show the "frustration, anguish, and disappointment" with her speech that she carefully hid from her public (Gitter "Deaf-Mutes" 191). In fact, Keller experienced a period of severe depression after beginning speech training, the second of three such periods in her childhood and youth (Herrmann). (The first occurred when she started English lessons with Sullivan, and the third when she graduated from Radcliffe.)

Keller's speech was widely criticized by those who heard it. A typical comment comes from a hearing librarian who, in 1907, told a group of deaf people visiting the Library of Congress that at a lecture of Keller's she had attended when Sullivan was ill and unable to interpret, Bell attempted to interpret Keller's voice but was unable to follow her for more than a few minutes, so the audience sat through the lecture with no idea what Keller was saying (L[ong]). Of the scores of negative remarks on Keller's speech, perhaps the most telling comes from Eleanor Roosevelt in 1961:

> I find it hard to understand Miss Keller's speech today but ... sometimes I think one does not actually have to understand her words because the spirit shines through the expression of her face and her eyes that are so full of beauty. (Roosevelt 7)

That's a breathtakingly patronizing statement, even if we overlook the creepy comment about Keller's beautiful eyes, which were in fact glass.

So why did Keller continue not only to speak in public but also to present herself as having overcome muteness and to preach oral education to all deaf children? Part of the answer must be found in Keller's personality: from childhood, she was naturally willful and stubborn, used to getting her own way. These character traits, however, like so much of her personality and so many of her opinions, were carefully hidden from the public so that she would be seen, like Bridgman, as "cheerful, reverent, and unselfish" (Gitter Imprisoned Guest 109–10) and thus garner the sympathy necessary to make her an effective fund-raiser, first, as a mere child, for the Perkins Institution and later for the American Foundation for the Blind.

After Howe's retirement from Perkins and when Bridgman was no long young and adorable enough to function as an effective fundraiser, the Institution came under the direction of Howe's protégé and son-in-law, Michael Anagnos, whom Howe had picked up as a youth on a trip to Greece. It was Anagnos, then, who exploited Keller as a child, publicizing her education and using her to raise funds for a Kindergarten when she only ten years old. Keller seems to have enjoyed the work and the attention it brought, and she certainly appreciated this opportunity of forming social contacts. During her college years and shortly after graduation, she had hoped to make a living as a writer, but the public was interested in only one story — how she "overcame her handicap" in childhood — and once that story was told, the reading public was disinclined to buy her books on other subjects. When the American Foundation for the Blind was established in 1921, Keller entered into a mutually beneficial relationship with the group by which Keller and Sullivan got the "income and a meaningful public life" that they had known as fundraisers for Perkins, while the AFB got national recognition from the famous Helen Keller (Nielsen "Was?" 27). Keller worked for the AFB until her death more than forty years later, acquiescing to the trade-off of concealing much of her character for the benefit of an income, first from the AFB payroll and later from her own appearances on the vaudeville stage.

Among the things Keller had to give up were her wishes to work for socialism and pacifism. Among the things she found herself obliged to do was to continue with her speech. By the early twentieth century, any public interest in sign language, or any sort of manual communication, had given way to repulsion (Freeberg 31–34; Nielsen "Was" 32). In addition, any arrangement in which Keller would fingerspell a lecture or even an interview with Sullivan as interpreter would invite suspicions of fraud, which had already surfaced during Keller's childhood when many people believed Sullivan was conning them. Keller would be no good to the AFB if she did not speak. Once she became identified as the deaf-blind woman who spoke, turning back would have left both her and Sullivan destitute.

The Deaf community of the 1890s and early twentieth century was unaware of how much the need to earn a living factored into Keller's choices and, even if they had understood that, would they have excused her for public statements like these, given below? The first excerpt is from Keller's infamous address to the American Association to Promote the Teaching of Speech to the Deaf at their meeting in Philadelphia at the new Mt. Airy campus of the Pennsylvania Institution in 1896, when Keller was only 16.

> I cannot understand how anyone interested in our education can fail to appreciate the satisfaction we feel in being able to express our thoughts in living words. Why, I use speech constantly, and I cannot begin to tell you how much pleasure it gives me to do so. Of course I know that it is not always easy for stranger to understand me, but it will be by and by; in the meantime I have the unspeakable happiness of know that my family and friends rejoice in my ability to speak ... We shall speak, yes, and sing, too, as God intended we should speak and sing.

Keller claimed, here, to know God's intentions for deaf people – who could argue with that? In a letter reporting on this speech, Keller reported that "Every one said I spoke very well and intelligibly" (Story, letter to Hitz 15 July 1896) and she appears to have believed these kind words. And why shouldn't everyone have told her so? After all, her appearance did more than anything else to bolster the Association's cause.

A second excerpt is from an open letter regarding the establishment of oral training under Nebraska law, written in 1913 when Keller was 33:

> The disaster of deafness is incalculable, and every little that is done to lessen it is precious. Surely the lack of speech is the most grievous loss caused by deafness, and no pains should be spared to prevent dumbness from being added to the already great burdens which the deaf child must carry through life. ... I was able to make myself understood [in two recent speaking engagements] by many people, and my success has strengthened my convictions that the gift of speech, however imperfect, is a priceless blessing to the deaf. (Nebraska Parents)

For someone whose speech was not widely or easily understood, to say that her own "success" was sufficient evidence for establishing oral education for all deaf children is simply monstrous. Again, the word "blessing" suggests that speech is God-given.

In a third example, taken from a 1929 article Keller wrote for *The American Magazine* when she was 49, she appears to know not only God's intentions but what it means to be human when she calls deafness "an inhuman silence" (Keller "If" 63).

One would suppose that the Deaf community responded promptly and vigorously to Keller's public pronouncements, but one would be mistaken. The Deaf world's newspaper editors, columnists, and contributors, as well as principals of deaf schools, all hesitated, at first, to condemn her. While these leaders of the Deaf community castigated Bell, Horace Mann, and Samuel Gridley Howe, they held their fire against Keller (Gitter Imprisoned 292). Did they fear that the public would regard them as unkind to the sweet little deaf-blind girl? Or did they truly regard young Keller as lacking any meaningful responsibility for her behavior? It's difficult to understand what various writers were thinking.

In 1891, Job Williams, the hearing principal of the American Asylum in Hartford, which still supported sign-language education, wrote in the American Annals of the Deaf and Dumb that he had thought reports of Keller's speech must be "grossly exaggerated" but, after meeting her, found that her speech as "so distinct that I failed to understand very little of what she said" (Williams "Miscellaneous" 163) — or, to unpack his syntax, he understood most of what she said, and of course few people were more accustomed to deciphering deaf speech than a hearing teacher at a deaf school. Williams is careful to avoid appearing to endorse oralism, however, by emphasizing that Keller is a "prodigy" and that her command of spoken English depended upon her prior knowledge of the language, which she gained through the finger alphabet.

A year later, Edward Allen Fay, Vice-President of Gallaudet College, who was not only an advocate of sign-language education but was also regarded in his time as a master signer, asserted in the Annals that twelve-year-old Keller spoke "freely and fully" and that she was able to lipread even such an odd sentence as "Are you a politic maiden?" ([Fay] "Miscellaneous" 38.3:239). He, too, avoids giving aid and comfort to oralism by stating that touch is more effective than sight for lipreading.

When Keller visited Gallaudet College that same year (when she was in DC as a guest of the Volta Bureau), a student who met her wrote in her diary, "She expressed herself with equal readiness by fingerspelling and vocal speech," adding that a hearing friend described Keller's voice as "unnatural, but not more so that that of deaf persons generally" (qtd. in [Fay] "Miscellaneous: A Visit" 171). The unnamed student went on to write of her sympathy for Keller, using the adjective "pathetic" in its older sense of "arousing compassion": "it was pathetic to observe her use of expressions which implied the possession of both sight and hearing." Contrast that statement to the response among Gallaudet students today to Keller's habit of referencing sights and sounds she could only have had second hand. Tonya Stremlau, who taught Keller's autobiography in the 1990s, reported that students were annoyed by Keller's remarks on, for example, bright sun shine and bird song, wishing she had, instead, explained to her readers how she would actually have sensed a lovely spring day.

During the early 1890s, the Deaf papers not only reported favorably on Keller's oral training, but also reported on her "breakdowns" with sympathy and tact. For example, The Silent Worker reprinted a letter from The Deaf-Mutes' Journal in 1892 reporting that Keller was in danger of "sink[ing] into confirmed melancholy and helplessness," adding that the cause was likely overwork ("Helen Keller Broken"), then retracted it ("We are very glad") and printed a letter of denial from Keller reporting, "Yes, truly I am happy, and growing happier each day that I live" ("From Helen Keller"). The next year, Fay told his readers that reports of Keller's breakdowns were all refuted by Sullivan ([Fay] "Miscellaneous" 38.1:79), which he appeared to take at face value.

In addition to such reports on Keller's health and speech, *The Silent Worker* reprinted dozens of articles from hearing papers on topics such as Keller's comprehension of music, her preparation for college, a meeting with Thomas Edison, her views on mainstreaming for the blind, and her public statements on war and socialism. Only the occasional piece was critical, like that about the librarian who sat through one of Keller's uninterpreted talks without a clue as to what she was saying. That particular piece was written by Ella Florence Long, a Gallaudet graduate whose husband, J. Schuyler Long, is better known today for having compiled the first sign language dictionary.

The one consistently critical voice in the Deaf press during these years was that of a hearing man with no connection whatever to the Deaf world but whose views were well received by editors who, perhaps, were glad that someone else was articulating their doubts for them. This person was William Wade, an elderly wealthy Pennsylvanian who, on a whim, sent nine-year-old Helen a mastiff and thus began a relationship with her and other deaf-blind people that led to publication of The Deaf-Blind, a roster of all known deaf-blind people in America, which went through several editions. By 1897, Wade had become both suspicious of Sullivan and critical of her character as Keller's teacher. He believed that Sullivan was fraudulently prompting Keller and, illogically, asserted that she was overworking the girl, endangering her health (Herrmann 119) — why would she have to overwork Helen if she was the source of Helen's answers?

Wade was also concerned about Sullivan's moral character and wanted to replace her as Helen's tutor with his own daughter (Herrmann 119). Keller later — upon Wade's death, actually, when he couldn't refute her version of events — referred to these matters as "a grave misunderstanding brought about by meddlesome persons whom he trusted" (Keller "In Memoriam" 49). Whatever the case really might have been, Wade's concerns induced him to criticize many aspects of Keller's success, including oralism, in Deaf newspapers. In 1904, for example, Wade was claiming that "no pure oralist ever read my lips" and that those deaf who did read his lips successfully were "thoroughly versed in Manual spelling and signs" (Wade "Mr. Wade on Lipreading"). By 1911 Wade had become more strident, referring to oralism as "Chemically Pure Oralism" or "C.P.O," and calling it "accursed rot" (Wade "A letter from Mr. Wade"). No wonder *The Silent Worker* called him "our friend."

Wade's rants and Ella Florence Long's criticism of Keller's speech during the several years following Keller's graduation from Radcliffe in 1904 were but a taste of the more explicit criticism to be published when Keller was no longer an adorable child or lovely young lady. Some sympathy persisted: for example, John P. Walker, writing for The Silent Worker in 1913, attempted to explain away Keller's letter to the Nebraska Parents by asserting that "she knows that under present conditions, many of those who leave us must fall short of proficiency" ([Walker] "Opinions"), though Walker could not possibly have known any such thing. Within a few years, however, Walker was reporting on the "universal complaint" that Keller did not visit deaf schools when she was in their areas on lecture tours. Explaining this behavior, he now engages in sarcasm, speculating that "Perhaps, after she has gotten a little competency," that is, sufficient income, "she will start out and pay us all a little visit" ([Walker] "Later"). Further edging toward the negative is Walter Glover's 1916 article in which he quotes reports from two hearing South Carolina newspapers about the poor quality of Keller's speech and goes on quote a deaf local that "Miss Helen Keller's work has not helped oralism much," but he backs off from direct criticism by opining that "some one has placed her in the hands of a mercenary organization that is starring her for the dollars" (Glover).

As late as 1913, however, the *Annals* gave Keller a forum to attempt to placate the Deaf community with some remarks on the usefulness of sign language (Christie 125) but the attacks on Keller would soon become continuous, and they would come from a new group of Deaf leaders: Deaf woman columnists. Women like Cora Coe, Augusta Barrett, Ella Florence Long, and the incomparable Alice Terry, all educated at Gallaudet, found themselves after graduation throughout the country at state deaf schools with a lot of free time and a lot of rage. These women didn't share the gentlemanly restraints of their male peers and they went after Keller with relish. Even the most sympathetic to oralism, Cora Coe, used Keller as an example of oralists not being honest with deaf people about the quality of their voices [C[oe]).

Among these women writers, it was Alice Terry, the "Little Mother of the Deaf," whose attacks on Keller were the most reasoned, sharply worded, and persistent. Terry was incensed by Keller's appearances on the vaudeville stage with Sullivan, now working under her married name, Mrs. Macy. The money made from these performances must have seemed immense to the average deaf worker, who did not realize that Keller and Macy came back from each tour poorer than they had started out, due to Keller's profligate spending. Terry began one of her "California" columns, in 1915, thus:

> It was Barnum, the great circus man, who said that the public loves to be humbugged ... he set about humbugging it too, with "miraculous" returns financially. It is not necessary for me to comment here on the returns of the Macy-Keller Lectures. The newspapers have emblazoned the profits in enormous figures.
>
> As Miss Keller is deaf and gained her education thro the self-same manual method (excepting braile [sic]) that we did, we feel quite a natural interest in her. But in most every city where she has stopped we have not been privileged to meet her, personally, to interest her in our cause [that is, the cause of maintaining sign education for deaf children].... I sincerely hope that she will yet condescend to form a real acquaintance with us.
>
> But meanwhile, would it not be just as well for our State Associations to go further and protest at the public exhibition of blind, deaf and mute persons doing so-called "decent speaking and lip-reading" on the public platform?
>
> Such we have had in the Macy-Keller Lecture Tours. And it is safe to say no public demonstration ever worked greater in jury to the deaf as a class.... Whether or not the public could understand Miss Keller's difficult articulation, it really didn't matter, for they were so moved with compassion, so

wrought up at the vocal "Miracle" of the famous girl as to suffer partial paralysis of reason.... The public forgets, or does not know, that Miss Keller was NOT educated by the Oral Method. Nor can other deaf-mute children receive even a fair amount of knowledge by that one single method. (Terry "California")

It was not only the signing deaf, like Terry, who were appalled at Keller's vaudeville appearances. Alexander Pach reported, in 1922, that the "extreme oral wing have frowned on Miss Keller's going into vaudeville," citing Bell and an unnamed principal of an oral school who sat through her performance with a "glacial demeanor" (Pach). (Pach ended this installment of his "With the *Silent Worker*" column suggesting that Keller should get married, a comment that will seem sexist to us but that certainly paralleled Keller's own dreams.)

Deaf opposition to Keller's vaudeville performances was widespread and particularly vehement. For example, an anonymous writer in 1920 pointed out with delicious sarcasm that Keller's vaudeville act comes on top of many other achievements, including a college degree from Radcliffe, graduate courses at Harvard, several books, and "even ... an airplane flight"! ("Helen Keller in Vaudeville") The French Deaf writer, Yvonne Pitois, who was nearly as well known in her own country as Keller and who was in fact a close friend and biographer of Keller, called the shows "painful, offensive, and exhibitionistic," "unfortunate eccentricities" that Pitois hoped would be forgotten (Hartig 23, 24).

While opposition to Keller's vaudeville appearances frequently touched on matters of dignity, as these examples show, most Deaf people were more concerned about the message she was sending on the merits of oral education. In 1919, Terry noted the irony of Keller's "success" with oralism:

In her book, "The World I live in" [sic], Helen Keller says, in the preface, that she cannot write as she wants to, but must write as editors want her to. She would like to give her views on education, the tariff, labor, and other big issues of the day. But editors do not want that; instead, they ask her to confine herself to her own soundless and sightless world.... Can't you see through that? Can't you see that her well-advertised attempts at articulation have not converted thoughtful people to the extent that they seek her views on the important issues of the day. (Terry "Sound – Why Not Let It Alone?")

One other habit of Keller's garnered repeated complaint in the Deaf papers during this period, and that was how she appeared to be snubbing Deaf people, clubs, schools, and organizations. In 1903, when she was finishing up her degree, Keller wrote, "Above all must I interest myself in affairs which concern the deaf and the blind" (Keller "My Future"), but she made little, if any attempt to carry out this plan; there is no record that she even acknowledged E. M. Gallaudet's presence at her graduation ceremony (Lash 313). We saw that Alice Terry had complained on this point in 1915 and that John P. Walker called this a "universal complaint" a year later. Keller's own letters mentions visits to and from "friends" who are deaf, but these deaf people never seem to have names (Nielsen Helen Keller: Selected Writings 101, 172). Resentment simmered through the following decade. Augusta K. Barrett, in one of her "Angelenograms" columns, for example, complaining that Keller and Sullivan Macy failed to respond to an invitation to luncheon at an upscale Los Angeles eatery with a group of "deaf ladies." As usual, Barrett, who was a founding member of the O.W.L.S. at Gallaudet, blamed it on Keller's handlers and tossed in a complaint about her oralism to boot:

> It seems that those in charge of her do not encourage any contact with the deaf tho it was by means of the Manual Alphabet of the deaf that the light first entered the mind of the little blind-deaf child, the foundation for her later achievements. (Barrett)

When Keller declined an honorary degree from Gallaudet College, extended by President Percival Hall in 1939, no one seems to have been surprised as it passed without mention.

Any mention of Keller in the Deaf press after the 1920s is not only a rarity but also entirely lacking in substantive comment. For example, The Silent Worker reported the death of Keller's companion, Polly Thompson, in 1960 (Lange "With the Foreign Deaf) and the celebration of her birthday at the Jewish School for the Deaf in Tel Aviv in 1961 ("Israel Honors"), and Deaf Life published a story in 1990 on a statue commemorating Anne Sullivan Macy (Jacobsen). Holcomb and Woods' 1989 Deaf Woman provided only a short article giving the basic facts of her life, and Lang and Meath-Lang's 1995 Deaf Persons in the Arts and Sciences likewise avoided controversy in their slightly longer entry. Jean Christie's entry on Keller in the 1987 Gallaudet Encyclopedia of Deaf People and Deafness usefully provides two paragraphs on the "sign language – voice training controversy," couched in neutral language (Christie 125). Sharon Woods and Henning C. F. Irgens, in an article about the Holcomb-Woods reference work, point out that Keller's success had mostly to do with the socio-economic status of the family she was born into. And that's about it.

As for scholarship from outside the Deaf community, we have not been well served by present-day Keller scholars, who appear not to understand that Keller was deaf and or that her influence on deaf education was enormous. Dorothy Herrmann, for example, indexes "work for the blind and deaf" but all cited pages have to do with work for the blind. Lash's dual biography of Keller and Sullivan stumbles repeatedly when dealing with anything deaf, confusing the Annals with the oralist Association Review and referring to the American Asylum as "The Hartford Institution for Deaf Mutes," to name just a few of his blunders. Only Kim Nielsen, frequently cited in this paper, occasionally addresses Keller's role in Deaf history, citing Long and Terry, for example, to show the "hostile distance between herself and the Deaf community" (Nielsen "Was?" 29).

Those of us who want to use Keller and her writings to open a window on anything from the history of deaf education to Deaf women columnists of the early twentieth century can start with Nielsen's work but must expect to do most of the spade work ourselves.

REFERENCES

Barrett, Augusta R. "Angelenograms." *The Silent Worker* 37.9 (1925): 425-28.
Christie, Jean. "Helen Keller." *The Gallaudet Encyclopedia of Deaf People and Deafness*. New York: McGraw-Hill, 1987.
C[oe], C[ora] E. "A Heart-to-Heart Talk." *The Silent Worker* 28.6 (1916): 108-09.
[Fay, Edward Allen]. "Miscellaneous: Helen Keller." *American Annals of the Deaf and Dumb* 38.1 (1893): 79.
[Fay, Edward Allen]. "Miscellaneous: A Visit from Helen Keller." *American Annals of the Deaf and Dumb* 38.2 (1893): 170-72.
[Fay, Edward Allen]. "Miscellaneous: Helen Keller." *American Annals of the Deaf and Dumb* 38.3 (1893): 238-40.
Freeberg, Ernest. *The Education of Laura Bridgman: The First Deaf and Blind Person to Lean Language*. Cambridge, Massachusetts: Harvard University Press, 2001.
Fuller, Sarah. "How Helen Keller Learned to Speak." *American Annals of the Deaf and Dumb* 37.1 (1892): 23-30.
Gitter, Elizabeth. "Deaf-Mutes and Heroines in the Victorian Era." *Victorian Literature and Culture* 20 (1992): 179-96.
Gitter, Elizabeth. *The Imprisoned Guest: Samuel Howe and Laura Bridgman, the Original Deaf-Blind Girl*. New York: Farrar, Straus & Giroux, 2001.
Glover, Walter. "South Carolina's Views and Comments on Miss Helen Keller." *The Silent Worker* 28.10 (1916): 183-85.
Hartig, Rachel. *Crossing the Divide: Representations of Deafness in Biography*. Washington: Gallaudet University Press, 2006.
"Helen Keller Broken Down." *The Silent Worker* 5.8 (1892): 5.
"Helen Keller in Vaudeville." *The Silent Worker* 32.7 (1920): 174.
Herrmann, Dorothy. *Helen Keller: A Life*. New York: Knopf, 1998.
Holcomb, Mabs, and Sharon K. Wood. *Deaf Women: A Parade through the Decades*. Berkeley: DawnSignPress, 1989.
"Israel Honors Helen Keller." *The Silent Worker* n.s. 13.5 (1961): 9.
Jacobsen, Pamela D. "In Memory of the Great Teacher." *Deaf Life* 3.5 (1990): 8-13.
Keller, Helen. "From Helen Keller." *The Silent Worker* 5.9 (1892): 8.
Keller, Helen. "If You Have Friends, You Can Endure Anything." *American Magazine* September 1929: 62-63, 168-72.
Keller, Helen. "In Memoriam: William Wade." *Outlook for the Blind* Autumn 1913: 47-48.
Keller, Helen. "My Future as I See It." *The Ladies' Home Journal* 20 (1903): 11.

Keller, Helen. *The Story of My Life*. New York: Dell, 1961.

Lang, Harry, & Bonnie Meath-Lang. *Deaf Persons in the Arts and Sciences: A Biographical Dictionary*. Westport, Connecticut: Greenwood P, 1995.

Lange, Paul. "With the Foreign Deaf." *The Silent Worker* n.s. 13.1 (1960): 18.

Lash, Joseph P. *Helen and Teacher: The Story of Helen Keller and Anne Sullivan Macy*. New York: Delacorte, 1980.

L[ong], E[lla] F[lorence]. "Stray Straws." *The Silent Worker* 20.2 (1907): 25.

Nebraska Parents' Association to Promote the Oral Education of the Deaf. *Opinions upon the Nebraska Law*. s.l.: The Association, [1913].

Nielsen, Kim E. "Was Helen Keller Deaf?: Blindness, Deafness, and Multiple Identities." In *Women and Deafness: Double Visions*, ed. Brenda Jo Brueggemann and Susan Burch (Washington: Gallaudet UP, 2006): 21-39.

Nielsen, Kim E., ed. *Helen Keller: Selected Writings*. New York: New York University Press, 2005.

Pach, Alexander L. "With the Silent Workers." *The Silent Worker* 34.7 (1922): 254.

Perry, Ralph Barton. Introduction. *Keller, Story of My Life*: 11-15.

Roosevelt, Eleanor. Foreword. *Keller, Story of My Life*: 7-8.

Stremlau, Tonya. Personal correspondence.

Sullivan, Annie M. "How Helen Keller Acquired Language." *American Annals of the Deaf and Dumb* 37.2 (1892): 127-54.

Terry, Alice T. "California." *The Silent Worker* 28.2 (1915): 26.

-----. "Sound – Why Not Let It Alone?" T*The Silent Worker* 31.7 (1919): 113, 130.

Wade, William. "A letter from Mr. Wade." *The Silent Worker* 23.4 (1911): 67.

-----. "Mr. Wade on Lipreading." *The Silent Worker* 16.7 (1904): 103.

[Walker, John P.] "Later On, Perhaps." *The Silent Worker* 28.10 (1916): 192.

-----. "Opinions." *The Silent Worker* 25.10 (1913): 190.

"We are very glad." *The Silent Worker* 5.9 (1892): 4.

Williams, Job. "Miscellaneous: Helen Keller." *American Annals of the Deaf and Dumb* 36.2 (1891): 162-64. Rpt from The Hartford Courant 20 Feb 1891.

Wood, Sharon Kay, and Henning C. F. Irgens. "Does 'Herstory' Speak for the Deaf Community?" *Deaf American Monographs* 47 (1997): 75-78.

DEAF-WORLD Positional Identity Negotiations

BRYAN ELDREDGE, PH.D.

THIS PAPER EXAMINES THE ROLE OF DISCOURSE IN THE ESTABLISH-ment and maintenance of positional identities in the Deaf-World. Positional identities are those that mark persons as certain kinds of members of a group (e.g. shaman, orator, wacko, etc.). As with other social groups, there is a hierarchical relationship among positional identities within the DEAF-WORLD. Certain positions carry more power, prestige, and privilege than others. As a result, the processes that elevate people to or prevent their ascension to more prestigious and more powerful positions are of great significance.

This paper demonstrates a number of practices that Deaf people use to assert and ascribe elite identities, positions within the Deaf world that other Deaf people respect. The most significant of these are discursive practices by which individuals display a form of "super competence" in ASL. The most significant feature of super competence is the adroit use of a particular cluster of formal features that index the ASL storytelling style and the positional identity associated with its use. We will get back to this notion of super competence and its relationship to the storytelling style in a while, but first let's see a claim to an elite positional identity in action.

This study is taken from ethnographic fieldwork I conducted along Utah's Wasatch Front, primarily in Utah County, during the late 1990s and early 2000s. During the course of that fieldwork, I relied heavily on my training as a linguistic anthropologist to collect naturally-occurring, contextually-situated discourse as my primary data source.

As part of the fieldwork I recorded a conversation among a number of Deaf individuals during a dinner for single adults in Utah County held at an

LDS chapel. The only married person at the table was Wayne, an ecclesiastical leader who was getting to know the young single members of his congregation. Their discussion reveals some significant ways that positional identities can be signified.

In this exchange Wayne asked two deaf siblings about the presence of deafness in their family, a topic that was carried on until most everyone at the table was asked how it was they became deaf, which always solicited accounts of the presence of other deaf family members (Eldredge, 2004). The one exception to the questioning was Wayne, who started the line of questioning. The reason no one questioned Wayne is not immediately obvious, and what was initially less obvious to me is why Wayne offers an unsolicited explanation whose referential content would appear to threaten his claim to a Deaf identity. Careful analysis, however, uncovers some important insights into Wayne's identity as well as to how the way Wayne uses ASL says more about him that what he says with it.

As the younger people were recounting their relationships to other Deaf members of their families, Wayne broke into Jared's account (this interruption begins in line 32, but he did not get recognized so he started again in line 34 below).

Translation:
30   Jared: I'm the only deaf person in my family. Really, there's no hard-of-hearing [people] or anything.
        ^Wayne: I was born. . . .(*Unacknowledged.*)
33   Josh: (*To John or Ron*) He's [Jared] mental.
        Wayne: I was born hearing but my mother became crazy. She stuck her fingers in my ears and flipped me head over heels again and
36   again. That's what made me deaf.

Unlike the other responses, Wayne's account is clearly farcical. In his account Wayne claimed that he was born hearing but became deaf when his mother, in a fit of insanity, stuck her fingers in his ears and repeatedly swung him head over heels (lines 34–36).

In contrast to the others' responses, Wayne gives no factual information about when or how he became deaf or whether he has any Deaf relatives. Instead, he gives the kind of information the others avoid — the cause of his deafness, but the information is false (line 34-36). He was not born hearing, nor was his deafness caused by his insane mother's swinging him in circles with her fingers in his ears. The entire account is *clearly* a lie, and that is to Wayne's benefit because it presents potentially damaging information. Being born hearing opens the door to the possibility of early enculturation into hearing ways and perhaps very late exposure to the DEAF-WORLD. But in this case, Wayne's story did just the opposite. With it Wayne staked a strong claim to an elite status within the DEAF-WORLD. He managed this positive outcome because, as I will explain, the *way* he told his lie overpowered its referential content.

The effectiveness of Wayne's telling lies in his story's humor, despite the fact that it may not seem funny at all to outsiders. Beyond its absurdity, there is nothing particularly funny about the *content* of Wayne's brief narrative. To Deaf people the story is funny because it presents a *visual image* of Wayne's mother deafening him by placing her fingers in his ears and swinging him around. And as I have suggested, Wayne's telling does more than elicit laughs; it asserts an identity beyond simply being Deaf. The bizarre visual imagery uses a combination of classifiers and role shifting — the features in ASL that take maximal advantage of the signing medium — that creates a visual image reminiscent of Vaudeville sight gags. This indexes the storytelling style, which in turn links Wayne to elite, storytelling status.

Careful analysis of the brief narrative (lines 34-35 above) reveals the mastery that Wayne displays. The transcription of these lines appears below. (As a reminder, a complete transcription key appears as Appendix A.)

Transcription:
>Wayne: POSS-1st BORN HEARING. POSS-1st MOTHER BECOME CRAZY. (As mother) <(2h)CL-1"stick fingers in ears" (2h)CL-1"swing me around in circles" .... (H1)CL-2"legs flipping around"> BECOME DEAF (H2)..>

Translation:
>Wayne: I was born hearing but my mother became crazy. (*As his mother.*) She/I stuck her/my fingers in my/his ears and flipped me/him head over heels again and again. That's what made me/him deaf.

Note that three of the twelve signs comprising Wayne's story are classifiers (in bold). The three classifiers, **(2h)CL-1"Stick fingers in ears," (2h)CL-1"Swing me around in circles,"** and **(H1)CL-2"legs flipping around"** come in succession and immediately follow his role shift to take on his mother's perspective and persona. The second and third classifiers are performed at the same time, one on either hand. This simultaneous word production in the signing space is impossible in spoken languages, and its visual nature, the physical "picture" it creates, is the basis for the story's humor. (Note that the onset and end of Wayne's role shift, where he takes on and departs from the role of his deranged mother, is indicated by < and > respectively.)

The *timing* of the three classifiers and the role shift in the story is more important than their mere presence. The classifiers (see figures 5-2, 5-3, and 5-4) appear precisely at the point of the story that purports to tell how Wayne became deaf. They form the punch line, bringing the story a visual humor that is characteristic of storytelling.

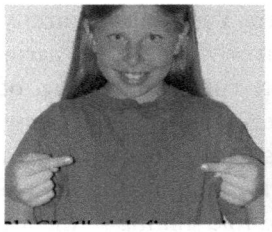 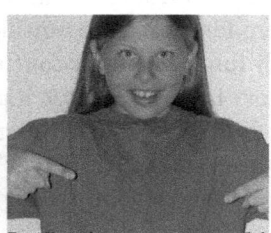 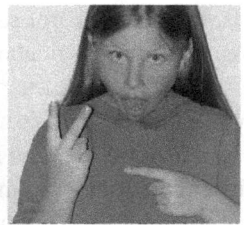

Figure 5-2: The classifier (2h)CL-1"stick fingers in ears."

Figure 5-3: The classifier (2h)CL-1"swing me around in circles."

Figure 5-4: The classifier (H1)CL-2"legs flipping around."

As we have seen, Wayne's narrative presents some culturally salient symbols that indicate that he holds an elevated position in the Deaf-World. Specifically, his telling exemplifies the storytelling *style* in its use of classifiers and role shifting. In terms of Peircean semiotics, the formal elements of Wayne's story act as *sign vehicles* or *signs*, are "something which stands to somebody for something is some respect or capacity" (Peirce, 1985:5). In this case, Wayne's signing indicates that he holds an elite status.

STYLES AS INDICES

Among the actions that index elite status is the production of certain valorized sign styles or types of signing, and some styles do this better than others. Deaf-World language ideology holds that Deaf people are by definition competent with conversational ASL. In contrast, elite Deaf people demonstrate high-level proficiency, or *super competence*, in the styles associated with storytelling.

As Hanks (1996) explains, "Speech of all kinds has stylistic dimensions" (1996:184), but "to say that all language has style is not to say that it is all the same" (1996:185). A given speech style is "a cluster of formal characteristics (phonetic, lexical, and syntactic)" (Urban, 1985:313) and when those characteristics come together in an instance of talk, that talk is taken as an instance, or token, of the style. Urban explains,

> In semiotic terms, a speech style is a general regularity or "type" as opposed to an occurring instance or "token." That is, a speech style is a general form that is recognizable apart from specific instances in which it is used. As a

type, a speech style must be viewed as an alternative linguistic norm, rather than as an individual's deviation. (1985:312)

Styles are familiar to virtually all language users. We name them things like chants, songs, yelling, lecturing, nagging, and so on. These broad categories are the styles Hanks describes. The tokens, then, are the instances of a particular style as when children sing "Ring around the Rosies" or any of the new songs they might create. We recognize the patterned qualities of these new songs, and it is this recognition that allows us to call them songs.

We consider the "everyday" or "conversational" style as the unmarked form and all other styles are marked to varying degrees by how much they differ from the conversational style. Unmarked styles exhibit what Urban (1985) calls "expressive restriction," which contrasts with "formal amplification" in marked style. The marked styles stand out as something out of the ordinary for everyday conversation and are appropriate to some other set of circumstances. As with any language community, Deaf people recognize various styles in ASL. I have identified a number of these styles and have listed them in table 1.

Style	Characteristics	Uses
Everyday ASL or "Heritage ASL" (Bahan, Hoffmeister, & Lane, 1996)	The unmarked form in which Deaf people see nothing unusual. Natural, relaxed, flowing, expressive. Includes nonmanual signals including facial expressions and body movement. Communication is clear. Signers maintain frequent eye contact with addressees, ensuring comprehension and uninterrupted flow of communication. Lack of MCE affixes and initialized signs associated with MCE (this despite the fact that even ASL's forerunner LSF incorporated numerous initialized signs). Exhibits substantial variation in breadth of vocabulary and in topics of discussion.	Used in "everyday" settings, including introductions, greetings, chats, and one-on-one and group discussions. Used between intimates and nonintimates alike.

Storytelling	Tremendous eye contact between storyteller and audience, with the intent of drawing in the audience. Includes a much larger number of classifiers whose use is often as much the central part of the story as is the referential content. Role shifting/direct address common, often in conjunction with classifiers. Often storytelling is done entirely in various roles and using classifiers almost exclusively. Feeds the story and constantly checks for comprehension. Generally flows faster. Signers move more than in everyday ASL. Entertaining because of the content and the form. Humor often lies in sign play. Idealized as a more pure form of ASL.	Used in formal performances, commonly used in residential schools with Deaf adults telling stories to students. Common in Deaf "bull sessions" and in dealing with personal experiences.
Joke Telling	Large expressions. Much in common with storytelling, including the use of classifiers and role shifting/direct speech. Honorific pronouns used sarcastically. Deals with personal experiences less often than storytelling. Good deaf jokes require experience in the Deaf culture and a high degree of ASL skill.	Used between friends or nonintimates.
Poetry	Rhythmic. Eye contact has functions beyond maintaining connection with audience. Eye gaze often associated with role shifting and very often only acknowledges the audience at the very end. This may be in part because establishing eye contact invites the addressee to convey a lack of understanding which demands redress. Attempts to clarify break established rhythms that are significant feature of poetry.	Used as entertainment at formal and semiformal events, in classrooms, etc.

Sign Play or "Handshape Stories"	These creative verbal art performances come in two basic varieties: Single-handshape and sequential-handshape stories. Single-handshape stories use only signs sharing the same or closely related handshapes, or they use a handshape (such as ILY for "I love you"). That shape is applied to all the signs of the story. Sequential-handshape stories create a narrative out of signs using handshapes that resemble the first letter of a particular sequence (e.g., alphabetical order, numerical order, or the spelling of a particular word, like G-O-L-F). Statements such as "I have a good handshape story" almost always key these stories.	Sign play of this sort are performed in bull sessions. They are a favorite of Deaf adults to perform for deaf children. They are also performed at formal or semi-formal events as entertainment.
Formal ASL	Slower, bigger, more English influence, more formal signs (two-handed, older forms, etc.), more full fingerspelling, lack of slang, profanity, and vulgarity.	Used by teachers in formal classes and workshops (see lectures), and other situations, such as job interviews, in which there exists a significant and obvious power differential.
Lectures	Slower, bigger, more English influence, more formal signs (two-handed, older forms, etc.). Signer tends to stay in one small area.	Used by teachers in formal classes and workshops.
Master of Ceremonies	Very exaggerated, huge signing space (results in slower production), dramatic, acting. Signer moves back and forth, making eye contact with various audience members. Honorific pronouns common. English-like question forms often employed.	Used by masters of ceremonies or hosts at awards banquets, pageants, etc.

Reverent	More graceful and restrained, more two-handed and formal signs, honorific second and third person pronouns used. Subject matter is normally serious and/or spiritual. Humor is very limited (usually based on irony, may not be recognized as a joke right off).	Used in formal sermons and sometimes by teachers in Sunday school classes.
Prayer	Eyes closed, head often bowed slightly. Similar to reverent signing in many respects: second and third person honorific pronouns, slow deliberate sign formation, etc.	Used in public and sometimes private settings including church meetings, blessings on food, and the performance of religious ordinances.
Yelling	Hard, faster, stronger, bigger space, abrupt, quick, abrupt, facial expressions (often accompanied with a vocalization, if not actual production of words).	Used in heated arguments, often during sporting events, domestic disputes, etc. Linked to anger. Often considered appropriate, or at least justified, when the angry person appears to have been wronged.
Foreigner Talk	Simplified form with slower, greatly exaggerated signs. Heavy reliance on iconic signs. Frequent brief pauses accompanied by nonmanual signal (i.e., facial expression and eye gaze) to check the addressee's comprehension. Over mouthing of English words and possibly speech often accompany the signing. Syntactically simple.	Used with novice signers or non-signers.

Table 1: ASL Styles

Styles are important to identity negotiations because each instance ("token") of a style ("type") is linked to a social position. Each style is necessarily related to specific sets of contexts and meanings. Each token points to other tokens of the same type and highlights the social context(s) in which the style is appropriate (Urban 1985). Styles are indexically linked to particular contexts, including particular users. Therefore, a person who invokes a style invokes for him or herself the status and/or position of those who typically use that style.

To see this in action, let's return to Wayne's claim that his mother made him Deaf so I can do a little bit of theoretical housekeeping. Specifically, I need to acknowledge that one might reasonably argue that Wayne's use of classifiers, being a part of ASL, really only indicates competence in ASL. To a certain extent, this is true. It is also true that classifiers (as well as role shifting) are not limited in use to the storytelling style. Their use in everyday discourse does mark signing as ASL because they constitute a clear contrast to linear English, as do other formal elements, including agreement verbs, aspectual inflections, directional verbs, spatial pronouns, and deictics.

The evidence that Wayne's story signals more than mere ASL fluency lies in *the combination* of classifiers, role shifting, and other elements to key the storytelling style, however briefly. The classifiers alone do not indicate an elite status. Multiple formal elements that key the storytelling style also link Wayne to the elite. The role shift Wayne undertakes to express his mother's act is a significant ingredient to the storytelling style. In a sense, taking on the role of another person moves one from "telling" something to "performing" it. Wayne's shift to his mother's role is evident in the locative relationships expressed by the classifiers — specifically a body classifier that represents his mother's fingers being placed in his ears. The classifier's placement in relation to Wayne's body shows the location of his own ears. The classifier is placed in the signing space in front of him, not near his own ears because he has adopted the vantage point of his mother; his fingers have become hers and his head is positioned relative to (i.e., in front of) his mother. This is the kind of reported speech or "direct discourse" described above, and its use indexes the storytelling style.

Although these role shifts often allow signers to employ classifiers, as in the present case, they do not always do so. The two do not necessarily go together. They are conceptually linked within DEAF-WORLD ideologies of language because they both constitute the picture-like qualities which Deaf people value so highly. They both take advantage of the signing medium in ways that are touchstones of "pure" ASL, which in turn is associated with more "authentic" Deaf persons that storytellers epitomize. This is the first of the two indexical linkages I discussed above: classifiers and role shifts index storytelling and "pure" ASL.

Wayne could have given this explanation without performing the role shift. For example, he could have altered the form of the first two classifiers — (2h)CL-1"stick fingers in ears" and (2h)CL-1"swing me around in circles" — so that their location was near his own ears rather than in the signing space in front of him (see figures 5-5 and 5-6). He then could have just deleted the final classifier — (H1)CL-2"Legs flipping around" — which is a redundant description of his being swung around. The resulting construction would allow Wayne to completely omit the shift to his mother's perspective.

Figure 5-5: (2h)CL-1"Stick fingers in ears" as himself.

Figure 5-6: (2h)CL-1"Swing me around head over heels" as himself.

Figure 5-7: The ASL verb TO-PUT-in-ears.

He could then have added the pronoun PRO-3rd ("she") and, as in the previous example, produced the classifier (2h)CL-1"Swing me around in circles" near his own ears and then deleted the final classifier in the series (H1)CL-2"Legs flipping around." The resulting construction contains only one classifier (in bold) and no role shift.

Possible Form B:

    Wayne: POSS-1st BORN HEARING. POSS-1st MOTHER BECOME CRAZY. POSS-3rd FINGER-topic TO-PUT-ear. PRO-3rd (2h)CL-1"swing me around in circles" BECOME DEAF.

Wayne might have used any number of combinations of these changes to create different ways to tell the story, all without resorting to a role shift. In reality, removing the role shift necessitates a change in classifier form. The classifiers are performed from the mother's perspective, which means they must agree spatially with her position relative to his. To tell what happened without assuming her role results in different spatial relationships that require changes in form.

It is interesting to note that the alternative forms I proposed to exclude the role shift can be translated essentially the same way as the original: "She stuck her fingers in my ears and flipped me head over heels again and again. That's what made me deaf." Here you can see the importance of the storytelling style. Neither of my alternative constructions change the referential content much, but there is a clear functional difference. Those familiar with ASL and DEAF-WORLD practices will recognize that each of these alterative forms I have just described might seem odd or unnatural. Few fluent ASL signers would find any of these variant forms as comfortable as the one Wayne used, and none of them are as humorous. It may appear that my examples stretch the point, but in practice, none of these *possible* variations is likely. You just would not find Deaf people describing this event this way, and that's why Wayne does it the way he does. It is not that there is no other way to tell it; there is just no other *reason* to do so. The only reason for Wayne to tell this absurd story at all is because it is funny as an ASL story. It gets its humor through its exploitation of the spatial nature of sign. The only possible reason to give such a story using any style but storytelling would be to evade the issue of Wayne's deafness onset — to be uncooperative — and that would only serve to raise suspicion about Wayne's identity.

THE SIGNIFICANCE OF STORYTELLING

The storytelling style in ASL indexes its users with one of the highest positional identities in the DEAF-WORLD, that of storyteller. Storytelling in ASL is a performance style most clearly marked by highly adept use of ASL classifiers and role shifting. They are often used together, along with the other characteristics described in Table 1.

The skillful use of the ASL storytelling style does more than link the signer to the DEAF-WORLD; it connects the user to an elevated position within it. This is an intricate semiotic process involving indexical associations among structural elements and the storytelling genre, as well as the simultaneous valorization of those forms and the position of storytellers within the DEAF-WORLD. Analysts have already noted the connection between the particular characteristics of the storytelling style. Rayman (1999), for example, has noted that role shifting is an important aspect of ASL storytelling; role shifting and classifier use are what distinguish it from storytelling in English.

Role shifting appears in other signed languages as well, and its prevalence probably results from the potential of the spatial medium to exploit it (Lucas & Valli, 1987; Mandel, 1977). Morgan explains that role shifting is like direct discourse or reported speech shifts in spoken language. The difference being that in sign languages signers exploit these shifts to report actions *and* the words from another person's perspective (Morgan, 1999). The actions and words are closely linked because they are produced simultaneously, and they are both visual in signed languages. Movements of the body perform both talk and gesture, and the division between the two is sometimes unclear (Emmorey, 1999).

The ASL storytelling style has special historical and cultural significance. It is tied up in DEAF-WORLD ideologies about language and was illustrated in the way my informants talked to me about their language, something that space does not allow me to illustrate here. Kroskrity (1998) finds a similar phenomenon wherein kiva speech — speech of modern pueblo peoples used in the performance of religious rituals, usually done in rooms called kivas — as the site wherein pure forms of Tewa (a traditional language of pueblo peoples) are retained as a form of resistance to the creeping shift to Hopi — and English — in other realms of discourse.

The link to storytelling also tells us about storytellers. Kroskrity notes that for the Tewa, "The model of the ritual speech foregrounds the importance of the positional, rather than the personal, identities and the use of appropriate role-specific speech" (1998:112). In this case, Tewa speakers invoke a particular style to foreground their authority among members of the community. This authority results from their status and is reflected in their use of a speech style appropriate to that status. A similar, though slightly different, foregrounding occurs in the Deaf case where storytelling is valorized as a more "pure form." Kroskrity notes that Tewa speakers can foreground the role individuals embody, thereby distancing the individual from responsibility for the speech.

Similarly, Deaf signers skillfully use particular forms to index the storytelling style. However, rather than distancing themselves, Deaf storytellers assert their status as storytellers, a respected and influential position within the DEAF-WORLD. They position themselves as "more than entertainers; they are the culture's oral historians and teachers, and their stories have messages embedded in them about DEAF-WORLD values" (Lane et al. 1996).

In the DEAF-WORLD, storytelling has long been an important means of transmitting culture (Rutherford, 1989, 1993; Stokoe, 1995) both in the referential content and through the replication of valorized discourse forms. Because most deaf children have hearing parents who are usually moderately competent at best in ASL, the residential school setting has been a key site for culturally-Deaf people — both adults and acculturated Deaf children, such as those whose parents are Deaf — to pass on stories, and equally important *the storytelling style*, to new generations of Deaf people, stories which teach newcomers how "to be Deaf" (Padden & Humphries, 1988).

In describing styles and the effects of their use, Greg Urban says, "A style is not just an instance of language usage....It characterizes a potentially infinite set of such instances...more or less independently of the semantic meanings" (1991:107). Urban further argues that these styles are themselves both iconic and indexical signs, meaning that they have meaning because they both look like previous instances of the style and the style is linked to identities. In Heather's case, her signing style links her directly with the core of the DEAF-WORLD.

Two Indexical Linkages

I explained earlier that the storytelling style is most commonly recognized by its intense combination of classifier predicates and roleshifting. Classifier predicates and role shifting are similar to spatial verbs and pronouns (which I have said are shibboleths of ASL) in that they each take advantage of the spatial nature of signing. However there are some significant differences. The most important is the presence of spatial pronouns and spatial verbs that ASL's grammatical rules require. Classifier predicates and role shifting are not required, although grammatical rules do affect the ways they are used. The omission of spatial pronouns and spatial verbs results in one of two things: either the sentence is ungrammatical, or the sentence is something other than ASL (usually signed English). This is not true of classifiers and role shifting. The implication is that the use of spatial pronouns and spatial verbs indicates competent ASL use and, consequently, culturally Deaf personal identities. On the other hand, the proficient use of optional classifiers and role shifting, or the lack thereof, indicates positional identities in the DEAF-WORLD.

The storytelling style marks individuals as elite members of the DEAF-WORLD through a semiotically complex process involving the conjoining of two indexical linkages. First, the use of classifiers, role shifting, and associated forms marks one as elite because these linguistic forms are indexically linked to the traditional storytelling genre. Second, talented storytellers hold a special status as cultural elites. They embody notions of the "authentic" Deaf person. The two indexical linkages are stated more plainly below:

First Indexical Linkage:	Second Indexical Linkage:
Classifiers, role shifting, and associated forms are linked to the storytelling style, and those proficient with them are linked to (and sometimes seen as) storytellers.	The storytelling style is linked to an elite status, giving storytellers elite positional identities.

These relationships can be further illustrated as in figure 5-1 below, in which the symbol ⇓ means "are indexically linked to."

Classifiers & Role Shifting
⇓ (1st)
Storytelling & Storytellers
⇓ (2nd)
Elite Identities

Figure 5-1: Two Indexical Linkages.

The application of these processes involves a somewhat paradoxical circularity that is often considered weakness in argumentation but one that is inherent to indexical relationships: those who effectively exploit the most complex spatial resources of the linguistic medium, namely classifiers and role shifting, are indexically linked to storytelling. At the same time, classifiers and role shifting are considered the highest form of language use because they are the forms that the best storytellers use. Thus is the nature of indexical relationships — one thing points to another and vice versa.

Beyond Question
It is too strong a statement to say that Wayne presents this account of becoming deaf solely to assert his identity. I think he was trying to be funny as well. But the assertion of his identity is a result and I would be wrong to suggest that Wayne was not aware of this effect. Undoubtedly, the story is intended to be funny and it is. It is the nature of the humor that makes it a classic example of a Deaf story. It is visual or, as Danny suggested, "like pictures." Wayne's use of role shifting and classifiers takes full advantage of the visual medium to create a form of *visual* humor.

Equally important is the fact that Wayne's visual humor expresses an idealistically Deaf perspective. Rayman argues that Deaf people's experiences as visual people affects them, saying "The visual orientation to the world shapes their culture and the modality of their language that may in turn promote the value of vivid depictions in storytelling" (1999:80). The joke's focus on the visual represents a Deaf center in much the same way De'VIA art and Deaf poetry, with their similar attention to the visual, embody a Deaf worldview.

Evidence of Success
The question that remains is to what extent Wayne's story achieves its aims. There is evidence in the exchange(s) that followed the story to suggest that it does serve to establish, or at least to reinforce, his position within the DEAF-WORLD. For example, the others never did ask Wayne the real story of how he became deaf. They didn't ask him about his family connections either, and this despite the fact that Wayne started that line of questioning. Why not? Simply because the manner of his telling says enough about him to render the questions irrelevant. And while no one pursues these questions further, the conversation that follows his narrative further reinforces Wayne's position.

Below I again present a translation of the exchange with Wayne's lie. This time, I have included the discourse that follows so we can examine the evidence that Wayne's positional identity is made clear. Ron's response to Wayne's narrative (lines 37-38) shows that Ron misunderstood the initial telling and inaccurately believed that Wayne was talking about swinging around on a type of swing set.

Translation:

36 Wayne: I was born hearing but my mother became crazy. She stuck her fingers in my ears and flipped me head over heels again and again. That's what made me deaf.
Ron: [Obstructed] (*Misunderstanding.*) She swung you all the way around? On a swing?
39 Wayne: (*Slower.*) My mother... became crazy. You know her index fingers? She stuck them in my ears, like this, and flipped me head over heels again and again, you see?
42 Ron: (Leans back, shakes head [rolls eyes?].)
Wayne: (*Shrugs.*) She's still crazy.
45 (Lisa laughs. Ron shakes his head. Lisa changes positions while laughing, fans herself.)
Mandy: (*To Ron, smiling broadly.*) Can you imagine learning to sign from him?
48 Ron: (*To Mandy as just prior self.*) I sat here looking at him. He said she stuck her fingers in his ears, and I knew he was kidding me. Geez!
Mandy: (To Ron.) Hey... (Unacknowledged.)
51 Ron: (*To Josh.*) [Obstructed] His mother was crazy and she stuck her fingers in his ears and flipped him head over heels again and again. (Josh and Jared join the others in laughing.)
54 Ron: (*To Wayne as recent self.*) I sat here watching you say that... (*As self.*) You are nuts.
Josh: That's funny.

In-depth analysis of the video reveals that none of them gave any indication that they grasped the story's meaning on that first telling, despite the fact that Wayne is using ASL, just as everyone else at the table has been. This is not a case of code switching between languages, yet there is a *qualitative* difference between the kind of ASL Wayne uses here and that used by the others. Apparently his shift makes it difficult to understand. I can only speculate on the reasons Ron might have misunderstood Wayne's story (line 37). He was sitting to Wayne's immediate left, which may have limited his peripheral vision a bit. Perhaps the absurdity of the story may have caused him to doubt whether Wayne actually said what he did. Or possibly the form itself inhibited his comprehension, with its use of classifiers whose antecedents are not clearly established. Not coincidentally, three other people at the table, including both Lisa and Mandy, were watching the story unfold, and none of them appear to have understood it to the first time.

It is possible that Wayne tells his story in part to demonstrate that his ability to use the language exceeds the others' ability to comprehend it. Perhaps he *intends* it to be difficult for them to understand, creating a kind of intentional linguistic opacity at the positional level. This motive looks a little devious and unlikely, so I do not insist on it. I do, however, think it is important to consider the possibility, which is made ever so slightly more probable by the exchange that takes place when Ron reveals that he misunderstood Wayne's story (lines 37-38).

When it becomes clear that Ron has misunderstood the story, Wayne clarifies it for him. However, instead of just repeating it, he shifts to something akin to "foreigner talk" (lines 39-41). The most salient changes in his shift are that he slows down and adds several very brief pauses accompanied by nonmanual signals (such as facial expression) that ask the addressee to indicate his comprehension (which in turn is usually given through nonmanual signals like head nods). Wayne's retelling also repeats a key sign, (2h)CL-1"stick fingers in ears." Below is my transcription of Wayne's initial telling followed by Ron's clarifying question and Wayne's retelling. A translation of the sequence appears below that. Note the repetition in Wayne's explanation as well as the addition of another role shift, both of which are marked in bold.

Transcription:

    Wayne: POSS-1st BORN HEARING. POSS-1st MOTHER BECOME CRAZY. (As mother) <(2h)CL-1"stick fingers in ears" (2h)CL-1"swing me around in circles" .... (H1)CL-2"legs flipping around"> BECOME DEAF   (H2).................................>
                                               y/n   y/n
    Ron: [Obstructed] CL:2"swing in circles on a swing"? SWING?
          t
    Wayne: (Slower) MOTHER..... BECOME CRAZY, MOTHER

    <(2h)BCL-1"stick fingers in ears"> (Looks at Ron for comprehension. As himself.)
                                            y/n
    <(2h)BCL-1"fingers" (2h)CL-1"stick fingers in ears"> (As his mother.)

    <(2h)CL-1"stick fingers in my ears", (2h)CL-1"swing me around by her fingers in my ears"..... (H1)CL-2"legs flipping around" (Nods.)
     (H2)................................>

Translation:
> Wayne: I was born hearing but my mother became crazy. She stuck her fingers in my ears and flipped me head over heels again and again. That's what made me deaf.
> Ron: [Obstructed] She swung you all the way around? On a swing?
> Wayne: (*Slower.*) My mother... became crazy. You know her index fingers? She stuck them in my ears, like this, and flipped me head over heels again and again, you see?

I noted above that Wayne's second telling includes some repetition of key signs (lines 39-41), which amounts to additional explanation of the classifiers used to represent his mother's fingers being placed in his ears. In this explanatory account he not only holds (pauses) the classifiers (produced simultaneously, one on each hand) and shifts them towards Ron, he actually repositions them so as to indicate more clearly their locative relationship by placing them near his own ears — thereby shifting out of his role as his mother — and then shifts back by placing his fingers in the signing space in front of him, repeating the classifier. To summarize, in order to clarify his role shift and classifier use, he adds yet another of each.

Wayne's simplified repetition resembles foreigner talk, but there is a significant difference. He doesn't exchange complex vocabulary items for common ones, nor does he delete words or complex structures. Instead, he sticks with the complex classifiers but this time he slows them down and explains them so Ron understands not just what he said but *how* he said it. Wayne adds additional classifiers, from different perspectives, to clarify the antecedents of the classifiers in his original telling. It strikes me that this approach is not unlike a practice I use in teaching my ASL classes.

In foreigner talk, the goal is primarily the transmission of propositions, but in classroom situations the goal is to teach the meaning of a vocabulary item (or a structural element) to the students. Wayne is a fairly experienced ASL teacher, so his use of this technique is not surprising. Yet it is significant in that he is not merely clarifying; he is teaching, sharing his knowledge of complex classifier usage and role shifting. This creates a distinct power differential because Wayne has this knowledge and Ron needs to be taught it: Wayne controls Ron's comprehension and he clarifies Ron's misunderstanding by simplifying his own signing to a form reminiscent of that used in teaching outsiders. He marginalizes Ron by emphasizing a difference in abilities between Ron and himself, but the marginalization is from the elite sphere rather than from the DEAF-WORLD.

The other people at the table who were watching Wayne's story unfold appeared to have only understood it after this retelling as well. Wayne's explanation prompts some specific responses. For example, it is at this point that Mandy asks Ron if he could imagine learning to sign from Wayne. Ron responds to Mandy's question by adopting a similar approach to the one Wayne just used.

Transcription:

Mandy: (To Ron, smiling broadly.) CAN PRO-1st IMAGINE LEARN

y/n
SIGN FROM PRO-3rd-[Wayne]?

Ron: PRO-1st <(As self just prior.) LOOK-AT-3rd[Wayne]

(2h)CL:1"stick fingers in ears", HANDS [Obstructed].> (As present self.)

<'pshaw' SICK PRO-3rd[Wayne]>.

This is worthy of further examination. Ron's response is like a story and it recounts what just happened — all of which Mandy witnessed — and he does so through the use of a role shift (in bold). Unlike Wayne's shift, in which he assumes the role of another person, Ron assumes the role of himself, a self in the just-completed past. This shift from his present self to a past self does two things. First, it demonstrates his ability to use role shifting, which might be called into question by his failure to understand Wayne.

Second, it serves to mark a boundary between the current self and the one who at first did not understand Wayne's story. This distancing is a way of diminishing responsibility for the failure, putting it behind him, as it were. Having established this boundary, Ron next employs the classifier that caused him trouble and which served as the crucial point of the story.

Transcription:
Ron: (To Mandy as self just prior.) <PRO-1st LOOK-AT-3rd[Wayne]> (2h)CL-1"stick fingers in ears" (Pause.) HANDS [Obstructed]. 'pshaw' SICK PRO-3rd[Wayne].
Translation:
Ron: (To Mandy as self just prior.) I sat here looking at him. He said she stuck her fingers in his ears, and I knew he was kidding me. Geez!
Having recreated the scene of the telling, Ron says that he realized that it could not be true during Wayne's retelling.

Josh and Jared miss out on this entire exchange because they take up a side conversation just as it begins. Their discussion concludes just as Ron finishes his explanation to Mandy, and Ron takes advantage of this by turning to Josh and again repeating Wayne's story.

Transcription:
Ron: (To Josh.) [Obstructed] MOTHER CRAZY, (As mother.)
<(2h)CL-1"stick fingers in ears" (2h)CL-1"swing him around by her

fingers in his ears" (H1)CL-2"legs flipping around."
(H2)...>

Translation:

Ron: (To Josh.) [Obstructed] His mother was crazy and she stuck her fingers in his ears and flipped him head over heels again and again.

Ron uses essentially the same classifiers and role shifts Wayne used, the ones he failed to comprehend just a moment before. By using Wayne's forms, Ron acknowledges their centrality to the humor of the story. This serves to repair the damage his misunderstanding caused in three ways. First, it allows him to use similar and identical forms, demonstrating to those who saw Wayne schooling him (as well as to Wayne) that he is competent with ASL. Second, by using a form of reported speech, Ron "inhabits the discourse he reports" (Urban, 1996:50) serving "to associate [himself] more closely with the quoted speaker or entity." Last, Ron's use of classifiers and role shifting diverts the attention from his inability to understand the forms and places the attention on the unlikelihood of the referential content. Ron implies that he failed to understand the narrative, not because of its form, but because the story is patently absurd.

Things Left Unsaid

The elements I have examined thus far in this interaction are by no means the only ones used in this discussion. I have taken an action-centered approach to analysis, focusing primarily on individuals' behaviors that are semiotically significant. There is also significance in what they did not do. For instance, even though Wayne's joking explanation for his deafness is clearly untrue, no one asks him to give the real cause of his deafness. The reason is simple: in the process of telling his story, he has made his identities very clear, both personal as a DEAF-WORLD member and positional as a storyteller, and, therefore, as an elite member. Establishing and revealing these identities was the point of the original line of questioning, despite its reference to causes of deafness.

Speaking of things that aren't said, I have never seen any Deaf person ask another person, "Are you culturally Deaf?" The significance that the literature attributes to the Deaf/deaf distinction would make such a question reasonable. Instead, Deaf people ask simply YOU DEAF YOU? Which translates out to either "Are you Deaf?" or "Are you deaf?" Interestingly, the difference between the two translations is determined largely by the response. That is the question elicits information relative to identity from which the person asking the question formulates his or her perceptions about that responder's identity. This fact is fairly well understood. What is less widely understood is that how one says it is often more important than what one says, as Wayne's narrative illustrates. At that table, no one asks anyone "Are you culturally Deaf?" or "How culturally-Deaf are you?" although that is primarily the information they appear to be after.

But I want to make it clear that the exchange between Wayne, Ron and the others did not occur between someone clearly Deaf and someone clearly not Deaf; the primary participants have some quite obvious claims to being Deaf. This highlights the ongoing nature of the identification process. Identities are not achieved all at once. They are continually reasserted, renegotiated, and reclaimed, and both personal and positional identities are simultaneously negotiated. These negotiations are a part of everyday life, and these negotiations' outcomes have real consequences.

CONCLUSION

Discourse practices have a great deal to do with the creation and projection of positional identities in the DEAF-WORLD, just as they do with personal identities. Demonstrations of communicative competence serve to index people as DEAF-WORLD members. Displays of super competence index elite status. This group of elite Deaf people enjoys numerous benefits from their status, including political and cultural power, but these benefits should not be mistaken for the defining characteristics of the elite; they are simply benefits. The benefits come through the demonstration of super competence that is most clearly marked by highly adept use of ASL classifiers and role shifting. Those whose actions successfully index them to the storytelling tradition enjoy elite status as the most authentic Deaf people and as custodians of pure ASL. But a successful claim on this status doesn't preclude future negotiations any more than a wedding precludes marital discord. In both cases, it may be only the beginning.

REFERENCES

Bahan, B., Hoffmeister, R., & Lane, H. (1996). *A Journey Into the DEAF-WORLD*. San Diego: Dawn Sign Press.

Eldredge, B. (2004). The Role of Discourse in the Formation and Maintenance of Deaf Identity and the Deaf-World. (Unpublished doctoral dissertation.). The University of Iowa, Iowa City.

Emmorey, K. (1999). Do Signers Gesture? In L. S. Messing & R. Campbell (Eds.), *Gesture, Speech, and Sign* (pp. 133–159). Oxford: Oxford University Press.

Hanks, W. F. (1996). *Language and Communicative Practices*. (J. Comaroff, P. Bourdieu, & M. Bloch, Eds.). Boulder, CO: Westview Press.

Kroskrity, P. V. (1998). Arizona Kiva Speech as a Manifestation of a Dominant Language Ideology. In B. B. Schieffelin, K. A. Woolard, & P. V. Kroskrity (Eds.), *Language Ideologies: Practice and Theory* (pp. 103–122). New York: Oxford University Press.

Lucas, C., & Valli, C. (1987). From Signer's Perspective: A Comparative Sign Language Study. In W. H. Edmondson & F. Karlsson (Eds.), SLR '87: *Papers from The Fourth International Symposium on Sign Language Research at Lappeenranta, Finland July 15-19, 1987* (pp. 129–152). Hamburg: Signum-Press.

Mandel, M. (1977). Iconic Devices in American Sign Language. In L. A. Friedman (Ed.), *On The Other Hand: New Perspectives in American Sign Language* (pp. 57–108). New York: Academic Press.

Morgan, G. (1999). Event Packaging in British Sign Language Discourse. In E. Winston (Ed.), *Storytelling and Conversation: Discourse in Deaf Communities* (Vol. Volume 5, pp. 27–58). Washington, DC: Gallaudet University Press.

Padden, C., & Humphries, T. (1988). *Deaf in America: Voices From a Culture*. Cambridge, MA: Harvard University Press.

Peirce, C. S. (1985). Logic as Semiotic: The Theory of Signs. In R. E. Innis (Ed.), *Semiotics: An Introductory Anthology* (pp. 1–23). Bloomington: Indiana University Press.

Rayman, J. (1999). Storytelling in the Visual Mode: A Comparison of ASL and English. In E. Winston (Ed.), *Storytelling and Conversation: Discourse in Deaf Communities* (Vol. Volume 5, pp. 59–82). Washington, DC: Gallaudet University Press.

Rutherford, S. (1993). *A Study of American Deaf Folklore*. Burtonsville, MD: Linstok Press.

Rutherford, S. D. (1989). Funny in Deaf. Not in Hearing. In S. Wilcox (Ed.), *American Deaf Culture* (pp. 165–82). Burtonsville, MD: Linstok Press.

Stokoe, W. (1995). Deaf Culture Working. *Sign Language Studies*, 86(Spring), 81–94.

Urban, G. (1985). The Semiotics of Two Speech Styles in Shokleng. In E. Mertz & R. J. Parmentier (Eds.), *Semiotic Mediation* (pp. 311–329. New York). Academic Press, Inc.

Urban, G. (1991). Grammatical Parallelism and Thought. In *A Discourse-Centered Approach to Culture*. Austin: University of Texas Press.

Urban, G. (1996). *Metaphysical Community: The Interplay of the Senses and the Intellect*. Austin: University of Texas Press.

Toward True ASL Dictionaries: New Developments in Handshape Similarity

KAREN ALKOBY

DESPITE THE ORALISM MOVEMENT, ASL WAS DISCOVERED TO BE A natural language in the 1960s. Previous research has arrived at the consensus that handshape is one of the phonemes of ASL and one of the most recognizable. However, there is little consensus about the number of distinct handshapes in ASL and there is even less consensus about similarity among handshapes. Understanding handshape similarity is important because it is an essential building block toward the development of true ASL dictionaries. True ASL dictionaries would permit people to look up definitions of signs based on ASL phonemes without the use of English. Similarly, using handshapes to look up a sign is essential to the development of true, bilingual ASL/English dictionaries, where it is just as possible to find the English equivalent of a sign as it is to find the sign corresponding to an English word.

Work on handshape similarity initially blossomed in the 1970s, but withered without producing consistent results, due in part to the costly nature of the research. Previous studies involved human subjects performing a large number of comparisons to measure human perception of handshapes. Another impediment was the lack of a realistic 3D representation that respected the natural physiology of the human hand.

In contrast, an analytic model of handshape similarity predicts human perception of handshapes based on the physical positioning of the hand joints in space. Once definitively established, an analytic model has the potential to determine the similarity of additional handshapes without needing to conduct costly perceptual tests.

This paper discusses the creation and initial evaluation of an analytic model of handshape similarity. Initial results are very promising. The model grows more accurate as handshapes are added to it.

HANDSHAPE

Handshape is the most apparent and complex parameter of a sign and it is the first one that people think of when preparing to make a sign [1, 12]. The handshapes in ASL are composed of letter handshapes, number handshapes, and classifier handshapes [3].

As of today, there is no consensus about the number of distinct handshapes in ASL. Determining handshape similarity is a closely related problem to the determination of the number of handshapes.

Work on handshape similarity initially blossomed in the 1970's [5, 10], but withered without producing consistent results, due in part to the costly nature of the research. Previous studies involved human subjects performing a large number of comparisons to establish human perception of handshapes. Another impediment was the lack of a realistic 3D representation that respected the natural physiology of the human hand.

ISSUES AND BENEFITS

ASL was recognized as a language in the 1960s and the study of ASL as a language is still a nascent discipline. The current inconsistencies and controversies in handshape usage may have been caused by the oralism movement and the use of various manual codes of English. There are numerous challenges in handshape studies that need to be pushed to the next level. These include the problem of expanding a search handshape query when an exact match will not work and determining how to compensate for errors in user's memory recall of a handshape.

A tool that would help in solving these and other questions in handshape studies would be an analytic model of handshape similarity that computes a mapping of the physical positioning of the hand joints in space to human perception of similarity. This paper describes the creation and initial evaluation of an analytic model of handshape similarity. The benefit of such a model is that, once established, it can predict the similarity of additional handshapes without needing to conduct costly perceptual tests. It is an essential building block toward the development of true ASL dictionaries.

PLAN OF WORK

This section is an outline of the plan for developing a methodology for computing the similarity of selected ASL handshapes based on the physical (three-dimensional) aspects of handshape production, namely joint rotation. Achieving this will require five steps:
- Card Sort I, to establish a baseline of human perception of a group of handshapes
- Model Development, to analyze the card sort data and create candidate models,
- Model Prediction, where each model computes the similarity of a new, larger set of handshapes,
- Card Sort II to determine the human perception of the larger set of handshapes and
- Model Evaluation, which looks at how well each model predicted human perception.

The remainder of the paper discusses each of these steps in detail followed by results and a discussion of future work.

Card Sort I

This step establishes a new baseline through user tests and establishes a perception-based similarity among an initial set of handshapes. This step involves card sorting sessions using the same group of handshapes that previous researchers used [5, 10]. Card sorting offers several advantages, including being simple, relatively cheap and quick to execute [7]. It can help to reveal users' mental model of an information space. It is an excellent way to gather users' perspective on the handshapes to help classify objects in terms of human perception.

Having 30 partcipants is the minimum for getting a reasonably consistent fit. [11]. Because Stungis had indicated that Deaf and hearing people seem to perceive handshape differently in terms of producing handshapes, this initial card sort interviews 30 Deaf participants and 30 hearing participants.

Thirty Deaf participants completed card sorting sessions at Deaf Expo on October 8, 2005 in Chicago, Illinois. Thirty hearing participants were recruited from students in the ASL/English Interpretation Program at Columbia College Chicago. They completed card sorting sessions during the first week of April 2006. This study passed the DePaul University Institutional Review Board #KA080405CTI-R1.

The session began with obtaining informed consent. Deaf participants viewed the informed consent in ASL on a videotape and hearing participants read the information as written English text. Each participant then completed a very short background questionnaire.

The actual session started with a very short practice period to familiarize participants with the card-sorting technique. The participants were instructed to sort the cards into piles based on similarity and were free to make as many or as few piles as she or he saw fit. After the practice session, the participant sorted the 20 handshapes. See Appendices A and B for the practice cards and actual cards.

Model Development

Model Development occurred in two parts. The first part identifies statistical measure(s) that consistently and accurately summarize the similarities in the card sort data. Consistency measures identify the most appropriate statistics for the card sort data.

The next step is to compare the card sort data to previously recorded three-dimensional joint values to develop a method that assigns similarity measures to the three-dimensional handshape data [2].

Statistical Analysis Methods

The Pearson's correlation between the card sorting sessions at Deaf Expo and the card sorting sessions at Columbia College is r = .86. One notable difference between the two groups is that all participants at Columbia College placed almost every card into one of the piles, but many Deaf Expo participants did not place all the cards into piles.

Two commonly-used statistics that analyze similarity as clusters are Multi-dimensional Scaling (MDS) and Cluster Analysis; these were used in both of the previous studies [5, 10]. Both methods require the use of a distance (or similarity) measure which is created from the raw card sort data. Figure 1 contains the results of using MDS to visualize the Deaf Expo data.

Figure 1: MDS of Deaf Expo

Unfortunately, the MDS of the Deaf Expo data exhibits severe inaccuracies in visualizing the similarities. For example, participants at Deaf Expo grouped "Baby O" and "X" handshapes together into the same cluster 17 times out of 30 times. However, the MDS visualization places the "BabyO" handshape closer to the "E" handshape, which was only paired with "BabyO" 10 times out of 30 times. The stress (measurement of goodness of fit) after several iterations of the MDS procedure was between fair and poor. Therefore, MDS is not an effective statistic for visualizing this data, and it was not used to visualize any additional sets of data.

The second method, Cluster Analysis, displays the data as a tree. See Appendices C and D. In a cluster hierarchy tree, each handshape appears as a leaf node. Handshapes that have a greater similarity are linked at a lower level. Cluster analysis seems more effective for finding handshape similarity in the card sort results, but it is important to determine the goodness of fit. This requires the use of cluster validity measurements. Cluster validity evaluates and assesses the results of a clustering algorithm. There are two types of cluster validity: external and internal criteria. An internal criterion examines how accurately a cluster tree represents the distance in the original data. External criterion examines the amount of agreement between two cluster trees. The cophenetic correlation is as an internal measure [4] and the Rand statistic is an external measure [9].

In a hierarchical cluster tree, any two objects in the original data set are eventually linked together at some level. The level of the connection is the cophenetic distance. Examining the match between the cophenetic distances in a tree and the original card-sort distances is one way to measure how well the computed clustering represents the original distance data.

The Rand statistic is a measure of the goodness of fit between two clustering trees. It computes the probability that two pairs belong either to a same cluster or to different clusters in both trees [9]. This measurement allows comparison across different levels and number of clusters found within a classification.

The cophenetic correlation for both clusterings were quite high (Deaf-Expo c = .8924, Columbia c = .9596). So the cluster analysis does accurately summarize the original data. The Rand statistic between the two clusterings was also quite high (R = .84). The high value of the Rand statistic in addition to the high Pearson's correlation would tend to indicate that the Deaf and hearing participants seem to perceive similar patterns in handshape similarity.

Assigning similarity metrics to joint rotation data
The goal of this second part of model development is to create candidate models for directly computing handshape similarity from physical three-

dimensional aspects of the human hand. Twenty joint values are necessary to create a convincing simulation of the poses that the fingers and thumb can assume[8]. Some joints rotate in either abduction-adduction capabilities (spread-close) or flexion-extension motion (bend-open). See Figure 2. The DIP in each finger is highly correlated with the PIP in the same finger. The thumb structure is a little more complex than the fingers but it functions in basicly the same way.

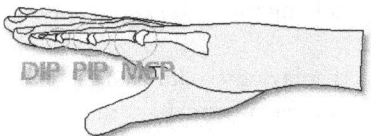

Figure 2: Joints in the fingers

Four candidate models were developed. All four candidate models apply a cluster analysis on either the entire set of handshape data or to a selected subset of it. The entire set of data uses 20 joint values for each handshape. The subset of data also uses joint values, but excludes the DIP of the fingers for a total of 16 joints values. Each handshape pair creates a distance in either 20- or 16-space and these are used in the cluster analysis.

The first two candidate models are Geometric Descriptors which use geometric values. Model 1 uses the entire data set but Model 2 uses the large subset of the values. The last two models are Linguistic Descriptors. These models get their name from the fact that range of geometric data is converted into the range from 0 to 1, analogous to the binary designations used in linguistics. Model 3 uses the entire data set of data but Model 4, the last model, derives its values from the selected subset of 16 joints mentioned previously [1, 6].

Tables 1 and 2 summarize the ability of each model to match the card sort data. The cophenetic correlation for each of the candidate models is shown in Table 1. The candidate models that include the DIP joints yield a higher cophenetic correlation.

Cophenetic Correlation			
Linguistic Descriptors	With DIP	Model 1	.7451
	Without DIP	Model 2	.7211
Geometric Descriptors	With DIP	Model 3	.7383
	Without DIP	Model 4	.6824

Table 1. Cophenetic correlations for the candidate models

Table 2 shows the result of computing the Rand Statistic between the clusterings from each of the candidate models and the clusters from the card sorting sessions. Interestingly, omitting the DIP joints yields a slightly better match.

Rand	Geometric Descriptors		Linguistic Descriptors	
	With DIP	Without DIP	With DIP	Without DIP
Combined Deaf Expo & Columbia	.7947	.8263	.8158	.8316

Table 2. Rand results for the candidate models

Model Prediction

In this step, each candidate model will compute (predict) similarity measures from three-dimensional joint data. This step will introduce five additional handshapes to the original 20 handshapes. Each of the candidate methods will compute similarity measures for the 25 handshapes. Figure 2 shows the five new handshapes, which are 'S', 'Vbent', 'Lhook', '8' and '3bent.'

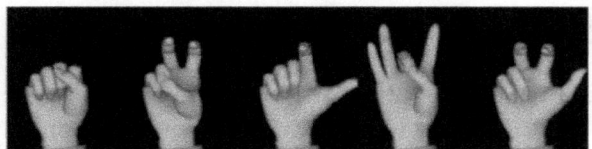

Figure 2. Additional 5 handshapes

Card Sort II

The second set of card sorting sessions uses the same procedure as Card Sort I, but includes the additional five handshapes together with initial handshapes. Because the outcome from the first card sessions showed little difference between Deaf and hearing groups, Card Sort II included only Deaf participants. Thirty one interviews with Deaf participants took place during the month of February of 2007 at a Deaf Duppies (Deaf Urban Professionals) event in Chicago and at the Western Suburban Association of the Deaf (WSAD).

Model Evaluation

This last stage assesses the predictive validity of the candidate models by comparing the similarity measures computed by the model to the empirical results of Card Sort II. To satisfy the goal of predictive ability, it was necessary obtain improvement in both internal and external criteria when additional handshapes were added. The results from each of the candidate models were compared to the results from Card Sort II using both cophenetic correlation and the Rand statistic. As a final check, the five new handshapes were deleted from the Card Sort II data, reclustered, and compared with the initial card sort sessions.

ASSESSMENT OF THE CANDIDATE MODELS

For the linguistic descriptors model without DIP joints, the cophenetic correlations improve. However, for the models that use Geometric Descriptors to represent handshapes, the cophenetic correlations indicate that it is better to include all 20 joint angles (see Table 3).

Rand Statistic	Geometric Descriptors		Linguistic Descriptors	
	With DIP	Without DIP	With DIP	Without DIP
	Model 1	Model 2	Model 3	Model 4
Card Sort I	.7383	.6824	.7451	.7211
Card Sort II	.7510	.6997	.7218	.7343

Table 3. Cophentic Correlation

The Linguistic Descriptor approach is particularly promising because it shows an efficiency model that the Geometric Descriptor approach did not. When the DIP angles were omitted from the Geometric Descriptor, it performed poorer. But when the DIPs were omitted from the Linguistic Descriptor model, the cophenetic correlation improved, and its Rand statistic (agreement with user perception) was the best of all the models; see Table 4.

Rand Statistic	Geometric Descriptors		Linguistic Descriptors	
	With DIP	Without DIP	With DIP	Without DIP
	Model 1	Model 2	Model 3	Model 4
Card Sort I	.7947	.8263	.8158	.8316
Card Sort II	.8633	.7600	.8667	.8867

Table 4. Rand Statistic

In Card Sort II, the cophenetic correlation and the Rand statistic improved for the Linguistic Descriptor without DIP joints. Therefore, the Model 4 is the best candidate for predictive ability. This model is particularly promising because it appears that it produces better results when incorporating additional handshapes in the model. However, all four of the candidate models should still be evaluated and validated with a still larger number of handshapes.

As a check, a final cluster analysis was performed on the data gathered from Card Sort II after the five new handshapes were removed. The cophenetic correlation of the result is extremely high (c = .9202). The Rand statistic between the Card Sort II subset and the combined set of Deaf Expo and Columbia from Card Sort I is .87. This indicates that the addition of new handshapes did not affect the overall perception of handshape similarity.

FUTURE WORK

Using a cluster analysis with the properly chosen representation appears to produce better results as the number of handshapes increases. A next step would be to introduce additional handshapes to create a large set of approximately 40 handshapes to further test all of the candidate models.

The handshape similarity concept has the potential to create effective computerized ASL/English dictionary searching. Finding a next handshape similarity can be addressed either due to misidentifying or memory error recall which can be rectified in "fuzzy" searches for ASL signs. For example, one may misidentify the handshape for the sign DOUBT by selecting "3-bent" handshape, because it is very similar to V-bent. If a search on a "3-bent" handshape yielded no desired results, the user could elect to expand the search by considering similar handshapes. This fuzzy search would look for handshapes that were closest in appearance to the "3-bent" handshape.

APPENDICES

a) Practice cards   b) Actual cards

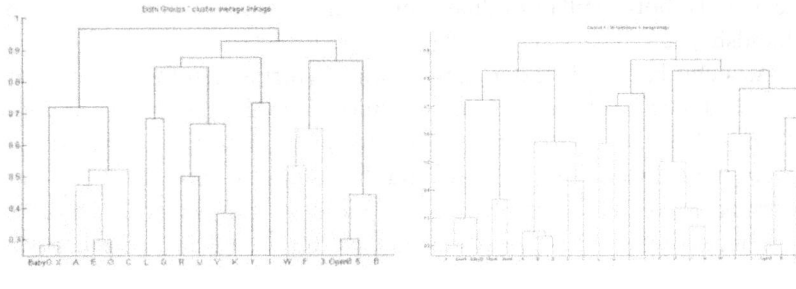

c) Card Sort I 's Cluster Tree   d) Card Sort II's Cluster Tree

REFERENCES

[1] Brentari, D. (1998). *A Prosadic Model of Sign Language Phonology*. Cambridge, MA: MIT Press.
[2] Davidson, M.J., Alkoby, K., Sedgwick, E., Berthiaume, A., Roymeico, C., Christopher, J., Craft, B., Furst, J., Hinkle, D., Konie, B., Lancaster, G., Luecking, S., Morris, A., McDonald, J., Tomuro, N. , Toro, J., Wolfe, R. (2000, November 4, 2000). *Usability Testing of Computer Animation of Fingerspelling for American Sign Language*, Presented at the 2000 DePaul CTI Research Conference, Chicago, IL.
[3] Grieve-Smith, A. B. (1998). Sign Synthesis and Sign Phonology. Paper presented at the Proceedings of the First Annual High Desert Linguistics Society Conference, Albuquerque: HDLS.
[4] Halkidi, M., Batistakis Y., and Vazirglannis, M. (2002, June 2002) *Cluster Validity Methods: Part I*. SIGMOD Record Vol. 31, No. 2, 40-44
[5] Lane, H., Boyes-Braem, P. , & Bellugi, U. (1979). A feature Analysis of handshape. In Klima & Bellugi (Ed.), *The Signs of language* (pp. 164-180). Cambridge, MA: Harvard University Press.
[6] Liddell, S., & Johnson, R.E. (1989). *American Sign Language: The phonological base*. Sign Language Studies, 63, 195-277.
[7] Maurer, D., and Warfel, Todd. (Retrieved 04/07/2004). Card sorting: a definitive guide, from http://www.boxesandarrows.com/archives/card_sorting_a_definitive_guide.php
[8] McDonald, J., Toro, J., Alkoby, K., Berthiaume, A., Chomwong, P., Davidson, M., Konie, B., Lancaster, G., Lytinen, S., Roychouhuri, L., Furst, J., Sedgwick, E., Tomuro, N. & Wolfe, R. (2000). *An Improved Articulation Model of the Human Hand*. Proceedings of the ISCA 15th International Conference on Computers and Their Applications (CATA-2000) 427-430.
[9] Rand, William. (1971) Objective Criteria for the Evaluation of Cluster Methods, Journal of American Statistical Association. Vol. 66, Number 336 in Theory and Methods Section
[10] Stungis, J. (1981). Identification and discrimination of handshape in American Sign Language. Perception and Psychophysics, 29, 261-276.
[11] Tullis, & Wood (2004, June 7-11, 2004). How Many Users Are Enough for a Card-Sorting Study? Paper presented at the Proceedings UPA 2004', Minneapolis, MN.
[12] Valli, C., & Lucas, C. (1995). Linguistics of American sign language: An introduction (2nd ed.). Washington, D.C.: Gallaudet University Press.

Deaf Wannabes: Technologies of Deafness and The Fetishizing of Hearing

KRISTEN HARMON, PH.D.

AT THIS CONFERENCE, WE HAVE BEEN DISCUSSING "DEAFHOOD," AND so this presentation may seem to be quite a departure from our ongoing discussion of cultural and sociolinguistic definitions of Deaf identity. However, I see this as fitting in with the ongoing dialogue about what it means to be colonized, and how we might go about de-colonizing our minds and bodies. Part of doing so could entail the examination of the inverted assumptions made about Deaf identity and the deaf body within deaf fetishes; desiring a d/Deaf body has implications for the psychology of colonization.

First, I need to explain the title: by "technologies of deafness," I mean that set of constructs that are used to mimic or to create a simulacrum d/Deaf people. As Paddy Ladd mentioned in his keynote address, all too often, ASL is studied, in a hearing context, as being made by "signing machines." A Deaf person's experience and worldview is not often included within this flattened construct. I use the term "technologies" in a similar fashion to describe the particular ways in which "Deaf wannabes" copy or mimic what they perceive as "signs" of a culturally Deaf person or a physically deaf person, i.e. a "deaf voice."

Like many others in the Deaf community, I first learned about the presence of this internet-based interest group through Trudy Suggs's article, "Deaf Wanna-bes" in *The Tactile Mind: Quarterly of the Signing Community*. By the spring of 2008, over seven hundred active and inactive members had exchanged over two thousand messages within this English language discussion group. Members mostly consisted of British and Northern European people, followed by a good number of Americans. Being a curious person by nature, and an ethnographer by training, I joined the group.

When I first logged on, I braced myself, envisioning a group of balding men who shared pictures of hearing aids like pornography, men who also had fetishes for other forms of disability, for diapers, for canes, for braces (and in one notable posting, all of the above). I envisioned swinging couples who shared erotic sex play fantasies of a "hearing-impaired" girl who asks her partner to "speak up" as she cannot hear too well. There is that, yes. And yet, the narratives, the reasons for wanting to be deaf, or to be perceived as deafened or culturally Deaf are not always that simple, and not always that prurient.

These deviant desires — for deafness or disability — are only partially explained by a large body of views on the fetish. Perhaps the presence of such desires point to a Cartesian culture talking to itself about body integrity; what happens if the mind doesn't fit the body? In any case, this paper focuses primarily upon the ways in which the fetishizing of hearing vis a vis deaf bodies is necessary for deficit thinking: incorporating or desiring an "Other" who is perceived as lacking draws upon the very same systems of privilege and pathology that sustain audism.

In regards to members of "disability fetish" internet interest groups like this one, there are said to be three categories of members: devotees, pretenders and wannabes. *Devotees* are "nondisabled people who are sexually attracted to people with disabilities, typically those with mobility impairments and especially amputees; *Pretenders* are non-disabled people who act as if they have an ability by using assistive devices (e.g. braces, crutches, and wheelchairs) in private and sometimes in public so that they 'feel' disabled or are perceived by others as having a disability; *Wannabes* actually want to become disabled, sometimes going to extraordinary lengths to have a limb amputated" (emphasis in original) (Bruno 243–244). In this particular variation on disability fetishes, devotees are those who are fascinated by wearers of hearing aids or other assistive technology; pretenders are those who pretend to be deaf, often with the assistance of hearing aids, and finally, wannabes are those who, in their own terms, "cross the bridge" by "self-deafening."

In this particular group, there is considerable overlap between devotees and pretenders; many of the devotees post pictures of hearing aid wearers as well as chronicle their own experiences with wearing hearing aids in private and in public. Devotees/pretenders tend to be male, professional, educated, and judging from self-disclosure, white. They also tend to have more erotic sex play regarding use and sight of hearing aids; they also tend to self-identity as having "fetishes." This tendency is in keeping with the findings that fetishists, or rather, people with paraphiliac fixations, tend to be heterosexual men (Aguilera 260, Seligman and Hardenburg 107).

The wanna-bes, interestingly enough, tend to be women, and particularly young women. A surprisingly large percentage of the wanna-bes already have some degree of naturally-occurring hearing loss, and of those, many express interest in exerting some level of control over the process. Still others intentionally deafen themselves for reasons that are more aligned with identity, and this will be explored at more length later.

Let me briefly note that this is part of a much longer project that references the following:

1. Freud on fetishes
2. Homi Bhabha on racial/cultural fetishes and the mimicry of the "Other"
3. Marx and the commodity fetish (and in this case, I argue, hearing aids and cochlear implants)
4. Controversial sexologist John Money's conceptualization of disability-oriented paraphilias
5. DSM-IV fetish criteria and recently proposed categories such as "Body Integrity Identity Disorder" (cf. Michael First)
6. Body modification and transsexualism
7. Overdetermination of gender roles and limits

With that larger context in mind, let me now elaborate on the three categories of deaf-fetishists.

For the pretenders and some of the devotees, the use of a hearing aid encodes disability by projecting it upon their own bodies. For example: "Yes I'm most DEAFinitely turned on by the feel and sight of myself in hearing aids...In fact I'm convinced I perform far better sexually when I have them in! This belief is essential to my fetish" (as qtd. in Suggs 68[1]).

There's an odd tension between the overtly sexual and then the asexual — yet furtively erotic — nature of many email exchanges between group members, particularly in relation to sensation and to the "thing-ness" of deafness and hearing loss, e.g. body aids are seen as "ultra cool" on "girls" and pictures of such are requested ("Deaf WannaBes" 54[2]). As Aguilera pointed out in relation to the "Dragonworks [Amputee] Devotee Community," "pictures were relatively soft-core, and could in fact barely be called pornography at all...notably less explicit than mainstream pornography... In the written stories too, there seemed to be a surprising lack of actual sex" (256, 257).

As with the amputee fetishists Aguilera interviewed, the fetishists in the "Deaf Wannabe" group generally use the group as a source of hearing-aid and fetish-related erotica, of sorts, rather than as a "hook up" site, though, to be sure, such liaisons do happen. Instead of overt sexual or erotic identification with deafness, new members typically express profound relief and delight for having found that he or she "is not the only one in the world" who has felt this way. A few pretenders and devotees do make it immediately clear that they are sexually attracted to hearing aids and to women wearing hearing aids, but these are not the majority.

The hearing aid, it seems, demarcates reality as a corporeal being; as such the hearing aid acts as a prosthesis — the assistive device that allows for the mechanism behind the metaphor — to the trope of deafness as being somehow more "real." As another member, a wannabe who has already induced hearing "gain," puts it: "I really do like the quiet life" (as qtd. in Suggs 52). Another member, in a lengthy and meditative posting, notes that one of the greatest joys with induced hearing loss is a peaceful quiet, where there's no noise in the home or in the office, where traffic is no longer bothersome, and the supermarket is no longer an intrusively noisy place; instead, the country air is more noticeable and more relaxing. He goes on to note that the other senses are heightened as a result, and he enjoys being able to switch on and off — like a radio — his hearing (through the use of hearing aids) ("Deaf WannaBes" 158). Tellingly, this member opposes the work life, the life of the market and the business-place with the more sensory, and more "in-touch" reality of life in a sensory body, disconnected, "unplugged," as it were, from the noises that make up social reality for hearing people in a capitalist society.

For some, particularly women who wear hearing aids or who "gain hearing loss," the use of hearing aids for a "real" purpose takes on implications for identity formation. As one woman wrote, when she found out she had a diagnosed hearing loss (after repeatedly shooting a rifle without ear protection), "I wanted to always wear a hearing aid, and to have a proper hearing loss to justify it...By now I had simulated deafness in one ear for many years, and I knew this was what was right for me...Getting tested and having a severe hearing loss was like heaven" (as qtd. in Suggs 50). She goes on to state that "now everyone back home knows I'm partly deaf and need a hearing aid, and from the start of my working career I have been known as a hearing aid wearer" (as qtd. in Suggs 50). She, like another woman who had induced loss, does not see sign language as the end goal: they, and quite a few others, induce enough loss so that sign language isn't a necessity but is instead a fun option ("Deaf WannaBes" 82). Here, as with a good number of others, identity is not about a culturally-grounded Deaf identity, it is about a sensory experience and a way of being in the (hearing) social world.

In similar fashion, some members note that they do not want a "real" hearing loss, meaning a hearing loss that would necessitate life in a different body, in effect. In this way, their use of hearing aids fit the use of fetish as "'a fantasy instrument for embracing not only sexuality or desire but also an escape from reality'" (as quoted in Lowenstein 140). Marx might recognize the impulse here towards the fetishization of a commodity, where social relations are conflated with the product : "Value, therefore, does not stalk about with a label describing what it is. It is value, rather, that converts every product into a social hieroglyphic. Later on, we try to decipher the hieroglyphic, to get behind the secret of our own social products; for to stamp an object of utility as a value is just as much a social product as language" (Marx 449). As a consequence of this conflation, the political relationships are also obscured; who is exploiting whom?

This commodification of the hearing aid was aptly described by one of the members; this member described aids as looking like wrinkled and deformed bits of plastic. However, they are transformed by the wearer into something seductive and compelling ("Deaf WannaBes" 139). Indeed.

Yet, because the pretender and devotee fetishes tend not to harm the physical body, and because this use of hearing aids reflects consensual behavior and/or a private decision, does this mean that such co-opting of the deaf apparatus, i.e. hearing aids, is innocuous? As Kath Duncan, a double congenital amputee and activist suspects, "the distance between the biomedical gaze and the adoring one...is not so very far. The devotee gaze is enabled by dominant, powerful, envisioning of different bodies" (Duncan and Goggin). As a possibly scopophiliac gaze (by way of Freud), the first source of pleasure arises from "using another person as an object of sexual stimulation through sight. The second...comes from identification with the image seen" (Mulvey 441). While scopophilia and the resultant gaze rests upon homologous oppositions due to the phallic principle, and as such, does not easily explain (or invites a too facile explanation of) women's use of hearing aids, the significant point here is that the "pleasure in looking has been split between active/male and passive/female" and signification only comes about through attachment to an idealization (Mulvey 442).

The idealization seems less about the disabled body, per se, and more about the use of prosthesis as a trope; that instead of correcting a deficiency, the use of hearing aids supplies a deficiency, and in doing so, "fill[s] a gap, but...also diminish[es] the body and create[s] the need for itself" (Jain 44). So this use of hearing aids endlessly refers back to the medical definitions of impairment, but it is the idealization of subject position as well as the supernumerary nature of sensate body (with a prosthesis) that fuels the machine behind the gaze.

However, "elective deafness" flips the trope by making the body the prosthesis to the mind by way of deafness, and in doing so, internalizes the scopophiliac gaze in unexpected ways. There is a significant population in "Deaf WannaBes" and other similar interest groups who want to significantly, severely, or profoundly deafen themselves, and very intentionally so. Techniques are shared on how to deafen, and warnings are given out to avoid lethal doses of certain ototoxic drugs. The experience of not only deafening but also of getting fitted for earmolds and hearing aids are described in exquisite, almost erotic detail: "I allow the fine needle to touch my eardrum, and with a slight push, and a nice sound of scrunching paper, it's through" (as qtd. in Suggs 55). The level and kind of hearing loss are described, in an informative yet with excited tones; those who self-deafen describe the process of "tuning" their ears to the frequency characteristics of the desired loss ("Deaf WannaBes" 35).

The organic body becomes the machine, the prosthesis for the mind, or the identity, that sees itself as *gendered* deaf, so to speak. And, significantly, while there are some men who intentionally deafen themselves, the majority of wannabes are women, and particularly young women. After describing a very active social life, including "clubbing," one young woman writes, "But deep down I have an irrepressible need to develop a bilateral hearing loss. This is my Nirvana. I'm not deaf, but I am hard of hearing in both ears. For me it is good, and I think my hearing loss is probably just as much as I want it to be without become [sic] seriously deaf or isolated" (as qtd. in Suggs 63). In this sense, variations on the spectrum between "disabled" and non-disabled are incorporated more like technologies of gender, where gender also exists as a spectrum, with variation. After much soul searching, a male wanna-be writes that he could no longer deny his true self (Deaf WannaBe" 158). Here, the trope centers around "true" fit between body and mind, a Cartesian split that can only be remedied through adaptation of the body. This use of the body as prosthesis for the mind suggest that "the body itself is artifice," a "side effect of its extensions" (as qtd. in Jain 38). However postmodern and cyborgian this sounds, the narratives on "Deaf Wannabees" do not take on a celebratory, or even resistant, stance. Instead, there is a sense of hushed anguish in many of these narratives, e.g.

> I want to be deaf. Genuinely, properly (and — as I see it — wonderfully) deaf...I want to live my life in a world which is almost silent, maybe completely silent, without hearing aids...I want to be deaf. So badly. I don't know why, but I do know this is very real...a voice inside me has been telling me for a long time that I want — I need — to be deaf...I want to live life as a deaf girl and woman...I'm quite lonely with this very, very private thing but I just know that I need to do it to become the person I aspire to be" (as qtd. in Suggs 83).

This young woman later notes a history of self-mutilation. There's some evidence of a history of self-mutilation in other wannabe narratives, particularly those of women who want to transition into being deaf or deafened as a private, bodily matter, not as a social, or public, matter.

In addition to being a prosthesis for the mind, the body is used as a text to "communicate something that is difficult or impossible to articulate in conventional modes" (Potter 2). Many, but again, not all, of these wannabes make the parallel between their sense of bodily mismatch and the experience of transsexuals. The same man who wrote in with a request for samples of "deaf voices," notes that until "wannabes" are recognized by the medical establishment and resources are made available — including operations for those who desire amputation — every person who wants disability will have to do it on his own ("Deaf WannaBes" 608).

There is precedence for such a view of the body, with the cyborgian body and with the "plastic" body — altered and alterable through plastic surgery — a body whose "corporeal identity is always in a state of potential transition" (Jordan 327-328). This uneasy alliance between currently accepted body modification and then the outer limits of such "human intervention in altering...appearance" has more to do with same territory that "decadent fetishism" covers, or rather, that celebratory and triumphalist set of narratives centered in cultural fetishism, where transformation of the body transgresses beliefs about gender, sexuality, and the body (Jordan 327, Fernbach). Such celebratory narratives are relatively rare on the "Deaf WannaBe " list, but there are some, and these narratives seem out of context, allied with, but not, as other members would have it, indicative of a "true" pretender/wannabe/devotee. If anything, the wannabes seem to be wanting to return to a pastoral ideal of the body itself: the desire to not be disturbed by sounds and people is often expressed, and sign language is not necessarily the primary goal ("Deaf WannaBes" 650).

There's a revealing disconnect between the ways in which the body is conceptualized; in the ideology of healthy bodies, it is heretical to demand that the body be adapted for disability and not corrected, healed, or improved upon. And yet, for the purposes of "elective," corrective, or cosmetic surgery, the natural body is a "body-in-transition...[which fits] easily within 'the cultural landscape of modernity: consumer capitalism, technological development, liberal individualism, and the belief in the makeability [sic] of the human body'" (as qtd. in Jordan 332). Similarly, the cyborgian, contemporary, body is "plastic," a "rhetorically contested substance" (Jordan 328). Confronted with the notion of "adopting" deafness, paradigms of the body collide.

Other wannabes, particularly CODAs (Children of Deaf Adults) or hard of hearing people use the trope of belonging to describe their desires for deafness. To wit: one CODA writes in with the statement that her family is centered around Deaf pride, but as a hearing person, she has never felt like she belonged; because of the fact that her mother would be proud of her desire to be deaf, this member feels that her true identity is also to be physically deaf in addition to being culturally Deaf ("Deaf WannaBes" 501).

Significantly, the desire to become deaf in order to "join" the Deaf community is relatively uncommon, enough so that a few Deaf people who joined the list out of outrage or curiosity felt compelled to recommend that anyone who wants a truly Deaf experience learn sign language for the purposes of communicating with "real" Deaf people ("Deaf WannaBes" 228). Members of the group do express some interest in learning sign language, but there is no consistent correlation between a signing, Deaf identity and the desire to become deaf.

One unanticipated commonality among a significant portion of this population is that quite a few already had a naturally-occurring hearing loss. These members interacted somewhat uneasily with the pretenders, though both shared a great deal of information amongst themselves about hearing aids and various adaptive devices. The motive for inducing additional hearing loss was rather simple for these members, and judging from what was written, did not seem to have much erotic overlay; often members in this grouping noted the desire to take control over the process rather than waking up surprised by additional loss ("Deaf WannaBe" 108). These wannabes tended to be surprisingly matter-of-fact and determined. A few wanted to eradicate tinnitus that comes about from nerve damage, though it was pointed out on the list that inducing hearing loss has to be done precisely in the "desired frequencies" as it is difficult to avoid tinnitus.

At times, the juxtaposition between the eroticized interests of the pretenders, the fascination expressed by the devotees, and then the more "serious" consequences of intentional deafening, created an uneasy dialogue between this group of people brought together by a common need or desire for deafness. At one point, the juxtaposition is jarring: a long and heartfelt personal narrative about the effects of (a "natural" and progressive) hearing loss was followed by a long, and rather eroticized, description of various techniques and tools for inducing deafness, including a discussion of "thresholds of pain."

The Deaf community discovered the presence of this list and Deaf individuals joined the list to express their outrage along with raising pertinent points about the political relationships that are obscured in the act of "elective deafness": "Enjoying yourself now, eh? Changing your identity from hearing to HoH for 'kicks'? Do you realize that d/Deaf people can't even try to change themselves from d/Deaf to Hearing even if their lives counted on it?" ("Deaf WannaBes" 794). In this sense, the "acquiring of hearing loss" returns to its initial status as a commodity fetish, albeit a more complex one than hearing aids. "A commodity," Marx argued, "is therefore a mysterious thing, simply because in it the social character of men's labour appears to them as an objective character stamped upon the product of that labor; because the relation of the producers to the sum total of their own labor is presented to them as a social relation, existing not between themselves, but between the products of their labor" (446). Becoming d/Deaf does not just have sensory value but also social and political, not to mention linguistic, implications.

What is problematic with this group, however, is the valorization of the Deaf community (and deaf people in general) without recognizing the historical forces of social, economic, and linguistic oppression; to ignore this history of stigma and negative eugenics is to denigrate the struggles of a community and to erase an entire group of people from ethical consideration. Also problematic is the ways in which hearing privilege marks a body and mind (deciding that one does not want to be hearing any more does not automatically remove one from the effects of that same privilege). Finally, the repetition of stereotyped perceptions of deaf people through the use of a "deaf voice" (along with advice on how to "fake" a failing audiogram in order to get services) once again, in tiresome reiteration, depends upon "lack" as the essential definition of a d/Deaf person.

And yet, not very many of the list members are interested in learning sign language and/or joining the Deaf community. Most desire the deafened, "deviant" body, or the apparatus affiliated with such a body. Motivations vary, but what is significant is that this desire is a fairly new phenomenon. What is significant is that by desiring deafness, or a deaf sensory world, the technology and "plasticity" of the body have caught up with our narratives of bodily integrity and identity.

ENDNOTES

1. The quotations in Suggs's "Deaf Wanna-bes" article (The Tactile Mind: Quarterly of the Signing Community Spring 2003) are a verbatim recording of the original postings on "Deaf Wannabee."
2. Despite the public nature of the group, no identifying information other than the posting number is used.

REFERENCES

Aguilera, Raymond J. "Disability and Delight: Staring Back at the Devotee Community." *Sexuality and Disability* 18.4(2000): 255-261.
Bhabha, Homi. *The Location of Culture*. New York: Routledge, 1994.

Bruno, Richard L. "Devotees, Pretenders, and Wannabes: Two Cases of Factitious Disability Disorder." *Sexuality and Disability* 15.4(1997): 243-260.

"Deaf WannaBee" Group. Yahoo.

Duncan, Kath, and Gerard Goggin. "'Something in Your Belly' — Fantasy, Disability, and Desire in My One-Legged Dream Lover. *Disability Studies Quarterly* 22.4(2002): 127-144. March 2006. <www.cds.hawaii.edu/dsq>

Fernbach, Amanda. "Fetishism and the Future of Gender." 12 Jan. 2006. http://www.ias.uwa.edu.au/__data/page/17737.fernbach.htm.

First, Michael. "Desire for Amputation of a Limb: Paraphilia, Psychosis, or a New Type of Identity Disorder." *Psychological Medicine* 35(2005): 919-928.

Jain, Sarah. "The Prosthetic Imagination: Enabling and Disabling the Prosthesis Trope." *Science, Technology, and Human Values* 24.1(1999): 31-54.

Jordan, John W. "The Rhetorical Limits of the 'Plastic Body.'" *Quarterly Journal of Speech* 90.3(2004): 327-358.

Lowenstein, L.F. "Fetishes and Their Associated Behavior." *Sexuality and Disability* 20.2(2002): 135-147.

Marx, Karl. *The Portable Karl Marx*. Ed. Eugene Kamenka. New York: Viking Penguin, 1983.

Money, John, and Kent Simcoe. "Acrotomophilia, Sex, and Disability: New Concepts and Case Report." *Sexuality and Disability* 7.1-2(1984): 43-50.

Mulvey, Laura. "Visual Pleasure and Narrative Cinema." In *Feminisms: An Anthology of Literary Theory and Criticism*. Eds. Robyn Warhol and Diane Price Herndl. New Jersey: Rutgers University Press, 1997. 438-448.

Potter, Nancy Nyquist. "Commodity/Body/Sign: Borderline Personality Disorder and the Signification of Self-Injurious Behavior." *Philosophy, Psychiatry, and Psychology* 10.1(2003): 1-16.

Seligman, Linda, and Stephanie A. Hardenburg. "Assessment and Treatment of Paraphilias." *Journal of Counseling and Development* 78(2000): 107-113.

Suggs, Trudy. "Deaf Wanna-Bes." *The Tactile Mind: Quarterly of the Signing Community* Spring(2003): 43-86.

Visual Histories: Recording, Preserving and Disseminating and Analyzing Deaf Stories

PATRICIA DURR

BORROWING A TRADITION ESTABLISHED BY DR. PADDY LADD OF HONoring a Deaf individual before presenting, I have selected to honor Meta Noveck. Meta was a Deaf Jewish survivor whom I was blessed to meet for a few hours during the late 1980s when Lexington School for the Deaf invited her to share her experiences in concentration camps during WWII. It was through talking to Meta about her experiences that I came to realize that I had always looked at the Holocaust largely through the male dominant lens and always from a hearing lens. I had never been introduced to or really considered what a Deaf woman's experience must have been like during this time. I am most grateful to Meta for having shared her story and for tugging at my heartstrings over the years. She inspired me to write a play later in her honor.

The primary purpose of this paper is to promote the importance of visual testimonies for Deaf cultural studies programs. With the advent of videotaping technology, oral testimonies have now begun to be referred to visual testimonies and are ideal for capturing the stories of Deaf people who use sign language. Ethnographic studies are a very important part of understanding people and their cultures yet appears to be a somewhat underutilized field of study within Deaf cultural studies. Presently, visual testmonies with Deaf interviewees tend to be largely used for sign language linguistic analysis and they have not been explored for historical, social and political understandings.

The chief values in conducting Deaf visual testimonies are that they afford for the documenting, preserving, and disseminating of these materials, which in turn enrich our understanding of Deaf history, Deaf culture, and the Deaf perspective via analysis of these works.

THE FIRST VISUAL HISTORIES

The National Association of the Deaf (NAD) Motion Picture Project under the stewardship of Roy Stewart and leadership of George W. Veditz recognized the importance of the medium of film to preserve sign language and Deaf history and raised $5,000 in donations for this aim. In 1910 at the Ninth Convention of the NAD and the Third World's Congress of the Deaf, Veditz stated, "We possess and jealously guard a language different and apart from any other in common use: a language which nevertheless is precisely what all-wise Mother Nature designed for the people of the eye, a language with no fixed form or literature in the past, but which we are now striving to fix and give a distinct literature of its own by means of the moving picture film." From 1910 to 1920, the NAD filmed several Deaf and Hearing individuals attending a convention and signing speeches, addresses, sermons, jokes, poetry, and a song. The most famous of them all is Veditz's 1913 "Preservation of Sign Language," in which he proclaims sign language as the "noblest gift God has given us deaf people," and emphasizes the importance of film in preserving ASL and Deaf culture (see figure 1).

Figure 1. George Veditz, NAD "Preservation of Sign Language" 1913. "A-s l-o-n-g a-s we have deaf people on the earth, we will have signs and a-s l-o-n-g a-s we have our f-i-l-m-s, we will be able to p-r-e-s-e-r-v-e our beautiful sign language in its original p-u-r-i-t-y. It is my hope that we all will cherish and defend our beautiful s-i-g-n l-a-n-g-u-a-g-e a-s t-h-e n-o-b-l-e-s-t g-i-f-t God has given us deaf people."

Figure 2. Dr. John Hotckiss NAD "Memories of Old Harford" 1913.

The oldest known Deaf visual history produced in the U.S. is Dr. John Hotchkiss' "Memories of Old Hartford" (see figure 2). This testimony is sadly often overlooked and undervalued, but it is rich with texture, details, and great spirit. The two excerpts pay homage to Laurent Clerc, the founder of the American School for the Deaf with Thomas Gallaudet. The first quote explains Clerc's bilingual method of instruction which he brought with him from France and the second details his humble wish. More than just a moving document to be analyzed for language use in that time period, this visual history tells us much about our ancestors, our educational legacy, our cultural values and beliefs, our norms of behavior, our traditions and possessions and artifacts; in short it is a treasure trove filled with Deaf cultural information waiting to be unlocked and appreciated to the fullest within the field of ethnographic and Deaf cultural studies.

Excerpts from of Dr. John Hotchkiss' "Memories of Old Hartford" (1913)

> "He told us of the significance of literacy, grammar, and word order. He selected two sentences to demonstrate this. The first, which he fingerspelled completely was, "We live to eat" and the other was "We eat to live."
>
> And with his very elegant and grandiose signing (and some what lengthy delivery), he explained the difference with great preciseness and clarity.
>
> We children could clearly see how different the meaning was based on a simple verb change by switching the terms "live" and "eat."
>
> (Hotchkiss imitating Clerc's signing style)
>
> "I, you and you and you, we do not live solely to feast upon food and eat and eat. No, not at all. We live for better things than that. But it is true that each of us must eat in order to give us fortitude and good health to enable us to live and do good." …
>
> "Another time, Clerc was admiring the monument that Deaf people throughout America had paid for to be made in honor of Thomas Gallaudet, which you yourselves over the past few month have been contributing to have restored to its original luster. While Clerc was studying this monument, a few boys happened upon him and asked, 'will there be such a tribute in your honor some day in the future?" to which Clerc replied, "oh, I don't know, perhaps.' 'On what spot would you want such a monument to be set?" a boy asked. Clerc answered, 'well, I don't know but I think I would like it right there. It would be fitting if it were along side Gallaudet's as I was his colleague and friend throughout life. So too should the two statues stand side by side keeping us united even after death.' And so after a few years passed, the Deaf people of this nation gathered up $3,000 to pay for a platform and bronze bust of Clerc to be erected in the very place he, himself, had selected several years before."

This precious testimony has a wealth of material, knowledge, and cultural values to be discovered and examined within the field of Deaf cultural studies and ethnographic studies. Thankfully NAD realized and capitalized on the value and importance of film in order to record Deaf people's lives and stories much as the tape recorders helped to document and preserve spoken languages with no written form. However, it is unfortunate that the Motion Picture Project was not sustained or resurrected after 1920.

DEAF SURVIVORS OF WORLD WAR II

Fortunately other institutions have recognized the importance of Deaf testimonies, especially those relating to World War II. The USC Shoah Foundation Institute has over 52,000 videotaped interviews, of which five are of Deaf survivors and one is of a hearing woman with Mother-Father Deaf (CODA). Yad Vashem, the Holocaust Martyrs' and Heroes' Remembrance Authority in Israel, has conducted several visual testimonies with Deaf survivors and two are available on line with Hebrew voice over and English captions. NTID/RIT and Gallaudet University have done several interviews with Deaf survivors. These testimonies are captioned and up on the NTID/RIT website at www.rit.edu/deafww2 (see figure 3) under videos. The Yale Fortunoff Video Archives for Holocaust Testimonies holds more than 4,300 interviews of survivors; of these, ten were of Deaf survivors and one hearing woman who had Mother-Father-Sister Deaf. (Text summaries of these interviewers are available at the website above. For a detailed bibliography of books, articles, and videotapes about Deaf people and WW II, visit RIT's Librarian Joan Naturale's bibliography listing at: http://wally.rit.edu/pubs/guides/deafwartestimonies.htm.)

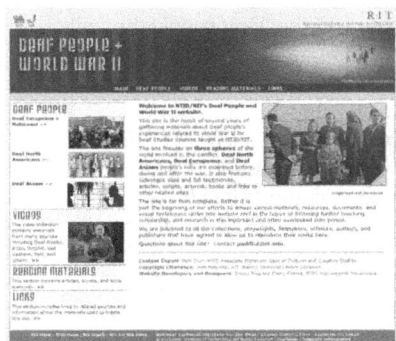

Figure 3: Screen from www.rit.edu/deafww2

Figure 4: Ingelore Honigstein as a youth

Unfortunately it is feared that a great many visual testimonies recorded by family members, lay people or organizations have been lost, misplaced, or overlooked. Furthermore, there is a significant problem in gaining access to some visual testimonies, as some interviewers prefer to keep the materials to themselves. The RIT Wallace Memorial Library has been amassing the materials above into one centralized collection to help facilitate the sharing and use of these valuable Deaf related visual histories.

In order to illustrate the power of Deaf visual testimonies several excerpts were shared during the Deaf Studies Today 2008 conference presentation. It should be noted that all of the quotes below are translations from the testimonies, which were given in American Sign Language by survivors who learned ASL later in life, and do not fully or adequately represent the original message and delivery. In cases where the voice interpretation does not accurately reflect the original message, I have taken the liberty of correcting the text to match the signed testimony. Hopefully, you will be able to spend some time with the visual testimonies by watching the ones we have on-line at the www.rit.edu/deafww2 site and/or by going to the RIT Deaf Studies Archives in the Wallace Memorial Library.

INGELORE'S STORY

Ingelore Honigstein (see figure 4) is a vibrant Deaf German woman who shared a personal and brutal sexual attack she experience at the hands of two Nazi youth:

> "One day the streetcar was running late, very late, and I was not supposed to get back to my school after eight in the evening. I walked very quietly up the street. Two Nazi youth, military students from the academy nearby, came up behind me. They grabbed hold of me and took me to their room and there they raped me repeatedly. The first one told me exactly what he wanted me to do and that I had to do everything he wanted and then the second one did the same. I screamed and they clasped their hands over my mouth and told me not to make any noise. I suffered horribly. I had so much blood all over my legs, trickling down. It was terrible. I could not even walk. It was terrible, horrible pain I was experiencing. That happened when I was already 15 years old. It was just at the beginning of December.
>
> I went back to the school, but they would not open the door for me. They refused. I pounded and pounded. I said, "It's Ingelore, let me in. Please open the door." All the lights were out and the building was dark. Finally, the door opened and I was allowed to come in. The door closed behind me and the caretaker saw all the blood all over me. She took care of me and cleaned my up and she said, "What happened to you?" I explained everything to her and I said, "I do not want to go back to that house. I do not want to go back to that job again.

When I was healed, it was time for Christmas vacation so I took a train back home. I was going to stay there for a while and then come back to school the same way. I got to my house and my mother looked at me and she knew immediately that something was wrong. I was not smiling. I had become very serious. It is as if I aged and became older, but my mother never knew what had happened to me. I was ashamed to tell her."

Ingelore then goes on to chronicle her immigration to the U.S. with her parents, discovery of the pregnancy that results from the attack at the age of 16 and her subsequent abortion. The full testimony of Ingelore as well as her hearing son, Frank Stiefel, are available at www.rit.edu/deafww2 under video and NTID. Her son is now in the process of making a documentary of Ingelore's story.

DORIS' STORY

Doris Fedrid is another Deaf Polish survivor, which NTID interviewed. Doris grew up Deaf and became blind later in life after the war. She hid in over twenty hiding places during the war and was in a ghetto as well as a labor camp. One of the excerpts shared during the presentation discussed the type of work details she experienced.

> "During the war, I had had a bad back. A doctor later told me the cause was from all the stooping I did washing clothes. I would do this work the entire day. I remember my knuckles would swell terribly, but I had to do it. In Germany, they would use double the soap and back then we did not have gloves. All of the women who worked this job had the same problems with their hands. My mother was very worried about me. My father stole butter from his work and I would use the butter on my hands to help soften them and make them feel better. It did help. I would also leave them wrapped in cloth.

> (Interviewer – What type of work / wash were you doing?) I washed uniforms. We would use the soap and scrub them on the washboards to get them clean. That was before washing machines were invented. Now you can just pour the soap in the machine and it does all the work for you. It is so easy now. Back then, we had these big bars of soap that we used. Do you know what that soap was made out of, Jewish people?"

Doris's testimony is rich with detail and meaning. Her facial expression, body language, and words emphasize the hardship and terror of the times in which she lived. One powerful example being when she shares how her mother prepared for the worst:

> My mom actually had poison that she held on to. I remember seeing it. It was a dark color, it was black. She always kept it with her in case they every

caught us. She would take it and then it would be over. It was in case the Nazis came to kill us, we'd take the poison and die peacefully and quietly.

Several short excerpts were shared regarding Doris' hiding places. Her hearing parents had hidden her over twenty-two times. Below she describes a very tight spot-hiding place in which she had to be alone due to the size limit:

> "Well actually, when you opened the bathroom door there was an area right behind that door and it was like a vent. Here I will show you with the paper what it looked like. This is what it looked like and the door would shut on top of this. It was a very small space. I slid in on my back face first with my arms in front of me. It was not good. I only hid there once. It was very uncomfortable and hard to get out of. It was one of the worse hiding spaces and I stayed there all day. There was no light whatsoever. It was completely in the dark. No food. No way to use the toilet. I just mostly slept and waited.
>
> I remember I could feel people walking around inside. It was the Nazi army stamping around. I could feel them searching the house. It was very scary. I'll never forget this..."

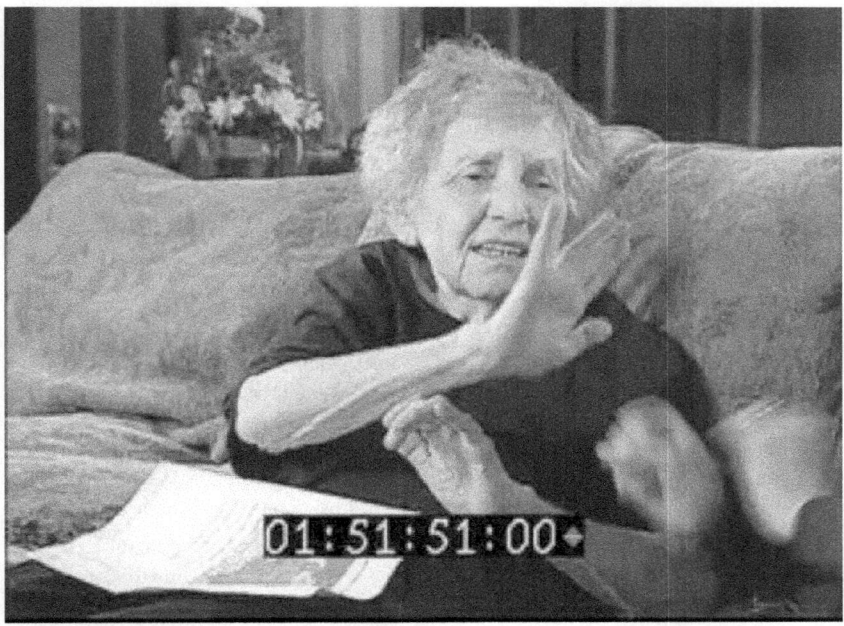

Figure 5: Doris Fedrid

There was always constant fear of the round ups in the Lviv ghetto. Here Doris describes one such akton (deportation) in the ghetto, which swelled to 200,000 and eventually shrunk to 200-300 people surviving after the liquidation and eventual liberation:

"Here is what the house looked like. It was an old couple's house and up in this section was where the daughter lived. This is where the old couple lived, and this is where their daughter lived. She moved out of this room and then we came and hid in this room. They had built a fake wall. They had cut a hole in it and to hide the wall where they had cut the hole, they put like kitchen utensils, bread pans, and stuff like that. They would put a bench up and have pails of water on either side of the bench.

People would go into the wall and then we would shut it behind us and just remain there. I remember hearing the Nazi army actually walking around looking around for us, but we just remained quiet and stayed there overnight. I remember my mom. She was wondering what was going on so she looked out of the wood slats, but she was told not to do that. Of course, I mean that would put us under risk. I remember the babies crying and just trying to keep everybody quiet. It was really difficult and it was very scary. We were there for about three days and then finally we were able to get out. I remember when we got out I looked around the neighborhood and people were gone.

When I got out, I also saw a little girl hiding behind this desk and I called my mom over to look at it. What we had to do was move the desk and we got the little girl out. She was so quiet and so scared. She had said that her parents were taken by the Nazi army. We got her grandmother to come and take her. Her grandmother held her in her arms and the girl just sobbed. She was only three-years-old. She had a little bow in her hair. She had a really nice dress on and big blue eyes. She was only three."

Another clip describes a different hiding place they used while in the ghetto to try to avoid selection.

"Well there was a stove and we had to remove the stove. Then there was a like kitchen counter that we had to remove and we had to build an area underneath the floor, some stairs there. Once those were finished, we covered that over. First and foremost before we covered it though we put a big door on the ground and then we put a cloth and then we added sand to make it really hard. We added carpet over the top of that to make sure that when the army came through the house, they would not notice any difference. We made it soundproof. We did not want it to sound hollow.

Next to it, we cut out a hole in the wall and then put the kitchen counters back and then the stove back and made everything look as though everything was being used. We would use tape to adhere the pots and pans to the stove and things to the kitchen counter. There were table and some chairs and we used the chairs to climb into the hiding space."

On another occasion the group was betrayed by a fellow Jew and deported to the Janowska labor camp only to find that later, the same person would be deported and incarcerated with them also. The money he had gained by turning them in would be of no help to him and his family once behind the camp's fences and guards. Within the camp, Doris's father was separated from her and her mother and they endured very hard work detail and several illnesses. Once when a selection was about to begin and Doris was worried about being sent on to the nearby death camp at Belzec, she made a suggestion that could have been deadly:

> "We saw a lot of people going in this place. There were about 500 people I think we saw over there, and I told my mom that I wanted to join them. My mom said, "No! No! Absolutely not!" You do not know what they do in there. There was a pipe that came out of the roof and my mom showed me the pipe and she said what they do is they seal it and then they use gas to kill all of the people in there."
>
> (Interviewer – This was in the camp right?) 'Yes, it was in the camp.' The building really was a hospital building and a lot of people would go in there. They would bribe their way into the infirmary because they thought their life would be spared, but instead they got killed — gassed!

Doris describes the liquidation of the camp and their final hiding place:

> "I remember the last time we were in the camp, it was July 22nd. Something was going on, people were talking about something and I saw people standing around, very solemn. They were getting ready to do the appels. People were standing around wondering if their name was going to be on the list. Anytime they called my name, someone would touch me and I would raise my hand. Then there was a mass exodus that night, everyone was trying to escape.
>
> There was an old house that they had liquidated and down in the basement it was flooded with water. That is where we stayed to wait out the army. You could see people going on with their daily chores. I could see people going to the bathroom. I remember we were there Thursday, Friday, and then Saturday morning there seemed to not be anything going on. The coast was clear and we were able to make our escape. Sylvia was with us and the four of us were able to leave.
>
> My father went to scope out a hiding place. He explained to us what to do in the pastime, so we went to hide in the forest until my father came back at nightfall and got us. My father had found a chicken coop, where they had made a shallow pit that we could hide in. It was like a shallow pit and then they had sand over the top of it. They used bird feed sacks to cover that area. We were not able to go out at all. There was a woman that lived there that owned the property and she would come and give us information. She usually did that at night and then we would stay there all day. We were only able to eat once a day and we only ate potatoes."
>
> We also had mice up in the ceiling as well. My father put paper up there to try to prevent them from coming down, but you could hear them running around and scattering through the ceiling.
>
> Sometimes when my parents would find out information, they would relay information to me via my palm, the palm of my hand. They would just form

the outline of letters in the palm of my hand like this, and they would use the Polish language to relay this information to me and sometimes they would use my back."

Doris and her parents would spend over a year hiding in the chicken coop. When they learned that the Russians had liberated the area, they had to crawl about because their muscles were so weak from lack of use. As with many other survivors, the end of the war did not begin a time of tranquility as many Jews, especially those from Poland, found that they were not welcome home and faced the threat of death from their own countrymen. Doris' testimony is rich in its description of her life before, during and after the war and her immigration and settlement in the U.S.

WIENER / RATTNER STORY

The fascinating story of the Wiener / Rattners, a family of Deaf Austrians, has been documented by the Yale Fortunoff Video Archives for Holocaust Testimonies with their visual testimonies of Hilda Rattner and her daughter Nelly. A score later, NTID documented Nelly's younger sister, Lilly, by producing a sit down full-length interview as well as a short documentary about the family called "EXODUS: A Deaf Jewish Family Escapes the Holocaust" (see figure 6). Hilda, her two Deaf children (Nelly and Lilly) and her Deaf brother, Richard, along with their hearing mother were able to get out of Nazi occupied Austria in 1940 only to be detained at Ellis Island for five month because of their being deaf with the threat of being returned to Europe. Thankfully they were able to gain entry into the U.S. with the support of several Jewish agencies and individuals but the children's father Isadore Rattner, who had separated from Hilda before the war, did not survive the Holocaust. The NTID produced visual history and documentary can be viewed at www.rit.edu/deafww2.

Visual Histories: Recording, Preserving and Disseminating and Analyzing Deaf Stories 527

Figure 6: Still from the documentary *Exodus*

The Yale Fortunoff Video Archives for Holocaust Testimonies are very valuable Deaf visual histories as they are rich with information. Since it is not permitted to stream these visual histories on the Deaf People and World War II website, NTID was grateful for being permitted to show excerpts from three of the Deaf survivors in this collection who are no longer living, one of which was Hilda Rattner, mentioned above. While this is one of the shortest visual histories amongst the Deaf survivors in the Yale Fortunoff Video Archives for Holocaust Testimonies, it is packed with meaning and significance as Hilda says volumes with her facial expression and emphasis:

> "It took us about two months to get to America. It was a long time. Luckily I had two brothers who had already moved to America. If it weren't for them, we surely would have been killed (signs – throats slit).
>
> (Interviewer – And did your parents leave also?)
>
> My father had already passed away before. My mother was with us. He was sick and died.
>
> I was very happy in Austria. I cried when we had to leave. I loved Austria. This was before. Once the Nazis came I was disgusted and wanted nothing to do with Austria anymore.
>
> You understand my point? After I arrived in America, about ten years later, someone nudged me and asked if I'd like to visit Vienna. At first I was unsure but decided to go. When I arrived and my friends saw me, they all burst out crying. They begged me to stay. "We want the Jewish people to

come back," they said. (Interviewer – Oh, you went back to Vienna and you did too (too Nelly who is off camera). Yes, But I replied, "No way. You think after being forced to flee this country I am going to come back and live here, no, no!" I loved them all. I was happy to see them. They all said how sorry they were. But what are you going to do? Stay, no way. Oh, how they begged but I said, "No, I am going back to my new homeland." I am so thankful to America and so I said goodbye to Austria."

Studying survivors' stories within the full context of their lives helps us to more fully appreciate the impact that the war and the Holocaust had on their families. As a result of the documentary and Lilly Rattner allowing the US Holocaust Memorial Museum to scan many photographs of Deaf Austrian life and social gatherings before the war, she has come to learn more about her father's fate and to see primary documents detailing how difficult it was for her family to get out.

META'S STORY

And now we come to one of the testimonies of the very first person who introduced me to the Shoah from a Deaf Jewish person's perspective. Meta N. is the woman who first shared a brief snapshot of her story with my class many years ago at Lexington and when I made the play in her honor, Dr. Simon Carmel informed me that Meta had been videotaped by Yale and was part of their Yale Fortunoff Video Archives for Holocaust Testimonies along with several other Deaf survivors. When I was finally able to see the videotape, we had to send it out for captioning as Meta, as many interviewees will do adjusted to the communication / language of her interviewer. In this case it was a hearing, non-signing interviewer with a sign language interpreter present also. Meta responds largely in spoken English with some German when recalling names of places or titles and some gestures, ASL and fingerspelling. Meta had survived four concentration camps and while her testimony is somewhat difficult to follow, she provides some valuable first hand information about the Deaf experience within the Holocaust:

> (Interviewer – And who was in charge of this camp?) An S.S. commander. I forget the name. No, I don't remember the name. He never knew I was deaf. I was very careful myself. MY heart was beating. OH! (Interviewer – What did you think would happen to you if he knew that you were deaf?) Oh, yes. In the beginning of December or whatever, a few deaf people were there, and the S.S. commander said, "We want to take you to another place that's better. If children want to go to school some with their mothers can go. Old people, deaf people, other handicapped people, yes." And I didn't want – I just was very quiet and stayed put and in the background. I was the only deaf person who remained, who stayed back. All the rest went. The

commandant never knew for three years about me. Only the young were left behind and the rest went. I was the only deaf one. Gosh! I told myself, "I am going to be brave." I was going to "think strong."

Like several other Deaf survivors, Meta also had a friend who would help her know when to step forward during roll call and warned her and/or aided her in situations where to hear was a matter of life or death.

WILLIAM'S STORY

William F.'s story is another outstanding visual history within the Yale Fortunoff Video Archives for Holocaust Testimonies collection as it details the amazing story of a Deaf Hungarian Jewish man, his marriage to a Deaf Jewish woman in Czechoslovakia, their attempt to flee to Palestine, their shipwreck, "rescued" to be put into a concentration camp in Italy, their voyage to the U.S. and being placed in a refugee camp in Oswego, NY with the threat of being returned to Europe after the war. In the excerpt below, William explains what happened after a ship that was smuggling over 1,200 Jews to Palestine during the war hit an unknown island and sunk. He and his wife were the only Deaf passengers:

> "We had — the ship...had broken. (Interviewer – Crashed?) Yes, the ship crashed and was destroyed. People were very afraid for their lives. The island was not far, so we had to get off. The water was coming into the ship and was about to sink. Some people knew how to swim; some didn't. And so we made this rope, we rigged this rope up for people who didn't know how to swim could grab onto the rope hand over hand until they reached the island. So we went to this island, and there was nothing there. It was barren. So, you know, how were we going to sleep at night? So I went back to the ship via this rope. And the ship was on its side by this time it had not sunk. And I took things like food and wood and the things that we needed for sleeping...
>
> We — I made, uh, an S.O.S. I drew this from a blanket that was taken from the ship. And I used shoe cream — shoe and made this S.O.S
>
> After nine days the group was "rescued" by Italy, one of the Axis Powers along with Germany and Japan, and placed in a camp (Ferramonti) in Italy.
>
> "In the morning there'd be like, black soup, like, coffee. There was cornbread. One each. Vegetables mixed in water. It was really poor-quality food. And morning and afternoon was all the food that we got. We were fed twice a day. I was very thin. You could see my ribs, and I was very bony. Almost —
>
> You could have played it like a washboard. (Interviewer – Did they live in fear?) Yes, I was. At that time, there was a lot of bombing going on. And my pants were hanging. And an airplane went by and they had shot a hole into my pants and started a fire. There was a big hole in my pants. And we

were very afraid. We went into where the toilet was and lay down. And it was smelly and filthy, but it didn't matter. We had to be safe, and so we lay there. One woman who was pregnant was sitting, and she was struck in the stomach, and her womb just exploded, and it went all over the floor, and it was very smelly.

And there were many people who died all over the camp. Their faces were white.

(Interviewer - Who was bombing? Americans? Italy?)

I don't know. Germany. I don't know. We were very afraid. There was a wall.

And I was near the wall, and a bullet went right by me. And I was--luckily, I was saved. God helped me, but I was very afraid. I was very, very scared. My wife was crying. I wasn't with her at that time, but she told me she was very afraid also. We suffered terribly. There were people dead everywhere. But thank god. God saved me. I don't want to really talk about the situation. I don't sleep well at night when I think about the situation. So I just want to have a new life now.

William's story is one of perseverance, good fortune and marvel. We are incredibly grateful that Yale University conducted these testimonies, as many of the interviewees are no longer living. They also had Dr. Carmel conduct three of the interviews of survivors who are still living and since both the interviewer and interviewee all use ASL, communication complications do not surface in those testimonies.

LEOPOLD'S STORY

Sadly, the Shoah is not the only genocide the world has seen. In an effort to collect, preserve and share modern day genocides from a Deaf perspective, the visual history of Leopold Myasiro was conducted by Argiroula (Roula) Zangana and videotaped by Ryan Commerson (see figure 7). Leopold is Hutu and grew up in Rwanda where he was a witness to the genocide and civil war there. While he is a member of the dominant culture, while many Hutus took machete blades against Tutsis, Leopold did not participate in the atrocities and spent much of the four month in 1996 when the massacres were happening in hiding. While some testimonies of Deaf survivors in World War II report how Deaf non-Jews actively turned them in or demonstrated anti-Semitism towards their fellow Deaf Jews, Leopold reports that the Deaf of Rwanda were more committed to protecting each other regardless of which tribe they were members of:

"The Free Radio broadcast a lot of negative information about Tutsis. You understand that the deaf can not hear the radio so the deaf did not get access to these hate messages. Maybe some would pick it up in school but most, like myself for example, were never taught to hate Tutsis. My classmate sitting next to me might be a Tutsi and I simply saw him as a fellow human being.

Whereas in the hearing schools they tended to teach everything including the teaching of history. This is where the conflict between the Tutsis and Hutus comes up – the on-going struggle between these tribes. Since the making of the war, the revolution in '59 – this information would be taught and studied in the hearing schools; whereas, those of us in the deaf schools would know nothing about it. We ate and sat together. There was no discussion amongst the deaf children about who was Hutu or Tutsi. We deaf were completely innocent to this hatred until hearing people would explain it to us and we were like, 'Oh, ok now I understand.' But we still could not easily go ahead and kill our brethrens."

Figure 7. Leopold Myasiro

I met one of my former classmates who had stayed in his rural area, which had no deaf community there. This is perhaps why he could find no support. The hearing people did not care that he was deaf and would strike the machetes against anyone indiscriminately. This is why he still has many injuries, wounds scars from machete attacks. But within the Deaf community there is a bond and a comfort level – no one cares if someone is Tutsi or Hutu.

It is true that some deaf people died. Perhaps they lived in the rural area far from a large deaf community and only a few deaf people lived in their region. Understand that most deaf do not live close to one another.

Except for in larger cities where they look for work. This is how they often come together to share room and board. Having a job means they can afford the rent and can chip in together. This is how some deaf people were able save each other. It did not matter what tribe you were from, you shared and helped each other. When the war came, deaf hid and helped each other. They could not kill their mate. They had a connection to each other. This is how they were very lucky to survive."

Leopold goes on to explain how Hutu Deaf people did not only refrain from participating in the genocide but some were active in protecting their Tutsi Deaf friends:

"One deaf person told me how he saved some deaf Tutsis. The army showed up at this deaf Hutu man's home because they knew he was friendly was Tutsis and wanted to make sure he was not hiding anyone. So the man gave them some kind of cover story that there were no Tutsis there even though they were right under the bed. They could have been killed. He decided to bribe the army in order to get them to leave. This happened repeatedly until the war was over and they left. So they are still alive today. That is how they were lucky to be saved."

While the above is second hand information, Leopold serves as a witness of the genocide while he was in hiding at his home, separated from his family and fearful that he would be seized up to join the Hutus or targeted by the Tutsi:

"My village is very close to the river Nyabarongo. This was a popular place to dump the dead bodies in and I would watch this flood of bodies flow down stream. And many birds would enjoy this feast. Like vultures, those larges birds would come and eat the dead. I sat and watched and felt so badly. I wondered are some of my friends still alive or not? I had many classmates and friends who were Tutsis and I wondered if they are living or not. I wondered if they survive and we meet again, could we reconnect as friends or would they be suspicious of me. You know what I mean? One name can be used to label all, you know what I mean? I would sit, watch and wonder, what is to come later? That is a hard area to predict."

Having testimonies of Deaf individuals who have lived through world events and can describe them in ASL and share these events from a Deaf perspective contributes a great deal to our understanding of world events, history, society, politics, language, and humanity — or inhumanity.

IMPACT OF VISUAL HISTORIES

> "Ethnological phenomena are the result of the physical and psychical character of men, and of its development under the influence of the surroundings."
> Franz Boas, Anthropologist

An essential part of our work within the field of Deaf cultural studies is to bring students to the threshold of their own understanding of the human condition via the reviewing of visual histories. In 2005, I conducted a qualitative study involving twenty-two students to assess the impact of Deaf related testimonies of survivors of the Holocaust on NTID Deaf, hard of hearing, and hearing students in my World War II and Deaf People classes. Dr. Susan Foster, an ethnographic researcher at NTID/RIT, and I developed five qualitative questions for the students to respond to. Students were asked to describe their feelings in response to the visual testimonies they had viewed. At that time we did not have all the ones we presently have. Despite the low number of visual histories we had at this time, their impact was clearly measurable. Throughout our ten-week quarter, students were shown Deaf related testimonies (some were of hearing family members) but most were of Deaf survivors themselves using ASL or gestures with English captions. At the end of the quarter, students were asked to comment on the feelings they experienced while watching the visual histories, what they learned, what surprised them, if they thought deaf and hearing people experienced the Shoah differently, and whether or not they felt differently when watching deaf survivors versus hearing survivors.

Note: In order to preserve the original authenticity of the respondents and not wanting to tamper with their responses, their statements have not been edited nor their English corrected.

Question 1: Feelings and Examples

Students were asked "Take a moment to think about when you viewed the videotaped interviews. Now write down words that describe your feelings while you viewed the tapes. Can you give an example of a story that really brought out each of these feelings?"

While all of them remarked on having strong negative feelings in response to the testimonies, they were also able to report a great many positive feelings as a result of seeing the Deaf survivors share their stories with such love and strength.

	Fall '05	Winter '05
Negative Feelings	15	21
Terms Used	Nauseated, sad (3), disappointed, terrified, bad, stunned (2), shocked (2), guilty, tearful, upset, dreadful	Sad (2), heartbreaking, depressing, gross, painful, disgust, anger (2), disbelief, horrified, frustrated, bad (2), cruel, frustration, shocked, sorry (2), want to hit or beat the Nazis up (2)
Positive Feelings	11	8
Terms Used	Awed, interested, eager, proud, wow (surprised), amazing, bit of humor, heart-touching, relieved, happy, impressive	Impressed (2), hope, relief, inspired, surprised, amazement, thankful

Table 1: Reported feelings from viewing Deaf related testimonies

Question 2: Learned and Examples

The second question asked of the students was "What did you learn from these interviews that you didn't know before? Be sure to give an example from an interview." The students' qualitative answers were long and well thought out. I have selected a few here so you can see examples of their own statements as to what they learned from these visual histories.

> "I learned that deaf people were forced to be sterilized even though they are not Jewish – part of the eugenics movement. Even that if they had children, they would not know if their child would be deaf or hearing the Nazis were not willing to take that chance. Being deaf is almost like being Jewish, because they were disabled and not seen to be supporting the greater good of the country. Being both Jewish and deaf (also others such as black, gypsy, etc.) was an automatic death sentence during that time and were sent to the camps immediately."

> "Actually, I learned many things from the interviews that I had never known before. Take Hilda and Lilly's story for example. I did not know that Hilda, Lilly and their family was stuck on the Ellis Island near New York City all because they were deaf and because America didn't want them to enter their country because they were viewed as a burden to the society. I was stunned that they were stuck on that tiny island for five months straight with nothing to do except to wait and wait! Unfortunately, there were no history documented that any deaf people were stuck there on the island during the World War II, so that was why nobody really knew anything about it. I am little ashamed of America because they should have welcomed Hilda and Lilly's family with a wide-open arms into their country. But however, they were extremely lucky that they didn't get sent back to Europe whereas they

might be sent to the concentration camps! Not only that, I learned a lot from a fresh new perspective of the Holocaust and the World War II from the deaf person's perspective. It all made it more realistic to me."

Question 3: Surprising

The third open-ended question was "What was the most surprising thing you learned from the interviews?" While some students elected to restate their answer in question number two, many of them cited specific testimonies and situations that surprised them the most. In this answer we could see a pattern of common values and understandings on the part of our students.

Surprises that were most often cited have been summarized and listed.
- The fact that any Deaf Jewish people could survive
- Signing was dangerous and deadly
- Deaf people had been forcibly sterilized
- A few Deaf people were helped by SS members
- Luck played a big role in survival
- Family members either went to great efforts to help their Deaf family member or others abandoned them
- Some Jewish boys were dressed as girls to prevent them from being caught and revealed to be Jews
- The Nazis had been bad to Deaf people too (not just against Jewish people)
- People were willing to help Deaf people
- Deaf people used a variety of methods to conceal their being Deaf - truly making them silent (no voice / no signing)
- Deaf people would take great risks to leave Europe only to be rejected by the US due to their being Deaf
- Nazi passport pictures were shown in profile to emphasize the "Jewish features" (nose and ear size/shape)
- Migrating to Shanghai, China as a last resort (the only place not requiring a passport and still accepting Jewish immigrants during the war)
- Many survivors love and cherish their new homeland (U.S.) despite any difficulties entering
- Some Deaf non-Jewish people were pressured to join a Hitler youth type group
- How realistic the Deaf testimonies made the Holocaust for the students

While all of the students statements are valuable and important just a few have been selected for your review to emphasize how much is gained by sharing these visual testimonies with our students and by asking them to in turn share what they glean from them.

Student A: "In my opinion, I believe that all of the interviews of the deaf survivors' stories are all equally shocking and stunning. What surprised me in general was that those deaf survivors were so lucky to have made it out alive. They got lucky many times. They escaped the death's shadows several times. Oftentimes the deaf people had a slim chance of surviving under Hitler's regime. Hitler and his people didn't like the deaf people because they believed that they were useless to the society. Also, I wanted to note that I was surprised when I listened to Lilly telling stories how his father was sent to the gas chambers in the concentration camp because the soldiers saw her father using sign language chatting with his deaf buddies in the camp. The soldiers didn't like the deaf persons there in the camps so they decided to send them off all because their flying hands were "too noticeable, disturbing, and perhaps too annoying". It helped me picture an imagery of the deaf people just standing around and chatting in the concentration camps to help kill the time. It made it seem so realistic, and that time made me stunned the most."

Student B: "The most surprising thing from all the interviews is that the Nazis actually let the survivors that were interviewed live. The one that touched me most was the interview with William F. I myself am Hungarian and I always thought that the Hungarian were on the Germany side. His story about the escape from Europe, his ship wreck on the island and later captured by Italy where the SS soldier had a deaf sister himself and let William be with his deaf wife and let them work together. It seemed more of a romance between him and his wife and the story of a SS soldier not being like the others letting them live together. Unlike any other concentration camp I think they got lucky."

Student C: "One of the most surprising things that I learned from the videos was the extent that parents would go to in order to protect their children. The greatest example was that Stanley Teger's mother dressed him as a girl so that he would not be forced to have his genital area examined by the Nazis. If the Nazis found that a boy had been circumcised, it was an indication that the boy was Jewish. I'm sure that Stanley's mother's decision to hide him under the guise of a girl saved his life."

Student D: "I was surprise that NN was forced to join with Hitler Youth group, I think they threaten her to join in. That is really scaring for someone to threaten a German to join in Hitler Youth Group. I was surprise when Stanley got hit on his head by a soldier guns, and his mother try her very best to protect her own sons (communicating) like told him to be quiet she would squeeze his hand that is the signal of be quiet. I was surprised when father (Lore's father) said that to go ahead and abortion the baby because they don't want no half nazi mixed wit jews as of the baby get older, he or she would probably think what kind of father I had and hurted my mother. Therefore I was surprise because I'm against abortion but in her story I understand her situations."

Question 4: Different Experiences

When asked "Do you think deaf people experienced the holocaust differently than hearing people? Why or why not?" This student wrote:

> "I believe that Deaf people experienced the holocaust differently than hearing people did. I think that way because usually they probably did not know what was going on, such as when her Deaf mother (De Jong) was taken away and tossed into the truck. I would imagine how scary it would be to be tossed into a truck with no one who knew I was Deaf and being unable to communicate with anyone in the truck. It would be like sitting ducks with out knowing what I would be facing next. Maybe it was harder for them when the Germans were yelling out directions and it would have taken more time for Deaf people to figure out what the Germans wanted, thus maybe the Germans may have gotten frustrated with Deaf people who were slow so they ended up shooting them before they were taken to the gas chambers. It also may have been more difficult for Deaf people to freely learn about what was going on around there because they usually had to refrain from using sign language."

Another student commented:

> "I do believe that Deaf people's experiences in the Holocaust were different from those of hearing people. Overall I think that Deaf people experienced a heightened sense of confusion. I can't imagine what it must have felt like to be crammed into a cattle car, taken on a journey hours long, and then be forced to be separated from your loved ones, let alone to be forced to do all of that without having a clue as to what was being communicated around you! All of the prisoners who were taken to the camps must have been in a mass state of panic and confusion, but I think it was far worse for the Deaf prisoners. At least the hearing prisoners would be able to understand what was being screamed at them and demanded of them. I also think that Deaf people must have felt much lonelier than their fellow hearing prisoners. Unless two Deaf people happened to be assigned to the same barrack, than a Deaf person would most likely not have anyone with whom to communicate, or to share their emotions and misery."

The other qualitative responses for this question were similar to the above, demonstrating how students personalized the Holocaust experience and developed empathy and sympathy for the plight of their deaf ancestors.

Question 5: Feel Differently
For the final question, "did you feel differently when you watched the interviews with deaf survivors than when you watched the interviews with hearing survivors? If so, what do you think made you feel differently?" Several students had difficulties assessing this question. Two students reported not feeling differently with these explanations:

> "No – re: deaf culture. No I don't really feel differently, because I'm not so serious about the deaf culture because I have just trying my best to learn deaf culture so however, they seems to be the same thing, because they said

things almost the same thing when they saw things happened with their own eye and actions.

Another respondent who said 'no' stated,

"I did not feel any difference after watching both hearing and deaf survivors. They all have a sad and somewhat similar story. They all share a part of history in their own eyes. They all are equals. So no I did not feel any difference and I have experience in both deaf and hearing culture being that I was raised mainstream and only knew maybe 4 hard of hearing students until I arrived at NTID. At NTID I learned there is no difference between us just the language and a little culture but we are all still equal and similar."

However, all the other Deaf, hard of hearing, and hearing students indicated that they did feel differently when watching the Deaf survivors versus the hearing ones and attributed this largely to language delivery, facial expression personal relevancy and the ability to put one's self in the interviewee's shoes:

Student A: "Yes, I felt a big difference when watching the interviews by deaf survivors than I did with hearing survivors. With hearing survivors, I felt some kind of distance from them because we have different kinds of lives and a different kind of communication methods. Thus, I was able to relate to them lesser. As for the deaf survivors, I instantly felt closer to them and understood how they felt about their experiences by looking at their face expressions and emotions on their faces. I was able to relate with them more because they are deaf like me and understood them better. Also, watching the deaf survivors discuss about their experiences made it all seem so realistic with me. But both of the deaf and hearing survivors' tales touched me equally."

Student B: "Yes, I felt differently when I watched the interviews with deaf survivors than when I watched the interviews with hearing survivors because I'm deaf myself, and I felt more connected with these deaf survivors. Especially see them signing and I could understand them well from visualizing things better. Watching deaf survivors interviews impacted me harder because it's all about the miracles. For hearing survivors, it's more common, but deaf survivors are more like WOW because they have a disability and they could be killed immediately."

Student C: "I felt differently when I watched the interviews with deaf survivors, because I can relate to them being deaf, and we still suffer persecution sometimes of being deaf. Some people can't accept that we're deaf."

Student D: "Yes. I think deaf people would tell more than hearing people. Deaf people can tell about the life and I would interested in that story about how to survive through the war. I feel differently that deaf people can tell elaborately, exactly pattern. Hearing people do different way that they talk and I am lost what hearing people lecturing."

Clearly, visual testimonies can be and should be a very significant part of Deaf Cultural Studies programs. While the classes used textbooks, websites, discussions, and general World War II videotapes to learn about the subject matter, it is most likely that these visual histories and the visits from living survivors will stand out the most in their minds for years to come.

CONDUCTING VISUAL HISTORIES

Typical videos of Deaf people telling their personal histories have been examined more for sign production and grammar (linguistics) than for content and meaning. We wish to maintain and advance linguistic and socio-linguistic analysis of Deaf visual histories, while simultaneously urging researchers to examine how we make sense of the Deaf experience via identify values, norms of behavior, traditions, and material cultures that are revealed within these testimonies. It is vital that we record, preserve analyze and disseminate our Deaf experiences / perspectives and in doing so may we do our ancestors, elders, peers and future members honor and justice.

Key things to keep in mind when undertaking visual histories:
- Develop a rapport with the interviewee/narrator
- Videophone / preliminary interview
- Write up notes while fresh in your mind
- Research historical background
- Have maps and images ready in advance
- Ask for their materials to be filmed/scanned
- Question vs. interrogate (make interviewee comfortable and don't contradict or argue; asking gentle, guiding, and clarification questions)
- Be aware of how your gender, age, language, background etc may affect interviewee/narrator
- When possible do voice-over after the interview; don't record live voice interpretation. This allows interpreter to study the interview and meet with interviewer for clarification and preparation before recording voice interpretation
- Identify a repository / archives to donate the visual history to for others to be able to access the materials
- Get signed release from the interviewee and the interviewer (also for the voice interpreter if needed)

There are many useful sources of materials on conducting visual histories:
- The Smithsonian Folklife and Oral History Interviewing Guide by Marjorie Hunt (2003)
- http://www.folklife.si.edu/explore/Resources/InterviewGuide/InterviewGuide_home.html

- Step by Step Guide to Oral History by Judith Moyer (revised 1999): http://dohistory.org/on_your_own/toolkit/oralHistory.html
- "Oral History Manual" by Sommer and Quinlan (2002)

Articles regarding Deaf survivors and visual testimonies:
- "Oral History and Deaf Heritage: Theory and Case Studies" by Dr. Schuchman in Looking Back (1993)
- "Deaf People in Hitler's Europe: Conducting Oral History Interviews with Deaf Holocaust Survivors," by Dr. Ryan in The Public Historian (2005)
- "Creating a Video Library: An Oral History Project" by Amy Cohen and Yona Diamond Dansky in Perspectives (1992)

Graeme Turner in *Film as Social Practice* stated "Film is a social practice for its makers and its audience; in its narratives and meanings we can locate evidence of the ways in which our culture makes sense of itself." While speaking more of narrative films than visual history, what he speaks of is especially true for Deaf visual histories. Typical videos of Deaf people telling their personal histories have been examined more for sign production and grammar (linguistics) than for content and meaning. We wish to maintain and advance linguistic and socio-linguistic analysis of Deaf visual histories, while simultaneously urging researchers to examine how we make sense of the Deaf experience via identifying values, norms of behavior, traditions, and material cultures that are revealed within these testimonies. It is vital that we record, preserve analyze and disseminate our Deaf experiences / perspectives and in doing so may we do our ancestors, elders, peers and future members honor and justice.

> "The purpose of anthropology is to make the world safe for human differences." Ruth Benedict, deaf anthropologist

REFERENCES

Biesold, Horst. *Crying Hands: Eugenics and Deaf People in Nazi Germany.* Washington, DC: Gallaudet University Press, 1999.

Deaf People in Hitler's Europe. Ed. Donna F. Ryan and John S. Schuchman. Washington, DC: Gallaudet University Press, 2002.

Durr, Patricia, prod. Exodus: A Deaf Jewish Family Escapes the Holocaust. Rochester, NY: RIT, 2006. www.rit.edu/deafww2

Elizabeth Feldman de Jong: Jan. 11, 1995. Kalb, Edie, interviewer. Videocassette. Survivors of the Shoah Visual History Foundation, 2003. www.rit.edu/deafww2

Fedrid, Doris. NTID/RIT Holocaust Survivors Series, Interview with Patricia Durr. Rochester, NY: RIT, 2007. www.rit.edu/deafww2

Helga G. Holocaust Testimony: Oct. 25, 2001. Carmel, Simon, interviewer. Videocassette. NTID at RIT, Yale Fortunoff Video Archives for Holocaust Testimonies, Yale University, 2001.

Herta M. Holocaust Testimony: October 27, 2000. Carmel, Simon, interviewer. Videocassette. Yale Fortunoff Video Archives for Holocaust Testimonies: Yale University, 2000.

Hilda R. Holocaust Testimony: April 13, 1986. Schiff, Gabriele, and Lilian Sicular, interviewers. Brenda Marshall, Interpreter. Videocassette. Yale Fortunoff Video Archives for Holocaust Testimonies, Yale University, 1986.

Hotchkiss, John, "Memories of Old Harford," NAD Films, 1913.

Honigstein, Ingelore. NTID/RIT Holocaust Survivors Series, Interview with Patricia Durr and Joshua Berman. Rochester, NY: RIT, 2007. www.rit.edu/deafww2

Hunt, Majorie. *The Simthsonian Folklife and Oral History Interviewing Guide*, Washington, DC: Smithsonian Institution Center for Folklife and Cultural Heritage, 2003. http://www.folklife.si.edu/explore/resources/interviewguide/interviewguide_home.html

"In Der Nacht." 403. Deaf Mosaic. Gallaudet University. Washington, DC. Fall 1988. www.rit.edu/deafww2

Meta N. Holocaust Testimony: April 13, 1986. Forman, Miriam, and Lilian Sicular, interviewers. Brenda Marshall, Interpreter. Yale Fortunoff Video Archives for Holocaust Testimonies: Yale University, 1986.

Moyer, Joyce. *Step by Step Guide to Oral History* (revised 1999). http://dohistory.org/on_your_own/toolkit/oralHistory.html#http://dohistory.org/on_your_own/toolkit/oralHistory.html

Nelly M. Holocaust Testimony. Videocassette. Yale Fortunoff Video Archives for Holocaust Testimonies: Yale University, 1986.

Ryan, Donna F. "Deaf People in Hitler's Europe: Conducting Oral History Interviews With Deaf Holocaust Survivors." *The Public Historian* 27.2 (Apr. 2005): 43-52.

Schuchman, John S. "Oral History and Deaf Heritage: Theory and Case Studies." *Looking Back: A Reader on the History of Deaf Communities and their Sign Languages*. Ed. Harlan Lane and Renate Fischer. Hamburg: Signum, 1993.

Shirey, Lilly Rattner. Interview with Patricia Durr and Joshua Berman. An Interview with Lilly Rattner Shirey, Rochester, NY: RIT, 2006. www.rit.edu/deafww2

Sommer, Barbara and Mary Kay Quinlan. *The Oral History Manual*. Walnut Creek, CA, AltaMira Press, 2002

"Stanley Teger." 309. Deaf Mosaic. Gallaudet University. Washington, DC. Jan. 1987. www.rit.edu/deafww2

Veditz, George, "Preservation of Sign Language," NAD Films, 1913.

Veditz, George, "President's Message," *Proceedings of the Ninth Convention of the National Association and the Third World's Congress of the Deaf*, Colorado Springs, Colo. August 6 to 13, 1910.

William F. Holocaust Testimony: April 13, 1986. Tobin, Phyllis, and Miriam Forman, interviewers. Brenda Marshall, Interpreter. Videocassette. Yale Fortunoff Video Archives for Holocaust Testimonies: Yale University, 1986.

Is There a Place on Children's Educational Television for ASL?

DEBBIE GOLOS, PH.D.

ONE OF THE MOST PRESSING CONCERNS REGARDING THE EDUCATION of deaf and hard of hearing (D/HH) children is their lack of academic success as measured by their literacy skills. Most deaf children finish high school reading below a fourth grade level (Allen, 1986; Holt, 1993). This is largely due to the fact that 90% of children who are D/HH have hearing families who need to learn sign language in order to communicate with their children. Like learning any new language, learning sign language can be a lengthy process. The result is that many D/HH children enter school with limited language exposure.

It is known that early delays in oral language in hearing children can have a negative impact on reading comprehension and overall academic achievement (Beimiller, 1999). This has also been found to be true in research on deaf children. According to Morford and Mayberry (2000), "Individuals who are exposed to languages at earlier ages consistently outperform individuals exposed to languages at later ages on tests for second language acquisition of both signed and spoken language" (p. 111). Research has also demonstrated a significant correlation between sign language skills and reading skills. Deaf children of Deaf parents (DOD), who have been exposed to ASL from birth, develop literacy skills that allow them continuously outperform deaf children with hearing parents on vocabulary tasks and language skills (Mayberry, 1993).

Deaf children of hearing parents (DOH) need early intervention to help them increase their early language skills and hearing parents need ways to begin engaging their children in literacy activities at a young age in order to narrow the reading gap between deaf and hearing children. Using educational videos or television programs is a promising method of for engaging deaf children in both language and literacy activities at an early age.

Since 1970, educational television has been used as a supplemental tool to help hearing children develop emergent literacy skills. Programs such as *Sesame Street, Blue's Clues, Reading Rainbow* and *Between the Lions* have been a successful medium for educating preschool hearing children. One of the targeted populations of such programs has been minority and bilingual populations (Fisch & Truglio, 2001). Research on educational television programming such as *Sesame Street*, (Rice, Huston, Truglio, & Wright, 1990) *Between the Lions* (Rath, 2002), and *Blue's Clues* (Crawley, Anderson, Wilder, Williams, Santomero, Evans, & Bryant, 1999), has demonstrated that watching these programs improves literacy and cognitive skills for preschool, hearing children.

Deaf and hard of hearing children could also greatly benefit from this rich educational medium. However, the majority of these programs are inaccessible to deaf children because they are designed with hearing children in mind and are accessible to children only in spoken English. The purpose of this study is to determine whether preschool deaf and hard of hearing children engage in literacy related behaviors while viewing an educational video in ASL, and if so, what types of behaviors they engage in.

This study is part of a larger mixed methods study that measured vocabulary gain of targeted vocabulary after multiple viewings on an educational video in ASL.

THEORETICAL FRAMEWORK

The three theories guiding this study are: emergent literacy, linguistic interdependence, and active viewing. The emergent literacy perspective posits that language and literacy skills develop simultaneously rather than sequentially (Teale & Sulzby, 1989; Sulzby & Teale, 1991). Researchers of language and literacy development of deaf children have also begun to adopt an emergent literacy perspective (Williams, 2004).

The theory of linguistic interdependence supports an additive approach to bilingual education and posits that knowledge from the first language transfers to knowledge of learning a second language (Cummins & Swain, 1986). An additive approach, as defined by Baker (2001), fosters the learning of a second language without reducing or replacing the first language or first culture. Researchers suggest that this applies to Deaf children as well, and recommend that an additive approach be used in Deaf education (C. Erting, 1992; L. Erting, 2001). Thus, a combination of an additive approach to bilingual education with the emergent literacy perspective, would advocate that children be exposed to both language and literacy from birth, in both their first and second languages.

The third theory that guides this study stems from educational television research. The active viewing theory (Anderson & Lorch, 1983) suggests that children are not passive viewers of television as previously believed. Theorists who support the active viewing theory propose that how much children pay attention to television is affected by the effort they expend to comprehend the television program. They explain that there is a "causal relationship from comprehension to attention" (p.14). As applied to this study, the active viewing theory would predict increased active viewing to reflect an increase of video comprehension.

REVIEW OF THE LITERATURE

It is important to examine both the research that has been conducted related to emergent literacy development of Deaf and hard of hearing children and research related to educational television programs for hearing children.

Relationship between ASL and English

Although the processes involved in deaf children learning how to read have yet to be understood (Musselman, 2000), research on deaf children has produced some common themes. One theme that has emerged is the relationship between knowledge of American Sign Language (ASL) and its impact on learning English. Current research reflects that there is a significant correlation between ASL skills and reading skills (Padden, 1996; Mayberry, 1993; Padden & Ramsey, 1998; Prinz & Strong, 1998; Singleton, Supalla, Litchfield, & Schley, 1998). Deaf children of Deaf parents, who have been exposed to ASL from birth, develop literacy skills that allow them to continue to outperform deaf children with hearing parents on vocabulary tasks and language skills (Mayberry, 1993; Mayberry & Eichen, 1991).

Research has yet to explain the specific mechanisms that enable Deaf children with Deaf parents to perform better on reading tasks than deaf children of hearing parents. Some propose that there are more reasons other than just early exposure to sign language (Marschark & Harris, 1996). It could be because they were exposed to ASL at a later age (Padden & Ramsey, 1998), or because Deaf parents provide them with a home rich in communication from birth that incorporates both language and literacy (Musselman, 2000). To help answer this question, researchers have begun to study the various ways Deaf adults engage in language and literacy activities with their Deaf children.

Language development

Oral language development is an essential component of literacy development (Snow, Tabors, & Dickinson, 2001). Research suggests that children with larger spoken vocabularies have higher literacy rates (Hart & Risely, 1995) and that oral language development begins at birth. For deaf children, oral language is in the form of a visual modality, ASL. Research indicates that deaf adults modify their use of ASL with infants (e.g. using exaggerated expressions, gestures and modified signs) to help facilitate oral language development (C. Erting, Prezioso, & Hynes, 1994; Holzrichter & Meier, 2000; Maestes y Moores, 1980).

Fingerspelling

Fingerspelling is the use of the manual alphabet to spell out words on the hands such as proper names. Fingerspelling is a tool that can be used to help children develop literacy skills. In fact researchers advocate that fingerspelling can be used as a bridge to connect children's knowledge of ASL to their knowledge of English print (Padden & Ramsey, 1998). Studies with Deaf parents and their babies reveal that Deaf parents begin fingerspelling to their children from birth (Blumenthal-Kelly, 1995; C. Erting, Prezioso, & Benedict, 2000; C. Erting, Prezioso, & Hynes, 1990).

Children's fingerspelling development

Padden and Ramsey (1998) discovered that children do not necessarily have to know how to read the printed alphabet in order to understand a fingerspelled word. This may be one reason that Deaf children of Deaf parents attempt to fingerspell at a very young age. Akamatsu (1983) conducted a study of three Deaf children (ages 3;8 to 5;2) with Deaf parents. Some of these children's initial attempts at fingerspelling often represented the shape of a fingerspelled word as a single lexical unit rather than individual letters (Akamatsu, 1983; Padden, 1991).

In studies documenting fingerspelling development, several researchers observed that the first words children fingerspell are their names and that this occurs around age three (Maxwell, 1998; Padden & Lemaster, 1986). However, this could be related to fingerspelling input from parents. In a case study of their own daughter, Berrigan and Berrigan (2000) observed their child fingerspelling the entire alphabet at 30 months. This indicates that it is possible that the more parents fingerspell from birth the earlier children will begin fingerspelling.

Fingerspelling and storybook reading

Because there is not an equivalent sign for every printed English word, deaf children must learn to connect concepts to signs and signs to print (Maxwell, 1984). Researchers have focused on strategies Deaf adults use during storybook sharing. Parents label objects in the environment through sandwiching: they point to an object, sign the object, fingerspell the object and then point to it again (Blumenthal-Kelly, 1995). This strategy carries over when parents interact with their children and English print. In addition to fingerspelling, parents combine pointing to print, and signing in a variety of ways (Maxwell, 1984; Andrews & Taylor, 1987; C. Erting et al., 2000; Akamatsu & Andrews, 1993). Padden and Ramsey (1998) refer to this as chaining. This also occurs when working with deaf children who have had minimal sign language exposure (Mather, 1989).

There is a discrepancy in the research as to when the deaf children make a connection between fingerspelling and print. It appears that if younger children are exposed to fingerspelling (C. Erting et al., 2000; Berrigan & Berrigan, 2000), they are able to develop this skill. In Berrigan and Berrigan's study (2000), their daughter was able to recognize numbers and letters on shirts, license plates and store names and would initiate conversations about them by age 2 (Berrigan & Berrigan 2000). In contrast, Padden (1991) found that deaf children were not able to understand the relationship between fingerspelling and print until around age three.

One explanation could be related to vocabulary development. Anderson and Reilly (2002) studied ASL development in 100 DOD ranging in age from 8-35 months. Results revealed that that by 11 months, the children had a vocabulary of 17 signs. By 34 months children had a mean vocabulary size of 402 signs. They found that vocabulary size rather than age was a factor in developing fingerspelling skills. Once the child's vocabulary reached 400 signs (as measured by the ASL-MCDI test), children were attempting both fingerspelling words as well as letters.

Whatever the reason for differences in variability of children's fingerspelling and literacy development, the more adults expose children to sign, fingerspelling and English print from birth, the greater the possibility that children will begin to develop these skills at a young age. This research was taken into account when developing the educational video for this study. To create a design to measure the effectiveness of this video, it is also essential to examine the research related to educational television.

Educational television and comprehension

The program *Blue's Clues*, which was designed to encourage audience participation, was analyzed by Crawley and colleagues (1999). They discovered that comprehension improved after episode repetition. In addition, they analyzed verbal behaviors such as: answering questions, commenting on or questioning the content of the video, and imitating dialogue and nonverbal behaviors such as nodding, pointing, imitating behaviors, and other. Results revealed that both verbal and nonverbal interactions (especially answers and imitations) greatly increased with episode repetition (Crawley et al., 1999).

There has been no research conducted to date on the effects of engagement and attention of any instructional sign language video geared toward preschool deaf children. Research has shown that hearing children attend to educational videos and that children's attention and engagement increase with multiple viewings of the same program (Crawley et al., 1999, 2002).

Research has yet to be conducted to test whether this is also the case for deaf and hard of hearing children. There exists little, if any, evidence whether either deaf or hearing children will attend to or engage in an educational video that uses sign language as its primary means of communication. There is one study that suggests children might attend to a video in sign language. Fisch, Brown and Cohen (2001) studied children's comprehension of television programs that used only nonverbal communication. They showed two segments from a television series to 135, hearing 3-5-year-olds. Each segment contained an educational message that was conveyed through, "anthropomorphic chickens that communicated in noncomprehensible 'chicken talk.' Results indicated that children were able to comprehend the educational message of the story and that comprehension increased when the messages were visually concrete. This study suggests that it might be possible for children who do not know sign language to comprehend a story in sign language if concrete visual images accompany the signs.

Educational television and emergent literacy skills

Educational researchers have been examining the effects of educational television programs for the past 30 years. Most of the programs that have been analyzed air on PBS, particularly *Sesame Street, Between the Lions* and *Reading Rainbow*. Research indicates that watching *Sesame Street* and *Reading Rainbow* positively influences children's literacy skills, particularly vocabulary (Rice, Huston, Truglio and Wright, 1990; Wright & Huston, 1995; Wright et al, 2001; Graham, Vandergriff & Burke, 2001).

That hearing children can learn literacy skills from educational television programs indicates the possibility for deaf and hard of hearing children to learn literacy skills from educational television programs as well. To elicit engagement of participants while viewing a video, it is also important to take into account successful strategies that are incorporated into educational television programs.

STRATEGIES USED IN EDUCATIONAL TELEVISION

Formative research on *Sesame Street* reveals that children respond to interactive elements that allow the children to participate in the program. Reports from observational data from the *Sesame Street* Research Department (1999) reveal that when watching "Elmo's World," children counted along, moved along, and imitated actions.

Over the past 30 years, *Sesame Street* programs have incorporated techniques such as giving the child an opportunity to supply answers before the characters do and the use of characters who hesitate or make mistakes that viewers can correct (Fisch & Truglio, 2001). Additional techniques that *Sesame Street* researchers have found successful are as follows: making sure program content is comparable to children's real life situations; providing repetition and reinforcement either within or across different episodes; and providing the same content presented in different contexts (Fisch & Truglio, 2001). If similar techniques were used in an educational video in ASL, it might encourage engagement of the child viewers.

Each of the categories of literature reviewed provides insight into different aspects of creating and testing an instructional video in sign language. However, there are many gaps in the research. For each of these three fields of study: literacy, bilingual education, and educational television, we have a limited research base related to the deaf population. There have been few instructional videos made for deaf children. Of those that have been made, there is minimal research to support whether deaf children will engage in an instructional video where the primary means of communication is sign language. Without this information, we are unsure whether an instructional video would be a valuable tool for helping deaf and hard of hearing children develop emergent literacy skills. This study is part of a larger study designed to determine whether preschool deaf and hard of hearing children will engage in and learn from an instructional video in ASL.

METHODS

Research Design

The focus of this study is to report on descriptive findings related to literacy related behaviors preschool children engaged in literacy related behaviors during multiple viewings of an instructional video in ASL and how frequently these behaviors occurred. Findings are also reported from extensive field notes collected during observations of video viewing.

Participants

The 25 participants of this study ranged in age from 3 to 6-year-olds and were deaf and hard of hearing children who use sign language as a mode of communication (Mean X = 4 years, 10 months). Of the total 25 participants, 15 were boys and 10 were girls. Eight of the participants had Deaf parents (all from a residential program) and 19 had hearing parents (see Appendix A). Fifteen of the children were attending preschool at three different self-contained programs in the state of Colorado. Ten children were attending a residential school for the deaf in the mid-west (see Appendix A). Fifteen additional children began the study, but were not included in the analysis due to an absence during the week of testing.

Deaf children have a variable background. Many different factors influence deaf children's language such as: age of intervention, age of identification, parents' level of sign language, when parents started learning sign language and children's hearing status. Some children have Deaf parents who have been exposed to ASL from birth while others have hearing parents who have had limited exposure to sign language. By choosing participants from both of these groups, I hoped that they would be representative of the general deaf population.

SETTING

Data for this project were collected in four different preschool classrooms and one elementary classroom over a span of four months. Three of the programs were self-contained programs and one was a residential program. In each of the classrooms, there were 10-15 children ranging in age from 3 years, 0 months to 6 years, 10 months. Each of the teachers in the self-contained programs was a non-native signer. Each of the self-contained programs subscribed to a Total Communication philosophy and both manual communication and spoken language were used within the classrooms. A Total Communication approach can be described as an English-only classroom since the focus is one English with support of manual communication (rather than a signed language such as ASL), "English is the primary language to be developed and maintained and there is limited use if any of ASL" (Allen, 2002, p. 4).

The fourth program was a residential school for the deaf. The school subscribed to a bilingual/bicultural philosophy of providing language acquisition and facilitating proficiency in two languages, American Sign Language (ASL) and English. Programs that subscribe to this philosophy aim to incorporate both the children's first language and culture into the curriculum and strive for students' competency both in ASL and written English

(Grosjean, 1992). Participants from the residential school came from four different classrooms. Two of the teachers were Deaf and two of the teachers were hearing. The two classrooms with hearing teachers had deaf aides in the classrooms.

MATERIALS

Based on the research reviewed, an instructional video was developed to be used to determine whether or not children would engage in an instructional video in sign language. The video is structured so that targeted skills are repeatedly presented throughout the program. Each time they are repeated, various methods are employed to convey the targeted concept (Beck, McKeown, & Kucan, 2002). Examples of additional strategies that are used are as follows: chaining techniques, (Andrews & Taylor, 1987; C. Erting et al., 2000; Blumenthal-Kelly, 1995), showing ASL and English at the same time (Mather, 1989), asking viewers to sign along with the characters, repetition and reinforcement of targeted skills (Fisch & Trugilio, 2001), and providing Deaf role models.

Vocabulary

While literacy, language and cultural skills were all part of the video curriculum, targeted vocabulary was frequently incorporated in the video because exposure to vocabulary impacts oral language development (Teale, 1984) and literacy development (Hart & Risely, 1995; Beck, McKeown & Kucan, 2002). Also, vocabulary development in both first and second languages is essential for bilingual populations (Calderón, 2005). This also applies to second language learners who are deaf (Padden, 1996; Mayberry, 1993; Padden & Ramsey, 1998; Prinz & Strong, 1998; Singleton, Supalla, Litchfield, & Schely, 1998).

Ten vocabulary words were targeted and incorporated into the video. Five of these words were emphasized for instruction. I chose to target five vocabulary words based on Calderón's (2005) recommendation to pre-teach three to six vocabulary words prior to read-alouds. Following Rupley, Logan, and Nichols' (1999) recommendation to teach words in sets that are conceptually related, each of the 5 vocabulary concepts emphasized for instruction were related to a farm theme. They were also each repeated throughout the video an average of 24 times each using signs and an average of 8 times each using fingerspelling. Each of the targeted vocabulary words was displayed as print on the screen an average of 15 times throughout the video. However, characters only called direct attention to each of these target words approximately five out of the 15 times.

PROCEDURES

Once parents signed a parental consent form, the teachers in the programs sent home a survey. Baseline data of the participants were collected using a survey of demographic information. Baseline measures were used to determine the children's hearing loss, age of identification, the age at which the intervention program began, and parental signing skills. Parents also reported their children's television and video viewing habits, including frequency and type of programs watched.

Children viewed the video three times within one week. At each of the sites, I went into the classroom to bring the group of children to watch the video. In one of the self-contained programs and the residential school, children sat in a row on the floor in front of the television. In the other two programs, children sat in chairs in front of the television because the TV/VCR cart was too high for them to see from the floor.

Throughout each video viewing, I remained quiet unless one of the children directly asked me a question. If asked a question, I generally either redirected the child so as not to give the answer or told the child that we would discuss it at a later time. If the children asked me to sign along with the video (e.g. "Debbie, sign corn"), I did so.

MEASURES

Baseline measures
Background information (i.e. age of identification of hearing loss, degree of hearing loss, parents signing skills, type of intervention) about the children's families were obtained through a parental survey. Parents were also asked to provide information regarding their children's television and video viewing habits (i.e. hours of TV watched per day, programs viewed etc.).

Children's active viewing behavior
Children were observed and videotaped during three viewings of the videotape to determine their active viewing behavior. Active viewing was defined as the degree to which a child attends to and engages in watching a video. Engagement was defined as the degree to which a child physically responds to the video through movement, makes comments or reacts to the video through facial expression (Crawley et al., 1999). Comments related to the video were further broken down into the following literacy related categories: attention to text, predicting, sequencing, comments on characters in the video and copying dialogue. In examining literacy behaviors during

video viewing, I defined these behaviors as acknowledgement of either pictures or print in the video. I included pictures in this category based on Sulzby's classification scheme (1985). In this video, the main character, Peter, presents pictures representative of what happened during their trip to the farm. First, he asks the audience to help him sequence the pictures, then they add text to the pictures and place them in the book, and finally he reads the story. During this segment, Peter asks the children in the video as well as the viewing audience which picture is next. This is a sequencing skill. If after watching the video once, the participants mentioned what picture, word or sentence would appear next, which is predicting. Copying dialogue was defined as participants signing exactly what characters in the video signed. For the purpose of this paper, only literacy related engagement behaviors will be reported.

DATA ANALYSIS

In this study, I used an extensive descriptive analysis of coding engagement behaviors which will be described below. In order to have a better understanding of engagement and attention behaviors that occurred during the video viewings, it was helpful to have a more detailed picture of the participants of the study. After considering students' differences in sign language background, literacy skills, age, and school attended, I chose to describe four participants in detail who I felt best reflected the variability of participants in this study.

For each of these focal participants, I coded the data into background information, engagement behaviors, and interaction between me and the child. I cross referenced the background surveys filled out from parents, transcripts of the video, field notes taken during video viewing, pre-posttest gains and attention results. I then looked for examples from each of these categories that best represented each of the children.

Videotape transcription
Each group of children watched a total of 135 minutes of video. For each group the entire 135 minutes was recorded on a digital camcorder. Each child's spontaneous signed and spoken conversations were transcribed and their behaviors were also documented. Transcription was completed in Microsoft Word and color-coded for the following five categories: pointing to the television screen, signing of a targeted vocabulary word, fingerspelling of a targeted vocabulary word, conversation related to the video, and movement related to the video. Additional behaviors and conversations were transcribed but not coded. The categories of movement and con-

versation related to the video were further broken down into subcategories. Literacy related behaviors were counted both in the categories of conversation related to the video and signing or fingerspelling of targeted vocabulary. Each transcription was separated into Day 1, Day 2, and Day 3, and each coded category was then counted for frequency of occurrence. Totals were entered into a Microsoft Excel database and totals of each category were documented as well. Each category was totaled and the difference between Day 1 and Day 3 were calculated.

Coding of engagement behaviors. Each behavior was transcribed from the video viewings into five categories: pointing to the screen, signing targeted vocabulary words, conversation related to the video, fingerspelling targeted and vocabulary words. From the transcriptions, I color-coded the five categories into red, yellow, blue, green and pink. I then counted how many times each behavior occurred during each video viewing for each child (see Table 1). Then each category was totaled and the difference between Day 1 and Day 3 were calculated. Twenty percent of the transcriptions were coded by a second researcher following these same methods. Differences between the two coders were checked for reliability. The original coder counted a total of 324 engagement behaviors and the reliability coder counted a total of 301. The correlations between the original coder and the reliability coder were 97% with an average difference between the coders' scores of three and maximum difference of six

RESULTS

Engagement behaviors

Table 1 presents the coding of three different types of engagement behaviors: signing targeted vocabulary words, conversation related to the video, and fingerspelling targeted vocabulary words. Each category was totaled and the difference between Day 1 and Day 3 were calculated. The percent difference between Day 1 and Day 3 are also listed in Table 1.

As Table 1 represents, there was a dramatic increase from first day to the third day in the signing of targeted vocabulary words. Signing targeted vocabulary increased 287% from the first day of 70 times to 271 on the third day. Similarly, additional comments had a large increase at 130% from the first day of 291 to the third day at 669. While children fingerspelled the words less often, the number of times vocabulary were fingerspelled still increased 170% from Day 1 at 20 times to Day 3 at 54 times.

After further breaking down the category of comments related to the video into: attention to text, predicting, sequencing, comments on the characters in the video, I found that participants' attention to text in the video increased from 12 instances on Day 1 to 29 instances on Day 3. Predicting story elements also increased from each video viewing starting at 5 on the first day, 21 on the second and 31 on the third. Sequencing information only increased once between Day 1 and Day 2 from 5 to 6 times, but doubled on the third day from 6 to 12 times.

Types of Engagement	Day 1	Day 2	Day 3	Difference Day 1–3	Percent Increase Day 1–3
*Pointing to screen	55	74	74	19	35%
**Signing targeted vocabulary	70	157	271	201	287%
*Comments	291	426	669	378	130%
**Fingerspelling targeted vocabulary	20	14	54	34	170%
Movements	146	203	226	80	55%

Table 1: Engagement Behaviors Totals. Note: *Refers to categories that included some literacy related behaviors; **Refers to categories in which all behaviors were literacy related.

STUDENT PROFILES

The participants I describe are: Maria, Greg, Gary, and Elisa. Maria and Greg are from two different self-contained programs, both of which subscribe to a Total Communication philosophy. They have hearing parents and at the time of the study had minimal exposure to ASL. Gary and Elisa attend a residential program that uses ASL as a means of instruction. They both have Deaf parents and have been exposed to ASL from birth.

Maria

Maria was four years old and eleven months at the time of the study. On the first day she did not display any engagement behaviors, such as signing along or copying any movements. During the second video viewing, she signed one of the targeted vocabulary words. She also signed two nontargeted vocabulary concepts: "game" and "story." Signing these two concepts reflected her ability to predict what would happen in the video. There is a segment of the video where they play "Word Game." Maria signed the word "game" right before the word game was going to start. She also signed the word "story" right before the storytelling portion of the video was going to take place. On the third day, she signed targeted vocabulary 24 times as opposed to none the first day and one the second day. Similarly to Day 2, she predicted what would happen next three times. This was the first day that she fingerspelled words in addition to signing them. She fingerspelled three of the targeted vocabulary.

Greg

Greg was five years old and ten months at the time of the video viewings. His teacher reported that he had just received a cochlear implant. The first day he did not sign or fingerspell any of the targeted vocabulary words but he commented vocally 34 times. Greg's behaviors related to literacy increased on Day 2. He signed targeted vocabulary words 25 times and fingerspelled them five times. In addition to signing and finger spelling targeting vocabulary, he exhibited other literacy related behaviors such as predicting skills and attention to text. Greg also asked me if he could act out the video, which I allowed. Not only did he want to act it out but he encouraged the other children to do so as well. During the third video viewing, Greg signed targeted vocabulary words 27 times and finger spelled targeted words 7 times. Similar to Day 2, Greg asked if he could act out the video again. His comments reflected this because most of them were direct imitations of the dialogue in the video.

Elisa

Elisa was one of the oldest of the participants that I tested from the residential group. She was six years old and eight months at the time of the testing. On Day 1 Elisa signed the targeted vocabulary words twice and finger spelled them 6 times. Elisa's behaviors indicated her interest in literacy, particularly her engagement with print in the video. At one point, she pointed to the sentence, "We ate corn," waved to me and signed that it was wrong. She finger spelled the word, "ate" and laughed and said it should be "eat." I told her that ate meant, "finish eats" (English translation: We *ate*). Then she signed the sentence, "We finish eat corn."

On the second day, her engagement behaviors increased. Her comments reflected an understanding of literacy elements in the story, such as acknowledging important events, characters, and predicting what would happen next. She read the sentences again and signed the sentence about eating the corn correctly as, "We finish eat corn." She also named all of the characters by their name signs.

On the third day, she exhibited engagement behaviors related to literacy such as attending to print, predicting, and sequencing. For example, she read all of the sentences when Peter made the book. She also acknowledged the printed sign, "Peter's Place." She was the only child who did this.

Gary

Gary was one of the youngest children that I tested. He was three years and three months at the time of the study. On Day 1, he signed targeted vocabulary words twice and signed 15 comments about the video. Gary's literacy related behaviors included acknowledgement of characters and recognition that print has meaning. At the beginning of the viewing, he signed the word, "Rabbit," which is what he called the character Rika. During book making section, he turned to me and signed, "Write what?" asking me what they were writing. Most of his comments during this segment were labels of colors on the screen. Gary was sitting on a rug and when he saw a color he would jump up and sign, "Green!" very excitedly.

During the second video viewing, he signed targeted vocabulary words six times. He seemed to be most interested in Rika's character (calling her a rabbit), which he commented on several times. Similar to Day 1, most of his comments were related to the colors which he signed with great enthusiasm.

On the third day, his engagement behaviors increased dramatically. While he only signed targeted vocabulary words twice on Day 1 and six times on Day 2, he signed them 12 times on Day 3. His behaviors related to literacy included talking about characters and acknowledging events in the story. While he commented on the Rabbit character again, his comments expanded to, "Point, point Rabbit where? There Rabbit there! Rabbit wake up! During the sequencing of pictures, he also pointed and acknowledged that they were choosing pictures in the correct order by signing "Right (correct)." Again he named all of the colors.

DISCUSSION

The purpose of this study was to examine what types of literacy related behaviors preschool deaf and hard of hearing children would engage in while viewing an instructional video in American Sign Language and the frequency with which these behaviors occurred. As aligns with the theory of active viewing (Anderson & Lorch, 1983), results of this study indicate that deaf and hard of hearing children between the ages of 3 to 6 will actively engage with an instructional video in ASL. Some of these engagement behaviors are literacy related behaviors such as: sequencing, predicting, signing and fingerspelling targeted vocabulary and attending to text printed on the screen. In addition, there was evidence that these behaviors increased after watching the video multiple times.

Children viewing the video identified the sequencing of pictures in a variety of ways. Sometimes they pointed to them (often walking up to the screen and pointing) and other times they said the key word for what happened in the picture (e.g. corn for "We ate corn," or tractor for, "We rode on a tractor"). By Day 3, participants sequenced items 12 times. While the fact that this occurred at all is positive, there is more potential for this skill to be developed. In the video, the main character Peter points to 1 of 5 pictures, but there is not a close-up of the picture he points to. If there was a close-up of the pictures, this could help to facilitate the development of sequencing skills.

In addition to sequencing skills, there were 29 occurrences on Day 3 of children reading or attending to the text. One example of this was when children signed the targeted vocabulary word after seeing it in print (without a picture). For example, when the character Rika writes the sentences on the screen. Elisa read the print and signed the sentence incorrectly, "We eat corn." when the printed English read, "We ate corn." After Day 1, each time that sentence appeared across the next three days, she signed it correctly as "We finish eat corn," which translates into "we ate corn." These results suggest that she learned a past tense form through watching the video (with interaction from an adult).

The student profiles reflect the variability among participants in signing background, age, and engagement behaviors. Even though there were many differences between these children, it seems clear from their profiles that they all enjoyed interacting with the video. Gary, the youngest participant, appeared to like both the visual aspects of the video (e.g. colors) and Rika's character. Greg on the other hand was most interested in becoming physically involved with the characters and storyline of the video, and Maria was most engaged in learning new vocabulary and talking about events in the story. Elisa seemed most engaged in the printed text and showing me what she remembered from the previous viewing.

Their engagement behaviors also reflect the variability in their literacy skills. Whether it was acknowledging that print had meaning, signing or fingerspelling a targeted vocabulary word or reading a full sentence, each of these children interacted with print in one way or another. Many of them also sequenced pictures, predicted what would happen next or talked about characters in the story. Regardless of their age or signing background each one of these children individually found their own way to connect with the video and many of these connections were literacy related.

According to the emergent literacy perspective, children should be exposed to both language and literacy from birth and can learn these skills simultaneously (Teale & Sulzby, 1989; Sulzby & Teale, 1991). For Deaf children following both an additive approach to Bilingual Education knowledge of their first language transfers to their second language and they should be exposed to information in their first language (ASL) and their second language (English) from an early age (C. Erting, 1992; L. Erting, 2001). Regardless of signing skills, the children in this study attended to and engaged with both English and ASL). Given that deaf and hard of hearing children are significantly behind hearing peers in reading ability (Allen, 1986; Holt, 1993) and that this video is appropriate for children with a wide variety of exposure to ASL and English, the video could be used as means to facilitate literacy skills in this population. This could in turn help narrow the gap between deaf and hearing children's reading skills.

Results of this study also reinforce using both a bilingual-bicultural approach and an emergent literacy perspective in Deaf Education. The curriculum and design of this video align with an additive approach toward bilingual education (MacSwan, 2005; Dickinson, Snow & Tabors, 2001; Au, 2000; Au, 2002; Johnson, Liddell & Erting). The video also aligns with an emergent literacy perspective showing preschool children both languages (ASL and printed English) simultaneously (Teale & Sulzby, 1989; Sulzby & Teale, 1991). Both parents and educators could use this video in the home and/or school in a variety of situations to foster language, literacy, and cultural aspects essential to deaf children's identity development and education.

IMPLICATIONS FOR FUTURE PRACTICE

The results of this study provides both teachers and parents with a potential new medium of instruction with which to expose deaf and hard of hearing children to emergent literacy skills. The participants in this study varied in their signing skills, literacy skills, educational exposure, hearing loss, and exposure to ASL. This study reveals that even when children have limited exposure to ASL, they will still attend to and engage in a video in ASL with no sound and learn from it.

For deaf children with hearing parents, this is particularly informative. It takes time for hearing families to learn to sign. These children could benefit from watching the video by themselves in their homes by being exposed to English print through their first language, ASL while their families are learning to sign. They could also benefit from watching the video with other family members in the hopes that it would maximize children's learning and simultaneously help families improve their ASL skills.

According to research on *Between the Lions* (Linebarger, 2000), children learned more when the teachers interacted with children during video viewing and provided additional supplementary activities than when children only watched the video. If a parent or teacher were to answer questions or initiate dialogue, and/or stop the video in ASL for discussion with their children while watching the video, children could learn more. In addition, if adults encourage the children to sign along, there could be an increase in engagement behaviors which could also facilitate learning. Overall the attempted interaction with the researcher indicates that results could be increasingly positive with intentional interaction with an adult.

There are currently limited curriculum materials incorporating bilingual (ASL/English) strategies targeted for preschool deaf and hard of hearing children. This video could be used in educational settings as a means of supplementing instructional practices related to literacy skills such as reinforcing vocabulary development in both ASL and English. Teachers could show either partial or complete segments of the video to children individually or in groups to target literacy skills such as vocabulary development, letter recognition, print awareness, comprehension, sequencing skills and/or understanding of story elements.

IMPLICATIONS FOR FUTURE RESEARCH

There are multiple possibilities for future research. For example, there is an increasing body of research that reveals different strategies that Deaf adults use to help children make connections between ASL and English print (Akamatsu & Andrews, 1993; Padden & Ramsey, 1998; Andrews & Taylor, 1987). This study suggests that these same strategies can be used in the medium of television with positive results. These strategies could be further analyzed by examining the amount of time each targeted vocabulary word appears versus the levels of difficulty of signed, fingerspelled and printed vocabulary. While vocabulary was targeted in the current curriculum, other essential components of emergent literacy could be targeted and assessed in future videos including book and print knowledge, letter knowledge, sequencing and comprehension skills.

This study was limited to a small sample size. In addition to increasing the number of deaf and hard of hearing participants, it would also be informative to repeat this study with hearing children. Using hearing children would allow for a greater sample size and for a design which could include a control group. If this medium was found to be effective with hearing children, not only could it benefit development of literacy skills in hearing children, it could also foster cross cultural understanding and appreciation of bilingualism in Deaf education through a visual-gestural modality.

The student profiles in this study provided essential information not revealed in the descriptive and statistical analyses. Conducting more case studies of a variety of both deaf and hearing participants viewing instructional videos both in the home and in school would allow for more in depth qualitative analysis both of engagement behaviors including literacy related behaviors and the development of emergent literacy skills based on children's signing skills, literacy skills, and age.

There is a great need for research related to preschool deaf and hard of hearing children and literacy, bilingual education, and educational television. This study is a step toward beginning to fill one of those gaps. As these results indicate that there is a place for ASL in educational television programming. There are unlimited possibilities for instructional videos in sign language and it is a medium which can be a beneficial, supplemental tool to help facilitate the development of preschool deaf and hard of hearing children's ASL and emergent literacy skills. This study may inspire additional researches to explore the benefits of instructional videos in ASL.

APPENDIX A

Name	Parental hearing status	Age at time of study	Type of academic program	Gender	Years parents signed	Mode of communication in the home	Child's hearing loss	Child's use of aides
Greg	DOH	5;10	self-contained	M	5.5	Speak/sign same-time	sever/profound	hearing aides, CI
Mark	DOH	4.08	Self-Contained	M	-	-	-	-
Mike	DOH	5.10	Self-Contained	M	5	Speak/sign same time	Moderate-severe	Hearing aides
Ella	DOH	6.3	Self-Contained	F	5	Speak/sign same time	Profound moderate	Hearing aides
Cole	DOH	3.8	Self-Contained	M	5.5	Speak/Sign same time	profound	Hearing aides, CI
Zeek	DOH	4.11	Self-contained	M	1.5	Speak/Sign same time	moderate	Hearing aides

Name	Parents	Age	Setting	Sex	Signing since	Communication	Hearing loss	Amplification
Stan	DOH	4.1	Self contained	M	4 yrs	Speak/sign, ASL	profound	Hearing aides/CI
Duke	DOH	5.02	Self contained	M	Since birth	Combination	Severe-profound	Hearing aides
Aaron	DOH	4.11	Self-contained	M	--	--	--	--
Zane	DOH	3.4	Self contained	M	3 yrs	Speak/sign	Profound	CI
Maria	DOH	4.11	Self contained	F	1 year	Signed English	Severe-profound	Hearing aides
Julie	DOD	5.7	Residential	F	Since birth	ASL	moderate	no
Lucian	DOD	4.2	Residential	M	Since birth	ASL	profound	no
Chuck	DOD	4.8	Residential	M	Since birth	ASL	profound	Hearing aides
Anica	DOD	4.10	Residential	F	Since birth	ASL	moderate	Hearing aides
Gary	DOD	3.3	Residential	M	Since birth	Combination of modes	moderate	Hearing aides
John	DOH	3.25	Residential	M	1.5 year	ASL, speak/sign	profound	no
Avery	DOH	5.4	Self Contained	M	NA	Talk/sign	Severe-profound	CI
Elisa	DOD	6.8	Residential	F	Since birth	ASL	profound	Hearing aides sometime
Aidan	DOH	6.10	Residential	M	4 yrs	Speak/sign	Severe-profound-moderate	Hearing aides
Annie	DOD	6.8	Residential	F	Since birth	ASL	Severe-profound	no

Appendix A: Participants in study. Note: DOD = Deaf children with Deaf parents, DOH = Deaf children with hearing parents, CI = cochlear implant

REFERENCES

Akamatsu, C. (1983). Fingerspelling formulae: A word is more or less than the sum of its letters. In W. Stokoe & V. Voterra (Eds.), SLR, '83. *Proceedings of the 3rd International Symposium on Sign Language Research*. Sign Language Research. Rome, Silverspring: CNR/Linstok Press.

Akamatsu, C. T., & Andrews, J. F. (1993). It takes two to be literate: Literacy interactions between parent and child. *Sign Language Studies*, 81, 333-360.

Allen, B. (2002). ASL-English bilingual classroom: The families' perspectives. *Bilingual Research Journal*, 26, 1-20.

Allen, T. (1986). Patterns of academic achievement among hearing impaired students: 1974 and 1983. In A. N. Schildroth & M. A. Karchmer (Eds.), *Deaf Children in America* (pp. 161-206). Boston: College-Hill.

Anderson, D., & Reilly, J. (2002). The MacArthur Communicative Development Inventory: Normative data for American Sign Language. *Journal of Deaf Studies and Deaf Education*, 7, 83-106.

Anderson, D. R., & Lorch, E. P. (1983). Looking at television: Action or reaction? In J. Bryant & D. R. Anderson (Eds.), *Children's understanding of television: Research on attention and comprehension* (pp. 1-33). New York: Academic Press.

Andrews, J., & Taylor, N. (1987). From sign to print: A case study of picture book "reading" between mother and child. Sign *Language Studies*, 56, 261-274.

Baker, C. (1991). *Foundations of Bilingual Education and Bilingualism*. Multilingual Matters: UK. 2001.

Beck, I. L., McKeown, M. G., & Kucan, L. (2002). *Bringing words to life: Robust vocabulary instruction*. New York: Guilford.

Beimiller, A. (1999). *Language reading and success: From reading research to Practice: Volume 5*, Cambridge, Mass: Brookline Books.

Berrigan, D., & Berrigan, S. (2000). Bridget & books: Fingerspelling, reading — and sleeping — with print. *Odyssey*, 1(4), 6-9.

Blumenthal-Kelly, A. (1995). Fingerspelling interaction: A set of deaf parents and their deaf daughter. In C. Lucas (Ed), *Sociolinguistics in Deaf communities*. Washington, DC: Gallaudet University Press.

Crawley, A. M., Anderson, D. R., Wilder, A., Williams, M., Santomero, A. (1999). Effects of repeated exposures to a single episode of the television program Blue's Clues on the viewing behaviors and comprehension of preschool children. *Journal of Educational Psychology*, 91, 630-637.

Crawley, A. M., Anderson, D. R., Wilder, A., Williams, M., Santomero, A., Evans, M. K., & Bryant, J. (2002). Do children learn how to watch television? The impact of extensive experience with Blue's Clues on preschool children's television viewing behavior. *Journal of Communication*, 264-280.

Cummins, J., & Swain, M. (1986). *Bilingualism in education*. London: Longman Group Inc.

Erting, C. (1992). Deafness & literacy: Why can't Sam read? *Sign Language Studies*, 75, 7-112.

Erting, C. J., Prezioso, C., & Hynes, M. O. (1990). The interactional context of deaf mother-infant communication. In V. Volterra & C. Erting (Eds.), *From gesture to language in hearing and deaf children*. Berlin: Springer-Verlag.

Erting, C., Thumann-Prezioso, C., & Benedict, B. (2000). Bilingualism in a Deaf family: Fingerspelling in early childhood. In P. Spencer, C. Erting, & M. Marschark (Eds.), *The Deaf child in the family and at school*. Mahway, NJ: Lawrence Erlbaum Associates.

Erting, L. (2001). Booksharing the deaf way: An ethnographic study in a bilingual preschool for deaf children. Dissertation Abstracts International, (UMI No.3035993).

Fisch, S. M., Brown-McCann, S. K. & Cohen, D. (2001). Young children's comprehension of educational television: The role of visual information and intonation. *Media Psychology*, 3, 365-378.

Fisch, S., & Truglio, R. T. (2001). *"G" is for growing: Thirty years of research on children and Sesame Street*. New Jersey: Lawrence Erlbaum Associates, Inc.

Graham, W., Vandergriff, & Burke (2001). *Evaluation of Reading Rainbow: Badger's Parting Gifts*. Portsmouth, NH: RMC Research Corporation.

Grosjean, F. (1992). The bilingual and the bicultural person in the hearing and deaf word. *Sign Language Studies*, 77, 307-320.

Hart, B., & Risely, T. (1995). *Meaningful differences in the everyday experiences of young American children*. Baltimore: Brookes Publishing Company.

Holt, J. (1993). Stanford achievement test — 8th edition: Reading comprehension subgroup results. *American Annals of the Deaf*, 138(2), 172-175.

Holzrichter, A., & Meier, R. (2000). Child-Directed signing in American Sign Language. In C. Chamberlain, J. P. Morford, & R. I. Mayberry (Eds.), *Language acquisition by eye* (pp. 25-40). Hillsdale, NJ: Erlbaum.

Johnson, R. E., Liddell, S. K., & Erting, C. J. (1989). *Unlocking the curriculum: Principles for achieving access in deaf education*. Washington, DC: Gallaudet Research Institute.

Linebarger, D. L. (2000, July 21). Summative evaluation of *Between the Lions*: A final report to WGBH educational foundation. Retrieved March 1, 2003, from http://pbskids.org/lions/about/pdf/BTL-Summative.pdf.

Marschark, M., & Harris, M. (1996). Success and failure in learning to read: The special case (?) of deaf children. In C. Cornoldi, & J. Oakhill (Eds.), *Reading comprehension difficulties: Processes and interaction*. Mahway, NJ: Lawrence Erlbaum Associates.

Mather, S. (1989). Visually oriented teaching strategies with Deaf preschool children. In C. Lucas (Ed.), *The sociolinguistics of the Deaf community*. NY: Academic Press.

Maxwell, M. (1984). A deaf child's natural development of literacy. *Sign Language Studies*, 44, 191-224.

Maxwell, M. (1988). The alphabetic principle of fingerspelling. *Sign Language Studies*, 61, 377-404.

Mayberry, R. I. (1993). First language acquisition after childhood differs from second-language acquisition: The case of American Sign Language. *Journal of Speech and Hearing Research*, 36, 1258-1270.

Mayberry, R., & Eichen, E. (1991). The long-lasting advantage of learning sign language in childhood: Another look at the critical period for language acquisition. *Journal of Memory and Language*, 30, 486-512.

Morford, J. P., & Mayberry, R. I. (2000). A reexamination of "early exposure" and its implication for language acquisition by eye. In C. Chamberlain, J. P. Morford, & R. I. Mayberry (Eds.), *Language acquisition by eye* (pp. 111-30). Hillsdale, NJ: Erlbaum.

Musselman, C. (2000). How do children who can't hear learn to read an alphabetic script? A review of the literature on reading and deafness. *Journal of Deaf Studies and Deaf Education*, 5, 9-31.

Padden, C. (1991). The acquisition of fingerspelling by deaf children. In P. Siple & S. Fischer (Eds.), *Theoretical issues in sign language research Vol. 2: Psychology* (pp. 191-210). Chicago: University of Chicago Press.

Padden, C. (1996). Early bilingual lives of deaf children. In I. Parasnis (Ed.), *Cultural and language diversity: Reflections on the Deaf experience* (pp. 99-116). Cambridge, MA: Cambridge University Press.

Padden, C., & Le Master, B. (1985). An alphabet on hand: The acquisition of fingerspelling in deaf children. *Sign Language Studies*, 47, 161-172.

Padden, C., & Ramsey C. (1998). Reading ability in signing Deaf children. *Topics in Language Disorders*, 4, 30-46.

Prinz, P., & Strong, M. (1998). American Sign Language (ASL) proficiency and English literacy within a bilingual Deaf education model. *Topics in Language Disorders*, 4, 47-60.

Rath, L. K. (2002). Get wild about reading: Using *Between the Lions* to support early literacy. *Young Children*, 57, 80-87.

Rice, M. L., Huston, A. C., Truglio, R. T., Wright, J. C. (1990). Words from *Sesame Street*: Learning new vocabulary while viewing. *Developmental Psychology*, 26 (3), 421-428.

Rupley, W. H., Logan, J.W., and Nichols, W. D. (1998/1999). Vocabulary instruction in a balanced reading program. *The Reading Teacher*, 52, 336-346.

Singleton, J., Supalla, S., Litchfield, S., & Schley, S. (1998). From sign to word: Considering modality constraints in ASL/English bilingual education. In Prinz, P. (Ed.) ASL proficiency and English literacy acquisition: New perspectives. *Topics in Language Disorders* 18(4), 16-29.

Snow, C., Tabors, P., & Dickinson, D. (2001). Language development in the preschool years. In D. Dickinson and P. Tabors (Eds.), *Beginning literacy with language: Young children learning at home and in school* (pp. 1-26). Baltimore: Brookes Publishing Co.

Sulzby, E. (1985). Children's emergent reading of favorite storybooks: A developmental study. *Reading Research Quarterly*, 20, 458-481.

Sulzby E., & Teale, W. (1991). Emergent literacy. In R. Barr, M. L. Kamil, P. Mosenthal & P. D. Pearson (Eds.), *Handbook of Reading Research, Vol. II* (pp. 727-758). New York: Longman.

Teale, W. (1984). Reading to young children: Its significance for literacy development. In H. Goelman, A. Oberg, & F. Smith (Eds.), Awakening to literacy (pp. 110-21). Portsmouth, NH: Heinemann.

Teale, W. H., & Sulzby, E. (1989). Emergent literacy: New perspectives on young children's reading and writing development. In D. Strickland & L. Morrow (Eds.), *Emerging literacy: Young children learn to read and write* (pp. 1-15). Newark, DE: International Reading Association.

Williams, C. L. (2004). Emergent literacy of deaf children. *Journal of Deaf Studies and Deaf Education*, 9, 352-365.

Wright, J., & Huston, A. C. (1995). Effects of educational TV viewing of lower income preschoolers on academic skills, school readiness, and school adjustment one to three years later. Report to Children's Television Workshop. Center for Research on the Influences of Television on Children: University of Kansas, Lawrence.

Wright, J. C., Huston, A. C., Murphy, K. C., St Peters, M., Pinon, M., Scantlin, R., & Kotler, J. (2001). The relations of early television viewing to school readiness and vocabulary of children from low-income families: The early window project. *Child Development*, 72, (5), 1347-1366.

Deaf Wiki Project

JORDAN EICKMAN, PH.D. & SERGEI SIMEONOV

DEAFWIKI IS MODELED AFTER WIKIPEDIA, THE WELL-KNOWN ENCYclopedia. DeafWiki was created using Mediawiki, an open source software program. The intent behind creating DeafWiki is to establish a Deaf-produced, Deaf-centered source of information that covers everything about Deaf people and the Deaf community in the world. DeafWiki's aim is to provide free and reliable content about Deaf people and the Deaf community from the Deaf point-of-view.

DEAFWIKI CONTENT

DeafWiki content will be available in both signed and written languages. DeafWiki's content emphasis is on signed language content. Obviously, signed content will be presented in video format.

Each country will contribute content in its own signed and written languages. For example, American-produced content will be in American Sign Language (ASL) and written English, French-produced content will be in Langue des Signes Française (LSF) and written French, and so on.

DeafWiki is intended to be both editable and edited by the Deaf community. MediaWiki, an existing wiki tool is available to edit written articles. DeafWiki's next goal is to enable editing of signed content videos within a web browser. This goal presents a technological hurdle that is discussed later in this paper.

DeafWiki content will be moderated to ensure it remains Deaf-centered and factual. The purpose behind having an on-line, editable DeafWiki is to enable Deaf people world-wide, especially from developing countries, to contribute content without much financial or technical difficulties. Only access to a computer, a webcam, and an internet connection is needed to contribute to DeafWiki. Today, these items are readily available for a low cost in a variety of settings (at home or work, Deaf clubs, Internet cafes, libraries, etc.)

DEAFWIKI ORIGINS

Gergin Simeonov's story
Inspired by the fame and success of Wikipedia, Gergin Simeonov decided to initialize a website for Deaf people. Before the DeafWiki website was founded, Simeonov undertook a search to see if a similar website existed. Upon discovering there was none, he voluntarily established DeafWiki because he knew the importance of sharing information among Deaf people. Simeonov launched the current DeafWiki website in May 2006.

Jordan Eickman's story
Simultaneously, Jordan Eickman was working on a research project on the history of Deaf community pillars and mapping these histories using ArcGIS, a Geographic Information System software program. After Eickman's presentation on this project at the 2006 Deaf History International conference, Joe Murray, a World Federation of the Deaf board member, suggested to Eickman that a Wikipedia-type website be started to collect Deaf-related data.

After both men's return to CSUN from Europe, they met again and exchanged their respective experiences and activities. Eickman saw the potential for DeafWiki to be an extremely effectively tool for gathering research data directly from Deaf people through both signed and written languages. Simeonov then invited Eickman to work as partners on the Deaf-Wiki project as both had skills, resources, and strengths that would complement the other and benefit the DeafWiki project.

OUR SHARED VISION

After further and extensive discussion, both men developed a vision of what DeafWiki could become and developed a plan to make this vision become a reality. DeafWiki is visualized as becoming a new gateway for Deaf-centered research and a free-content, complete and reliable Deaf-produced encyclopedia covering Deaf people and anything else that may concern the Deaf-World and Deaf people's lives. DeafWiki will also allow new research and information systems protocol dealing with vlogs and data presentation given in signed languages to be developed.

What to include in DeafWiki?
DeafWiki is a Deaf-centered information source that includes:
- Deaf-centered academic and community research projects and data collections
- Deaf travel guides
- Deaf history guides
- Additional categories (the possibilities are limitless)
- An area for Deaf community discussion

Who can contribute to DeafWiki?
Three possible ways to contribute to DeafWiki are as an individual, as a group, and as part of a research project.

Individual contributors
Individual contributors are people who add content to DeafWiki on their self-initiative and their own time. They can share their knowledge and life experiences, and volunteer adding content on general Deaf topics in an ethical way (ie: appropriately citing paraphrased and quoted sources, and not violating copyrights or plagiarizing).

Group contributors
Group contributors are people who are based within the same city, state, region, or nation. The geographic distance between group members dictates which scale the group operates in. For example, one group within a nation that is small in size such as Luxembourg could easily cover the whole nation. However, in nations that are larger in size, the same group would focus only on a region, state, or city, depending on the size of the nation.

Group contributions can focus on one of two broad themes. The first is focusing on contributing geographic-based Deaf information from a group's city, state, region, or nation. The second is to focus on general Deaf information applicable world-wide. Additionally, for both themes, a group can add similar information from adjacent or nearby areas where there is no existing DeafWiki group.

Group contributions are made in the appropriate signed and written languages of the group's country. Each group is expected to be self-operating and self-funding.

Each group selects its own leader who will coordinate its contributions with DeafWiki and consult with DeafWiki on technical and format issues.

DeafWiki wants to empower each group to take its own initiative and to identify Deaf people who are experts within their geographic scope and encourage them to make contributions.

Research projects

Research projects can be organized to take advantage of DeafWiki's worldwide data collection capabilities. However, research projects must have aims consistent with DeafWiki's Deaf-centered position and be willing to share data and final reports or products with DeafWiki and the world-wide Deaf community. Projects that do not meet these criteria will not be allowed.

As with group contributions, each research project will select a leader to coordinate with DeafWiki on technical and format issues.

Exchanging info between countries/regions

Each of the three aforementioned different types of contributors should focus on making DeafWiki established as a source of Deaf-centered, reliable and correct information about Deaf people. DeafWiki encourages information sharing, which creates increased awareness of Deaf people and preserves Deaf history and community-based news items and information within that country/region/state/city.

Collaborating

There are many ways to collaborate and make contributions to DeafWiki:
- Teachers with students, Deaf mentors with Deaf youth, and Deaf organization leaders with volunteers all can pair up.
- Cooperation on the local, national, and international levels can take place.
- Contributors can organize DeafWiki data collections, making information logically organized and easy to locate. The data collections will become integrated into a coherent whole body of information.

Who benefits from DeafWiki?

Various groups of people will benefit from DeafWiki. Naturally, Deaf and hard of hearing people will benefit the most. This includes Deaf people involved in academics, international travel and other special-interest groups.

Hearing parents of deaf children, hearing Deaf community allies such as Children of Deaf Adults (CODAs), ASL/English interpreters, teachers of deaf children, ASL/Deaf Studies students, other hearing people working with Deaf people, and the non-signing hearing community (the media and laypeople) will also benefit.

Deaf people will benefit from DeafWiki by being able to exchange information about their local Deaf communities. Also, as Bienvenu (2008) said during the 2008 Deaf Studies Today! conference, it's time for the centralization of Deaf identity by Deaf people to occur. DeafWiki certainly can contribute to that process by being the Deaf community's "flagpost-in-the-ground" containing information about our Deaf identity and Deaf views.

Hearing people will benefit from DeafWiki by being able to learn the correct information about Deaf people and the Deaf community and to be referred to the proper Deaf authorities on Deaf-related topics.

DEAFWIKI'S TIMELINE

The DeafWiki project has already initiated operations, with the DeafWiki website up and running at www.deafwiki.org. Articles can be added and edited.

The next step and challenge for DeafWiki is editable video. DeafWiki wants to make video editing within web browsers possible. Three problems have been encountered regarding this feature.

The first problem is that at the time of our presentation at the Deaf Studies Today! 2008 conference, it was thought that intellectual property ownership became an issue if we used YouTube, a well-known and existing on-line video "cache" to place videos on-line and establish links within the DeafWiki website to videos stored at YouTube. Upon subsequent inspection of YouTube's Terms of Use (see http://www.youtube.com/t/terms, specifically sections 5 (particularly 5A-5C) and 6 (particularly 6C), it appears that using YouTube as a "cache" is possible.

However, it is still preferable that DeafWiki develops our own "cache" so that video and information contributed by the Deaf community remains within the ownership of both DeafWiki and the contributor of each video/information source. In essence, what is contributed to DeafWiki stays within DeafWiki and the Deaf community. The second problem is that the development of a programming code to enable editing, inserting, or deleting small amounts of signed content within a video and within a web browser is needed. The third problem is that the development of a programming code to directly upload signed content is needed.

The rationale behind developing both types of code is to allow Deaf community members worldwide to be able to modify videos and add their own signed content without having to obtain/use expensive video editing programs and to be able to upload their contributions onto the DeafWiki server.

DEAFWIKI DURABILITY

It is our intent to make DeafWiki durable, current, factual, and ever-lasting. This way, the information database will remain Deaf-centered, consistent, and maintain continuity.

Keeping DeafWiki alive

To keep DeafWiki alive, we need to share, distribute, and educate. The main goal is to ensure DeafWiki continues to thrive and to make people aware of and become educated by DeafWiki's Deaf-centered information database covering Deaf people and Deaf culture. Figure 1 shows the current DeafWiki front page.

Figure 1: DeafWiki website front page (http://deafwiki.org/index.php5?title=Main_Page)

The current front page is a work-in-progress. Signed content will be added to replace the introductory text. Content categories will be added as the number of contributions increases.

Figures 2 and 3 are shown with the intent of demonstrating how Deaf-Wiki can be used to share data from a Deaf community research project.

Figure 2 displays a map contributed from data collected as part of Eickman's Deaf community pillars project and mapped using Google maps within DeafWiki.

Deaf Wiki Project 573

Figure 2: DeafWiki mapping feature sample (http://www.deafwiki.org/index.php5?title=Template:Geo-Deaf_community_pillar_maps-Schools_for_the_deaf)

Figure 3 is an example of a visual mapping of a Deaf community pillar location using Google maps.

Figure 3: DeafWiki hybrid mapping feature sample (http://www.deafwiki.org/index.php5?title=Template:Geo-Schools_for_the_deaf-Europe)

DEAFWIKI'S FUTURE

The DeafWiki project is currently seeking financial support by pursuing grant opportunities and sponsorships.

DeafWiki's future belongs to you, the Deaf community. Local teams world-wide need to be established to bring information to DeafWiki. Deaf people everywhere are encouraged to participate and contribute. The Deaf-centered knowledge we, as the world-wide Deaf community, impart to the world will truly benefit the next Deaf generation.

REFERENCES

Bienvenu, M. J. (2008, April 11). Expedition for a (Deaf) theory. Presentation made at the 2008 Deaf Studies Today! Conference at Utah Valley State College, Orem, Utah.

DeafWiki. (2008, June 20). Main page. Retrieved June 20, 2008 from http://deafwiki.org/index.php5?title=Main_Page

DeafWiki. (2008, March 12). Template:Geo-Deaf community pillar maps-Schools for the deaf. Retrieved April 11, 2008 from http://www.deafwiki.org/index.php5?title=Template:Geo-Deaf_community_pillar_maps-Schools_for_the_deaf

DeafWiki. (2008, May 14). Template:Geo-Universities with Deaf Studies programs-Europe. Retrieved May 14, 2008 from http://www.deafwiki.org/index.php5?title=Template:Geo-Universities_with_Deaf_Studies_programs-Europe

YouTube, LLC. (2008). Terms of use. Retrieved April 30, 2008 from http://www.youtube.com/t/terms

www.ingramcontent.com/pod-product-compliance
Lightning Source LLC
Chambersburg PA
CBHW071956150426
43194CB00008B/897